STRATEGIC MARKETING

Creating Competitive Advantage

Second Edition

Douglas West, John Ford, and Essam Ibrahim

OXFORD UNIVERSITY PRESS

OXFORD
UNIVERSITY PRESS

Great Clarendon Street, Oxford OX2 6DP

Oxford University Press is a department of the University of Oxford.
It furthers the University's objective of excellence in research, scholarship,
and education by publishing worldwide in

Oxford New York

Auckland Cape Town Dar es Salaam Hong Kong Karachi
Kuala Lumpur Madrid Melbourne Mexico City Nairobi
New Delhi Shanghai Taipei Toronto

With offices in

Argentina Austria Brazil Chile Czech Republic France Greece
Guatemala Hungary Italy Japan Poland Portugal Singapore
South Korea Switzerland Thailand Turkey Ukraine Vietnam

Oxford is a registered trade mark of Oxford University Press
in the UK and in certain other countries

Published in the United States
by Oxford University Press Inc., New York

First published 2006

Second edition 2010

British Library Cataloguing in Publication Data

Data available

Library of Congress Cataloging in Publication Data

Data available

Typeset by MPS Limited, A Macmillan Company
Printed in Italy by L.E.G.O. S.p.A.

ISBN 978–0–19–955660–1

5 7 9 10 8 6 4

Dedicated to Lynda, Alexandra, Olivia, and Valerie and the memory of my parents.

DCW

This book is dedicated to my wife, Sarah, and my children, Lisa, Kimberly, John, and Jamie.

JBF

I dedicate this book to the memory of my father, Mr Bakr, and my two beloved daughters, Wasyla and Sondos. A smile on their faces was like a magic word for me to continue when it was hard.

EI

Preface

What is new in this second edition is that the book has been completely overhauled and updated. Nevertheless, the approach and framework remains exactly the same as in the first edition with cost-differentiation and the 'WWHD' framework, respectively.

The strategic approach of the book continues to be Porter's tried-and-tested cost-differetiation. Yes, organizations often need to reduce costs *and* differentiate rather than choose between the two. However, as an approach, it remains second to none in capturing the essence of marketing strategy.

The book continues to utilize the popular WWHD framework consisting of the four questions:

1. Where are you now?
2. Where do you want to be?
3. How will you get there?
4. Did you get there?

As with the first edition, we came to the conclusion that choosing a different framework would only be for the sake of being different. It works, and in our view it does not need fixing, and the application of strategy to the marketing mix at the 'How will you get there stage?' continues to be a feature of the book.

Each chapter contains two mini cases and one longer end-of-chapter case with questions for class discussion or assignment work. There are also three much longer end cases with questions that integrate the central themes of the book which are placed within the context of the marketing strategy 'blueprint'. The cases cited are for illustrative purposes only and are not in any way tied to any judgments about marketing strategy.

Hopefully some sense of the multinational nature of this endeavour will come through. All three of us have lived and worked abroad and we reside in different parts of the world, albeit two of us in the UK. It was for this reason that we decided against having an 'international marketing strategy' chapter which we thought would largely be redundant given our combined national and cultural dimensions and with the application of examples and cases from around the world.

What's new? Each chapter has been revised to incorporate advances in the field. Several chapters have undergone more extensive changes to reflect changes in technology as well as to plug some gaps identified by readers and reviewers of the first edition. The changes are too numerous to mention in their entirety, but we would point out a complete revision of several chapters such as Chapter 4, 'Strategic Marketing Decisions, Choices, and Mistakes', Chapter 7, 'Relational and Sustainability Strategies', Chapter 11, 'Marketing Communications Strategies', Chapter 12, 'E-marketing Strategies', and Chapter 13, 'Social and Ethical Strategies'. In terms of new content, additions include new work on portfolio analyses, cool brands, experiential marketing, and financial measurement. In addition, all the mini end-of-chapter and end-of-book cases are new. Each of these changes, and many others not mentioned, will hopefully assist in gaining a thorough understanding of the theory and application of marketing strategy and the underlying issues involved. The Online Resource Centre continues to provide a wealth of additional materials for everyone interested in marketing strategy and also provides links to additional resources.

Turning to readers, the book is designed for post-graduate students and undergraduates in the final year of their studies. It is not intended as an introduction to marketing. This is the second and updated edition of our account of strategic marketing and we hope that you enjoy it.

DCW

Acknowledgements

A wider team supports the production of a book such as this and there is always a risk in attempting to acknowledge the contributions of others that some people will be missed. Nonetheless the attempt to acknowledge must be made. We would like to give our thanks to the staff at Oxford University Press who have had a significant affect on the shape of the book and its evolution. In particular thanks to Nicki Sneath and Kirsty Reade for their encouragement, advice, and professional management of the process of this second edition. Also, our thanks to Sacha Cook for helping us see it into print in the first place. As well, there has been a small group of anonymous reviewers who have provided guidance on the book's structure and updating of the content. Thanks also to John Pearson and Leyland Pitt who provided a great deal of help and advice. There are also many people we would like to thank who have helped us track down specialist content. In particular we would mention Kari Aarvala, Melody Bartlett, Timo Kiravuo, Nicola Simpson, and Tim Pile. We would additionally like to take the opportunity for some special mentions with the cases. Thanks to Paul Beuttenmuller, Marc Fetscherin, and Levanchawee (Lily) Sujarittanonta for their outstanding work in developing two of the end-of-book cases. We also utilized three illustrative end-of-chapter cases which were developed by nine graduate students who worked under the supervision of Professor Hope Corrigan at Loyola College of Maryland, namely: Allison Broglie, Kathryn Cook, Mike Guest, Anastasia Kadantseva, Pamela Mooring, Corey Mull, Shalva Sikharulidze, Amy Wisner, and Christine Zeitschel. Many thanks for their first-rate work and for Professor Hope's supervision. We would like to thank our research and business colleagues and students over the years who have helped shape our thinking. Finally, we each owe a special debt to our wives and children who have been constant sources of encouragement and support throughout.

Outline contents

Contents

Online resource centre

Visit the *Strategic Marketing* Online Resource Centre at

http://www.oxfordtextbooks.co.uk/orc/west2e/

to find an extensive range of teaching and learning resources, including:

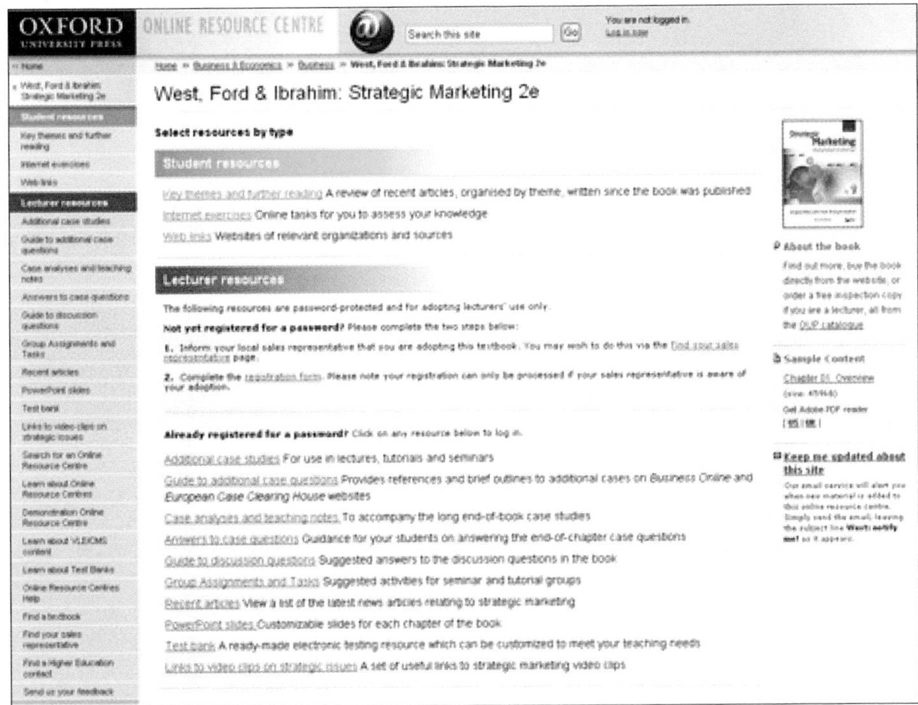

For students:

- Key themes and further reading—providing information on the latest developments in the field of marketing
- Internet exercises—a variety of tasks and assignments to be carried out online
- Annotated web links—websites of relevant organizations and sources for each chapter

For lecturers (password protected):

- PowerPoint® slides—for use in lecture presentations and handouts
- Case analyses and teaching notes—for use alongside the case studies
- Guide solutions—tips on how to answer the discussion questions
- Group assignments and tasks for each chapter
- Additional case studies
- Answers to case questions
- Guide to additional case questions
- Test bank of questions—can be used for assessment purposes
- Recent articles—ideas for further sources links to video clips on strategic issues

Part I Introduction

I. Introduction

1. Overview and strategy blueprint
2. Marketing strategy: analysis and perspectives

II. Where are we now?

3. Environmental and internal analysis: market information and intelligence

III. Where do we want to be?

4. Strategic marketing decisions, choices, and mistakes
5. Segmentation, targeting, and positioning strategies
6. Branding strategies
7. Relational and sustainability strategies

IV. How will we get there?

8. Product innovation and development strategies
9. Service marketing strategies
10. Pricing and distribution
11. Marketing communications
12. E-marketing strategies
13. Social and ethical strategies

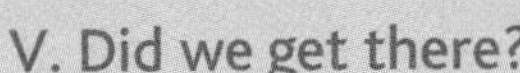

V. Did we get there?

14. Strategy implementation, control, and metrics

1

Overview and strategy blueprint

LEARNING OBJECTIVES

- Be able to define marketing strategy
- Understand the essential differences between the main approaches towards marketing strategy
- Review the structure of the book
- Assess the importance of marketing strategy to a business and identify the kinds of things that can go wrong

CHAPTER AT A GLANCE

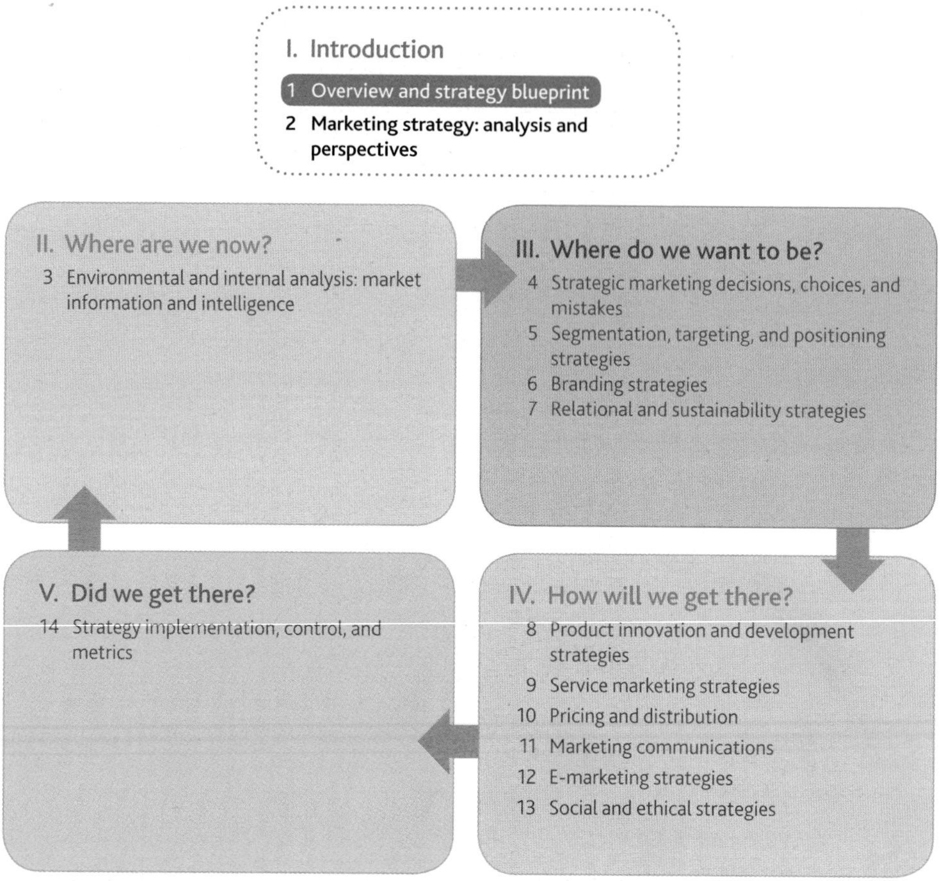

Introduction

Marketing plays a vital role in the marketing process. Look at arguably one of the most successful companies in recent years—Apple. Their design team work closely and intently with engineers, marketers, and manufacturing contractors in Asia. They do their homework. For example, when they figured out how to put a layer of clear plastic over an iPod's core, they were able not only to speed up the manufacturing process, but also to give an iPod tremendous depth of texture.

The first commercially distributed personal digital devices were SaeHan Information Systems 'MPMan' and the Diamond Rio Digital Player (see Figure 1.1), which were introduced to the market in 1998. Both represented technological breakthroughs, yet were clunky and unwieldy and lacked seamless software integration. Whereas the Apple iPod, which was introduced in 2001, was a triumph of marketing strategy. Apple adopted a market-oriented strategy based upon design, ease of use, and software integration. This resulted in market leadership and the establishment of a profitable and sustainable market position against significant competition from major companies such as Sony by continuously creating and

Figure 1.1 The Diamond Rio Digital Player

Source: Diamond Multimedia Legacy.

developing a competitive advantage, based upon their iconic designs and focus on customer expectations.

Competitive marketing strategy is 'a market-oriented approach that establishes a profitable competitive position for the organisation against all forces that determine competition by continuously creating and developing a sustainable competitive advantage (SCA) from the potential sources that exist in a firm's value chain' (see Mini Case Study 1.1). The key elements are:

- **Market-orientated:** the strategy is based upon the needs and wants of the marketplace. Given that the marketplace is often global, companies need to consider international expansion and acquisition strategies (Yip, Rugman, and Kudina, 2006) as well.
- **Establishes a profitable market position:** the end goal of the strategy is to make a profit in the for-profit sector or to meet alternate metrics such as in the not-for-profit sector. In the latter case, for example, a road-safety campaign based on a particular marketing strategy might 'make a profit' if there is a decline in road injuries and deaths attributed to it.
- **Forces that determine competition:** these are all the complex mix of ingredients that create the marketing 'whirlwind', such as government regulation, global competition, or the extent of buyers' knowledge and understanding of a particular market.

- **Continuously creating an SCA:** marketing strategy is not about one-off transactions. The aim is to reach a point where an organization finds a place in the market that fits its available marketing resources (see Mini Case Study 1.1). Few (if any) organizations can just rest on their laurels, so the idea is find a spot where, if need be, the primary challenges can be tackled. Not all organizations have to do this on a continuous basis, of course, but if they had to, an organization with a sound competitive marketing strategy would be able to do so. A simple example: you might make the best tomato ketchup in the best-recognized glass bottles, but if the market moves towards plastic 'squeezy' bottles, you need to be able to adapt.
- **Potential sources that exist in a firm's value chain:** competitive marketing strategy relates to what value any organization wants to create using its available marketing resources.

MINI CASE STUDY 1.1 Dumb networks

IBM (nicknamed 'Big Blue') has not been immune to the economic downturn and has laid off thousands of workers in 2009 and been criticized by the media in the US for exporting jobs to Asia. However, it also gave out bonuses to nearly 400,000 employees and earned over $12.3 billion on $103.6 billion in revenue, with a 44.1 per cent gross profit margin.

IBM's earnings are based upon a strategic shift by former CEO, Lou Gerstner, who steered the company away from hardware towards services and software in the early 1990s. Since the dotcom bubble burst, the company has stopped making disk drives, leased the ThinkPad division to Lenovo, and uncompromisingly moved into global consulting and data analytics, spending $50 billion on the acquisition of over ninety consulting, data, and R&D businesses. Most notably, they purchased PwC's consulting arm and Cognos, a leading business data company. The position today is that the company produces about 4,000 patents a year and a third of the $6 billion R&D budget goes into long-term research. The basic strategy is to develop a codified and tacit knowledge framework based on problem-solving technologies that can be applied across different industries. Part of IBM's strength has always been that it has a cultural history of selling and focuses on salesmanship: its senior managers are often drawn from the selling side of the business.

IBM's strategy is to turn its selling spotlight onto leading high-margin problems faced by businesses and local and central governments. It is currently receiving considerable attention from the media with its 'Let's build a smarter planet' campaign, which features a number of IBM staff saying that they are 'IBMers' and working on such things as smarter cars, cities, classrooms, energy grids, food supplies, grocery stores, and shipping.

The thread connecting all these things is 'dumb network' problems, which refers to the extent to which processes and objects are not working effectively. Cars and shipping burn fuel inefficiently and pollute, energy grids operate on the basis of overcapacity and oversupply, cities suffer gridlock several times a day, and classrooms don't always get the best out of children. By consulting across a range of dumb network problems, the company is able to develop expertise and offer solutions from one industry to another. No doubt, part of the attraction of the advertising by IBM is to appeal to and encourage its staff. Indeed, employees are encouraged to suggest any dumb network that IBM might be able to work smarter.

» IBM is not alone in the use of technology and in particular the use of data and data analysis to drive a corporate SCA. Companies such as Cisco, GE, and HP are all working on projects that improve efficiency, reduce pollution and/or energy use, and generally improve the planet. After all, that's what the market wants.

The trade press has reported a number of IBM's successes along the dumb-to-smart network. For example, the company and its subcontractors have helped alleviate the Stockholm rush hour using overhead cameras with optical character recognition (OCR) software with unheard-of precision to facilitate tolls by time of day with quite small graduated charges. The system clearly operated well and after the six-month experiment, it was passed by referendum.

Stockholm was left with reduced congestion and pollution, buses that could better keep to their schedules, and a friendlier place for pedestrians. Also, major investments in transport infrastructures could be put on hold. Research has shown that one of the biggest factors has been people making more efficient trips into the city. Rather than just pop into the supermarket whenever they wanted to, they would combine the trip with the school run, for example.

The IBM sustainable competitive advantage might appear to be rooted in the relatively newer consulting skills of the business, but perhaps the key is the link back and synthesis with the old 'Big Blue'. The key to developing smart networks out of dumb ones is the use of technology such as data storage, RFID sensor chips, digital video for sharp motion capture, powerful processors and software, and huge computing capacity. The old SCA has been combined with the new consulting one to provide an extremely powerful value proposition to the market.

It will be essential to dissect the various definitions of marketing strategy in some detail to establish the book's platform, and this will be undertaken in the next chapter. However, it is worth pointing out that Peter Drucker—the eminent management consultant and writer who looked at the organization of businesses, government, and the non-profit sector, and saw marketing as the decisive activity—would probably have argued that the definition above was too long. For example, his definition of marketing was a succinct: 'marketing is the business as seen from the customers' (Darroch, 2009, p. 10). Perhaps it's a bit like getting dressed? Sometimes it's appropriate to put on something formal, but sometimes it's best to dress down.

The **dress-down** version of the book's marketing strategy above might be: **'marketing strategy enables an organization to understand the environment and achieve its objectives in using its resources to meet the needs of its customers'**. Strategies are basically about the allocation of people and capital. The essentials of marketing strategy are: (1) understanding the external environment; (2) establishing the organizational purpose and objectives; and (3) assessing the internal environment in terms of resources and capabilities. Ultimately, it's about optimizing strategies that plug the gap between the environment and what the organization wants to achieve and its ability to do so. For example, as the car market inexorably moves towards smaller cars, some manufacturers are better placed with their resources and competencies to provide a fit. In particular, car manufacturers with expertise and offerings of relatively small cars are in the best place, whereas those companies producing relatively big cars will need to figure out how to use their current resources to best meet current and evolving needs. It's all about the environment, the organization's mission and objectives, and the organization's internal resources and competencies. The role of marketing strategy is to find the pre-eminent fit to enable the organization to survive and continue in business.

Thinking First

The book takes rational 'Thinking First' as the basis for marketing strategy, which is an approach that is primarily logical, sequential, and linear. Thinking First (see Figure 1.2) is about analysing a strategic marketing problem and developing the solution (the strategy) through a carefully thought-through and largely sequential process. **Instant views and decisions are not made, though it can help to see the 'big picture' occasionally.** It can involve some inspiration and insight, but the process is largely one of painstakingly doing your homework to arrive at a solution.

Thinking First is closely connected to a market-driven approach, such as Tesco's and BMW, which stand apart by their devotion to customer value and their culture, process, and abilities. Volvo is generally an example of a company at the forefront of customer satisfaction practices (Dahisten, 2003) given that their policy is 'Customer satisfaction is the way we measure quality.' Recognizing the need for a greater extrinsic focus to provide greater customer satisfaction insight, Volvo has added a more proactive approach to its research. Principally, qualitative research has been added to the mix with much greater direct customer contact involving engineering teams, senior managers, and dealers. Interactions with customers on the Web and through local workshops in different markets are being made so that customers' shifting perceptions of issues, such as on safety, are being more strongly tracked. Lost-sales analyses have been instigated to capture the perceptions of customers who decided not to buy Volvo.

Marketing is an activity that continues to rely largely upon the successful generation, dissemination of, and response to market intelligence (see, for example, Matsuno and Mentzer, 2000). Competitive marketing strategy is part and parcel of a market-driven approach, however, it is rarely quite as rational as Thinking First suggests; logic and rationality provides only

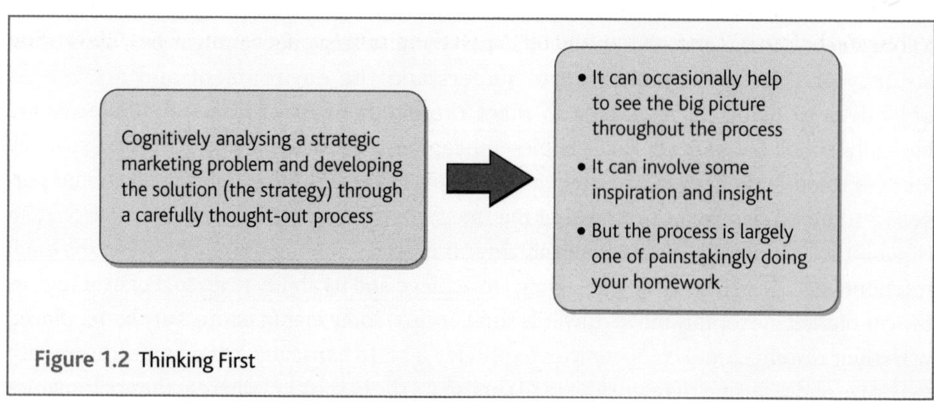
Cognitively analysing a strategic marketing problem and developing the solution (the strategy) through a carefully thought-out process
• It can occasionally help to see the big picture throughout the process
• It can involve some inspiration and insight
• But the process is largely one of painstakingly doing your homework

Figure 1.2 Thinking First

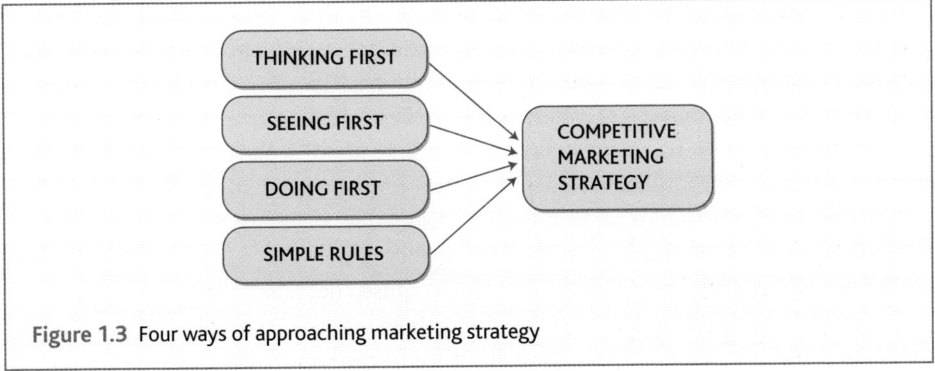

Figure 1.3 Four ways of approaching marketing strategy

one perspective. Decisions can be taken from a variety of perspectives and the main alternatives are (see Figure 1.3):

- Seeing First
- Doing First
- Simple Rules.

Each of these will now be considered in turn.

Seeing First

Seeing First reminds us that the importance of **seeing that the overall decision is sometimes greater than thinking about individual elements.** As Mozart observed, the best part of creating a symphony was to, 'see the whole of it at a single glance in my mind' (Mintzberg and Westley, 2001). Seeing First is basically **insight** and insight often only comes after a period of preparation, incubation, illumination, and verification in the cold light of day (Wallas, 1926). So, the best way of Seeing First might be after a process of rational analysis! The 'eureka' moment has often been known to come after sleep, as rational thought is generally switched off during sleep (see Figure 1.4). Thus, Seeing First is a cognitive process but it relates to the whole picture, rather than to a sequential analysis.

Some inspirational leaders can certainly scan the signals in the environment, sense what is going on before it is articulated, and rely upon their intuition (Gofee and Jones, 2000). For

- Seeing the overall decision is sometimes more important than thinking about it
- Insight often only comes after a period of preparation, incubation, illumination, and verification in the cold light of day
- The 'eureka' moment

Figure 1.4 Seeing First

example, Franz Humer, the CEO of Roche, is someone who easily detected changes in climate and ambience and sensed underlying currents of opinion. Such leaders are skilful at sensing and keeping on top of changes within the company and in the environment. However, sensing skills can be dangerous if overly relied upon. It is especially difficult to sense how far you can lead when it comes to major change. For example, the respective leaders in the Kyoto Protocol talks had many difficulties in sensing how far they could take the process without losing support. The danger of not being able to distinguish key issues from the peripheral is another danger. A leader might be able to sense a whole range of issues, but not be able to sift out the really important ones. This might lead to confused decision-making.

Are some organizations more likely to See First than others? According to Hamel (1999), there are two kinds of companies: **stewards** and **entrepreneurs**. Stewards are the incumbents who conserve by 'polishing the silver', cutting costs, outsourcing, and selling off bad business units. Entrepreneurs are the revolutionary wealth creators who capture the future riches. In this sense, they are capable of 'Seeing First'. In most industries, newcomers such as Amazon.com, Google, Facebook, and SanDisk are creating much of the new wealth.

Stewards have only one option to survive—they have to 'out-entrepreneur' the entrepreneurs. Hamel's challenging solution for big companies is to move from what he sees as resource 'allocation' to resource 'attraction' by developing internal markets for ideas, capital, and talent. Places like Silicon Valley are 'refugee camps' for frustrated entrepreneurs who could not get a hearing elsewhere. In Silicon Valley, if an idea has merit, it will attract capital and talent—there is no CEO to allocate resources.

Can the Silicon Valley approach be grafted onto big rational-thinking companies? According to Hamel, the answer is a resounding 'Yes' and he cites several good examples such as GE Capital, Monsanto, Royal Dutch/Shell, and Virgin. The principles employed by these big companies involve ideas, capital, and talent.

A flow of new ideas is essential for wealth creation and the best way to encourage this is to reward internal entrepreneurs handsomely. For example, Shell invites internal entrepreneurs to present their business plans to a wide cross-section of senior executives in the hope that at least one might say 'yes'. The second aspect relates to **capital**. Silicon Valley's venture capitalists are prepared to relax traditional financial screens. Taking the example of Shell again, the company has created a panel to which innovators can present a business case at any time. Silicon Valley's **talent** market is the third element of wealth creation that can be adapted internally by big companies. Every CEO in Silicon Valley knows that employees need exhilarating work or they will 'turn in their badges'. Shell lists their jobs on their intranet and anyone, with two-months' notice and within reason, can go and work on anything that interests them. The bottom line is that if highly creative and ambitious people feel trapped in 'dead end' positions, they will leave and if they do so they may create wealth somewhere else and not for your organization.

Even if larger companies do start to See First more easily through developing their flow of ideas, capital, and talent, many companies still face a problem as the competition from the 'left field' has grown more intense since the mid-1990s. As a result of consumer tastes, globalization and unrelenting technological change, competitive boundaries have blurred significantly. Take the case of BT, which has formed partnerships with such companies as Accenture, Computacenter, CSC, HP, Intel, Microsoft, Nortel, Vodafone, and ddfdf to provide integrated solutions to its customers. With Intel, BT is conducting joint research and development (R&D) to improve wireless services and with ddfdf, it is developing networked contact centres to reduce the costs of maintaining service quality.

How can firms See First and diagnose the likelihood of a new entrant from an unexpected place? According to Geroski (1999), a couple of observations can be made. One is that successful unexpected entrants are not like aliens in the marketplace. They behave rationally by **applying basic product and/or process innovations** and generally use **sound business planning**. However, the second observation is that **incumbents often have problems seeing outside their immediate competitive environments** and rarely cope with unexpected entrants.

Producers of similar products are known as **complementors** and these are the firms **most likely to mount unexpected entrances into your marketplace**. On the other hand, they also offer the best opportunity to form alliances with and to mount your own unexpected entrances into other firms' markets. For example, book publishers, cinema chains, newspaper groups and magazines, and TV companies are complementors—they all compete for our sedentary leisure time and 'feed off' each other for content and publicity. Having a related competency is another route to unexpected entrance. For example, Racal and Ericsson's understanding of cellular technology in the defence sector enabled them to enter as competitors in telecommunications, and Nike's expertise in athletic shoes has enabled it to branch out into sportswear, sports equipment, and managing sports events. Similarly, supermarkets have skills in managing cash transactions, which has enabled their entrance into financial markets such as banking services.

To maintain control of your market Geroski (1999) recommends five steps:

1. Begin by identifying who might take advantage of the flows of information from your market.
2. After that, you need to imagine that you were the potential new entrant and think coherently about them.
3. Then organize your thoughts coherently from the point of view of attacking your own market position.
4. Think through the what, who, and when aspects of market entry and assess the required competencies.
5. Finally, pre-empt potential entrants by introducing the new process or product developed in (4) yourself!

Summary

'Seeing First' has most relevance with new ventures or dramatic changes of direction. The reality with Seeing First is that, invariably, you need to do your homework. That is, you also need to be able to Think First. Mozart may have been able to See First before he wrote his symphonies, but the application of this to marketing strategy is less obvious. You might occasionally have luck with Seeing First, but for the most part, marketers need to examine the trends and the evidence and be able to develop some sense of what is important within the mass of actions and events. A more accessible alternative approach is to see the 'Big Picture', which does involve Thinking First. Successful marketing strategy requires the ability to move from tactical detail to a 'Big Picture' overview of the market to place their strategy in context.

Doing First

When you cannot think it through and you do not see it, what do you do? 'Doing First' is when marketing managers **experiment and learn from the mistakes and successes**. The process is: **(1) do something; (2) make sense of it; and (3) repeat the successful parts and discard the rest** (see Figure 1.5). Instead of marketing strategy, the reality is often that 'doing' drives. For example, many companies that have successfully diversified their businesses have done so by a process of figuring out what worked and what did not.

Take the case of Manchester United Football Club. Of all the English football clubs, Manchester United's performance on (and off) the pitch has been tremendous. According to Szymanski (1998), its success is rooted in its exceptional 'brand image' which has been developed over the century. Manchester United entered the football league in 1892, staved off bankruptcy ten years later, and thereafter has rarely looked back. As an institution, it entered the collective psyche in the 1950s and 1960s when Matt Busby's 'Babes' dominated the game and in between, the Munich air crash of 1958 stunned the nation. The club's success has not been based on the outcome of strategic marketing planning. Instead, it has been based on the vagaries of fortune and the maintenance of its brand character over time through investment in its management, facilities, and players. In recent years, the club won several Premier League Championships and FA cups. Manchester United is the 'Coca-Cola' of English football. Even when its pitch performance has been below that of its rivals, it has been able to attract higher attendances to its fixtures than its rivals.

The key aspect of football economics is that there is no significant link between profits and league position. As clubs improve their league position, their profits are just as likely to go up as down. The reason is simple. Better league performances lead to higher revenues with better attendance, higher ticket prices, and TV rights. However, increased expenditure on wages leads to sustained league performances. Thus, to move up the league, and stay there, a football club has to spend out on the better players in order to consistently win matches. Consequently, successful clubs cannot harvest profits—they are forced to maintain spending to replace players over time. So, how has Manchester United managed to combine profitability with pitch performance?

Among the fans, the decision to support the club is straightforward. As the leading brand name, a costly information search by fans for the best club to follow is reduced. Fans know that the games will be entertaining and the likelihood of winning will be high. Additionally,

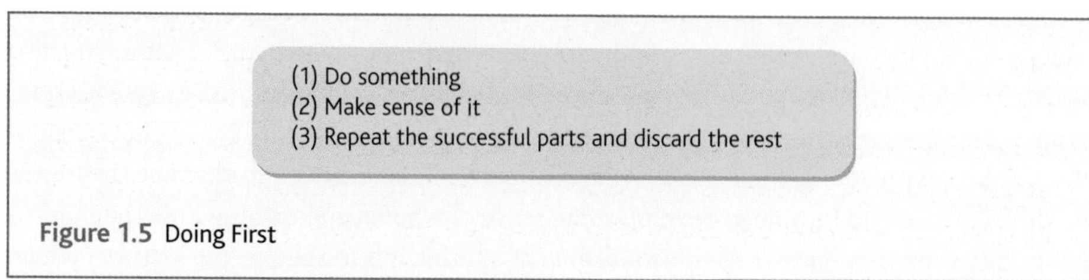
(1) Do something
(2) Make sense of it
(3) Repeat the successful parts and discard the rest

Figure 1.5 Doing First

fans often make lifetime 'once-for-ever' decisions on which clubs to support. Manchester United has demonstrated its commitment to maintaining its quality over time, much like Nescafé does. Both these factors are essential to fans shunning their local teams in favour of Manchester United. A final factor is that the choice of which team to support for many football fans is often random. Fans unable to make an immediate choice are influenced by which teams are doing well at the time of the decision, and over the century, Manchester United has been one of the most successful teams. Manchester United is well supported because it has always been well supported and that is the value of a strong brand.

Summary

'Doing First' is a credible and viable strategic approach (see Mini Case Study 1.2). There are often so many circumstances and issues that it is virtually impossible to disentangle the best course of action or outcome. Doing First enables organizations to try out marketing strategies and with careful monitoring, assess the results. This is the way to test the boundaries of stretching a brand, the viability of new kinds of distribution channels, and so on, and so on. However, Thinking First is still a necessity in establishing how you will define and measure the success of any Doing First strategy.

MINI CASE STUDY 1.2 Doing First with Skype

In the second half of 2005, eBay Inc. acquired Luxembourg-based Skype Technologies SA for around $2.6 billion in cash and eBay stock. The aim was to provide people across the world with an e-commerce platform embracing Skype, eBay, and PayPal. The core of the original idea was for eBay to employ Skype to generate further trade on the auction site. Skype would enable sellers to talk directly to buyers online, which would be particularly useful for high-value items such as cars and antiques, where a basic listing failed to scratch the surface deep enough and the lack of discussion between buyer and seller presented a barrier.

Skype provides voice communication to anyone with an Internet connection and subscription anywhere in the world, and video if they have a webcam. This is known as VOIP (Voice over Internet Protocol) and the software is straightforward to install and calls are free between fellow Skype users. Additional relatively low-cost calls to landlines and mobiles can be bolted on along with voicemail, call forwarding, instant messaging, and videoconferencing. When eBay purchased Skype, it had about 54 million registered users across the world. This has grown to over 405 million largely by word-of-mouth and it's essentially the market leader in nearly every country where it operates.

However, the idea of changing the way people communicate, shop, and do business online failed to come to fruition. Skype has revolutionized how many communicate, but the revolution to shopping on eBay failed to materialize. The intention had been that buyers would be able to talk to sellers seamlessly and get the deeper information that they need to buy. On the other side, sellers could more easily build up relationships with customers and close sales for such things as antiques, used cars, business, and »

» industrial equipment. It might also provide a way of increasing market penetration and dominance in the economies of Brazil, Russia, India, and China (BRIC), where vast distances presented barriers to a lot of commerce in which bargaining was a powerful driver in transaction. Factoring in fees for Skype communications combined with PayPal would also make for a powerful combination. Creating a PayPal account for each Skype account would make it much easier for users to pay for Skype fee-based services and in turn have synergies with PayPal by adding to the number of accounts and increasing payment volume. Overall, combining the different Internet platforms of eBay, PayPal, and Skype with their obvious synergies and complementary elements appeared to make a great deal of sense.

Fast forward to the news that eBay had decided to float Skype as a stand-alone company in 2010. What did investors make of this decision? Shares in eBay immediately increased in price. Why? There was certainly considerable logic to the original acquisition of Skype in 2005 and the brand has proved to be a very successful Internet business and has quickly moved beyond the early adopter phase to become a mainstream consumer and business technology. The problem was that the synergies envisaged with eBay failed to materialize. Buyers and sellers didn't use it in the volumes anticipated. The basics of the auction process involving the hands-off relationship between buyers and sellers and the anonymous competition between the bidders prevailed. To most eBay investors, Skype was a distraction to the core of the business and had tied up too much capital.

Had eBay made a mistake? Hindsight is a wonderful thing. It was only by undertaking the acquisition and observing the buyers' behaviour that the lack of synergy with Skype was revealed. Did it make sense in the first place? Undoubtedly, the answer is 'Yes'. What is more, Skype has proved to be an Internet phenomenon with a bright future—it's just that for the foreseeable, it won't pivot around eBay.

Postmodern

A completely different view of strategy is provided by the postmodern school. Underpinning the approach of postmodern marketing strategy is the proposition that **buyers are increasingly sophisticated and cynical about 'regular' marketing**.

Wright (1985) has argued that consumers have to interpret and withstand marketers' sales appeals and that they develop knowledge and coping tactics to do so. **Persuasion knowledge** helps consumers identify how, when, and why marketers try to influence them and helps them to respond adaptively to attempts at persuasion to achieve their own goals (Friestad and Wright, 1994). Developing this notion that consumers have developed **schemer schema** or intuitive theories about marketers' attempts to influence them, they draw marketers' attention to **folk** models of persuasion. These observe that consumers learn about persuasion in many ways: from everyday social encounters, from observing marketers and other persuaders, and from media commentary on marketing and advertising tactics.

The diffusion of psychological concepts and language into our culture also plays a role, as does formal education in schools about marketing issues. Developing over time, consumer's persuasion knowledge is an important factor shaping their response to attempts to persuade (O'Donohoe, 2001). Individuals develop context-specific persuasion knowledge in situations that they frequently encounter. Marketing persuasion knowledge has migrated widely. Thus, when commercial television first appeared in 1955, its persuasive attempts were novel and powerful. Moving black-and-white commercials inside people's homes had never been experienced before. However, since then, cultural knowledge about television advertising and other marketing techniques have developed in greater depth. This knowledge has been based on the first insights that people had about the early commercials, in shared conversations as well as what they learnt from the occasional commentaries of professionals on marketing. Passing between and within generations, there is now a high degree of understanding of how marketing 'works' and postmodern marketing strategy argues that if you ignore this, you run the increased risk of failure.

One of the leading proponents of the postmodern view, Stephen Brown (2001) argues that customer-centric marketing has gone too far and now places many companies in the position of Uriah Heep: 'unctuous, ubiquitous and unbearable'. His view is that **people do not want the truth, the whole truth, and nothing but the truth**. They certainly do not expect truth from marketers. People want marketing to be about glitz, glamour, and to be mischievous and mysterious. Marketing should be fun, but any nastiness is forbidden. Contemporary consumers find marketing's obsession with love, honour, and obey embarrassing. They would prefer a lovable rogue to the Disneyfied version that is the norm of today. **Retromarketing** harks back to the 'good old bad days' when marketers were pranksters and proud of it. To undertake a retro strategy, marketers need to practice TEASE: 'tricksterism', entertainment, amplification, secrecy, and exclusivity (see Figure 1.6).

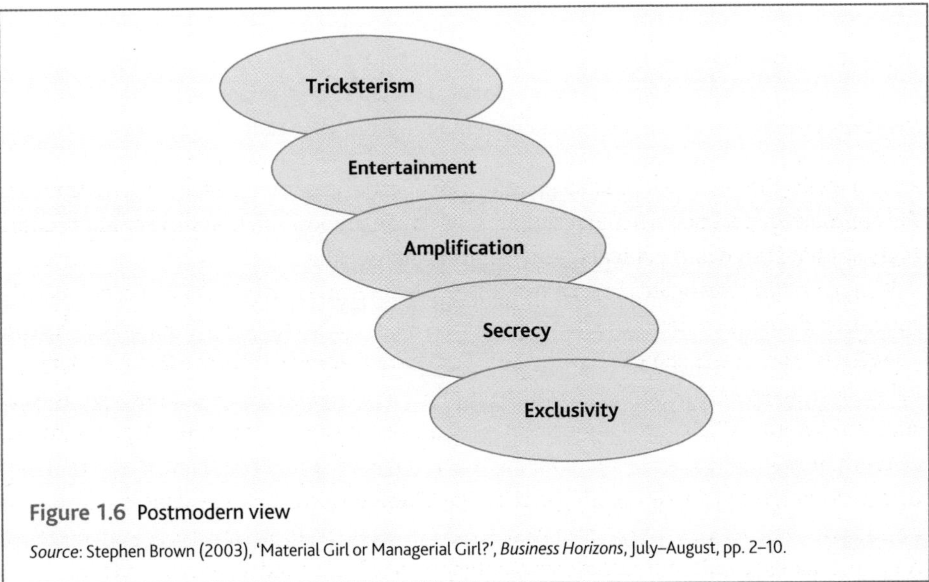

Figure 1.6 Postmodern view

Source: Stephen Brown (2003), 'Material Girl or Managerial Girl?', *Business Horizons*, July–August, pp. 2–10.

Tricksterism has to be played as a postmodern joke. Tango's numerous attempts to trick its customers, leaving them 'Tango'd', qualifies, especially its bogus hotline for customers to notify the company of knockoffs of the brand that were not fizzy. It turned out to be a new non-carbonated version of the drink and owned by Tango.

Entertainment is one of the major elements in retro's armoury, according to Brown. The idea here is that marketing has forgotten how to 'flirt'. The surreptitious and ambitious Web-based promotions to promote Spielberg's *AI* were highly entertaining. It involved using a Web-search discovery of a murder and a 'body' of clues provide a perfect example of entertaining consumers rather than boring them.

Amplification is about ensuring that the hot ticket or cool item is talked about and especially that the talking about is talked about. The idea is to turn a tiny advertising spend into a mega-budget monster. Examples include Benetton, the Citroën Picasso, Calvin Klein, and Pizza Hut paying to place its logo on the side of a Russian rocket.

Secrecy in retro is the opposite of upfront and above board. It is best seen in 'secret' recipes for Coca-Cola, Heinz Ketchup, Kentucky Fried Chicken, and Mrs Fields Cookies, but can also be found in cosmetics and hideaway holiday packages.

Exclusivity is central to retro. 'Get it now while supplies last' replaces 'There's plenty for everyone'. It is practiced, for example, by Beanie Babies, De Beers diamonds, Disney's videos, Harley, Harry Potter, the Honda Odyssey, and Mazda Miata. The end result is less inventory and consumers who luxuriate in feeling that they are the lucky few.

In a later contribution, Brown (2003) offers another view of postmodern marketing strategy, illustrated by an assessment of the marketing of Madonna. He argues that her phenomenal success relies upon the fact that people like to be shocked more than in her ability to shock them, as they enjoy being affronted and expressing outrage at her transgressions. As such, her marketing model is antithetical to the traditional 4P model, being based upon what he coins to be the 'Seven Ss' of subversion, scarcity, secrecy, scandal, sell-ebrity, storytelling, and sublimity.

Subversion relates to Madonna's contemptuous disregard for her audience. Her approach is very much 'forget the consumer' and 'the customer isn't king'. With her 2001 'Drowned World' tour, she regularly swore at the audience, refused to perform any of her greatest hits, and ended the show with a giant video-clip telling the audience that she wasn't coming back and that they should go home.

Scarcity conveys her attempts to restrict supply to the marketplace. Rather than raise supply in response to demand, Madonna has done the opposite. She has only had five major tours in twenty years and performs on stage for about 90 minutes.

Secrecy recounts Madonna's carefully manufactured mystery. She constantly changes her image, has ambiguous lyrics and cryptic song titles, has married twice in extreme secrecy and has 'predictably unpredictable' offstage behaviour.

Scandal is an essential ingredient in marketing Madonna. She is a master at scandal-selling, that is, carefully timing a scandal to coincide with the launch of a new product. Her 2000 video 'What it Feels Like for a Girl' was banned on the basis of the amount of violence depicted in the film and the song duly went to number one in a chorus of cash registers.

Sell-ebrity refers to Madonna's ability to sell the selling of scandal rather than just selling scandal alone. For example, when she attended the Academy Awards with Michael Jackson on a 'date', it was clear to both the media and the public that the whole event was simply a stunt to publicize their latest projects.

Storytelling or the creation of legends is an essential part of Madonna's marketing prowess. She has created a rags-to-riches myth that people buy into, along with a parade of personalities that go with her changing plots from 'Monroesque movie siren' to 'earth mother hippie chick'.

Sublimity relates to Madonna's ability to straddle different worlds, including sacred and profane, gay and straight, parent and child, street chic and haute couture, material and ethereal and commerce, avant-garde and mainstream.

Summary

'Postmodern Marketing Strategy' can provide considerable insight into markets. Most markets, be they business-to-consumer or business-to-business, have enormous levels of 'savvy'. Buyers are smart and have a good appreciation of the motives and methods of marketing strategies. The vast majority of marketers set out to create genuine value for their customers but strategies faced with increased suspicion and cynicism need increasingly to take into account the postmodern perspective. The endpoint of the strategy needs to engage, be interactive, and take into account the buyer's perspective. A significant minority of creative customers or groups continually adapt, modify, or transform goods and services as with people who 'pimp' their cars or work with open code software (Berthon et al., 2007).

Simple Rules

Marketing strategy as Simple Rules is about **selecting a few key marketing strategic processes, crafting a handful of Simple Rules, and 'jumping in', rather than avoiding uncertainty** (see Figure 1.7). In many respects, the approach is related to 'Doing First', except

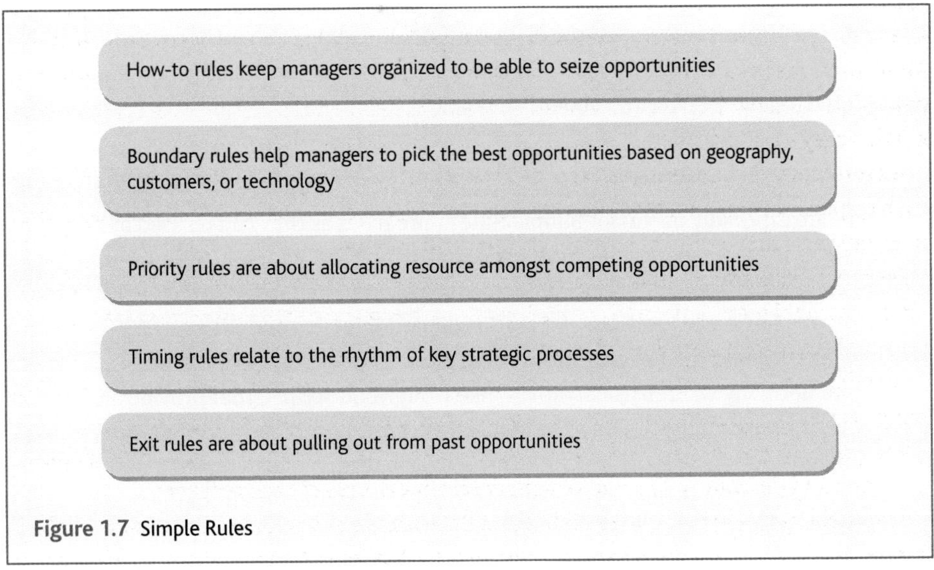
How-to rules keep managers organized to be able to seize opportunities
Boundary rules help managers to pick the best opportunities based on geography, customers, or technology
Priority rules are about allocating resource amongst competing opportunities
Timing rules relate to the rhythm of key strategic processes
Exit rules are about pulling out from past opportunities

Figure 1.7 Simple Rules

that the rules are predefined. Companies like Vodafone and Yahoo! have excelled without the traditional advantages of superior resources or strategic positions.

According to Eisenhardt and Sull (2001), the key to their success has been the use of Simple Rules:

How-to rules are about keeping managers organized enough to be able to seize opportunities. For example, Dell applies a rule that when any customer segment's revenue reaches $1 billion, the segment must be split into two halves.

Boundary rules help managers to pick the best opportunities based on either geography, customers, or technology. Thus, when Cisco decided on an acquisitions-led strategy, its boundary rule was that any company acquired would have a maximum of seventy-five employees, of whom 75 per cent had to be engineers. When Miramax decides on a film project, it has to satisfy four boundaries: the film must revolve around the human condition, such as love; the main hero must be flawed in some way; there must be a clear beginning, middle, and end; and a firm cap on production cost must be established (e.g., the films *The Queen* (2006, with Pathé and Granada Productions); *Venus* (2006); *There Will Be Blood* (2007, with Paramount Vantage); *Brideshead Revisited* (2008, with Warner Independent Pictures and Recorded Picture Company); *The Boy in the Striped Pyjamas* (2008)).

Priority rules are about allocating resources among competing opportunities. For example, Intel allocates manufacturing capacity based on a product's gross margin.

Timing rules relate to the rhythm of key strategic processes. For example, many Silicon Valley companies set timing rules for NPD. When developers approach a deadline, they are often forced to drop features in order to meet the schedule.

Exit rules are about pulling out from past opportunities. New initiatives might be dropped if set sales and profit goals are not being met. Such rules can be quite specific. At the Dutch hearing-aid company, Oticon, product development is halted if any key team-member decides to leave for another project.

How many rules are optimum? Ideally, companies should develop between two to seven rules and nothing complex—marketing strategic rules should be easy-to-follow directives. It is better to have fewer rules when the market is unpredictable and you need flexibility. Also, when the rules go stale, they need to be changed. The basic tenet is that when business is complicated, marketing strategy should be simple.

Scenarios and Simple Rules

Scenarios are especially useful for Simple Rule approaches as they can be used as triggers—that is, when events happen, the rules come into place. For example, Microsoft famously implemented a scenario to develop and introduce its Explorer Web browser when Internet activity reached a crucial level. However, according to Schnaars and Ziamou (2001), writing scenarios has become an idiosyncratic process, much like writing a novel.

They are normally written as narratives, like Hollywood scripts, that provide an image of some kind of future end-state. Such **scenarios are based on plots with beginnings, middles, and ends**. Another characteristic is that scenarios are usually written in sets of three or four. The final element is that most scenarios provide a progression from the present to the future, rather than provide a single-point forecast. They weave a plot that connects as a series of interrelated events. While there is a great deal of variety in the nature of scenario writing, when viewed as an aggregate, four steps can be observed:

1. The starting point for most scenarios is normally to identify the key drivers that will affect the issue at hand and thereby generate a list of trends or factors.
2. The next stage is normally to rank or combine all the identified drivers into a smaller, more meaningful set that can be used for structure. One popular scheme ranks by uncertainty and impact using a PESTLE (political, economic, social, technological, legal, and environmental; see Chapter 3) environmental scan analysis. A PESTLE can be used to identify the kinds of issues facing an organization over a defined period (say, five years). These issues can be scored on two scales: certainty and importance from 1 (low) to 5 (high) (see Figure 1.8).
3. Write the scenarios: three scenarios remain the most popular ('best guess', 'base case', and 'middle ground'). However, drilling down to just two scenarios overcomes the problem of focusing on middle ground. Good practice is to identify the most likely scenario.
4. Finally, a single marketing strategy has to be created to cope with the identified scenarios. One of the key problems in scenario writing is the 'reduction problem' of reducing the multitude of plausible scenarios to just 2 to 5. The best way of doing this is to keep the initial analysis simple and to combine trends and events into logical themes. It is not as easy as it sounds.

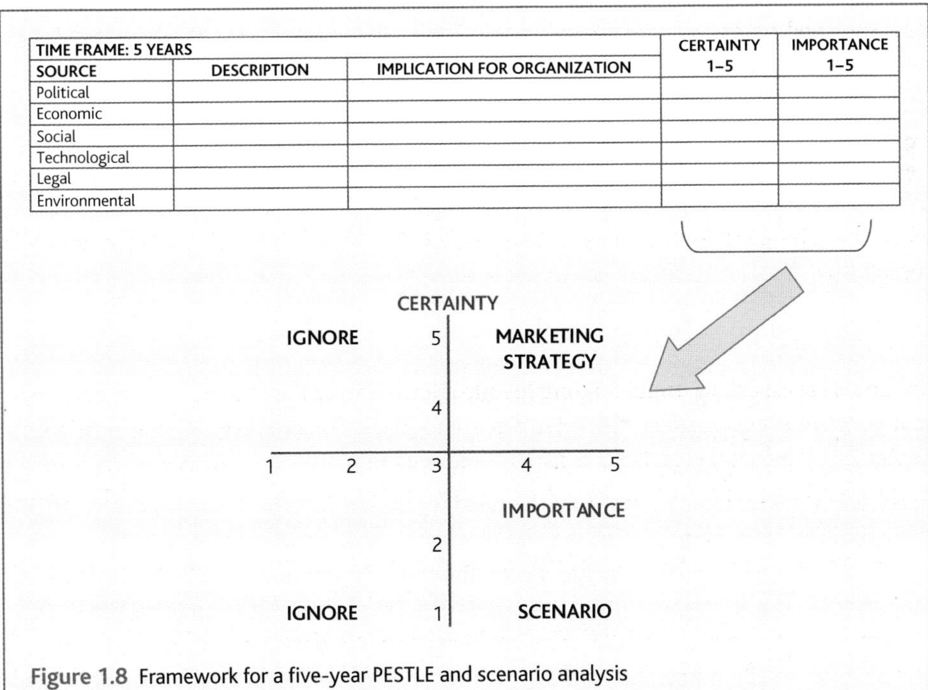

Figure 1.8 Framework for a five-year PESTLE and scenario analysis

Summary

Overall, 'Simple Rules' is an approach particularly well suited to complex markets. How do you identify the Simple Rules to use? You need to Think First and establish your business model and propositions. Once you have done this, you can identify, establish, and put your simple marketing strategy rules into place. To do this, the much-neglected Thinking First art of scenarios can be utilized. Scenarios are often misunderstood as part of competitive marketing strategy, but can aid a Simple Rules marketing strategy.

Market-oriented strategy

Market-driven firms, such as Tesco and BMW stand apart by their devotion to customer value and their culture, process, and abilities. Many firms attempt to adopt a market-oriented strategy, but according to Day (1998), many adopt one of three less successful orientations: the 'self-centred', the 'customer compelled', and the 'sceptical'. **Each orientation is a form of myopia that inhibits organizations from realizing the potential from their marketing strategy**.

Successful organizations are the most prone to the **self-centred trap** as they take their place for granted. Generations of managers emphasize maximizing returns and have an increasingly inward focus, until the original value proposition is distorted beyond recognition. IBM's orientation of the 1980s is a classic example: its strong profitability masked a total loss of focus as the company became distant, arrogant, and unresponsive. By 1990, it had squandered its trust with customers with IBM-compatible competitors educating them on the alternatives.

Customer-compelled organizations try to be all things to their markets. This trap leaves most organizations unable to set priorities on which markets to serve. Compelled by customers, each function acts separately and tries to find new segments, features, or points of differences. Thus, IBM attempted to satisfy large and medium-sized customers in every industry in the early 1990s with a total offering that was incoherent.

The **scepticism trap** is a curious backlash to the customer focus. The assertion is that customers cannot envision breakthrough products and seldom ask for products that they later come to value. Customer research leads to bland offerings and is a distraction to the real work. For example, Motorola's research on the cellular phone concept was met with discouraging customer feedback. While such examples abound, Day considers that they miss the point. Truly breakthrough products require an intimate understanding of customer behaviour, latent needs, changing requirements, and deep-seated dissatisfaction with current alternatives. Thus, the potential fax-machine market of the early 1970s, was estimated based on the need for urgent written messages given existing technologies.

The desire to satisfy customers has a common-sense appeal as well as being likely to lead to greater loyalty and higher future profits than otherwise. Lots of companies have extensive and rigorous customer satisfaction measurements, but **it is not always clear that the right variables are being measured or that the data are being used in anything other than a reactive way**. The focus for many firms has been 'internal' (preventing dissatisfaction), rather than 'external' (increasing satisfaction). Too great an internal focus can lead to getting stuck in a customer satisfaction rut (Dahisten, 2003).

Volvo is generally regarded as a company at the forefront of customer satisfaction practices. Product quality is seen as equivalent to customer satisfaction within the company as noted in their policy: 'Customer satisfaction is the way we measure quality.' However, interviews amongst managers have revealed divergent views about what constitutes customer satisfaction. For example, Dahisten (2003) found one manager who asserted that customer satisfaction 'equals no mistakes', whereas another saw it more closely aligned with customer delight by defining it as: 'Positively surprise the customer'. Other views were that it was, 'having the right range of attributes in the product profile', and somewhat tautologically, customer satisfaction 'is what is being measured'.

Unfortunately, there is a range of variables that can influence customer satisfaction and measurement itself can sometimes take precedence. Volvo's measures are primarily quantitative (as with other car manufacturers) and it only uses qualitative occasionally, such as when designing new vehicles. Topics surveyed include satisfaction with the car, sales, and workshop experience. Owners are the primary subjects and comparisons made to rival brands to show Volvo's position. A huge amount of data is produced and largely analysed in a descriptive way. Managers rarely question the validity of the data. The data are used in an action-oriented approach, rather than a knowledge-enhancing one. Actions are generally focused on the short-term and mainly on complaints.

Recognizing the need for a greater extrinsic focus to provide greater customer satisfaction insight, Volvo has added a more proactive approach to its research. Principally, qualitative has been added to the mix with much greater direct customer contact involving engineering teams, senior managers, and dealers. Interactions with customers on the Web and through local workshops in different markets are being made so that customers shifting perceptions of issues, such as on safety, are being more strongly tracked. Lost-sales analyses have been instigated to capture the perceptions of customers who decided not to buy Volvo. Product development projects capture customer satisfaction issues at the development stage, rather than only at production. This has been exemplified by Volvo's recent SUV, the XC90, which was developed from the beginning with customer satisfaction in mind with the aid of a group of female customers in California.

Summary

'Market-Driven Marketing Strategy' has its weaknesses, but remains the primary approach. Marketing is an activity that continues to rely largely upon the successful generation, dissemination, and response to market intelligence (see, for example, Matsuno and Mentzer, 2000). Marketing strategy, as suggested in this book, is part and parcel of a market-driven approach.

The book's perspective

In reality, marketing strategy is neither completely deliberate nor cognitive or completely emergent as practised by leading exponents such as the General Electric Corporation (GEC) (see Mintzberg, 1990; and Ocasio and Joseph, 2008). As such, the book's thesis is that marketing strategy is endemic. The central structure of the book is thus unashamedly on the 'deliberate' Thinking First side, resting on four central questions:

1. Where are we now?
2. Where do we want to be?
3. How will we get there?
4. Did we get there?

This is the most widely used competitive marketing strategy framework. Figure 1.9 identifies how the chapters fit the framework. The particular value of the where/where/how/did framework is that the four stages neatly define the necessary mindsets and place the associated key tools to develop the marketing strategy.

Another way of looking at the book's structure is provided in Figure 1.10, which sets out a strategy **blueprint**. You can see that the key tools at **phase one** provide an audit, a starting point with an environmental scan. Every organization has to grapple with thousands of activities in their markets every day and so the starting point of any marketing strategy must be to get a definite understanding of the key ones to include in the plan (events that are important and likely to happen) by using a scanning tool such as PESTLE to identify the key activities and those that might feature in a scenario, along with a five forces analysis (see Chapter 3). These tools can be applied in a variety of ways and finally placed within the context of strategic fit with a tool such as a SWOT (strengths, weaknesses, opportunities, threat) or TOWS analysis (see Chapter 3).

Phase two sees the narrowing of marketing **strategy** in terms of portfolio analysis, objectives, segmentation, targeting, and positioning. These are the crucial and central decisions

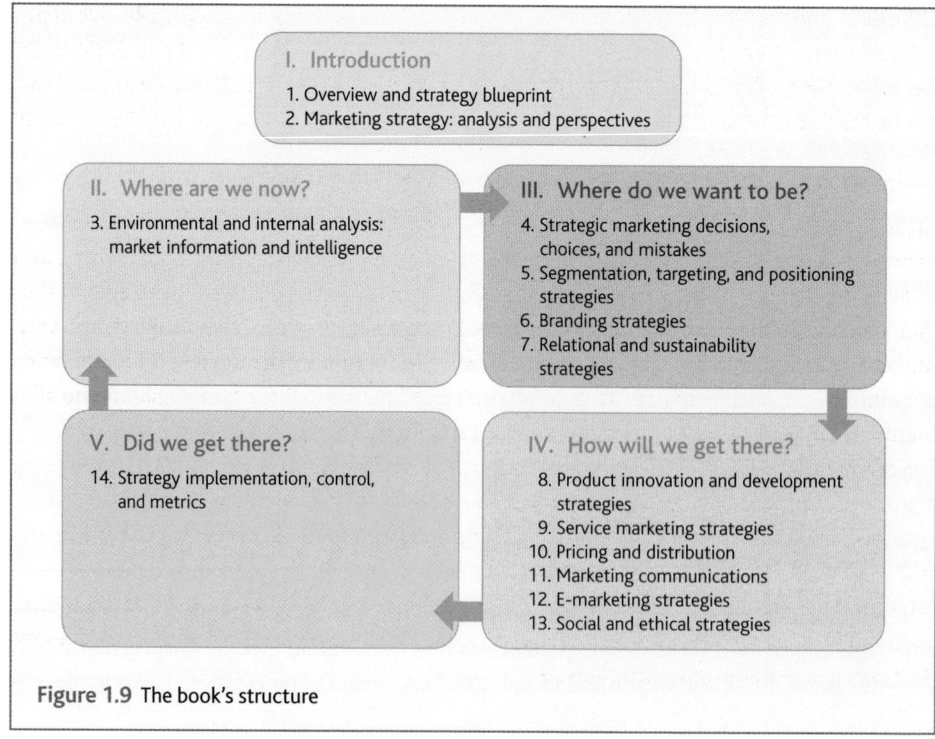

Figure 1.9 The book's structure

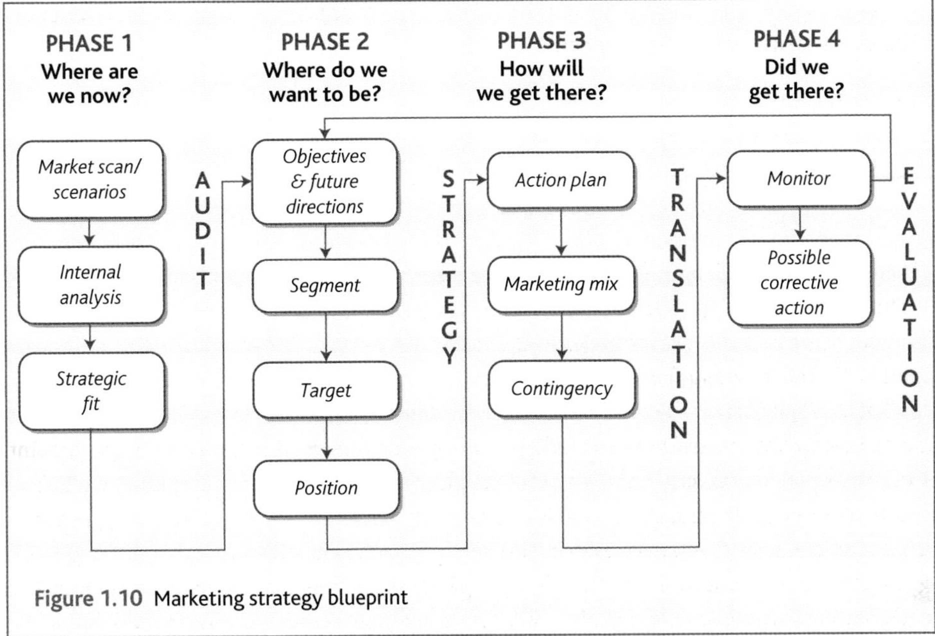

Figure 1.10 Marketing strategy blueprint

in the development of any competitive marketing strategy. They are linked to the audit in that where you are now will greatly affect where you want to go. For example, if the audit identifies that the market is largely unattractive, it will affect the portfolio analysis, then the objectives and future direction may focus upon seeking new segments, distributive channels, or geographic markets and this will affect subsequent targeting and positioning. On the other hand, if the market is highly attractive, the objectives will likely be to stay with the existing market and products or services leading to market share or customer loyalty objectives.

The concern of **phase three** is how will we get there? This involves the **translation** of the strategy to the marketing mix. The focus here is on product innovation and development, branding, services, pricing and distribution, marketing communications, e-marketing, and social and ethical strategies. In the book, each of these is examined from a strategic, rather than a tactical perspective. Good practice would suggest that organizations set aside a contingency in case either the strategy or tactics (or both) do not work out and additional funds are needed. This rarely happens but at least 10 to 20 per cent of the budget should be allocated for the 'just in case'.

Finally, having decided on how to get there, the question of 'Did we get there?' is reviewed in **phase four**. Here, the organization needs to undertake an evaluation based upon a dashboard of metrics (Farris et al., 2006), which may cover such elements as share of hearts and minds and markets, margins and profits, product and portfolio management, customer profitability, channel management, pricing strategy, advertising and promotion, and finance. Corrective action may be required if things are going badly, which will necessitate a review of the chosen objectives and future direction.

What to choose

Considering marketing strategy overall, the key issue is to recognize what approach is **appropriate**. Both Thinking First and Seeing First are largely **cognitive**, whereas Doing First and Simple Rules are largely **experiential** in nature. On the other hand, both Doing First and Thinking First are largely ongoing and formative, whereas Simple Rules and Seeing First are largely immediate in their application. 'Largely' is the key word here as there are elements of experience, cognition, immediacy, and longer timescales in all four approaches.

Thinking First/Market Orientation works best when the issues are clear, the data are reliable, the context is structured, thoughts can be pinned down, and discipline can be applied. On the other hand, Seeing First works best when many elements have to be creatively applied, commitment to solutions is key, and communications across boundaries are needed (e.g., in new product development (NPD)). Doing First or Simple Rules work best when the situation is novel and confusing, complicated specifications would get in the way, and a few simple relationship rules can help move the process forward.

Throughout, the postmodern orientation needs to be continually borne in mind to provide a check on how, in reality, buyers will interpret the final offering, but the book essentially takes a 'Thinking First' view of competitive marketing strategy from a market-driven perspective. Thus, it nods more towards the Igor Ansoff (1991) synoptic and deliberate approach to strategy than the more incremental and emergent approach advocated by Henry Mintzberg (1990).

How important is marketing strategy?

From a study of 160 companies carried out between 1986 and 1996, Nohria et al. (2003) provide some interesting insights into the importance of strategy to any business. They found that companies that outperformed their rivals **excelled at the four primary management practices of strategy, execution, culture, and structure**. These were then supplemented by any two out of four secondary management practices of talent (holding onto talented employees), innovation (industry-transforming), leadership (finding leaders committed to the business and staff), and mergers and acquisitions. They called this winning combination the '4 + 2 formula' for business success, and it was found to provide a 90 per cent chance of sustaining superior performance.

Winners develop and maintain a performance-oriented culture. Home Depot, for example, gives associates (a term applied to all employees) a sense of ownership of the stores. Store managers are allowed to determine their own layout and there is no sense of a command-and-control leadership. Nohria et. al (2003) found that 90 per cent of winners linked pay to performance. With regard to structure, winners built and maintained fast, flexible, and flat organizations. Procedures and protocols were used, but winners trimmed as much red tape as possible for everyone, including vendors and customers.

Surprisingly, while winners were found to excel in the four primary areas, it did not make any difference which two secondary areas they chose (talent, innovation, leadership, and mergers and acquisitions) and there was no improvement if they went beyond 4 + 2.

How do you articulate marketing strategy? A marketing strategy statement needs to be succinct and to the point and it should ideally be possible to summarize it in about 30 to 40 words. If few people in an organization can do this then it is likely that the organization has failed to articulate its marketing strategy strongly enough or, more likely, that they do not have one. There is often confusion over how strategy differs from other organizational 'directional statements'. A quick snapshot of the hierarchy would be:

- **Mission:** why the organization exists.
- **Values:** what the organization believes in and how it behaves.
- **Vision:** where the organization wants to go to.
- **Strategy:** what the competitive 'game plan' will be.

Conclusion

Developing a marketing strategy is a largely subjective activity. This book suggests that Thinking First is the best model to adopt, based on a rational and linear thinking perspective. Nevertheless, while Thinking First dominates our view of marketing strategy, there are alternative approaches. Seeing First suggests taking a single glance at the organization and its market to produce the key flash of insight of the central strategy. For example, the flash of insight from Sir Stelios Haji-Ioannou and his easyGroup was that the market wanted 'simple' (see Figure 1.11). Here is a list of 'simple' business units by date of introduction:

- 1995: easyJet
- 1999: easyInternet café
- 2000: easyCar
- 2001: easyValue.com
- 2001: easyMoney.com
- 2003: easyCinema.com
- 2004: easyBus.co.uk
- 2004: easyHotel.com
- 2004: easy4 men
- 2004: easyJobs.com
- 2004: easyPizza.com
- 2004: easyMusic.com
- 2005: easyCruise.com
- 2005: easyMobile.com
- 2005: easyWatch.com
- 2007: easyVan
- 2007: easyOffice.co.uk

Figure 1.11 The easyGroup

Source: With the kind permission of easyGroup.

On the other hand, Doing First recognizes that Seeing First is rarely straightforward. Quite often in strategy, there is no clear way forward and so the best solution is to make a decision and to try and make sense of it—then repeat the successful bits—and leave out the rest. A number of companies have undertaken acquisition and mergers (A&M) on the basis of Doing First. Sometimes they work (e.g., Vodafone and AirTouch Communications) and sometimes they do not (e.g., Daimler Benz and Chrysler), and it is not always clear what makes the difference. Often it is culture, but it can be resources or market issues and it is only by trying out A&M that such aspects are revealed, such is the complexity of the activity. There is a difference between acquiring a company, where the acquirer takes charge (sometimes called a takeover, which may be friendly or hostile), and merging, where both companies integrate on a largely equal basis.

Simple Rules are especially relevant to complex markets, where triggers can be established to set strategies in motion. Thus, a tea manufacturer might decide to introduce a herbal tea range if the market reaches a certain size or a rival does something similar. Once the manufactuerer establishes the rules for this, the rules are not matters for debate, but should be followed to the letter.

Postmodern strategy offers a completely different view to Thinking First. The postmodern view of marketing is that the scientific twentieth century of marketing is waning in impact as buyers know many of the 'tricks of the trade'. Even on the business-to-business side, buyers are more aware of the techniques and practices of marketing and as a consequence are more wary. Faced with cynical and suspicious buyers, the argument is that the tried and trusted tools of marketing no longer have such saliency and there are certainly numerous examples where more irreverent approaches to the marketing of mainstream products have been successful, such as with Tango. Postmodernism reminds us that Thinking First and the logical and rational development of marketing strategies can neglect the all-important question of how the intended audience will respond to the strategy. For example, a claim that a dishwasher tablet is 'new and improved' (even if true) may be greeted with derision. Having said that, there is nothing that stops a Thinking First approach arriving at a postmodern solution to a problem, if that is what is deemed best.

Marketers appreciate that there are constraints on our ability to make optimal choices. All decision-making is in a state of 'bounded rationality' owing to complexity, limited time, and inadequate mental computational power (Buchanan and O'Connell, 2006). Strategy has been shown to be a fundamental component of business success, along with execution, culture, and structure. Things can go badly wrong, such as with poor vertical communications or conflicting priorities, and they often do.

Summary

This chapter has taken a somewhat 'left field' and alternative view of strategy. The book is devoted to a Thinking First and rational view of marketing strategy; this opening chapter has taken the opportunity to review and discuss alternative approaches that are less mainstream. A bit like learning to walk before you can run, Seeing First or Doing First are approaches to decision-making that normally need a prior understanding of Thinking First. You need to know the rules before you can break them. You can then break all the rules once you know what they are!

KEY TERMS

Doing First Making experimental strategic-marketing decisions and learning from mistakes and successes.

Postmodern A reaction to the 'modern' marketing practices of the twentieth century, favouring a more ironic, cynical, and less scientific view of marketing.

Scenarios Plausible written narratives based upon problems that exist in some small form today that may become unexpectedly important marketing problems in the future.

Seeing First Appreciating the wider strategic picture with one glance based upon insight.

Simple Rules Identifying market triggers that set in motion key changes in strategy.

Thinking First Rationally addressing marketing strategy problems with a view to finding a solution.

DISCUSSION QUESTIONS

1 Examine the pros and cons of the Seeing First approach to strategy.

2 Imagine a chocolate manufacturer is going to launch an ice cream based on its leading brand. It has decided there are too many uncertainties to be sure of the outcome and so is just going to 'do it' and see what happens. What kinds of things might it measure to see what did and did not work?

3 Would it be fair to say that there are more examples of postmodern approaches to strategy in consumer rather than in business markets? If so, why?

4 Write a short (single) scenario on one of the following markets with implications for marketing strategy:

(a) The personal digital audio player.

(b) An electric car.

(c) Convenience food.

ONLINE RESOURCE CENTRE

Visit the Online Resource Centre for this book for lots of interesting additional material at: **www.oxfordtextbooks.co.uk/orc/west2e/**

REFERENCES AND FURTHER READING

Ansoff, Igor. H. (1991), 'Critique to Henry Mintzberg's "the Design School: Reconsidering the Basic Premises of Strategic Management"', *Strategic Management Journal*, 12 (6), pp. 449–61.

Beer, Michael, and Russell A. Eisenstat (2000), 'The Silent Killers of Strategy Implementation and Learning', *Sloan Management Review*, 41 (4), pp. 29–40.

Berthon, Pierre R., Leyland F. Pitt, Ian McCarthy, and Steven M. Kates (2007), 'When Customers Get Clever: Managerial Approaches to Dealing with Creative Customers', *Business Horizons*, 50, pp. 39–47.

Brown, Stephen (2001), 'Torment Your Customers (They'll Love It)', *Harvard Business Review*, October, pp. 83–8.

Brown, Stephen (2003), 'Material Girl or Managerial Girl?', *Business Horizons*, July–August, pp. 2–10.

Buchanan, Leigh, and Andrew O'Connell (2006), 'A Brief History of Decision Making', *Harvard Business Review*, January, pp. 33–41.

Collis, David J., and Michael G. Rukstad (2008), 'Can you Say what your Strategy is?' *Harvard Business Review*, April, pp. 82–90.

Dahisten, Frederik (2003), 'Avoiding the Customer Satisfaction Rut', *MIT Sloan Management Review*, Summer, pp. 73–8.

Darroch, Jenny (2009), 'Drucker on Marketing: An Interview with Peter Drucker', *Journal of Academy of Marketing Science*, 38 (8), pp. 8–11.

Day, George S. (1998), 'What Does it Mean to be Market-driven?' *Business Strategy Review*, Spring, pp. 1–14.

Different Voice (2006), 'Leadership in Literature: A Conversation with Business Ethicist Joseph L. Badaracco, Jr.', *Harvard Business Review*, March, pp. 47–55.

Eisenhardt, Kathleen M., and Donald N. Sull (2001), 'Strategy as Simple Rules', *Harvard Business Review*, January, pp. 107–16.

Farris, Paul W., Neil T. Bendle, Philip E. Pfeiffer, and David J. Reibstein (2006), *Marketing Metrics: 50+ Metrics Every Executive Should Master* (Upper Saddle River, NJ: Wharton School Publishing).

Friestad, Marian, and Peter Wright (1994), 'The Persuasion Knowledge Model: How People Cope with Persuasion Attempts', *Journal of Consumer Research*, 21, pp. 1–31.

Geroski, Paul A. (1999), 'Early Warning of New Rivals', *Sloan Management Review*, 40 (3), pp. 107–16.

Gofee, Robert, and Gareth Jones (2000), 'Why Should Anyone be Led by You?' *Harvard Business Review*, September–October, pp. 63–70.

Hamel, Gary (1999), 'Bringing Silicon Valley Inside', *Harvard Business Review*, September–October, pp. 70–84.

Herbold, Robert J. (2002), 'Inside Microsoft: Balancing Creativity and Discipline', *Harvard Business Review*, January, pp. 73–9.

Mason, Katy, and Lloyd C. Harris (2005), 'Pitfalls in Evaluating Market Orientation: An Exploration of Executives', *Long Range Planning*, 38 (4), pp. 373–89.

Matsuno, Ken, and John T. Mentzer (2000), 'The Effects of Strategy Type on the Market Orientation–Performance Relationship', *Journal of Marketing*, 64 (4), pp. 1–16.

Mintzberg, Henry (1990), 'The Design School: Reconsidering the Basic Premises of Strategic Management', *Strategic Management Journal*, 11 (3), pp. 171–95.

Mintzberg Henry, and Frances Westley (2001), 'Decision Making: It's Not What You Think', *MIT Sloan Management Review*, 42, Spring, pp. 89–93.

Nohria, Nitin, William Joyce, and Bruce Roberson (2003), 'What Really Works', *Harvard Business Review*, July, pp. 42–53.

Ocasio, William, and John Joseph (2008), 'Rise and Fall—or Transformation? The Evolution of Strategic Planning at the General Electric Company, 1940–2006', *Long Range Planning*, 41 (3), pp. 248–72.

O'Donohoe, Stephanie (2001), 'Living with Ambivalence: Attitudes to Advertising in Postmodern Times', *Marketing Theory*, 1 (1), pp. 91–108.

Schnaars, Steven, and Paschalina (Lilia) Ziamou (2001), 'The Essentials of Scenario Writing', *Business Horizons*, 44 (4), pp. 25–31.

Szymanski, Stefan (1998), 'Why is Manchester United so Successful?' *Business Strategy Review*, 9 (4), pp. 47–54.

Tourish, Dennis (2005), 'Critical Upward Communications: Ten Commandments for Improving Strategy and Decision Making', *Long Range Planning*, 38, pp. 485–503.

Wallas, G. (1926), *The Art of Thought* (New York: Harcourt Brace).

Wright, Marian (1985), 'Schema Schema: Consumers' Intuitive Theories about Marketers' Influence Tactics', in *Advances in Consumer Research*, 13, Richard J. Lutz (ed.) (Provo, UT: Association for Consumer Research), pp. 1–3.

Vilà, Joaquim, and J. Ignacio Canales (2008), 'Can Strategic Planning Make Strategy More Relevant and Build Commitment over Time? The Case of RACC', *Long Range Planning*, 41, pp. 273–90.

Yip, George S., Alan M. Rugman, and Alina Kudina (2006), 'International Success of British Companies', *Long Range Planning*, 39, pp. 241–64.

END OF CHAPTER 1 CASE STUDY The Pelican College

Note: This case is fictitious; any resemblance to personal or business names is purely coincidental.

Introduction

You have been appointed to a position as a trainee consultant for Ace Strategies (Manchester). You receive a contract with your base salary and benefits, and an expense account. Arriving at 8.30 a.m. on your second day at Ace Strategies, you learn that your first job is to develop an initial speculative proposal for the 'The Pelican College' that will be used as the basis for future discussions when you meet the College representatives at the end of the week. The value of the account has yet to be decided.

Market overview

The Pelican College is a private institution founded in 1954, which see itself as one of the few in the market that offers quality training with a strong benefit to industry (but note that the overall private business-training sector has a poor image). The price of tuition is £2,300 to £7,100, with the average being around £5,000). Such private colleges generally appeal to students requiring quick results and/or speciality training.

The Pelican College employs about 120 people and enrols approximately 4,000 students annually in Birmingham, Leeds, Manchester, and Oxford. They staff four full-time placement people, delivering an average placement of graduates of 87 per cent. The Pelican College offers a solid service in that, once you have graduated from the College, their placement officers continue to assist graduates in finding suitable upgrade positions as the students feel they have outgrown their positions. They also employ career counsellors who assist students in deciding which course would be most beneficial. The Pelican College takes pride in not placing a student in a course in which they are not likely to succeed or find work.

Market

Currently, female students represent roughly 80 per cent of Pelican College students. There are three primary groups of targets:

- graduates with no or minimal work experience;
- people who have completed or have not completed GCSE or A level exams, but have a number of years of work experience and are seeking to upgrade their skills; and
- individuals who have been away from the workforce and are seeking a means of getting re-employed.

People's requirements

No or minimal work experience

Many students graduate or leave school without much work experience and have little idea of what they are going to do for a living. Those interested in college or university often find that they do not have the appropriate prerequisites for the course that interest them.

Individuals requiring upgrading

Lots of people find that they are stagnating in their current position and it may be that they are seeking more fulfilment, greater career opportunities, and/or more money. Also, they may be required to upgrade in order to prosper within their existing employ, whether it is to keep up with technology or their peers.

Re-entering the workforce

This category mainly consists of women who have been away from work for some time due to family considerations. As a result of the family growing up, boredom, divorce, or the need for income and/or self-improvement, they will often look for a refresher, upgrade, or basic skill course as a tool to enter/re-enter the workforce.

For someone who has been away for some time and lacks self-confidence, this can be a difficult first step. The entire process of seeking a school and/or work, can be very intimidating, especially after several rejections. Regulations on most courses stipulate that individuals must have certain prerequisites or must take entry exams. Applicants have been known to break down and cry or excuse themselves during such tests to go to the lavatory and never return.

Strategic direction of Pelican

Graduate market

- Capitalize on the Pelican College course benefits, which include shorter courses that provide students with the essential skills to obtain immediate employment in their area of interest.
- Emphasize that the Pelican College offers counselling on courses best suited to the applicant and that the course components resemble those that the student is likely to encounter within the new work environment.
- Communicate that classes are small, allowing for personal attention when necessary and that each class is designed to be self-paced.

In addition, it should be very clear to prospective students that Pelican College has a placement service with a very good record of performance. Concentrate on courses (see Table C1.1) which are likely to appeal to young graduates with no or minimal experience.

Upgrade market

- Once again, capitalize on the immediacy of Pelican College course benefits. With this category, day and night course flexibility should be communicated.
- Address the 'Achilles' heel' of people who are frustrated with their current situation and who want to make a change but believe that they would have to invest several years in extended education to obtain the necessary tools to do so.
- Perhaps appeal to individuals wanting to grow within their current field (i.e., the secretary wanting greater income could look at the Legal Secretary or Medical

Secretarial course). A legal secretary could look at a Professional Legal Assistant course. A business person may want to take an IT skills course to keep up with their peers and/or technology, an accounting clerk may want to take Advanced Accounting, and so forth. The placement service/record and individual counselling should not be ignored with this group.

Re-entry market

The strategy for this group should be designed to appeal to individuals who are lacking self-confidence and are not likely to respond to strategies appropriate for the upgrade market. These individuals are likely not to know where to start, despite a gnawing need to do something. The positioning should combine Pelican College's image and performance benefits, providing the prospect with a sense of hope and confidence. This group might be viewed as a new product introduction.

TABLE C1.1 Summary table of courses and markets at Pelican College

		Courses				
		Male %	Female %	Lack work experience %	Upgrade (work experience) %	Re-entering work force %
Travel and tourism	26	20	80	20	40	20
Administrative secretary	18	5	95	–	60	40
Legal secretary	20	10	90	40	–	60
Medical secretary	20	5	95	–	100	–
Professional legal assistant	44	25	75	–	100	–
IT & web skills	5	25	75	30	70	–
IT & accounting	13	35	65	25	–	75
		New courses being considered				
Personal assistant		–	100	25	75	–
Law office management		50	50	50	–	50
Advanced accounting	13	35	65	70	30	–

QUESTIONS

Despite its continued success, the Pelican College has appreciated for some years that while it has formulated a good overall value proposition for its market, it is unsure about how to formulate its future marketing strategy:

1. Should Pelican go with Thinking First, Seeing First or continue, as they seem to have been, with Doing First? What about the postmodern approach?
2. A lot of Pelican's younger students are really cynical about marketing. Might TEASE or the Seven Ss have a role to play? Would a combination of approaches work?

Source: This case was prepared by Douglas West of the University of Birmingham as the basis for analysis and class discussion and not to illustrate either effective or ineffective handling of an administrative situation.

2

Marketing strategy: analysis and perspectives

LEARNING OBJECTIVES

- Outline the importance of marketing strategy for corporate success
- Provide a historical review of strategy concept and explain how the concept has migrated from military planning to the business field
- Review the definitions of corporate strategy, business unit strategy, and functional strategies
- Review the nature and different definitions of marketing strategy
- Discuss the possible orientations of marketing strategy and define what competitive marketing strategy is
- Review the strategic 'linear' models/frameworks for strategy development

CHAPTER AT A GLANCE

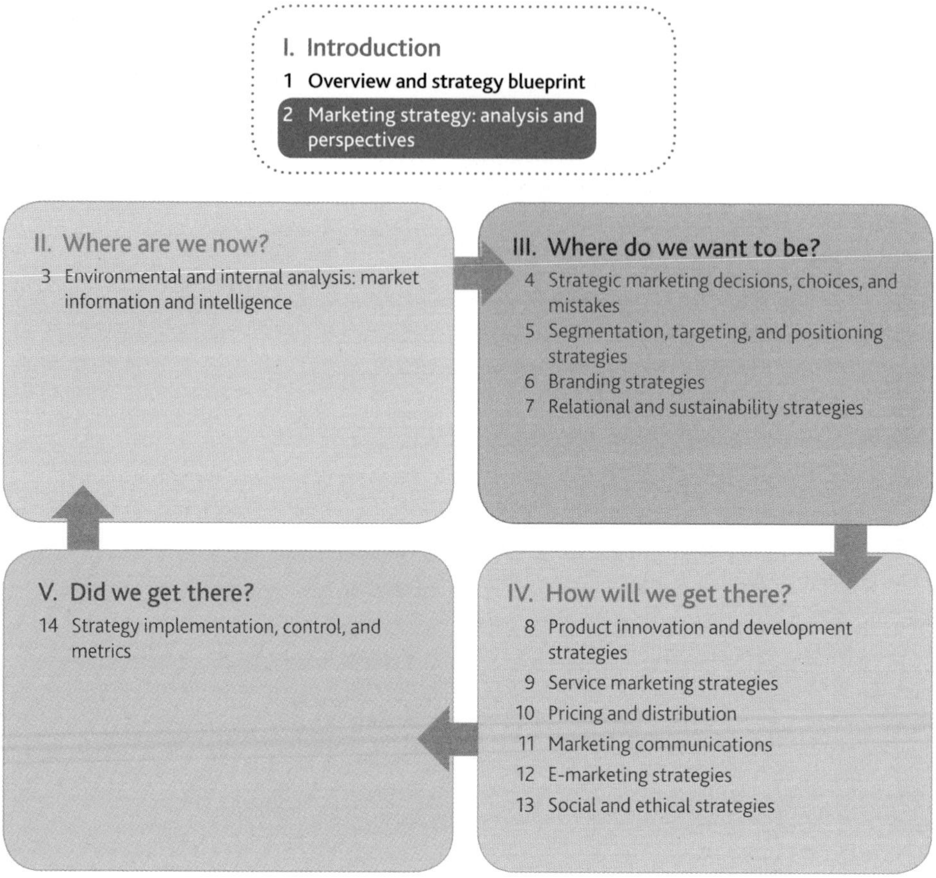

I. Introduction
1 Overview and strategy blueprint
2 Marketing strategy: analysis and perspectives

II. Where are we now?
3 Environmental and internal analysis: market information and intelligence

III. Where do we want to be?
4 Strategic marketing decisions, choices, and mistakes
5 Segmentation, targeting, and positioning strategies
6 Branding strategies
7 Relational and sustainability strategies

IV. How will we get there?
8 Product innovation and development strategies
9 Service marketing strategies
10 Pricing and distribution
11 Marketing communications
12 E-marketing strategies
13 Social and ethical strategies

V. Did we get there?
14 Strategy implementation, control, and metrics

Introduction

Marketing strategy has been the subject of considerable research in both the business and marketing literature over the past four decades. It has become an area of primary concern to all organizations, depending critically on a subtle understanding and analysis of the market. Its importance becomes even greater in today's ever-challenging and fast-changing business environment. According to Cravens et al. (2009), the development of marketing strategy in the complex and challenging business environment requires forming a strategic vision and selecting the market targeting and positioning strategy for each market target. At the centre of the process is the understanding of the marketing environment and competitive space.

The development of marketing strategy is essential for success not only in developed markets, where the competition can be intense and with every player attempting to gain market share, but also in emerging markets where the elements of product, price, communications, and distribution are recognized as valuable sources for competitive advantage. This importance becomes even more vital in the case of developing markets, where local producers are coming under increasing pressure to become more competitive in order to face the intense competition from their foreign counterparts.

In fact, increasing competition from abroad, coupled with environmental uncertainties, present a formidable challenge to the business community in these markets to formulate and implement their marketing strategy more effectively. No doubt, the presence and success of many global companies such as McDonald's, Toyota, Vodafone, Coca-Cola, and HSBC in several emerging markets have forced local companies to search for new competitive advantages through the effective use of their marketing resources. Ward and Lewandowska (2008) note that organizations aspiring to encounter the difficulties of fast-changing market environment and increasing global competition need strategic decisions to be founded on well-conceived strategies. Clearly defined and well-developed marketing strategies and plans are a must if the organization is to achieve its objectives in the markets in which it competes.

Marketing strategy in a changing environment

One of the greatest challenges facing marketing managers in today's changing business environment is the development of the critical strategic thinking and analytical skills required to adapt quickly and effectively to the environmental and market changes. According to Cravens et al. (2009), selecting strategies for fast-changing markets begin with the identification and evaluation of potential market changes and the strategy implications. Emerging from this process should be a strategic vision for the future. This vision provides the basis for developing strategic targeting and positioning changes based on the implications of the vision (e.g., changes in market boundaries and structure). Targeting and positioning strategy matches customer value opportunities against the organization's core capabilities (new product management, customer relationship management, and/or value chain management).

Fodness (2005) noted some strategic marketing initiatives of many well-known companies in response to environmental and market changes:

- Samsung parlaying its vast knowledge of consumer electronics into a cohesive strategy for designing digital devices for the home—many of which lead their product-market category.
- P&G emerging as a growth company after adding lateral marketing and seeking innovation from outside sources (new products, new markets, and new technologies).
- Retailer TK Maxx targeting 'something new every day' strategy at customers for whom shopping is like hunting.
- IBM rejecting traditional market research techniques in favour of listening to customer stories to really understand their markets.
- Hewlett-Packard extending beyond their traditional industry boundaries to open up new markets and to deliver new value to customers with HP PhotoSmart.

There is strong evidence that the credit crunch and economic downturn of 2008–9 have forced a number of organizations to walk out of the market because of their weak/slow response to environmental change, and the lack of adequate adaptability skills to face these challenges. The success of large and small organizations in such market situations depends primarily on the management ability to understand the marketing environment in which they operate, and on their ability to think critically and act strategically to adapt quickly to any market changes. Trim and Lee (2008) note that the strategic marketing concept should be viewed as all-embracing, flexible, and adoptable. It requires that marketing managers ensure that the organization achieves a sustainable competitive advantage through a structured approach to planning and strategy development.

Strategy concept and definitions

Originally, the word *strategy* comes from the Greek word *strategos*, strictly meaning a general in command of an army; it is formed from 'stratos', meaning army and 'ag', meaning to lead. Therefore, the concept of 'strategy' was first introduced and defined in ancient military dictionaries. Strategy is defined in military literature as 'a plan of attack for winning the battle' or 'a plan for beating the opposition'. Similar definitions are used today in the business field. Researchers are still examining the effective application of strategy in the military field (Frentzel et al., 2000). The militaristic roots of the term strategy are well documented, with some key components of the military view of strategy having been transferred to business usage. In reflecting upon the link between military and business usage of the strategy concept, it has been claimed that the discourse and practice of strategy is distinctively a mechanism of power, whether seen from a military or business perspective (Horton, 2003).

The word 'strategy' appeared for the first time in the business literature in 1952 in a book by William Newman. At that time, strategy was implicitly regarded as a plan for achieving organizational goals. Since then, there have been several attempts in business literature to present the concept of strategy. Most notable are the pioneering works by Ansoff (1965), Andrews (1971), and Hofer and Schendel (1978). The contributions of those writers and others can be classified into three categories. In the first category are writers who produced analytical or rationalistic models, which while precise, are neither sufficiently comprehensive nor useful enough for practice. In the second category are those who were more eclectic and introduced a range of frameworks that collectively define the underlying notion of strategy in business management. Finally, some writers have been primarily 'verbal' in presenting their understanding of strategy.

The increasing pace of environmental change over the past three decades forced management to make their strategies explicit and to change them frequently. Responding to such circumstances, academic interest in strategy has grown rapidly. Cummings and Daellenbach (2009) state that there has been much debate in business literature about 'what strategy really is', and whether one view of what it is is better than another. Therefore, it is not surprising today to find a profusion of books and articles on strategic planning, corporate strategy, business strategy, and marketing strategy—a fashionable word in business language.

Strategy has been defined in a very short manner as 'the means an organization uses to achieve its goals'. Whilst this definition describes strategy as a means to achieving a company's objectives, it does not establish a distinct boundary between strategies and tactics, and it seems to ignore the influence of business environment on strategy development. It is also not clear in this definition what type of organizational decisions can be regarded as strategic and what distinguishes these decisions from other operational decisions. This question is central in any discussion of strategy. Cummings and Daellenbach (2009) raise a similar question: is strategy just plans made by senior strategists; or can even the smallest micro-activity be strategic—and if so, how do we know which are strategic and which are not? For example, how could we describe the decision by Dell to use a business model of selling directly to the consumer? Should it be regarded as a strategic decision or something else?

Taking two dimensions together, strategy can be defined as the overall plan for deploying an organization's resources to establish a favourable position in the market, while a tactic is a scheme for a specific action. It appears from this definition that one of the core tasks of strategy is identifying how a firm can deploy its resources in its market to satisfy its long-term goals and how it will organize its activities to execute this strategy. Honda UK, the Japanese car producer, announced a shutdown of its UK plant in Swindon for four months during 2009. This move was viewed by some experts as an operational decision in response to the downturn in the UK car market. Others have seen this move as a rather strategic decision that aims to redeploy the company's resources from a less profitable market (then) to more attractive areas.

Adding a competitive dimension, Wilson and Gilligan (2005) defined strategy as the broad statement of the way in which the organisation sets out to achieve its objectives. Included within this would be a series of decisions for the markets in which the organisation will operate, the type of products/services it will offer and the basis of the competitive stance.

From a multi-angular view, Mintzberg and Quinn (1996) proposed five definitions of strategy (5Ps)—strategy as plan, ploy, pattern, position, and perspective—and looked at some of the interrelationships between these five definitions. The preceding definitions reflect that successful strategies are typically characterized by four key ingredients:

1. They are directed toward unambiguous long-term goals.
2. They are based on insightful understanding of the external environment.
3. They are based on intimate self-knowledge by the organization or individual of internal capabilities.
4. They are implemented with coordination and effective harnessing of the capabilities to achieve the competitive position targeted.

Having reviewed the concept of strategy in terms of its dimensions, ingredients, and characteristics, three types of strategy can be specifically defined in relation to organizational structure. Varadarajan and Jayachandran (2000) note that strategy exists at multiple levels in an organization: *corporate*, *business unit*, and *functional* levels. Figure 2.1 shows this hierarchical relationship.

Corporate strategy

Corporate strategy describes a company's overall direction in terms of its general attitude toward growth and the management of its various businesses and product lines to achieve a balanced portfolio of products and services. Additionally, it is (a) the pattern of decisions regarding the types of business in which a firm should be involved; (b) the flow of financial

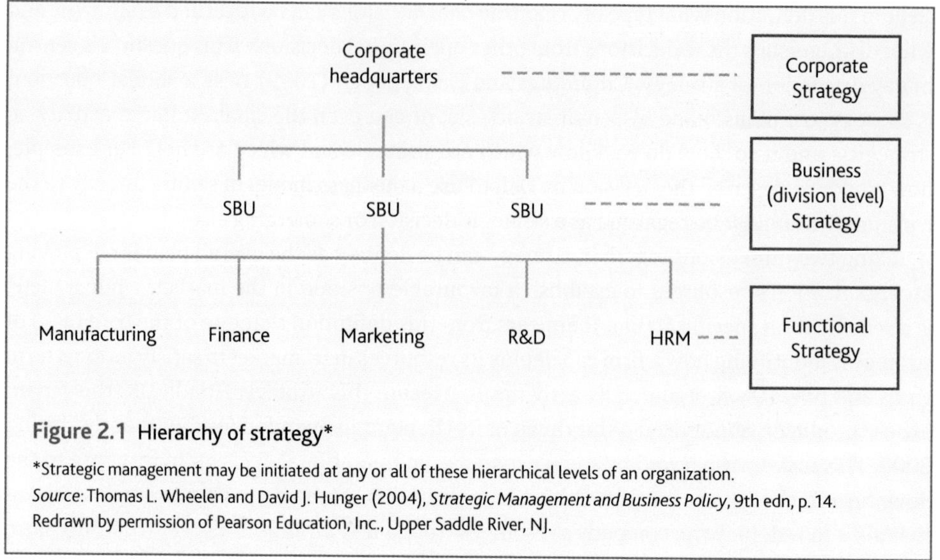

Figure 2.1 Hierarchy of strategy*

*Strategic management may be initiated at any or all of these hierarchical levels of an organization.
Source: Thomas L. Wheelen and David J. Hunger (2004), *Strategic Management and Business Policy*, 9th edn, p. 14. Redrawn by permission of Pearson Education, Inc., Upper Saddle River, NJ.

and other resources to and from its divisions; and (c) the relationship of the corporation to key groups in its environment. In a drastic change to the company corporate strategy, AT&T decided to obtain local access for its long-distance customers and chose to acquire the country's biggest cable operators, TCI and Media One, for $110 billion. These acquisitions put AT&T directly into the booming Internet business. This was a significant advantage of the company's corporate strategy.

Business strategy

Sometimes called competitive strategy, business strategy is usually developed at divisional level and emphasizes improvement of the competitive position of a corporation's products or services in the specific industry or market segment served by that division. Just as corporate strategy asks what industry the company should be in, business strategy asks how the company or its SBUs should compete or cooperate in each industry. In order for AT&T to achieve its corporate objective described above, should the company purchase more cable companies (very expensive), form strategic alliances with cable companies (many of them are not interested), or should it try something different? Business strategies should also integrate various functional activities to achieve divisional objectives.

Functional strategy

Financial strategy is concerned with maximizing resources productivity. Within the constraints of the corporate and business strategies around them, functional departments, such as marketing, finance, R&D, and production, develop strategies to pull together their various activities and competencies to improve performance. But where should a function be housed? Should it be integrated within the organization or purchased from an outside

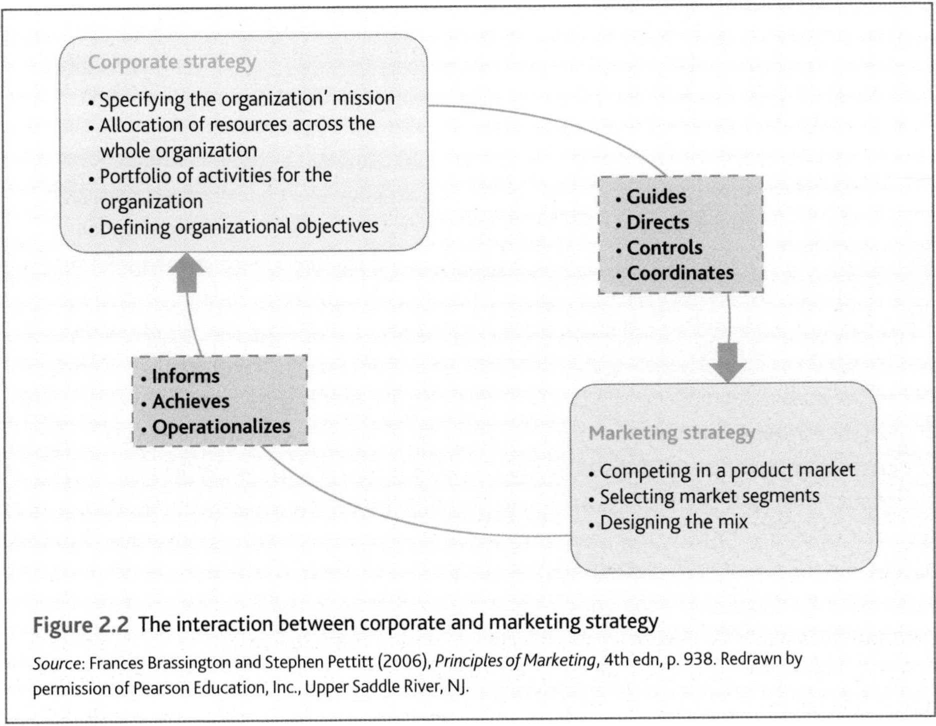

Figure 2.2 The interaction between corporate and marketing strategy

Source: Frances Brassington and Stephen Pettitt (2006), *Principles of Marketing*, 4th edn, p. 938. Redrawn by permission of Pearson Education, Inc., Upper Saddle River, NJ.

contractor? Some voices suggest that organizations should purchase from outside only those activities that are not critical factors to the company's distinctive competencies. Otherwise, the company may give up the capabilities that made its success in the first place. Therefore, outsourcing decisions are at the top of the agenda of major corporations. A recent survey in the US showed that 94 per cent of the US firms outsource at least one activity. The outsourced activities found are general and administrative (78 per cent), human resources (77 per cent), information systems (63 per cent), distribution (66 per cent), manufacturing (56 per cent), marketing (51 per cent), and finance and accounting (18 per cent) (Wheelen and Hunger, 2004).

The three levels of strategy form a hierarchy of strategy development within any large corporation. They interact closely and constantly and must be well integrated for corporate success. Figure 2.2 illustrates how corporate and marketing strategy interact together to achieve the overall objectives of an organization.

Marketing strategy: nature and definitions

In the early 1980s, marketing strategy was seen as being an indication of how each element of the marketing mix will be used to achieve the marketing objectives. According to this view, marketing strategy was defined as 'the broad conception of how product, price, promotion and distribution are to function in a co-ordinated way to overcome resistance to meeting marketing goals' (O'Shaughnessy, 1995). This definition gave a complete reliance on the marketing mix and, therefore, the utilization of the mix elements is the marketing strategy. It shows how the key features of the firm's offerings (4Ps) are intended to achieve the marketing and company objectives.

Later, this view was broadened to incorporate other marketing concepts (e.g., segmentation and positioning, product life cycle, market share, and competition) when defining marketing strategy. Utilizing these concepts/bases, marketing strategy has typically been seen as being part of the long-term planning of the marketing function. Utilizing the concept of segmentation and positioning, marketing strategy was defined as a means that identifies the target markets toward which activities are to be directed and the types of competitive advantages that are to be developed and exploited in each target market (Dibb et al., 2006). This definition advocates the use of segmentation and targeting concepts and, hence, the competitive advantages are directed to specific market segment/s. The marketing targeting strategy aims to select groups of consumers (or organizations) that the management wishes to serve in the product market. Once the company's target markets are identified and their relative importance to the firm is determined, the management will be in a position to select/design the company's positioning strategy. The market positioning strategy is the employment of the organization's product, distribution, price, and promotion activities to position the company's offerings against the competitor's offerings in meeting the needs and wants of the target market. The positioning strategy provides the unifying concept for deciding the role of each component of the marketing mix.

Earlier, Ries and Trout (1981, p. 219) stated that:

> positioning strategy is thinking in reverse. Instead of starting with yourself, you start with the mind of prospect. Instead of asking what you are, you ask what position you already own in the mind of prospect.

Thus, the concept of positioning goes beyond image creation, which merely identifies the attributes that are strengths, to provide guidance on which attributes should be used in the positioning/repositioning strategy.

The above definitions seem to belong to the school of thought that sees 'marketing' as an organizational function, and believes that marketing strategy is one of the firm's functional strategies, which is developed within the marketing department and aims to achieve marketing goals only. The differences between the definitions could be attributed to the different dimensions of marketing strategy being defined.

Acknowledging the role marketing can play to contribute towards the organization's strategic directions in a market, Baker (1992), at a very simple level, defined three principal marketing strategies: differentiated, undifferentiated, and concentrated. The definitions of these three marketing strategies seem to be similar to those of Porter's generic strategies (i.e., low-cost, differentiation, and focus) which normally occur outside the marketing department.

Another approach to defining marketing strategy, which recognizes the contributions of marketing in the organization's strategic directions, is the use of Ansoff's classical matrix that combines the two dimensions of 'products to offer' and 'market to target'. According to this approach, four strategies are defined: *market-penetration strategy*, *market-development strategy*, *product-development strategy*, and *diversification strategy*. When market and product are combined, this will produce a *market-penetration/development strategy* by which a company can capture a large share of an existing market for its current products or develop markets for its current products. Producers of consumer products such as P&G, Unilever, and Colgate-Palmolive are very experienced in using advertising and other communication tools to implement a market-penetration strategy to gain the dominant market share in a market. By means of a *product-development strategy*, a company can develop new products for existing markets or develop new products for new markets. The Sara Lee Corporation uses its successful brand name 'Sara Lee' to promote other products such as premium meats and freshly baked food products (see Mini Case Study 2.1).

MINI CASE STUDY 2.1 A bird in hand is worth two in the bush

It's easy to lose sight of how much can be gained from looking after the customers you already have when you are always pursuing new ones.

Most marketers work hard at chasing and seducing new customers. But many of us are playing the field too much and are missing the value of our existing customers. The great thing about encouraging the costumers we already have to use more of our product or service is that it can be done on a shoestring. How? By using every bit of the brand that touches our customers, from packaging to the Web, not just as a communication tool, but to actively promote usage.

The first way of growing business from exiting costumers is to keep them interested in your product or service. Take the example of the online network Linked In—a sort of Facebook for business people. The risk with this service is that people stop using the site after the novelty has worn off. A clever new feature on Linked In's home page now suggests people you may want to connect to. In my case it was scarily accurate, and this morning I linked to four interesting new contacts and so spent time on the site again. And as you accept or reject recommendations, the system gets smarter as to whom to suggest.

Another way of growing is to build your brand's share of usage with those customers you already have. In many markets consumers have a 'repertoire' of several products they use, with the task being to become one of their favourites. A good example of such a market is breakfast cereals. Most of us have several boxes of cereal, with a couple being used regularly and the others stuck at the back of a cupboard. One such brand was Weetabix, which had been tried by many people, but was a daily breakfast for few. So the brand used the idea of the 'Weetabix Week' to suggest different and interesting ways of eating Weetabix as a tasty and healthy breakfast. This idea is now communicated at the back of the pack, encouraging people to try new ways of eating the product at the moment they are consuming it. The brand's website has been transformed from a communication vehicle into an active sales booster, by highlighting the Weetabix Week. It has suggestions for a month of different breakfast ideas that you can print, and you can even sign up for daily email alerts.

Finally, you can try extended usage: encouraging customers to use your product in new ways. Hellmann's, the mayonnaise brand, grew its business by making recipe suggestions on its website and on packaging, suggesting to costumers that they use the brand as a cooking ingredient, not simply in sandwiches. The marketing team set itself an objective of getting every customer to use 'one cup more' of Hellmann's a year, with this being enough to increase sales by 5%.

The attraction of chasing after something new is always strong, whether or not you're talking about marketing. But as any life coach will tell you, making the most of what you already have can ultimately be more fulfilling and rewarding.

Source: David Taylor. This article first appeared in *The Marketer* (June, 2008), p. 13, the magazine of the Chartered Institute of Marketing.

Adopting a similar approach, it is possible to suggest numerous marketing strategies that exist in the categories of product line, pricing, distribution, and promotion. For example, combining promotion and distribution, a company can choose between a *push* and *pull* marketing strategy. Most of the large fast-moving goods (FMG) companies follow a push strategy by spending a great amount of money on a particular trade sector to gain/hold a shelf space in major retail outlets (Wheelen and Hunger, 2004). Also, with pricing and distribution, a company may adopt either a *skim-pricing marketing strategy* or a *penetration-pricing strategy*. Adopting a skim-pricing strategy enables the company to direct its products/services to the upmarket segment, charging differentiated (high) prices to customers who are willing (and can afford) to pay a premium for top-quality products/services (e.g., BA which arguably targets particular segments of the market and charges them premium price). By adopting *penetration-pricing strategy*, the company aims to direct its offerings to several market segments, charging lower prices in order to gain market share (e.g., KLM offers a wide range of prices that suit the majority of airline travellers).

Pulling these themes together, it could be argued that marketing strategy provides the concepts and process for gaining a competitive advantage by delivering superior value to a business's customers. Sharma (2004) describes marketing strategy as a means that aims to improve the strategic performance of an organization through the use of sub-strategies such as the development of new products, the development of new segments and/or customers, specialized delivery arrangements, after-sales service improvement, market forecasting, and market-share analysis.

Marketing strategy development

From the above definitions, one could argue that the development of marketing strategy can occur at three main levels of a firm. At the top level, the core strategy of the company is selected, and marketing objectives and the broad focus for achieving them are identified. At the next level, market segments and targets are selected and the company's differential advantage in serving the customer targets better than the competition can is identified.

Taken together, the identification of targets and the definition of differential advantage constitute the creation of the competitive positioning of the company and its offerings. At the functional level, a marketing department capable of putting the strategy into practice must be created. The marketing department, at this stage, is responsible for designing the marketing mix programmes that can convey both the positioning and the products/services to the target market (Hooley et al., 2004). Applying this structural concept of marketing strategy development to British Airways (BA), it is possible to see that at the first level, the company's core strategy and marketing objectives have been set to ensure that BA is the customer's first choice through the delivery of an unbeatable travel experience. At the next level, BA has elected to provide an overall superior service and good value for money in every market segment in which it competes. At the third level, BA's marketing mix programmes have been designed to support its product/service positioning at the forefront of the globalization of the airline industry. BA's marketing strategy is geared to sustaining a significant presence in the world market by emphasizing a consistent quality of customer service and the delivery of value for money.

TABLE 2.1 Selecting and developing marketing strategies for different market and competitive situations

	Important issues	Major actions/decisions
Product-market definition and analysis	• Evaluating the complexity of the product-market structure • Establishing product-market boundaries	• Defining product-market structure • Customer profiles • Industry/distribution/ competitor analysis • Market size estimation
Market segmentation	• Deciding which level of the product-market to segment • Determining how to segment the market	• Selecting the basis of segmentation • Forming segments • Analysing segments
Define and analyse industry structure	• Defining the competitive area • Understanding competitive structure • Anticipating changes in industry structure	• Sources of competition • Industry structure • Strategic group analysis
Competitive advantage	• Deciding when, where, and how to compete	• Finding opportunity gaps • Cost/differentiation strategy/focus • Good/better/best brand positioning strategy
Market targeting and positioning strategies	• Deciding market scope • Good/better/best brand positioning strategy	• Selecting targets • Positioning for each target • Positioning concept • Marketing mix integration

Source: David W. Cravens (1994), *Strategic Marketing*, p. 325. Reproduced by permission of McGraw-Hill Education, Inc.

Cravens (1994) suggested a stepwise approach to the development of marketing strategy for different markets and competitive situations. This approach is shown in Table 2.1, which presents the sequential steps to developing a marketing strategy, a summary of the important issues to be considered at each step, and the major actions/decisions that are required.

Marketing strategy orientation

It is useful at this point to shed light on the different orientations of marketing strategy. Should the development of marketing strategy be orientated by consideration of customers, competitors or both? During the 1960s and 1970s, academics and practitioners gave much consideration to customers and emphasized the importance of understanding and satisfying customers' needs and wants. In the late 1970s, competitor orientation was seen as preferable to a customer orientation. In the early 1990s, it was argued that organizations need to pay equal attention to both customers and competitors, that is, to adopt a *marketing orientation*. The contributions of marketing orientation to corporate success have been the subject of several studies that are discussed later in the chapter (see, e.g., Kohli and Jaworski, 1990, 1993; Narver and Slater, 1990; Slater and Narver, 1994, 2000; and Slater et al., 2004).

Ward and Lewandowska (2008) examined which particular orientation of marketing strategy (customer or competitor) would be most effective in which particular business environment, and suggested that a firm's emphasis on a particular orientation may yield different results in different business environments or industry situations. Their study found that a customer-orientated marketing strategy seems to be most effective in turbulent environments, while a competitor-orientated strategy would be best suited to placid-clustered environments and business conditions which are favourable and thus attract greater competition. Therefore, the focus on the aspects of the marketing orientation (customer versus competitor) for marketing strategy development should be determined based on the environmental conditions in which these aspects would best work.

The role of the marketing concept (orientation) in strategy development and corporate success

Marketing has been traditionally defined as 'a social process by which individuals and groups obtain what they need and want through creating, offering, and freely exchanging products and services of value with others' (Kotler and Keller, 2006). Marketing in this definition has been seen as a process of exchanging benefits (for more information about marketing as exchange process you can consult the classical article by Bagozzi (1975), who argues that the core of marketing is 'exchange').

From a different perspective, marketing has been defined as 'organisational activities that facilitate and expedite satisfying exchange relationships in a dynamic environment through the creation, distribution, promotion and pricing of goods, services and ideas' (Dibb et al., 2006). This definition seems to belong to the school of thought that describes 'marketing' as a set of specific activities undertaken by the marketing department at the functional level to achieve marketing goals only. However, Varadarajan and Jayachandran (2000) note that the 'marketing' function in organizations, besides being responsible for the content, process, and implementation of marketing strategy at the product-market level, plays a significant role in the strategy development process and the determination of strategy content at the business and corporate levels. The strategic role of marketing arises from the boundary-spanning nature of the marketing function (i.e., its interactions with consumers and competitors).

According to this view, marketing has an important role to play in strategy development and corporate success not only at the functional level, but also at the business and corporate levels. Marketing, therefore, can be described and categorized as **operational marketing**—that is, the classical commercial process of achieving a target market share through the use of tactical means related to the 4Ps, and **strategic marketing**—that is, to specify the firm's mission, define objectives, elaborate a development strategy, and ensure a balanced structure of the product portfolio (Lambin, 2000). Strategic marketing has been seen in a specific way by Trim and Lee (2008) as an intelligence focused and led process that has both an internal and an external dimension, which utilizes the skills of competitive intelligence officers who work with marketing managers and strategists to establish trust-based relationships throughout the partnership arrangement, which [...] ultimately results in the organization fulfilling its mission statement.

One of the major themes of strategic marketing is the development and implementation of the 'marketing concept'. It must be emphasized here that the marketing concept is not a second definition of marketing. The marketing concept is:

> a way of thinking—a management philosophy guiding an organisation's overall activities. This philosophy which holds the key to achieving organisational goals consists of the company being more effective than competitors in creating, delivering, and communicating customer value to its chosen target'. (Kotler, 2000)

As suggested by Nwokah (2008), the marketing concept defines a distinct organizational culture or business philosophy that puts the customer at the centre of the firm's thinking about strategy and operation. It also defines the set of activities developed by organizations to permanently monitor, analyse, and respond to market changes such as consumer preference, faster technological growth, and growing competitive rivalry.

Foley and Fahy (2009) argue that in response to the operationalization problem of the marketing concept, the seminal work of Kohli and Jaworski (1990) developed the three pillars of the marketing concept into precise aspects (manifestation) of what they call a 'market orientation', and for the first time, organizations were given a useful template for assessing how market-orientated they are. Since then, marketing orientation has become a popular term in the marketing literature that is frequently used as an indicator of the extent to which a firm implements the marketing concept. Marketing orientation holds that the key to achieving organizational goals such as market share, sales growth, and/or profitability, depends on identifying the needs and wants of the target market and delivering the desired satisfaction more effectively and efficiently than competitors. According to Nwokah (2008), a marketing-orientated firm is one that presumably has superior market-sensing and customer-linking capabilities, and these capabilities are presumed to assure it higher profits to outperform those organizations that are less market-orientated.

How significant is the adoption of a *market orientation* on the firm's strategy and business performance? While this question has been extensively examined in the marketing and strategy literature, the results of empirical research vary. The pioneering work by Kohli and Jaworski (1990, 1993) found that a market orientation provides a unifying focus for the efforts and projects of individuals, thereby leading to a superior performance. Similar results were found by Narver and Slater (1990), who concluded that a market orientation has, in some cases, a substantial positive effect on profitability. Subsequent research by Slater and Narver (1994, 2000; and Slater et al., 2004) found that a market-orientated culture provides the foundation for value-creating capabilities which enables businesses to consistently deliver superior value (that is, competitive advantage which leads to the achievement of superior performance) to customers. Other studies (e.g., Diamantopoulos and Hart, 1993; Greenly, 1995; Mavondo and Farrell, 2000; Hooley et al., 2003) have produced inconsistent results. Ward and Lewandowska (2008) provided a complete review of research studies that examined the relationship between marketing orientation and corporate success.

Despite the credibility and importance of the market orientation, Mason and Harris (2005) claim that it is still not being fully realized by practitioners. While many perceive their companies to be orientated to consumers, the evidence is contrary and the development of a genuine market orientation remains elusive. This study indicated that executives often develop skewed, inaccurate, or incomplete assessments of the market orientation of their company. Foley and Fahy (2009) also suggest that the proof of a positive relationship between market orientation and performance is not manifest. There is also a poor understanding of how market orientation affects strategy—and ultimately performance.

Competitive marketing strategy: various perspectives

What is competitive marketing strategy? Should it be viewed and defined as a typical marketing strategy which is orientated by the consideration of competition in the marketplace? Or should it be defined as a 'business' competitive strategy that is driven by the market orientation? The answer to this question requires some critical analysis and discussion of the definitions of both 'competitive strategy' and 'marketing strategy' before establishing what 'competitive marketing strategy' is.

Within the hierarchy of strategy development, the business unit strategy sits between the high level of corporate strategy and the detailed strategies for individual functions. Doyle and Stern (2006) pointed out that while corporate strategy sets the broad direction for the company, the business 'competitive' strategy details how a sustainable competitive advantage can be achieved, allowing the strategic business unit (SBU) to contribute to the overall corporate objectives. Aaker (2005) also noted that business strategy, which is sometimes termed competitive strategy, can be defined in terms of six elements or dimensions: (1) the product market in which the business is to compete; (2) the level of investment; (3) the functional area strategies needed to compete in the selected market; (4) the strategic assets or skills that underlie the strategy and provide the SCA; (5) the allocation of resources to the business units; and (6) the development of the synergistic effects across the businesses.

While this view refers implicitly to the competitive dimension of business strategy, other writers have been more explicit in defining business strategy as a competitive strategy. El-Morsy (1986), for example, suggested that:

> competitive strategy is a business strategy that discerns the basic forces affecting competitive conditions and their underlying structural causes, identifying the particular strengths and weaknesses of the firm vis-à-vis each underlying structural cause and determining offensive and defensive tactics for creating and maintaining a competitive position over time.

Also, Wheelen and Hunger (2004) noted that:

> business strategy which is often called competitive strategy focuses on improving the competitive position of a company's products or services within the specific industry or market segment that the company or business unit serves.

Two alternative orientations of competitive strategy can be reviewed (see Mini Case Study 2.2).

MINI CASE STUDY 2.2 Brand extension or ego trip?

Success in a new market will be out of reach unless your brand offers something new and relevant while avoiding stepping on the competition's toes.

Extending your brand beyond its original market remains a hot topic for many marketing teams. The most famous example of stretching a brand has to be Virgin, which sells everything from bridal gowns to business-class travel. Or maybe Apple. Its iPod or iPhone extensions have helped quadruple the share price over the past two years.

But diversifying successfully is a tricky business. More than half of all brand extensions fail, joining the likes of Cosmopolitan yoghurts, Bic perfume and Levi's suite in the overcrowded diversification graveyard. So what can we do to avoid betting on a dud? First and foremost we need to focus on bringing something new, different, and relevant to serve. This sounds obvious, but many companies get too big for their brand boots. They hope that simply slapping a popular name on an average product or service will guarantee success. This kind of brand ego trip can be expensive.

When we look more closely at Virgin, we find that for every successful extension such as Virgin Atlantic, there were also several flops. Virgin Vodka and Virgin Jeans both lacked the style credentials and differentiation to compete. Low price in an already flooded market was not enough to make it in those lifestyle categories. In contrast, Dove brought something new to the deodorant market when it successfully moved beyond soap bars to moisturising anti-perspirant. It also spent several years before the deodorant launch ensuring that the product offered effective enough protection to match the best on the market. Of course, Dove brand was already famous for the skin-friendly properties it was bringing to this new niche.

Apple's iPod and iPhone both built on the brand's reputation for beautifully designed and intuitive interface. Transferring brand benefits to new products and markets improves the chances that people will trust your new offer. It also means that the extension will further reinforce your brand. Many unsuccessful Easy Group extensions, such as men's cosmetics and pizzas, have had little connection with the original airline brand values of a no-frills service with cheaper prices for booking early.

Remember to be careful who you take on in a new market. Smart companies respect the competition because they will fight the new kid on the block with vigour. Procter & Gamble had the product technology and trusted brand, Pampers, to launch a successful baby shampoo. But the company still held back because the competitive response from market leader Johnson & Johnson would have led to a costly battle that just wouldn't have paid off.

So our watchword for new market ventures should not be 'What can the new market do for our brand?' but rather 'What can our brand do for the market?'

Source: David Taylor. This article first appeared in *The Marketer* (March, 2008), p. 13, the magazine of the Chartered Institute of Marketing.

Marketing-orientated competitive strategy

A marketing-orientated competitive strategy allows marketing to decide the direction pursued by a business, as well as adopt a supporting role in relation to strategy. Marketing can help to establish a match between firms and their environment by deciding: (1) what kinds of business firms may enter in the future; and (2) how the chosen field of endeavour may be successfully conducted in a competitive environment, by pursuing product, price, promotion, and distribution perspectives to serve target markets.

A marketing-orientated competitive strategy recognizes some alternative approaches for achieving differential advantage over competitors, such as concentrating on particular market segments, offering products which differ from other competitors' offerings, using better approaches to distribution and promotion activities, and putting more emphasis on price or non-price aspects. IKEA has been transformed from a local mail-order furniture business into one of the key retail furnishing businesses in the world by having a clear differential advantage over competitors and providing value-for-money products. The success of the company derives from the unique benefits it offers to customers and its consistent implementation of an effective marketing-orientated competitive strategy. Successful implementation of a marketing-orientated competitive strategy requires a sound organizational structure that places a major emphasis on the marketing concept as an overall business philosophy.

Technology-orientated competitive strategy

This strategy involves serving high-income markets with a flow of new, preferably unique, high-performance, and high-technology products. Microsoft, Mercedes-Benz, and Sony are typical examples of the large corporations that pursue technology leadership in their respective industries. Competitive strategies adopted by those companies have been developed to flag up their substantial investment in technology and R&D activities. Technological innovation provides an opportunity to develop an advantageous position for the longer term. The power of technology as a competitive weapon lies in its ability to alter competition through changing industry structure. In fact, technology and competitive strategy are inseparable and technological decisions are of fundamental importance to businesses as a valuable source of competitive advantage.

From the above definitions of competitive strategy and the previously discussed definitions of marketing strategy, it can be concluded that **competitive strategy** is a business strategy that exists at the SBU level and deals primarily with the question of competitive position, while **marketing strategy** is arguably seen as a functional strategy that is limited to the actions of specific functions within an organization. The differences between competitive and marketing strategies are shown in Table 2.2.

Several points can be noted from this table. Competitive strategy, in most cases, is developed at a higher strategic level (the SBU) than marketing strategy, which develops at the operational level of functional areas. Competitive strategy development involves four key factors: determination of mission statement; evaluation and selection of generic strategies; objectives setting; and policy-making. On the other hand, marketing strategy development involves choosing the target market/s, assessing the competitors' marketing strategies, and designing the marketing mix strategies. Responsibility for competitive strategy development is borne by all managers in the company, by following bottom-up or top-down planning as modes of strategy formulation. Responsibility for marketing strategy development is borne by the marketing manager in the marketing department.

TABLE 2.2 Illustrative comparison of business and marketing strategies

	Corporate and business units strategy	Marketing strategy
Perspective	Organizational and/or competitive focus, often with a heavy industry orientation	Customer and/or product focus, often with a heavy end-user orientation
Decisions	• Mission determination • Allocation of business resources to business units • Acquisition/diversification • Elimination of business units • Product development and management • Selection and implementation of SBU strategies	• Identification of market opportunities • Choice of target market(s) • Marketing programme positioning strategy • Product, distribution, price, and promotion strategies
Strategic focus	• How to gain and keep strategic advantage • How to determine business strategies • How to organize the business for planning/control	• How to divide product/markets into segments • What segment(s) to serve • How to position for each segment
Information needs	• Financial performance • Business opportunity assessment • Market performance and forecasts • Competitors' strategies and performance	• Financial performance by market target and product type • Customer/prospect description and requirements • Market position and forecasts • Competitors' marketing strategies and performance

Source: David W. Cravens (1994), *Strategic Marketing*, p. 92. Reproduced by permission of McGraw-Hill Education, Inc.

From these points, it could be suggested that an organization's development of a functional strategy is dictated by the SBU strategy of its parent. For example, a business unit following a competitive strategy of differentiation through high quality requires a manufacturing functional strategy that emphasizes an expensive quality assurance process, a human resource functional strategy that emphasizes the hiring and training of a highly skilled workforce, and a marketing functional strategy that emphasizes a distribution channel 'pull' using advertising to increase consumer demand, rather than 'push' using promotional allowances to retailers. However, if a business unit is to follow a low-cost competitive strategy, a different set of functional strategies would be needed to support the business strategy. As a company may decide to adopt different competitive strategies in different regions of the world, functional strategies may have to vary accordingly (Wheelen and Hunger, 2004). Ford, for example, has a different set of functional strategies in the Middle East than the ones adopted in the UK. Ford is seen as a differentiated car producer in the Middle East, while this is not the case in Britain.

Based on this critical analysis and discussion of the definitions of both 'competitive strategy' and 'marketing strategy', one might argue that the inclusion of the two terms *competitive* and *marketing* with strategy in one definition could be seen as the first referring to the type/level of strategy, while the second refers to the orientation of the strategy. Accepting this view, competitive marketing strategy can be defined either as: (1) a business strategy that is guided/driven by the market orientation; or (2) a marketing (functional) strategy with competitive orientation.

In the competitive orientation of marketing strategy, the marketer observes what rival firms are doing, anticipates their moves, and sets objectives for ways to surpass them. In the marketing orientation of business (competitive) strategy, marketing plays a pivotal role for strategy development by linking the organization to its environment. Because of marketing's position at the boundary between the organization and its customers, channel members and competition forces, it becomes central to the business (competitive) strategy planning process and is seen as a responsibility of the entire business, rather than as a specialized function. Hart (2003) pointed out that marketing can no longer be the sole responsibility of a few specialists. Rather, everyone in the firm must be charged with the responsibility for understanding marketing because the formulation and implementation of market-driven business strategy requires marketing skills in designing, developing, managing, and controlling strategic alliances. The absence of a strong marketing orientation culture may have a significant impact on the competitiveness of the firm and several potential problems may arise. Authors like Wilson and Gilligan (2005) claim that there is a strong interdependence between strategic planning and marketing which, in their view, can be used to develop an effective competitive strategy.

The view adopted in this book has been influenced by the previously discussed perspectives on marketing strategy, which recognize marketing as a business philosophy. It is believed that competitive marketing strategy cannot be reduced to a lower level of strategy development, nor be seen as a functional strategy developed to serve the 4Ps. It should rather be seen as a marketing-orientated business strategy. Based on this view, the following definition of competitive marketing strategy could be suggested.

Competitive marketing strategy is a market-orientated approach that establishes a profitable competitive position for the firm against all forces that determine industry competition by continuously creating and developing a sustainable competitive advantage (SCA) from the potential sources that exist in a firm's value chain.

Planning frameworks for the strategy-making process

Strategy is the outcome of an organization's planning activities. These activities are undertaken through a process in which strategy is developed, approved, implemented, and evaluated. This process of strategy making has been described over the years in such terms as, 'budgeting', 'long-range planning', 'strategic planning', 'strategic market planning', 'strategic management', and 'strategic market management'. These terms are often used interchangeably. However, they can be put in a historical context as four key phases in the evolution of the management planning discipline (Wheelen and Hunger, 2004). The discussion in this section focuses only on the third and fourth phases.

Strategic planning

Strategic planning and associated concepts were born amid a flurry of optimism and industrial growth in the 1960s and early 1970s. There are several reasons for this, perhaps the most notable of which is that, largely because of the growing and continuously buoyant markets of the 1950s and 1960s and the turbulence of the early 1970s, many managers needed to find a radically different approach to the running of their business (Porter, 1987).

Ansoff (1965) was one of the first scholars in the strategy field to define strategic planning (which he then referred to as strategic decisions). Strategic planning was later defined as the process which defines the long-term objectives of a company and the means by which these objectives are to be achieved. However, planning horizons may vary from one company to another and from industry to industry. For example, in a retail company, a three-year plan may be appropriate. In companies operating in the oil industry, however, planning horizons may be as long as ten to fifteen years. The above definition may also give the impression that strategic planning and strategic thinking are similar. They are not.

Whereas strategic thinking involves creative and entrepreneurial insights into a company and its environment, strategic planning has often degenerated into frameworks for the systematic and comprehensive analysis of known options. Strategic thinking is a shaping process in which a reflective conversation with a situation takes place in order to reduce the complexity of such a situation, while strategy-making is a process of continuous adaptation between the industry environment and organization capabilities. For example, the management of Hewlett-Packard (HP), after a careful study of trends in the computer and communications industries, found that the company needed to stop thinking of itself as a collection of stand-alone products with a primary focus on instrumentation and PC hardware. Instead, the top management felt that the company needed to become a customer-focused and integrated provider of information appliances, highly reliable information technology infrastructure, and e-commerce services. A comprehensive framework of strategic planning, which illustrates the firm's internal and external appraisal of its environment, is shown in Figure 2.3.

Strategic planning as a model of strategy making has its supporters (e.g., Ansoff, 1991, 1994; Kaplan and Beinhocker, 2003). Wheelen and Hunger (2004), for example, pointed out that strategic planning is strongly related to improved financial performance of businesses, evidenced by a survey of the high-growth *Inc. 500* firms, which revealed that 86 per cent of them undertook strategic planning; of those, 94 per cent reported improved profits. The validity of the model, however, was subject to many criticisms (e.g., Mintzberg, 1990, 1994a, 1994b; Mintzberg and Lampel, 1999). Ocasio and Joseph (2008), for example, claim that the role and importance of strategic planning in corporate practice remains a subject of controversy for both academics and practitioners. The contribution of strategic planning to firm innovation and competitiveness was often questioned, and the critiques culminated with Mintzberg's writings on the subject, which focused on the failings of formal planning processes. Also, Whittington and Cailluet (2008) pointed out that the debate in this area, which focused on whether strategic plans are effective in setting strategic directions and whether firms that undertook strategic planning out-performed no-planning companies, was mixed.

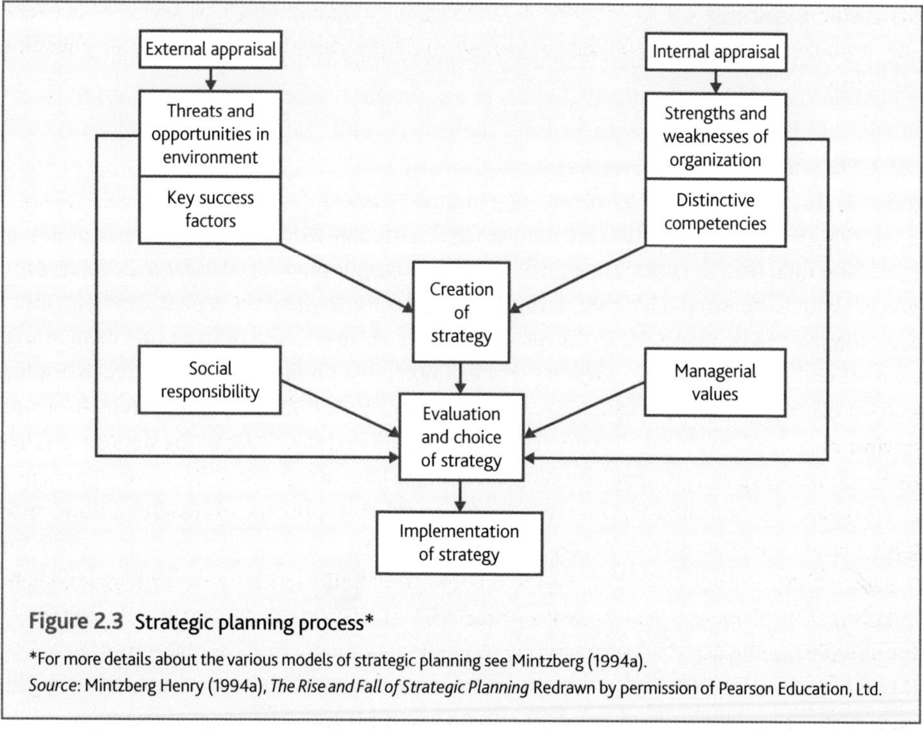

Figure 2.3 Strategic planning process*

*For more details about the various models of strategic planning see Mintzberg (1994a).
Source: Mintzberg Henry (1994a), *The Rise and Fall of Strategic Planning* Redrawn by permission of Pearson Education, Ltd.

Despite this controversial debate, Eppler and Platts (2009) note that strategic planning processes are still among the most demanding tasks that managers need in today's complex marketplace. It can be an overwhelming challenge to take into account, simultaneously, the developments of technologies and societal trends, the behaviour of competitors, customers and regulators, all within a changing legal, environmental, and financial framework. When this is compounded with time pressure, environmental uncertainty, and constant distractions and internal tensions, making sound and effective strategic decisions becomes essential and requires these decisions to be made in a systematic and orchestrated manner. Vilà and Canales (2008) also believe that many companies still find that their approach to strategic planning has a major impact on the usefulness of what results from the planning process. They suggest that strategic planning, which guides discussion between managers at different organizational levels, can play an important role in stimulating the collective process for shaping the development of effective and sustainable strategic goals and priorities.

Strategic market planning was added to the lexicon of strategic concepts by Abell and Hammond (1979). The inclusion of the word 'market' in strategic planning serves to emphasize that strategy development needs to be driven by the forces of market environment rather than by internal factors. Strategic market planning could be defined as the managerial process that entails analysis, formulation, and evaluation of strategy and that enables an organization to achieve its objectives by developing and maintaining a strategic fit between the organization's capabilities and the threats and opportunities arising from its changing environment.

Strategic marketing planning

There is also a need to distinguish strategic **market** planning from strategic **marketing** planning. Whereas the first prepares an organization to develop a strategic response to its changing market environment, strategic marketing planning is concerned with functional decisions related to the marketing mix elements. In that capacity, marketing competes with other functional areas for the firm's resources. However, there is still a significant role to be played by marketing in the strategic planning process. While the primary responsibility of strategic market planning is always to look outward and keep the business in tune with its expected environment, the lead role in meeting this responsibility is played by marketing. As a general management responsibility, marketing embraces the interpretations of the environment and the crucial choices of which customers to serve, which competitors to challenge, and with which product characteristics the business will compete.

Baker (1992) distinguished strategic marketing planning from marketing planning by stressing that the latter is seen as dealing primarily with the marketing mix, while the former is seen as planning for all aspects of an organization's strategy in the marketplace. Based on this view, strategic marketing planning is described as the establishment of the goal or purpose of an SBU and the means by which this is to be achieved.

In fact, marketing has a presence at the three organizational levels of any corporation. At the corporate level, marketing can influence organizational culture; while at the SBU level, marketing guides the company's competitive positioning; and, finally, at the operational level, marketing is responsible for the development of 4Ps tactics.

The concepts and practicalities of strategic and tactical marketing planning and their relationship to strategic planning are comprehensively covered in the marketing literature, and there is a wide agreement about the process and content of strategic marketing planning and its contribution to the development of the organization's overall strategy (Varadarajan and Jayachandran, 2000).

After all, the concept and processes of strategic planning still attract academics' interest and remain visible in the business literature (Ocasio and Joseph, 2008). It remains a pervasive and influential phenomenon in the business world, perhaps more so than ever. Since 1996, Bain & Co's survey of management tools has regularly reported strategic planning being used by around 80 per cent of its responding companies, and in 2007 found it the most popular tool for all, with an eleven-year record of 88 per cent of companies using it (Whittington and Cailluet, 2008).

Strategic management

Strategic management was introduced in the late of 1970s in response to a number of criticisms associated with strategic planning. The concept of strategic management was created to highlight the importance of strategy implementation, evaluation, and control. Strategic management stems from an assumption that the planning cycle is inadequate to deal with the rapid rate of change that can occur in the environment facing the firm. Strategic management was defined as a set of managerial decisions and actions that determine the long-run performance of a corporation (Wheelen and Hunger, 2004). To cope with strategic surprises and fast-developing threats and opportunities, a firm's strategic decisions need to be made outside the planning cycle (Aaker, 2005).

In the business literature, Ansoff et al. (1976) were among the first academics to transform the concept of strategic planning into strategic management. In the world of business during the 1980s, General Electric Corporation (GEC), one of the pioneers of strategic planning, led the transition from strategic planning to strategic management. Because strategy formulation and implementation are now considered to be of equal importance, and interdependent (a key concept of strategic management), it has been suggested that all the largest companies in the world have to take strategic management seriously. Figure 2.4 shows the strategic management process and its four basic elements: environmental scanning, strategy formulation, strategy implementation, and evaluation and control.

Research on the validity and credibility of the strategic management model has produced conflicting views. While many research studies revealed that strategic management, in general, leads to improved performance far more often than it results in no change or even in poorer performance, others have criticized the concept and its benefits to business organizations. Cummings and Daellenbach (2009) assessed the development and evolution of strategic management in the past forty years and reported that, while strategic management should have grown up years ago to overcome its theoretical and application problems, it still has distinctive contributions to business thinking and practice.

The concept of **strategic market management** emerged as an extension of the term strategic management to emphasize that strategy development should be informed by the market environment rather than being internally orientated. The concept emerged to underline the fact that the process must be proactive rather than reactive. Strategic market

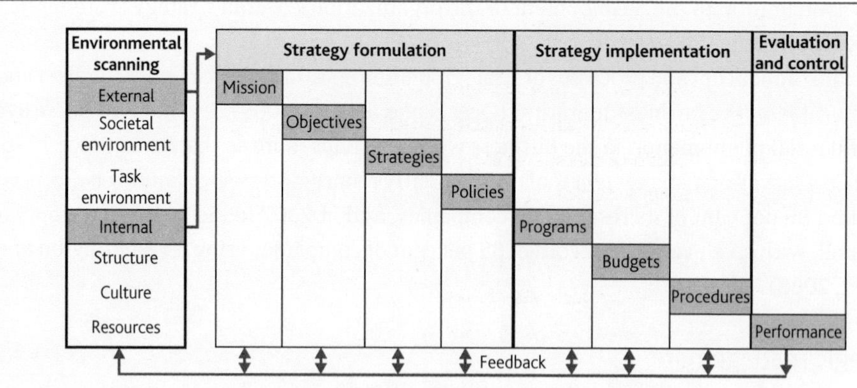

Figure 2.4 Strategic Management Framework

Source: T. L. Wheelen (1981), 'Strategic Management Model', adapted from 'Concepts of Management', presented to society for Advancement of Management (SAM), International Meeting, Richmond, VA, 1981.

management has been defined as a system designed to help management in developing, evaluating, implementing, and changing business strategies. This system will: (1) provide vision to businesses; (2) monitor and understand a dynamic environment; (3) generate strategic options; and (4) develop strategies based on sustainable competitive advantages (Aaker, 2005). The content of that system is shown in Figure 2.5.

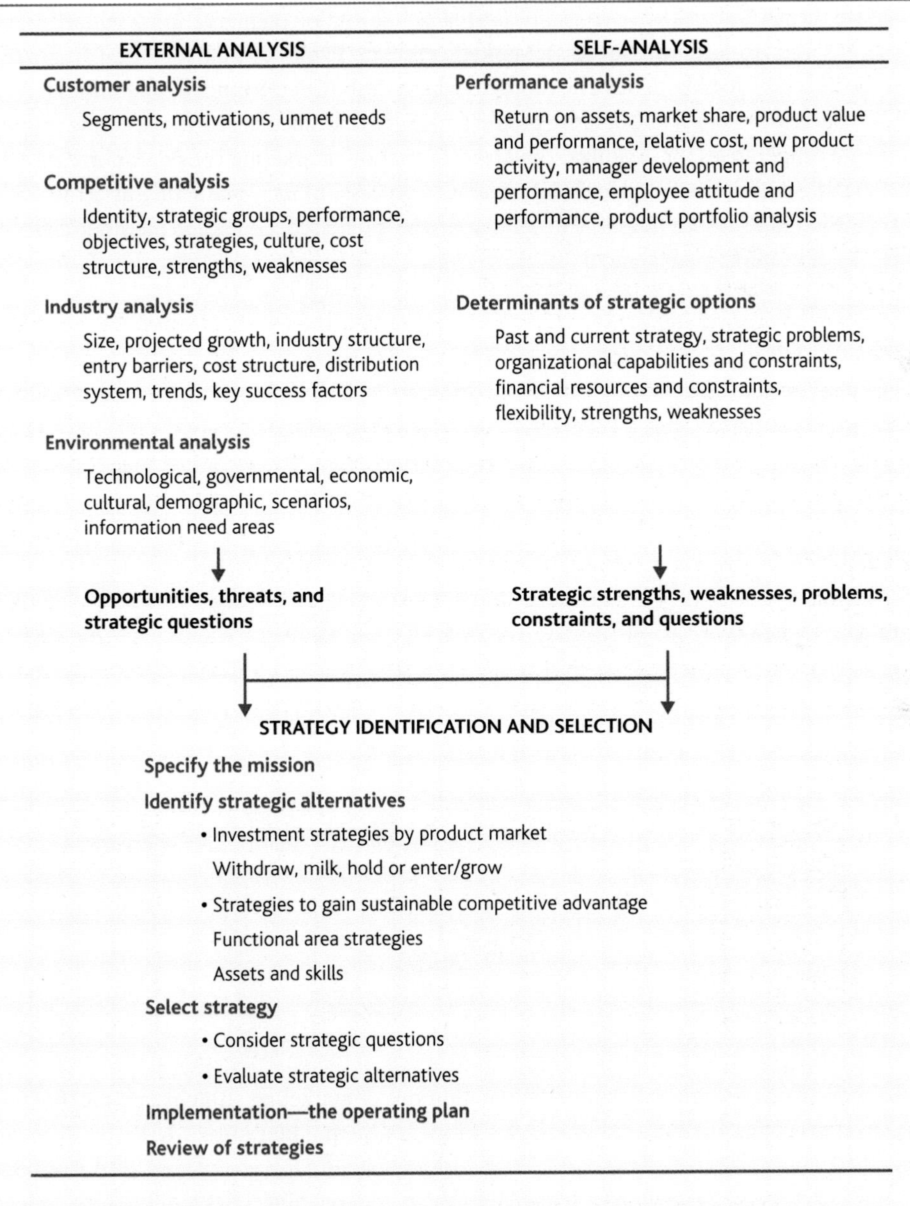

Figure 2.5 Overview of strategic market management

Source: David A. Aaker (2005), *Strategic Market Management*, p. 20. Redrawn by permission of John Wiley & Sons, Inc.

Strategic marketing management

The concept of strategic **marketing** management was originated to highlight the lead role of marketing as the primary link between the organization and its environment, and also to appreciate the pivotal importance of marketing in formulating and directing the implementation of the organization strategies. The role of marketing in strategy development and implementation and its contribution to business performance have been acknowledged in the marketing and strategy literature (see the section on marketing orientation and its contribution to corporate success). Marketing is likely to play an analytical and diagnostic role in the search for competitive advantages where the business's unique capabilities match the key success factors of one or more product markets. And since strategic marketing activity generates imperatives for organizational transformation, marketing considerations are also the starting point for the strategic management process. In fact, marketing as a relatively mature discipline has the potential to contribute viewpoints, concepts, and methodologies to the field of strategic management.

Conclusion

The current view of the development of marketing strategy is consistent with the early literature about the marketing concept, which recognized marketing as not only a set of functions but also as a guiding philosophy for all of an organization's activities. At the functional level, the major task of a marketing manager is to influence the level, timing, and character of demand in a way that will help to achieve the organization's marketing objectives. The marketing manager is the organization's primary link to the customer and the competition and must, therefore, be concerned in particular with the development of the organization's positioning strategy and marketing mix programmes.

At the strategic (SBU) level, marketing as a business philosophy can play a significant role in guiding all of an organization's activities. Therefore, it has been suggested in this book that competitive marketing strategy is not an upgraded version of the marketing strategy that is oriented by competitors, but rather:

> a market-oriented approach that establishes a profitable competitive position for the firm against all forces that determine industry competition by continuously creating and developing a sustainable competitive advantage (SCA) from the potential sources that exist in a firm's value chain.

Summary

This chapter has reviewed the nature and definitions of marketing strategy, a topic that has received extensive analysis and discussion in the marketing literature. Marketing strategy is typically seen as having developed through three sequential steps/phases. First, the core strategy of the company will be selected, and the marketing objectives and the broad focus for achieving them will be identified. Second, market segments and targets (both customers and competitors) are selected, and the company's differential advantage in serving the customer targets better than the competition is identified. Together, the identification of targets and the definition of differential advantage constitute the creation of the competitive positioning of the company and its offerings. Finally, a marketing manager capable of putting the strategy into practice must be elected. At this stage, the marketing department is concerned with establishing the marketing mix programmes that can convey both the positioning and the products/services themselves to the target market.

KEY TERMS

Business strategy Is usually developed at the strategic business unit (SBU) level and emphasizes improvement of the competitive position of a corporation's products or services in the specific industry or market segment served by that SBU.

Competitive marketing strategy Is a market-orientated approach that establishes a profitable competitive position for the firm against all forces that determine industry competition by continuously creating and developing a sustainable competitive advantage (SCA) from the potential sources that exist in a firm's value chain.

Corporate strategy Describes a company's overall direction in terms of its general attitude toward growth and the management of its various businesses and product lines to achieve a balanced portfolio of products and services.

Functional strategy Is concerned with maximizing resource productivity. Within the constraints of the corporate and business strategies around them, functional departments, such as marketing, finance, and production, develop strategies to pull together their various activities and competencies to improve performance.

Market positioning strategy Is the employment of the organization's product, distribution, prices, and promotion activities to position the company's offerings against the competitor's offerings in meeting the needs and wants of the target market. The positioning strategy provides the unifying concept for deciding the role of each component of the marketing mix.

Marketing concept Is 'a way of thinking—a management philosophy guiding an organisation's overall activities. This philosophy which holds the key to achieving organisational goals consists of the company being more effective than competitors in creating, delivering, and communicating customer value to its chosen target' (Kotler, 2000).

Marketing targeting strategy Is a strategy that aims to select groups of consumers (or organizations) the management wishes to serve in the product market.

Strategic market planning Is defined as the managerial process that entails the analysis, formulation, and evaluation of strategy and that enables an organization to achieve its objectives by developing and maintaining a strategic fit between the organization's capabilities and the threats and opportunities arising from its changing environment.

Strategic marketing 'Is an intelligence-focused and led-process that has both an internal and an external dimension, which utilizes the skills of competitive intelligence officers who work with marketing managers and strategists to establish trust-based relationships throughout the partnership arrangement, which ... ultimately results in [the] organisation fulfilling its mission statement' (Trim and Lee, 2008).

Strategic thinking Strategic thinking involves creative and entrepreneurial insights into a company and its environment. It is a shaping process in which a reflective conversation with a situation takes place in order to reduce the complexity of this situation.

DISCUSSION QUESTIONS

1 Evaluate the concept of strategy and explain its components and levels. Also, discuss the relationship between corporate and marketing strategies. Provide illustrative examples to support your discussion.

2 Marketing can be viewed as a business philosophy that guides the organization's overall activities and as a function responsible for a particular set of activities. Discuss these complementary views.

3 Discuss the strategic marketing management process and assess the extent to which you agree/disagree that this process is of real value to large organizations.

4 Using examples to support your argument, discuss the key issues facing a small company when developing and implementing its marketing strategy to support its expansion into different markets.

5 Do you think that all companies need to practice the marketing concept to some extent? Are there companies which do not need this orientation? Which companies need it most?

ONLINE RESOURCE CENTRE

Visit the Online Resource Centre for this book for lots of interesting additional material at: **www.oxfordtextbooks.co.uk/orc/west2e/**

REFERENCES AND FURTHER READING

Aaker, David A. (2005), *Strategic Market Management* (New York: John Wiley & Sons, Inc.).

Abell, Derek F., and John S. Hammond (1979), *Strategic Market Planning: Problems and Analytical Approaches* (Englewood Cliffs, NJ: Prentice Hall, Inc.).

Andrews, Kenneth R. (1971), *The Concept of Corporate Strategy* (New York: Dow Jones-Irwin, Inc.).

Ansoff, Igor H. (1965), *Corporate Strategy* (New York: McGraw-Hill, Inc.).

Ansoff, Igor H. (1991), 'Critique of Henry Mintzberg's "The Design School: Reconsidering the Basic Premises of Strategic Management"', *Strategic Management Journal*, 12 (6), pp. 449–61.

Ansoff, Igor H. (1994), 'Comment on Henry Mintzberg's Rethinking Strategic Planning', *Long Range Planning*, 27 (3), pp. 31–2.

Ansoff, Igor H., Roger P. Declerck, and Robert L. Hayes (1976), *From Strategic Planning to Strategic Management* (New York: John Wiley & Sons, Inc.).

Bagozzi, R. (1975), 'Marketing as Exchange', *Journal of Marketing*, 39 (4), pp. 32–9.

Baker, Michael J. (1992), *Marketing Strategy and Management* (London: Macmillan Press Ltd).

Brassington, Frances, and Stephen Pettitt (2006), *Principles of Marketing Strategy*, 4th edn (Upper Saddle River, NJ: Pearson Education, Inc.).

Cravens, David W. (1994), *Strategic Marketing* (New York: Richard D. Irwin).

Cravens, David W., Nigel F. Piercy, and Artur Baldauf (2009), 'Management Framework Guiding Strategic Thinking in Rapidly Changing Markets', *Journal of Marketing Management*, 25 (1/2), pp. 31–49.

Cummings, Stephen, and Urs Daellenbach (2009), 'A Guide to the Future of Strategy?' *Long Range Planning*, 42 (1), pp. 234–63.

Diamantopoulos, A., and S. Hart (1993), 'Linking Market Orientation and Company Performance: Preliminary Work on Kohli and Jaworski's Framework', *Journal of Strategic Marketing*, 1 (2), pp. 93–122.

Dibb, Sally, Lyndon Simkin, William M. Pride, and O. C. Ferrell (2006), *Marketing: Concepts and Strategies* (New York: Houghton Mifflin Company).

Doyle, Peter, and Stern Philip (2006), *Marketing Management and Strategy* (Harlow: Prentice-Hall, Inc.).

El-Morsy, Gamal E. M. (1986), Competitive Marketing Strategy: A Study of Competitive Performance in the British Car Market (Unpublished PhD, University of Strathclyde, UK).

Eppler, Martin J., and Ken W. Platts (2009), 'Visual Strategizing: The Systematic Use of Visualization in the Strategic-Planning Process', *Long Range Planning*, 42 (2), pp. 42–74.

Fodness, Dale (2005), 'Rethinking Strategic Marketing: Achieving Breakthrough Results', *Journal of Business Strategy*, 26 (3), pp. 20–34.

Foley, Anthony, and John Fahy (2009), 'Seeing Market Orientation through a Capabilities Lens', *European Journal of Marketing*, 43 (1), pp. 13–20.

Frentzel, Y. William, John M. Bryson, and Barbara C. Crosby (2000), 'Startegic Planning in the Military', *Long Range Planning*, 33, 402–29.

Greenly, G. E. (1995), 'Market Orientation and Company Performance: Empirical Evidence from UK Companies', *British Journal of Management*, 6 (1), pp. 1–13.

Hart, Susan (2003), *Marketing Changes* (London: Thomson Learning).

Hofer, Charles W., and Dan Schendel (1978), *Strategy Formulation: Analytical Concepts* (St Paul, MN: West Publishing Company).

Hooley, Graham, John Saunders, and Nigel F. Piercy (2004), *Competitive Positioning: The Key to Market Success* (Harlow: Prentice-Hall International Ltd).

Hooley, G., J. Fahy, G. Greenly, J. Beracs, K. Fonfara, and B. Snoj (2003), 'Market Orientation in the Service Sector of the Transition Economies of Central Europe', *European Journal of Marketing*, 37 (1/2), pp. 86–106.

Horton, Keith S. (2003), 'Strategy, Practice, and Dynamics of Power', *Journal of Business Research*, 56 (2), pp. 121–6.

Kaplan, Sarah, and Eric D. Beinhocker (2003), 'The Real Value of Strategic Planning', *Sloan Management Review*, 44 (Winter), pp. 71–6.

Kohli, Ajay K., and Bernard J. Jaworski (1990), 'Market Orientation: The Construct, Research Propositions, and Managerial Implications', *Journal of Marketing*, 54 (April), pp. 1–18.

Kohli, A. K., and Bernard J. Jaworski (1993), 'MARKOR: A Measure of Market Orientation', *Journal of Marketing Research*, 57 (November) pp. 467–77.

Kotler, Philip (2000), *Marketing Management: Analysis, Planning, Implementation and Control* (Englewood Cliffs, NJ: Prentice Hall, Inc.).

Kotler, P., and Kevin Lane Keller (2006), *Marketing Management*, 11th edn (Upper Saddle River, NJ: Pearson Prentice Hall, Inc.).

Lambin, Jean-Jacques (2000), *Market-driven Management: Strategic and Operational Marketing* (Basingstoke: Macmillan Business).

Mason, Katy, and Lloyd C. Harris (2005), 'Pitfalls in Evaluating Market Orientation: An Exploration of Executives', *Long Range Planning*, 38 (4), pp. 373–91.

Mintzberg, Henry (1990), 'The Design School: Reconsidering the Basic Premises of Strategic Management', *Strategic Management Journal*, 11 (3), pp. 171–95.

Mintzberg, Henry (1994a), *The Rise and Fall of Strategic Planning* (Englewood Cliffs, NJ: Prentice Hall, Inc.).

Mintzberg, Henry (1994b), 'Rethinking Strategic Planning Part I: Pitfalls and Fallacies', *Long Range Planning*, 27 (3), pp. 12–21.

Mintzberg, H., and J. Lampel (1999), 'Reflecting on the Strategy Process', *Sloan Management Review*, 40 (Spring), pp. 21–30.

Mintzberg, Henry, and J. B. Quinn (1996), *The Strategy Process: Concepts, Contexts, Cases* (Harlow: Prentice-Hall International, Inc.).

Mavondo, F. T., and M. A. Farrell (2000), 'Measuring Market Orientation: Are there Differences between Business Marketers and Consumer Marketers?' *Australian Journal of Marketing*, 54 (4), pp. 223–44.

Narver, John C., and Stanley F. Slater (1990), 'The Effect of a Market Orientation on Business Profitability', *Journal of Marketing*, 54 (October), pp. 20–35.

Nwokah, Gladson N. (2008), 'Strategic Market Orientation and Business Performance: The Study of Food and Beverages Organisations in Nigeria', *European Journal of Marketing*, 42 (3/4), pp. 279–86.

Ocasio, William, and John Joseph (2008), 'Rise and Fall—or Transformation? The Evolution of Strategic Planning at the General Electric Company 1940–2006', *Long Range Planning*, 41 (3), pp. 248–72.

O'Shaughnessy, John (1995), *Competitive Marketing: A Strategic Approach* (London: Routledge).

Porter, Michael E. (1980), *Competitive Strategy: Techniques for Analyzing Industries and Competitors* (New York: The Free Press).

Porter, Michael E. (1987), 'Corporate Strategy: The State of Strategic Thinking', *The Economist*, (May 23), pp. 21–8.

Ries, A., and J. Trout (1981), *Positioning: The Battle for Your Mind* (New York: McGraw-Hill Book Company).

Sharma, Bishnu (2004), 'Marketing Strategy, Contextual Factors and Performance: An Investigation of their Relationship', *Marketing Intelligence and Planning*, 22 (2), pp. 128–43.

Slater, Stanley F., and John C. Narver (1994), 'Market Orientation, Customer Value, and Superior Performance', *Business Horizons*, 37 (2), pp. 22–8.

Slater, Stanley F., and John C. Narver (2000), 'The Positive Effect of a Market Orientation on Business Profitability: A Balanced Replication', *Journal of Business Research*, 48, pp. 69–73.

Slater, Stanley F., John C. Narver, and Douglas MacLachlan (2004), 'Market Orientation, Innovativeness, and New Product Success', *Journal of Product Innovation Management*, 21, pp. 334–47.

Trim, Peter R. J., and Yang-Im Lee (2008), 'A Strategic Marketing Intelligence and Multi-organisational Resilience Framework', *European Journal of Marketing*, 42 (7/8), pp. 731–45.

Varadarajan, Rajan P., and Satish Jayachandran (2000), 'Marketing Strategy: An Assessment of the State of the Field and Outlook', *Journal of the Academy of Marketing Science*, 27 (2), pp. 120–43.

Vilà, Joaquim, and J. Ignacio Canales (2008), 'Can Strategic Planning Make Strategy More Relevant and Build Commitment over Time? The Case of RACC', *Long Range Planning*, 41 (3), pp. 273–90.

Ward, Steven, and Aleksandra Lewandowska (2008), 'Is the Marketing Concept always Necessary? The Effectiveness of Customer, Competitors and Societal Strategies in Business Environment Types', *European Journal of Marketing*, 42 (1/2), pp. 222–37.

Wheelen, Thomas L., and David J. Hunger, (2004), *Strategic Management and Business Policy* (New York: Pearson Education, Inc.).

Whittington, Richard, and Ludovic Cailluet (2008), 'The Craft of Strategy', *Long Range Planning*, 41 (3), pp. 241–7.

Wilson, Richard M. S., and Colin Gilligan (2005), *Strategic Marketing Management: Planning, Implementation and Control* (Oxford: Elsevier Butterworth-Heinemann).

KEY ARTICLE ABSTRACTS

Eppler, Martin J., and Ken W. Platts (2009), **'Visual Strategizing: The Systematic Use of Visualization in the Strategic-planning Process'**, *Long Range Planning,* 42 (2), pp. 42–74.

This article is one of the most recent contributions to the field of strategic marketing management, which discusses how visualization can be used in the strategic planning process.

Abstract: This study postulates that visualization can improve the quality of the strategic planning process by addressing many of its cognitive, social, and emotional challenges. It also highlights the benefits of visual methods for strategizing, and illustrates these benefits with five case studies covering the entire strategizing process, from analysis to implementation. The study follows a conceptual framework to group and position interactive visual representations of information along the strategic planning process. The key lesson the study provides for executives is that visualization should not just be seen as an attractive way to communicate the outcome of the strategic planning process and to monitor its progress, but should also be seen as a powerful process enabler that can enable strategizing as a joint managerial practice.

Ocasio, William, and John Joseph (2008), **'Rise and Fall—or Transformation? The Evolution of Strategic Planning at the General Electric Company 1940–2006'**, *Long Range Planning,* 41 (3), pp. 248–72.

This is another case study-based article that examines the history of the evolution of strategic planning practices at the General Electric Company (GE) during six CEO regimes.

Abstract: The study distinguishes strategic planning—a system of strategy formulation, decision-making, and control—from particular planning technologies such as SBU planning. It discusses how an integrative system of strategic planning was first established in GE in the 1950s which was originally called long-range planning, later strategic planning, and after the abandonment of SBU planning it was labelled GE's operating system. The study concludes that the history of strategic planning at GE has several implications for their contemporary strategy making.

Varadarajan, Rajan P., and Satish Jayachandran (2000), **'Marketing Strategy: An Assessment of the State of the Field and Outlook'**, *Journal of the Academy of Marketing Science,* 27 (2), pp. 120–43.

This is an interesting paper that offers a comprehensive literature review and provides an illustrative assessment of the state of the field of marketing strategy research and outlook.

Abstract: The study develops and follows an organizing framework that served as a road map for assessing different research streams in marketing strategy. The paper found that significant strides in conceptual development and empirical research of marketing strategy have been achieved in a number of areas over the past years. The study concludes that marketing is likely to play a more important role in charting the strategic direction of the firm.

Vilà, Joaquim, and J. Ignacio Canales (2008), **'Can Strategic Planning Make Strategy More Relevant and Build Commitment over Time? The Case of RACC'**, *Long Range Planning,* 41 (3), pp. 273–90.

This is a case study-based article which illustrates the major implications of the company's approaches to strategic planning on strategy development.

Abstract: This study specifically assesses the practice of the strategic marketing planning process at the RACC automobile club. The paper shows that the planning process is a powerful tool in the hands of top management, and also discusses how active participation in the process can contribute to middle managers' awareness of key principles, issues, and strategic goals. The study suggests that active participation assists managers to make strategy relevant and to prepare their minds for necessary adaptations during the implementation stage. The paper concludes that an upfront and clear definition of the purpose for the planning process has a major say in the ultimate outcome that the firm reaches.

Ward, Steven, and Aleksandra Lewandowska (2008), **'Is the Marketing Concept always Necessary? The Effectiveness of Customer, Competitors and Societal Strategies in Business Environment Types'**, *European Journal of Marketing*, 42 (1/2), pp. 222–37.

This is a useful study that examines whether there is a link between the chosen strategy and the environment in which the strategy will be implemented.

Abstract: This study tries to identify which particular strategies will work best in which particular business environments. The study suggests that the choice of marketing strategy needs to be carefully considered so that it is appropriate for a set of environmental conditions or business conditions. The findings of this study showed general support for its hypotheses that different environmental situations provide suitable conditions for a customer-, competitor- or societal-orientated strategy.

END OF CHAPTER 2 CASE STUDY

VisitScotland: marketing strategy for a sustainable tourism destination

VisitScotland is a Non-Departmental Public Body, reporting to the Scottish Government. It is a national organization with fourteen VisitScotland Network Offices and over a hundred Tourist Information Offices. VisitScotland, as Scotland's National Tourism Organization, has a strategic role to develop Scottish tourism in order to get the maximum economic benefit for Scotland. It exists to support the development of the tourism industry in the country and to market Scotland as a quality destination. It does not control the tourism sector in Scotland, nor does it have a direct role in running attractions or accommodations. Rather, VisitScotland seeks to provide leadership and coordination for the industry. The core objectives of VisitScotland are to:

- attract visitors by building a successful Scottish tourism brand
- engage and work in partnership with the tourism industry
- enhance the visitor experience
- provide strategic direction to the industry
- produce quality assurance and niche market schemes, including the Green Tourism Business Scheme (GTBS), to which individual businesses sign up.

To achieve these objectives and others, VisitScotland has identified what people are specifically interested in doing whilst on their visit in Scotland, and, as a result, promote Scotland according to these interests, highlighting events, identifying the best time of the year for these interests, and promoting added-value offers from relevant tourism businesses. »

For focus, these interests have been grouped together in what is called Scotland's Product Portfolio:

- **Active** (golf, hill/long walks, climbing, cycling, fishing, water sports, etc.)
- **Freedom/touring** (touring, gardens, island hopping, wildlife, etc.)
- **Culture and heritage** (history, traditional culture, performing arts, visual arts, literary, music, film, museums)
- **Cities** (shopping, nightlife, food and drink, etc.)
- **Business tourism** (conferences, meetings and incentive travel, etc.)

VisitScotland has also defined Scotland's key tourism markets and their contributions to the industry in 2007 as follows: (a) **UK leisure** tourism market, including Scots themselves and people visiting friends and relatives—this category generates around 50 per cent of total tourism revenues; (b) **Overseas leisure** tourism market, which generates around 25 per cent of total tourism revenues; and (c) **UK and overseas business** tourism, which generates 25 per cent of total tourism revenues.

Having defined Scotland's product portfolio and its key markets, VisitScotland is targeting and directing its marketing activities at various segments in its three key markets, including **Youth, Seniors, Families, City-breakers,** and **Business Tourists**. Extensive consumer research by VisitScotland across these segments shows that the most important factors for tourists in their choice of Scotland as a leisure destination are scenery, natural environment, sightseeing, and the friendly attitude of local people. The criticisms most commonly mentioned are the weather, exchange rate, and the quality and cost of transportation and accommodation.

In March 2007, the Scottish Tourism Minister, Patricia Ferguson, delivered a speech at the beginning of Scottish Tourism Week. She said that:

> Tourism is one of the leading sectors of our economy. With record investment being pumped into the industry and overseas visitors at an all-time high we are already outperforming the rest of the UK. We want to motivate everyone in Scotland, because tourism is everyone's business and this week should help us do that.

The chair of VisitScotland said:

> Scottish Tourism Week is an excellent opportunity to highlight how one of Scotland's largest and most sustainable industries helps support our economy. It is great to see our industry taking the lead in this way. Hundreds of countries are competing for the same visitors and we need to leave people feeling that there is always more to do in Scotland if we want to succeed in growing tourism revenues by 50 per cent in ten years.

Recent trends in the tourism market

From its extensive market research, VisitScotland recognizes that the tourism market is changing. It confirms that today's travellers want: customized and flexible travel to a destination; special-interest holidays and special experiences; an authentic experience; and good value for money. Other key trends identified are the increasing prevalence of late Internet booking, strong trends towards shorter breaks, and higher awareness and interest in environmentally friendly tourism destinations.

Building on these trends, VisitScotland has undertaken a number of scenario-planning work. This paints a picture of what the Scottish tourism market could look like in 2015.

This picture suggests that the main opportunities for growth could come from the UK market, along with Europe and North America. Therefore, VisitScotland is committed to the Scottish Government's ambition to develop tourism in Scotland in a sustainable way, both through its own activities and advice for the tourism industry in Scotland.

In promoting the country, a whole new marketing strategy was built to promote Scotland and its product portfolio as a strong brand that reflects what visitors want to buy. This new customer-focus strategy permeates all that VisitScotland does and is the most telling feature on the new approach. The brand is built around attributes people associate with Scotland—the brand essence: enduring, dramatic, and human—and is captured in UK marketing in a proposition that a visit to Scotland is a unique and powerful personal experience. The marketing of Scotland is also done on a geographic basis, where areas and places have particular resonance with visitors—for example, Loch Lomond, Edinburgh Castle, Loch Ness, The Highlands, etc. Most promotions link both geography and products from the portfolio—for example, Freedom and Heritage trails. Other marketing activity, using the same brand and product portfolio building blocks, focuses on the time of year—for example, the Edinburgh Festival during the summer.

Over the past years, this approach to marketing has been successful in giving Scotland a distinctive voice in the very crowded tourism market. VisitScotland is continuing with such marketing activities and is concentrating on refining the approach through a better understanding of the market, analysis of competition, effective segmentation, and customer relationship management (CRM). But, more importantly, is the promotion of Scotland as a sustainable tourism destination, a concept that many other tourism destinations are adopting (see Appendix C2.1 below listing websites of countries that have been involved in programmes of sustainable tourism, including Ireland, Sweden, Australia, New Zealand, Spain, and Costa Rica).

Planning for the future, VisitScotland, together with the Scottish Government and other tourism industry partners, have outlined an ambition to develop the value of tourism in Scotland by 50 per cent by 2015. However, is this sustainable? Is it sustainable for the Scottish economy, community, and environment?

Sustainable tourism in its purest sense is an industry which attempts to make a low impact on the environment and local culture, while helping to generate income, employment, and the conversation of local ecosystems. It is responsible tourism, which is both ecologically and culturally sensitive. Genuinely, sustainable tourism requires that all the benefits and costs—economic, environmental, and social—of tourism activities be taken into account in the planning and development process. Sustainable tourism will ensure that Scotland's key tourism assets, natural heritage, and built heritage and communities will survive and thrive. VisitScotland wants Scotland to be Europe's most sustainable destination. Becoming a sustainable tourism destination will give Scottish tourism businesses a competitive edge by generating greater community support for tourism, achieving cost savings, and creating marketing opportunities.

VisitScotland is aware that many of the visitors are attracted to Scotland because of the clean, unspoiled environment, and diverse wildlife; and this is something that they would like to build on. If Scotland is to be promoted as Europe's most sustainable tourism destination, there is a need to ensure that tourism growth doesn't result in the degradation of the very environment which is one of Scotland's unique selling points. Therefore, and to meet its ambition, VisitScotland does not necessarily need to be creating a lot of additional accommodation or visitor attractions. Instead, they should consider improving the current product portfolio, extending the season beyond the peak months, and ensuring that the whole industry is as green as possible to protect the environment that many of the visitors come to see. VisitScotland has to work with tourism businesses to promote sustainable tourism for socially orientated and environmentally conscious visitors.

In order to achieve the ambition of growth in a sustainable way, VisitScotland needs to have an integrated marketing strategy, bringing the marketing activities of VisitScotland and those of the private sector in line behind a common brand concept. In developing such a marketing strategy, there needs to be a higher level of awareness of what is happening in the marketplace, of consumer trends, what competitors are doing, and how this intelligence could be used to deliver improved products and services. The whole approach to tourism development in Scotland must be sustainable—economically, socially, and environmentally.

As part of the development process, VisitScotland would like to appoint a consultancy team to reassess its current marketing activities and make suggestions as to how they might develop/advance their marketing strategy to meet the ambition of developing tourism in Scotland by 50 per cent by 2015, and in the mean time promoting Scotland as a sustainable tourism destination.

Source: This case was prepared by Essam Ibrahim of the University of Edinburgh as the basis for analysis and class discussion and not to illustrate either the effective or ineffective handling of an administrative situation.

Appendix C2.1: Useful websites of other tourism destinations

Scotland

- VisitScotland at: **http://www.visitscotland.org**
- GTBS at: **http://www.green-business.co.uk/**
- Sustainable tourism at: **http://www.greentourism.org.uk/GTBSFacts.html**

Rest of the UK

- VisitLondon at: **http://www.visitlondon.com/people/green/index**
- Visit Somerset at: **http://www.visitsomerset.co.uk/site/places-to-stay/green-tourism-business-scheme**
- Devon at: **http://www.devon.gov.uk/index/culturetourism/sustainabletourism.htm**

Other

- Australia at: **http://www.tourism.australia.com/**
- Costa Rica at: **http://www.visitcostarica.com/ict/paginas/home.asp?ididioma=2**
- Ireland at: **http://www.visitireland.com/index.html**
- New Zealand at: **http://www.tourismnewzealand.com/**
- Spain at: **http://www.spain.info/TourSpain?Language=en**

- Sweden, the global leader for environment and social responsibility, according to *The State of Responsible Competitiveness 2007—Making Sustainable Development Count in Global Markets'*, report at:
    - **http://www.accountability21.net/publications.aspx?id=878**
    - **http://www.visitsweden.com/**
    - **http://www.visitsweden.com/Default38775.aspx**

QUESTIONS

Drawing upon your reading of this chapter on marketing strategy, the information contained in this case study, and on your own observations, you are required to help VisitScotland in developing an effective marketing strategy that will help them achieve their ambition of developing tourism in Scotland by 50 per cent by 2015, and in the meantime market Scotland as a sustainable tourism destination. In developing the required marketing strategy, you have to produce a detailed long-term action plan for the marketing mix elements.

The suggested marketing strategy should present:

1. A situation analysis that assesses the current marketing activities of VisitScotland in response to the current trends of sustainable tourism and the travellers' growing interest in environmentally friendly tourism.
2. A detailed competitor analysis that assesses how other tourism destinations are dealing with and/or capitalizing on sustainability issues in their marketing activities.
3. A brief profile of the three target segments identified in this case. You are required to define the characteristics of these segments and identify the 'might be' travellers' concerns and interests in relation to sustainable tourism destinations.
4. A detailed and justified set of recommendations and suggestions for VisitScotland on how to market Scotland as a sustainable tourism destination to the three segments of the tourism market.

Part II Where are we now?

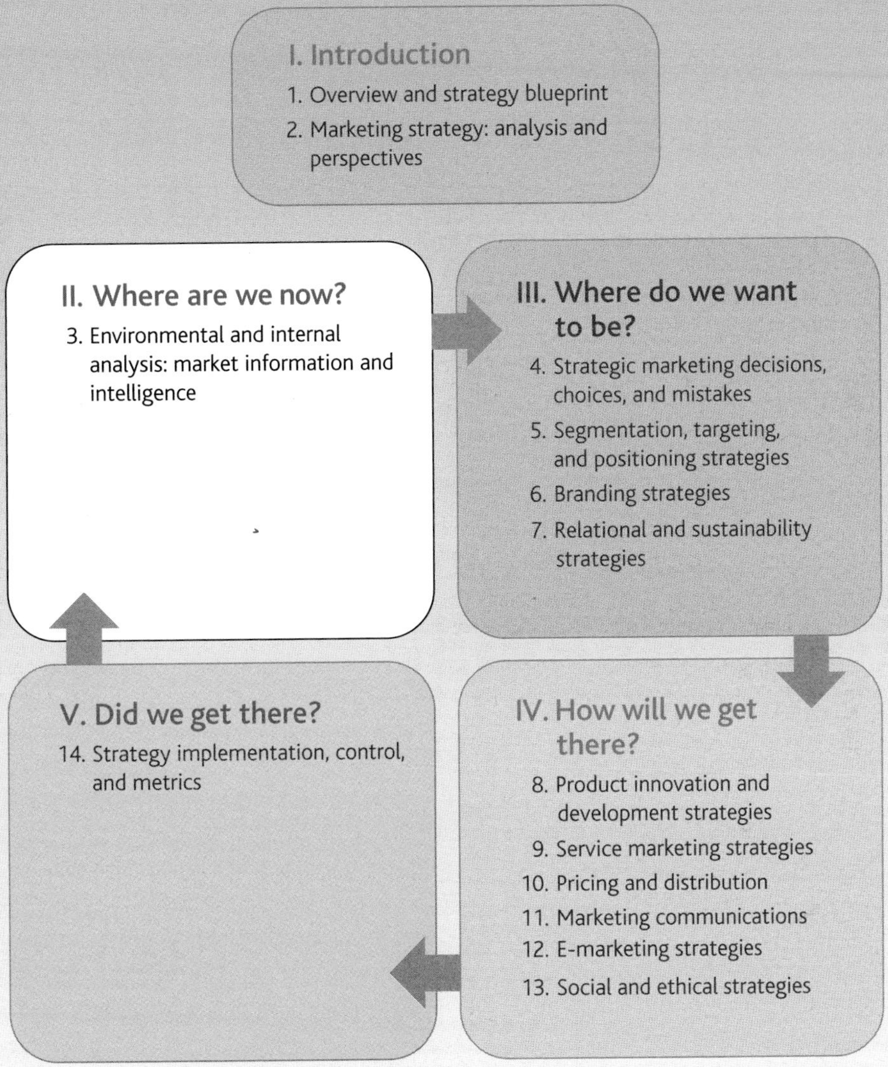

I. Introduction

1. Overview and strategy blueprint
2. Marketing strategy: analysis and perspectives

II. Where are we now?

3. Environmental and internal analysis: market information and intelligence

III. Where do we want to be?

4. Strategic marketing decisions, choices, and mistakes
5. Segmentation, targeting, and positioning strategies
6. Branding strategies
7. Relational and sustainability strategies

IV. How will we get there?

8. Product innovation and development strategies
9. Service marketing strategies
10. Pricing and distribution
11. Marketing communications
12. E-marketing strategies
13. Social and ethical strategies

V. Did we get there?

14. Strategy implementation, control, and metrics

3

Environmental and internal analysis: market information and intelligence

LEARNING OBJECTIVES

- Provide an overview of the three stages (areas) of the strategic marketing management (SMM) process
- Define the marketing environment and discuss the various types of market information required for market scanning and analysis
- Review the analytical models/frameworks that can be used at the strategic analysis stage
- Outline the potential outcome of the strategic marketing analysis stage and the possible implications for the subsequent stages of the SMM process and future strategic choices

CHAPTER AT A GLANCE

I. Introduction
1 Overview and strategy blueprint
2 Marketing strategy: analysis and perspectives

II. Where are we now?
3 Environmental and internal analysis: market information and intelligence

III. Where do we want to be?
4 Strategic marketing decisions, choices, and mistakes
5 Segmentation, targeting, and positioning strategies
6 Branding strategies
7 Relational and sustainability strategies

IV. How will we get there?
8 Product innovation and development strategies
9 Service marketing strategies
10 Pricing and distribution
11 Marketing communications
12 E-marketing strategies
13 Social and ethical strategies

V. Did we get there?
14 Strategy implementation, control, and metrics

Introduction

Building on the discussion in Chapter 2, where the analytical frameworks of strategic marketing planning/management were briefly reviewed, this chapter and Chapter 4 discuss in greater detail the first two stages of the strategic marketing management (SMM) process for strategy development, namely, strategic analysis and strategic choice. The remaining chapters of the book are devoted to the third stage of the SMM process, namely, strategy implementation. In other words, the remaining chapters of the book will discuss the implementation aspects of the marketing mix and marketing activities. Porter's generic strategy typology (low cost, differentiation, and focus) forms the backdrop to the discussion in the book. Although other typologies of generic strategy are available in the literature (e.g., Utterback and Abernathy, 1975; Miles and Snow, 1978), Porter's typology is still the one that has received wide acceptance and appreciation from both academicians and practitioners. The SMM process involves three subsequent stages—*strategic analysis*, *strategic choice* and *strategy implementation* (see Figure 3.1)—(there has been a typical academic debate between two key scholars in the area of strategy: namely, Ansoff in support of and Mintzberg against the validity of the SMM model; see: Ansoff, 1991, 1994; Mintzberg, 1990, 1994a; Mintzberg and Lampel, 1999).

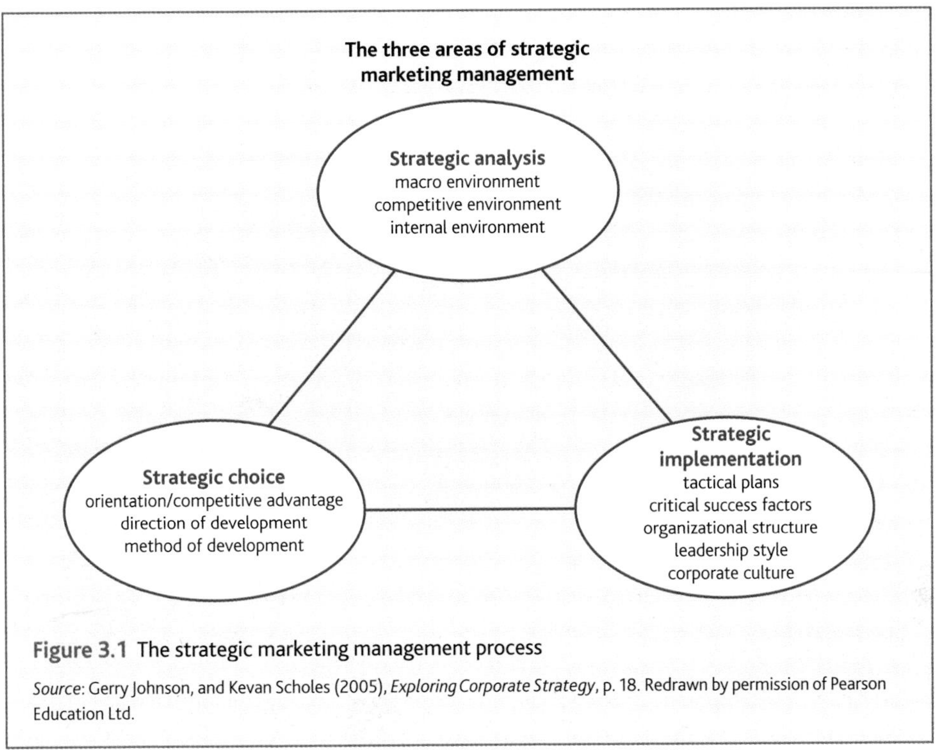

Figure 3.1 The strategic marketing management process

Source: Gerry Johnson, and Kevan Scholes (2005), *Exploring Corporate Strategy*, p. 18. Redrawn by permission of Pearson Education Ltd.

Johnson and Scholes (2005) described the three stages of the process as follows. **Strategic analysis** is concerned with understanding the strategic position of the organization in terms of its external environment, internal resources and competencies, and the expectations and influence of stakeholders. **Strategic choice** involves understanding the underlying bases guiding future strategy, and generating strategic options for evaluation and selecting from among them. **Strategy implementation** is the translation of strategy into organizational action through organizational structure and design, resource planning, and the management of strategic change.

The marketing environment and its components

Any organization is a creature of its environment. Trim and Lee (2008) note that the strategic marketing concept is viewed as all-embracing, flexible, and adoptable. It requires that marketing managers ensure that the organization achieves a sustainable competitive advantage in its environment through a structured approach to planning and strategy formulation. Strategy formulation is, therefore, seen as the development of long-range plans for the effective management of the environmental opportunities and threats while taking into account the organization's strengths and weaknesses. Strategic analysis, as an integral stage of strategy formulation, involves the collection and analysis of relevant types of information about the environmental forces and trends on the one hand, and organizational resources and capabilities on the other hand.

The firm's marketing environment involves two distinct levels, the internal environment, consisting of variables within the organization but not usually within the long-run control of top

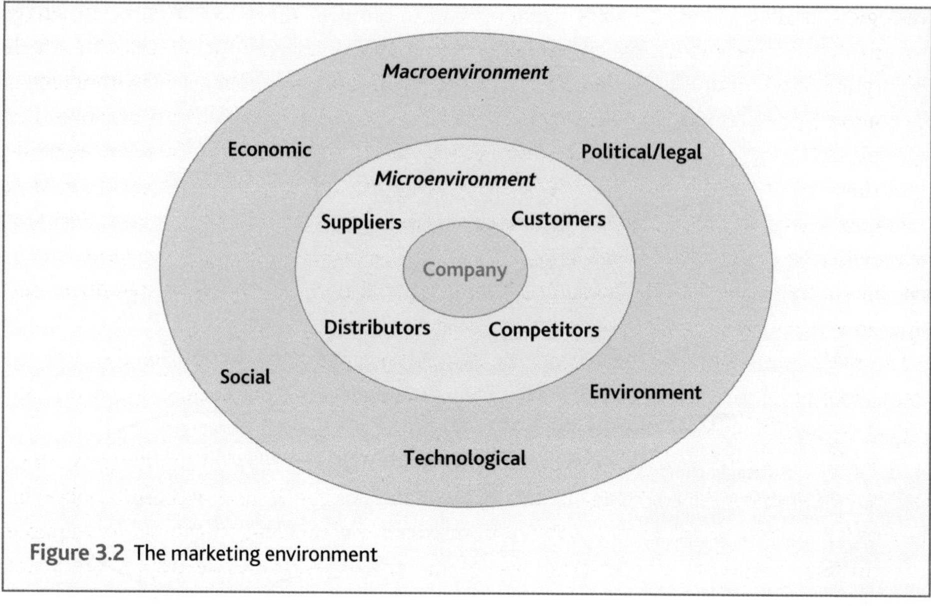

Figure 3.2 The marketing environment

management; and the external environment, consisting of variables outside the organization and not typically within the short-run control of top management. The external environment is further divided into two sub-environments: the 'macro' or remote environment; and the 'micro' or competitive environment. The potential output of analysing the external environment is the detection of opportunities and threats, both present and potential, which face the organization, while the key output of analysing the internal environment is the identification of strengths and weaknesses that exist within the organization's culture and structure (see Figure 3.2 for the marketing environment and its components).

Strategic analysis of the external marketing environment

To be successful over time, an organization must be in tune with its external environment. There must be a 'strategic fit' between what the environment wants and what the organization has to offer, as well as between what the organization needs and what the environment can provide. While most airline companies saw the horrific event of 9/11 as a major threat affecting the whole industry and started to slow down their businesses, a low-cost airline, easyJet responded differently. Two months after 9/11, it was reported that the market share of easyJet was not only in good shape but actually increasing. A step towards achieving such a strategic fit is scanning and analysing the variables and forces that exist in the two sub-levels of the external environment: remote and competitive.

Strategic analysis of the macro (remote) environment

The 'macro' or remote environment includes general forces that do not directly touch on the short-run activities of the organization but that can, and often do, influence its long-run strategic decisions. These variables generally affect, but in different ways, every single organization in the marketing environment regardless of the industrial sector in which the organization operates. The number of strategic variables in the macro environment is enormous, given the fact that each country has its own unique set of macro variables. For examples, although China, Thailand, Taiwan, Hong Kong, and Japan are part of Asia's Pacific Rim, they have different views on the role of business in society. It is generally believed in China, for example, that the role of business is primarily to contribute to national development, whereas in Hong Kong and Thailand the role of business is primarily to make profits for the shareholders. Needless to say, such differences may translate into different trade regulations and varying degrees of opposition to the foreign competitors.

The variables in the macro environment are enormous and can be clustered in various ways, the most notable being the PESTLE model (political, economic, socio-cultural, technological, legal, and environment; see Table 3.1).

To remain competitive, organizations (large and small) are required to analyse the various variables in the external environment and examine the possible impact of these variables on the firm's activities. Johnston et al. (2008) pointed out that most organizations are required to anticipate changes in their external marketing environments and be prepared to adapt their marketing/business activities accordingly. Every organization has to anticipate how its environment might change in the short, medium, and long term. Such anticipated changes will have a direct impact on marketing decision-making. Table 3.2 is a simple framework organizations can use to describe and measure the possible impact of each variable in the organization's macro environment.

In a dynamic environment where changes occur in unpredictable ways, the challenge for an organization is to collect relevant information on which to base its decisions. Johnston et al. (2008) note that the strategy formulation process is a process that allows a firm to make decisions about its activities with the purpose of matching its internal competencies and the external environment. This means that within the context of the strategy formulation process, firms need to find ways of collecting and analysing information about its external environment, as well as dealing with the unpredictability of their future external environment. Obtaining relevant information is the first stage in the process of strategy formulation, and organizations should, therefore, systematically scan and analyse the external environment.

Dibb et al. (2006) defined environmental scanning and analysis as follows. **Environmental scanning** is the process of collecting information about the forces and trends in the environment. Scanning involves observation, perusal of secondary sources such as business, trade, government, and general interest publications. Motorola, the mobile handset producer, has its intelligence department to monitor the latest technology developments introduced at scientific conferences, in academic journals, and in trade gossip. This information helps it build 'technology roadmaps' that assess where breakthroughs are likely to occur, when they can be incorporated into new products, how much money their development will cost, and which of the developments is being worked out by competition. **Environmental analysis** is the process of assessing and interpreting the information gathered through market intelligence and environmental scanning.

The role marketing can play in environmental scanning relies on the specific activities of market research and marketing audit. The **marketing audit** involves a formal review of the

TABLE 3.1 PESTLE framework for environmental analysis

Political factors
Political stability
Regime orientations
Government stability
Pressure groups
Trades union power
Economic factors
Business cycles
Interest rates
Inflation rates
Investment levels
Unemployment
GNP trends
Patterns of ownership
Social-cultural factors
Demographics
Lifestyles
Social mobility
Educational levels
Attitudes
Consumerism
Technological factors
Levels and focuses of government and industrial R&D expenditure
Speed of technology transfer
Product life cycles
Legal factors
Legislative structures
Anti-trust laws
Trade policies
Employment legislation
Foreign trade regulation
Environment factors
Sustainability legislation
Green issues
Energy supply

organization's products, markets, customers, and forces and trends in the external environment. Marketing research has been successfully used by companies such as Procter & Gamble and Microsoft to identify new market opportunities. Procter & Gamble, for example, create a market advantage by spending a great amount of money on advertising and promotion to build entry barriers in the face of a new entrant. This company and others believe that market research is an especially useful tool in directing incremental improvements to existing products.

In scanning and analysing the macro environment, Johnson and Scholes (2005) suggested a stepwise approach which involves an initial audit of environmental influences followed by

TABLE 3.2 PESTLE for environmental scanning and analysis

Source	Description	Implication	Certain	Impact
Political				
Economic				
Social				
Technological				
Legal				
Environment				

a series of increasingly focused steps that are designed to provide the strategist with a clear understanding, not just of the current state of the environment, but also of how it is most likely to develop. Another approach has been suggested by Wheelen and Hunger (2004), who put together the variables of the macro environment and the competitive environment to form a matrix. This approach enables the strategic managers to estimate how future developments of the macro variables may affect the firm via their impact on forces in the firm's competitive environment.

Despite the difficulties of environmental scan and analysis that act as deterrents to the formulation and implementation of an effective scanning system, there are several principal benefits. The essence of strategy formulation is relating a company to its environment. The competitive dimension of the environment is strongly influential in determining the competitive rules of the game, as well as the competitive strategy that is to be pursued. For example, it has been claimed that businesses following a differentiation strategy tend to scan the environment primarily for opportunities and closely monitor customer attitudes, while firms following a cost leadership strategy tend to scan the environment primarily for threats and closely monitor competitors' activities. Organizations usually develop their strategies on the basis of environmental analysis and scanning to find the 'strategic fit' between external opportunities and threats, on the one hand, and internal strengths and weaknesses, on the other. IKEA's experiment with housing trends in Europe in the late 1990s was presumably the result of its ability to identify a possible market opportunity and also its attempt to capitalize on its skills in developing kit-form products at reasonable prices for customers.

In responding to the macro environmental variables, organizations may accept environmental forces as uncontrollable and remain passive and/or reactive towards this environment, or, if they believe that environmental forces can be shaped, they may adopt a more proactive direction. See Mini Case Study 3.1 for some examples of how business organizations in the UK have used marketing techniques to react to the world recession and economic downturn during the 2008–9 financial crisis. The following section discusses how organizations can deal with and react to environmental uncertainty through scenario analysis and planning.

MINI CASE STUDY 3.1 Brand value—Cash is King

Cash flow is crucial to surviving any economic downturn, but it will dry out fast if your organisation devalues the brand cutting marketing spend.

Warren Buffet 'the sage of Omaha', once remarked that 'you only know who's swimming naked when the tide goes out'. Well, the tide has now gone out to reveal that many apparently reputable brands have been swimming naked for a long time. The banks, insurance companies and rating agencies were the first to bare all. Cynical disregard for customers and staff have led to disaster, and many of these brands have paid the ultimate price.

Now brands in the 'real' economy are also blushing. Over-geared, over-hyped and over-priced brands such as Starbucks, Coca-Cola, BMW, L'Oréal and M&S are all suffering as recession-hit consumers reappraise the benefiters of conspicuous consumption. Their value has plummeted because they have fallen out of touch with consumers' wants and needs. In contrast, brands such as Wal-Mart, McDonald's, Avon, Johnson & Johnson, Budweiser, Ford and HSBC are doing well. It's no coincidence that they're all middle-of-the-road brands that have had to reinvent or reposition themselves in tough markets. All have re-evaluated customer relationships, products, or services and the price-value equation.

In the last big recession many brands were badly hit as consumers switched to cheaper alternatives. In 1993, Marlboro realised it had stretched consumer loyalty too far and dropped its price overnight by 25 per cent. While this caused short-term panic on Wall street, a huge fall in Philip Morris's share price and suggestions that this was 'the end of branding as we know it', it simply rebalanced the price-value equation and consumers flooded back. A salutary lesson for out-of-touch brands.

In recessions, price elasticity curves shift. Functional attributes, including price, rapidly come to the fore. Image attributes decline in relative importance. Conduct attributes remain critical but not at any price. Getting the balance right is virtual in recession. But in the struggle to adapt, only brands with strong values maintain their brand value. Consider Innocent—an expensive brand, but one that delivers on function, image, and conduct. I expect it will adapt sensitively to allow for thinner purses, while maintaining its value system, and so hold up well in recession.

There are a few simple rules to surviving the downturn. The first and most important is that cash is king. As one 'witty' accountant once remarked 'turnover is vanity; profit is sanity; cash flow is reality'. Without cash flow, brands will simply not survive. This forces many finance officers to consider cutting marketing budgets. These are often poorly justified and so it may be the right thing to do. But when marketing communications are well defined there is strong evidence that maintaining marketing budgets in recession leads to greater value.

In 1998, consultancy PIMS showed that of 1,000 consumer brands surveyed, those that cut marketing spend during the 1991–93 recession made higher profits during recession but lost market after it. Maintainers ended up with higher brand values after recession. Brands must maintain their values and investments if they want to emerge unscathed from the recession. Just be sure you have the cash to keep your brand alive.

Source: David Haigh. This article first appeared in *The Marketer* (December 2008/January 2009), p. 15, the magazine of the Chartered Institute of Marketing.

Environmental uncertainty scenario analysis

Johnston et al. (2008) suggest that the perception of environmental uncertainty results from a combination of incomplete information about the environmental events, trends and changes. It could also result from the lack of understanding of what the information means, lack of understanding of the causal relationships, and the inability to develop a response to environmental changes or to predict the effect of a response. Therefore, managers have to make strategic decisions with varying degrees of incompleteness of information about the future of the organization's external environment. One option for dealing with the future is anticipatory action based on the awareness of possible futures. This is the essence of scenario analysis which enables the firm to evaluate the effect of change in multiple variables, and the uncertainties that each holds, thereby allowing the firm to consider strategic actions.

Aaker and McLoughlin (2007) note that scenario analysis provides an alternative for investing in information to reduce environmental uncertainty. Scenario analysis provides a conceptual framework by which organizations can understand the external environment as it unfolds. It basically accepts the uncertainty as given and uses it to provide a description of two or more future scenarios. By creating a number of market context scenarios and evaluating their likelihood and impact, scenario analysis can be a powerful tool to deal with complex environments. Trim and Lee (2008) emphasized that scenario analysis and planning enable staff to find unique solutions to complex, ongoing problems, and if coupled with simulation exercises that are used to develop individuals' decision-making skills, can reinforce the organization's resilience value system by making key decision-makers aware of the changes occurring in the environment and what the likely impact will be should a certain impact materialize. Scenario analysis forces managers to build a strategic monitoring system that enables the organization to formulate robust defensive strategies in times of uncertainty. For example, Shell was among the first to practice scenario planning in the late 1960s and was one of the few companies ready when the oil crisis hit in 1973 (Kachaner and Deimler, 2009).

There are two types of scenario analysis. The first type is strategy-developing scenarios—its key objective is to provide insights into future competitive contexts, then use these insights to assess existing business strategies and stimulate the creation of new ones. This type of scenario analysis can help create contingency plans to save organizations from unexpected events or disasters. It can also suggest investment strategies that allow organizations to capitalize on future opportunities caused by new trends in the market or technological breakthrough. In the second type of scenario analysis, which is 'decision-driven scenarios', a strategy is proposed and evaluated against several scenarios. The key objective is to challenge the strategies, thereby helping to make decisions and suggesting ways to make the strategy more robust in withstanding competitive forces. If the decision, for example, is to enter a new market with new technology, alternative scenarios could be developed about product acceptability in the marketplace, competitor response, and the stimulation of customer applications.

In either type, scenario planning will involve three sequential stages, as suggested by Aaker and McLoughlin (2007). These are: the creation of scenarios, relating these scenarios to existing or potential strategies, and assessing the probability of each scenario. When developing scenarios, it is useful to create them based on probable outcomes: for example, pessimistic scenario, optimistic scenario, and the most likely one. The combination of these can result in several possible scenarios. It is important for organizations to reduce the number of scenarios created by identifying a small set that ideally includes those scenarios that are credible and those that are substantial enough to affect strategy development. Having developed a fewer number of credible scenarios, an organization has to relate them to existing and new strategies. Even if the scenario analysis was not motivated by a desire to formulate new strategies, it is useful to examine what strategies would be optimal for each scenario. Estimating scenario probabilities is the last step of the scenario planning process, by which the organization can evaluate the possible outcome of alternative strategies based on a rich combination of several environmental variables.

Scenario analysis, however, has not been without criticism. Verity (2003) suggests that scenario analysis is not widely used because its methodological applications are confusing to infrequent users. Matching the methodology and the level of analysis to the business issue is difficult and a large number of resources are required. In addition, it is often difficult for organizations to communicate the outcome of scenarios to those not involved in the process.

Strategic analysis of the micro (competitive) environment

The 'micro' or competitive environment includes those forces or groups that directly affect, and are affected by, an organization's major operations. An organization's competitive environment is often referred to as the industry in which the organization competes. A fundamental stage in strategy development is the anticipation and analysis of the major structural elements of the industry. Such structural elements of any industry are identified by Aaker (2005) as industry size, growth, competitive structure, cost structure, channels, trends, and key success factors. The analysis of the industry's environment, however, should include not only the characteristics and trends of the industry but also the forces that influence such characteristics and trends. Many analytical models and frameworks have been suggested for analysing the micro (industry) environment in which any organization operates. In a linear model, Cravens (1994) focuses on the most important aspects that should be examined when analysing the industry environment (see Figure 3.3).

Industry can simply be defined as a group of firms producing similar products or services. From a competitive perspective, industry can also be defined as a group of competitors producing products or services that compete directly with each other. However, one of the most difficult problems in industry analysis is defining the specific industry to which the company's product belongs. This might be because no clear boundaries exist between industries in terms of product lines or geographical area. In practice, many organizations compete for customer's money, e.g. Coke versus Pepsi versus crisps versus a lottery ticket versus a hamburger versus whatever consumers can spend their money on, at the same price. Kotler (2000) suggested that instead of looking at industry as an aggregate group of companies that produce similar products, industry can be looked at as different sets of companies that satisfy the varying needs of customers. Using an illustrative example, industry can be defined and analysed in terms of four levels of competition within an industry:

- **Industry definition based on brand competition:** here, Ford might compete against Fiat, Toyota, and Honda but not against Mercedes.

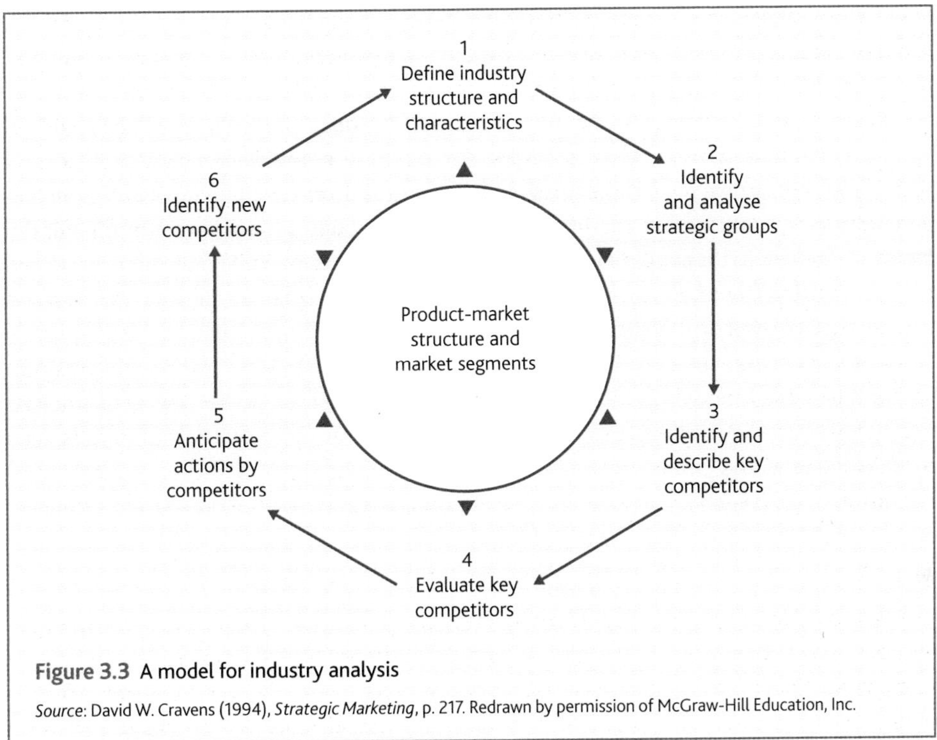

Figure 3.3 A model for industry analysis

Source: David W. Cravens (1994), *Strategic Marketing*, p. 217. Redrawn by permission of McGraw-Hill Education, Inc.

- **Industry definition based on product competition:** here, Ford might compete against all automobile manufacturers.
- **Industry definition based on form competition:** here, Ford might compete against not only other automobile manufacturers but also manufacturers of motorcycles, bicycles, and trucks.
- **Industry definition based on generic competition:** here, Ford might compete against companies that sell major consumer durables, foreign holidays, and new homes.

The potential companies (new entrants) that may come on the scene should also be considered when undertaking industry analysis. Ten years ago, no one would have imagined that Asda might compete in product lines other than food, beverage, and grocery goods. Today, Asda displays under one roof a variety of clothing products, appliances, and financial products alongside its conventional grocery goods. Although identifying the potential new entrants to an industry is not an easy task, they can often be expected to come from the following groups:

- firms not in the industry but which could overcome entry barriers
- firms for which there is obvious synergy from being in the industry
- firms for which competing in the industry is an obvious extension of the strategy
- customers or suppliers who may integrate backwards or forwards.

Another way for analysing the micro environment, which takes full account of the competitive forces that shape the industry structure, is Porter's **five forces model** (1979). According to

Porter's view, the state of competition in an industry depends on five basic competitive forces, the collective strength of these forces determining the ultimate profit potential of the industry and the ability of firms in an industry to earn rates of return on investment in excess of the cost of capital (Porter, 1985). The five forces and the elements related to each force are shown in Figure 3.4.

In his recent publication, Porter (2008) noted that understanding the competitive forces and their underlying causes reveals the roots of an industry's current profitability while providing a framework for anticipating and influencing competition and profitability over time. If the forces are intense, as they are in such industries as airlines, textiles, and hotels, almost no company earns attractive return on investment. If the forces are benign, as they are in industries such as software, soft drinks, and toiletries, many companies are profitable. Industry structure

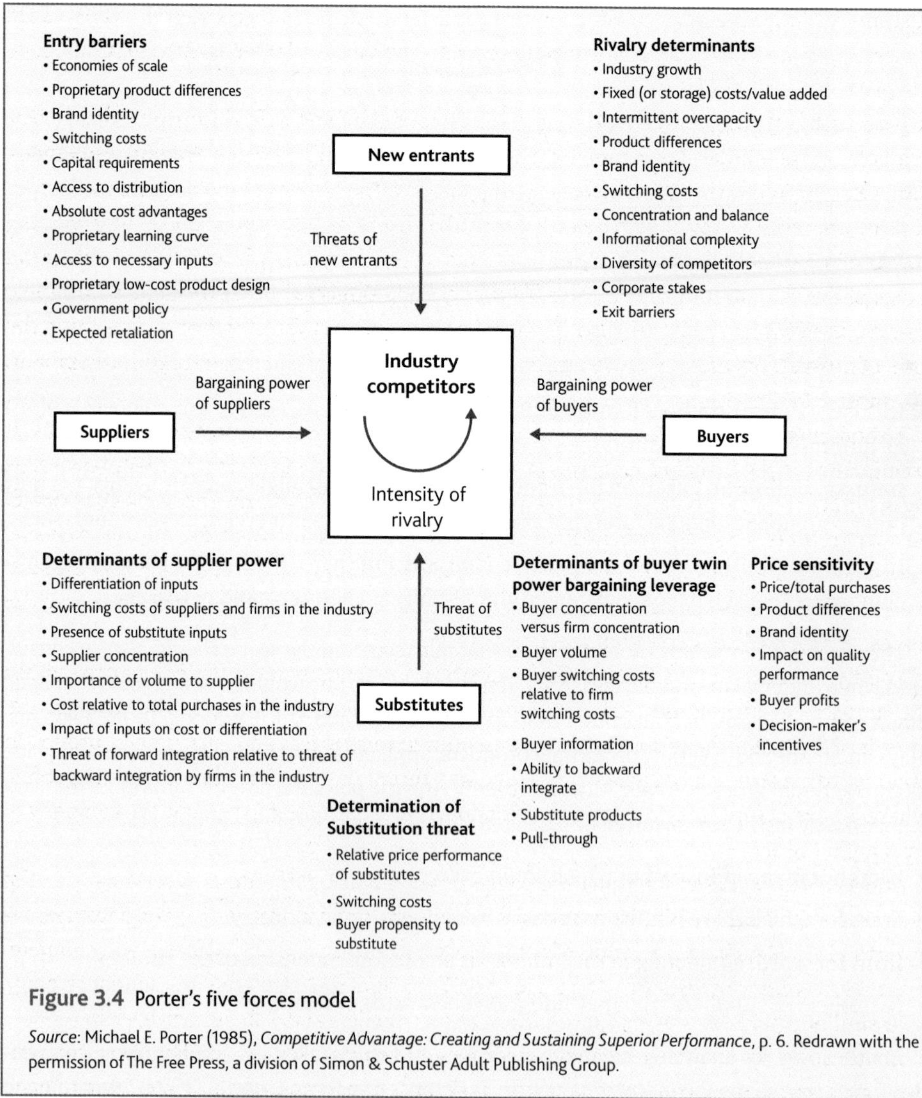

Figure 3.4 Porter's five forces model

Source: Michael E. Porter (1985), *Competitive Advantage: Creating and Sustaining Superior Performance*, p. 6. Redrawn with the permission of The Free Press, a division of Simon & Schuster Adult Publishing Group.

drives competition, not whether an industry produces a product or service, is emerging or mature, high-tech or low-tech, regulated or unregulated.

To illustrate the link between the five forces and strategy development, Porter (1980) pointed out that the goal of competitive strategy for a business unit is to find a position in the industry where the company can best defend itself against these competitive forces or can influence them in its favour. A strategist can analyse any market by rating each competitive force as high, medium, or low in strength. Looking at the sportswear industry in the UK, for example, the five forces could be rated as follows. Competition among existing rivalry is high as key players such as Adidas, Reebok, Nike, and Puma compete closely and strongly in the market. The threat of new entrants might be seen as low, since the UK market has reached the maturity stage and sales growth is not as high as it used to be. The threat of substitute could also be seen as low because other available products do not appeal to customers. The bargaining power of buyers could be rated medium in strength as buyers are interested in buying trendy sports products (well-known brands) but they cannot influence the price in their favour.

Porter (2008) suggested that the configuration of the five forces differs by industry. For example, in the market for commercial aircraft, fierce rivalry between dominant manufacturers Boeing and Airbus and the bargaining power of the airlines that place large orders for aircraft are strong, while the threat of entry, the threat of substitutes, and the bargaining power of suppliers are more benign. In the movie industry, the proliferation of substitute forms of entertainment and the power of the movie producers and distributors who supply movies, the critical input, are also important. The strongest force or forces determine the level of profitability of an industry and become the most important for strategy development. The most salient force, however, is not always obvious.

Although widely used, Porter's five forces model has been subject to several criticisms. It is claimed that the principal criticism of Porter's work is methodological in that many of his points do not appear to be justified. O'Shaughnessy (1995) criticizes the five forces model on two grounds. First, there is little to suggest that Porter's list is necessarily an exclusive or exhaustive one. Second, Porter gives no indication of how to operationalize any analysis based on these forces. In fact, there is no indication of how to assess the relative power of the forces, or how to determine what reactions to take.

The five forces model suggests that competition extends beyond the companies within the industry to include new entries, substitutes, suppliers, and buyers. The stronger the force is, the greater the restrictions on companies to raise prices and earn greater profits. In other words, a strong force may be regarded as a threat because it is likely to reduce profits, whereas a weak force may be viewed as an opportunity because it may allow the company to earn higher profits.

Another approach for analysing the competitive 'micro' environment is to categorize the various competitors within the industry into strategic groups. **Strategic group analysis** is essential for identifying the group of companies with which the organization will compete. A strategic group can be defined as a group of firms pursuing the same or a similar strategy with similar resources. For example, although McDonald's and Subway are both in the fast food industry, they may have different objectives and strategies, and thus belong to different strategic groups. They generally have very little in common and pay little attention to each other when planning competitive actions. Burger King, however, has a great deal in common with McDonald's in that both have a similar strategy of servicing low-priced fast food targeted for sale to the average family.

A firm's strategy can be distinguished using several dimensions that differentiate it from the strategies of other firms in the industry. Such strategic dimensions include those strategic decision variables that best distinguish the business strategies and competitive positioning of the firms within an industry. Two approaches are frequently used for forming strategic groups. The first is a two-dimensional analysis by which a firm selects two strategic variables or characteristics that differentiate the companies within an industry and draws them on the vertical and horizontal axes. The second approach is a multidimensional analysis by which the difficulty of selecting the best two strategic factors can be overcome by incorporating several strategic variables. Figure 3.5 shows an illustrative example of seven strategic groups in the world car industry.

The strategic group approach is an analytical device designed to aid in industry structural analysis. It is an intermediate frame of reference between looking at the industry as a whole and considering each firm separately. We should emphasize here that strategic groups are not equivalent to market segments of segmentation strategies but are defined on the basis of the broader concept of strategic posture. While segmentation analysis focuses on the characteristics of customers and products as the basis for dividing the market, strategic group analysis uses the characteristics of firms and producers as the basis for division.

The benefits of identifying strategic groups are twofold. The first is that the height of the barriers to entry and exit can vary significantly from one group to another. The second

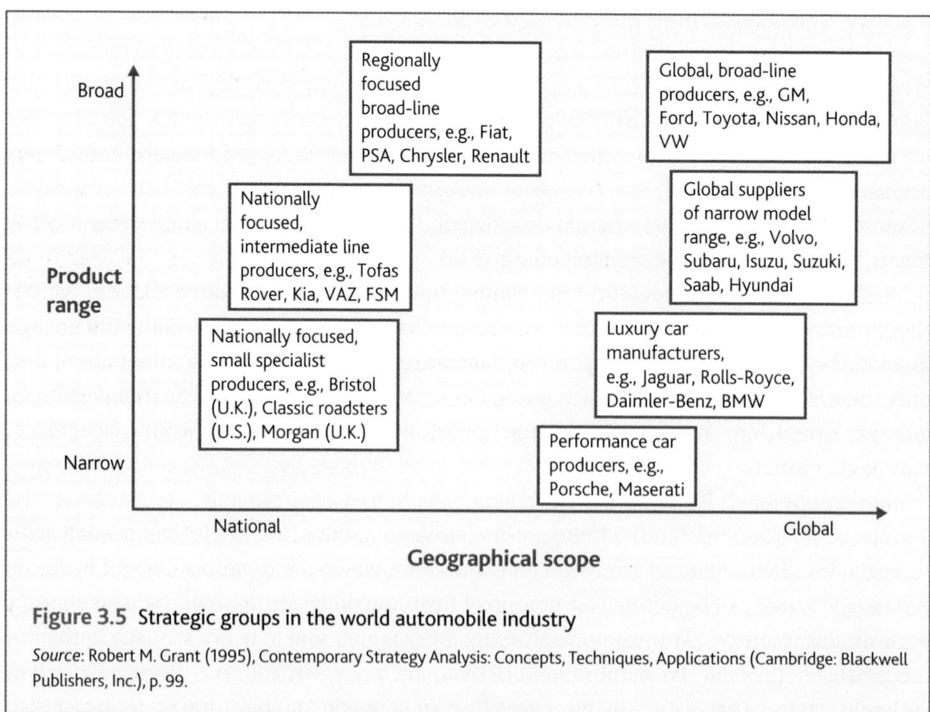

Figure 3.5 Strategic groups in the world automobile industry

Source: Robert M. Grant (1995), Contemporary Strategy Analysis: Concepts, Techniques, Applications (Cambridge: Blackwell Publishers, Inc.), p. 99.

is that the choice of a strategic group determines which companies are to be the principal competitors. Despite these benefits, a number of criticisms have been made. Issues related to identifying appropriate dimensions upon which to develop groups, their number, and the dynamic versus static analysis of strategic group formation remain problematic. While the strategic group is a useful concept, the value of that analysis is as a descriptive rather than a predictive tool. It is unlikely to offer much insight into why some firms in an industry are more profitable than others.

Competitor analysis

Another central aspect of strategic analysis is perceptive competitor analysis. The objectives of undertaking competitor analysis are twofold. First, a company may have to develop a profile of the nature and success of the likely strategy changes each competitor in the market might make. Second, the company may also have to anticipate other competitors' probable response to the range of feasible strategic moves other firms could initiate and each competitor's probable reaction to the array of industry changes and broader environmental shifts that might occur. Competitor analysis is necessary for a company to survive, grow, and remain competitive. Competitor analysis is seen as a set of activities which examines the comparative position of competing organizations within a given strategic sector. The set of activities that organizations might undertake when analysing competitors are:

- identifying the company's competitors
- understanding competitors' objectives
- identifying competitors' strategies
- assessing competitors' strengths and weaknesses
- estimating competitors' reactions
- selecting competitors to attack and those to avoid.

The key to identifying competitors is to link the industry perspective of competition and market perspective of competition by mapping out product/market segments. Such a map is the competitive arena in which a company can identify actual and potential competitors (Kotler, 2000). In identifying the company's competitors, a company should not be restricted to its current competitors, but also take into account potential competitors. Aaker and McLoughlin (2007) noted that, among the sources of potential competitors are firms that might engage in market expansion, product expansion, backward integration, forward integration, and the export of the asset of skills. Shell, for example, has introduced mini-supermarkets to its forecasts to compete with supermarket petrol stations and 24-hour opening for convenience. This has been countered by Tesco with the introduction of 24-hour opening in selective sites around the country.

Having identified the principal competitors, a company needs then to focus on each competitor's objectives. What drives each competitor's behaviour? Companies might begin by assuming that each competitor aims for profit maximization. In practice, however, profit maximization is an unrealistic objective which, for a wide variety of reasons, many companies are willing to sacrifice. The management of Ryan Air, 'the no-frill airline', may have decided in the first three years of its launch not to adopt profit maximization as a strategic objective;

instead, they were interested in achieving a sustainable market share in the domestic and Western European market. Therefore, one must assume that each competitor has a variety of objectives, each of which has a different weight. These objectives might typically include cash flow, market share growth, technological leadership, or overall market leadership. Gaining an insight into this mix of objectives allows the strategist to arrive at tentative conclusions about how a competitor will respond to a competitive thrust. For example, a firm like Volkswagen pursuing market share growth in the world car market is likely to react far more quickly and strongly against a price cut or a substantial increase in advertising spending than a firm like Microsoft, aiming for technological leadership.

The starting point for understanding competitors' strategies is identifying each competitor's assumptions. These assumptions generally fall into two major categories: (a) the competitor's assumptions about the industry and other companies; and (b) the competitor's assumptions about itself. A competitor's assumptions about the industry and other companies may well be subtly influenced by, as well as reflected in, its current strategy. Knowing a competitor's assumptions will guide a firm to identify the basis of the competitor's strategy; for example, the competitor may see itself as socially aware, an industry leader, a low-cost producer, or as having the best salesforce. These assumptions will influence how the competitor behaves, the way it reacts to events, and how it formulates its own competitive marketing strategy.

Having defined the competitors' assumptions, the firm is in a position to develop statements of the current strategy of each competitor. This strategy is most usefully thought of as a key operating policy in each functional area of the business. The firm needs to know each competitor's product features, quality, customer services, pricing policy, distribution coverage, salesforce policy, and advertising and other promotion programmes. The firm has also to estimate competitors' future strategies. These strategies may simply follow the general direction already established, particularly if there are no major external influences requiring them to change their strategies. Nevertheless, it is not wise to assume that an existing strategy will continue to be effective. Competitors' current actions may only signal probable future actions.

By this stage, it should be apparent that the identification and evaluation of competitors' strengths and weaknesses is at the very heart of a well-developed marketing strategy. Understanding a competitor's strengths and weaknesses provides insight into the firm's ability to initiate and/or react to strategic moves, respond to environmental or industry events, and pursue various strategies. The Japanese car producers were able to dominate the world automobile market during the 1970s and 1980s by analysing and understanding competitors' strategies and appreciating competitors' strengths and weaknesses. Such a thorough understanding enabled them to provide customers with better value than the competition.

As a first step, companies can gather secondary data on each competitor's goals, strategies, and performance over the past few years. They can also conduct primary marketing research with customers, suppliers, and dealers in order to understand more about competitors' strengths and weaknesses. According to Aaker (2005), competitor's strengths and weaknesses are based upon the existence or absence of assets or skills. Thus, to analyse competitors' strengths and weaknesses, it is necessary to identify the assets and skills that are relevant to the industry. For example, an intangible asset like Nike's well-known brand could present a major strength, as could a skill like the company's ability to manufacture top quality goods. Conversely, the absence of a unique asset or distinctive skill can present significant weaknesses. The knowledge of a competitor's weaknesses can often be used to great effect by a strategist. Wilson and Gilligan (2005) listed several factors that make a competitor vulnerable such as lack of cash, low margins, poor growth, and limited market share.

A growing number of companies have used benchmarking to assess and trace competitors' strengths. Benchmarking has become a powerful tool for increasing a company's competitiveness. It is a process for measuring products, services, and practices against those offered by leading competitors. The UK Customs and Excise department won the 1996 European best practice benchmarking award for an innovative adaptation of benchmarking to meet the requirements of a public sector organization market testing the value of its activities. Research suggests that benchmarking can actually generate broadly based change in organizations thinking and action and lead to a better understanding of competitors' strengths.

A company's survival depends on anticipating the actions and reactions of rivals. How a competitor is likely to behave in future should be examined from two sides: first, how a competitor is likely to respond to any changes taking place in the external environment; and second, how the competitor is likely to respond to specific competitive moves other organizations might make. Four common reaction profiles among competitors in terms of type and time of response have been identified by Kotler (2000):

- **the laid-back competitor:** does not react quickly or strongly to a given assault
- **the selective competitor:** might react to certain types of assault and not others
- **the tiger competitor:** react swiftly and strongly to any assaults
- **the stochastic competitor:** does not exhibit a predictable reaction pattern.

It has been suggested that firms can build competitive advantage by focusing on the actions and response profiles of their rivals in a market. A firm's response profile can simply be predicted from the manner in which it interprets and processes information.

While competitors can surely be threats, the right competitors can strengthen rather than weaken a firm's competitive position in the market. Companies that learn to live with competitors and even benefit from them will clearly be better positioned for the future. Microsoft and Apple Macintosh are examples of two companies competing in the same market (the PC market) and contributing to the market development and improving customer knowledge. A good competitor is not one that performs the beneficial functions and challenges the firm not to be complacent, but one with which the firm can achieve a stable and profitable industry equilibrium without protracted warfare. Bad competitors, on the other hand, have the opposite characteristics (Porter, 1985). In terms of the strategic benefits of a competitor, Porter (1985) identified four general categories: increasing competitive advantage, improving current industry structure, aiding market development, and deterring entry.

Competitive intelligence

In order to undertake competitor analysis that will be of value, a company needs to collect relevant information in an effective manner. Such information should be collected, organized, interpreted, disseminated, and used in a systematic way. Specifically, two basic categories of information are required for marketing strategy development: information about the company itself and relevant information about the company's environment and its competitors. The latter set of information is generally collected through an intelligence system.

Juhari and Stephens (2006) claim that the concept of intelligence has a rich history of more than 200 years. Calof and Wright (2008) referred to the British tea industry as an example that has its history in collecting competitive intelligence when Mr Wickham, who worked as an agent for the English East India Company, was sent to China to gather intelligence and he relayed the importance of tea and its potential to contribute to the British economy.

The concept of intelligence as part of marketing strategy has long been suggested as an effort to improve the organization's competitiveness and its strategic management. The intelligence process has been proposed by many authors under different labels, including environmental scanning, strategic intelligence, competitor analysis, competitive intelligence, and market intelligence. Calof and Wright (2008), for example, pointed out that 'competitive intelligence' is regarded as a system of environmental scanning which integrates the knowledge of everyone in the company. The term encompasses marketing, structural, strategic, and other organizational elements. Trim and Lee (2008) stated that competitive intelligence can be viewed as a process for supporting both strategic and tactical decisions, and in order to support these decisions, organizations need to have processes in place to gather and analyse reliable, relevant, and timely information that is available in vast amounts about competitors and markets. Day and Shoemaker (2006) have brought the concept of peripheral vision, which is also similar to competitive intelligence, as it was with Davenport and Harris (2006), who introduced the competitive analytics concept.

Most of these works have positioned competitive intelligence as a necessary activity for strategic planning/management. Dishman and Calof (2008) believe that the term 'competitive intelligence' may imply the true meaning and purpose of intelligence: that is, to gain strategic advantage. Competitive intelligence includes competitor intelligence as well as intelligence collected about customers, suppliers, technologies, environments, and/or potential business relationships. Calof (2008) identified the objective of any competitive intelligence system as helping organizations sustain and develop distinct competitive advantages by using the entire organization and its networks to develop actionable insights about the various components of the business environment. It uses a systematic and ethical process involving the planning, collection, analysis, communication, and management of the information that has been gathered.

The competitive intelligence system first identifies the vital types of competitive information and the best sources of this information. The system then continuously collects the data from the field. The information should be checked for validity and reliability before key information is communicated to relevant decision-makers. The process and functions of a competitive intelligence system are shown in Figure 3.6.

The effectiveness of any intelligence system is dependent on the frequency of collecting, interpreting, and disseminating the information required about the organization's marketing environment and competitors. Assessing the organizations' intelligence capabilities has been the subject of several studies. For a complete list of these studies, consult Fleisher et al. (2007). For example, Dishman and Calof (2008) found that the practice of competitive intelligence, while strong in the area of information collection, is weak from a process and analytical perspective. Tarraf and Molz (2006) examined the existence of the intelligence system as a business activity in small businesses and found that, while large corporations

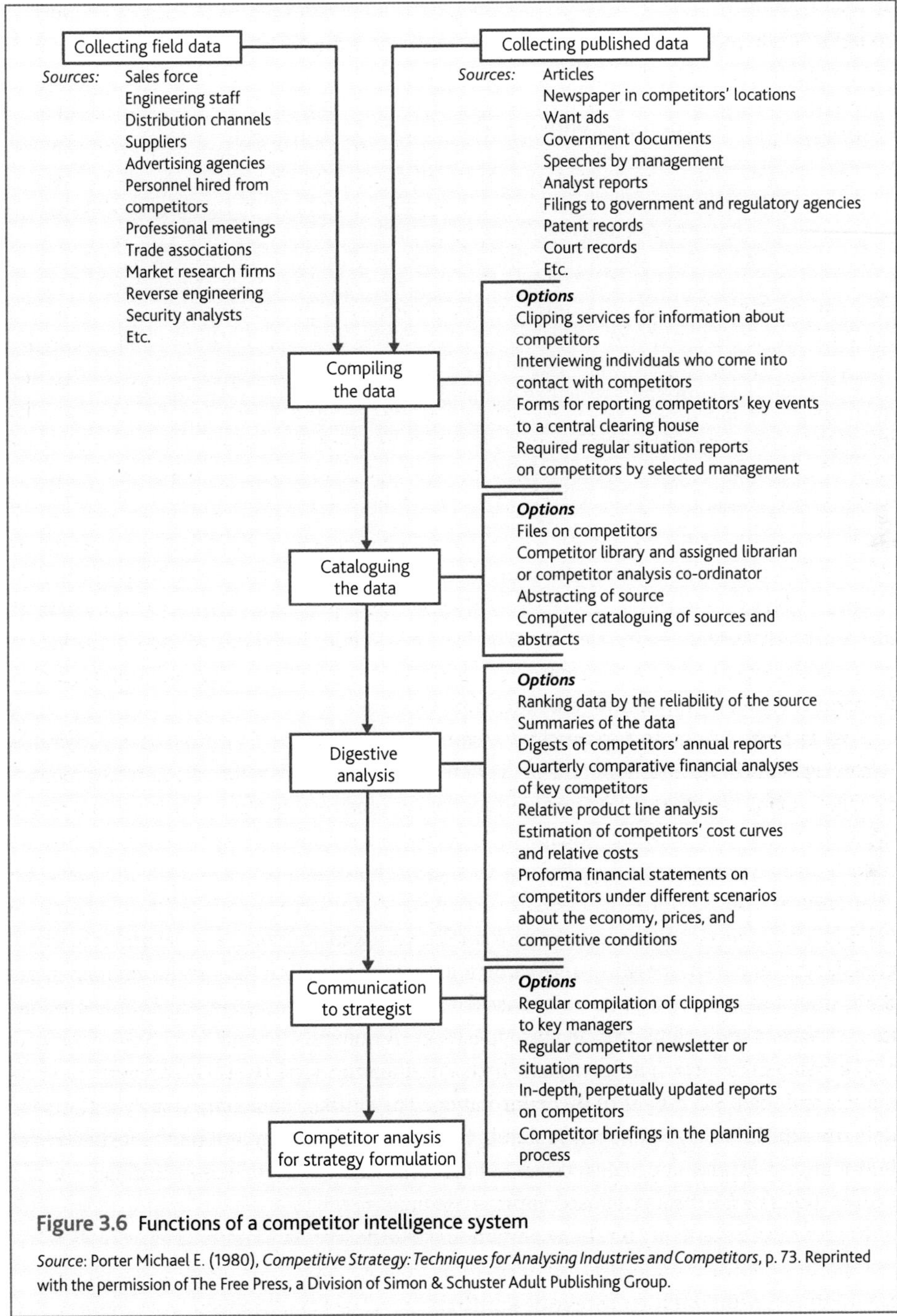

Figure 3.6 Functions of a competitor intelligence system

Source: Porter Michael E. (1980), *Competitive Strategy: Techniques for Analysing Industries and Competitors*, p. 73. Reprinted with the permission of The Free Press, a Division of Simon & Schuster Adult Publishing Group.

normally have an intelligence department, smaller companies may assign specific executives to watch specific competitors. Calof and Wright (2008) examined the effectiveness of competitive intelligence practice from interdisciplinary perspectives and those of practitioners and academics.

Strategic analysis of the internal environment

Internal analysis aims to provide a detailed understanding of those aspects of the organization that are of strategic importance. Although the external information and analysis are essential to success, they are not sufficient to achieve the required success unless they are accompanied by a thorough analysis of the organization's internal environment. The internal appraisal has a pivotal role in formulating marketing strategies and plans with which a firm can trace its success. It has been claimed that differences in performance among companies may be best explained, not through differences in industry structure identified by industry analysis, but through differences in the firm's assets and resources and their application (Hunt and Derozier, 2004). It has also been claimed that a considerable amount of thinking in the 1980s focused upon the nature and structure of the organization's external environment and upon the ways in which this environment is the principal influence on strategy development. More recently, however, it has been argued that the significance of the external environment has been over-emphasized and that a more appropriate focus for strategy development is the organization's resource base (Collis and Montgomery, 2008).

Resource-based approach to internal analysis

The resource-based approach to internal analysis is a well-recognized framework for strategy development (see Figure 3.7). Figure 3.7 illustrates the role of the firm's resources as the foundation for marketing strategy formulation. This framework shows how a firm's resources and capabilities can create a competitive advantage.

The elements of this framework are: (1) defining the firm's resources that present internal strengths and weaknesses; (2) the organization's combined resources form a number of capabilities; (3) these resources and capabilities provide a sustainable competitive advantage; (4) this sustainability derives from linking the organization's unique resources to different types of strategies that exploit these resources and capabilities across time; and (5) the characteristics of resources and capabilities (i.e., durability, transferability, and replicability) are important in sustaining competitive advantage and in identifying resource gaps. Research on the resource-based approach has shown that a company's sustained competitive advantage is primarily determined by its resources and capabilities. The resource audit identifies the unique resources available to an organization to support its strategies. Some of the resources may be unique because they are difficult to imitate, e.g. a world class brand, patented products, or location. A study by Hunt and Derozier (2004) has argued how resource-advantage theory—an evolutionary, disequilibrium-provoking process theory of competition—can ground business and marketing strategy.

In addition to the resource-based approach to analyse the internal environment, strategic managers can adopt/apply one or a combination of other distinct approaches.

Value chain approach to internal analysis

This framework was developed by Porter (1985) as a way of examining the nature and extent of the synergies, if any, among the internal activities of a firm. According to Porter, every firm is a collection of activities that are performed to design, produce, promote, deliver, and support its product. All of these activities can be represented in five primary

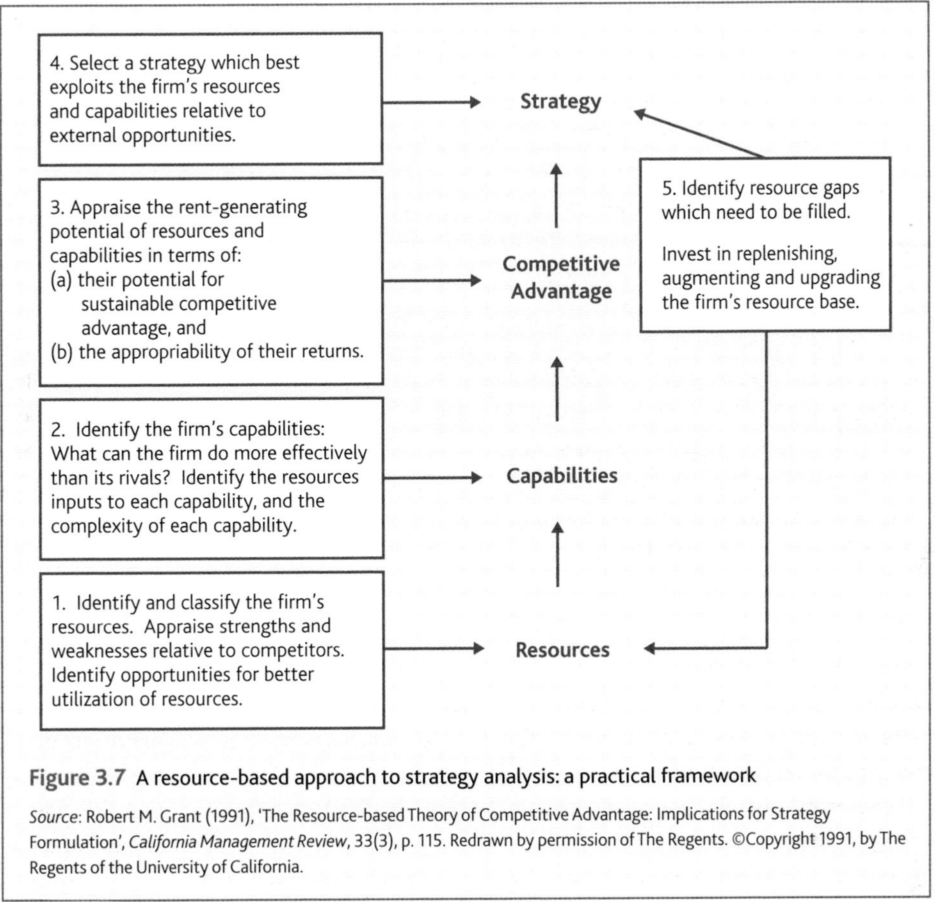

Figure 3.7 A resource-based approach to strategy analysis: a practical framework

Source: Robert M. Grant (1991), 'The Resource-based Theory of Competitive Advantage: Implications for Strategy Formulation', *California Management Review*, 33(3), p. 115. Redrawn by permission of The Regents. ©Copyright 1991, by The Regents of the University of California.

activities and four support activities using a value chain concept (see Figure 3.8). The main idea of a value chain is that it is a systematic way of examining all the activities a firm performs and how they interact to differentiate a firm's value chain from its competitors' value chains. Trim and Lee (2008) note that:

> The value chain concept forces managers to think about supply chain operations and building and maintaining trust-based relationships. Upstream activities need to be adequately evaluated—if, that is, economies of scale are to be realised and new investments in infrastructure are to yield the return expected.

Value chain analysis has been widely used as a means of analysing the internal activities of an organization and relating them to an assessment of the competitive strength of the organization. One of the key benefits of value chain analysis is the recognition that organizations are much more than a random collection of machines, money, and people because these resources are of no value unless deployed in activities and organized into systems which ensure that products and services are produced and valued by the final customer/user.

Because most companies produce several products or services, they may have a different value chain for each of the company's product lines. Thus, the internal analysis of the

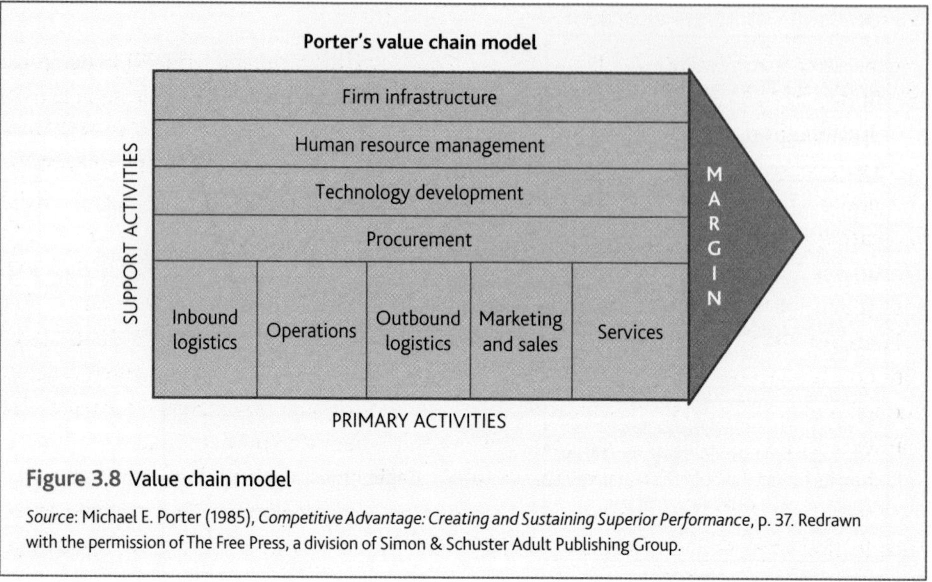

Figure 3.8 Value chain model

Source: Michael E. Porter (1985), *Competitive Advantage: Creating and Sustaining Superior Performance*, p. 37. Redrawn with the permission of The Free Press, a division of Simon & Schuster Adult Publishing Group.

company involves evaluating a series of value chains. The internal analysis of an organization can be undertaken as follows:

- examination of each product line's value chain in terms of the various activities involved in producing that product
- examination of the linkages within each product line's value chain
- examination of the potential synergies among the value chains of different products.

In addition to the above, it should be noted here that much of the value creation occurs not only inside the organization but also in the supply and distribution channels. For example, the quality of a passenger car is not only influenced by the activities undertaken within the manufacturing plant but also determined by the quality of spare parts, components, and the performance of distributors.

Evaluation of functional areas

One of the simplest approaches for analysing an organization's internal environment is functional analysis. A company's skills and resources can be organized into a competence profile according to the typical business functions of marketing, finance, R&D, and productions, among others. The firm's resources include not only the financial and physical resources in each functional area but also the ability of people in each area to formulate and implement the necessary functional objectives, strategies, and policies. The resources include the knowledge of analytical concepts and techniques common to each area and the ability of the people to use them effectively. Used properly, these functional resources serve as strengths to support strategic decisions. In addition to the functional resources, the organization's culture and structure should be regarded as key parts of the organization's internal environment.

Performance analysis approach

The most notable classical work being done in relation to this approach is the **PIMS program** (Profit Impact of Market Strategy) conducted by the Strategic Planning Institute in the US to help pinpoint relevant internal strategic factors for business corporations. The PIMS program was designed to discover empirical principles that determine which strategy variables, and under which conditions, produce what results in terms of return on investment (ROI) and cash flow. Specifically, PIMS research has identified nine major strategic variables that account for 80 per cent of the variation in profitability (ROI) among businesses in the database (Buzzell and Wiersema, 1981; Buzzell and Gale, 1987).

There are many other ways to evaluate the performance of a business. While the most common is the financial measure, other non-financial measures can also provide better understanding of long-term business health. A number of such non-financial measures are market standing, product value, management development, and productivity.

It should be noted here that an organization's strategic objectives may change over time, and so should the financial measures used for assessing business performance. For example, at the introduction stage of a new product, the key measure to use may be sales growth, whilst at the maturity stage, ROI may be used to assess the company's success. Given the importance of both financial and non-financial measures, Kaplan and Norton (1992, 1996) introduced a new, and arguably a comprehensive, method that measures and evaluates a company's performance, namely the **balanced scorecard**. This method recognizes four perspectives by which to integrate the financial and non-financial measures of a company's performance: the *financial perspective*, the *customer perspective*, the *internal business perspective*, and the *innovation and learning perspective*.

Apart from categorizing the internal variables into financial or non-financial, strategic managers must look within their companies to identify the internal strategic factors that have the greatest effect (positive or negative) on the company's performance. In other words, strategic managers should identify the internal variables that may be significant strengths or weaknesses. A variable is a strength if it provides a competitive advantage; is of value to the customer; and the firm does or has the potential to do particularly well relative to the abilities of existing or potential competitors. On the other hand, a variable is a weakness if it is also of value to a customer but the firm does it poorly or does not have the capacity to do it well, although its competitors have that capacity (Wheelen and Hunger, 2004). In evaluating the significance of these variables, strategists should ascertain whether they are a company's particular strengths or weaknesses, which will help determine its future performance. One way of doing this is to compare the measures of these variables with similar measures of: (a) the company's past performance; (b) the company's key competitors; and (c) the industry as a whole.

When using the financial statements to measure a company's performance, strategists should be aware that multinational corporations follow the accounting rules of their home country and, therefore, their financial statements may be somewhat difficult to understand or to use for comparisons with competitors from overseas. For example, British firms such as M&S and BP use the term 'turnover' rather than 'sales revenue'. See Mini Case Study 3.2 on how marketing and finance can work together to restore the commercial credibility of organizations.

MINI CASE STUDY 3.2 Business partnering—cosy up to commercial colleagues

Marketing and finance are all too often at daggers drawn. So why should we bother to work together.

Finance is tired of getting a bad rap and wants to get on better with other departments. Business partnering is the name of the game, according to the Chartered Institute of Management Accountants, which is studying the relationships of its members with other departments. There is an extensive body of evidence that shows our marketing departments need to get closer to finance in order to restore our commercial credibility. McKinsey and Booz Allen recently interviewed scores of marketing directors: both organizations observed a professional discipline struggling to come to terms with the modern business world. Marketers know that they haven't got all the answers, and they acknowledge that they need help.

This is not something that can be solved by sending marketing teams on a half-day commercial awareness seminar. Nor will it be solved by taking our finance director to the pub twice a year, although that might help. Finance people are often seen as bean-counters in ivory towers. Kept at arm's length and dismissed as unimaginative, they can be rather prickly. It need not be like that. I have worked with marketing and finance teams on partnering skills and, with a clear agenda it is possible to achieve big changes.

Skills are the first stop. Both marketing and finance need to augment their specialist skills—it's a mistake to provide general knowledge. What is needed is specifically tailored skill development. We have found that allowing marketing and finance to learn together in a simulated real-firm environment can improve the practical knowledge of both groups in a way that classroom training cannot. Automation is next. The data needed by the financial analysts from marketing usually has to be pulled out of several systems. Many analysts spend much of their working day cutting and pasting spreadsheets and preparing PowerPoint from the data. By automating routine data work, the analysts gain valuable time.

Provision of specialist tools and support is another quick-win area. Although spreadsheets are an important tool for all analysts, more specialist tools are needed to analyse and model marketing. These marketing analysis tools are now becoming available from specialist software firms.

Finally, reviewing the allocation of marketing budgets and headcount can be very revealing. Often, levels of spending in some areas of the department's activity are higher than can possibly be justified, whereas other areas of marketing are starved of resources. Again, instigation of budget and headcount reallocation necessitates top executive support.

Getting up close and personal is something that marketing and finance can and should do. Companies with cosy finance-marketing relations are reporting better results, fewer surprises, and improved inter-departmental trust. It works on a personal level, too. People from both departments find their jobs more interesting and enjoyable, to say nothing of improving their career prospects.

Source: Robert Shaw. This article first appeared in *The Marketer* (December 2007/January 2008), p. 15, the magazine of the Chartered Institute of Marketing.

'Strategic fit'—the conclusion of external and internal strategic analysis

In any model of strategy development, a successful strategy arises from a firm's strategic analysis of emerging opportunities and threats in the external environment, while taking into account the firm's internal strengths and weaknesses. Cravens et al. (2009) note that the development of marketing strategy requires forming a strategic vision and selecting and implementing the market targeting and positioning strategies. At the centre of the process is understanding the marketing environment and competitive space. For this purpose, the organization's strategic analysis of the remote and competitive environments must be concluded by developing what is known as an 'Environmental Impact Matrix' in which major opportunities and threats are identified, their potential impact are assessed/weighted, and their implications for strategy development are accounted for (see Table 3.3).

Similar to the conclusion of the organization's strategic analysis of its external environment, the analysis of the organization's internal environment can also be concluded by developing what is known as a 'Strategic Capability Profile' in which the potential strengths and weaknesses of the organizational resources and capabilities are identified, assessed, and weighted (see Table 3.4).

SWOT analysis (looking at strengths, weaknesses, opportunities, and threats) is usually suggested as a systematic way for integrating internal analysis and external analysis to find a 'strategic fit' between what the environment wants and what the organization has to offer, as

TABLE 3.3 Environmental Impact Matrix:

Factor	Impact of factor	Potential opportunity or threat
The macro environment		
Political/legal	Increased legislation on product liablity	Mild threat (–1)
Economic	Recession in key overseas markets	Major threat (–4)
Technological	Little innovation likely from competitors	Neutral impact (0)
Socio-cultural	Increased awareness of environmental protection issues	Significant opportunity (+5)
The competitive environment		
Competition	Intense rivalry in industry/market place	Critical threat (–5)
Buyers	Convergence of customer requirements worldwide	Significant opportunity (+5)
Suppliers	Few suppliers dominate industry	Critical threat (–5)
Threat of new entrants	Industry barriers to entry are low	Threat (–3)

Source: Reprinted with permission of the authors.

TABLE 3.4 Strategic capability profile (A) based on resource audit

Internal area	Resource/competence	Evaluation
Strategic capability profile (A) based on resource audit		
Physical resources	New facilities incorporating latest technology	Major strength (+4)
Human resources	Highly trained technical staff Top scientists recruited	Minor strength (+2)
Financial resources	High gearing	Mild weakness (–2)
Strategic capability profile (B) based on value chain activities		
Intangibles	Strong corporate image in the marketplace Well-established brand names	Significant strength (+5) Significant strength (+4)
Inbound logistics/ procurement	Over-reliance on a limited number of suppliers	Significant weakness (–4)
Outbound logistics	Ineffective warehouse automation	Weakness (–3)
Human resource management	High levels of absenteeism/poor industrial relations record	Significant weakness (–4)

Source: Reprinted with permission of the authors.

well as between what the organization needs and what the environment can provide. Trim and Lee (2008) describe the SWOT method as a well-established analytical device that is used to appraise an organization's current situation, and can be extended by linking the results of the analysis to scoring procedures and then placing the results in matrices to enhance the strategic decision-making process. SWOT analysis, or situation analysis, is an important foundation for any plan helping to produce realistic and meaningful strategic recommendations for an organization's future directions. Situation analysis provides an appraisal of the difference between the company's current performance and its past stated objectives in the light of the relevant set of information obtained from the company's external and internal environments (Dibb et al., 2006). The four headings of SWOT analysis can be very useful for summarizing many of the elements of the internal analysis and combining them with the key issues arising from the external environment analysis. In fact, SWOT analysis aims to identify the extent to which the current strategy of an organization and its more specific strengths and weaknesses are relevant to, and capable of, dealing with the changes taking place in the business environment.

SWOT analysis is a particularly well-known model and frequently used as a strategic tool. However, this tool has been subject to several criticisms because of its apparent limitations. One of the principal criticisms made about it is that the application of this tool has generally become of no real value in practice. The most common reason for this is the managers' tendency to list strengths, weaknesses, opportunities, and threats in a 'bullet-point format' without paying sufficient attention to their real significance. The result is what academics call 'a balance sheet approach'.

External elements \ Internal elements	Organizational strengths	Organizational weaknesses
	Strategic options	
Environmental opportunities (and risks)	**SO**: Strengths can be used to capitalize or build upon existing or emerging opportunities	**WO**: The strategies developed need to overcome organizational weaknesses if existing or emerging opportunities are to be exploited
Environmental threats	**ST**: Strengths in the organization can be used to minimize existing or emerging threats	**WT**: The strategies pursued must minimize or overcome weaknesses and, as far as possible, cope with threats

Figure 3.9 SWOT/TOWS Matrix

Source: Adapted from Heinz Weihrich (1982), 'The TOWS Matrix—A Tool for Situation Analysis', *Long Range Planning*, 15 (2), p. 60. © Elsevier.

Another criticism, made by Weihrich (1982), is that, having conducted the analysis, managers frequently fail to identify the strategic choices that the outcomes demand. Weihrich (1982) proposed a SWOT (TOWS) matrix which, while making use of the same inputs as the SWOT matrix, recognizes them and integrates them more fully into the strategic management process. This matrix (shown in Figure 3.9), illustrates the alternative ways in which an organization can use its strengths to capitalize on opportunities or to minimize threats and invest in available opportunities to overcome its weaknesses. The SWOT/TOWS matrix is a very useful tool for creating a series of strategic alternatives that decision-makers in an organization might not otherwise have considered.

Finally, once the analytical tool has been chosen for its strategic analysis, an organization needs to review its inputs on a regular or ongoing basis to identify how these inputs are changing and the implications of the changes on the future directions of the marketing strategy development.

Conclusion

The formulation of marketing strategy is the development of long-range plans for the effective management of the major factors and key trends in an organization's marketing environment. Therefore, the development of a marketing strategy should be based on a thorough understanding and effective use of environmental opportunities and threats, while taking into account the organization's strengths and weaknesses. Increasing environmental uncertainty, coupled with increasing pressure on organizations to create and sustain a distinctive competency, means that the scanning and analysis of the internal and external environment will become an important part of every marketer's job. To remain competitive, companies need to consider various methods of gathering, evaluating, and disseminating intelligence to those who need it. The availability of market information and competitive intelligence is essential for the development and success of any marketing strategy in today's business environment.

Summary

This chapter has discussed in greater details the first part (or stage) of the SMM process, namely strategic analysis. Strategic analysis is concerned with understanding the strategic position of an organization in terms of its external environment, its internal resources and competencies, and the expectations and influence of stakeholders. Strategic analysis is central for the development of marketing strategy. Without it, strategic managers could be wrongly guided and the strategy formulated might not be in tune with the key trends in the organization's marketing environment. For proper conduct of strategic analysis, different sets of market information and competitive intelligence should be gathered, scanned, and analysed. This analysis aims not only to identify the possible opportunities and threats in the external environment but also to identify the organization's internal strengths and weaknesses. Many analytical models and frameworks are available to support such an analysis and strategic managers should make their choice based on their understanding of how to operationalize the selected model. To conclude their strategic analysis and to inform the subsequent decision of strategic choices, strategic managers should attempt to find a strategic fit between external opportunities and internal strengths while working around external threats and internal weaknesses.

KEY TERMS

Environmental analysis Is the process of assessing and interpreting the information gathered through market intelligence and environmental scanning.

Environmental scanning Is the process of collecting information about the forces in the environment. Scanning involves observation, perusal of secondary sources such as business, trade, government, and general interest publications, and marketing research.

Scenario analysis Is the process of exploring different assumptions about the environment and its future. It involves the development of a few plausible scenarios, the formulation of strategies appropriate to each scenario, the evaluation of scenario probabilities, and the assessment of the resulting strategies across scenarios.

Strategic analysis Is concerned with understanding the strategic position of the organization in terms of its external environment, internal resources and competencies, and the expectations and influence of stakeholders.

Strategic choice Involves understanding the underlying bases guiding future strategy, and generating strategic options for evaluation and selecting from among them.

Strategic group approach Is an analytical device designed to aid in industry structural analysis. It is an intermediate frame of reference between looking at the industry as a whole and considering each firm separately.

Strategy implementation Is the translation of strategy into organizational action through organizational structure and design, resource planning, and the management of strategic change.

DISCUSSION QUESTIONS

1 Using examples throughout, describe and discuss how the marketing environment can impact on an organization operating within an industry of your choice.

2 With reference to a firm of your choice, discuss the implications of the advances in information technologies for improving the exercise of market scanning and analysis.

3 Discuss the purpose of competitive analysis and explain the major steps an organization might undertake to conduct such an analysis. Support your discussion with examples and the relevant model/frameworks.

4 It has been argued that an effective strategy is the one that is based upon the identification of sustainable competitive advantages. Making reference to the Japanese car producers in the UK, discuss a number of competitive advantages associated with the development of their marketing strategies.

5 As a newly appointed strategist, you are asked to identify and discuss relevant models and frameworks that could be used in analysing an organization's internal environment. Select one of these models and undertake an internal audit for a company of your choice.

ONLINE RESOURCE CENTRE

Visit the Online Resource Centre for this book for lots of interesting additional material at: **www.oxfordtextbooks.co.uk/orc/west2e/**

REFERENCES AND FURTHER READING

Aaker, David A. (2005), *Strategic Market Management* (New York: John Wiley & Sons, Inc.).

Aaker, David A., and Damien McLoughlin (2007), *Strategic Market Management*, European edn (Chichester: John Wiley & Sons, Ltd).

Ansoff, Igor H. (1991), 'Critique of Henry Mintzberg's "The Design School: Reconsidering the Basic Premises of Strategic Management"', *Strategic Management Journal*, 12 (6), pp. 449–61.

Ansoff, Igor H. (1994), 'Comment on Henry Mintzberg's Rethinking Strategic Planning', *Long Range Planning*, 27 (3), pp. 31–2.

Buzzell, Robert D., and Bradley T. Gale, (1987), *The PIMS Principles* (New York: The Free Press).

Buzzell, Robert D., and Frederik D. Wiersema (1981), 'Successful Share-Building Strategies', *Harvard Business Review*, January–February, pp. 135–44.

Calof, Jonathan L. (2008), 'Selling Competitive Intelligence', *Competitive Intelligence Magazine*, 11 (1), pp. 39–42.

Calof, Jonathan L., and Sheila Wright (2008), 'Competitive Intelligence: A Practitioner, Academic and Inter-disciplinary Perspective', *European Journal of Marketing*', 42 (7/8), pp. 717–30.

Collis, David J., and Cynthia A. Montgomery (2008), 'Competing on Resources', *Harvard Business Review*, (July–August), pp. 140–50.

Cravens, David W. (1994), *Strategic Marketing* (New York: Richard D. Irwin).

Cravens, David W., Nigel F. Piercy, and Arthur Baldauf (2009), 'Management Framework Guiding Strategic Thinking in Rapidly Changing Markets', *Journal of Marketing Management*, 25 (1/2), pp. 31–49.

Davenport, T. H., and J. G. Harris (2006), *Competing on Analytic* (Boston, MA: Harvard Business School Press).

Day, G. S., and P. Shoemaker (2006), *Peripheral Vision: Detecting the Weak Signals that will Make or Break your Company* (Boston, MA: Harvard Business School Press).

Dibb, Sally, Lyndon Simkin, William M. Pride, and O. C. Ferrell (2006), *Marketing: Concepts and Strategies* (Boston, MA: Houghton Mifflin Company).

Dishman, Paul L., and Jonathan L. Calof (2008), 'Competitive Intelligence: A Multiphasic Precedent to Marketing Strategy', *European Journal of Marketing*, 42 (7/8), pp. 766–85.

Fleisher, C. S., S. Wright, and R. Tindale (2007), 'A Chronological and Categorised Bibliography of Key Competitive Intelligence Scholarship: Part 4', *Journal of Competitive Intelligence and Management*, 4 (1), pp. 34–107.

Grant, Robert M. (1991), 'The Resource-Based Theory of Competitive Advantage: Implications for Strategy Formulation', *California Management Review*, 33 (3), pp. 114–35.

Hunt, Shelby D., and Caroline Derozier (2004), 'The Normative Imperatives of Business and Marketing Strategy: Grounding Strategy in Resources-advantage Theory', *Journal of Business and Industrial Marketing*, 19 (1), pp. 5–22.

Johnson, Gerry, and Kevan Scholes (2005), *Exploring Corporate Strategy*, (Harlow: Prentice-Hall Europe Ltd.).

Johnston, Michael, Audrey Gilmore, and David Carson (2008), 'Dealing with Environmental Uncertainty: The Value of Scenario Planning for Small to Medium-sized Enterprises', *European Journal of Marketing*, 42 (11), pp. 1170–8.

Juhari, A. S., and D. P. Stephens (2006), 'Tracing the Origins of Competitive Intelligence throughout History', *Journal of Competitive Intelligence and Management*, 3 (4), pp. 61–82.

Kachaner, Nicolas, and Michael S. Deimler (2009), 'Stretching the Strategy Process', *Strategic Decision*, 25 (1), pp. 17–20.

Kaplan, Robert S., and David P. Norton (1992), 'The Balanced Scorecard—Measures that Drive Performance', *Harvard Business Review*, January–February, pp. 71–90.

Kaplan, Robert S., and David P. Norton (1996), 'Using the Balanced Scorecard as a Strategic Management System', *Harvard Business Review*, January–February, pp. 75–85.

Kotler, Philip (2000), *Marketing Management* (Englewood Cliffs, NJ: Prentice Hall, Inc.).

Miles, Raymond E., and Charles Snow (1978), *Organisational Strategy, Structure and Process* (New York: McGraw-Hill, Inc.).

Mintzberg, Henry (1990), 'The Design School: Reconsidering the Basic Premises of Strategic Management', *Strategic Management Journal*, 11 (3), pp. 171–95.

Mintzberg, Henry (1994a), *The Rise and Fall of Strategic Planning* (Englewood Cliffs, NJ: Prentice Hall, Inc.).

Mintzberg, Henry (1994b), 'Rethinking Strategic Planning, Part I: Pitfalls and Fallacies', *Long Range Planning*, 27 (3), pp. 12–21.

Mintzberg, H., and J. Lampel (1999), 'Reflecting on the Strategy Process', *Sloan Management Review*, 40 (Spring), pp. 21–30.

O'Shaughnessy, John (1995), *Competitive Marketing: A Strategic Approach* (London: Routledge).

Porter, Michael E. (1979), 'How Competitive Forces Shape Strategy', *Harvard Business Review*, March–April, pp. 137–45.

Porter, Michael E. (1980), *Competitive Strategy: Techniques for Analyzing Industries and Competitors* (New York: The Free Press).

Porter, Michael E. (1985), *Competitive Advantage: Creating and Sustaining Superior Performance* (New York: The Free Press).

Porter, Michael E. (2008), 'The Five Competitive Forces that Shape Strategy', *Harvard Business Review*, January, pp. 79–93.

Tarraf, P., and R. Molz (2006), 'Competitive Intelligence at Small Enterprises', *SMA Advanced Management Journal*, 71 (4), pp. 24–35.

Trim, Peter R. J., and Yang-Im Lee (2008), 'A Strategic Marketing Intelligence and Multi-organisational Resilience Framework', *European Journal of Marketing*, 42 (7/8), pp. 731–45.

Utterback, James M., and W. J. Abernathy (1975), 'A Dynamic Model of Product and Process Innovation', *Omega*, 3 (6), pp. 639–56.

Verity, J. (2003), 'Scenario Planning as a Strategy Technique', *European Business Journal*, 15 (4), pp. 185–95.

Weihrich, Heinz (1982), 'The TOWS Matrix—A Tool for Situation Analysis', *Long Range Planning*, 15 (2), pp. 54–66.

Wheelen, Thomas L., and David J. Hunger (2004), *Strategic Management and Business Policy* (New York: Addison-Wesley Publishing Company, Inc.).

Wilson, Richard M. S., and Colin Gilligan (2005), *Strategic Marketing Management: Planning, Implementation and Control* (Oxford: Elsevier Butterworth-Heinemann).

Wright, S. (2005), 'The CI Marketing Interface', *Journal of Competitive Intelligence and Management*, 3 (2), pp. 3–7.

KEY ARTICLE ABSTRACTS

Brews, Peter, and Purohit Devavrat (2007), **'Strategic Planning in Unstable Environments'**, *Long Range Planning*, 40, pp. 64–83.

This article shines a new light on strategic planning, with emphasis on the multi-dimensionality of the strategic planning process in unstable environments.

Abstract: This is another empirical study that uses a multinational survey of 886 firms to examine how planning increases environmental instability. The paper suggests that certain planning dimensions such as generative and transactive planning are strongly associated with environmental instability. However, other planning dimensions such as symbolic and rational planning are more strongly associated with firm size than with environmental instability. The study confirms that planning does have potential to produce positive effects on the performance of companies.

Cravens, David W., Nigel F. Piercy, and Artur Baldauf (2009), **'Management Framework Guiding Strategic Thinking in Rapidly Changing Markets'**, *Journal of Marketing Management*, 25 (1/2), pp. 31–49.

This is a very interesting article that develops and discusses a new management framework to guide strategic thinking in changing markets.

Abstract: The study offers some valuable views/suggestions for managers and executives to cope with the complex and rapidly changing business environment. The proposed framework aims to guide managers in obtaining information, the perceptive interpretation of strategic issues and trends, and the choice of the right strategic initiatives. The development of the framework has been based on conceptual logic and empirical findings from multiple disciplines, including marketing strategy and strategic management.

Johnston, Michael, Audrey Gilmore, and David Carson (2008), **'Dealing with Environmental Uncertainty: The Value of Scenario Planning for Small to Medium-sized Enterprises'**, *European Journal of Marketing*, 42 (11), pp. 1170–8.

This is a useful article that discusses environmental uncertainty and the value of scenario planning for small to medium-sized enterprises (SMEs) operating in a volatile environment.

Abstract: The article provides a thorough review of the literature of strategy formulation, environmental uncertainty, and scenario planning in the context of managerial decision-making. The paper notes that the strategy formulation process is about matching an organization's internal competencies with the external environment it anticipates in the future. And since the future external environment cannot be predicted, especially in volatile markets, the challenge for managers is to make their strategic decisions under varying degrees/types of environmental uncertainty, and the best way to do this is through scenario analysis and planning.

Wirtz, Brend W., Alexander Mathieu, and Oliver Schilke (2007), **'Strategy in High-Velocity Environment'**, *Long Range Planning*, 40, pp. 295–313.

This is an empirical study that draws from industrial economics and the resource-based view to conceptualize strategy in high-velocity environments.

Abstract: This study investigates industries such as information and communications technologies and biotechnology as high-velocity environments in which demand, competition, and technology are constantly changing. The study examines the positive/negative effects of such environment characteristics on the business perfomance of organisations. The article has been concluded with some useful directions for future research.

END OF CHAPTER 3 CASE STUDY
British Airways and the credit crunch in the aviation industry

Introduction

The airline industry in the UK is highly concentrated and can be divided into two main sub-sectors; scheduled airlines (e.g., British Airways, BMI), and budget airlines (e.g. easyJet, Ryanair). Historically, scheduled airline carriers have enjoyed little in the way of price competition and have been able to dominate their chosen markets by controlling prices, as people's inspiration to fly and the need for business travel due to globalization meant that demand was on the upward curve. The advent of low-cost carriers in the mid 1990s, an idea which was taken from the American Southwest low-cost airline, has increased competition by giving consumers more choices. The introduction of carriers such as Ryanair did, of course, force companies through the industry to re-evaluate their strategies in order to be able to compete effectively. Intense competition and the rise in the number of carriers have increased demand as the price of aviation fell, making it a more affordable luxury.

The notable difference in price between budget carriers and scheduled airlines resulted in a reduction in their short-haul traffic, a situation exacerbated by the horrific attack of September 11, 2001. Although the growth rate in the industry has been steadily on the rise since its formation, events such as 9/11 and the Gulf War were testing times for the industry, which saw a significant decline after 9/11 and an impact on transatlantic flights. According to Datamonitor analysis, the growth rate of the UK airline industry has been relatively weaker than its counterpart in other parts of Europe. For example, between 1999 and 2003, the UK airline industry shrank, with a compound annual growth rate of –2.2 per cent. However, it was expected that the airline industry value would increase at the rate of CAGR 4.6 per cent by 2008.

It has been argued that scheduled airlines are at a mature stage of the industry life cycle compared to low-cost carriers, which are said to be at a growth stage. Therefore, it is expected that low-cost carriers will have a better chance in the future compared to scheduled airlines. Scheduled airlines were, therefore, advised to look more carefully at their marketing strategy in order to stay competitive.

British Airways is one of the major airlines in the UK, with more than 200 destinations in ninety different countries. Through the OneWorld Alliance and other alliances, BA offers its customers seamless flights to more than 500 destinations around the world. BA has seven classes, or seat bands, that it offers to its customers to meet their needs (i.e., First class, Club World, Club Europe, World Traveller Plus, World Traveller, Euro Traveller, Domestic). It is also recognized as one of the major cargo airlines in the world.

British Airways is engaged in the operation of international and domestic scheduled and charter air services for passenger travel, freight and mail, and for the provision of ancillary services. The company dominates the UK airline market by serving more passengers than its rivals of BMI, easyJet, and Ryanair. The difference between the volume and value share held by British Airways is reflective of the international long-haul scheduled service focus of its business.

British Airways Plc owns 17 per cent of Qantas, 9 per cent of Iberia, and 100 per cent of BA. The company's global position helped it to gain access to most of the regions around the world where there is demand for air travel. BA enjoys a strong network presence both in the domestic and the international market, which means that BA can generate a traffic feed for both domestic and international flights. Due to its established brand name and its engagement in alliances like OneWorld, BA has managed to serve customers in more than 130 countries to travel to more than 500 destinations around the world. The company is also trying to get involved in further alliances to increase its parameters (BBC News). BA's frequent flyer and loyalty programmes have also helped the company to retain its customers. As BA focuses on highly profitable business segments, it has launched different classes or seat bands. The airline offered improved amenities, including sleeper seats in an attempt to lure business travellers at the expense of economy class travellers.

The company had previously implemented a procedure of cost cutting by reducing its number of jobs and making annual cost savings. BA has also standardized its aircraft fleet, reducing costs and complexity even further. According to Datamonitor, the company generated $13.93 billion for the fiscal year ended 2004. Its net income was $240 million in the fiscal year of 2004, up 110.5 per cent from the fiscal year of 2002. In the year ending March 2004, BA achieved a cost saving of $869 million and a reduction in manpower of 13,082, against a target of $650 million and 13,000 in manpower, respectively (Key Note Ltd).

In addition to this, a number of initiatives have been implemented by BA to enhance its air travel service. Employing a mix of people from different backgrounds has led BA to improve its customer service. Capitalizing on technology has also enabled BA to introduce some new and innovative ideas. For example, effective from September 2004, customers using 'Manage your Booking' can now check online for their flight without the need to register with BA-registered staff. BA's Skyflyer Solo programme takes special care through the airport processes for children who travel on a flight by themselves. The timetable for BA flight schedules can be accessed and downloaded from anywhere in the world on to PDA and PCs. Moreover, the construction of Terminal 5 at Heathrow Airport enabled BA to timetable more takeoff and landing slots, which will give the company an opportunity to fly to more destinations.

Despite the apparent success in implementing these initiatives, the continuing threat of terrorist attacks, coupled with the fluctuation in foreign currency exchange rates have affected the number of business travellers and resulted in reducing BA's business and earnings. Also, the increasing concern for a sustainable environment and the company's effort to abide by the new environmental regulations have increased BA's expenditure and hence affected its revenue. Adding to these, and more importantly, was the credit crunch and economic crisis of 2008/2009, which is expected to affect the company and its business very significantly.

The credit crunch and the aviation industry

The effect of the credit crunch on the airline industry has been significant, as rising oil prices pushed up ticket prices. Coupled with cutbacks in spending due to the recession, this meant extinction for some of the smaller airlines and the beginning of a difficult financial period for the likes of BA and other flag carriers in Europe such as Air France-KLM and the Italian airline, Alitalia.

The aviation industry had already seen a number of casualties prior to the arrival of the credit crunch in the UK, primarily all business class airlines. The first of the casualties was the business class airline Maxjet, which placed the blame on an unsuccessful attempt to raise further capital. The American-based airline filed for bankruptcy in December 2007, and blamed the difficulties they faced on increasing competition, soaring oil prices, and the decline in consumer spending. Their small number of aircraft (only five) also hindered the company's ability to compete efficiently, although this was common in business-class only airlines. This particular reason may be seen as another cause for the failure of such small companies, which were up against established airlines such as British Airways which benefited from economies of scale. Many analysts had predicted the downfall of companies in this line of business and noted that this was due to their business models being similar. The collapse of Maxjet was soon followed by the collapse of another business class airline—Eos. In April 2008, Eos ceased trading, saying it had insufficient cash to continue operations. Similarly, they blamed difficult trading conditions on the reduction in passengers willing to buy or consume luxury goods/services.

Closer to home in the UK, **Ryanair** had a different take on the credit crunch as chief executive Michael O'Leary delivered a buoyant economic forecast, predicting that this budget airline would reap the benefits of the recession as people down-traded, which he stated would make travel on Ryanair more appealing. There was even talk on the possibility of expansion through the creation of a sister company to launch a low-cost long-haul airline, if aircraft were to become available at reduced rates due to the pending bankruptcies of many within the industry.

Ryanair's optimistic outlook had even seen them stating that they hoped to take advantage of the fuel prices in October 2008, which were at near $70 a barrel, down from the record $140 a barrel in July 2008. They hoped that if oil prices remained at below $80 a barrel, then profits would soon recover and possibly even force competitors to further increase fares, as some had already hedged oil prices for the next year at a significantly higher rate than Ryanair. This scenario would further widen the price gap between Ryanair's already lower fares and competitors. The other attempts to increase revenue and profitability included the suspension of several less profitable routes, some temporarily and others permanently.

However, by no means was Ryanair immune from the credit crunch, as it reported that profits had fallen a massive 47 per cent in the first half of the 2008 financial year due to the doubling of fuel prices. This led Ryanair to request a probe by the Office of Fair Trading (OFT) into the

50 per cent increases it was facing from Belfast and Glasgow Prestwick Airports, which they stated were Air BP's unjustified attempts to impose monopolies in these airports.

Another example is Irish airline, Aerlingus, which expanded rapidly due to the success of its low-cost business model, making it Europe's third largest airline in terms of passenger numbers. However, the company's performance has been affected by the current business conditions of the recession as its total revenue was down from £631.8 million in 2008, to £555 in the first half of 2009 (**http://www.aerlingus.com/Corporate/Half_year_results_2009_presentation.pdf**). The company was enjoying a successful period before the credit crunch as both revenues and profits doubled over the course of the previous five years before the financial crisis, and so it was believed that it was in a strong position to overcome the uncertain period as numerous companies around it folded.

The impact of the credit crunch on British Airways

(*Source*: BBC News, available at: **http://www.news.bbc.co.uk/go/pr/fr/-/1/hi/business/8062844.stm**)

One of the most notable examples of the negative effect of the credit crunch on airlines has been seen in British Airways. In May 2009, BA announced its biggest loss since the company was privatized in 1987. BA reported a pre-tax loss of £401 million for the year ending 31 March, after seeing its profits hit by the economic downturn in terms of a weak pound and higher fuel costs. Although revenues increased to almost £9 billion, BA faced a near-£3 billion fuel bill. The airline made a revised profit of £922 million in the previous year.

Chief Executive Willie Walsh said he saw 'no signs of recovery anywhere. It is difficult to avoid the impression that at least part of BA's agony, its descent in just twelve months from record profits to record losses, was of its own making.' Fuel costs rose 44.5 per cent after the price of oil soared in 2008. The weaker pound also contributed to rising costs, as fuel is bought in US dollars. But BA said it expected lower fuel prices to reduce its fuel costs by about £400 million in the year ahead.

The results also included redundancy-related costs of £78 million. BA said it had cut more than 2,500 jobs since the summer of 2008 and that it was in talks with unions about 'pay and productivity changes'. BA offered staff the option of taking unpaid leave or working part-time. Walsh said he would work for no pay in July 2009. He stated that, 'I certainly want to make a contribution in recognition of the extremely challenging position we face.' Walsh earns £735,000 a year. Finance Director Keith Williams, who is paid £440,000 a year, will also forgo his pay for the month of July 2009.

Despite BA's claims that it has been a victim of the global economic downturn, analysts say the airline is not entirely blameless for its poor results. One of BA's biggest problems is the 13 per cent drop in the number of the airline's real earners—the business travellers. Travel writer Simon Calder said that BA had been particularly hit by a fall in premium traffic—business class and first class passengers—which was down 13 per cent. The premium traffic, which accounts for half of BA's income, has simply dried up. BA bases its business on the fact that there will be plenty of businesses wanting to fly, but businesses are simply cutting back. Although the airline is doing all it can to keep them flying, including a recent offer of 'Buy One Get One Free', it is much harder for BA to take on the likes of easyJet and Ryanair when it comes to offering cheap economy seats. easyJet in particular is deliberately punting for business passengers forced to travel on a budget.

Another big problem is an old one. BA's fuel bills soared by 44.5 per cent in 2008. The real problem here is that the world's airlines buy their fuel in dollars, and the exchange rate against the pound was not good for BA. Another problem behind BA's loss was said to result from a lamentable rise in costs, including engineering and aircraft costs, landing fees, and staff costs. However, in 2009, BA said that it had seen a 'significantly better' operational performance, and that it had received record customer satisfaction ratings.

BA confirmed that the outlook for the airline industry was tough and it would not be paying dividends this year. It plans to reduce capacity by 4 per cent over the winter of 2009 by grounding as many as sixteen aircraft. BA is not the only airline suffering in the global recession, as higher fuel prices and a drop in demand for air travel have affected the whole industry. In May 2009, the Emirates group reported a 72 per cent fall in profits, and Air France-KLM revealed a net loss of £505 million in the three months to 31 March 2009, compared with a £534 million loss in the same period a year earlier.

The impact on the airlines soon passed through onto airports as it logically would, but the reduced number of flights flying through UK airports was not the sole reason for hitting airport profit margins so sharply. BAA Airport Ltd, which owns and operates numerous airports worldwide, including seven British airports, is one of the world's largest airport companies and has played an integral role in making 'London one of the world's best connected cities', which in turn has vastly contributed to the British economy. BAA's ownership of so many airports, in fact, has recently been up for review by the UK competition commission, which is forcing it to sell three airports to reduce fears that the monopolistic position held by BAA could have adverse effects on airlines, which in turn would be passing additional costs onto passengers.

The majority of BAA's income is derived from charging landing fees to airlines. Prior to the credit crunch, BAA's income was increasingly coming from retail outlets in its airports through business activity such as duty-free stores. Its financial performance had been significantly affected over the course of 2008 due to the general economic crisis. It blamed the fall in profits on airlines cutting routes, increased fares due to tax and fuel hikes, and increased security checks, which raised operation cost. The fall in the number of passengers travelling was seen across the country, particularly in airports such as Glasgow International, which is very much dependent on leisure travel. This fall in passenger numbers was attributed to individuals cutting back on their leisure travel in an attempt to reduce outgoings.

Although the demise of the airline industry had primarily been put down to the sudden hike in oil prices, the recovery would not be as straightforward as the oil price fall may have suggested. Although oil prices had fallen dramatically within the course of three months, most of the damage had already been done. Companies had predicted that oil prices would continue to rise and had already hedged oil prices at higher prices, meaning that the recent reduction in oil prices would be near impossible to pass instantly onto passengers.

Source: This case was prepared by Essam Ibrahim of the University of Edinburgh as the basis for analysis and class discussion and not to illustrate either effective or ineffective handling of an administrative situation.

QUESTIONS

1. Use the analytical models illustrated in this chapter to analyse the macro environment of BA, paying particular attention to the economic environment, and assess the emerging opportunities and threats to the airline industry.
2. Analyse the competitive environment in which BA operates, and advise the management on how to cope with what seems to be fierce competition in this market.
3. Identify and critically evaluate the key capabilities and core competences of BA, and advise the company on ways to capitalize on its strengths to overcome weaknesses and how to invest in opportunities to avoid threats.

Part III Where do we want to be?

I. Introduction

1. Overview and strategy blueprint
2. Marketing strategy: analysis and perspectives

II. Where are we now?

3. Environmental and internal analysis: market information and intelligence

III. Where do we want to be?

4. Strategic marketing decisions, choices, and mistakes
5. Segmentation, targeting, and positioning strategies
6. Branding strategies
7. Relational and sustainability strategies

IV. How will we get there?

8. Product innovation and development strategies
9. Service marketing strategies
10. Pricing and distribution
11. Marketing communications
12. E-marketing strategies
13. Social and ethical strategies

V. Did we get there?

14. Strategy implementation, control, and metrics

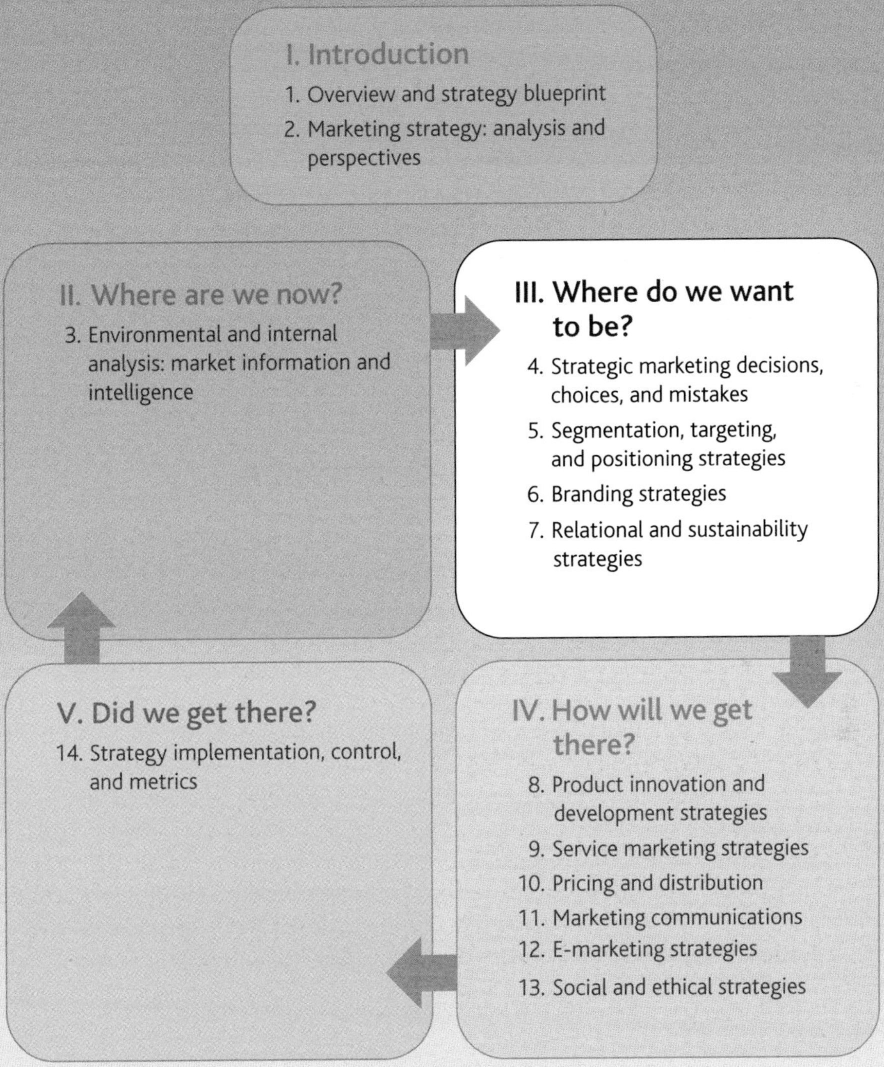

4

Strategic marketing decisions, choices, and mistakes

LEARNING OBJECTIVES

- Outline the hierarchy of strategic choices and decisions at three organizational levels
- Discuss strategic decisions at the corporate and SBU levels, such as selection of directional strategy and choice of generic strategy
- Discuss the strategic marketing decisions, including products to offer, markets to target, and competitive position strategies
- Review the analytical models and frameworks that can be used to help in the strategic choice and decisions stage

CHAPTER AT A GLANCE

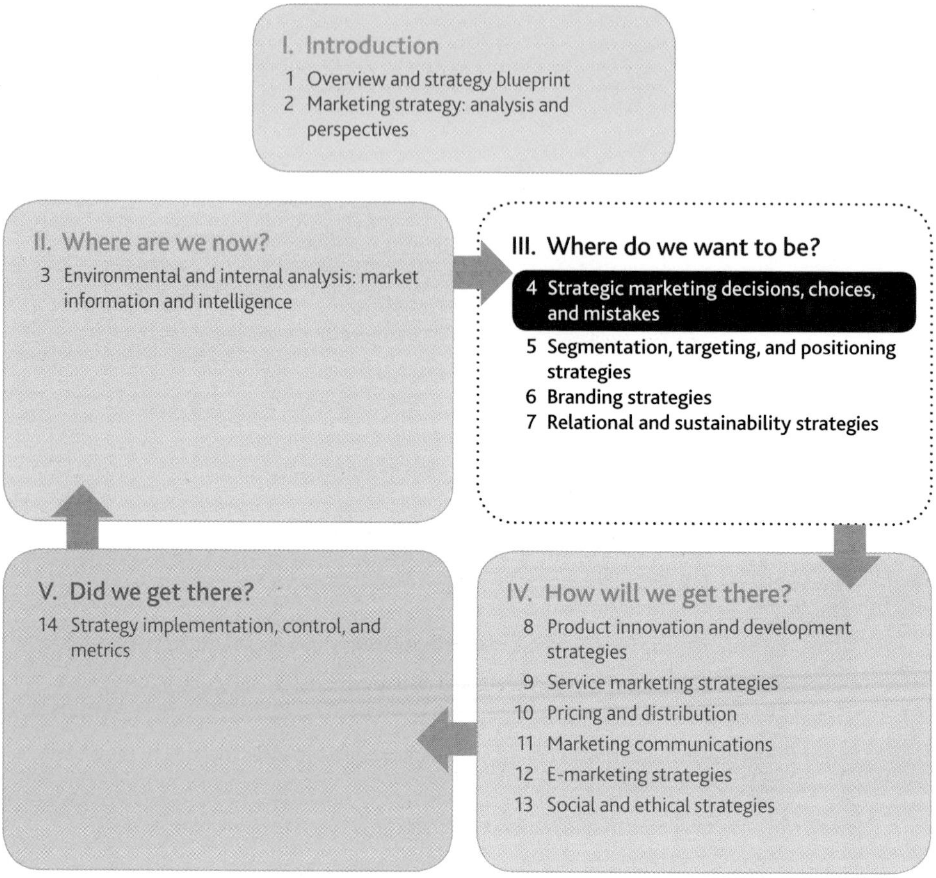

Introduction

Companies aspiring to meet the challenges of today's rapidly changing markets and increasing competition require strategic management decisions to be founded on well-conceived strategies. Well-justified decisions and clearly defined strategies are vital if the firm is to achieve its goals and objectives while optimizing the use of its resources (Ward and Lewandowska, 2008). The primary thrust of this chapter is to discuss in greater detail the second stage/area of the Strategic Marketing Management process (SMM), that is, strategic choice and decisions. *Strategic choice* involves understanding the underlying bases guiding future strategy, and generating strategic options for evaluation and selecting from among them (Johnson and Scholes, 2005). Drawing upon the conclusion of the strategic analysis stage, managers will have to identify and assess the alternative ways in which their organization can use its strengths to capitalize on opportunities or minimize threats, and invest in available opportunities to overcome its weaknesses. The key task is to generate a well-justified set of strategic options and choose from them the ones that will contribute to the achievement of the corporate strategic goals and objectives. The focus at this stage of the SMM process

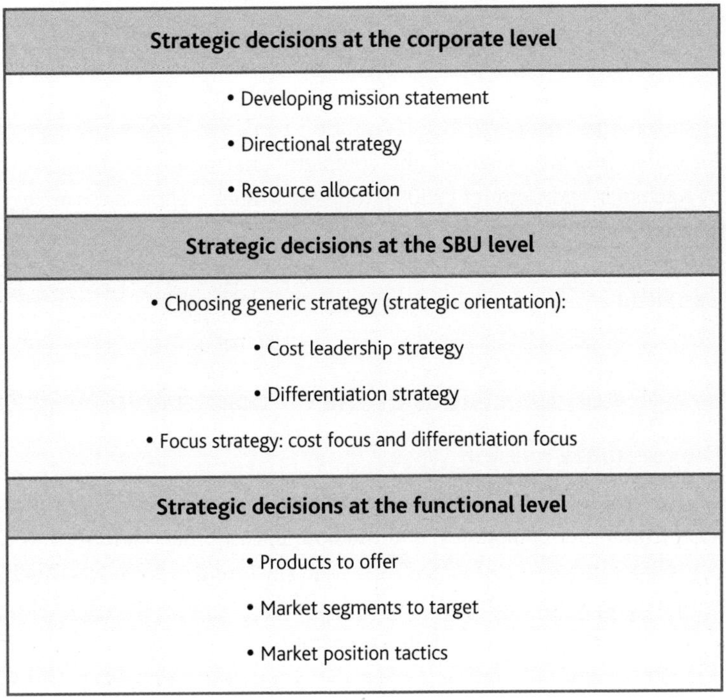

Strategic decisions at the corporate level
• Developing mission statement • Directional strategy • Resource allocation
Strategic decisions at the SBU level
• Choosing generic strategy (strategic orientation): • Cost leadership strategy • Differentiation strategy • Focus strategy: cost focus and differentiation focus
Strategic decisions at the functional level
• Products to offer • Market segments to target • Market position tactics

Figure 4.1 Hierarchy of strategic choice and decisions

is on defining the path to enhanced competitive advantage, identifying the critical business initiatives that will drive relative advantages, and identifying the internal rules of the game that will best support the realization of strategies and position the company to outperform competitors and to meet or exceed the market's expectations for growth, profitability, and asset utilization (Kachaner and Deimler, 2009). Figure 4.1 shows the hierarchy of strategic choice and decisions at the three organizational levels: corporate, SBU, and functional level.

Hierarchy of strategic choice and decisions

Having analysed the organization's marketing environment (see Chapter 3) and identified the external opportunities and threats, and internal strengths and weaknesses, strategic managers at different organizational levels are required to translate the outcome of such analysis into a number of alternatives and choose from them the most appropriate options. Strategic decisions at the corporate level involve developing a mission statement, choosing a directional strategy, and allocating resources among SBUs. Strategic managers at the SBU level have to make decisions regarding the choice of a generic competitive strategy (i.e., cost leadership, differentiation, focus) based on the unique competitive advantages the SBU has. Strategic choice and decisions taken at the functional level are related to the various functional areas within the organization (i.e., marketing, finance, R&D, production, etc.). Within the marketing area, strategists should consider decisions such as products to offer, market segment(s) to target, and market position strategies. The collaboration between different organizational levels and the integration of the proposed strategic options are necessary for generating well-justified and completely harmonized strategic decisions. As suggested by Kachaner and Deimler (2009), the best strategic options normally result from collaboration across various organizational levels—for instance, between the executives and line managers, staff and line managers, and between different functional areas and the strategy department.

Strategic choice and decisions at the corporate level

Defining the corporate mission

The mission statement is a brief description of the unique purpose of the organization, what distinguishes it from other companies, and the boundaries of its operations. It defines the primary direction of the organization and forms the key foundations upon which objectives and strategies are based. The creation of a mission statement is crucial in strategy development since it represents a vision of what the organization is or should attempt to become. The mission statement is important from an internal and external point of view. Inside the firm, it serves as a focal point for individuals to identify the organization's direction and ensure unanimity of purpose within the firm, thereby facilitating the emergence of an organizational culture. Outside the firm, the mission statement contributes to the creation of firm identity, i.e. how the company wants to be perceived in the marketplace by its customers, competitors, and general public (Wilson and Gilligan, 2005; see, also, Hamel and Prahalad (1994) about their exercise with fifteen officers of a large company who mistook their mission statement with those of their competitors, pp. 132–3).

A survey by David (1989) on 181 US companies, identified nine components that are frequently included in mission statements. These are: customers, products or services, location, technology, concern with survival, philosophy, self-concept, concern with public image, and concern with employee. The survey also found that the company's mission is shaped by five elements: the company's history, management preference, market environment, the organization's resources, and its distinctive competencies. While the corporate mission is defined in the early stage of strategy development process, it should be reviewed and updated as shifts in the strategic direction occur over time.

A good mission statement is one that can be seen to exhibit certain characteristics, is short on numbers and long on rhetoric, while still remaining succinct. Below is an example of a mission statement, which has been framed with a very narrow view:

> We shall build good ships—at a profit if we can—at a loss if we must—but always good ships.'
> (*Newport News Shipbuilding*, since 1886)

Another example of a mission statement, which gives a much broader frame of reference, has been developed by Scottish Power:

We aim to be recognised as a highly rated utility-based company trading in electricity, other utility and related markets, providing excellent quality and service to customers and above average returns to investors.

Choosing the directional strategy

Every corporation must decide its intention and orientation towards growth by asking three fundamental questions:

1. Should we expand, cut back, or continue our businesses unchanged?
2. Should we concentrate our activities within our industry boundaries or should we diversify into other lines of business?
3. If we want to grow and expand nationally or internationally, should we do so via self-development or through external acquisition, mergers, or strategic alliances?

Wheelen and Hunger (2004) pointed out that executives at the corporate level normally choose a directional strategy from three general directional orientations, often called grand strategies (see Table 4.1):

- growth strategies expand the corporation's activities
- stability strategies make no change to the existing activities
- retrenchment strategies reduce the corporation's level of activities.

Having chosen the general directional orientation of the corporation (growth, for example), strategic managers can then consider one or more specific sub-strategies such as concentration or diversification. They might decide to concentrate their efforts on one product line or one industry, or diversify into other market segments or even different industries. Such decisions should be based on a high degree of objectivity rather than subjectivity. Jackson (2008) noted that a successful growth strategy requires careful preparation to identify attractive markets/industries and new sources of competitive advantage. Porter (2008) pointed out

TABLE 4.1 The directional (grand) strategies

Growth strategies	Stability strategies	Retrenchment strategies
Concentration • Vertical growth • Horizontal growth	Pause/Proceed with caution No change Profit	Turnaround Captive company Sell-out/divestment Bankruptcy/liquidation
Diversification • Concentric • Conglomerate		

Source: Thomas Wheelen and J. David Hunger (2004), *Strategic Management and Business Policy*, 9th edn, pp. 10, 14, and 138. Redrawn by permission of Pearson Education, Inc., Upper Saddle River, NJ.

that it is a common mistake to assume that fast-growing industries are always attractive. Growth sometimes tends to mute rivalry because an expanding pie offers opportunities for all competitors. A high growth rate with low entry barriers will draw in new entrants. Even without new entrants, a high growth rate will not guarantee profitability if customers are powerful or substitutes are attractive. Porter (2008) stressed that a narrow focus on growth is one of the major causes of bad strategic decisions.

For a successful growth strategy involving acquisition, companies need to get both the strategy and timing right, which may require adjusting the strategy in the light of opportunities that arise. Ford made a strategic decision in the mid 1990s to acquire Jaguar and Aston Martin Lagonda, the two British car companies, in order to achieve quick growth/expansion. This decision was seen (then) as one that enabled Ford to have a wider presence in the passenger car market by serving new upmarket segments. More recently, Ford took a decision to give up these two companies—maybe to concentrate their resources on those market segments Ford knew better.

Corporate managers may select stability rather than growth as a directional strategy by making no changes to the corporation's current activities. This strategy is generally more popular in small businesses where owners find a profitable niche and enjoy their success in serving customers within this segment. While useful for small businesses in the short run, the stability strategy can be risky in the long term. For example, Tesco, the UK's largest superstore, with its wider presence and intense competition not only in the high street but also in small towns, has threatened smaller retailers such as bakers and butchers.

The corporate manager may choose to pursue a retrenchment strategy if the organization has a weak competitive position in one or more of its markets resulting in less acceptable profits. This situation puts pressure on the company to improve its performance by eliminating those product lines or SBUs that are dragging down the overall performance of the company. This strategy was adopted by BMW in 2000 after six years of owning Rover, the British car manufacturer. BMW had invested $3.4 billion in Rover over six years but failed to turn it into a profitable business. Eventually, BMW decided to sell Land Rover to Ford and the rest of the company to a British venture capital firm (MG Car Company).

Allocating resources between the SBUs

Large corporations with multiple products and/or strategic business units must decide how to allocate their resources (financial, human, time, and other resources) between SBUs to ensure the organization's overall success. Portfolio analysis is probably one of the most widely used strategic tools for allocating resources between SBUs. Portfolio analysis, which since the 1960s has had a colourful history in the business literature, is a key tool for assessing the strength of the position of SBUs in the market and allocating resources between them. Market attractiveness is largely determined by forces outside a firm's control, while a business unit's competitiveness can be shaped by the firm's strategic choices. Portfolio planning relates attractiveness and competitiveness indicators to inform the organization's strategic decisions by suggesting a balanced mix of products and businesses that will ensure growth and profit performance in the long term. A survey of *Fortune 1000* by Haspeslagh (1982) found that portfolio-planning approaches are widespread among large, diversified, industrial companies and are being increasingly used. Another survey, this time by Reimann and Reichert (1996) on the *Fortune 500* firms, found that the various methods of portfolio analysis were still used in strategy formulation by at least 27 per cent of corporations. However, it must be noted here that the popularity of portfolio analysis has dropped over the past decade for a number of reasons that will be outlined later in the chapter. The use of strategy tools, in general, has been the subject of a study by Knott (2008) to explore how practicing managers use various strategy tools as a source of inspiration in strategy activity. Mini Case Study 4.1 illustrates how organizations can use their available resources to achieve their marketing objectives.

MINI CASE STUDY 4.1 Make way for the heroes

Cutting spend on growth areas that will never take off can allow your bestselling products to flourish when times get tough.

In today's tough economic climate, getting the most bangs for your marketing buck is crucial. How can we ensure that the marketing department delivers value for money? One way to work how to optimize your budget could be to spend a big pile of cash on developing a fancy econometric model. A simpler, cheaper and equally effective solution is to focus on doing fewer things and doing them better.

Taking a long, hard, and dispassionate look at how you are spending your valuable resources isn't very sexy, but you'll need to review your marketing budget if a recession starts to bite. And it's not just about cash. The way your company expends the time and energy of its people is just as important as the way in which it spends its money. Defining objective criteria is important, as many investment decisions are clouded by factors that have nothing to do with the bottom line. These factors include pet projects to which people are emotionally attached, knee-jerk reactions to competitive activity and sheer inertia—the attitude that 'this is the way we have always done things around here'.

You can define as many criteria as you want in order to help you focus, but two are often enough. The first should relate to your strategic objectives. This can be done at a brand level, by looking at the desired changes in brand image and usage. Or it can be done at a whole-company level. The second criterion is, of course, profitable business growth. With these two criteria in place, you can move onto evaluation. A good place to start is with a review of your current portfolio of products or services. On the one hand you should be able to highlight a few 'hero' products: those that have strong customer appeal, good strategic fit and that result in big, profitable sales figures. But you are also likely to throw up a few 'dwarves': small products with small sales and little chance of ever growing. Getting rid of these dwarves may be painful, but it can free up valuable resources that can then be ploughed back into the core business. Market leaders use this strategy all the time—Lynx poured millions into it's launch of razors in an attempt to compete with Gillette, but decided to kill the product line and focus on its core body spray businesses. IBM offloaded its PC division to Lenovo so that it could focus on its more profitable consulting and services business. And when Texas Pacific Group (TPG) bought Burger King, it cut out underperforming franchises and ditched badly selling products to boost the core business.

Another option is simply to starve the dwarves by removing all funding and management time from them. The likely result is that they will die a natural death. If that sounds harsh, consider this: if you don't get ruthless with your non-core products, you may end up watching someone else—such as TPG—do it for you.

Source: David Taylor. This article first appeared in *The Marketer* (April 2008), p. 13, the magazine of the Chartered Institute of Marketing.

Portfolio planning takes two forms: (a) product portfolio analysis; and (b) business portfolio analysis. Below are some methods of portfolio analysis that are widely used by strategic managers:

- The Boston Consulting Group (BCG) matrix, which focuses on market share and market growth (see Figure 4.2)
- General Electric's (GE) business screen, which places the SBUs in the nine cells matrix using the attractiveness of the industry and the position of business (see Figure 4.3).
- The Shell directional matrix, which uses two dimensions: prospects for section profitability and firm's competitive capabilities (see Figure 4.4)
- Abell and Hammond's model, which is an expansion of the GE model and Shell directional matrix, and evaluates SBUs using two dimensions: business position and market attractiveness.

The BCG matrix is probably one of the most popular tools used by strategists for allocating resources between SBUs. In many respects, it is inferior to more discursive portfolios such as the GE business screen, but for many businesses it is seen as the simplest way to portray the corporation's portfolio of investments. The BCG matrix can be used with the product life cycle concept to provide a useful strategic framework for resources allocation. Figure 4.2 illustrates four positions a business unit (SBU) can attain in a market/segment based on the market share it has and the growth rate of the market/segment. Figure 4.2 also illustrates the movement of cash between different SBUs and the desired movements of businesses over time. SBUs are expected to change their positions in the market (the four quadrants of the matrix) over time. They generally start as 'problem children—wildcat' and with successful

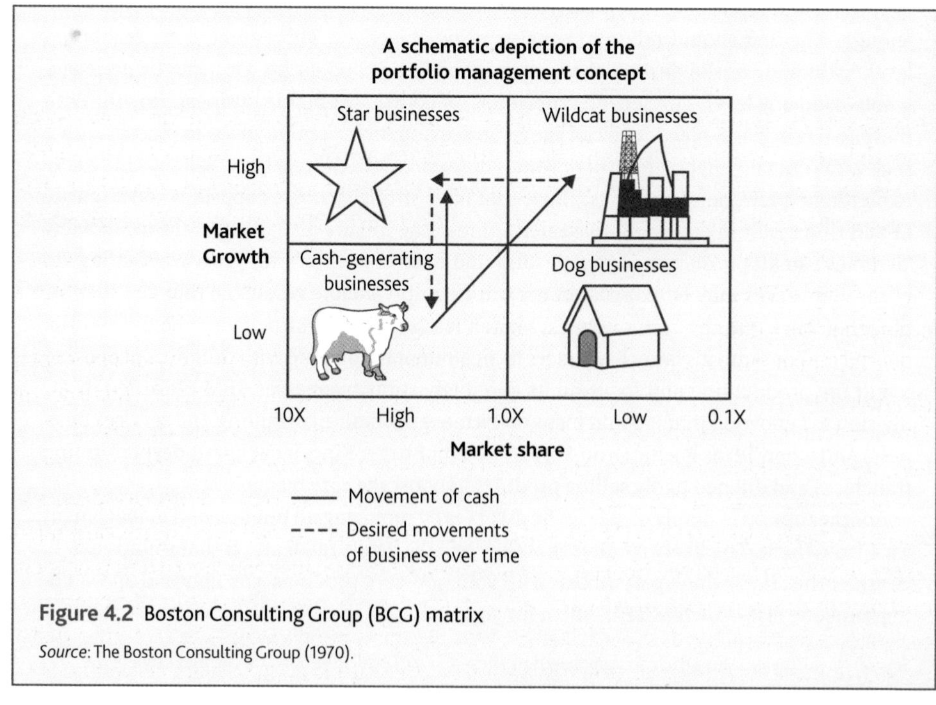

Figure 4.2 Boston Consulting Group (BCG) matrix

Source: The Boston Consulting Group (1970).

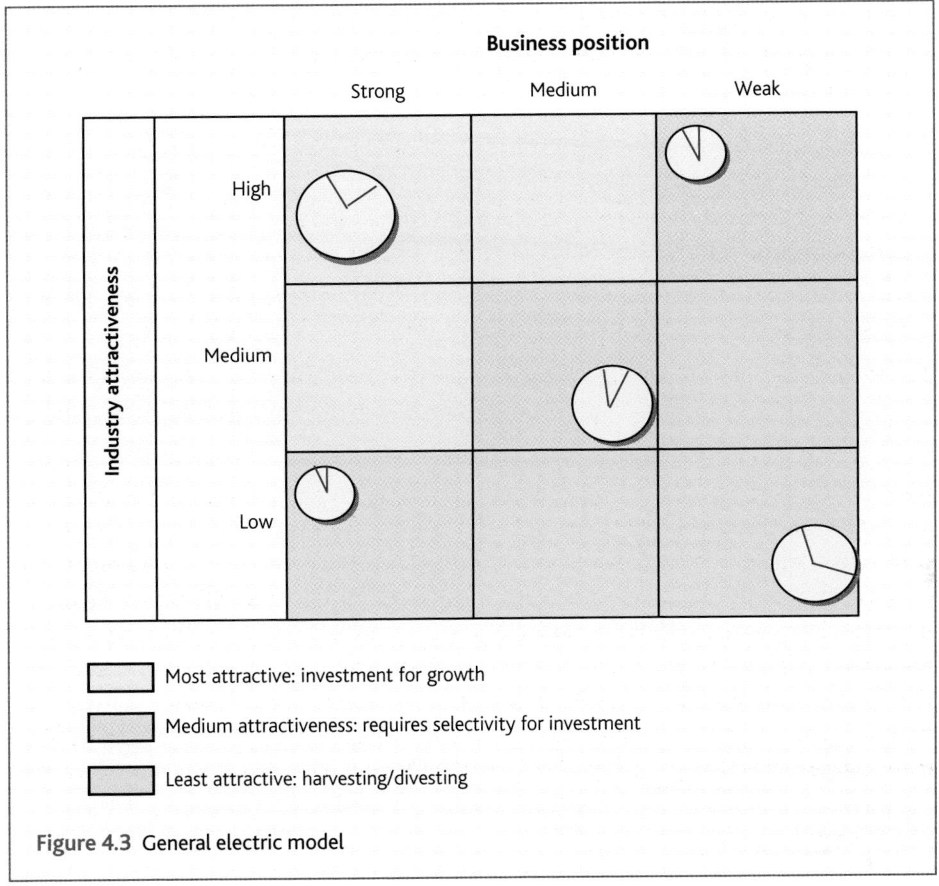

Figure 4.3 General electric model

management they move into the 'stars' category. Eventually they become 'cash cows' as the growth level of the market starts to slow down. Finally, when they begin to lose their market shares, they move into the 'dogs' stage. It has been suggested that each SBU should set up its strategic objectives based on its position in the BCG matrix. Build/Growth will, arguably, be an appropriate strategic objective for the 'stars', while Hold/Harvest will be appropriate for the 'cash cows'. Investment can be selected for the 'problem children', while divestment will be appropriate for the 'dogs' who are seen as having no potential.

The BCG matrix is a well-known tool with many advantages in: (a) helping organizations plan the desired movement of business over time; and (b) planning the movement of funds from the SBUs where there is less need for them to other SBUs where they are desparately needed. However, several limitations of this tool have been identified. The use of *high* and *low* to define the rate of market growth and level of market share is too simplistic and only one product can appear on the left-hand side as having the highest relative market share. In addition, the cut-off point of 10 per cent growth is far too high for most businesses. Furthermore, market growth is only one indicator of an industry's attractiveness and market share is only one measure of a company's competitive position. It is fair to say that the BCG has many pitfalls for it to be recommended as the sole portfolio tool, but its popularity made it worth focusing upon by many corporations.

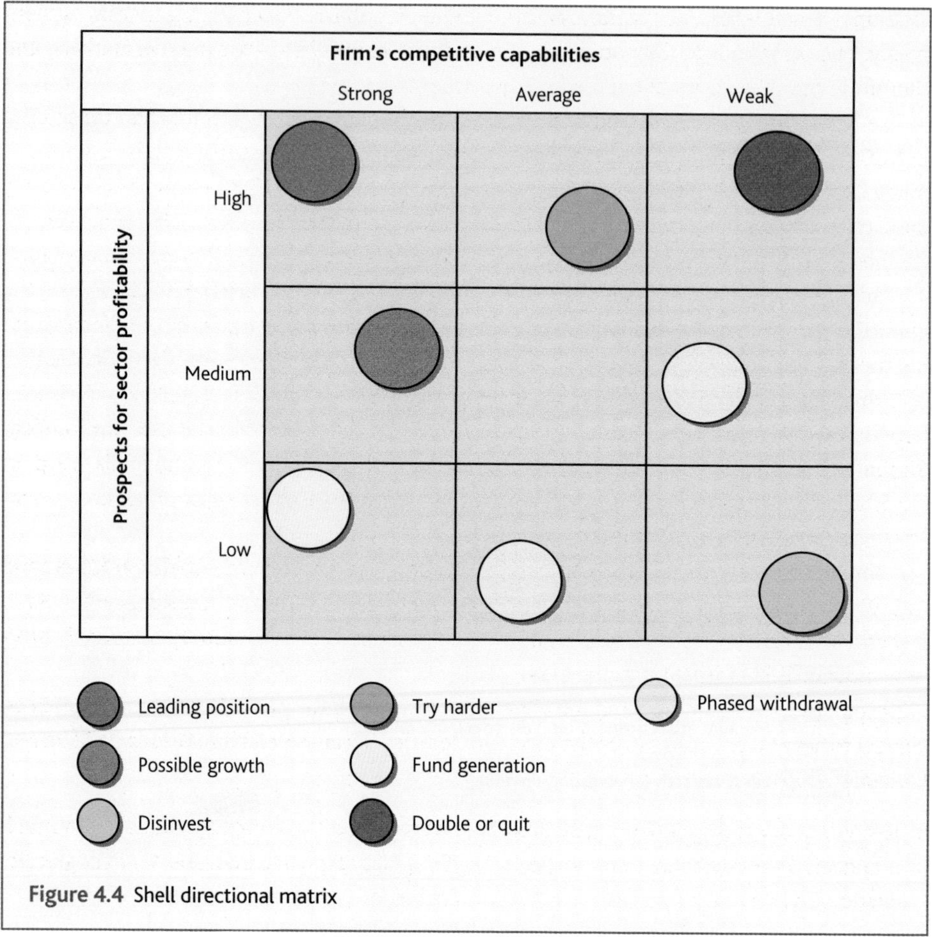

Figure 4.4 Shell directional matrix

In an attempt to overcome the limitations of the BCG matrix, a few alternative models have been suggested. General Electric's business screen is another portfolio planning tool, which is slightly more complicated than the BCG matrix. It is a multifactor model that includes nine cells based on long-term industry attractiveness and the competitive position of a firm. The definition of industry attractiveness covers market growth rate, industry average return, industry size, plus other possible opportunities and threats. On the other hand, a business's competitive position includes such factors as market share, profitability, a firm's size, product quality, brand image, and other possible strengths and weaknesses (see Figure 4.3).

As Figure 4.3 shows, the individual strategic business units are plotted in the matrix as circles, and each circle represents the size of the market (in terms of sales, for example) rather than the size of the SBU, with the pie slices within each circle representing the market share of the SBU in this market. The nine cells of the GE matrix fall into three categories, each of which needs a different investment strategy. For example, the three cells at the top left of the matrix are considered the most attractive, that require an investment strategy for growth. The three cells that run diagonally from the top right to bottom left are seen as having a medium attractiveness, hence they require a greater emphasis placed on selective investment policy. The three cells at the bottom right of the matrix are the least attractive markets, and therefore require a policy of harvesting/divestment.

The advantage of the GE model lies in the use of many more variables than those used in BCG matrix, and the recognition that the attractiveness of an industry can be assessed in many different ways than simply by using growth rate. It also allows strategists to choose any industry variables they justifiably feel are more relevant to their organizations. However, the GE model has its shortcomings. The nine cells matrix can be quite complicated to understand and might impose some difficulties for managers to reach a meaningful conclusion. Also, the quantification of industry attractiveness and a business's competitive position, while simplifying the analysis, are simply generated based on subjective rather than objective judgements.

A third approach to portfolio analysis is the Shell directional 3 × 3 matrix, which uses two dimensions: the firm's competitive capabilities and the prospects for sector profitability. Similar to GE matrix, each dimension is divided into three categories, and SBUs are plotted within the matrix to allow top management to identify the most appropriate investment strategies for each SBU (see Figure 4.4).

A similar matrix to the Shell directional model has been produced by Abell and Hammond (1979) to depict relative investment strategies. Although it is almost the same as the Shell directional matrix, Abell and Hammond's model uses different terminologies, namely business position and market attractiveness.

Despite the wide adoption and the apparent attraction of the portfolio analysis, it has been subject to several criticisms over the past two decades because of its limitations (Wilson and Gilligan, 2005):

- It is generally too simplistic in structure, and may lead the company to place too much emphasis on market share growth and entry into high-growth businesses, or to neglect its current businesses.
- Its practical value is based on developing an appropriate definition of the industry and market segments in which an SBU competes.
- It suggests a standard strategy for each competitive position, which in some cases seems impractical.
- It uses subjective judgements of top management, and its results, therefore, are sensitive to the ratings, and weights can be manipulated to produce a desired plot in the matrix.
- It is not always clear what makes an industry attractive or where a product is in its life cycle.

However, it should be noted here that portfolio analysis has gained a wide adoption because it offers some advantages (Haspeslagh, 1982):

- It encourages managers at the corporate level to think strategically, and adopt a more proactive approach to management.
- It motivates managers to evaluate the internal and external environment of each business unit to set long-term objectives and allocate resources between them.
- It furnishes companies with a greatly improved capacity for strategic control when portfolio planning is applied intelligently.

- It stimulates the use of externally oriented data to supplement management's judgement.
- It recognizes the importance of the fund generation ability of each SBU to inform the allocation of resources between the SBUs.

Another planning approach that gained widespread adoption by large corporations and/or business units is business models. A **business model** describes the set of coordinated activities a company performs to deliver goods and services to customers in order to ensure overall success (Wheelen and Hunger, 2004). Originated in the 1990s, the term 'business model' was used to show how the new technology and global trade are changing how companies must do business. Every successful company operates according to an effective business model, and by systematically identifying all of its constituent parts, the company can understand how the model fulfils a potent value proposition in a profitable way. With that understanding, the company's executives can judge how the same model could be used to fulfil a radically different customer value proposition, and what they need to construct a new model, if required, to capitalize on that opportunity.

Johnson et al. (2008) claim that business model innovations have reshaped entire industries and redistributed millions of dollars of value in the US business environment. Retail discounters such as Wal-Mart and Target, which entered the market with pioneering business models, now account for 75 per cent of the total valuation of the retail sector. Also, low-cost airlines grew from a slice on the radar screen to 55 per cent of the market value of all airline carriers. Johnson et al. (2008) referred to a survey conducted in 2005 by the Economist Intelligence Unit, which reported that over 50 per cent of CEOs believe that business model innovation will become more important for success than product or service innovation. Another survey conducted by IBM in 2008 on corporate CEOs echoed these results.

While established companies can often launch new products and services that outperform competitors without fundamentally changing their existing business models, there are some circumstances that require a new business model to be invented. Johnson et al. (2008) identified five of these strategic circumstances:

1. The opportunity to address the needs of potential customers who are shut out of a market because existing solutions are too expensive or too complicated for them.
2. The opportunity to capitalize on a brand new technology or leverage a tested technology by bringing it to a whole new market.
3. The opportunity to bring a job-to-be-done focus when one does not yet exist. A job focus allows companies to redefine industry profitability.
4. The need to fend off low-end disrupters.
5. The need to respond to a shifting basis of competition.

Strategic choice and decisions at the SBU level

What is an SBU? It is a single business or interrelated businesses that can plan separately from the rest of the corporation. An SBU competes in a specific industrial sector or marketplace and has a manager responsible for the strategic planning and profit performance of the SBU, who also controls factors affecting profit. The key strategic decisions taken at the SBU level relate to the selection of a generic competitive strategy. A generic strategy specifies the fundamental approach to the competitive advantage a firm is pursuing, and provides the context for the decisions to be taken in each functional area.

Identifying a generic competitive strategy

Managers at the SBU level normally choose a generic strategy that exploits the company's internal strengths and external opportunities, and utilizes its competitive advantage over its competitors. An appropriate selection and formulation of a generic competitive strategy will best position the company's offerings against competitors' offerings and give the company the strongest possible competitive advantage within its industry. Porter (2008) suggests that generic strategy can be viewed as building defences against competitive forces or finding a position in the market where the forces are weakest.

In the strategy literature, different typologies of generic strategy have been suggested (Utterback and Abernathy, 1975; Miles and Snow, 1978; Porter, 1980). For instance, Utterback and Abernathy (1975) proposed cost-minimizing and performance-maximizing strategic business types that may be positioned at the opposite ends of the spectrum. Miles and Snow (1978) proposed four business types of competitive strategy: 'reactor', 'defender', 'analyser', and 'prospector'. Porter (1980) pulled all these types of strategy together and suggested three generic types of competitive strategy: cost leadership, differentiation, and focus.

While Porter (1980) originally proposed focus as a third generic strategy, he introduced differentiation focus and cost focus as two variants of focus strategy in his subsequent book *Competitive Advantage* (1985a) (see Figure 4.5). In his later book, *The Competitive Advantage of Nations* (1990), Porter dropped focus as a separate generic strategy and began viewing it instead as a category of competitive scope.

Porter's generic competitive strategies

Cost leadership is a low-cost competitive strategy that aims at the broad mass market and requires aggressive construction of efficient-scale facilities, vigorous pursuit of cost reduction

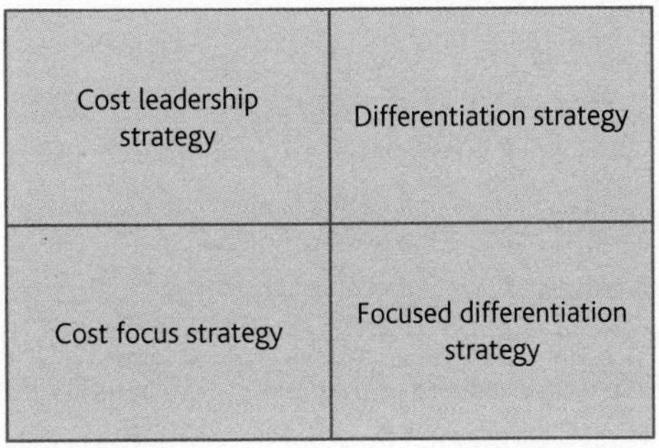

Cost leadership strategy	Differentiation strategy
Cost focus strategy	Focused differentiation strategy

Figure 4.5 Porter's generic strategy

Source: Michael E. Porter (1985), *Competitive Advantage: Creating and Sustaining Superior Performance, p. 12*. Redrawn with the permission of The Free Press, a Division of Simon & Schuster Adult Publishing Group.

from experience, tight cost, and overhead control, avoidance of marginal customer accounts, and cost minimization in areas like R&D, service, sales force, and advertising. Because of its lower cost, the cost leader is able to charge a lower price for its products than its competitors and still make a satisfactory profit. Having a low-cost position also gives a company a defence against rivals. Its lower costs allow it to continue to earn profits during times of heavy competition. Its high market share gives it great bargaining power with its suppliers because it buys in larger quantities. Its low costs serve as a barrier to entry, as few new entrants will be able to match the leader's cost advantage. As a result, cost leaders are likely to earn above-average return on investment (Porter, 1980). Note that sometimes cost leadership is confused with setting low prices. Certainly cost leaders are more able to make a profit at lower prices than rivals, but it is not necessarily part of the strategy. For example, Dell has a cost advantage with its direct business model. However, its prices are by no means the lowest.

Differentiation is a generic strategy that involves the creation of a significantly differentiated offering, for which the company may charge a premium. This speciality can be associated with design or brand image, technology feature, dealer network, or customer service. Differentiation is a viable strategy for earning above-average returns in a specific business because the resulting brand loyalty lowers customers' sensitivity to price. Buyers' loyalty also serves as an entry barrier—new firms must develop their own distinctive competence to differentiate their products in order to compete successfully (Porter, 1980).

What to choose? Differentiation strategy is more likely to generate higher profit than is low-cost strategy because differentiation creates a better entry barrier. However, low-cost strategy is more likely to generate increases in market share.

Cost focus is a low-cost strategy that focuses on a particular buyer group or geographic market and attempts to serve only this niche, to the exclusion of others. In using a cost focus strategy, the company seeks a cost advantage in its target segment. This strategy is based on the belief that a company that focuses its efforts can serve its narrow strategic target *more efficiently* than can its competitors. However, a focus strategy does necessitate a trade-off between profitability and overall market share (Wheelen and Hunger, 2004).

Focused differentiation is a strategy that concentrates on a particular buyer group, product line segment, or geographic market. The target segments must have buyers with unusual needs or else the production and delivery system that best serves the target segment must differ from that of other industry segments. In using a focused differentiation strategy, the company seeks differentiation in its target segment. This strategy is valued because of the belief that a company that focuses its efforts can serve its narrow strategic target *more effectively* than can its competitors.

Focused differentiation and cost focus strategies are not the same. Whilst cost focus exploits differences in cost behaviour in some segments, differentiation focus exploits the special needs of buyers in certain segments (Porter, 1985a). Another comparison can be made between overall differentiation and differentiation focus strategies. These two are perhaps the most often confused strategies in practice. While the overall differentiator bases its strategy on widely valued attributes, the differentiation focuser looks for segments with special needs and meets them better.

Stuck in the middle Porter (1980) suggested that a company must pursue only one of the generic strategies, otherwise it will get 'stuck in the middle' with no competitive advantage because the cost leader, differentiators or focusers will be better positioned to compete in every segment. Few empirical studies suggested that commitment to only one of the three generic strategies would result in higher performance than if a company fails to stick to a single strategy. However, other research noted that companies which compete using both a low-cost and a differentiation strategy will perform better than those businesses primarily competing with either a low-cost or a differentiation strategy. The cases of the Japanese car producers of Toyota, Nissan, and Honda are the best examples of companies which pursued both a low-cost and a high-quality position. However, this case is often temporary and requires strict conditions because differentiation is usually costly.

MINI CASE STUDY 4.2 Cheap and nice, not cheap and nasty

Cheap need not be synonymous with nasty if you find out what your customer really wants and ensure that is exactly what you give them.

Back in the 1990s most companies followed the advice of Harvard Business School's Professor Michael Porter when defining their marketing strategy. They took one of the two main routes to growth: cost leadership or differentiation. Many of today's successful businesses are making money by doing these things. But how can it be possible to keep prices low, differentiate on service and quality, and still make money? The answer is a ruthless focus on giving customers more of what they want and less of what they don't.

Take the fast-growing chain of business hotels and meeting venues Chateauform. The company started a decade ago with a single venue outside Paris, but now has a string of hotels encircling the city, as well as properties in Italy, Belgium, Spain, and Switzerland. The secret of the company's success is a host of innovative features that deliver a double whammy of lower costs and better service for clients. The beautiful properties are in small, quiet villages that are less than an hour from the airport, but miles away from the bright lights of Paris. This means dramatically lower real estate costs, but also ensures that the teams of executives staying on site remain on site, bonding and doing business rather than going out on the town.

Chateauform's rooms don't feature costly plasma screen TVs, mini-bars or flashy furniture. Instead they provide a case of small Evian bottles outside your room and mobile phones you can use during your stay. Finally and most importantly, the company hires a husband-and-wife team, who share in the profit, to run each property. This delivers a unique level of personal client service as well as better staff retention, which in turn drives down cost. The result is more of what business customers want from a meeting venue, and a highly competitive price.

The 'cheap and nice' approach works just as well with products as it does with services, as shown by the stunning success of the Nintendo Wii gaming console. The company has cleverly focused on a sizeable segment of consumers, including women and older people (in gaming terms, anyone over 25) who were not interested in paying for the Playstation's processing power, which is designed to deliver more realistic graphics of gangsters spilling blood and guts. Instead, Nintendo created a much simpler machine, at a lower price, along with milder games that were more about mental stimulation and fun than violent role-play.

» Having been a poor third-player behind Sony and Microsoft, Nintendo has leapt into leadership position. So forget Professor Porter's 'either or' model of marketing strategy, and look instead for inspiration from the immortal lyrics of the Spice Girls. Ask your costumer to 'tell me what you want, what you really really want'—and then strip out everything else and give them what they want.

Source: David Taylor. This article first appeared in *The Marketer* (September 2008), p. 13, the magazine of the Chartered Institute of Marketing.

Criticism of Porter's generic strategies

Although widely acknowledged by academics and practitioners as one of the most accepted methods for defining, categorizing, and selecting competitive strategies, Porter's typology has been criticized in many ways. It is argued that, while Porter's generic strategies might be appealing to organizations, they have practical limitations. Pretorius (2008), for example, noted that Porter's generic strategy often proves inadequate for use by distressed firms because it assumes that companies operate 'normally' in a competitive environment. Managers of troubled organizations facing turnaround situations need to analyse the complex factors involved, and cannot depend on Porter's typology of generic strategy alone. Akan et al. (2006) also identified many gaps in Porter's typology which hinder managers' attempt to implement these generic strategies. One of these gaps is the lack of identifying what tactics are associated with each of the three generic strategies. Also, it is not clear what tactics will warrant higher levels of organizational performance. Another criticism is related to Porter's presentation of the generic strategies. His presentation seems to give an impression that it is up to SBUs to choose from them, although the appropriate selection of a generic strategy will be dependent on the firm's resources and capabilities, the industry life cycle, and the state of competition in the market. Table 4.2 illustrates the commonly required skills and resources and the common organizational requirements for each of Porter's generic strategies.

From a marketing perspective, Baker (1992) argued that Porter's three generic strategies are typical marketing strategies that have been presented by marketers for the past thirty years. Porter had only rebranded such marketing strategies using different names. Cost leadership invariably depends upon standardization and so is equivalent to an undifferentiated marketing strategy. Differentiation is identical in both models. Cost focus and focus differentiation are both variants of a concentrated marketing strategy and involve niche marketing.

Support for Porter's generic strategies

Despite the above criticisms, other scholars have defended the concept and its application. Herbert and Deresky (1987), for example, emphasized that the generic strategies form a simplified system and offer several important advantages for guiding the choice of a competitive strategy.

- They highlight the essential features of separate, situation-specific strategies, capturing their major commonalties so that they facilitate the understanding of a broad strategic pattern.
- They provide guidance at the corporate level on decisions concerning business portfolio management and resource allocation.

TABLE 4.2 Requirements for generic competitive strategies

Generic strategy	Commonly required skills and resources	Common organizational requirements
Overall cost leadership	• Sustained capital investment and access to capital • Process engineering skills • Intense supervision of labour • Products designed for ease of manufacture • Low-cost distribution system	• Tight cost control • Frequent, detailed control reports • Structured organization and responsibilities • Incentives base on meeting strict quantitative targets
Differentiation	• Strong marketing abilities • Product engineering • Creative flair • Strong capability in basic research • Corporate reputation for quality of technological leadership • Long tradition in the industry or unique combination of skills drawn from other businesses • Strong co-operation from channels	• Strong co-ordination among functions in R&D, product development, and marketing • Subjective measurement and incentives instead of quantitative measures • Amenities to attract highly skilled labour, scientists, or creative people
Focus	• Combination of the above policies directed at the particular strategic target	• Combination of the above policies directed at the particular strategic target

Source: Michael E. Porter (1980), *Competitive Strategy: Techniques for Analysing Industries and Competitors,* pp. 40–1. Redrawn with the permission of The Free Press, a Division of Simon & Schuster Adult Publishing Group.

- They assist business-level strategy development by suggesting priorities and providing broad guidelines for action.

From the preceding arguments, it is fair to say that although Porter's generic strategies have been subject to some criticisms, the concept itself describes the generic strategic approaches available to organizations. It goes beyond competitive analysis to show exactly what the different types of competitive strategies are, how a competitive strategy can be selected, what its effects on the competitive forces are, and finally, the advantages and disadvantages of each strategy.

Strategic choice and decisions at the functional level

Strategic decisions taken at this level are related to the various functional areas within an organization (e.g., marketing, finance, R&D, production, etc.). The development of the functional strategies and the coordination between them play a major role in creating and sustaining a firm's competitive advantage. This section focuses on the key strategic decisions taken within the marketing department in particular. These decisions include marketing objectives to support corporate strategy, products to offer, market segments to target, and market position strategies. Other strategic decisions of other functional areas (e.g., production, finance, R&D) are also outlined in this section.

Setting the marketing objectives

A company has to develop specific marketing objectives for the planning period. While a few businesses may decide to pursue a single objective, most companies will have a mixture of marketing objectives including sales growth, market share, innovativeness, customer satisfaction, reputation, and brand loyalty. Although marketing objectives are primarily developed to guide the overall marketing activities, they are also used for evaluation purpose to find out whether the chosen strategy has accomplished its purpose in the market. Key characteristics and guidelines for developing the appropriate set of objectives are:

- **hierarchical:** objectives should go from most to least important
- **quantitative:** in order to avoid ambiguity, marketing managers must turn objectives into measurable targets with respect to size and time
- **realistic:** objectives should be developed based on the result of a detailed analysis of the firm's capability, its competitive strengths, and external opportunities
- **consistent:** to avoid confusion, marketing managers have to pursue compatible marketing objectives. It is obviously unrealistic to aim for substantial gains in both market share and profitability at same time.

If a company's strategic objectives are inaccurately developed, either focusing too much on short-term goals or being so general that they provide little real guidance, there might be a planning gap between planned and achieved objectives. When such a gap occurs, strategic managers have to change their strategies to improve performance or adjust objectives downward to be more realistic.

Marketing strategy

Marketing is viewed in this book as an orientation that guides an organization's overall activities (see Chapter 2). However, this does not deny that marketing is a distinct function. At the functional level, the major task of marketing managers is to influence the level, timing, and character of demand in a way that helps the organization in achieving its long-term strategic objectives. The marketing manager is often seen as the organization's primary link to the market and must, therefore, be particularly concerned with the development of the firm's positioning strategy and the marketing mix programmes.

The development of marketing strategy has been discussed extensively in the marketing literature. For example, Hooley et al. (2004) pointed out that the development of marketing strategy can be seen at three main levels. At the first level, the core strategy of the organization is selected, where the marketing objectives and the broad focus for achieving them are identified. At the next level, market segments and targets are chosen and the organization's differential advantage is defined to better serve the target groups of customers than the competition. Taken together, the identification of targets and the definition of differential advantage constitute the creation of the competitive positioning of the organization and its offerings. At the third level, a marketing department capable of putting the strategy into practice must be created. The marketing department, at this stage, is concerned with establishing the marketing mix programmes that can convey both the positioning and the products/services to the target market.

Cravens (1994) suggested another approach to the development of marketing strategy. As shown in Table 4.3, this approach illustrates the sequential steps to developing a marketing strategy, a summary of the important issues to be considered at each step, and the major actions/decisions that are required.

Table 4.3 illustrates the role marketing can play in **creating competitive advantage**. This role, which has been discussed in the marketing literature since the 1970s, is seen as a fundamental step in developing a marketing strategy. In a classical article, Cook (1983) linked the concept of strategic marketing ambition to the marketing mix and suggested a new paradigm of marketing strategy development. In this study, an operational measure of differential marketing advantage and methods of analysis were introduced in an illustration of competitive investments, marketing strategy and differential advantage. In a later

TABLE 4.3 Selecting and developing marketing strategies for different market and competitive situations

	Important issues	Major actions/decisions
Product-market definition and analysis	• Evaluating the complexity of the product-market structure • Establishing product-market boundaries	• Defining product-market structure • Customer profiles • Industry/distribution/competitor analysis • Market size estimation
Market segmentation	• Deciding which level of the product-market to segment • Determining how to segment the market	• Selecting the basis of segmentation • Forming segments • Analysing segments
Define and analyse industry structure	• Defining the competitive area • Understanding competitive structure • Anticipating changes in industry structure	• Sources of competition • Industry structure • Strategic group analysis
Competitive Advantage	• Deciding when, where, and how to compete	• Finding opportunity gaps • Cost/differentiation strategy/focus • Good/better/best brand positioning strategy
Market targeting and positioning strategies	• Deciding market scope • Good/better/best brand positioning strategy	• Selecting targets • Positioning for each target • Positioning concept • Marketing mix integration

Source: David W. Cravens (1994), *Strategic Marketing*, p. 325. Reproduced by permission of McGraw-Hill Education, Inc.

study by Cook (1985), it was noted that marketing strategy is the manner in which the company resources are used in the search for a differential advantage. It was also emphasized that a marketing strategy should be formulated with reference to the market environment and competitive conditions in which an organization operates. Recently, Ward and Lewandowska (2008) examined which particular marketing strategies would work best in which particular business environment. In a survey of 217 companies in Australia, Singapore, the Netherlands, and China, they found that most marketing strategies appear to be useful in conditions of relatively stable environments such as placid-clustered environments. In turbulent environments, though, it does seem that concerns for customers should be the major focus of organizations, and therefore customer-orientated strategies seem to be most effective. Competitor-based strategies are best suited to placid-clustered environments, business conditions, which are favourable and therefore attract greater competition. Societal marketing-based strategies seem to be most effective in placid random and placid clustered environments.

Other functional strategies

Financial strategy

The primary job of any financial manager is to manage the organization's funds, ascertain the best sources and uses of funds, and control their use. Any financial manager must be knowledgeable about all these functions in order to formulate and implement an effective financial strategy. The principal goal of a financial strategy is to provide organizations with an appropriate financial structure and funds to achieve its overall objective. It can also provide competitive advantage through a lower cost of funds and a flexible ability to raise capital to support a competitive strategy. Wheelen and Hunger (2004) noted that a financial strategy usually attempts to maximize the financial value of the firm by establishing the trade-off between achieving the desired debt-to-equity ratio and relying on internal long-term financing via cash flow. Such a trade-off is a key issue in any financial strategy development, which would lead to the creation of competitive advantage for the firm.

Manufacturing strategy

The primary task of a manufacturing manager is to develop an effective production strategy and operate a system that will produce the required number of products or services with a certain quality, at a given cost, and within an allocated time. Manufacturing strategy can be defined as the management principles dictating how a product is manufactured, how resources are deployed in production, and how the infrastructure necessary to support manufacturing should be organized (Zahra and Das, 1993). Manufacturing strategy creates and adds value by helping a firm to establish and sustain a defensible competitive advantage, which is the unique position an organization develops vis-à-vis its competitors. The role manufacturing facilities can play in creating competitive advantage to organizations has been acknowledged in the business literature. Design for manufacturing (DFM), for example, can contribute to the creation of competitive advantage by serving as the basis for a differentiation or low-cost position in the marketplace. DFM can provide differentiation through speed of delivery, quality, and variety in combination with the former two. DFM can also contribute to a low-cost position by reducing scrap and rework, creating efficiencies in purchasing, assembly, and inventory, and by allowing a firm to move up the learning curve faster.

Manufacturing resources can also contribute to organizations' competitive advantages in two principal ways: either by gaining a first mover advantage, or by erecting mobility barriers. Either method requires an organization to attain a distinctive competence by the appropriate use of its production resources. The ability to rapidly alter the production process of diverse products can also provide an organization with a distinct competitive advantage. In other words, organizations owning flexible technology and adopting flexible manufacturing processes can react more quickly to market change to improve customer satisfaction and increase profitability. Thus, competitive strategy based on flexible manufacturing technology enables organizations to be better positioned in the marketplace. Wheelen and Hunger (2004) supported this argument, and stressed the importance of adopting a flexible manufacturing strategy as a way to react quickly against competitor's moves in the marketplace. Increasing competitive intensity in many industries has forced companies to switch from adopting a traditional mass production strategy to a continuous improvement strategy. Because a continuous improvement strategy enables firms to adopt the same low-cost approach as does a mass production strategy, albeit at a significantly higher level of quality, it is rapidly replacing mass production as 'the' manufacturing strategy.

Research and Development (R&D) strategy

The R&D manager is responsible for developing and implementing a company's technology strategy in the light of its overall objectives, strategies, and policies. The job of the R&D manager, therefore, involves: (1) choosing among alternative new technologies to use within the company; (2) developing methods of embodying the new technology in new products and processes; and (3) deploying resources so that the new technology can be successfully implemented. R&D strategy principally deals with three ingredients: basic R&D, which focuses on theoretical problem areas; product R&D, which concentrates on marketing and is concerned with product improvements; and process R&D, which concentrates on quality control and the improvement of production. Companies that depend on either product or process technology for their success are becoming increasingly concerned with the development of R&D strategies that complement business-level strategies.

Research suggests that focusing on quality improvement through an effective R&D strategy is one of the best ways for organizations to improve market position and profitability, and to gain a sustainable competitive advantage. Thus, the R&D strategy that aims to improve product quality must be recognized as a significant part of a company's competitive strategy.

Human resources management and other functional strategies

Strategies related to human resource management, information systems technology, and other areas within an organization are likely to play a significant role in creating and sustaining the competitive advantage. Human resources management, for example, is seen as a strategic tool to achieve the match between individuals and jobs available. This match will enhance job performance and employees' satisfaction and will properly equip employees to carry out the company's goals and objectives. Management development should be integrated with competitive strategy to enable the company to build its collective competence and to create the learning organization essential for future competition.

Information technology (IT) also has a role to play in creating and sustaining an organizations' competitive advantage. To be successful in its business environment, a company needs to have access to different types of information which adds value to strategic decision-makers. This information, when analysed, will strengthen the company's competitive advantage. Information technology is necessary to ascertain what the company's competitive advantage is and how able it is to convert advantage into strategic positions. In a study by Powell and Dent-Micallef (1997), it was found that information technologies alone were not enough to produce sustainable competitive advantage. Organizations have gained advantages by integrating IT with their firms' infrastructure of human and business complementary resources such as flexible culture, partnerships, integration of strategic planning and IT, and supplier relationships. For example, Dell integrated supply-chain management with customer-driven order processing, complete control over the building process, logistics, delivery, a strong relationship management system, disintermediation, and mass customization, etc. This led to a significant competitive advantage (none of their rivals have grown as fast). Dell has capitalized on first-mover status and has managed to stay ahead of the competition by employing IT as a strategy and seeking to develop strategic alliances with others such as Microsoft.

The recent development of Internet-based strategy is the best example of how IT can be used to create competitive advantage. Porter (2001), for example, stated that the Internet per se does not lead to competitive advantage. His premise was, however, that the Internet can be used as part of the business strategy and the business strategy itself is the driver for the creation of competitive advantage.

It is true that many companies do not grasp the strategic importance of IT, but those that do can capitalize on the benefits that employing a coherent IT strategy can give. Wheelen and Hunger (2004) noted the significant role of IT for an organization's business strategy, and gave several examples to illustrate how companies are increasingly adopting information systems strategies to provide business units with competitive advantage. Many companies are also attempting to use information technology to build closer relationships with their customers and suppliers through sophisticated systems.

Strategic decisions on products to offer and markets to target

Based on the analysis of the marketing environment and the company's overall objectives, marketing managers have to consider a number of marketing-related decisions for achieving these strategic objectives. Fundamental marketing decisions that should be considered at this stage are product/s to offer and market segments to target. While the topic of segmentation, targeting, and positioning is discussed in more detail in Chapter 5, this section presents some marketing-related options. Ansoff's 2×2 matrix (shown in Figure 4.6) is a useful framework that is frequently used to guide marketing managers in making such strategic decisions.

This matrix illustrates the four possible options available to any organization in relation to product/market strategy. **Market penetration** as a strategic option involves selling more of the organization's existing products in its existing marketplace, which means increasing the level of penetration in these market segments. Adopting this option will depend on competitors' activity and the likely development of existing market segments over the next

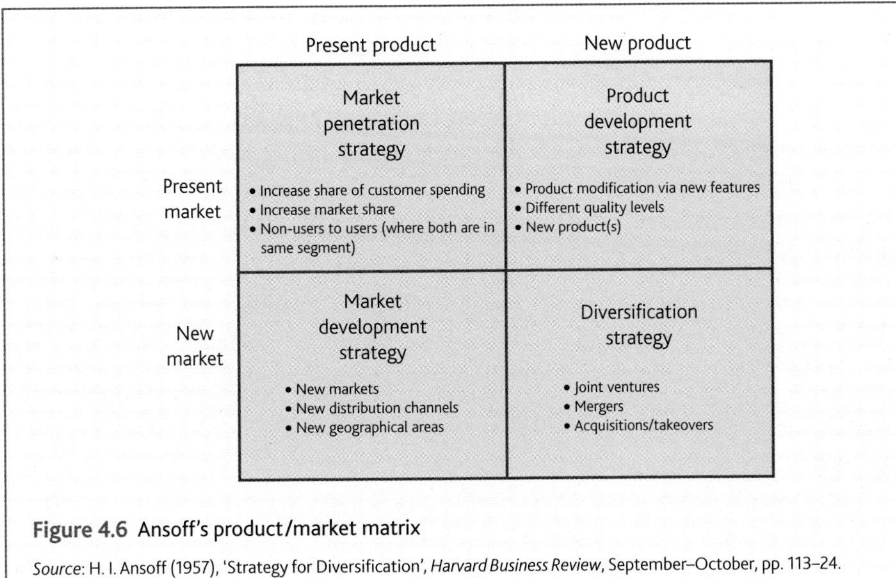

Figure 4.6 Ansoff's product/market matrix

Source: H. I. Ansoff (1957), 'Strategy for Diversification', *Harvard Business Review*, September–October, pp. 113–24. Reprinted with the permission of *Harvard Business Review*, by Harvard Business School Publishing Corporation.

two to three years. Market penetration is the least risky option of the four alternatives since the organization will be targeting market segments it already understands, using products or services it knows. Consumer product manufacturers such as Procter & Gamble and Unilever are experts in using their promotional activities to implement market penetration strategy to gain the dominant market share in a product category.

Product development involves developing additional or new products to serve existing market segments. The aim here is to expand the product range in the present marketplace in order to increase the level of sales. This strategic option is more risky than market penetration as it entails developing a new product where there is uncertainty as to how it will be perceived by existing customers. The development of a new product may also create a degree of cannibalization that might affect the net growth in the marketplace and issues of product rollover.

Market development takes place when the organization keeps its focus on the present product range, but searches for new market segments and looks at ways of marketing its existing products in these new segments. The degree of risk associated with this option is probably higher than with the above two options. It is not very likely that the existing products, without modification, will satisfy customer requirements in different market segments. Also, entering a new market will obviously require the organization to undertake an environmental analysis in order to understand the new market.

Diversification is probably the riskiest of the four alternatives as it involves the marketing of new products into new markets, though the potential return can be high. Producing new products will definitely require an increase in resources used, and reasonable investment. Serving new market segments will also need further analysis of the micro marketing environment, including customers and competitors.

It should be mentioned here that the choice between the four strategic options will be influenced by a number of external and internal factors (Aaker and McLoughlin, 2007).

External factors include the state of competition in the market and the critical success factors in the industry. Internal factors, on the other hand, include the product life cycle and the range of the company's product offerings. For example, it might be more risky for a firm in a fast-changing marketplace to stay with the penetrations strategy than to follow the market development strategy. Table 4.4 sets out the critical success factors in action.

Strategic choices and decisions for competitive tactics

A tactic is an operating action specifying 'how', 'when', and 'where' a strategy is to be implemented. Compared to strategies, tactics are narrower in scope and shorter in time horizon. Tactics may, therefore, be viewed (like policies) as a bridge between strategy formulation and implementation. Some of the tactics available to organizations are those dealing with timing 'when' and competitive market position 'how'.

Timing tactics

Organizations that move earlier than their competitors to produce and sell a new product, new design, or new model are classified as the *first mover*. A company that moves after the first mover is a *late mover*. Others may be classified as *early followers*. The three categories represent the timing tactics that a company has to consider and choose from in order to act or react against its competitors. The decision, as with any other strategic posture, depends on the company's resources, capabilities, and competencies. Furthermore, a company that has previously moved first does not necessarily have to be constantly proactive.

O'Shaughnessy (1995) identified the competitive timing movement depending on market share as a goal of the firm. In O'Shaughnessy's view, using market share as the goal, a firm seeks either market share protection or market share advancement. In the light of the chosen goal,

TABLE 4.4 Critical success factors in action

Critical success factors	Strategies	Performance indicators
Ability to achieve critical mass volumes through existing brokers and agents	• Develop closer ties with agents • Telemarket to brokers • Realign agents' compensation	• Policies in force • New business written • Percent of business with existing brokers
Be able to introduce new products within six months of industry leaders	• Underwrite strategic joint ventures • Copy leader's products • Improve underwriting skills	• Elapsed time to introduce • Percent of products introduced within six months • Per cent of underwriters having additional certification
Be able to manage product and product line profitability	• Segment investment portfolio • Improve cost accounting • Closely manage loss ratio	• Return on portfolio segments • Actual product cost/revenue versus plan • Loss ratio relative to competitors

Source: Richard M. S. Wilson and Colin Gilligan (2005), *Strategic Marketing Management: Planning, Implementation and Control*, p. 579, with the permission of Elsevier.

Goal	Move before competition	Move with competition	Move away from competition
Market share protection (hold defend)	i. Mix adjustments ii. Deterrent action	i. Imitate ii. Compensate	i. Merger ii. Acquisition iii. Collusion
Market share advancement (growth)	i. New areas ii. New segments iii. Additional channels iv. Penetration pricing	i. Capitalize ii. Leapfrog	i. New offerings ii. Reciprocal agreements

Figure 4.7 Competitive timing/direction matrix

Source: J. O'Shaughnessy (1995), *Competitive Marketing: A Strategic Approach*, p. 243. Redrawn by permission of Routledge.

the firm has to decide whether to *move before* the competition, *move with* the competition, or *move away from* the competition. When the chosen goal and the selected action are combined together in a matrix, a set of strategic options are available to a firm (see Figure 4.7).

While Figure 4.7 illustrates several tactics, they are neither exhaustive nor mutually exclusive, since some of them may be adopted simultaneously. Two issues should be clarified here. The first is to redefine the traditional typology of *hold, build, harvest*, and *acquire* as tactics rather than strategies. Build, hold, and harvest are the results of a generic strategy. Similarly, acquisition and vertical integration are not strategies, but means of achieving them. The second is the view of market share as an ultimate goal for the firm's competitive strategy. Some firms might go so far as to set the goal that all their business units should have the highest market share in their industries. This approach to strategy is dangerous. Market share is certainly relevant to competitive position; however, it is not per se important competitively; competitive advantage is. Pursuit of the higher market share for its own sake may guarantee that a firm never achieves a competitive advantage or that it loses the one it has. Such a goal also embroils managers in endless debates over how an industry should be defined to calculate shares, obscuring the search for competitive advantage, which is at the heart of strategy.

There has been a stream of research to identify sources of competitive advantage for the market pioneers, and to assess the impact on a firm's performance of being first mover. For the relationship between the order of market entry and market share, there seems to be general agreement that market pioneers have substantially higher average market share than late movers, and these share advantages are influenced by both business and industry characteristics. Empirical evidence indicates that both firm-based and consumer-based factors result in long-term market share advantages for pioneers relative to late movers, and therefore, the order of entry is a major determinant of market share.

For the relationship between the order of market entry and a firm's financial performance, research suggests that first movers tend to enjoy a long-term profit advantage over their rivals.

This high return is necessary to compensate the pioneer's heavy investment in designing new products.

Other advantages of being a first mover have been identified. The company can build its reputation as a leader in the industry, move down the experience curve to assume the cost-leader position, and earn temporarily excessive profits from buyers who value the product or service very highly. In terms of generic strategy, it has been suggested that pioneering firms will usually choose differentiation strategy, whilst a greater proportion of late movers will choose low-cost strategy.

Being first mover, however, has some disadvantages which, conversely, are the advantages enjoyed by late movers. These disadvantages are: pioneering costs, demand uncertainty, changes in buyer needs, technological discontinuities, and, finally, imitation risk.

Competitive position tactics

According to its position in the market, a company can implement its competitive marketing strategy by pursuing offensive or defensive tactics. An offensive tactic usually takes place away from a company's position in the marketplace, whereas a defensive tactic usually takes place within.

Although the two terms 'offensive' and 'defensive' are frequently defined in the business literature as two types of competitive strategy, they are viewed in this book as competitive tactics rather than types of competitive strategy. This is for two reasons. First, strategy by definition is formulated and implemented for a long period of time, but for a firm to be defensive or offensive this will depend on the state of competition in the market at any given point of time. The state of competition, by its nature, is more dynamic than static and, therefore, it is not required for a firm to be offensive or defensive at all times. Second, generic strategy is a way by which the entire firm's activities are engaged to achieve and sustain competitive advantage. Therefore, a firm's generic strategy (low-cost or differentiation) should be orientated by the goal of competitive advantage rather than by a set of defensive or offensive actions to protect or increase the market share in a market segment or geographical area. In other words, a firm can act offensively in one segment or geographical area and defensively in another. Below is a brief discussion of various competitive tactics in relation to four market positions.

1. **Market leader:** the firm with the largest market share and, by virtue of its pricing, advertising intensity, distribution coverage, technological advance, and rate of new product introduction, it determines the nature, pace, and bases of competition. To remain number one, leading firms may implement both offensive and defensive tactics.
2. **Market challenger:** a runner-up firm that is fighting hard to increase its market share. It may choose to adopt an aggressive stance and attack other firms, including the market leader. Therefore, it will normally implement offensive tactics.
3. **Market follower:** another runner-up firm that wants to hold its share without 'rocking the boat'. It may adopt a less aggressive stance and defensive tactics in order to maintain the status quo, but at the same time follow the leader.
4. **Market nichers:** firms that serve smaller segments not being pursued by other firms. By concentrating their efforts in this way, market nichers are able to build up specialist market knowledge and avoid expensive head-on fights with larger companies. We can

discriminate between segmenters and nichers in a few words. A segmenter tends to select a group of customers within the market whose needs can be met by a smaller section of the industry, whereas a nicher selects a group of customers within a market whose needs may be met economically by only one company.

Figure 4.8 illustrates an overview of how market leaders might defend their current position, how challengers might attempt to seize a share offensively, and how followers and nichers will act accordingly.

Competitive tactics for the market leader

If a company is to remain as the dominant player in a market, it needs to defend its position constantly. To do so, three major competitive tactics should be considered.

Expanding the total market

The market leader needs to search for *new users, new uses, and more usage*. Search for *new users* by attracting buyers who are still unaware of the product, or who are resisting it because of its price or its lack of certain features. Search for *new uses* by discovering and promoting new ways for the use of the firm's product. Search for *more usage* by encouraging existing users of the product to increase their usage rates.

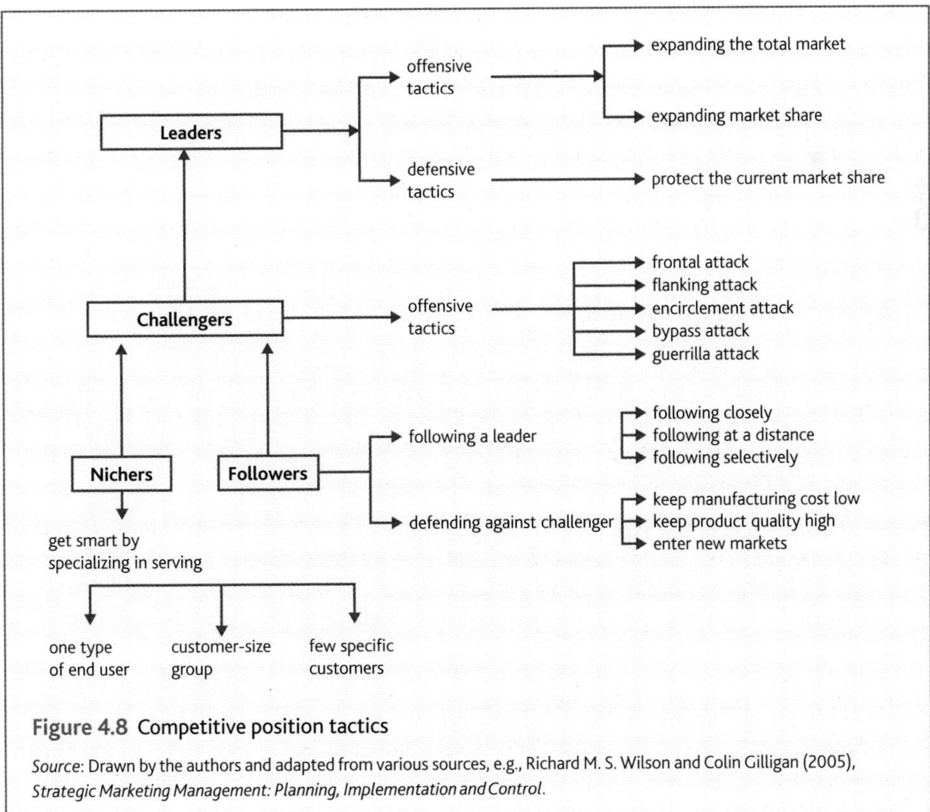

Figure 4.8 Competitive position tactics

Source: Drawn by the authors and adapted from various sources, e.g., Richard M. S. Wilson and Colin Gilligan (2005), *Strategic Marketing Management: Planning, Implementation and Control*.

Expanding market share

At the same time as trying to expand the total market, the market leader should not lose sight of the need to defend its market share. According to the saying, 'the best defence is a good offence', the market leader may adopt an offensive tactic to increase its market share over other competitors. This can typically be done in a variety of ways, including heavier advertising, improved distribution, price incentives, and new products. By doing this, the market leader increases its market share at the expense of other competitors and reaps the benefits of this increase in the form of higher profitability.

Protect the current market share

It has long been recognized that leaders are often vulnerable to attack. Therefore, a market leader has to adopt defensive tactics to protect its position. Porter (1985b) pointed out that defensive tactics aim to lower the probability of attack, or reduce the threat of attack to an acceptable level. Porter suggested three types of defensive tactics, such as raising structural barriers, increasing expected retaliation, and lowering the inducement for attack. Military analogies have frequently been used in the business literature to describe different types of defensive tactics:

- **Position defence,** in which a company builds fortifications around its current position, but simply defending a current position or product rarely works.
- **Flanking defence,** in which the company carefully checks its flanks and attempts to protect the weaker ones.
- **Pre-emptive defence,** where, in contrast to a flanking defence, the leader firm can be more aggressive, striking competitors before they can move against it.
- **Counter-offensive defence,** where despite its flanking or pre-emptive efforts, a market leader company could be attacked, so it needs to respond to minimize the threat. Counter-attack is particularly important in those markets that are crucial to the leader. Therefore, the leader must act decisively and swiftly.
- **Mobile defence,** involves more than aggressively defending a current market position; the leader extends itself to new markets that can serve as future bases for defence or offence.
- **Contraction defence,** when a firm finds its resources are spread too thinly and competitors are nibbling away on several fronts, so it opts to withdraw from those segments in which it is most vulnerable or in which it feels there is the least potential. It then concentrates its resources in other segments in order to be less vulnerable.

Competitive tactics for the market challenger

The challenger can attack the market leader, avoid the leader and, instead, challenge firms of its own size or smaller. The selection of who to challenge is thus fundamental and is a major determinant not just of the likelihood of success, but also of the cost and risk involved. Attacking a strong leader requires the challenger to meet three conditions. First, the assailant must have a sustainable competitive advantage (in cost or differentiation). Second, the challenger must be able to neutralize partly or wholly the leader's other advantages. Finally, there must be some impediment to the leader retaliating (Porter, 1985b). A number of possible attack tactics have been suggested in the marketing literature:

- **Frontal attack:** consists of opposing the competitor directly by using its own weapons, and without trying to use its weak point.
- **Flanking attack:** as an alternative to a costly and risky frontal attack, the challenger can focus its strength against the competitor's weaker flanks or on gaps in the competitor's market coverage.
- **Encirclement attack:** involves attacking from the front and sides. A challenger encircles the competitor's position in terms of products or markets or both.
- **Bypass attack:** the challenger chooses to change the rules of the game. It might diversify into unrelated products, move into new geographic markets, or leapfrog into new technologies to replace existing products.
- **Guerrilla attack:** the fifth tactic open to a challenger is in many ways best suited to smaller companies with a relatively limited resource base. The challenger might use selective price cuts, executive raids, intense promotional outbursts, or assorted legal actions.

Competitive tactics for the market follower

As an alternative to challenging for leadership, many companies are content to adopt a far less proactive posture and simply follow what others do. The market follower can learn from the leader's experience and copy the leader's products and strategies, usually with much less investment. Wilson and Gilligan (2005) identify three distinct postures for market followers, depending on how closely they emulate the leader:

- **Following closely,** with a similar marketing mix and marketing segmentation
- **Following at a distance,** so that the follower can flag up some areas of differentiation, and diminish the obvious similarities with the leader
- **Following selectively,** both in product and market terms so that the likelihood of direct competition is minimized.

Competitive tactics for the market nicher

A nicher is interested in one or two niches, but not in the whole market. The objective is to be a large fish in a small pond rather than a small fish in a large pond. The key idea in nichemanship is specialization. A market nicher can specialize in serving one type of end-user, specialize in serving a given customer-size group, or focus on one or a few specific customers. Although there are many advantages in niching, specialization can prove risky if the market changes in a fundamental way as a result of either greater competition or an economic downturn, leaving the nicher exposed. For this reason, there is a strong argument for multiple niching rather than single-sector niching.

Strategic mistakes and organizational failure

Mistakes and failure are facts of life that most organizations cannot escape. Cannon and Edmondson (2005) defined failure, in organizations or elsewhere, as the deviation from expected and desired results. This includes both avoidable errors and the unavoidable negative outcomes of some strategic decisions. Taking a strategic choice perspective, one might argue that organizational failure is a product of repeated strategic mistakes and unsuccessful interactions between the firm's management and its external environment. Porter (2004) noted that the reason why firms succeed or fail is perhaps the central question in 'strategy'. Neilson et al. (2008) argue that organizational failure and/or poor organizational performance is invariably down to ineffective strategy execution. These authors identified several areas and issues to support their argument, and put forward the idea of key building blocks to aid improvement. Closer understanding of strategy and strategic mistakes has as much to contribute to the understanding of organizational failure as the continued study of success. Therefore, it is important for organizations to identify, understand, and learn from their strategic mistakes in order to avoid organizational failure.

Wilkinson and Mellaho (2005) claim that academics offer little guidance to help managers predict or prevent strategic mistakes and organizational failure. They also claim that, while most managers know they are always at risk of facing organizational failure, they try to ignore the subject rather than actively seek to find the reasons for failure, guard against it or, at least, be prepared to learn from it when it does occur. The question is still open about the possible causes of strategy mistakes and organizational failure, and where they emerge from.

If strategy is defined as a means that helps to marshal and allocate an organization's resources based on anticipated changes in the market, failing to evaluate the environment properly represents the most fundamental strategic mistake managers can make. Inaccurate or improper evaluation of the environment in which the organization operates might lead to poor strategy formulation and implementation. There is no doubt that economic, social, and technological environments do change and these changes sometimes punish firms that fail to adapt/adjust their strategies accordingly. Although external forces can, to some extent, influence how the turnaround outcome—strategic success or failure—eventually unfolds, these forces are mediated by strategic manoeuvring within the firm. Many firms have suffered because they tried to adapt to environmental fluctuations that lasted for only a brief period of time, or have based their adaptation efforts on a faulty understanding of the environment or their own capabilities.

In this context, Porter (2004) notes that the threats to strategy are seen to emanate from outside a company because of changes in technology or the behaviour of competitors. Although this is true, the greater threat to strategy often comes from within. Thus, it is critical to our understanding of organizational survival and failure that we recognize three factors: (a) a firm's management; (b) its external environment; and (c) the way the firm's management interacts with its external environment. These three factors play a significant role in determining the organization's ultimate fate. A sound strategy, sometimes, is undermined by a misguided view of competition, by over-estimated organizational capabilities, and, especially, by the desire to grow.

Sheppard and Chowdhury (2005) suggested four essential points managers need to know in order to understand the link between strategy mistakes and organizational failure:

- organizational failure is not typically the fault of either the environment or the organization, but rather it must be attributed to both of these forces; or, to be more exact, failure is the misalignment of the organization to the environment's realities

TABLE 4.5 Strategic advice to managers to avoid failure

Strategic elements	What to do
Poor strategy performance	Do not confuse a sustained decline with a brief hiccup or a series of hiccups. This delineation is critical: if confusion leads to oversight or inaction on your part, it may lead to your firm's eventual death. Recognize a decline early and that there are elements of the firm's strategy that must be changed
Taking strategic actions	Be serious and judicious in understanding the situation you are up against and prioritize actions and execute your strategies accordingly
Mission statement	Know what your firm is all about: what basic customer needs your firm can serve well; the products you sell; the customers and market segments you serve. Develop a clear identity that sends a clear signal to customers
Addressing key stakeholders	Listen carefully to key stakeholders. Ask for their input and all-out support and mobilize them to rally around your firm's chosen course of action
Industry dynamics	Be careful about ambiguous and incomplete environmental data, as they might lead to incorrect interpretation of the industry dynamics. Because of constantly evolving industry dynamics, an incorrect reading does not let you manoeuvre the external forces well; rather it serves as a booby trap
Resources	Be steadfast and decisive in the acquisition and use funds needed to make the correct change in a timely fashion. The same change might need far more resources later, or the opportunity to change might have been lost for good
Strategic capabilities	Have marketing to connect with what customers want and the financial acumen to fund needed changes
Core competences	Make a dedicated effort to exploit where the firm can add value with rare, hard-to-imitate activities
Domain selection	Be familiar with your industry's domain without defining it too broadly. Be ready to quickly adjust your domain along with changes in customer needs. Do not stick to domains that have recently seen limited success
Implementation	Coordinate implementation of strategy elements to work together in an effective, decisive, and timely way

Source: Jerry Paul Sheppard and Shamsud D. Chowdhury (2005), 'Riding the Wrong Wave: Organizational Failure as a Failed Turnaround', *Long Range Planning*, 38, pp. 256. © Elsevier.

- because organizational failure involves the alignment or misalignment of the firm and its environment, it is by definition, about strategy
- because organizational failure deals with strategy, managers can make choices to accelerate it or avoid falling into its clutches
- because organizational failure can be avoided even after a decline—rapid or prolonged—the ultimate failure of the organization really stems from a failure to execute a turnaround successfully.

Baumard and Starbuck (2005), in a study on a very large European telecommunications firm, identified a number of strategic choices and decisions that might lead to strategic mistakes and failure:

- attempted growth into a new domain without adequate skills or experience might lead to strategy failure
- projections of over-estimated demand can also lead to strategic failure where organizations bore heavy fixed costs
- transferring an old business model to a new situation might result in strategic failure if the transfer was inappropriate
- launching a new product can increase uncertainty and mobilize resources with a low predictability of success
- designing new activities that are projections of core beliefs can be a version of escalating commitments to losing businesses.

To prevent strategic mistakes and failure recurring, or to initiate corrective actions to minimize the damage incurred while navigating through failure, Sheppard and Chowdhury (2005) produced a list of 'what to do' in the form of strategic advice directed to managers in order to avoid strategy and organizational failure (see Table 4.5).

Managers must draw lessons and learn from past strategic mistakes and failure. Understanding the causes for strategic mistakes and organizational failure requires companies to adopt a proactive approach and undertake a skilful search within and outside the organization.

Conclusion

Drawing upon the strategic analysis of the organization's internal and external environment, managers have to evaluate several strategic alternatives available to them and make strategic decisions that will define the future direction of their organization. The key task is to generate a well-justified set of strategic choices and select from them the ones that will strengthen the future position of the organization in the market(s) in which it has elected to compete. Figure 4.1 shows the hierarchy of strategic decisions taken at the three organizational levels: corporate, SBU, and functional. Strategic decisions that are expected at the corporate level are the creation of a mission statement, the selection of a directional strategy, and the allocation of resources between SBUs. The key strategic decision that should be taken at the SBU level is identifying the organization's strategic orientation for the future, that is, one of the three generic strategies (cost leadership, differentiation, focus). Strategic decisions, within the marketing area at the functional level, include products to offer, markets to target, and market position strategies. In this chapter, we presented and discussed each of these strategic decisions and reviewed some of the available literature to support our discussion.

Summary

This chapter has discussed in more detail the second stage/area of the Strategic Marketing Management (SMM) process, namely strategic choice and decisions. Strategic managers, at this stage, aim to understand the underlying bases guiding future strategy, generating strategic options and selecting from among them. They will have to use the organization's strengths to capitalize on external opportunities and/or minimize threats, and invest in available opportunities to overcome the organizations' major weaknesses. A number of strategic choices and decisions should be taken to contribute to the achievement of the overall corporate goals and objectives. The first set of these strategic decisions will be taken at the corporate level, the next set will be taken at the SBU level, and the final set will be taken at the functional level. This chapter has discussed the various sets of strategic decisions at each level and reviewed key analytical models that have been frequently used to inform the decision-making at each level.

KEY TERMS

Differentiation strategy Another generic strategy which involves the creation of a unique product or service for which the company may charge a premium. This speciality can be associated with design, brand image, technology feature, dealer network, or customer service.

Directional strategies The corporate directional strategies are those designed to achieve growth, stability, or reduction in a corporation's level of activities.

Focus strategy A generic strategy which involves concentrating the marketing effort on a particular segment and competing in this segment using cost factor or differentiation approach.

Low-cost strategy A generic strategy pursued by organizations which aims at the broad mass market and requires the aggressive construction of efficient-scale facilities, vigorous pursuit of cost reduction from experience, tight cost and overhead control, avoidance of marginal customer accounts, and cost minimization in areas like R&D, service, sales force, and advertising.

Mission statement Is a generalized statement that serves as a focal point for employees to identify the organization's direction and to ensure unanimity of purpose within the firm. It also contributes to the creation of organization identity and how it wants to be perceived in the marketplace by customers, competitors, and the general public.

Organizational failure From a strategic choice perspective, organizational failure is a product of repeated strategic mistakes and unsuccessful interactions between the firm's management and its external environment.

Strategic choice Involves understanding the underlying bases guiding future strategy, and generating strategic options for evaluation and selecting from among them.

DISCUSSION QUESTIONS

1 It has been argued that the core purpose of marketing strategy is positioning of the company's product in the market segment(s) in which it competes. Making reference to examples, discuss different approaches to marketing strategy development and explain how a company could have different positions in the same product market.

2 In terms of Porter's typology of generic strategy, discuss which generic strategies have been pursued by the Japanese carmakers in Europe. Do you think it would be possible for a car producer to compete in the global market pursuing two different generic strategies simultaneously?

3 It has been argued that an effective strategy is the one that is based on the identification of sustainable competitive advantages. Making reference to a couple of UK retail companies of your choice, discuss the competitive advantages associated with the development of their generic strategies.

4 For organizations holding each of the following market positions, what types of marketing strategies would you recommend as most appropriate and why:

- market leader
- market follower
- market challenger
- niche player?

ONLINE RESOURCE CENTRE

Visit the Online Resource Centre for this book for lots of interesting additional material at: **www.oxfordtextbooks.co.uk/orc/west2e/**

REFERENCES AND FURTHER READING

Aaker, David A., and Damien, McLoughlin (2007), *Strategic Market Management*, European edn (Chichester: John Wiley & Sons, Ltd).

Abell, D. F., and J. S. Hammond (1979), *Strategic Market Planning: Problems and Analytical Approaches* (Englewood Cliffs, NJ: Prentice Hall, Inc.).

Akan, Obasi, Richard S. Allen, Marilyn M. Helms, and Samuel A. Spralls (2006), 'Critical Tactics for Implementing Porter's Generic Strategies', *Journal of Business Strategy*, 27 (1), pp. 43–53.

Ansoff, H. I. (1957), 'Strategy for Diversification', *Harvard Business Review*, September–October, pp. 113–24.

Baker, Michael J. (1992), *Marketing Strategy and Management* (London: MacMillan Press Ltd).

Baumard, Philippe, and William Starbuck (2005), 'Learning from Failures: Why it May not Happen', *Long Range Planning*, 38, pp. 281–98.

Cannon, Mark D., and Amy C. Edmondson (2005), 'Failing to Learn and Learning to Fail (Intelligently)', *Long Range Planning*, 38, pp. 299–319.

Cook, Victor J. (Jr) (1983), 'Marketing Strategy and Differential Advantage', *Journal of Marketing*, 47 (Spring), pp. 68–75.

Cook, Victor J. (Jr) (1985), 'Understanding Marketing Strategy and Differential Advantage', *Journal of Marketing*, 49 (Spring), pp. 137–42.

Cravens, David W. (1994), *Strategic Marketing* (New York: Richard D. Irwin).

David, Fred R. (1989), 'How Companies Define their Mission', *Long Range Planning*, 22 (1), pp. 90–7.

Dibb, Sally, Lyndon Simkin, William M. Pride, and O. C. Ferrell (2006), *Marketing: Concepts and Strategies* (Boston, MA: Houghton Mifflin Company).

Hamel, Gary, and C. K. Parahalad (1994), *Competing for the Future* (Boston, MA: Harvard Business School Press).

Haspeslagh, Philippe (1982), 'Portfolio Planning: Uses and Limits', *Harvard Business Review*, January–February, pp. 58–73.

Herbert, Theodore T., and Helen Deresky (1987), 'Generic Strategies: An Empirical Investigation of Typology Validity and Strategy Content', *Strategic Management Journal*, 8 (2), pp. 135–47.

Hooley, Graham J., John Saunders, and Nigel F. Piercy (2004), *Competitive Positioning: The Key to Market Success* (Harlow: Prentice-Hall International Ltd).

Jackson, Stuart E. (2008), 'Strategic Opportunism', *Journal of Business Strategy*, 29 (1), pp. 46–8.

Johnson, Gerry, and Kevan Scholes (2005), *Exploring Corporate Strategy* (Harlow: Prentice-Hall Europe Ltd).

Johnson, Mark W., Clayton M. Christensen, and Henning Kagermann (2008), 'Reinventing your Business Model', *Harvard Business Review*, December, pp. 50–9.

Kachaner, Nicolas, and Michael S. Deimler (2009), 'Stretching the Strategy Process', *Strategic Direction*, 25 (1), pp. 17–20.

Knott, Paul (2008), 'Strategy Tools: Who Really Uses Them?', *Journal of Business Strategy*, 29 (5), pp. 26–31.

Kotler, Philip (2000), *Marketing Management* (Englewood Cliffs, NJ: Prentice Hall, Inc.).

Miles, Raymond E., and Charles Snow (1978), *Organisational Strategy, Structure and Process* (New York: McGraw-Hill, Inc.).

Miller, Danny (1992), 'The Generic Strategy Trap', *Journal of Business Strategy*, 13 (January–February), pp. 37–41.

Neilson, G. L., K. L. Martin, and E. Powers (2008), 'The Secrets to Successful Strategy Execution', *Harvard Business Review*, June, pp. 60–70.

O'Shaughnessy, John (1995), *Competitive Marketing: A Strategic Approach* (London: Routledge).

Porter, Michael E. (1980), *Competitive Strategy: Techniques for Analyzing Industries and Competitors* (New York: The Free Press).

Porter, Michael E. (1985a), *Competitive Advantage: Creating and Sustaining Superior Performance* (New York: The Free Press).

Porter, Michael E. (1985b), 'How to Attack the Industry Leader', *Fortune*, 111 (9), (29 April), pp. 153–66.

Porter, Michael E. (1990), *The Competitive Advantage of Nations* (New York: The Free Press).

Porter, Michael E. (2001), 'Strategy and the Internet', *Harvard Business Review*, March, pp. 63–78.

Porter, Michael E. (2004), 'What is Strategy?' in Susan Segal-Horn (ed.), *The Strategy Reader* (Oxford: Blackwell Publishing, The Open University), pp. 41–62.

Porter, Michael E. (2008), 'The Five Competitive Forces that Shape Strategy', *Harvard Business Review*, January, pp. 79–93.

Powell, Thomas C., and Anne Dent-Micallef (1997), 'Information Technology as Competitive Advantage: The Role of Human, Business, and Technology Resources', *Strategic Management Journal*, 18 (5), pp. 375–405.

Pretorius, Marius (2008), 'When Porter's Generic Strategies are not Enough: Complementary Strategies for Turnaround Situations', *Journal of Business Strategy*, 29 (6), pp. 19–28.

Reimann, B. C., and A. Reichert (1996), 'Portfolio Planning Methods for Strategic Capital Allocation: A Survey of Fortune 500 Firms', *International Journal of Management*, (March), pp. 84–93.

Sheppard, Jerry Paul, and Shamsud D. Chowdhury (2005), Riding the Wrong Wave: Organisational Failure as a Failed Turnaround', *Long Range Planning*, 38, pp. 239–60.

Speed, Richard J. (1989), 'Oh Mr Porter! A Re-appraisal of Competitive Strategy', *Marketing Intelligence and Planning*, 6 (5), pp. 8–11.

Treacy, Michael, and Fred Wiersema (1993), 'Customer Intimacy and other Value Disciplines', *Harvard Business Review*, January–February, pp. 84–93.

Utterback, James M., and W. J. Abernathy (1975), 'A Dynamic Model of Product and Process Innovation', *Omega*, 3 (6), pp. 639–56.

Ward, Steven, and Aleksandra Lewandowska (2008), 'Is the Marketing Concept Always Necessary? The Effectiveness of Customer, Competitors and Societal Strategies in Business Environment Types', *European Journal of Marketing*, 42 (1/2), pp. 222–37.

Wheelen, Thomas L., and David J. Hunger (2004), *Strategic Management and Business Policy* (New York: Addison-Wesley Publishing Company, Inc.).

Wilkinson, Adrian, and Kamel Mellahi (2005), 'Organisational Failure: Introduction to the Special Issue', *Long Range Planning*, 38, pp. 233–8.

Wilson, Richard M. S., and Colin Gilligan (2005), *Strategic Marketing Management: Planning, Implementation and Control* (Oxford: Butterworth-Heinemann).

Wright, Peter (1987), 'A Refinement of Porter's Strategies', *Strategic Management Journal*, 8 (1), pp. 93–101.

Zahra, Shaker A., and Sidhartha R. Das (1993), 'Building Competitive Advantage on Manufacturing Resources', *Long Range Planning*, 26 (2), pp. 90–100.

KEY ARTICLE ABSTRACTS

Stuart, E. Jackson (2008), **'Strategic Opportunism'**, *Journal of Business Strategy*, 29 (1), pp. 46–8.

This is an interesting study that provides organizations with some valuable views/advice to guide the success of their growth strategy. The paper shows how successful acquirers combine both strategic discipline and a willingness to react quickly to market opportunities—an approach the author called strategic opportunism.

Abstract: This article draws lessons from leading private equity investment groups, some of whom excel at this approach. The author uses the example of Snapple Beverage Corporation, a company that has been acquired four times since 1992, twice by private equity investors Thomas Lee and Triarc, and twice by corporate owners Quaker Oats and Cadbury Schweppes. Each owner brought different organizational priorities and different capabilities to add value to the business. The clear implication of this paper is that for a successful growth strategy involving acquisitions, companies need to get both the strategy and timing right. This may require adjusting the strategy in light of opportunities that arise, and taking steps to align organization priorities and incentives.

Mellahi, Kamel (2005), **'The Dynamics of Boards of Directors in Failing Organisations'**, *Long Range Planning*, 38, pp. 261–79.

This is a useful case study-based article that investigates how executives can early predict organizational strategic failure.

Abstract: This article addresses two questions: why do boards of directors often fail to detect warning signals during the early stage of strategy failure; and when they do detect warning signals, why do they tend to remain passive? The article aims to answer these questions through an in-depth study of the collapse of HIH. It also examines board dynamics over the different stages of strategy failure. The paper identifies the special challenges that directors confront at each stage of strategy failure and suggests initiatives the board should use to prevent or reverse strategy failure.

Obasi, Akan Richard S. Allen, Marilyn M. Helms, and Samuel A. Spralls III (2006), **'Critical Tactics for Implementing Porter's Generic Strategies'**, *Journal of Business Strategy*, 27 (1), pp. 43–53.

This is an interesting study that flags up some important gaps in the understanding of Porter's typology, which hinder the managers' attempts to implement Porter's generic strategies appropriately.

Abstract: This study notes that previous research has not identified tactics associated with each of the generic strategies. Furthermore, prior research has not determined which of these tactics are associated with higher levels of organizational performance. Thus, managers lack insight into which specific tactics to implement at the operational level of their organization when following a chosen generic strategy. The major contribution of this article is that managers will gain the knowledge of how to better tailor their strategy implementation to more effectively implement whatever generic strategy they attempt to use.

Woonghee, Lee, and Nam S. Lee (2007), **'Understanding Samsung's Diversification Strategy: The Case of Samsung Motors Inc.'**, *Long Range Planning*, 40, pp. 488–504.

This is another interesting case study-based paper which explores the strategic decision-making process at Samsung Motors Inc., and highlights how the company has survived the crisis in the world automobile market.

Abstract: This study follows the changes in Samsung's strategic management during and after the Asian economic crisis when SMI's first car rolled off the Pusan production line. Two questions are raised in this research: (1) How did Samsung come to invest in automobiles? and (2) How did the Korean crisis in general and the crisis in the automobile market in particular change Samsung's strategic decision-making process? The study found that non-economic influences prevailed over economic influences in the decision to pursue the diversification strategy, and that due in part to the strength of these influences, Samsung underestimated the market risk and overestimated the contribution its core competencies and synergy could make.

END OF CHAPTER 4 CASE STUDY Intelligent Finance (IF.com)

Introduction

The financial service industry provides goods and services that help people to manage their financial resources and fulfil their financial commitments. Financial institutions in the UK could be divided into two types, e.g. mortgage providers or insurance companies, or those that provide a combination of these products, e.g. retail banks and building societies. Within this sector, the introduction of the Internet has allowed for the creation of new Internet-based financial service providers, and a multitude of new organizations.

» As a result, the retail banking sector can be further divided into two groups of organization; online-only banks and the traditional high-street banks. Online-only banks offer various financial services to customers via the Internet only. Examples of this type of bank in the UK include Egg, Smile, IF, Cahoot, and many more.

Intelligent Finance (IF.com) is a retail bank operating in the UK via the Internet, and also recognized as a tele-net bank and offset mortgage provider. IF.com offers a wide range of products and services, including offsetting that not all other competitors are offering, which gives IF.com a position beyond threshold for best product performance. The company is a fully owned subsidiary of HBOS in its corporate set-up and purely handling financially savvy customers as an online retail bank. HBOS is a banking and insurance group with its main operations in the UK but also has operations in Australia, Ireland, and Spain. After the merger between the Bank of Scotland and Halifax, the HBOS group was the fourth biggest UK banking group in terms of market capitalization and one of the UK's biggest mortgage lenders. Over the five-year period between 2001 and 2006, operating income (net interest income and non-interest income) per share rose on average by 16.8 per cent per year for the listed UK retail banks. This figure partly overstates underlying growth since a part of this increase can be attributed to non-interest income in investment and insurance business due to equity gains from a bull market in equities during the same period.

The UK retail banking market

Before the world recession of 2008/2009, the market of retail banking in the UK was seen as a mature market. The market has all the characteristics of maturity with steady or falling profitability. Although the market has gone through a period of consolidation, it was still very fragmented and competitive. There are more than fifty retail banks competing in the UK market, but many of the brands are owned by major players, as illustrated in Table C4.1 below. The market has no clear market leader but five major players: HSBC, Royal Bank of Scotland (RBS), HBOS, Barclays, and Lloyds TSB.

A brief analysis of the financial service market in Britain illustrates that the relative market share of the UK retail bank loans in 2006 indicate that HBOS is the third biggest lender of the UK retail banks after Royal Bank of Scotland and HSBC. The relative market share in the UK retail bank equity in 2006, which reflects the financial strength of an institution and its ability to compete in the marketplace, shows that HSBC has 20 per cent more equity than RBS, followed by HBOS and Barclays, both with around 40 per cent of the equity of HSBC.

Retail banks in the UK are operating in a highly competitive marketplace, characterized by increasingly empowered and financially literate customers. This is combined with the proliferation of direct low-cost competition from well-recognized high-street names such as M&S, Tesco, and Virgin, and dedicated Internet banks, to make the trading environment ever more competitive. As customers are increasingly interacting through remote technological channels (e.g., by telephone and the Internet), the implications for bank–customer relationships are potentially of key importance. Whilst every UK bank has Internet banking capability, there appears to be uncertainty as to what is the best practice in the area of Internet banking. The relative novelty of Internet banking means that actual trends are still quite difficult to extrapolate. »

TABLE C4.1 Retail banking brands in the UK*

Parent company	UK retail banking brand
Allied Irish Bank	First Trust Bank
Allied Irish Bank	Hill Samuel
Bank of Tokyo-Mitsubishi	Mercantile Bank of India, London and China
Barclays	The Woolwich
Danske Bank	Clydesdale Bank
Danske Bank	Northern Bank
Danske Bank	Yorkshire Bank
Garanti Bank	Ottoman Bank
Grupo Santander	Abbey
Grupo Santander	Cahoot
HBOS	Bank of Scotland
HBOS	Birmingham Midshires
HBOS	Halifax
HBOS	Intelligent Finance
HBOS	Julian Hodge Bank
HBOS/Sainsbury's	Sainsbury's Bank
HSBC	First Direct
KBC Group NV	Brown, Shipley & Co.
Lloyds TSB	Cheltenham and Gloucester
Prudential Plc	Egg Banking plc
RBOS	Adam and Company
RBOS	Coutts
RBOS	NatWest
RBOS	Ulster Bank
RBOS/Tesco	Tesco Personal Finance
RBOS/Virgin	The One Account
SocGen	Hambros Bank

*This list represents the situation in 2006.

Tele-net banking

The Internet has revolutionized the value chains of many industries. In banking, with the explosion in the use of the Internet, there has been an unprecedented increase in the number of online or tele-net banks offering services through the telephone and the Internet. Arguably, the only advantage these banks have over traditional 'bricks and mortar' banks is their lower cost base in terms of not having any infrastructure costs, and as a result they are able to offer their customers better interest rates. What remains questionable is whether these tele-net banks are able to differentiate themselves using factors that are only applicable to online and tele-net banks. With low entry barriers, the differentiating factor for each player becomes even more difficult.

Traditional banks have been characterized by trust, solidity, and economies of scale. Corporate identity was always seen as a distinguishing factor in traditional banking. Consumers normally rely on the name and the values for which the organization stood and banking was not commoditized. It is more to do with trust and tradition than with speed and convenience. In other words, corporate identity was a differentiating factor for the traditional banking system. In the new arena of pure tele-net banks competing with traditional banks as well as other online banks, corporate identity plays a major role. The products and services of the online banks need to embody the image of the bank. Traditional banks have successfully made the transition into online banking by utilizing the inherent advantages of their large customer base, trust, and multi-channel access (KPMG, 2000), available at: **http://www.kpmg.co.uk/about/index.cfm**).

Banks like Barclays and HSBC have started their online banking as an offshoot of the traditional banking system by stretching the same values that they stand for into their online business, while banks like Egg.com and Smile.co.uk, which started as pure online banks, have not had the same advantage. This raises the question of how these pure online banks differentiate themselves and/or create a unique competitive advantage. Smile.co.uk, is a good example of an online bank that, from the very beginning, has tried to differentiate itself by building a brand that stands for a unique set of values. They have bagged awards consecutively for best customer service and best online bank, as well as associated the Smile brand with ecological issues in order to differentiate themselves from other online banks. They are actively differentiating their brand by associating it with ecological products such as Tree2mydoor, Ecotricity, and Gifting Direct. It seems from this example that the differentiating factors in the online banking market lie in having strong branding, unique product offerings, and superior customer service.

IF.com key product (offseting mortgage) strategy

There are three key players in the online banking market that offer offset products: Egg, First Direct, and IF. With comparable offsetting offerings, there is little to differentiate between the three. Offsetting, being introduced some years ago, has been seen as a cleaver method of mortgage payment, especially for people with high savings and paying capital gains on interest income on savings. However, customers with smaller savings are not very likely to get many advantages from offset products as the rates that are charged if the balance goes below initial deposit in the savings account are higher than the average rate in the market.

IF.com's offset product strategy, compared with other online banks that are offering this product seems to be focused on telling customers that the offset product is their key strength. In the case of other banks like Egg and First Direct, the offset product is embedded as a part of their mortgage offerings. Another observation on IF's website is the highly visual demo that can be shown for this product. This educates the customers who are looking for mortgages about the benefit of offset mortgages. The current strategy of IF.com is a vital tool to get the first mover advantage in a product category that is relatively new in the market. The increase of IF's customer base which led to the popularity of the offset product can be seen as a positive point as it creates an impression of IF.com as a pioneer in the field of offset mortgages.

IF.com competitive advantage

As mentioned before, the UK retail banking industry is a mature market, where the players are striving to create unique competitive advantage, mainly by trying to achieve differentiation through their marketing strategies. For a UK retail bank, competitive advantage can arguably emerge from eight sources, as categorized below:

- superior inputs
- superior knowledge base
- superior technology
- superior operation
- superior offerings and branding
- superior access
- superior segments
- superior customers.

Analysing these sources of competitive advantage in the case of IF.com, it is possible to discuss briefly the eight categories as follows:

1. **Inputs: Financing.** IF.com financing is provided by HBOS—an established financial institution—at rates comparable to those of other financial institutions, so it has no superiority over its direct competitors.
2. **Knowledge base.** IF.com activity of tele-net banking has been developed, fast creating some advantage; however, this has not been leveraged for supernormal returns as the knowledge base can shift, and later competitors can/will catch up.
3. **Technology.** IF.com initially had an early mover advantage, however, web-based technology is very difficult to protect with intellectual Property Rights (IPR), and the fast proliferation of technology seems to mean that no one will be able to achieve a sustainable advantage by leveraging technology.
4. **Business Operations.** IF.com was created independently of the existing HBOS structures, which means that IF.com is far less burdened by operational costs than it would be—had it been an 'add-on' to the existing HBOS structure. Being formed from scratch means that IF.com as a business organization is leaner, more responsive, and has far less 'fat' than a longer operating, established institution. This could be seen as a

source of some advantage, but as with most other aspects which may be sources of competitive advantage, it is likely to be seen by competition and whilst it is not as easily emulated as 'technology' other online banks are also seeking to optimize their business organizations.

5. **Branding and offerings.** IF.com brand is less recognized than the brands of its founders 'HBOS', and this might have affected the view of the brand as a competitive advantage. However, the bank offering of 'offset mortgage' was initially seen as a product advantage, but since similar products are now offered by many competitors, it is no longer considered a unique source of competitive advantage.
6. **Superior access.** Most customers (approximately 80 per cent) were introduced to IF.com via existing HBOS intermediaries. The use of HBOS intermediaries is seen as a key source of competitive advantage, which should be developed further and utilized aggressively.
7. **Superior segment.** The deregulation and aggressive marketing approach which is pervasive in the UK financial sector means that no bank has real, sustainable, competitive advantage that would have derived from having access to a superior segment, or leveraging resources in a way which would allow superior exploitation of a market segment. Whilst some have managed to grow market share, it has often been achieved by lowering margins.
8. **Superior customers.** Due to data protection legislation, it is difficult to define the types/profile of IF.com customers in order to conclude whether their demographic, loyalty, and socioeconomic status differs significantly from the customer base of other online banks.

The brand IF.com is not as strong compared to the HBOS brand, and its core competency is in being a technology channel for HBOS to support its traditional 'bricks and mortar' approach. Although IF.com has tried to differentiate through its products like the offset mortgages, this product has been easily imitated by competition. It is also a fact that 80 per cent of IF.com customers come through various intermediaries of HBOS, while 20 per cent only come directly through IF's website. This supports the notion that the trust customers have in the brand name of HBOS makes them more comfortable to bank with them than would new customers be who approached a tele-net bank solely for their financial needs.

When viewing IF.com through the customer intimacy framework of Treacy and Wiersema (1993) in relation to its competition, its pricing is on average a little lower than its competitors, especially in credit cards and is one of the lowest in mortgages. This gives IF.com a position in best total cost for customers slightly above threshold. IF.com provides a wide range of products and services, including offsetting that not all the competitors are offering, which gives IF.com a position beyond threshold for best product performance. The fact that 20 per cent of IF.com final customers come directly through the company's website suggests that IF.com is not very close to its customers and places the company at threshold in best customer relationship in the customer intimacy framework.

IF.com strategic directions

In the current volatile marketing environment and financial crisis, IF.com needs to consider a new future strategic direction in order to maintain/strengthen its competitive position in the UK. There are a number of strategic scenarios available to the company which could be implemented.

Continue with current strategy

IF could keep on capitalizing on its access to other subsidiaries' customers under the HBOS umbrella and keep on getting 80 per cent of new customers through intermediaries. But all the other subsidiaries have their own websites and seem to be competing with each other on anything else but price, and intermediaries do want something instead for pushing customers to IF.com. By keeping the current strategy, IF.com will have a difficult time due to being limited to tele-net banking as the only means of contact. Customers do want strong banking brands they can trust, with a tangible existence in tandem with the tele-net option, but not to be limited by tele-net only. Since IF.com has no 'bricks and mortar' and is a stand-alone brand, gaining new customers via their websites will remain a problem, and those who do come are likely to be opportunistic and looking for the lowest price. Building societies are likely to be consolidated to cut costs and will be looking for increased market share, especially in mortgage lending. The UK lending market is currently not growing, or growing at a slower rate than five years ago, which might impose some difficulties for IF.com in its attempt to attract new customers and gain market share.

Overall cost leadership

IF.com and its parent HBOS are one of the largest banks in the UK in terms of total assets and equity, thus a direct price war should be avoided, for even if HBOS were to beat the competitors to the lowest cost, the margins available would be severely reduced in the process. IF.com and HOBS would also receive fierce retaliation from competitors, especially those with a stronger equity base and a higher credit rating, such as HSBC, the Royal Bank of Scotland, and Barclays, which would most certainly not sit still while IF.com and HBOS are grabbing market share from them in the UK retail market. In addition, the fact that HBOS is a publicly listed company, means that its shareholders will not appreciate a fall in net earnings as would happen with the low-cost leadership strategy.

Differentiation strategy

The Internet is creating new ways of differentiation by enabling mass customization, which improves the response of companies to customer wishes. In the 1940s and 1950s, manufacturers used to build products and wait for customers to respond. Now they are more marketing-orientated and take directions from customers before manufacturing any products. Dell computer, for example, established its leadership position by creating an online ordering system that allows customers to configure their own products. This type of mass customization has not been fully implemented in the retail banking sector, although it is possible to tailor longer-term debt products (such as mortgages). This may be something that IF.com could look at. Some differentiation has already been achieved by products such as offset mortgages, but a more effective differentiation strategy has to run deeper.

Source: This case was prepared by Essam Ibrahim of the University of Edinburgh as the basis for analysis and class discussion and not to illustrate either the effective or ineffective handling of an administrative situation.

QUESTIONS

1. Identify and discuss the key success factors and strategic forces that drive the Internet-based retail banking market in the UK.
2. What are the major attributes that could differentiate IF.com from other key players in the UK Internet-based retail banking market?
3. Critically evaluate the strategic directions available to IF.com, and advise the management on how to strengthen the company's competitive position in the UK Internet-based retail banking industry.

5

Segmentation, targeting, and positioning strategies

LEARNING OBJECTIVES

- Examine the ways in which companies can segment markets
- Discuss ways in which marketers can measure the effectiveness of identified target segments
- Identify the various ways in which marketers can reach the identified market segments
- Provide an explanation for the importance of positioning the product in the head of the target consumer
- Present several important tools for perceptual mapping so that the reader can understand how to achieve a powerful position within the mind of the target consumer

CHAPTER AT A GLANCE

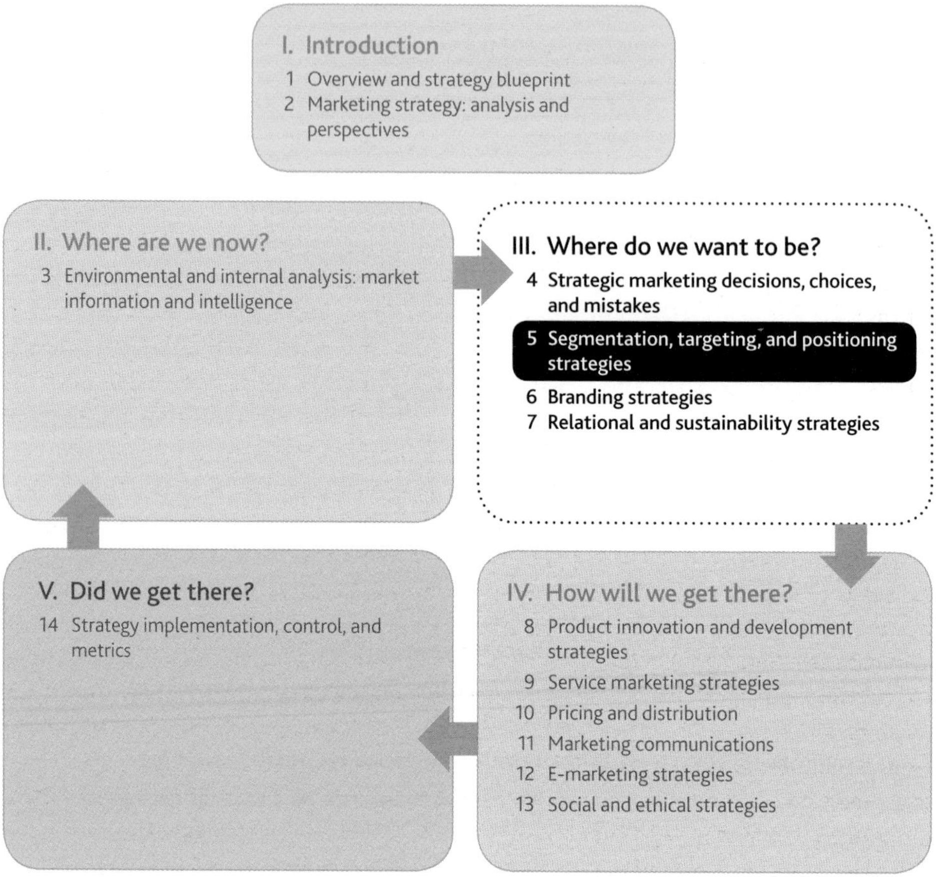

I. Introduction
1 Overview and strategy blueprint
2 Marketing strategy: analysis and perspectives

II. Where are we now?
3 Environmental and internal analysis: market information and intelligence

III. Where do we want to be?
4 Strategic marketing decisions, choices, and mistakes
5 Segmentation, targeting, and positioning strategies
6 Branding strategies
7 Relational and sustainability strategies

IV. How will we get there?
8 Product innovation and development strategies
9 Service marketing strategies
10 Pricing and distribution
11 Marketing communications
12 E-marketing strategies
13 Social and ethical strategies

V. Did we get there?
14 Strategy implementation, control, and metrics

Introduction

Market segmentation is vital for company success. Without a clear idea of the nature of the target segments, the firm is forced to use a scatter-shot approach to marketing strategic decision-making, with little chance for success. Dividing the market up into reasonable segments is only a starting point. The firm must then develop a series of strategic goals and strategies for effectively reaching those identified segments. Targeting requires the firm not only to aim at but hopefully to hit its target segments. The final important aspect involves the establishment of an important perceptual position in the mind of the consumer. The company whose brand comes immediately to mind when a need arises in a particular product/service class has a distinct advantage over its competitors. This chapter will present a series of possible foundations for effective segmentation and mechanisms for developing action plans for reaching those segments, and will discuss ways in which the marketing strategist can enhance their product/service position inside the mind of the targeted consumer. New thinking is presented in discussions on emotional segmentation and price-benefit position maps.

Foundations for effective segmentation

With the vast array of different wants and needs for any product or service class, it is unlikely that any company can have the luxury of appealing to an entire market. The buying requirements for this wide array of consumers would be widely varied. This might be possible in the early stages of a product or service form life cycle; however, as competition builds, the company is forced to give consumers a reason to prefer its product offerings to those of the competitors through differentiation. For this to be successful, it is necessary for the company to identify target segments of consumers and tailor their offerings to best meet the wants and needs of that particular group of consumers. It must be reiterated, however, that the initial requirement for effective segmentation is for the company to have clear strategic goals/objectives set within the umbrella of the corporate mission statement before target segments can be identified, targeted, and a positioning strategy developed.

Market segmentation involves the analysis of mass markets to identify subgroups of consumers with similar wants and buying requirements. These subgroups can range from quite large, down to 'segments of one'. It might be possible to focus successfully on each and every customer as a viable target market (particularly for business-to-business marketers, where markets are smaller by nature than for business-to-consumer marketers). The point is to maximize between segment differences while minimizing within segment differences using a variety of grouping variables. The firm is then in a position to tailor its offerings to best meet the desires of the consumers belonging to that segment. The point is for the firm to identify clusters of similar consumers that will allow for more efficient uses of resources and improve firm performance. The identification of a segment allows the firm to identify a profile of its typical desired customer, which in turn would allow the firm to develop a product configuration, pricing scheme, promotional campaign, and distribution coverage plan to best meet the needs of that identified typical consumer.

Criteria for identifying segments

The most important variables for identifying segments are as follows:

Geography

- Global
- Global regional
- National
- National regional
- City/state
- Neighbourhood/local
- Topography
- Climate

Demography

- Gender
- Age
- Education
- Income
- Occupation
- Religion
- Ethnicity
- Family size
- Stage of family life cycle
- Social status/class

Psychography

- Personality
- Lifestyle
- Values

Behaviour

- Usage rate
- Loyalty level
- Event creation
- Key benefits.

Each of these will now be discussed with illustrative examples.

Geographic bases for segmentation

Geography focuses on the 'where' issues. It ranges from **local/neighbourhood** to **global**, and could encompass any variation within the two extremes. Here, the main mechanism for segmentation is the nature of the geographic market being covered. **Local segmentation**, often used by small firms getting their start, keeps the market confined to a manageable area of coverage until a far greater understanding of possible niches is gathered. Since these firms are often not sure who their direct competitors are or will be, they opt for a group of nearby customers to reach. Picture the small restaurant getting its first connection to potential area customers with the placing of windscreen flyers or door-to-door leaflets to tell people that they are open for business.

Global segmentation would assume that the company sees the entire world as its appropriate playing field. This would indicate that the firm sees the broadest array of customers as its potential market. The danger of this approach normally entails the potential for cultural inappropriateness without some modification for different regions or nations. The other options are all variations limited by the amount of geographic coverage. Often companies will use geographic mapping programmes (like SPSS Maps) to address geographic segmentation by measuring potential trading area coverage. There are often assumptions made that if their best customers are located in a particular area, there may be important opportunities to build other strong customers in that coverage area. Kotler (2003) mentions the use by many companies of customer cloning, whereby the densest geographic areas are mapped and the company assumes that if the majority of customers are located in a particular area, then the best potential customers will come from that area.

Another aspect of geographic segmentation, which is often overlooked, is **topography**. The contour of the land within a geographic area may have a bearing on effective segmentation. Topography includes such elements as rivers, mountains, lakes, and valleys, which may affect population movement. The costs of overcoming physical obstacles may make a significant argument for effective segmentation. This might also apply to climactic conditions. Arid desert conditions as opposed to humid rainforest conditions can also be an appropriate mechanism for segmentation.

In practice, larger firms undoubtedly utilize a variety of different segmentation approaches, given different types of products. Campbell's soup had great success in the Upper Midwest of the US with its Cheddar cheese soup. But this product had little relevance for the US southwest as consumers in that region did not like the bland flavour of Cheddar cheese in a soup, so Campbell's put in jalapeno peppers to add a spice flavouring to it and found great acceptance for the product as a coating for tortilla chips.

MINI CASE STUDY 5.1 Should companies target children?

For many years, there have been complaints in the UK as well as in the US aimed at companies attempting to target their products to children. Nowhere is this more prevalent than with fast food and sweets producers whose products are considered to be 'junk food', with high sugar and fat content. Cereal companies have often been accused of hitting children with adverts during morning cartoon programmes which push children to pressurize their parents to buy these products for them when they are at Waitrose or Tesco. Of course, government regulators are concerned with controlling this as there is concern on both sides of the Atlantic regarding the ever-increasing level of youth obesity, as children are becoming less physically active and tending towards unhealthy lifestyles. To address the obesity concern, physical activity is often promoted through public service announcements, with 'get out and play' campaigns using famous sports figures to motivate children to get off the sofa and out onto the sports pitch. The problem is that while there are bans on adverts promoting unhealthy products to children (in the UK, this took effect in January of 2008), marketers are now using viral alternatives to reach these important consumers. Creative marketers are using websites to reach this target audience with fun and games, and mobile phone networks are reaching children with a variety of prize promotions. Coke and its Fanta brand have tried these types of campaigns in the US and the UK. Of course, these methods are in addition to the heavy use of cinema and TV product placements and celebrity tie-ins. If Miley Cyrus, star of the popular »

» Walt Disney Channel teen series, *Hanna Montana*, is eating some brand of junk food, it is pretty easy to see how many star-struck children might try to eat the same thing. Luckily, Walt Disney Co. has always been concerned about conveying the 'right' messages to children, but as the company's films are creeping out of the U ratings to PG and higher restrictive ratings to get bigger audiences, the potential is there to step slightly over the moral line.

Who has made a more visible use of food tie-ins for children than McDonald's, Burger King, and KFC? The 'Happy Meal' tying in of a variety of new movie-focused toys has been an issue for parents for many years. Children push to get the whole series of toys, and the parents are pressurized to buy many Happy Meals to get the whole series of toys for their kids. At least KFC has made the move to eliminate toys from children's meal packs. Hopefully, the others will follow suit. McDonald's makes use of its 'Kid Zone' on its website, which offers games for children mixed in with a variety of Happy Meal adverts, and even Cadbury's makes use of Bebo for the promotion of Crème Egg sweets.

In this day and age, it would appear that a better way to target your offerings would be to take the high road and opt to act in a socially responsible manner to get the parents of the kids to support your company. Of course, this means that food producers must seek new, healthier alternatives like cereals with lower sugar content and low-fat snack treats. Wendy's has taken the moral high road in the US, allowing parents to substitute oranges and apples and salads for fries, and McDonald's appears to be close behind as good citizenship is proving to be profitable. Finally, in November of 2008, an agreement was reached between some of the biggest fast food franchises in the UK to improve the fat and salt content of their products. Wimpy, Nando's, McDonald's, KFC, and Subway, among others, have committed to making their offerings healthier. So, the question that some are asking is whether the use of more 'creative' marketing campaigns to reach children should still be used if they are not breaking any laws and attempting to improve the overall quality of their products. It can be argued that it is always better to take the high ground in these matters.

Demographic bases for segmentation

Here, the overall market is subdivided using a series of demographic variables. One of the most obvious ways to segment demographically is by gender, but this is a complex term. **Gender** does not just address physical sexual makeup. It also contains a psychological component. How the individual sees themselves in terms of their sexual makeup and orientation is becoming less distinct in a variety of developed countries. Sex segmentation involves choosing males or females as the target audience. Certainly, there are a variety of products that have attempted this, from cosmetic companies to alcoholic beverages; however, it is more difficult now as one's feelings of masculinity/femininity affiliation may be a more appropriate segmentation tool. In the US, Virginia Slims cigarettes were orientated to women, but it was not clear that they did not have appeal to those males who felt a particular affinity for things of a feminine nature. Mini Case Study 5.2 focuses on this type of segmentation with the example of a vodka being marketed only to women.

MINI CASE STUDY 5.2 Vodka

There have been a number of examples over time of products that have been targeted specifically at women. One of the earliest examples was seen in the American market in the 1970s, with the promotion of the brand of cigarettes known as Virginia Slims and the obvious promotional tie-ins which included tennis tournaments with such stars as Billie Jean King, Chris Evert Lloyd, and Martina Navratilova. Since then, a number of products have targeted women in the US as well as the UK. Recent examples include the Dove and Wonderbra campaigns, which have asked for input from the target consumers themselves. In late 2008, Motorola introduced its female-oriented mobile handset known as the Moto Jewel, which was an attempt to follow the lead already set by Nokia and Samsung with products geared towards women. Now alcoholic beverage marketers are trying to market to women. Coors in the UK has created a group that will be designated as Eve to address the potential of marketing beer to women. This was prompted by the interest shown by women in two of Coors' products, Coors Light and Kasteel Cru, which had been primarily consumed by women. Of particular interest is a new Vodka product produced in Russia which is targeted only at women. The name of the product is Damskaya, which will be marketed in a purple-coloured bottle covered with a white dress, which reveals a label underneath which is imprinted with the words 'Ladies' Vodka'. Vodka is considered, along with Beluga caviar to be quintessential Russian products, and with all of the different types of vodka products that are aiming at different segments, it seems reasonable that a vodka marketed only to women would be a profitable idea. The product will be priced on the more expensive side, aimed at a more affluent woman, and the idea is that since women in Russia see vodka as a masculine drink, this brand may help them change their minds. The product will come in flavours like vanilla and lime, and the adverts will be geared toward the readers of up-market women's magazines like *Marie Claire* and *Vogue*.

Of course, gender is not just a sexual makeup issue as there is a psychological aspect to it, and while these products may be targeted towards women, there are certainly going to be men who will actually buy them as well. The concern that has been voiced is whether it is wise to target women if there are both men and women who will buy these types of products as there may be a chance of alienating potential consumers. Some believe that this kind of product has no benefit associated with it since there are already flavoured vodkas that appeal to women from Stolichnaya and other brands. The difference would be that the targeting will make use of the vehicles seen as preferred by the up-market target female consumer. The question is whether the perceptual positioning will resonate with the intended audience. There are also the usual problems associated with the marketing of alcoholic beverages, like the growing concern over high levels of alcoholism in Russia and the fact that there are a number of female alcoholics in the country.

Is the time right for a vodka marketed only to women? Will it be profitable? Wouldn't it be better just to take one of the existing products and add female colours and touches to it, effectively feminizing it? Wouldn't this have less of a chance to alienate any important constituencies?

Age is another basis for demographic segmentation. This can be clearly seen in the segmentation being done by Sony and Microsoft for its popular computer gaming systems and hand-held systems (Sony's Playstation and PSP and Microsoft's X-Box). The aim is to reach the computer-savvy youth with considerable discretionary income to spend on computer games, music CDs, and DVDs. Youth can clearly be seen in the segmentation of toys, music, cereals, clothing, electronics, and cellular telephones.

With globalization forces at work, there is an increasing opportunity for similarity of youth segments in terms of wants and needs driven strongly by world entertainment media (cinema, music, television). This would primarily apply to developed countries, as income levels in developing countries would not support these types of products and services.

Elderly consumers provide another promising avenue for product/service segmentation. With life expectancies significantly increasing in many developed countries, the elderly become increasingly lucrative as a segmentation vehicle. The US has seen a considerable increase in the segmenting of older consumers by fast-food franchisers as consumers looking for places to socialize with others and as potential employees. A wide range of health-related products are being aimed at increasingly older consumers with travel and leisure products/ services and low-fat and low-carbohydrate food/beverage products.

An interesting shift in focus was seen for Red Bull energy drinks in the UK, which had built a credible position in targeting what was considered the 'edgy youth' interested in nightclubs and extreme sports. The company shifted its segmentation target in 2004 to older consumers interested in golf, which would move the product into the mainstream. The company has plans to distribute Red Bull in UK golf clubs and will align itself with the European Professional Golfers Association Tour (Sweeney, 2004). Another attempt to shift focus can be readily seen in the recent relaunching of Burton Food's Viscount brand of biscuits. The new product is called Viscount Minis, and the new target is the younger woman who buys biscuits and confectionaries to share. This is a distinct departure from the more mature female consumers who were previously seen as the key segment for the company's biscuits.

An important approach to age segmentation involves the concept of a **cohort of society** moving through the ageing process together. While birth age is relatively easy to use as a basis for grouping potential consumers, it actually has little to do with consumer motivations. Defining moments and events in late adolescence/early adulthood (17 to 23 years of age) provides a set of fairly stable values that stay with members of the same generational cohort throughout their lives. *Advertising Age* (15 January 2001) presented six main generational cohorts in the US market: (1) the **GI Generation** (those born between 1901 and 1924) who are conservative and civic-concerned; (2) the **Silent Generation** (those born between 1925 and 1945) who are interested in conforming and raised families at an early age and are concerned with youthfulness and vitality; (3) the **Baby Boomers** (those born between 1946 and 1964) who believe that personal acquisitions are important, have high levels of disposable income, and who are concerned with value and do not want to be perceived as older; (4) **Generation X** (those born between 1961 and 1981) who are considered to be somewhat cynical, have great economic power, and who feel somewhat lost or alienated; (5) **Generation Y** (those born between 1976 and 1981) who are a subset of Generation X, interested in an urban style, like outdoor activities, and enjoy retro-style products; and, finally, (6) the **Millennials** (those born between 1982 and 2002) who are multicultural, interested in high-tech products, are well educated, and more used to violence and sex as a part of life.

It was noted by Jacqueline Scott and Lilian Zac (1993) that there have been many similarities in the life experiences of these kinds shared by both Americans and the British, which would suggest that similar cohorts could be effectively used for segmentation in the UK. This, however, may not work globally. An interesting recent study by Schewe and Meredith (2004) examined generational cohorts in a global setting and found that there are a number of countries which may not have the kinds of cohorts that have been found in the US. They argue that for cohorts to be formed, there are three requirements: (1) a telecommunications infrastructure that facilitates mass communications; (2) a population which is reasonably literate; and (3) a significant social impact of the events involved. Schewe and Meredith (2004) propose that these conditions can be met in all developed countries as well as in India, Eastern Europe, Lebanon, and China. They urge that underdeveloped nations are not fertile ground for cohort segmentation. They found through extensive research that there are distinctly different generational cohorts in Brazil and in Russia. These cohorts provide a valuable opportunity for segmentation.

The **level of education** can also be an effective basis for segmentation. The complexity of certain products makes them more appropriate for proper evaluation and usage by individuals with higher levels of education. There are certain products which are actually targeted at different levels of students from primary school (with such products as crayons, books, games, and snacks), to higher levels of education such as high school and college (with products like calculators, computers, apparel, music, and DVDs). The US has seen the advent of the SKIPPies acronym as descriptive of an important buying group (School Kids with Income and Purchasing Power). Firms like Coca-Cola, Nike, and Nabisco have all turned to in-school promotions to attract the teenage student segment.

Cort, Pairan, and Ryans (2004) report that one particularly successful in-school marketing programme used in the US is offered by Channel One. This in-school television network broadcasts a twelve-minute daily programme with two minutes of commercials to over 12,000 schools throughout the US and carries news and programming of interest to students. In return for allowing the programming during classes, the school receives television sets and receiving equipment. It is hoped that the advertiser utilization of the system will begin to build the seeds of brand awareness and loyalty in a unique environment with long-term consumer relationship potential.

A logical basis for segmentation is **level of income**, but in many countries, the larger concern is the individual's level of purchasing power. The important distinction in income is found in the difference between disposable income and discretionary income. For basic necessity types of products (food, clothing, and shelter), the starting point would be to examine disposable income, which is the income that is left over after taxes and creditors are paid. Discretionary income is what is left over from disposable income after basic necessities have been acquired. The remainder is then used to buy such products/services as fashion items/jewellery, cosmetics, and fragrances, and a variety of leisure-time products/services such as vacations and fitness club memberships.

Occupation can also serve as an appropriate basis for segmentation. There are a series of products/services that are aimed at homemakers as opposed to professionals, students, 'and white collar' workers (managers, executives, professionals) as opposed to 'blue collar' workers (labourers, tradespeople), retirees/pensioners, and the unemployed.

Religion is an important basis for segmentation, particularly when religious teachings/doctrine make the consumption of certain products mandatory or prohibited. Some products may never be allowed (beef for Hindus, alcoholic beverages for Muslims), while others may depend on the time of year or even day of the week. Acceptable articles and types of clothing may be dictated by religion (coverings to be worn by women in the Middle East). In the US, Manischewitz Company sells products which meet Jewish Kosher standards.

Ethnicity equates to the national country/culture of origin. In the United States, McDonald's has been particularly focused on race and ethnic heritage as a segmentation tool. Ads are run with Asian-American, African-American, and Hispanic-American settings, which include appropriately representative models, locales, music, and language. This can just as easily also apply to any national origin and cultural extraction. The key element would involve the use of effective representations of those cultures. In many developed countries, there are significant ethnic communities with considerable purchasing power which are effective targets for segmentation strategies. In Great Britain, there are considered to be seventeen different ethnic groups according to the *Labour Force Survey* published in 2003 (Marketing Pocket Book, 2004). The breakdown in thousands of individuals is shown in Table 5.1.

What these statistics clearly indicate is that there is a series of large ethnic groupings in Great Britain that may prove to be desirable bases for product/service segmentation. Palumbo and Teich (2004) suggest that minority and ethnic group segmentation must also consider the impact of acculturation since the amount of time that the individual has spent in the society will impact their outlook. Parallel strategies should be developed for targeting both acculturated ethnic groups and those not yet acculturated. The authors suggest that this is equally applicable in the US as in Western Europe, given the heavy influx of immigrants into these countries/cultures.

Family size is another segmentation variable worth considering. The existence of the extended family in many developing countries is an important consideration since there are various members of the family unit who can play a variety of roles in the product/service choice process. Kelloggs encountered problems in its advertisements aimed at Brazil when it showed a father and his child in a breakfast setting. It was not seen as representative of real life, since the father would not be the one normally getting the child his or her breakfast. In Brazil, the individual would be the grandparent. The ads were changed and were received much more favourably as a result.

Family life cycle stage reflects a variety of life conditions that have a potential impact on product/service purchase decisions. If the target segment is single as opposed to married, there may be a series of preferences linked to that life state. Examples can be found in food packaging of meals for one person as opposed to two or more, dating services, and fashion and hygiene products to help the individual find a date/partner. Later life stages include young married, married with no children, married with young children, married with older children, empty nesters (those married whose children have left home and are now on their own), and older married and those who are older but single again. These types of segmentation mechanisms are particularly useful in terms of leisure time activity choices as one's leisure time usage is heavily influenced by the nature of the home family situation.

TABLE 5.1 Population by ethnic group, 1995 and 2001 (in 000s)

	1995	2001
Black Caribbean	486	618
Black African	292	506
Black other	232	72
Indian	866	956
Pakistani	548	728
Bangladeshi	184	261
Chinese	123	180
Other Asian	173	250
White & Black Caribbean		271
White & Black African		65
White & Asian		145
Other mixed		30
Other	333	282
All ethnic minorities	3,237	4,364
White British		51,312
White other		1,690
White total	52,894	53,002
Total population	56,144	59,139

Automobile companies use life-cycle stage segmentation quite heavily. Vans are often chosen by families with young children since they have more space for carpooling several children at a time to a soccer game or to a school programme, while small sports cars with only two seats are aimed at singles or young marrieds.

In Great Britain, the 2003 National Readership Survey (NRS, Ltd) in its SAGACITY Life Cycle Groupings utilizes four distinct life cycle stages: dependent (mainly under the age of 24 and either living at home or a full-time student); pre-family (under the age of 35 and having established their own household but without children); family (under the age of 65 with one or more children in the household, representing as a group the main shoppers and primary income earners); and late (all adults whose children have left the home or those adults older than 35 without any children). For SAGACITY, these categories are then further divided into categories based upon previously discussed criteria (income and occupation). Here, life cycle stages are then divided into the white group (where the primary income earner works in the ABC1 occupation group) and the blue group (where the primary income earner works in the C2DE occupation group). Finally, in terms of the family and late categories, each is subdivided into two sub-categories in terms of income: better off and worse off. This combination approach leads to the identification of twelve separate and distinct categorizations for segmentation purposes. The theory here is that each subdivision reflects a group with different aspirations and behaviours.

Finally, **social class/status** can also be utilized as an effective basis for segmentation. There are six accepted grade definitions used in the UK reflecting social class (National Readership Survey, 2003): (1) A, **upper middle class** (3.5 per cent of the population), which reflects higher administrative, professional, and managerial occupations; (2) B, **middle class** (21.6 per cent of the population), which includes intermediate levels of each of the occupations mentioned above; (3) C1, **lower middle class** (28.5 per cent of the population), which counts junior levels of each of the above-mentioned occupations, along with supervisory and clerical positions; (4) C2, **skilled working class** (20.7 per cent of the population), including skilled manual labourers; (5) D, **working class** (16.5 per cent of the population), incorporating semi-skilled as well as unskilled workers; and (6) E, **those at the lowest level of subsistence** (9.2 per cent of the population), including state pensioners, widows (with no other earners), casual workers, and the lowest-grade workers (Marketing Pocket Book, 2004). Each of these groups has different wants, needs, expectations, and preferences. Demographic bases are the most used of all segmentation bases since they are the easiest to actually measure. Often they can be determined from readily available secondary data sources. When focusing on perceptual issues, segmentation mechanisms become a bit more complex.

Psychographic bases for segmentation

Psychographic bases for segmentation centre on perceptual issues. These segments are determined by combining individuals who are psychologically similar in their orientations. These distinctions are made based upon similarity of lifestyles, personalities, and values. Psychographics are often associated with the acronym AIO, which stands for activities, interests, and opinions, and segments which are exactly the same in terms of demographics may be significantly different in terms of their psychological makeup. This is an extremely important segmentation base due to its excellent potential for effective targeting of the segment due to an understanding of how the segment members live their daily lives and the opportunity to tie products and services to their particular values and aspirations.

Lifestyle reflects the ways in which the individual chooses to live their lives. What types of activities they enjoy, what life settings they desire, and who they surround themselves with are all components of lifestyle. A British company which has built its segmentation on lifestyles is the clothier, Ben Sherman, which has found a distinctive niche with a return to the look and styles of the 1960s (O'Loughlin, 2005). Two recent themes have been utilized: (1) the **Park Life** campaign (connecting their mod fashions to classic British icons like Big Ben and Hyde Park; and (2) the **Mods in the Mansion** campaign (tying affluent rock stars to country homes). In the United States, there are three main lifestyle groupings that are often chosen for segmentation: (1) the arts and culturally oriented consumer; (2) the sports enthusiast; and (3) the outdoors adventurer. The arts consumer is one who enjoys attending cultural events (e.g., the symphony, the opera, the ballet), which assumes a more educated, higher social grade, and a quieter type of individual, who needs cultural infusion to be happy. The sports enthusiast is seen as a younger, less educated individual, who is more outgoing and loud in voice and mannerisms. Finally, the outdoors person is one who enjoys the great outdoors. This individual enjoys a variety of ways to commune with nature, and is more apt to enjoy camping, hiking, jogging, and biking.

A recent study by Orth et al. (2004) attempted to use lifestyle patterns to segment beer consumers in the US. Using cluster analysis with lifestyle survey respondents, the authors identified eight different segments: (1) **TV-opposing moderates** (11 per cent of respondents who do things in moderation); (2) **unromantic thrill seekers** (9 per cent of the respondents who look for thrills but are not interested in social or romantic activities—predominantly male and younger); (3) **unexcited romantics** (9 per cent of the respondents who prefer quiet, leisurely, and romantic activities to thrills—predominantly females); (4) **lazy opportunists** (15 per cent of the respondents who prefer not to be active—predominantly older); (5) **interactive party animals** (15 per cent of the respondents who prefer activities which involve social interactions and shy away from activities which are done on one's own or are quiet—predominantly male and younger); (6) **introvert individualists** (14 per cent of the respondents who prefer to do things on their own); (7) **outgoing socializers** (12 per cent of the respondents who prefer social activities); and (8) **rushing adrenaline addicts** (16 per cent of the respondents who prefer activities involving excitement and motion).

Personality is another mechanism for segmentation. Kotler (2003) lists the four main variations of personality as: compulsive, gregarious, authoritarian, and ambitious. Here, the idea is to group people into roughly similar personality types with the underlying assumption that people will be more favourably disposed toward those of a similar personality profile. Personality has also been applied to products and services in the work of Jennifer Aaker (1997), who found that brands can be imbued with personality traits. Her research identified five different personality traits for brands: sincerity, ruggedness, sophistication, competence, and excitement. The idea is to match the brand personality with the consumer segment personality profile to establish a strong connection.

Another approach to psychographic segmentation involves the use of **core values**. The company tries to match its core values with those of its customer segments, building positive associations. The company stresses values in its products/services as well as in its corporate environment and culture, and the hope is that the segment will become loyal to the company because it embodies the core values of importance to the consumer. Core values are deep-set in the individual by life experiences and teachings, and are not able to be changed easily. The Body Shop, Ben and Jerry's Ice Cream, and Starbucks are all companies that try to resonate with the consumer by stressing concern for the environment, the use of natural materials, and human welfare. They hire people who embody these concerns, they infuse their store atmospheres and marketing communications with these values, and they back appropriate social causes, all indicating that not only their products fit with these values, but everything that they do as an organization is based on these values. This creates a powerful connection with the consumer and creates strong consumer loyalty. The work of Shalom Schwartz (1994) focuses on the identification of basic cultural core values. Schwartz identified seven cultural value types: (1) **conservatism** (where the stress is placed on maintaining the status quo and system order); (2) **intellectual autonomy** (freedom of thought, curious, creative, innovative); (3) **affective autonomy** (freedom of action, adventurous, free-spirited); (4) **hierarchy** (roles in society, social power, authority); (5) **mastery** (successful, ambitious, competent, confidence); (6) **egalitarian commitment** (loyalty, social justices, honesty, equality, responsibility); and (7) **harmony** (harmony of human beings and their natural surroundings, along with social harmony, peace, helpfulness). When a more global view of segmentation is taken by large corporations, there may be effective bases for global segmentation found in these basic cultural values.

A multi-based approach to segmentation incorporating both individual psychological values and demographics, known as the VALS typology, was developed by a company called SRI International. The organization, which presently oversees the VALS system, is SRI Consulting Business Intelligence (**http://www.sric-bi.com/VALS/**). For the US market, SRI identified eight separate groups for segmentation purposes: (1) **actualizers** (10 per cent of the population), who are successful individuals with high self-esteem, significant financial resources, and are very cognizant of their personal image as a representation of their character; (2) **fulfilleds** (11 per cent of the population) are highly educated, older individuals, concerned with maintaining order, satisfied with their life circumstances and make practical purchase decisions; (3) **experiencers** (13 per cent of the population) are impulsive, variety-seeking, younger, looking for more excitement, concerned with buying the latest fashions and electronics; (4) **achievers** (14 per cent of the population) are career-oriented, hard working, family-focused, buyers of prestige goods and services; (5) **believers** (17 per cent of the population) are nationalistic, patriotic, conservative, religious, community-oriented, interested in buying national products; (6) **strivers** (12 per cent of the population) are financial underperformers, who are concerned with betterment of their lives and living conditions without self-esteem problems; (7) **makers** (12 per cent of the population) who are do-it-yourselfers, with manual skills and like to be independent and self-sufficient, and like conservative governments that do not infringe upon individual rights; and (8) **strugglers** (12 per cent of the population) are elderly who are poor, lack skills, are relatively uneducated, are primarily focused on safety and security issues, and are wary consumers. The VALS system was a breakthrough in that it built on demographic variables and lifestyles and personal aspirations, and the eight categories provided marketers with new opportunities to build relationships with key consumer segments.

A similar approach has been taken in the UK with the Social Value Group typology as developed by Consumer Insight Ltd from its 2003 Survey. This survey is the largest survey of social changes that has been attempted in the UK, and the segments identified are based upon values, beliefs, and motivations and are linked to the various stages of Maslow's hierarchy of needs. The following are the segments which resulted from the 2003 Survey: (1) **self-actualizers** (15.9 per cent of the population), who are individualists, creative, people-oriented, relationship-oriented, looking for change without being judgemental; (2) **innovators** (9.1 per cent of the population), who are risk-takers, self-confident, want new and different products and services, and have clear goals in mind to achieve; (3) **esteem seekers** (22.3 per cent of the population), who are materialistic, looking to surround themselves with the kinds of trappings and having the kinds of experiences that would provide them with social status; (4) **strivers**

(15.1 per cent of the population), who are also concerned with personal image and status, but their concern is to gain status only in the eyes of their particular peer groups, and they tend to keep traditional values; (5) **contented conformers** (14.3 per cent of the population), who are concerned with being a part of the norm, so they go along with the crowd, which provides the security that they seek; (6) **traditionalists** (18.6 per cent of the population), who are conservative and do not like to take risks, who feel that traditional values and behaviours are safe and comfortable, and who are quiet and reserved; and (7) **disconnected** (4.7 per cent of the population), who live in the here and now, who are unhappy with their situations, and are somewhat apathetic. It is possible to see many similarities between the American VALS segments and the Social Value Group segments. The values and beliefs upon which these segments are built change very slowly, and are significant drivers of consumer purchase behaviour. These segments would seem to have important implications across Europe and the US. for those companies looking at identifying homogeneous segments on a global front.

Behaviouristic bases for segmentation

These bases are built around groups in which consumers have similar understandings of, uses for, and responses to particular products or services. **Usage rate** involves the amount that is normally consumed by the individual, and the normal categorizations are: light, moderate, and heavy users. The wants and needs of each group may be somewhat different from each other. The issue is that heavy users are far more important for most companies than others because they consume such high volumes and because they may be more likely to be loyal to a particular brand than moderate or light users. Rewards systems like frequent flyer miles are aimed at the frequent travellers to keep them coming back to the same airlines. Many hotels and motels aim at frequent business travellers by offering business travellers a wide variety of business services (in-room Internet access, business desks with fax/printer capabilities, free Wall Street Journals, free continental breakfasts, etc.). One interesting attempt to segment on usage rate can be seen by Interbrew UK, which launched its half-pint can of Stella Artois in 2005 to reach those who drink primarily on special occasions, rather than on a daily basis. Another example can be seen in their 2004 introduction of a draught beer dispenser for the home aficionado, which was created in a partnership with Philips Electronics.

Loyalty level is another effective base for segmentation. There are five different levels of loyalty: brand insistence, brand loyalty, split loyalty, shifting loyalty, and no loyalty (the switchers). **Brand insistence** is the highest level of loyalty, and it reflects the consumer who, when faced with the favourite brand not being available, will not buy any alternative brand. **Brand loyalty** is where the consumer will buy the favourite brand if it is available, but in the event that it is not available, another brand may be purchased instead. **Split loyalty** reflects having loyalty to more than one brand. Here, the consumer may want only two of the brands available in the product/service class, but either might be acceptable on any given occasion; the consumer who does not care whether the diet cola that they drink is Diet Pepsi or Diet Coke, but will not accept any other cola drink. **Shifting loyals** are those who are loyal to one brand for a period of time and then shift to another brand for a period of time. Finally, **switchers** are those who have no loyalty to any brand in that product or service class. These consumers are primarily deal- and variety-focused. Studying these different groups tells you quite a bit about your strengths as well as your weaknesses. Studying the brand insistent only tells you what you are doing right for that particular group of individuals. This will not provide any helpful insight into what you failed to do to attract others. Studying the brand loyal and the shifting loyals provides insight into who the brand's direct competitors are in the eyes of those consumers; studying the switchers tells you about what it takes to potentially attract consumers with deals and special promotions.

A 2002 study was published in *McKinsey Quarterly* by Stephanie Coyles and Timothy Gokey which cautioned that companies must be far more cognizant of changes in buying patterns because active management of migration patterns allows companies to stop potential customer defections and to shift consumers to higher levels of loyalty and consumption. The authors recognize six important loyalty profiles: (1) **emotive loyalists** (emotionally attached to the company and its products); (2) **deliberate loyalists** (who rationally choose the company and its products as the best possible choice); (3) **inertial loyalists** (who see the costs of switching away as too high); (4) **lifestyle downward migrators** (who may have experienced life changes and their needs are no longer being met); (5) **deliberately downward migrators** (who are prone to frequent reassessment of their needs and have found a better solution in some other company and its products); and (6) **dissatisfied downward migrators** (who are actively dissatisfied due to one or more bad experiences). The authors suggest that if one only studies the defectors, then they miss more subtle buying changes which can ultimately lead to defection, when it may be too late to get them back (Coyles and Gokey, 2002).

Another type of behaviouristic segmentation involves the **creation of special events**. The US florists, greetings card companies, and candy companies have long focused on special occasions. The creation of such special days of recognition such as Sweethearts' Day, Bosses' Day, Secretaries' Day, and even Mother-in-Laws' Day are all examples of segmentation on the idea of a special event as opposed to everyday occurrences. Some companies have chosen the opposite approach in focusing on those types of products and services that are used everyday without the need for a special occasion. Usually, this type of approach is used by the company that has nurtured a connection with a particular occasion but which wants to branch out into other use occasions. Another segmentation approach using events is to focus on critical events in the consumer's life. This is the type of segmentation used by jewellery companies to promote diamond engagement rings or anniversary gifts.

Benefit segmentation is based on the assumption that consumers can be grouped in terms of the key benefits that they seek from the use of certain products or services. There can be two or more different segments who buy the same products or services but seek different key benefits from the use of the products or services. For example, McDonald's may appeal to one group because its offerings are inexpensive, to another because of the taste of its food items, to another because it offers convenience, and to another because it offers an opportunity for socialization with peer group members. Some elderly consumers have become an important constituency for McDonald's because they like to have a chance to meet with friends regularly in a social setting and a breakfast or lunch meeting at McDonald's provides this opportunity. Other elderly consumers like McDonald's for meals because of the value menu items, given their limited income levels. Pomegranate growers have found that pomegranate juice contains high levels of anti-oxidants, which have been found to help the body ward off cancer. The key health benefits from the use of the product then provide an excellent special basis for segmentation. This anti-oxidant health benefit segmentation has also been successfully used by the growers/processors of blueberries, concord grapes, and the growers/bottlers of red wines. Anytime there is a new medical finding that shows how the use of a particular product can add years to one's life, a new segmentation mechanism will be created. This has been seen surrounding the cholesterol-reducing capabilities of oat bran, the heart-attack preventative use of aspirin, and the cold-preventative power of echinacea.

A recent study that appeared in the *British Food Journal* examined two important trends that affect British food consumption: convenience and health concerns. This study found that these are really not overlapping trends as convenience food items and health-oriented food items are most effectively segmented using distinctly different segmentation variables. The authors found that household size and region of residence were the most important segmentation variables for convenience-oriented food items, and they also found that gender and age were the most important segmentation variables for health-oriented food products (Shiu et al., 2004).

Strategic framework for segmentation

In order to transition from the foundation to the strategic considerations for segmentation, an excellent framework was provided by Palmer and Millier in a 2004 article. The principles of segmentation that they suggest are found in Figure 5.1. The framework is meant to be used by either B2C or B2B marketers. The segmentation can be done based on either who the buyer is or by what is being bought, and if it is based on who buys, then the segmentation criteria are

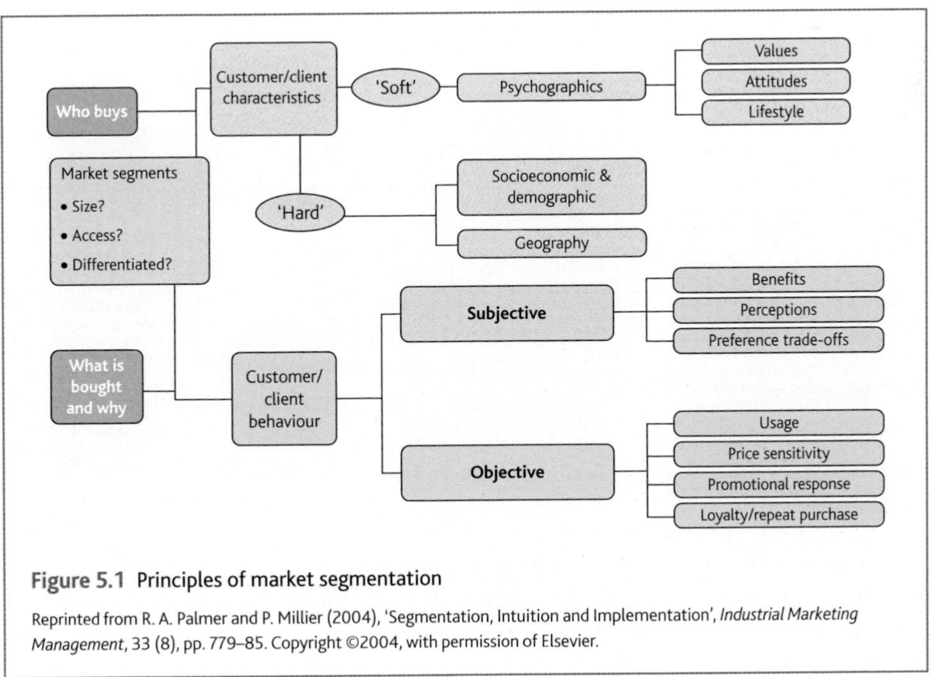

Figure 5.1 Principles of market segmentation

Reprinted from R. A. Palmer and P. Millier (2004), 'Segmentation, Intuition and Implementation', *Industrial Marketing Management*, 33 (8), pp. 779–85. Copyright ©2004, with permission of Elsevier.

separated by whether they are hard (based upon hard data categorizations—socioeconomic, demographic, or geographic) or soft in nature (values, attitudes, and lifestyles).

Since the point of segmentation is to identify a homogeneous group of consumers with a high probability of interest in the product/service offered, new and creative combinations of segmentation schemes are being attempted every day. A variety of tools to help the strategic marketer with segment identification will now be discussed.

Segmentation tools

The main tools used for segmentation are cluster analysis, conjoint analysis, discriminant analysis, and perceptual mapping. **Cluster analysis** is a group of multivariate techniques whose main purpose is to classify objects in such a way that within-group differences are minimized and between-group differences are maximized according to some grouping variable. These objects can be products or survey respondents. The goal is to create clusters that are similar within and distinctly different from one another, which are clearly the goals for consumer segmentation. The best starting point for clustering is to define clear and distinct customer needs. Often this can be preceded by qualitative mechanisms such as focus groups or in-depth interviews to examine a variety of different constituent groups to determine their needs and motivations. Once these needs are identified, then survey research instruments can be created and cluster analysis can be used to examine the nature of the respondents involved and the possibilities of grouping into meaningful and effective consumer segments. A rudimentary clustering example would involve asking a group of individuals to list in order of importance the attributes that are of concern to them in the choice of a particular product or service. What is interesting is that the overall lists of attributes that are part of the choice criteria will probably be quite similar across all of the lists, but where the differences will lie will be in the rankings of the relevant attributes. The rank orderings of attributes can then allow groupings of similar rankings. These subgroups with similar expectations regarding the important choice criteria comprise simple but quite relevant possible segments. Of course, computer analyses with more detailed data will lead to more sophisticated groupings, but the mechanism for clustering is seen as quite basic and logical.

Conjoint analysis, on the other hand, involves the use of a series of possible product/service attribute combinations to see which ones are actually preferred by survey respondents. In this case, the company chooses a series of possible variations of product attributes (e.g., three types of scent, four colours, three package sizes, three different prices), and a series of attribute combinations are generated in a partial factorial design (so that consumers only respond to a subset of all possible attribute combinations, making the process considerably more manageable for the respondent). The consumer can rank or rate the offerings in terms of preference, and from the various choices made, decomposition is utilized to develop a series of scores (utility part worths) for each variation of each attribute. From this analysis, the company can see what the optimal product configuration would be for each relevant consumer target segment. Coke often uses this type of analysis to assess the possibility of new can colourations (e.g., additional colours in addition to the normal red, white, and silver) or new product flavourings (e.g., Coke with lime, vanilla Coke, cherry Coke, Coke with lemon). The company can get a good idea of potential consumer reactions to product changes or new product offerings using this kind of tool.

The third approach to segmenting is **discriminant analysis**, which involves identifying a series of variables that help to discriminate the members of one or more groups from others in the dataset. The basic idea is to examine a series of possible differentiating variables that would explain and hopefully allow prediction of different possible group memberships. One way to use it would involve including in the analysis a variety of product/service attributes and demographic data which when combined could explain what makes buyers different from non-buyers of a particular product or service. It might also be used to examine non-users as opposed to light users, moderate users, and heavy users. The technique produces formulae that can be used to explain and predict group membership. In order to test the effectiveness of the models generated, all respondents are then classified according to the discriminating functions generated and the predicted group membership is compared to the actual group membership as a check for accuracy. If there were four categories involved (non-users, light users, moderate users, and heavy users), the prior probabilities would be 0.25 (1 in 4), so any classification scheme that does better than 0.25 would be an improvement over pure chance.

The fourth tool is **multidimensional scaling**, which involves a variety of different techniques that can visually demonstrate how particular consumers view the various offerings in a particular product or service class. These techniques are also often referred to as **perceptual mapping** because the goal is to differentiate spatially the perceptions of consumers relative to their preferences for or the similarities among a set of objects (e.g., companies, products, services) in terms of distances in multidimensional space. These techniques allow the researcher to determine what types of attributes are most distinctively associated with their products or services. It is certainly important for the consumer to have a clear idea of what the product stands for, and it allows the researcher to determine whether consumer perceptions match company management perceptions. The use of multidimensional scaling also provides important strategic direction if the company finds that a competitor is associated in the minds of the target market with attributes that are more appropriately associated with its own product. In this case, the company can try to communicate in advertisements to its target audience to educate them on the relevance of those important attributes with its products or services. As an example, if the company found that its competitor was seen as more environmentally friendly, the company could mount an advertising campaign to show how it is working to protect and maintain the environment.

Targeting

Once the firm has identified a series of potential market segments for consideration, the next step is targeting. Targeting involves the decision of the number of different segments to select and serve and the best action plans to reach the identified segments. The first consideration from a strategic standpoint is to decide on the type of pattern of coverage that the firm will utilize. According to one of the great marketing strategists, Derek F. Abell (1980), the firm faces the following choices: (1) **single-segment concentration** (where one product is geared towards one market segment in a niche strategy); (2) **selective specialization** (where the firm aims different product variants at different segments with the idea of one product per segment); (3) **product specialization** (where the firm aims a particular product variant to a variety of different segments); (4) **market specialization** (where the firm aims a variety of product variants at one particular market segment); and (5) **full market coverage** (where the firm uses undifferentiated marketing, aiming a variety of product variants across a variety of segments).

Measuring the effectiveness of target segments

Once the segments have been chosen, then how do we know whether they are viable or not? Kotler (2003) presents the most recognizable series of requirements for segments to be appropriate. He suggests that they must be: (1) **measurable** (e.g., size of segment, income, and purchasing power, and characteristics of the segment); (2) **accessible** (reachable by the firm and able to serve the segment effectively); (3) **substantial** (large enough and capable of generating sufficient profits); (4) **differentiable** (truly distinct from other segments in terms of composition and response to marketing stimuli); and (5) **actionable** (marketing programmes can be developed to effectively identify, attract, and serve the segment).

These criteria can be put to the test in almost every company due to the fact that there is a trade-off within most organizations that must be considered when segmenting markets, which involves production and marketing. In one case, unrestrained marketing might identify a wide range of distinct market segments, but while there may be demand for these segments, there may be no cost-effective way to develop the necessary product variations to address the needs of all of the identified segments. On the other hand, unrestrained product differentiation might identify a wide variety of product variations that could be produced by the firm, but there may be no demand for some or all of the identified segments. This mandates that marketing and production work together to find the most cost-effective product variants to serve the most promising consumer market segments. Take, for instance, the situation in the United States in 1985 between the Ford Motor Company Thunderbird and the imported Honda Accord. In an attempt to convince the consumer that he or she could have any type of Thunderbird that they could want (mass customization), they offered as many as 19,000 different possible product variations, but the problem would arise particularly in how the Ford service departments would deal with all of the possible variations when handling servicing problems on all of the different possible product variants. What kinds of inventories of parts would be required for all of these possible segments? There is no way that there were 19,000 different viable segments for this product. It would have been surprising if more than 50 distinct offerings were in demand. The Honda Accord being shipped in from Japan provided only 34 different product variations, which would suggest that they had clearly thought through the issue of viability of each of the identified consumer segments. This balancing of segmentation with differentiation is an effective integrated strategic approach to finding viable segments with cost-effective product/service variants.

Targeting improvement

There is concern that segmentation can produce a wide variety of segments which cannot effectively be reached with a targeting strategy. There is also the possibility that some market segments may be very difficult (in terms of time and money) to measure effectively. A 1999 article in *McKinsey Quarterly* presented some interesting suggestions for how marketing strategists can actually attempt to create segmentation strategies that can work, even if it is hard to determine who exactly is included in the segment (Forsyth et al., 1999). The authors suggest that before actually attempting to identify and reach target customers, a viable alternative approach could be to consider whether certain collective segment traits may be associated with profitable strategies. They provide three options for these profitable strategies: (1) **self selection**, which concentrates on enabling the customer to find and select the best product, as opposed to finding the appropriate customers (examples provided include different sizes of washing-up bottles and cereal packets) which is best suited for large customer bases with such small individual sales that mass customization is not viable; (2) **scoring models**, which involve the development of a series of questions to allow a quantitative scoring that would place customers in different categories, depending on what is most important for those customers (e.g., credit card companies that distinguish good-risk customers from bad-risk customers) to allow appropriate targeting strategies to best reach those particular categorized groups of customers; and (3) **dual-objective segmentation**, which attempts to convert unreachable segments into actionable segments through a series of reclassification approaches which attempt to reclassify outliers into different categories and then follow-up profitability analyses are run. The idea is to try to place those who do not cleanly fall into consumer target segments into other possible segments. It may be that the outliers become a separate segment themselves rather than becoming squeezed into inappropriate segmentation schemes, or that the outliers do not make sense for targeting at all. The idea is to step back sometimes from the comfortable segmentation approaches and look at things from a different angle to see if there are new possibilities that may work better than old ways.

Positioning

Positioning refers to the placing of the product or service in a particular perceptual position within the mind of the consumer. This would follow the processes described in segmentation and targeting. The idea here is that there is a specific consumer segment in mind and a specific plan to reach it, and now the idea is to ensure that the target consumer has a clear and distinctive image in mind regarding the product/service offerings being aimed at them that is consistent and positive.

Al Ries and Jack Trout, advertising executives with over fifty years of experience between them, made a strong statement in their landmark book, *Positioning: The Battle for Your Mind* (2001), that the real battle does not take place at the cash register when the consumer goes to the store to make their purchase, but in the mind of the consumer before they ever even go to the store. They argued that it is positioning that is the strategic key. If the consumer has a particular product or service name that automatically comes to mind when a need arises in that particular product or service category, that is the product or service that the consumer is most likely to buy. The point is to keep your product brand name automatically at the top of the choice possibilities (the favourite brand). As Ries and Trout explain, there is a ladder inside every consumer's head for each and every product and service class. All of the brands that compete that are known to the consumer are therefore placed on different rungs of that ladder. The strategic goal is to get to the top rung where the consumer has chosen a particular brand as the best or their favourite. Once the need arises in that class, the top rung brand is what will normally come to mind and will more than likely be purchased by the consumer.

For Ries and Trout, the key was to understand the ladder and develop strategies according to where on the ladder the particular brand was placed by the consumer. Being on the top rung of the ladder allows the firm to enjoy consumer franchise, which is a term that was reported to have been coined by Dr Peter Sealey, Global Marketing Director for Coca-Cola Corporation, who has since left Coke to become a consultant in California. **Consumer franchise** is the ability of the firm to keep its product, brand or company name foremost in the mind of the target consumer. It is considered to be a bankable asset since there is a psychological buffering built in for the firm that is on the top rung of the product/service class ladder. When bad news appears regarding a particular company, if the product or brand in question is on the top rung of the ladder (the favourite or preferred brand), the psychological process known as 'denial' can buffer the company because the consumer is put in a mental situation where it could not possibly be their favourite brand that could have done something wrong. We tend to assume that our judgement is infallible, and when something happens that questions that judgement, we step back and refuse to believe that we have made a mistake. This denial is a powerful protectant for the company.

A company which benefitted a great deal from this denial and the power of consumer franchise was Coca-Cola Corporation when New Coke was introduced with a completely different product formulation than had been used for the previous Coke product. As the groundswell built up against Coke, with loyal consumers asking why the formula had been changed, sensing a problem, Coke implemented a contingency plan and introduced Classic Coke. New Coke did not fare well in the marketplace, but Coke was not hurt because it had taken corrective action, and was protected by its consumer franchise, and never felt the negative effects either financially or in lost market share. To illustrate how powerful consumer franchise is as a buffer, one colleague to this day claims that everything was part of a carefully designed strategic plan to offer an additional brand product. But the delay from the introduction of New Coke to the introduction of Classic Coke would argue that this was not a carefully designed plan from the beginning but a mistake with little negative backlash. Of course, Coke had to take corrective action, but it was able to fare well, demonstrating the power of its consumer franchise. Of course, my colleague was born and raised in Atlanta, Georgia, where Coke is a major economic power, which might explain the perceptual basis for his argumentation!

Consumer franchise has two major components, a behavioural component and an attitudinal component. How does a company measure whether it is the favoured or preferred brand behaviourally? By examining its market share figures and sales, it can be seen whether the brand is the favoured brand or not. Attitudinally, the only way to know is to do consumer surveys. In this case, the consumer can be asked to indicate their favoured brand among a series of choices, or the consumer can be asked if a need arose in a particular product category, what brand would they choose? The key strategic aspect to remember here is that a downturn in brand image might not immediately affect brand sales. There is usually a lag. As a result, it is important for companies to track both their results in the marketplace and their brand images so that a problem in terms of brand image can be corrected before it has a negative impact on corporate performance. If only the behavioural side is tracked, then the company may be caught in a situation where it is not sure what is actually causing the problem in the first place. If bad press is caught and corrected before it has a chance to affect consumer perceptions, any future performance problems may be eliminated before they manifest themselves.

The positioning statement

A key element of positioning is the development of a positioning statement that will serve as the foundation for all of the positioning efforts. An example of a positioning statement for Virgin Atlantic is found in Figure 5.2. As can be seen from this example, there are three key components to the positioning statement: (1) the audience and context; (2) the value proposition; and (3) the action components that will be used by the company to deliver the value proposition to the audience in the context identified.

Of course, there are many ways in which a position statement can be poorly structured, so the criteria for successful positioning are found in the **four Cs of positioning** as shown in Figure 5.3. Any positioning statement to be effective must be clear (**Clarity**). There can be no misinterpretation in terms of whom the intended audience is and what the clear benefit/value will be for them. With the Virgin Atlantic example, it is very specific in its statement of which individuals are the target and into which context they fall. The positioning statement must also be consistent (**Consistency**), so that all messages sent regarding positioning must be consistent with each other in order that consumer confusion is eliminated or at least minimized. If Virgin Atlantic sends different messages to consumers in their communications over time, they will lack consistency and the message will be lost. Also, the message must be credible (**Credibility**), since whatever claims that the company makes must be believable to the target audience. If the customer does not believe that Virgin Atlantic has the personnel and equipment to be able to get them where they need to go on time, safely, and at a reasonable price, then no matter what is claimed, the claims will not resonate with the customer.

Finally, the positioning statement must be seen as competitive (**Competitiveness**), so that the target audience sees it as something being offered by the company to them that cannot be provided by their competitors. If the target audience does not see Virgin Atlantic as superior to

[Convince] Business and leisure air-travellers that Virgin is the best choice for air travel

[That] Virgin will get the traveller to where they need to go, safely, on time, and at a reasonable price

[Because] Virgin focuses on creating an environment where passengers love to fly and where employees love to work

Figure 5.2 Sample positioning statement: Virgin Atlantic

- **Clarity:** in terms of target market and differential advantage
- **Consistency:** maintain a consistent message
- **Credibility:** in the minds of the target customer—they must believe the claim
- **Competitiveness:** the differential advantage should offer the customer something of value competitors cannot provide (competitors should be named if possible)

Figure 5.3 The 4 Cs of positioning

Aston Martin offers ... truly unique and prestigious automobiles that are hand-finished to incomparable standards that epitomize the perfect balance of power and style, beauty and strength

Honda offers ... a variety of products of the highest quality at a reasonable price for worldwide customer satisfaction based upon the power of dreams which will lead to new insights and technologies in automobiles, motorcycles, power products, parts, and other fields of mobility

Figure 5.4 Examples of positioning statements

British Airways or other competitors, then the positioning will not be able to stick with the target audience. Two excellent examples of strong positioning statements can be found in Figure 5.4.

The next step will be to examine ways in which the company can assess its perceptual position inside the heads of its target audience. This involves the use of perceptual mapping.

Perceptual mapping

Perceptual mapping is the visual representation of the different competitive brand offerings/objects of interest in perceptual space. In other words, it represents a map of the various offerings within the minds of the target consumers. This is where 'perception equals reality' comes home to marketing strategists. The only thing that is important is what the consumer believes—not what management believes to be the case. This can only be determined via survey instruments. As was previously mentioned, the attitudinal component of consumer franchise is the often-neglected side as behaviour is the representation of what has already been done. The problem is that past behaviour is no guarantee of future purchase behaviour.

An excellent example of perceptual mapping can be seen in Figure 5.5 and Figure 5.6, which present two different views of the sweets market in the UK. Figure 5.5 presents a

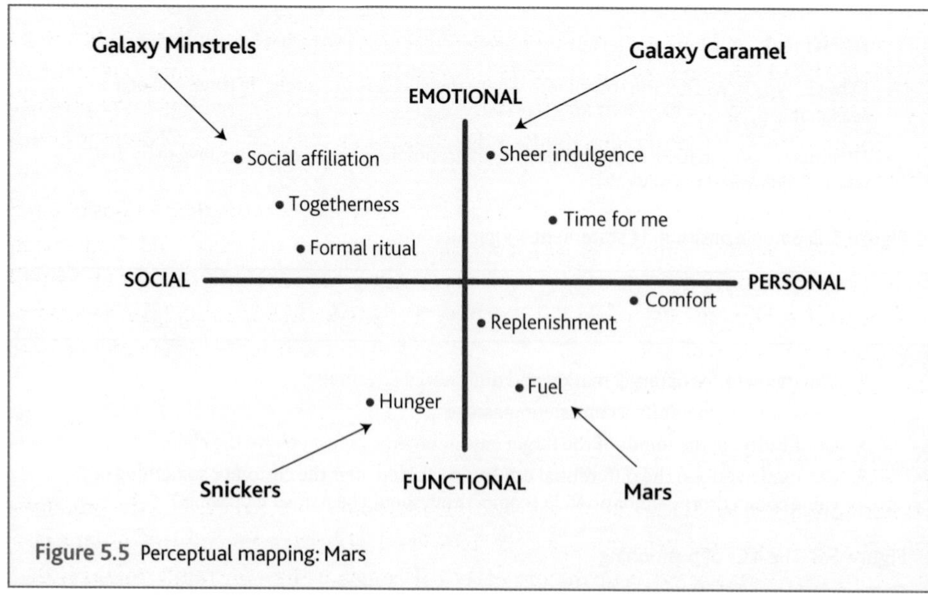

Figure 5.5 Perceptual mapping: Mars

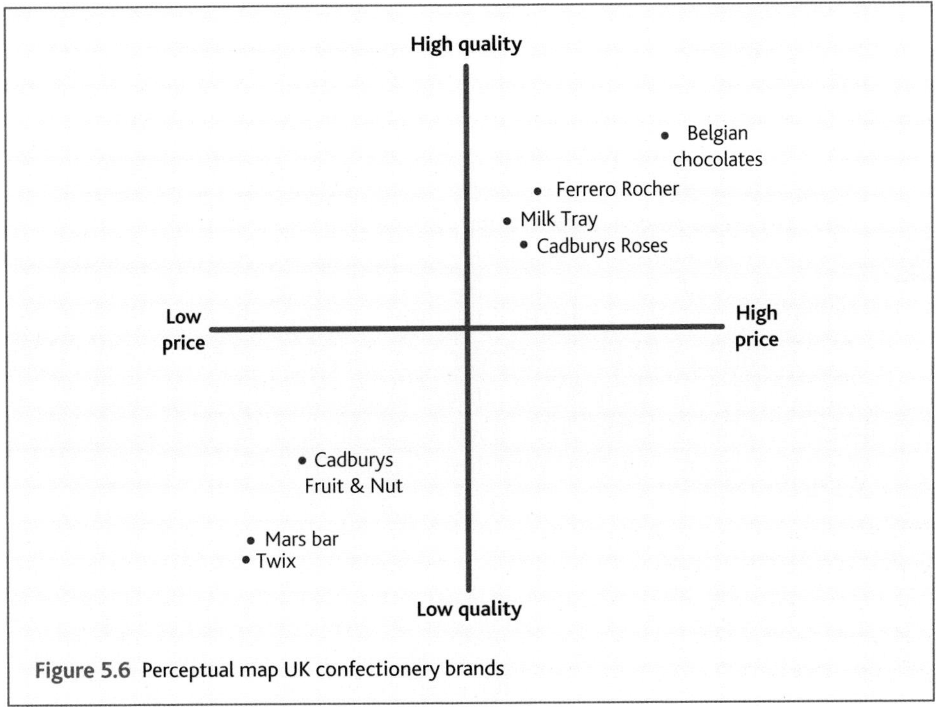

Figure 5.6 Perceptual map UK confectionery brands

perceptual map for Mars, in which four of its products are seen in perceptual space connected to key attributes in the mind of the target audience. As can be seen here, the two Galaxy products are aimed not functionally but emotionally. The Galaxy Minstrels are seen as more of a social product, while the Galaxy Caramel is perceived as more for personal benefit. The Snickers product is seen as functionally perceived to be a good mechanism for the satisfaction of hunger, while the Mars product is seen as something to use to get an energy boost when it is needed. These are very different perceptual positions that have been achieved, and the key is to strategically maintain the four Cs as long as the products are holding their own performance-wise but to take possible corrective action if performance is not what was expected.

Figure 5.6 shows a perceptual map of a variety of sweets given the perceptions of a particular market segment. Here, the perceptual axes are quality and price, and there appear to be two major groupings, given the particular product brands chosen for the study with the high-price, high-quality quadrant containing such brands as Rocher, Belgian chocolates, and Cadbury Roses, while the low-price, low-quality quadrant includes such brands as Mars, Twix, and Cadbury Fruit & Nut.

Positioning and the importance of consistency

As positioning reflects the position that the brand or product has achieved on the product or service class ladder, the key strategic issue associated with positioning is to present a clear and consistent message to the target audience. The company that constantly tinkers with its image stands the chance of confusing its target market. If strategic decisions are made which are inconsistent from period to period, the consumer is left with potentially mixed messages which become confusing and create cognitive dissonance. The often-seen use of brand extension creates a potential problem for strategic marketers as their company, which may have been clearly positioned in the past, begins to put its name on inconsistent products that set off alarm bells inside the heads of loyal customers. Look at the recent shift by Mercedes and Volvo to lower-priced product lines as a strong example. Can the company offer products at the top end and in the middle at the same time? The problems faced by Calvin Klein when selling jeans through Sears and at the same time selling extravagantly priced designer gowns should still resonate with the marketplace today. How can a company undermine its own distinctive perceptual niche? This potentially leads to strategic suicide. Harking back to the consumer franchise discussion reminds us that there is an attitudinal side which must be periodically tracked along with the behavioural side. Inconsistencies might not be reflected in a downturn in sales until much later, and then the problem becomes image reinstatement for the brand.

Sage positioning wisdom

Jack Trout revisited the issue of positioning in 1996 with Steve Rivkin in the book, *The New Positioning: The Latest on the World's #1 Business Strategy*. While this book was written a number of years ago, the need for it is as strong today as it was back in 1996. The critical message of the book was to report that many companies had run into positioning problems and needed to take corrective perception action. The authors suggested that this had occurred as a result of two major problems: (1) companies losing their focus in the mind of their target markets (through line extension and diversification); and (2) companies not noticing that their markets were changing underneath them. The answer to these problems is to reposition the product. This often means going back to basics and determining what it was that made the company successful in the first place and returning to these foundations. It may also mean determining how to make a passé product more relevant. All of this requires keeping in tune with the expectations and perceptions of the target market.

Trout and Rivkin (1996) present six positioning pitfalls that companies must be aware of and avoid: (1) the obvious factor (positioning is the search for what is obvious, and when the marketer feels that things need to be more complex or creative and clever, obvious is replaced by complex and confusing); (2) the future factor (constantly changing and modernizing strategy to deal with the future and its possible changes); (3) the cutesy factor (instead of telling things in a straightforward way, many companies like to get cute and creative); (4) the would-be-hero factor (the second-guessing of hard chargers in the company trying to get the CEO's attention who monkey with the positioning of the product); (5) the numbers factor (endless line extensions to maintain a healthy increase in sales to generate larger numbers); and (6) the tinkering factor (what are seen as improvements internally can often be seen as confusing by the target market).

What becomes obvious when examining these is that, ultimately, the real problem is that the company does not take a distinctive position in the mind of the consumer and then maintain it consistently.

The latest thinking: emotional segmenting and price-benefit position maps

Emotional segmenting

One of the most promising new approaches for segmentation is suggested by Daniel Yankelovich and David Meer in a 2006 *Harvard Business Review* article. According to the authors, psychographics, while very popular for segmentation, can certainly explain aspects of people's self-images, lifestyles, and attitudes, but the problem is that psychographics are not strong on being able to predict what these consumers' purchases will be in any particular product category. The authors suggest that careful segmentation is indeed valid, but they suggest that marketers should practice a 'smarter' form of segmentation based upon emotional connections. They provide six key questions that should allow the company to identify a better emotional segmentation foundation:

1. **What are we trying to do?** The point here is to see which of the company's strategic decisions can actually benefit from segmentation.
2. **Which customers actually drive profits?** Companies should start by ranking their customers in terms of profitability in order to concentrate the proper amount of attention on them, but the real key is to understand what actually makes them profitable as they are and to seek new customers that share some of the same characteristics.
3. **Which attitudes matter in the buying decision?** Understanding customer's lifestyles, attitudes, and self-images is helpful, but the marketer must realize that these change over time as the environment surrounding the customers and their particular values change.
4. **What are the customers actually doing?** Marketers should use tools like conjoint analysis to understand how willing customers would be to buy the product if certain attributes were added or removed or if the price was changed.
5. **Will this segmentation make sense to senior management?** If advanced statistical techniques are used by marketers without educating senior management on the benefits associated with their use, they may succeed in alienating this important internal support function.
6. **Can this segmentation register change?** Segmentation must be able to answer questions that arise as they arise, as attitudes and behaviours can change quickly since effective segmentations are always in flux.

In order to provide a proper foundation for perspective enhancement, Yankelovich and Meer (2006) present the Gravity of Decision Spectrum (see Figure 5.7), which allows marketers to evaluate the expectations that consumers bring to a particular transaction. The depth of gravity of decision then provides direction as to the necessary depth that will be required to understand the consumer's motives and concerns.

Price-benefit position maps

D'Aveni (2007) suggested an innovative approach to positioning by using price-benefit position maps. The author suggests that with this kind of chart, the marketer will understand exactly how much the customer will actually pay for a perceived benefit, and that this will

	Issues the business wants to solve	Consumers' concerns	What the segmentation should try to find out
Shallowest decisions	• Whether to make small improvements to existing products • How to select targets of a media campaign • Whether to change prices	• How relevant and believable new-product claims are • How to evaluate a given product • Whether to swich products	• Buying and usage behaviour • Willingness to pay a small premium for higher quality • Degree if brand loyalty
Middle-of-the-spectrum decisions	• How to position the brand • Which segments to pursue • Whether to change the product fundamentally • Whether to develop an entirely new product	• Whether to visit a clinic about a medical condition • Whether to switch one's brand of car • Whether to replace an enterprise software system	• Whether the consumers being studied are do-it-yourself or do-it-for-me types • Consumers' needs (better service, convenience, functionality) • Their social status, self-image, and lifestyle
Deepest decisions	• Whether to revise the business model in response to powerful social forces changing how people live their lives	• Choosing a course of medical treatment • Deciding where to live	• Core values and beliefs related to the buying decision

Figure 5.7 The gravity of decision spectrum

Souce: Daniel Yankelovich and David Meer (2006), 'Rediscovering Market Segmentation', *Harvard Business Review*, February. Reprinted with the permission of Harvard Business Publishing.

provide a potentially powerful tool for achieving competitive advantage. The point here is that if customers do not know what they are actually paying for, and, when this is combined with managers who do not know what they are charging for, then it will not be possible for the company to be able to understand its real competitive position. How can it then achieve any meaningful competitive advantage? The **price-benefit position map** builds on the primary benefit that customers will see as valuable to them, along with the prices of all of the various products in that specific product category. D'Aveni (2007) suggests the following steps in the development process: (1) **define the market** (identify the customer needs in question, choose the country or region of interest, and then decide on the specific segment or range of segments, brands or products, at the retail or the wholesale level to track); (2) **choose the price and determine the primary benefit** (the scope of the pricing analysis); and (3) **plot positions and draw the expected price line** (plotting the position of every company's product or brand in the selected marketplace according to its primary benefit and its price, and then drawing the line that best fits the data points on the map). What are the benefits to this perspective for strategic planning? First of all, the maps allow the marketer to see which benefits are most valued by customers. They also suggest where strategic gaps may be with unoccupied spaces in the marketplace. Another benefit is that it is possible for the strategist to see where there is a new opportunity available because of changes in the relationship between prices and primary benefits. Finally, this mapping allows for the anticipation of competitors' strategic moves. Other possible benefits include the ability to calculate the premiums that are achievable through intangible secondary benefits (which is particularly important for B2B marketers); the chance to see which benefits to develop and at what cost to meet changing needs of customers in terms of primary benefits; and, finally, market projections can be effectively built into the mapping to predict the strategic intent of rivals and potentially get the jump on them.

Conclusion

When companies approach the process of segmentation, targeting, and positioning as a series of logical steps in a process, they enhance their chances of success. Only in the rarest of circumstances is a company in the luxurious position of being all things to all customers, and as a result, the company must find appropriate target consumers, understand them, reach them effectively, and grab a position of importance on the product/service class ladder inside their heads. The company then has to avoid the lure of change for the sake of change and focus on consistency. This requires keeping up with the perceptions of consumers and continuing to build and maintain consumer franchise.

Summary

Segmentation involves the identification of a distinct subset of consumers within the overall marketplace that have a desire for the products/services that the company produces. This process should follow the careful development of strategic marketing goals/objectives. There are a variety of tools and techniques that can be used for segmentation across a variety of segmentation criteria. The firm must carefully assess the different segments and choose those that have the greatest potential for success. Once the firm has identified the various segment possibilities, the next step involves the assessment of the potential for each segment so that only those with the highest chances for success are chosen. Once the particular segments are chosen, the company must decide on how it will use the various pieces of the marketing mix to reach those segments. Targeting focuses on how to reach most effectively the various market segments. The last step involves the assessment of the particular perceptual space that the product achieves within the heads of the target segment consumers to ensure that the product is on the top rung of the product class ladder. The power of this position is found in the fact that when a need arises in the mind of the consumer, the product that commands the top rung of the mental ladder of competing products is the one most likely to be chosen for purchase.

KEY TERMS

Acculturation The exposure of a foreign visitor to a local culture and the impact that exposure will have on the visitor and their cultural makeup.

Cohort A group of consumers that go through life together and share common experiences.

Consumer franchise A term coined at Coca-Cola that refers to the ability to keep the company brand, product, or company name foremost in the mind of the consumer. It is comprised of a behavioural component and an attitudinal component.

Market segment A homogeneous subset of all consumers in a particular market.

Market segmentation The process of identifying appropriate separate subsets of consumers for targeting purposes out of all the consumers in that market.

Mass customization Each individual consumer is treated separately with a product configuration to suit the needs of each consumer.

Mass market All consumers are treated the same way with a single product configuration.

Perceptual mapping The use of a variety of tools to examine the various competing products and the positions that they command in perceptual space within the minds of the target market.

Positioning The process involved in placing the product into the mind of the consumer in terms of a position on the product/service class ladder.

Price-benefit position map A map which builds on the primary benefit that customers will see as valuable to them, along with the prices of all the various products in that specific product category.

Product differentiation Production-based orientation, which examines the various forms and variants of the product which the company can cost-effectively produce.

Psychographic segmentation Segmentation predicated upon the activities, interests, and opinions of a particular group of people. This will normally involve such variables as lifestyle and personality for segmentation purposes.

Targeting The use of the marketing mix elements to reach the consumers identified in the market segmentation process.

Topography Land contours that can affect the geographic grouping of appropriate target segments of consumers.

DISCUSSION QUESTIONS

1 Assess why market segmentation is vital for company success.
2 Review psychographic segmentation, and explain its role in marketing strategy.
3 What are the seven cultural values that were identified by Schwartz, and why are they important for marketing strategists?
4 Evaluate the various levels of loyalty, and explain how they can be used for segmentation purposes.
5 What are the four different tools for segmentation? How are they different from each other?
6 Assess the difference between market segmentation and product differentiation.
7 What is the value of the different patterns of target market coverage?
8 Critically evaluate the key criteria presented by Kotler to assess the viability of various target market segments under consideration.
9 Assess how a consumer franchise relates to the concept of positioning. Why is this relevant for marketing strategists?
10 Review the kinds of circumstances when there might be a need for repositioning.
11 Assess the benefits of emotional segmentation as opposed to psychographic segmentation.
12 What is a price-benefit position map, and why might it be useful to strategic marketers?

ONLINE RESOURCE CENTRE

Visit the Online Resource Centre for this book for lots of interesting additional material at: **www.oxfordtextbooks.co.uk/orc/west2e/**

REFERENCES AND FURTHER READING

Aaker, Jennifer (1997), 'Dimensions of Brand Personality', *Journal of Marketing Research*, 34 (3), pp. 347–56.

Abell, Derek F. (1980), *Defining the Business: The Starting Point of Strategic Planning* (Upper Saddle River, NJ: Prentice-Hall).

Christiansen, Clayton M., Scott Cook, and Teddy Hall (2005), 'Marketing Malpractice: The Cause and the Cure', *Harvard Business Review*, December, pp. 74–83.

Cort, Kathryn T., Judith H. Pairan, and John K. Ryans (Jr) (2004), 'The In-school Marketing Controversy: Reaching the Teenage Segment', *Business Horizons*, 47 (1), pp. 81–5.

Coyles, Stephanie, and Timothy C. Gokey (2002), 'Customer Retention is not Enough', *McKinsey Quarterly*, 2, pp. 81–9.

D'Aveni, Richard A. (2007), 'Mapping your Competitive Position', *Harvard Business Review*, November, pp. 110–20.

Forsyth, John, Sunil Gupta, Sudeep Haldar, Anil Kaul, and Keith Kettle (1999), 'A Segmentation you Can Act Upon', *McKinsey Quarterly*, 3, pp. 7–15.

Harrington, Richard J., and Anthony K. Tjan (2008), 'Transforming Strategy One Customer at a Time', *Harvard Business Review*, March, pp. 62–72.

Hemp, Paul (2006), 'Avatar-based Marketing', *Harvard Business Review*, June, pp. 48–57.

Keillor, B. D., and G. Tomas M. Hult (1999), 'The Development and Application of a National Identity Measure for Use in International Marketing', *Journal of International Marketing*, 4 (2), pp. 57–73.

Kotler, Philip (2003), *Marketing Management*, 11th edn (Upper Saddle River, NJ: Prentice-Hall).

Marketing Pocket Book (2004), (Henley: WARC).

O'Loughlin, Sandra (2005), 'Ben Sherman Brings U.K. Lifestyle to Spring', *Brandweek*, 46 (2) (10 January 2005), p. 9.

Orth, Ulrich R., Mina McDaniel, Tom Shellhammer, and Kannapon Lopetcharat (2004), 'Promoting Brand Benefits: The Role of Consumer Psychographics and Lifestyle', *Journal of Consumer Marketing*, 21 (2/3), pp. 97–108.

Palmer, R. A., and P. Millier (2004), 'Segmentation: Identification, Intuition and Implementation', *Industrial Marketing Management*, 33 (8), pp. 779–85.

Palumbo, Frederick A., and Ira Teich (2004), 'Market Segmentation Based on Level of Acculturation', *Marketing Intelligence & Planning*, 22 (4), pp. 472–80.

Phou, Ian, and Kor-Weai Chan (2003), 'Targeting East Asian Markets: A Comparative Study on National Identity', *Journal of Targeting, Measurement and Analysis for Marketing*, 12 (2), pp. 157–68.

Ries, Al, and Jack Trout (2001), *Positioning: The Battle for Your Mind*, 20th Anniversary Edition (New York: McGraw-Hill).

Robinette, Scott (2001), 'Best Practice: Get Emotional', *Harvard Business Review*, May, pp. 24–5.

Schewe, Charles D., and Geoffrey Meredith (2004), 'Segmenting Global Markets by Generational Cohorts: Determining Motivations by Age', *Journal of Consumer Behaviour*, 4 (1), pp. 51 Vol. 18, 64.

Schwartz, Shalom (1994), 'Beyond Individualism/Collectivism', in *Individualism and Collectivism: Theory, Method, and Applications*, Uichol Kim, Harry C. Triandis et al. (eds), Cross-Cultural Research and Methodology Series, Vol. 18, (Thousand Oaks, CA: Sage Publications), pp. 85–119.

Scott, Jacqueline, and Lilian Zac (1993), 'Collective Memories in Britain and the United States', *Public Opinion Quarterly*, 57 (3), pp. 315–31.

Shiu, Eric C. C., John A. Dawson, and David W. Marshall (2004), 'Segmenting the Convenience and Health Trends in the British Food Market', *British Food Journal*, 106 (2/3), pp. 106–18.

Sweeney, Mark (2004), 'Red Bull Targets Golfers in Shift to Mainstream', *Marketing*, (26 May 2004), p. 1.

Trout, Jack, and Steve Rivkin (1996), *The New Positioning: The Latest on the World's #1 Business Strategy* (New York: McGraw-Hill, Inc.).

Yankelovich, Daniel, and David Meer (2006), 'Rediscovering Market Segmentation', *Harvard Business Review*, February, pp. 122–31.

KEY ARTICLE ABSTRACTS

Schewe, Charles D., and Geoffrey Meredith (2004), '**Segmenting Global Markets by Generational Cohorts: Determining Motivations by Age**', *Journal of Consumer Behaviour*, 4(1), pp. 51–64.

Generational cohorts have been successfully identified and utilized in segmentation in American markets. This relevant article examines generational cohorts in a global setting, and the authors caution that while generational cohorts can be effectively identified in different country settings, they should not be approached as the same as those found in the United States.

Abstract: Marketing has long rested on the use of market segmentation. While birth age has been a useful way to create groups, it describes segments but in itself does not help in the understanding of segment motivations. Environmental events experienced during one's coming-of-age years, however, create values that remain relatively unchanged throughout one's life. Such values provide a common bond for those in that age group, or cohort. Segmenting by coming-of-age years provides a richer segmentation approach than birth age. This approach, known to work in America, is used in this paper to create generational cohorts in Russia and Brazil.

Orth, Ulrich R., Mina McDaniel, Tom Shellhammer, and Kannapon Lopetcharat (2004), **'Promoting Brand Benefits: The Role of Consumer Psychographics and Lifestyle'**, *Journal of Consumer Marketing*, 21 (2/3), pp. 97–108.

Reprinted with permission, Emerald Group Publishing Limited, **http://www.emeraldinsight.com/jbs.htm**

This paper presents a unique approach to the use of lifestyle patterns to segment beer consumers in the US. Using cluster analysis with lifestyle survey respondents, the authors identify eight different consumer segments.

Abstract: Because customers can vary greatly in their value composition, they may seek a range of different benefits from products and brands and hence will react differently to marketing communications emphasizing selected brand benefits. This study adapts a scale for measuring benefits that drive consumer preferences for craft beer. As part of this process, five dimensions of utility are identified, such as functional, value for money, social, positive, and negative emotional benefit. In order to support decisions on market segmentation and brand positioning, those dimensions of benefit are profiled against consumer brand preferences, lifestyle segments, demographic, and behavioural variables. Based on the results, guidelines for communication strategies are offered that address the benefits sought by specific segments more holistically.

Yankelovich, Daniel, and David Meer (2006), **'Rediscovering Market Segmentation'**, *Harvard Business Review*, February, pp. 122–31.

This is a very useful article which raises some serious questions about the basic assumptions behind psychological segmentation. Disappointing results have shown that marketers have tried to be too complex in their approach to psychological profiling, and the authors here suggest that knowing the real importance of a product or service to the consumer will help marketers to decide which of their particular expectations are most telling as to why they will want to buy that product or not.

Abstract: In 1964, Daniel Yankelovich introduced in the pages of the *Harvard Business Review* the concept of nondemographic segmentation, by which he meant the classification of consumers according to criteria other than age, residence, income, and such. The predictive power of marketing studies based on demographics was no longer strong enough to serve as a basis for marketing strategy, he argued. Buying patterns had become far better guides to consumers' future purchases. In addition, properly constructed nondemographic segmentations could help companies determine which products to develop, which distribution channels to sell them in, how much to charge for them, and how to advertise them. But more than forty years later, nondemographic segmentation has become just as unenlightening as demographic segmentation had been.

Today, the technique is used almost exclusively to fulfil the needs of advertising, which it serves mainly by populating commercials with characters that viewers can identify with. It is true that psychographic types like 'High-Tech Harry' and 'Joe Six-Pack' may capture some truth about real people's lifestyles, attitudes, self-image, and aspirations, but they are no better than demographics at predicting purchase behaviour. Thus, they give corporate decision-makers very little idea of how to keep customers or capture new ones.

Now, Daniel Yankelovich returns to these pages, with consultant David Meer, to argue the case for a broad view of nondemographic segmentation. They describe the elements of a smart segmentation strategy, explaining how segmentations meant to strengthen brand identity differ from those capable of telling a company which markets it should enter and what goods to make. And they introduce their 'gravity of decision spectrum', a tool that focuses on the form of consumer behaviour that should be of the greatest interest to marketers—the importance that consumers place on a product or product category.

Harrington, Richard J., and Anthony K. Tjan (2008), '**Transforming Strategy One Customer at a Time**', *Harvard Business Review*, March, pp. 62–72.

This insightful article addresses the limitations in B2B segmentation by examining how Thomson Corporation adopted more of a Procter & Gamble mind-set and found out exactly what their end consumers did with their products, since those who buy directly from them are not the ones who actually use the products themselves. Of particular benefit to Thomson was the adoption of the three-minute approach in which they combined observations with interviews to understand what end users were actually doing three minutes before and three minutes after use of the products.

Abstract: A decade ago, the Thomson Corporation, like most B2B companies, had a much better understanding of the people who purchased its newspapers, journals, and textbooks for their organizations than of the people who actually used them in their daily jobs. Facing an Internet shakeup of its market, Thomson realized it needed to bridge that critical knowledge gap. The company began systematically scrutinizing its end users as part of a new front-end customer strategy that would become the cornerstone of the firm's transformation. In this article, Thomson's CEO and a consultant who advised him, describe how the company adopted a user-centric mind-set—initially in the Thomson Financial Division and then throughout the organization.

END OF CHAPTER 5 CASE STUDY The metrosexual as segmentation target

The Metrosexual is a term that is certainly growing in companies as an attractive target population for segmentation strategies. This is the type of man who focuses on his looks and grooming and wants to convey just the right body image. The role model for the metrosexual is David Beckham, and whether he wears his hair long or short, he is seen as a fashion-trend leader who is not afraid of showing his softer side. The US image leader for the metrosexual is Tom Brady, the often-decorated quarterback of the National Football League Champion New England Patriots. These sports figures, along with such visible male icons as Brad Pitt, Jude Law, and Christiano Ronaldo, are seen as good representatives for men and adored by women. This cross-over appeal has opened up a new consumer segment, with young men concerned about taking the time to look their very best and to use cosmetic products to add to their looks. Obviously, this group would include gay men as well as heterosexuals, and it represents a growing segment of urban men who are cosmopolitan in outlook with plenty of discretionary income that they will be happy to spend on products and services that help them look and feel better. This growth has been seen in the US, the UK, Europe, Asia, and Australia, and it is presenting marketers with some interesting new possibilities. Women have long expressed a desire in these countries to have men unafraid to show emotion and be able to get in touch with their feminine side, and they have embraced in many ways the new 'sensitive' metrosexual.

The interest in grooming, appearance, and health is opening up a number of new opportunities for marketers who are paying attention. The growth in cosmetics use by metrosexuals is pronounced, and companies like Lancôme are turning to actors like Clive Owen to be the spokesperson for its new line of anti-ageing skin-care products. Nivea has been bombarding the sports channel airwaves with advertisements in the US to appeal to metrosexuals who are concerned about keeping their skin texture softer and more supple. This has also been seen in new opportunities for fashion items. The image of Daniel Craig in his tight bathing suit and designer tuxedo is drawing attention to the fact that men who are seen as macho can also be role models for metrosexuals. Nowhere has this been more obvious than in the enormous ads showing David Beckham in his tight white Armani briefs » across double-decker buses and on billboards. This has also spread to the use of spa treatments and even the use of waxing to get rid of chest hair. In Australia, there has been an increase in the number of waxing salons that now include such offerings as the Manzillian (Brazilian Male), where all the hair below the waist is removed to allow for a better appearance as well as more stimulating sexual encounters. This focus on appearance also stretches to health in keeping in shape and eating healthier things. What is interesting about this developing cohort is that the interests in exercising to keep fit are certainly high, but there is much greater interest in working out at the gym than in playing football or rugby to stay in shape.

How big is this market? Some believe that it is still only a small share of the male market, but the growth has been quite dramatic. Various research firms in the UK have reported that the market for men's grooming products (particularly such products as home moisturizers, waxing kits, and even manicure and pedicure kits) has reached anywhere from £800 to £900 million and should break through the £1 billion level by 2010. This is even spreading over into the area of cosmetic surgery as increasing numbers of men are opting for Botox treatments, tummy tucks, and even breast reductions. Looking good might get men in a variety of countries even to consider getting face lifts. Research in Australia and the US indicates that men are far more interested in these extreme methods to enhance their appearance than they were as few as five to ten years ago. Men are even learning to cook in many different countries to control what they eat and to appeal to their partners. This has opened many new opportunities for such ventures as cooking classes and culinary retailing to appeal to male consumers.

In the UK, Boots has begun to address this growing segment with the introduction of male grooming zones in its stores. They will use trained staff to provide answers to male grooming questions to help them pick the appropriate products for their needs. Boots has certainly seen a rapid growth in male skin-care product sales with consumers who are more informed and want specific products to meet their needs. Boots sees this segment as too large not to serve effectively, but there is always the concern lurking behind the scenes that traditional males may not like what they see at Boots and the focus on this segment. The answer, of course, is that if this growth is slowly taking over the old traditional male market, Boots had better be on the leading edge or else be left behind by others who have been more committed to reaching this growing customer base.

Well, have things gone a bit too far? It seems that a new product is on the horizon for metrosexuals. One recent development of note is the arrival of a slimming undershort for the concerned male. There will also be a slimming undershort product that will be coming out in the late summer or early fall of 2009. These products are expected to appeal to men who are concerned about making themselves look better without resorting to such extreme treatments as cosmetic surgery.

Source: This case was prepared by John Ford of Old Dominion University, Norfolk, Virginia as the basis for analysis and class discussion and not to illustrate either effective or ineffective handling of an administrative situation.

QUESTIONS

1. Discuss the metrosexual in terms of the various segmentation mechanisms discussed in the chapter.
2. Is the man girdle a product that will appeal to metrosexuals? Why or why not?
3. What market research would be necessary to gather to determine the viability of this product?
4. How would you target this kind of product to metrosexuals?
5. Would perceptual maps be helpful to marketers of this kind of product?
6. Talk about positioning issues for this product.

6

Branding strategies

LEARNING OBJECTIVES

- Provide an overview of the complex nature of branding
- Examine the ways in which consumers attach meaning to brands and the impact on company performance
- Discuss ways in which brand managers can streamline brand costs and improve brand profitability
- Identify the various ways in which brand managers can strategically create relationships between their brands and consumers and realize competitive advantages
- Present several strategic assessment tools that will aid the brand manager in assessing the nature of brand meaning and value and help in brand reinforcement and revitalization

CHAPTER AT A GLANCE

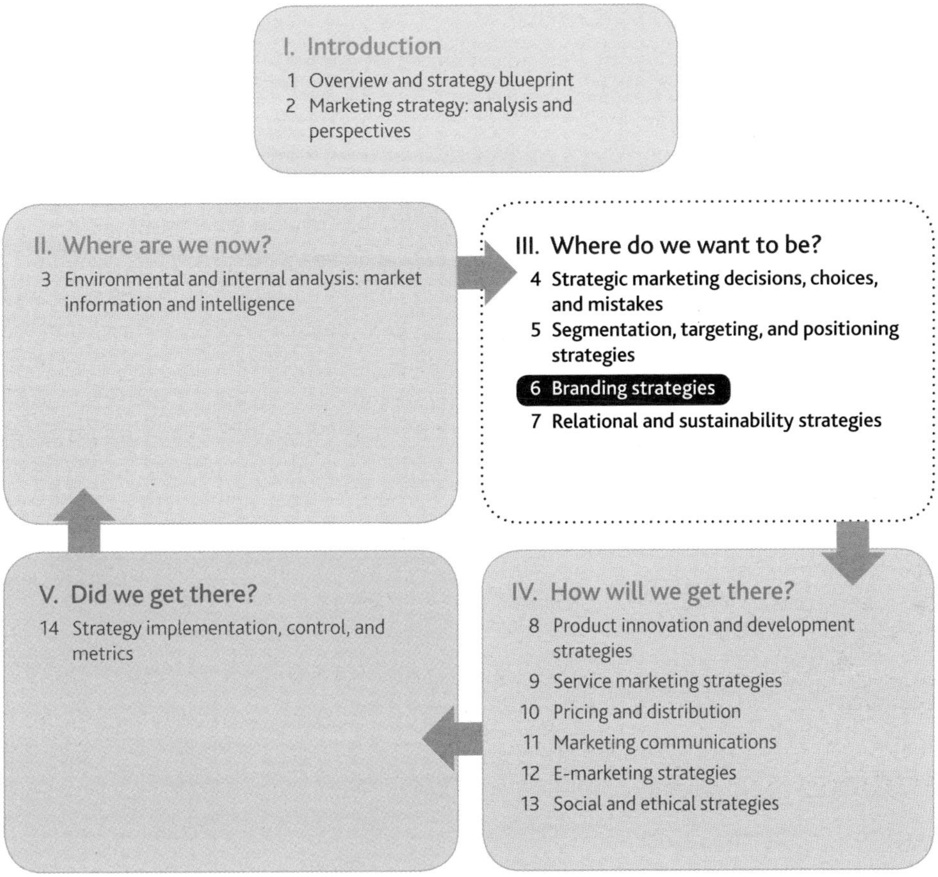

I. Introduction
1 Overview and strategy blueprint
2 Marketing strategy: analysis and perspectives

II. Where are we now?
3 Environmental and internal analysis: market information and intelligence

III. Where do we want to be?
4 Strategic marketing decisions, choices, and mistakes
5 Segmentation, targeting, and positioning strategies
6 Branding strategies
7 Relational and sustainability strategies

IV. How will we get there?
8 Product innovation and development strategies
9 Service marketing strategies
10 Pricing and distribution
11 Marketing communications
12 E-marketing strategies
13 Social and ethical strategies

V. Did we get there?
14 Strategy implementation, control, and metrics

Introduction

Branding is a major component of product strategy. The ability to develop and nurture effective brands is probably the single most important skill set within the marketer's professional tool kit. Brands communicate valuable information to the customer, and a thorough understanding of what the brand signifies to the customer is an essential part of marketing strategy. Whatever the company does can have an impact on customer perceptions of the brand, and the potential impact of corporate strategic decisions must be assessed, particularly in terms of consistency with the understanding and expectations of the customer. Daryl Travis (2000), the author of *Emotional Branding*, argues that a company's brand and its image are integrally linked—what the brand signifies to the consumer becomes inextricably linked to their perceptions of the company. The values inherent in the brand often merge with the company's values. The important thing to remember is that to the customer, perception is reality, and as a result, the firm must be careful to assess regularly the nature of its brand image and ensure that possible strategic actions will enhance and not potentially undermine its brands and ultimately its own corporate image.

What are the top brands today? Interbrand presents an annual assessment of brand value, which attempts to place a concrete financial figure on the value of a brand, but the list primarily focuses on the biggest brands in the global arena (see Figure 6.1 for the top twenty listing), but this is of little value to the small- to medium-sized entity trying to deal with the complexity inherent in brand valuations. What is particularly relevant in terms of differentiation and distinctiveness is the 'buzz' that is generated when the brand is considered by the public to be 'cool'. This kind of social caché keeps the brand top-of-mind, and the immense publicity value pays for itself many times over for the firm lucky enough to attain this perceptual position.

Superbrands, the UK-based organization which collects opinion data from a variety of different countries, released its CoolBrands listing in September of 2007, and its list of the top twenty cool brands is found in Figure 6.2. To qualify as a cool brand, the brand must meet the following six criteria in which it must be: (1) thought of as stylish; (2) perceived to be innovative; (3) seen as an original; (4) felt to be authentic; (5) desirable; and (6) considered as unique. These twenty brands were identified as the top brands out of some 5,500 brands that were considered. These companies have reached powerful perceptual positions that help

2008 Rank	2007 Rank	Company	Country	2008 value (£m)
1	1	Coca-Cola	US	36,032
2	3	IBM	US	31,905
3	2	Microsoft	US	31,892
4	4	General Electric	US	28,692
5	5	Nokia	Finland	19,426
6	6	Toyota	Japan	18,404
7	7	Intel	US	16,896
8	8	McDonalds	US	16,782
9	9	Disney	US	15,810
10	20	Google	US	13,831
12	12	Hewlett-Packard	US	12,706
13	13	BMW	Germany	12,592
14	16	Gillette	US	12,263
15	15	American Express	US	11,858
16	17	Louis Vuitton	France	11,676
17	18	Cisco Systems	US	11,516
18	14	Marlboro	US	11,512
19	11	Citi Corp	US	10,904
20	19	Honda	Japan	10,312

Figure 6.1 Top global brands by value

Source: Interbrand (2008), available at: **http://www.interbrand.com/best_global_brands.aspx?year=2008&langid=1000.**

1	Aston Martin
2	ipod
3	Youtube
4	Bang+Olufsen
5	Google
6	Playstation
7	Apple
8	Agent Provocateur
9	Nintendo
10	Virgin Atlantic
11	Ferrari
12	Ducati
13	eBay
14	Rolex
15	Tate Modern
16	Prada
17	Lamborghini
18	Green & Black's
19	iTunes
20	Amazon

Figure 6.2 Top 20 CoolBrands

Source: Superbrands (2008–9), available at: **http://www.coolbrand.co.uk.**

to reinforce the power of the brands involved. Given the excitement generated by products which are high-tech or Internet-related, it is not surprising to note that of the twenty brands listed, three are connected to the Apple Corporation (iPod, Apple, and iTunes) and four represent powerful online companies (YouTube, Google, eBay, and Amazon). There are also seven which represent global premium product manufacturers (Aston Martin, Bang+Olufsen, Ferrari, Ducati, Rolex, Prada, and Lamborghini), of which four are automobile brands.

This chapter will briefly examine the complex nature of brands and then present a series of strategic suggestions to help the brand strategist to create, maintain, and enhance this valuable company asset. The final section will provide a brief overview of the latest thinking regarding brands: lovemarks and BrandSimple.

Strategic brand marketing

The important questions that are raised in this chapter are:

1. How can we use brand strategy to reduce our overall costs? and
2. How can brand strategy differentiate our offerings and help to build a meaningful relationship with the target consumer?

Strategic brand management in light of Porter's strategic framework, therefore, requires a sophisticated understanding of industry cost structure, brand efficiency and brand profitability, and consumer perceptions of the brand and the potential for differentiation and sustainable competitive advantage. Both are important considerations and will be addressed in turn. The first step, however, is to review briefly the nature of branding and then lay the strategic foundation with an understanding of brand architecture.

The complex nature of brands

Branding represents one of the most important assets that the company can acquire, but it must be carefully managed. It is not just a logo or a name. A brand represents different things to different constituencies, and the key is to understand what goes on inside the heads of customers to effectively manage brand equity. The management of an array of products for multiple target groups of consumers raises difficult questions for brand managers without a sophisticated set of brand assessment tools and techniques.

Branding and functionality

So what exactly is a brand? At a base level, a brand is what identifies the company selling goods and/or services. It is information-laden and helps the consumer make the choice to fill a particular need among a series of similar offerings. However, as Berthon et al. (1999) explain, brands perform a series of functions for both the buyer and the seller. For the buyer, brands help: with product identification, which reduces search costs; to signal particular quality levels, which reduces perceived risks; and to provide social status, which reduces social and psychological risks. They suggest that there are also a series of benefits for the selling company in the form of:

- the facilitation of customer identification and purchase, which improves financial performance
- the breeding of customer familiarity, which aids in the introduction of new product offerings
- the ability to identify specific product offerings clearly, which aids promotional efforts
- the differentiation of company offerings from those of competitors, which enables the use of premium pricing
- the distinctiveness of the product offering, which allows for the identification of appropriate target segments and tailored communications/promotions
- the enhancement of brand loyalty, which promotes repeat purchases.

A brand is much more than just a signifier.

Brand identity

As David Aaker (1996a) explains in his best-selling book, *Building Strong Brands*, at its most basic level, the brand has a core identity which is its essence, and that remains constant.

There is also an extended identity, which focuses on a series of psychological and physical aspects that give it nuance and texture. A brand can be thought of as having a variety of important facets that should be considered in assessing the full nature of the brand.

First of all, a brand can be thought of as a product. Aaker (1996a, 1996b, 2004) suggests that this would entail such considerations as product scope, product-related attributes, quality/value associations with the brand, uses or applications for the brand, brand users, and brand country of origin. Companies can often be found in conflict involving the brand as product since the basic attributes and uses for the product should always be consistent with consumer perceptions and expectations engendered by the brand. So fit becomes important in this case between offerings and expectations given a particular brand. One only needs to look at such inconsistent offerings that tarnished brand names like Pierre Cardin offering wines, Bausch & Lomb, the eye-care specialty company, offering breath fresheners, and the BiC Corporation, makers of throwaway pens and lighters, offering ladies' stockings and pantyhose.

Another important facet of brand deals with the connections between the brand and the company which creates the brand. Aaker (2004), Keller (2000), and others suggest that a brand can also be imbued with organizational attributes (e.g., innovative, young, socially responsible, etc.) and certain expectations in terms of geographic coverage (e.g., local vs global). In this case, it becomes difficult for the consumer to actually separate the brand from the company behind the brand. As many brand specialists argue, the products produced by the company should always be tied back to the company and the associated brand so that a clear message is sent to the consumer which conveys the basic meaning and message associated with the brand. The Ritz-Carlton chain of hotels brings to mind service above and beyond the normal expectations and amenities that are at the highest standards of the hotel industry. Consistent with this would be such attributes as immediate attention from hotel staff, uniforms immaculate and consistent, bedroom amenities like Egyptian, high-count cotton sheets, room-darkening shades, sound proofing, and room décor and hotel facilities superbly presented.

A third level of branding can be seen in the brand possibly becoming synonymous with a particular person. This would include the brand potentially taking on a distinctive personality (e.g., compassionate, responsible, athletic, etc.) or creating the impression in the mind of the customer that they have an actual relationship with the brand (e.g., seeing the brand as a friend or a mentor, etc.). This personality connection was clearly seen in the Accenture ads which connected directly to the persona of Tiger Woods, known for drive, precision, preparation, and winning. In particular, Tiger was the symbol of the ultimate high performer, who served as an effective metaphor for Accenture's commitment to helping companies become high-performing businesses. More will be discussed about the Accenture branding scheme in the strategic assessment section later in this chapter. The unfortunate fall of Tiger from grace due to personal indiscretions caused Accenture to distance itself from Tiger, but the company enjoyed many years of positive association with the golfer until he lost favour in the eyes of the public.

The fourth possible level of branding is for the customer to see the brand as a symbol. This would entail the brand being connected with particular visual images (e.g., the McDonald's golden arches, the Nike swoosh, etc.), as well as the brand and its history or heritage (e.g., Jack Daniel's Tennessee whiskey and its black and white ads connecting the product

Figure 6.3 Jack Daniel's

The trademark 'Jack Daniel's' appears courtesy of Jack Daniel's Properties, Inc.
JACK DANIEL'S & the OLD NO. 7 Logo are registered trademarks of Jack Daniel's Properties, Inc.

to its storied heritage—see Figure 6.3). The idea here is to separate the product from others because it has distinctive imagery associated with it and/or because it must be good because it has been around for a long time.

Clearly, a brand means different things to different segments, and a better understanding of brand identity is an integral part of a successful brand management programme. The key is to understand the perceptions of the consumers relative to the array of company brands. Aaker (2004) emphasizes that successful brand companies have a clear idea of their brand identity, and a strategically branded identity serves as the basis for the development of a meaningful brand value proposition (based on functional and/or emotional benefits) which, when combined with the building of credibility in the eyes of the customer, help lead to a lasting and meaningful relationship between the brand and the customer that will, when effectively managed, lead to profitability.

Corporate vs product branding

One important distinction which needs to be made is that there is an significant difference between company or corporate branding and its effects versus the use of product brands or family branding. Obviously, when a company uses a distinctive corporate brand name, then everything that it does using that name must be consistent, as the name will become synonymous with a certain set of expectations. The unfortunate tendency is that once a brand is well known, the company will quickly begin to consider using that name awareness to leverage one or more additional offerings under that brand, but the problem is that when the next offering differs in any meaningful way from the previous offerings under that corporate brand, there can be problematic perceptions on the part of customers, who become confused about the cohesiveness across the various offerings. We see this being done by many companies, and the problem is that brand extension appears to be so much more cost-effective than product-specific branding.

The recent actions of Daimler, Volvo, and BMW highlight this potential problem with the pressure inherent on the companies to increase sales and profits, as lower-priced product variations have been introduced that raise important concerns for consumers when a comparison is made between these low-end products with their high-end counterparts. Why would someone who drives a Mercedes 500 SEL want to see a C-class product available at a fraction of the price? Part of the lure for Daimler is reaching a much larger number of consumers with its products, but how many top-end customers are going to want to see a product with the same Mercedes symbol everywhere? Part of the value is the status associated with the name, so how can the name maintain its high status when it is associated with a lower-quality product? One would expect that Daimler knew what it was doing when it put the Smart car under its own name as opposed to the Mercedes name, but the C-class of products at an 'affordable' price raises some serious questions about the potential for confusing the loyal Mercedes customer. This, of course, was exactly why Honda, Nissan, and Toyota introduced their high-end products in the US with the names Acura, Infiniti, and Lexus. These products were not consistent with their typical product offering and would have confused their target audiences.

The use of different brand names for different quality levels is a good way to handle this kind of perceptual issue. Toyota knew that the lower-end product, Scion, was also not consistent with the typical Toyota product perceptions, so offering the product under its own name protects the company brand from harmful perceptual effects. General Motors wanted a higher-quality offering than its typical car offerings and allowed Saturn to exist as a separate brand on its own. Unfortunately, with the recent economic downturn and the pressure on the corporation to turn a profit, the likelihood is that Saturn will be reduced to a brand within the GM stable of offerings, which would take away the product's distinctiveness and only confuse customers about what the corporate name really signifies. An excellent example of premium branding is found in Mini Case Study 6.1, which deals with the British Mackintosh and the need for brand re-energizing.

MINI CASE STUDY 6.1 Brand re-energizing: the case of the British Mackintosh

What could be more synonymous with the UK than the ever-present Mackintosh? Of course, this durable raincoat had fallen on difficult times from a branding standpoint as becoming seen as stodgy and boring. There is little question that the Mackintosh is well made, durable, and dependable. It traces its heritage back to 1823, with the development of waterproof material by Charles Mackintosh. The product became truly viable later in the 1800s, when the process of vulcanization allowed rubber to be combined with fabric in a way that made the new waterproof fabric more attractive and malleable. Since the brand has been around for over 185 years, it enjoys a strong brand heritage, which can effectively serve as a brand platform for distinction.

Brand distinction, however, does not necessarily mean brand excitement, and the brand leadership of Mackintosh astutely realized that they needed a bit more distinctiveness to increase brand demand. As a result, beginning in the late 1980s, the company started courting famous French designers to add a new elegance to its name recognition. Since the company has such a strong history and is associated with such a premium in its craftsmanship, these qualities were important as a selling tool to reach haute couture »

» designers like Hermès and Louis Vuitton. The company approached these prestigious fashion designers with the desire to allow Mackintosh to create fashionable rainwear, building on the quality and uniqueness of the Mackintosh name.

The success of its relationships with Louis Vuitton and Hermès has led to other profitable relationships with Balenciaga and Yamamoto, among others. This has added to its quality image and revitalized it as a fashionable name in clothing. While Mackintosh would put the designer names labels on its private branded creations for these fashion houses, it was not difficult to understand the connection back to Mackintosh through the readily visible use of the Mackintosh name on the handling and care instruction label sewn into every coat produced. This, in essence, provided effective co-branding opportunities for Mackintosh, infusing a new energy into their conservative brand in the trendiness and social value inherent in the various designer names, as well as for the fashion partners in enhancing the perceptions of manufacturing quality associated with goods connected to the Mackintosh name. This has produced a win-win scenario for both sides of the partnerships.

Another benefit from these relationships with designers has been the changes which have been effected on the basic Mackintosh products themselves. The success of different styles and colours has changed the company outlook and led to innovations in such features as more stylish outlines, more fashionable accessories, and availability in a variety of colours such as browns and greens. This represents quite a change from the very straight lines of the original product, available in a basic tan/beige colouring.

This new image as trendy and fashionable, while maintaining its high-quality and handmade distinctiveness, has allowed Mackintosh to add considerable energy to its once stodgy brand. Their unwillingness to locate plants in Asia has also allowed them a means for distinguishing themselves from key competitors who can no longer claim that they are only made in the UK. Now, by saying that they are truly British, they can live up to those claims.

Where corporate branding becomes particularly critical is when the company produces a great variety of products that are quite distinct from each other and wants to present itself as a good corporate citizen. The type of advertising that normally goes along with this positioning is patronage institutional advertising, and the concern is to promote the company as a good company to do business with because it is a reputable company that is a good citizen of the world. Take, for example, General Electric, which is a diversified conglomerate. Obviously, the company uses manufacturer branding which is known around the world immediately as soon as it is placed on the product. The savings are considerable in terms of making the various target audiences aware of the product, but the need to ensure product quality in terms of research and development somewhat offsets the savings. The key, however, is that if the company wants name recognition as a good company and not for what it makes, then it would need to focus not on its products but on its works for the public good. This is a situation in which companies can find themselves where they are not really known for their corporate image but as a series of individual brands. It might strategically be pertinent to have the extra boost of the corporate citizenry supporting the disparate group of brands. Since the company does not link its promotional efforts to its individual brands, it can promote itself as a corporate entity effectively. This provides the opportunity for a company like Unilever or Procter & Gamble to promote their corporate identity when they do not want to tie their individual brands together under the same perceptual umbrella.

The decision whether to brand each individual product on its own (as would be the case for the product-specific branding company) or to group all under the same name (for the manufacturer's brander) or for the company that wants groupings of products that are consistent under family brands (like Kellogg's or Kraft Foods), is a key one that requires a careful assessment of what the company name means to the target audiences so that the chance of confusing the target audiences is minimized. The next important consideration is how to value the brand.

Brand equity

Another integral strategic aspect of a brand relates to the concept of brand equity. Aaker first coined the term **brand equity** in his 1991 book, *Managing Brand Value*, and defined it as a set of assets (as well as liabilities) connected to the name and symbols of the brand that adds to (or detracts from) the value of the product or service to a company and/ or that company's customers. The point is to compare brand assets to brand liabilities and maintain a strong and viable brand equity valuation. The concept involves an assumption that there are really five types of assets that should be considered when examining the brand.

- The first of these is **brand name awareness**, and if the consumer is aware of the brand, then it will more likely be a candidate for their choice set, and familiarity certainly has the potential to generate positive feelings.
- The second is **brand loyalty**, which assumes that loyal customers will spread positive word-of-mouth and help attract a new set of customers. This also suggests that loyalty will allow the greater potential use of premium pricing, since this establishes a substantial barrier against new entrants.
- The third group of assets focuses on **perceived quality**, which is strongly associated with profitability.
- The fourth level involves **brand associations**, which involve the various connections and associations made by consumers about the brand.
- The last level of assets involves **intellectual rights** that support the brand, such as patents or trademarks.

These measures allow the brand manager to assess effectively the value of the brand as a firm asset, and the examination of brand value at regular intervals allows the brand manager to maintain a steady brand course and to take specific corrective action when downward trends are identified. Aaker (1996b, 2004) suggests that these measures can effectively be applied across a variety of products and markets.

An understanding of the complexity of brands is an essential starting point to the development of an effective marketing strategy from the perspective of brand management. Brand management involves a variety of different strategic brand choices and an assessment of the perceptual impact of those choices on various customer groups. For a small company with a single product or service offering, the branding decision is simpler than it would be for a company with a vast array of different product lines and product variants within each line. The main first decision is whether to tie the company name to the product or to create a distinct identity for the product that is separate from that of the company.

Most companies have more than one brand that they are managing, and the options they face are far more complex than those facing the startup business. The discussion will now focus on the strategic choices that will help the brand manager to improve the profitability of the brand and to differentiate the brand from its competition and aid in the creation and maintenance of relationships between the consumer and the brand.

Brand architecture: a strategic framework

Firms have many different options facing them when it comes to brand choices, and it is important to lay the groundwork. The best framework to date is the concept of **brand architecture**, which looks at the brand portfolio as a complex structure with a variety of different types of brand roles and relationships. The idea is that this structure is analogous to the structures designed by an architect. The term is an outgrowth of the work of Petromilli et al. (2002) and Devlin (2003). Thus, a new discipline has emerged which provides an excellent forum for strategic decision-making (Joachimsthaler and Aaker, 1997). Aaker and Joachimsthaler (2000a) present their brand relationship spectrum to demonstrate the various options that are possible for brand management (see Figure 6.4). The array of brand options stretches from the **house of brands** at one extreme, to the **branded house** at the other extreme. The house of brands involves a company that manages a disparate group of brands that stand on their own. Procter & Gamble, Colgate-Palmolive, and Unilever are all examples of companies which manage a house of brands. Each has the potential to own a particular niche market on its own merits and build strong brand relationships with specific target market segments. Virgin and BMW present examples of the branded house in that all of their offerings build on the name as a focal point for consumer expectation.

Another way of looking at this is the concept of **product-specific branding** as the mechanism used when a house of brands is utilized, and **manufacturer's branding** when a branded house is used. The point strategically is that the house of brands is an array of products with their own brands that stand alone and are separate and distinct from each other. Why might this be important for Unilever? Because the likelihood at this level of consumer products is that some new products will fail. Estimates have been shown to be as high as 80 per cent of all new products failing, and the strategic problem is that if a product fails, the company tied to the product will also be negatively affected by the failure. The failed brand would tarnish the overall brand reputation, which could be disastrous for the company involved. If one thinks about the strategic options in this case, the product can fail and not harm Unilever's reputation, but the drawback is that each product starts with no consumer awareness or understanding, and it will be necessary to launch the product effectively with all of the necessary marketing muscle to make the target market aware, interested, desirous, and then to get them to try the product and hopefully adopt it. This will require a major marketing expenditure outlay. Why is this worth the financial investment? Because at this level of consumer product, there is far less loyalty than there is at the higher end of the product spectrum. From a marketing standpoint, a stock out of the product is far worse than excess inventory, since not being able to meet consumer demand may potentially send the consumer to a competitor from where they might never come back again.

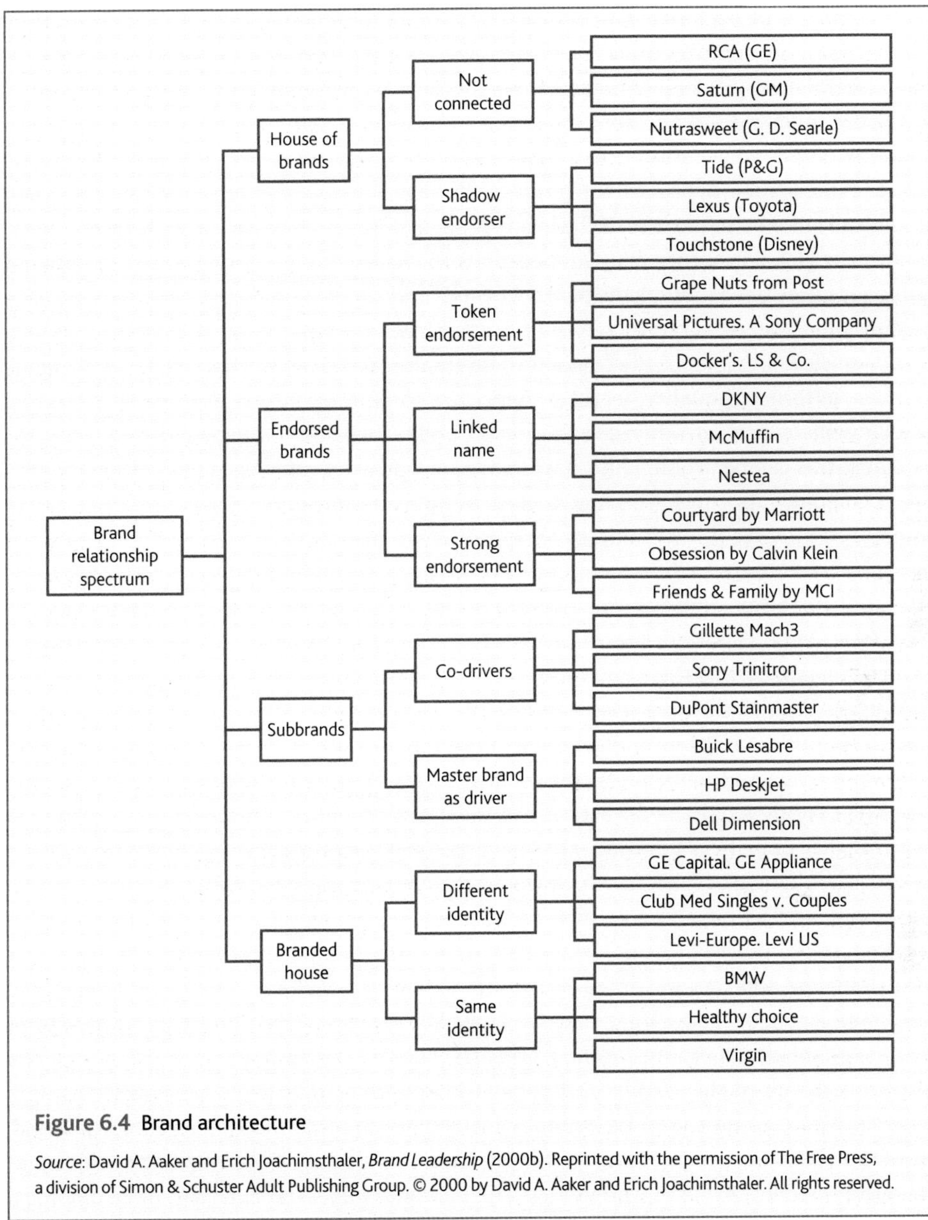

Figure 6.4 Brand architecture

Source: David A. Aaker and Erich Joachimsthaler, *Brand Leadership* (2000b). Reprinted with the permission of The Free Press, a division of Simon & Schuster Adult Publishing Group.

Another problem at this level is that consumers are far more deal and variety prone, so if they switch away from one of the company's brands, they will hopefully switch to another. The danger at this point is **cannibalization**, which is where the addition of a new brand does not increase the overall sales but shifts them among a now broader range of brands, which would be unprofitable for the firm. What is important to remember, however, is that marginal sales improvements might be beneficial, since they may improve overall company efficiency by improving capacity utilization rates, providing a basis for greater shelf-space allocation with a greater number of brands, and more chance that the consumer will buy one of the company's products if they want to try something new. As an illustration, Proctor & Gamble has 26 different types of laundry detergent in the US market to cover the range for consumers.

On the other side of the spectrum is the **branded house** or **manufacturer's brand strategy**. This is where all company products are tied to the same corporate name, and the power of the name will pre-sell the product offering. The manufacturer's brand can be geographically limited in the case of the local brand, like John Smith's brand of Yorkshire beer; or it can be global in nature, like Guinness or Stella Artois. From a positive side, the amount of money necessary to launch the product from a marketing/promotional standpoint will be somewhat less than the product-specific brand, since the company name is already known. The downside of this, since the company name is already known, is that whatever the name signifies in terms of quality, features, options, and performance will set the expectation level for whatever is introduced to the market under the same company name.

Where this can be problematic is when the new product offering is not consistent with other company offerings. The new C-class of Mercedes produced by Daimler-Benz is an attempt to move to a lower end of the product spectrum, but the issue is that this less expensive alternative, while potentially appealing to a much larger group of consumers, may confuse the existing customers who associate the premium-priced offerings with the Mercedes name. This is not the same type of offering that consumers have grown to expect from the company, and this may cause problems for the company and its brand as a result. Confusion in this case may lead to a loss of strategic advantage. The impression given here is that this is a cheaper alternative to the product-specific brand offering, and from a promotional standpoint, this is probably accurate; however, the downside here is that a product failure would be devastating to the overall company brand. The strategic need here for the company is to ensure that the quality of the product is as high as it can be to improve its chances of success, which would require a large investment into initial product development. The introduction of Diet Coke carried a major downside for Coca-Cola if it failed, so ten years of testing went into making sure that the product would be seen as consistent and appropriate for the loyal followers of the Coke brand. They did their homework well, and it became a huge success, especially given that the product is now the third most demanded cola product in the world after regular Coke and Pepsi.

Having discussed the extremes, there are other choices that might be possible as well. Another option is the **endorsed brand,** which builds on its connection to a known brand, but this connection can be strong or weak in nature. Another way of looking at this is the strategic possibility of having different groups of brands under the same corporate umbrella. This is sometimes referred to as umbrella branding. The point is that the company may have several different key brands under its ownership that represent different quality levels and do not detract from each other, but there are great strategic synergies in the connecting of the like products under the same brand umbrella. This is also sometimes referred to as family branding when the brands are all part of the same family of products. Examples would include food products like Post or Kellogg's cereal products. The endorsement in this case can range from very strong as in the use of Holiday Inn Express or Courtyard by Marriott hotels. The point is that the brand now has its own foundation but is tied to the endorser in such a way as to give the new brand greater credibility. At the other end of the spectrum, the endorsement can be much more tangential, like the Docker's brand of trousers that are owned by Levi Strauss, so the Levi's name is clearly secondary, and the hope is that the new brand will eventually be able to stand on its own.

Joachimsthaler and Aaker (1997) present a middle ground between these two endorsement extremes in what they call the linked name in endorsement, using such illustrative examples as the McMuffin sandwich or Chicken McNuggets for McDonald's. This is the real essence behind the idea of family branding, since all products have a common family link. So, what are the strategic benefits associated with this middle-ground option? Here, the company has the ability to avoid real customer confusion and potential alienation by tying together products or services of similar quality and consistency levels. This also allows the company to build name recognition synergistically around a like group of products. Imagine a company like Levi's which is so well known for denim jeans, but who wishes to branch out into other clothing products of a different type. Using the Levi's name as the focal point for the brand endorsement would too closely tie the name to the product offering. What may be preferable would be to use a token endorsement to alleviate the chance for serious damage if the product fails or is seen as too inconsistent.

Another strategic branding option involves the use of the **sub-brand**. This is a stronger connection than is involved in the endorsed brand. The point here is to connect the brand more closely to the parent brand. This can involve the tacit parenting of the company brand like HP Laserjet or Deskjet printers, where the hope is that HP is the key but Deskjet will be recognizable as well. This is also the kind of strategy followed by Sony with its Vaio computers. Sony is the key here, but the Vaio has the ability to develop its own recognition as well. If Vaio later becomes strong enough, it may become a co-driver, which is another option under sub-branding, where each name has more of an equal power and footing in the combined brand. This can be seen in Sony's television sets from the 1980s and 1990s when it introduced its Trinitron sub-brand. This involved a special colour gun in the TV which would present clearer and more vibrant colour since it mixed all colours with a single projection mechanism, as opposed to three different colour projections, as was done in most competing brand models. Trinitron was to be clearly connected to Sony but have separate added value as well. The main benefit was to have both equally add to the name recognition and value perceptions.

One other option of note is the **private brand**, which is where the manufacturer puts another company's name on the product for them. Why would it make sense for a manufacturer to put someone else's name on their products? There are several benefits, such as using their production equipment more efficiently, increasing their overall sales and their responsibility for the products ends with production, since the company that it is being branded has the responsibility for marketing the products. Thus, this is a great mechanism for retailers to gain brand followings as they have their own name which they hope will be preferred by their customers. The manufacturers and food processors involved in grocery chains like Tesco, Sainsbury's, and Waitrose who handle private branding for them are the same high-quality providers that also make their own branded merchandize available, so consumers can get good quality at value prices often when they buy private branded products. This allows the retailer to create relationships with target consumers that may be quite profitable over the long term.

Cost reduction: brand efficiency and brand profitability

As previously discussed, strategic brand decisions can have an important impact on firm financial performance, and there are a number of ways in which brand managers can improve brand performance from a cost and profitability perspective. Operational efficiencies can be achieved from such mechanisms as brand leveraging, co-branding, using new promotional vehicles, and promising new valuation mechanisms. It is also important for brand managers to begin to change their temporal brand focus from short term to long term, as brands have been found to have been weakened by constant price cutting and sale promotions at the expense of long-term brand-building advertising. Each of these will be discussed in turn.

Brand leveraging

Strong brands often produce above-average returns for shareholders, and there is great pressure on brand managers to use the name recognition that accompanies a strong brand to increase potential sales and profits by attaching the name to other company offerings (Court et al., 1999).

What are the potential advantages associated with brand leveraging? Brand extension is constantly luring businesses to tie new offerings to existing brands, since the name recognition is already there, and the costs to build awareness are considerably lower than would be associated with new startup names. Another point is the movement towards convergence with mergers and acquisitions and that leveraging involves a heavy focus on building relationships between customers and brands. After all, what the product has in terms of features and options is not as much an issue as the fact that they emotionally engage with the brand and feel a kinship.

Certainly, brand leverage success can be seen in the offerings of such brands as Walt Disney and Sony, but these companies make sure that the offerings are seen as perceptually consistent. Since the market for Disney is children and their parents, the idea of Disney putting its name on adult-content movies or alcoholic beverages would be ludicrous. Successful brand leveraging can be seen in the top-end electronic offerings of Sony, with its HDTVs, Blueray players, Walkman players, etc. This is also the case for Apple, with its high-demand specialty electronic products like Apple computers, iPods, and iPhones. What do these companies do that makes them successful? According to Court et al. (1999), they identify a 'golden thread' which can tie together a diversified group of businesses. There are significant economies of scale and scope, and shared resources which can provide significant mechanisms for improving profitability. One example they give is Disney and its focus on 'wholesome fun' and another is Sony and its elegance of design. These companies were also found to invest in the creation of a high-credibility brand personality that can be leveraged (Aaker, 2004; Keller, 2000). Examples of successful personality-based leveraging can be seen at General Electric, with its slogan of 'Bringing good things to life' and IBM's 'solutions for a small planet'. With the variety of products offered under the same brand umbrella, there are enormous opportunities for successful cross-selling/bundling of their various products.

While leveraging can produce economic benefits, there is also a downside to aggressive leveraging, as was found in the unsuccessful strategies employed by both BIC and Gucci. These companies were drawn into confusing extensions with product offerings that were inconsistent with their flagship products. Inconsistent offerings can confuse their loyal customers, and spreading out from their limited area of focus can be dangerous if the broadening occurs too quickly. Research has shown that the extent of damage done to the parent by a failed extension will depend to a certain extent on the involvement of the consumer with the parent brand, and in a sub-branding strategy, the damage is lessened to the parent when the brand extension is given another name in association with the parent brand (Keller and Lehmann, 2006). This would argue for the use of a co-branding strategy as opposed to a straight brand extension if the risk of potential failure is high. Sub-branding would also be warranted when the brand extension is quite a bit different from the parent brand product category and when fit between the extension and the parent is minimal. The sub-brand often acts as a buffer by shielding the parent from negative feedback (Keller and Lehmann, 2006).

Focused brands with leveraging potential are those that have slowly and continuously broadened their category definitions and resulting brand identities. McKinsey, the global consulting company, found that there is a significant relationship between company success and four organizational requirements: they must build brand stewardship (the brand should be considered a 'treasured asset'); brand leveraging must be explicitly built into corporate planning; they must nurture and develop a variety of supporting capabilities (like new business development and cross-selling); and develop and utilize appropriate performance metrics (Court et al., 1999).

Co-branding

One important way in which brand managers can reduce costs is through the pursuit of an appropriate co-branding arrangement, as previously discussed in the framework involving brand architecture. Co-branding involves the bringing together of two separate company brands to be marketed together to create a new joint-offering with additional value for the customer. Examples would include such successful pairings as British Airways and Hertz, Adidas and the New Zealand Rugby Union, Starbucks Coffee and Barnes & Noble Bookstores, and Kellogg's Cereals and Walt Disney. There are a number of operational benefits that can accrue to co-branding partners. Prince and Davies (2002) suggest that co-branding can make transactions more efficient through sharing of retail sites (e.g., Starbucks and Barnes & Noble). The authors suggest that Starbucks gets use of space in the bookstore and gets revenues from the high traffic of shoppers as a result. Barnes & Noble gets the benefit of lower expenses for overhead and up-front investments, which are being shared with Starbucks. Another example which they provide involves the site-sharing arrangement between Dunkin' Donuts and Baskin-Robbins. In this arrangement, they share the same space and share the expenses, while offering what are considered to be complementary products but with different peak activity times (doughnuts in the morning and ice cream in the afternoon and evening). Co-branding may be a viable strategic option, but it requires a careful assessment of the potential candidates for partnering. There will be spillover effects that will be incurred when the brands are combined in an alliance, but much of the potential downside would be driven by the lack of congruence in image or fit involved (Simonin and Ruth, 1998).

Abratt and Motlana (2002) suggest that co-branding is an effective mechanism for global brands to be successful in local markets. The local brands bring high local-brand equity to a global brand that may not have high local-brand equity. Co-branding then becomes a great tool for introducing new consumer products. The synergies that are created can often create an impression of greater value and reduce the financial risk associated with a normal new product introduction. They suggest that co-branding makes sense for acquisitions because the acquiring company develops a brand portfolio with a heritage that can help weak products.

Finally, is co-branding better than using just your own name in a brand extension? Desai and Keller (2002) suggest that while co-branding is helpful in the short term, in the longer term the profit impact may be inconsequential since the brand equity from the use of another brand does not necessarily add value to the parent brand. The real question then is who stands to benefit more, the parent brand or the brand partner?

MINI CASE STUDY 6.2 What makes brand alliances work?

Brand alliances can provide a number of ways in which the partners can benefit from image boosts to greater efficiencies and effectiveness. One such powerful brand alliance can be seen in the recent takeover of Wrigley by Mars, which will create the biggest sweets company in the world when it is finally approved in 2010. What makes this a particularly synergistic alliance is that both companies are known as well-run family businesses. The names of the original founders are represented in the brand themselves. They are also seen as complementary to each other, rather than as directly competitive. They also represent companies seen as similar in corporate values, with strong emphases on ethicality and respect for workers and their well-being, along with that of the environment; and both have long histories associated with building successful brands that have lasted for generations. Mars is known for global sweets like M&M's, Mars, Snickers, Starburst, Twix, and Milky Way, among many others, while Wrigley is known primarily for its chewing gum products like Juicy Fruit, Spearmint, Orbit, Doublemint, and Hubba Bubba, among many others.

Brand alliances can often be seen as a means to consolidation if both partners are faced with rapidly increasing costs as can be seen in the plan by British Airways and Iberia to merge. This would create the third largest airline in the world. Both companies have worked together for over ten years in code-sharing agreements, so they are well aware of values and management structures. They have similar visions and corporate philosophies which make the combination synergistic, much like that of Mars and Wrigley. This type of alliance where equals become partners allows the two companies to maintain their own individual brand identities and management structure for everyday operations, but the real benefits can be seen in the consistency of the two brands now being merged and the added value that brings with it. They will have a number of potential cost-savings opportunities involving ever-rising jet fuel prices, IT systems, and logistics, but they also see added benefit in their complementary routes and geographical coverage. A similar situation was seen recently in the United States with the merger of Delta and Northwest. This type of consolidation has been seen as particularly important in trying economic times, but the benefits that accrue will become even more valuable when economic conditions improve.

This, of course, assumes that there will be not only internal operating synergies between the brand partners, but also perceptual consistency in the eyes of consumers that will allow boosts for the co-brands. Some alliances do not provide this type of boost, as can clearly be seen by the failed Daimler-Chrysler merger, which brought a certain amount of credibility to Chrysler, but the opposing nature of the quality perceptions associated with Chrysler »

» probably did not do much good for Daimler. In fact, there is concern that the Chrysler focus on high volume has potentially clouded the view of Daimler, as it has downwardly expanded its Mercedes products to the lower-priced and lower-quality C-Class. The concern is that this may tarnish the image of the top-end products as the reach of the product will potentially eliminate some of the social caché associated with not seeing many able to afford a Mercedes automobile. The concern is that the weakness of the Chrysler brand can actually have a negative effect upon the stronger brand partner to the alliance. Of course, Daimler saw the error of its ways and divested Chrysler to a private equity group, but the question is whether the cultural change that occurred during the alliance will have a long-term negative effect upon Daimler and its Mercedes flagship.

Non-traditional communication/promotional channels

Joachimsthaler and Aaker (1997) studied successful European brands and found that European brand managers had found some interesting ways to streamline promotional expenses that had not been utilized effectively by their US counterparts. The authors found that European brand managers utilized a variety of efficient and effective promotional channels to build brand awareness as opposed to the normal mass-media, cost-inefficient mechanisms. They cite such examples as use of publicity (e.g., Body Shop's connection to environmental causes and firm actions to promote these causes); event sponsorship (e.g., Swatch's sponsoring of fashion, and social and sporting events, and Virgin's participation in Compuserve's UK Virtual Shopping Centre); membership-club development and maintenance (e.g., Nestlé and the Casa Buitoni Club); and theme-park development (e.g., Cadbury World and Legoland). Joachimsthaler and Aaker (1997) found that these companies were successful not only in finding more efficient ways to promote their brands, but also in enhancing the relationships between their brands and consumers, further solidifying their brand image and engendering loyalty as well as profitability.

A recent example of this type of enhancement can be seen in the efforts of Tommy Hilfiger in Britain. Following Hilfiger's success in the US in pairing rock stars and the Hilfiger brand, Tommy Hilfiger launched Tommy TV in 2008, using an online forum for aspiring rock stars to expand in a joint project with Sony BMG to help new talent to be seen and find potential record deals. New musicians can upload their auditions to YouTube. This connection between the Hilfiger brand and the sponsorship of concerts and music special events will now be emphasized as a series of new brand-stores are opened in Britain, Europe, and Asia.

New brand-valuation mechanisms

There are three recent approaches to asset valuation from a financial resource perspective that may aid brand managers to achieve greater efficiencies. One of these involves the measurement of advertising turnover and was suggested by Herremans et al. (2000). The authors suggest two ratios for analysis to tie brand asset valuation to the efficiency and effectiveness of marketing expenditures: **advertising turnover** and **brand ROI** (Return on Investment). The earlier discussion of brand equity provides mechanisms for overall brand valuation, but there are few mechanisms that allow the brand manager to evaluate marketing spending as it relates to the brand. The authors state that most brand valuation has been done for the purposes of external reporting, but little has really focused on valuations for internal strategic purposes. They argue that marketing investment and advertising investment are one and the same for brand valuation purposes since advertising makes up such a large part in brand building compared to any other marketing promotional mechanisms. As a result, they suggest a ratio, **advertising turnover**, which examines the relationship between advertising expenditures and brand value. This measure would therefore reflect how effectively the firm has converted advertising expenditures into brand value. Advertising turnover is calculated by dividing brand value by advertising expenditures on a year-by-year basis and examining trends.

Herremans et al. (2000) also suggest an additional measure for effective brand assessment, the **brand ROI**. They posit substitutions in the normal calculations for ROI to convert the focus to the brand. They assume the following formula for calculating ROI (sales/investment x net income/sales), and they substitute brand sales for sales and brand value for investment. Thus, the formula becomes:

$$\text{Brand ROI} = \frac{\text{Brand Sales}}{\text{Brand Value}} \times \frac{\text{Net Income}}{\text{Brand Sales}}$$

The first part of the formula reflects the brand turnover (brand sales/brand value), which shows the effectiveness of brand value conversion into sales; while the second part is the brand return on sales (net income/brand sales), which indicates how well brand sales convert into operating income.

The third and last of these new promising valuation measures is **brand health**, which was suggested by Berg et al. (2007). The authors found that many brand managers were making mistakes when approaching brand strength by relying too often upon problematic measures. In particular, Berg et al. (2007) chastise companies for overly narrow and passive management mechanisms. They say that brand managers often focus too heavily on brand awareness since there are weak connections between awareness and either customer commitment or brand health. Secondly, they argue that brand managers often miss the importance of customer satisfaction, which they found to be the strongest determinant of brand health. They also suggest that brand managers assume that current brand sales are a strong determinant of future relationships with customers, but the authors found in their research that sales are unreliable in predicting either commitment or relationship potential. Finally, the authors state that brand managers are often guilty of slack management of their brands. They tend to focus on crises, rather than maintain active and effective management practices.

Berg et al. (2007) present brand health as a useful tool for proper brand assessment. They suggest that the proper assessment of brand health involves the interrelating of five metrics which are all readily understood but rarely used as part of an integrated approach to brand measurements.

The first of these is **brand leadership**, which examines brand availability, brand reputation, and specific points of brand presence. This measurement is an attempt to answer whether consumers believe that the brand is available to them both now and in the future. The second measurement involves **brand liabilities**. This measure involves an examination of brand problems (e.g., negative associations, consumer reluctance, and any other brand weaknesses). The point of this measure is to come up with an evaluation of what things would be impeding customer commitment or what might be turning customers off about the brand. The third component is a measurement of **brand attractiveness**. In direct contrast to liabilities, this measure would focus on customer positive associations and attractions. Here, the company tries to measure whether customers are actually drawn to the brand. The fourth element is **brand distinctiveness**, which measures the ability of the brand to stand out from all others in a meaningful way. Finally, the last measure involves **brand satisfaction**, which examines the performance of the brand as compared with customer expectations. The real question here is how satisfied the customer is with the overall brand experience.

In their research, the authors found the following sets of interrelationships among the five components of brand health:

1. satisfaction is related to all components, and its importance reflects the relevance of the nature of the brand experience and its impact upon brand health
2. attractiveness is connected most strongly to satisfaction, but it is not connected to leadership
3. distinctiveness is related to satisfaction and attractiveness, but it is also not connected to leadership and
4. leadership is related to satisfaction and attractiveness, but it was not found to be related to distinctiveness and liabilities.

Berg et al. (2007) identify four revenue measures which are directly connected to customer commitment which they believe are relevant in any assessment of brand health:

1. the level of current customer spending
2. the risk of lost sales (likelihood of switching)
3. revenue momentum (intent to purchase additional products) and
4. the likelihood of referrals (producing new customers or sales).

Finally, the authors suggest that what will ensure brand success is the practicing of active brand management, and they offer the following questions as a mechanism for seeing how great the company's capacity is for active brand management:

- Is the brand fulfilling the addressable market?
- Can the brand position be defined distinctively?
- Does marketing = branding = advertising?
- Is branding being outsourced to an advertising agency?
- If there is a problem with customer satisfaction, who will sound the alarm within the company?
- Does brand tracking and budgeting go beyond advertising and promotion?
- Is it understood that brand building is a long-term process?

Short-term promotional mistakes by brand managers

Lastly, in keeping with the issue of brand mismanagement that was raised in the previous section, further problems with mismanagement have been identified in the research of Lodish and Mela (2007) in a recent *Harvard Business Review* article. Lodish and Mela suggest that brands have lost their luster for consumer-goods companies since they are too focused on short-term data and are not concerned about their brand's long-term health. They claim that too much reliance on price promotions at the expense of advertising and long-term brand building has severely weakened a number of once-powerful brands. They explain that there are three reasons why this has happened:

- there is a plethora of real-time sales data which can highlight short-term promotional effects
- there is also a corresponding lack of effective data regarding the assessment of long-term brand investments
- brand managers do not have a long life expectancy in their positions.

Lodish and Mela (2007) say that brand managers can learn from what Victoria's Secret recently learned. It was discovered that Victoria's Secret's TV advertisements did not result in sufficient short-term sales to allow the company to cover the cost of its ads. The benefits that were found for their advertisements were derived from the fact that the company found a connection between increases in its TV advertising and the company's ability to raise prices over the longer term. The TV ads have powerful benefits in their enhancement of the brand's strength over time. Of course, this links back to the argumentation that advertising must be seen in its cumulative effects as a long-term investment, rather than as merely a short-term discounting facilitator.

This section has focused on the cost side of brand management, but there is also the need to examine brand management from the perceptual side. The perceptions of brand, brand personality, and brand value are key strategic considerations that significantly improve brand strategic planning perspective in the pursuit of sustainable competitive advantage.

Differentiation: consumer perceptions of brand and sustainable competitive advantage

Brand management cannot focus on financial assessment alone. There is also an enormously important perceptual aspect. Companies are finding that brand management has an image and personality management component which must also be carefully assessed and tracked over time. This section will focus on such image-orientated strategic issues, which are: customer involvement with the brand; brand perceptual reinforcement and revitalization; the need for internal brand-marketing; and the overall assessment of the brand using the brand wheel.

Customer brand involvement and perceptual connections

Companies have found that the key to brand success is to build up strong relationships with customers by enhancing customer experiences with the brand, its personality, and its heritage (Joachimsthaler and Aaker, 1997). This involvement and relationship building can clearly be seen in innovative attempts to enhance customer experiences with the brand. Cadbury's theme park, Cadbury World, in Bournville, England, allows the customer to experience the brand in multiple ways, creating a link between brand, brand attributes, brand personality, and the customer. What was once just a factory tour has now become an entire theme park with the emphasis on Cadbury brand heritage via a chocolate museum, a restaurant, a tour of the plant, and a big chocolate sales store. Visitors learn about the history of chocolate (with characters portraying historic figures like Cortez, Montezuma, and King Charles II), as well as the history of John Cadbury and his company. This idea was so successful that it encouraged Hershey Chocolate to open its own version of this experience in New York City.

Another example can clearly be seen in the development of the H.O.G. chapters (clubs) by the Harley-Davidson motorcycles company. These *H*arley *O*wner *G*roups regularly get together to ride and celebrate the history and heritage of the motorcycles. Nestlé has also worked to develop customer groups with its Buitoni pasta products by creating the Casa Buitoni Club, which involves customers in the history of Buitoni and of pasta through visits to the Buitoni family home in Tuscany and a series of mailings of newsletters, Italian lifestyle literature, recipes, and discount coupons. Customers get continual positive brand reinforcement with the company's hope of building ever-increasing involvement with the customer.

Brand perceptual reinforcement and revitalization

Kevin Lane Keller (1999) suggests that brand management must always take a long-term perspective in terms of brand equity and valuation. Any strategic decisions made in the short term can affect the future potential of the brand by impacting brand awareness and image. Keller suggests that effective brand management requires a long-term perspective with continuous reinforcement of brand meaning and, when necessary, brand revitalization.

Reinforcement of brand equity occurs when marketing tactical decisions convey consistent meanings to consumers. A series of important questions raised by Keller (1999) in this regard are:

- What products are represented by the brand?
- What benefits are supplied by the brand?
- What specific needs are satisfied by the brand?
- How does the brand make those products associated with it superior?
- What distinct and favourable brand associations are made by consumers with the brand?

Keller (1999) warns that the most important consideration in brand reinforcement is the consistency of the support (in terms of both the type and amount) provided by the company to the brand. He emphasizes that price increase with inadequate marketing support is potentially disastrous. This is not meant to suggest that brand management should not make any changes to its marketing efforts for the brand, but that any changes keep the image integrity of the brand. Some companies have been forced to come back to old themes for advertising when new creative ideas did not register well with consumers from a perceptual standpoint. Kentucky Fried Chicken was forced to return to using Colonel Sanders to promote the product after eliminating his likeliness in favour of modernizing the company image. Change for the sake of change has the potential to undermine the brand's position in the head of the consumer. The reinforcement of brand meaning depends on the types of brand associations in the heads of brand consumers. These associations can be based upon either product-related associations (e.g., product design or production innovations which lead to an improved product which is not significantly different from what consumers expect); or, non-product-related types of associations (e.g., new advertising approaches and creative ideas that build a position for the brand that is perceived to be better while remaining consistent with the brand image).

There may certainly be times over the brand's lifetime that strategic chances will be taken that may not be successful and potentially undermine the vitality of the brand. In these instances, brand managers should consider revitalizing the brand. Revitalization requires a careful assessment of brand meaning and associations so that meaningful repositioning decisions can be made. This requires the implementation of a thorough **brand audit**. The brand audit is a comprehensive examination of the various sources of brand equity from the perspective of the company as well as the consumer. Keller (2000) introduced his own tool for effective brand auditing, the Brand Report Card, which involves ratings from one (extremely poor) to ten (extremely good) regarding honest answers to the following brand equity questions (Keller 2000):

- How well does the brand excel at delivering the benefits customers truly desire?
- How well does the brand remain relevant?
- How well does the pricing strategy reflect consumers' perceptions of value?
- How well is the brand positioned in the minds of consumers as compared with competing brands?
- How consistent are the brand's marketing programmes and the messages sent to the consumer?
- Does the brand portfolio and hierarchy actually make sense?
- How well does the brand utilize and coordinate a full range of marketing activities to build brand equity?
- How well do the brand's managers understand what the brand means to consumers?
- How well does the company give proper support to the brand, and how well has this support been sustained over the long run?
- How well does the company monitor the sources of brand equity?

Keller (1999) suggests that once a brand audit has been done, the important brand associations will be better understood and the firm will be able to take one or more of the following paths:

1. Expanding brand awareness (e.g., finding additional or new usage opportunities for the brand, like Arm & Hammer Baking Soda)
2. Improving brand image (e.g., strengthening positive associations and/or eliminating negative associations using such mechanisms as brand heritage/history)
3. Balancing both old and new target segments (e.g., bringing in a younger customer and keeping relationships with loyal older customers at the same time)
4. Retiring and/or consolidating brands (that no longer fit or would be too costly to revitalize, e.g. Procter & Gamble's merging of the White Cloud and Charmin toilet-paper brands and the Solo and Bold detergent brands).

The brand audit is a vital assessment tool for effective brand management.

Internal brand marketing

An interesting recent article proposed that financial services in the UK can effectively be differentiated through the use of internal marketing within the company to its own employees.

Papasolomou and Varonis (2006) found that when the company treats its own employees as customers, it enhances the potential for the creation of a service culture, which in turn will help to create a stronger brand. While this would seem to be pure common sense, it is remarkable how many companies—especially in consumer services—treat their employees as 'throwaways' rather than as essential to the company's success, which breeds poor morale, which in turn undermines the creation of a service culture and turn customers off. The authors suggest that in order to create a service culture, a company should view employees as internal customers, meet or exceed service standard expectations, provide training and development for employees to make service their first priority, and offer a series of employee incentives to improve performance.

Key brand assessment vehicles for differentiation purposes: the brand wheel

Given the complex nature of brands, a useful tool developed by Ward et al. (1999), can give the brand manager a reasonable view of his or her brand/brands without using inordinate amounts of complicated data acquisition and analysis. This is known as the brand wheel (see Figure 6.5). The first level, **features**, focuses on how the brand delivers its promise. An illustrative example of this could be seen in the global management consulting, technology services, and outsourcing company, Accenture. The company owns or maintains a series of tangible and intangible assets that it could point to which are used to deliver its promise. These assets

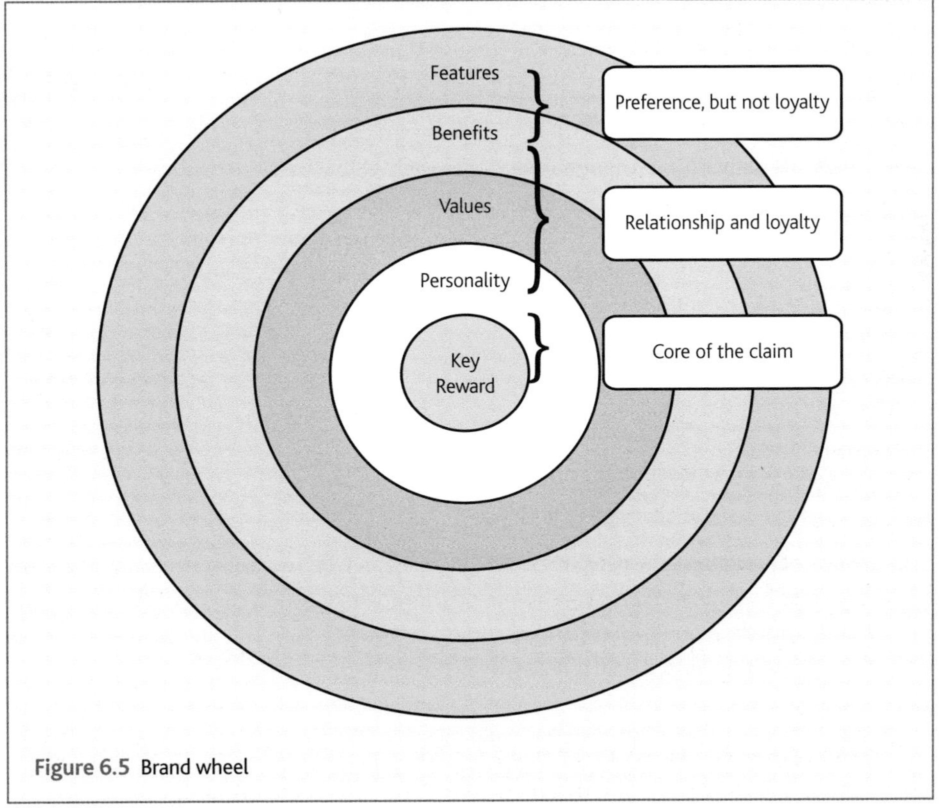

Figure 6.5 Brand wheel

would include such things as its various offices spread out across the world, its various trained staff members, its Web presences, and its consulting projects and research reference sources.

The second layer would involve the various **benefits**, which would incorporate the translation of these features into a series of benefits for its target audiences. Accenture would use its features to produce a series of benefits for its customers like: providing them with knowledge of relevant industries and target markets so that their customers would improve the effectiveness of their strategic decision-making, better access to select, trained personnel for hiring purposes, an enhanced information infrastructure to improve efficiency, effectiveness or improvement of firm security, and out-of-the-box creativity to provide new capabilities for future viability.

The third layer, **values**, would consider aspects of the firm in relation to its place in society. Now, the firm must be concerned with whether its brand conveys information about the nature of its community citizenship or social responsibility. This would then examine the ways in which the brand would be suggestive of a series of social values that would add to its brand worth. The key here is that many consumers are willing to pay a premium for products that are socially responsible (e.g., paying fair value for materials from developing countries and loyalty to companies that treat their workers well). In January of 2009, Coke announced that it was taking a much stronger position on environmental friendliness by stressing recycling on its Times Square Neon Advertisement billboard in New York City. Starbucks stresses the benefit of fair-traded coffee beans from smaller growers in developing countries. So, what is to be asked of the brand in terms of values focuses on such questions as what values are important to the company, whether it is an active charitable contributor, and whether it treats its workers and suppliers fairly. The point is to get a clear sense of what the company/brand stands for. On Accenture's website (**www.accenture.com**) the list of important company values is readily apparent. These are the six core values listed: (1) stewardship for the environment and the needs of stakeholders; (2) hiring and developing the best people for their business; (3) creating client value; (4) delivering exceptional service to their global client network; (5) developing an environment of respect for all individuals; and (6) inspiring trust through integrity.

The fourth layer is **personality**, which focuses on the particular personality traits that are associated with the company/brand. This is not something that is asked directly in a questionnaire. In order to examine this important aspect, the following are the types of questions that many companies use to identify associated traits:

- If this brand were a car, what would it be?
- If this brand were a person, who would it be?
- If this brand were a newspaper, which one would it be?
- If this brand were a lunch, what would it be?

In the case of Accenture, the company built a connection with the world-famous golfer, Tiger Woods, in its various ads and company promotions. It successfully tied Tiger's visible personality traits directly with the brand in the eyes of its various customers. Tiger was known for battling the odds regularly and epitomized such traits as drive, precision, preparation, and high performance. Tiger, when seen as the ultimate high performer, could become a symbol/metaphor for Accenture's commitment to helping its customer companies become high performers like Tiger. Accenture was building an automatic connection with Tiger in the mind of its customers. Unfortunately, Tiger's personal life became quite a mess when stories of infidelities came to light in

December 2009. This unfortunate turn of events forced the company to officially end its connection with Tiger Woods on 14 December 2009, opening up a need to build a connection with another personality. This demonstrates the risk that is borne by the company when it aligns itself with a famous figure, but it worked for Accenture for a number of years before Tiger fell from grace. Now they must find an appropriate replacement for the personality connection.

The final layer involves the **key reward**, and it is the central reason that people buy and/or use the brand, based upon the four earlier levels of the brand wheel. The identification of the most important of the brand-wheel levels is vital for understanding and nurturing the brand, and it may be that any one or a combination of the prior levels determines the key reward. It might be that it is the benefits layer or the personality where the key reward is found, or it might be the cumulative effects of all of the layers that create the key reward. It might be that overall excellence of service is the key, and in the case of Accenture, while personality and the connection to Tiger may be important, it's key reward would seem to draw on personality more than anything else.

An important distinction to make here is that features and benefits may create preference, but they will not necessarily ensure loyalty to the brand. Values and personality reflect the character of the brand and therefore offer the potential for loyalty. In the UK mobile phone marketplace, one of the current operators is trying to offer extremely attractive deals for customers, but there are conflicts in that a number of customers find themselves wary of the brand due to poor prior service and coverage.

So where does the brand manager go from here? The newest thinking presents new opportunities in the form of developing love for the brand and getting back to basics by simplifying the brand. These will now be discussed in greater detail.

The latest brand thinking

Lovemarks

One of the most interesting new views on branding is presented by Kevin Roberts, CEO for Worldwide Operations for Saatchi & Saatchi, in his 2004 book, *Lovemarks: The Future Beyond Brands* and later enhanced and expanded in his 2006 book, *The Lovemarks Effect: Winning in the Consumer Revolution*. It is Roberts' premise that branding itself is flawed, since brands are not actually making strong emotional connections with people. He claims that there are six reasons for this:

- brands are worn out from overuse
- brands are no longer mysterious
- brands can't understand the new consumer
- brands struggle with good old-fashioned competition
- brands have been captured by formula
- brands have been smothered by creeping conservatism.

The issue is to build an emotional bond with the consumer to such an extent that the consumer actually feels a love for the product. Roberts (2004, p. 70) believes that love goes beyond reason, and a love bond is an emotional attachment that transcends logic and reason. Roberts (2004) provides a comparison of brands and lovemarks as shown in Table 6.1 (adapted from Roberts).

TABLE 6.1 Brands vs lovemarks

Brand	Lovemark
Stands for information	Focuses on relationship
Recognized by consumers	Loved by people
Is generic	Is personal
Presents a narrative	Creates a love story
Promises quality	Presents a touch of sensuality
Is symbolic	Is iconic
Is defined	Is infused
Is a statement	Is a story
Is a set of defined attributes	Is wrapped in mystery
Is a set of values	Is a spirit
Is professional	Is passionately creative
Needs an advertising agency	Needs an ideas company

The Lovemarks approach has gained ground strategically and Roberts presents a series of brands that he believes have been elevated to lovemarks. These include among them IKEA, Singapore Airlines, Twinings, BBC, Snaidero, and Campbell's. In order for the Lovemark brand strategy to be integrated into marketing planning, it must have some robust metrics. A recent attempt to add metrics to lovemarks can be seen in a 2006 *Journal of Advertising Research* article by Pawle and Cooper. The authors developed a measure for emotion that combines qualitative analyses with quantitative measurement. They developed a grid for measuring the level of love on one axis and the level of respect on the other axis (see Figure 6.6). They developed scales for measuring emotional, social, cultural, and functional relationships between consumers and brands and combined these with qualitative projective techniques to gain insight into emotional relationships.

An example of the application of these techniques can be seen in Figure 6.7, which indicates the results of their assessment of the US cereals market. From their analysis, the only lovemark found was for Cheerios. This is extremely valuable and promising research. One key contention that the authors make which is supported by Roberts is that decisions are either rationally or emotionally made, and functional benefits which are rationally appealing are getting narrower and narrower over time, which in turn means that companies must offset these with ever-expanding emotional benefits. The way for companies to win over the consumer is to create an approach which makes the emotional connection and builds up a strong emotional bond. This will take precedent.

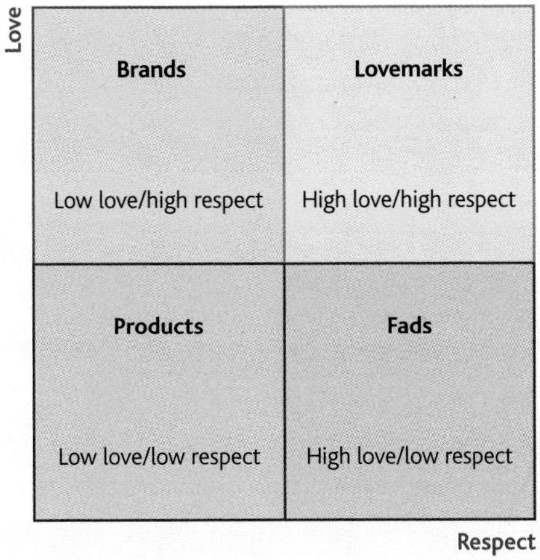

Love

Brands Low love/high respect	**Lovemarks** High love/high respect
Products Low love/low respect	**Fads** High love/low respect

Respect

Figure 6.6 Lovemarks measurement matrix

Source: John Pawle and Peter Cooper (2006), 'Measuring Emotion–Lovemarks, the Future beyond Brands', *Journal of Advertising Research*, (March), pp. 38–48.

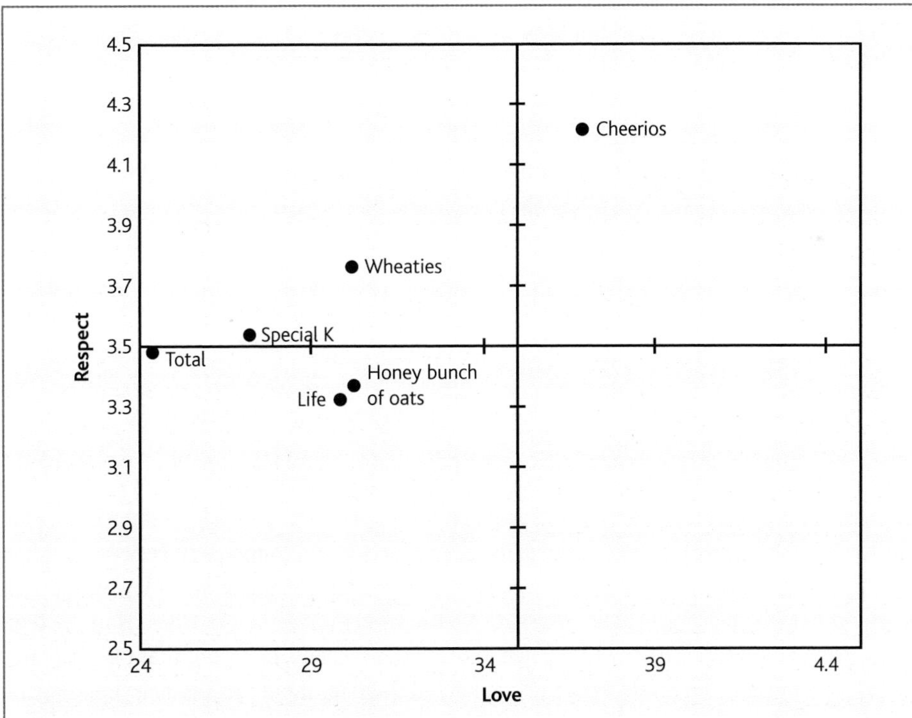

Figure 6.7 Lovemarks metrics: an example

Source: John Pawle and Peter Cooper (2006), 'Measuring Emotion–Lovemarks, the Future beyond Brands', *Journal of Advertising Research*, (March), pp. 38–48.

BrandSimple

Allen Adamson in his 2007 book, *BrandSimple: How the Best Brands Keep it Simple and Succeed*, suggests that the best brand strategies are ones in which the brand becomes clearly synonymous with the organization and embodies its values. Adamson argues that brands need to be simplified—not complicated. He suggests that companies too often overly complicate things by connecting too many different and distinctive nuances and messages to the various aspects of the brand, thereby doing nothing but confusing the public. Adamson suggests that when everything is simple and in synch, the message is clear and the door is now opened for a meaningful emotional connection between the consumer and the brand. How is this done? It is best handled by getting back to basics.

Adamson (2007), Aaker (2004), and many other important brand strategists (e.g., Keller, 1999 and 2000; Ries and Ries, 1998 and 2000) suggest that the basic foundation for everything begins with a simple **brand idea**. This is the basic concept or meaning behind the brand. It conveys in a succinct way the nature of the brand, and it serves as the focal point for all aspects of corporate branding strategy. Adamson (2007) says that many companies fail because they never establish a clear, distinct, and meaningful brand idea upon which to build the branding strategy. In the ideal scenario, the company embraces the brand idea, commits to it throughout the organization, and then maintains the simplicity of that idea in all brand signalling and ensures that it reiterates the **brand story** (the brand message derived from the brand idea) in all communications to its consumers. Anything which is not consistent with the brand story and basic idea should be eliminated. This serves to keep the brand message clear in the mind of the consumer. Adamson (2007) discusses the successes of such companies as Apple and FedEx, where the clear brand ideas allowed all aspects of the marketing mix to be able to reinforce that clear message not only to existing, but to potential customers as well. Adamson suggests that companies like American Express were forced to get back to basics and reposition themselves since the convoluted messages had become confusing for its customers. When Xerox starts offering personal computers, one begins to see where the basic brand idea was somehow lost throughout its corporate hierarchy. They really had no business being in the personal computer business when their basic brand idea was copiers.

Adamson (2007) describes the importance of a brand experience and stresses the need for consistency in all aspects of that experience for the consumer. He suggests that all messages that are connected to a brand should reflect the same values and focus. The simpler this brand message is in nature, the less the opportunity for creating dissonance in the mind of the customer in regard to the brand name. Adamson uses the recent mistake in brand experience by Audi to show how dissonance can negatively affect the overall brand experience. Audi has attempted to create a meaningful and consistent brand image for its products in the connections between product performance, appearance, styling, and social caché, but Adamson on his Web blog, BrandDigital/BrandSimple: The Blog, (18 December 2008) discussed the fact that Audi dived into the digital age using an Audi A4 Driving Challenge to reach digital consumers, but that the challenge fell short on a number of levels. While he applauded them for modernizing their branding, he discussed the fact that the challenge was not at all challenging in nature, and consumers saw it as nothing more than a weak attempt at self-promotion and advertising, which in turn resulted in negative effects on the overall Audi brand. Any attempt to add to/change/modify the brand experience must be carefully assessed for consistency to avoid consumer dissonance.

Conclusion

Strategic brand management requires an understanding of not only brand costs and profitability, but also of consumer perceptions of brand meaning, image, and value. Tactical brand decisions predicated upon cost savings and increased efficiencies must never be attempted without a clear understanding of the perceptual implications of those decisions, as brand perceptual inconsistencies may seriously undermine brand value and long-term brand equity. The company that regularly reassesses its brand equity will be in a better position to maintain its relevance with its target markets and ensure not only its long-term brand survival, but also its profitability and market leadership.

Summary

A brand is a complex entity that serves as a product and/or company identifier and provides utility for both buyers and sellers. A brand establishes important associations in the minds of target consumers, and these associations facilitate the building of a brand identity, meaning, and value. Customer perceptions of a brand are an integral part of brand management and must be carefully examined and brand refinements undertaken to maintain relevance to the consumer. Brand managers must be able to undertake thorough brand audits to understand what the brand truly means and how it is valued not only by the target customer, but also by firm management. Brand managers must constantly look for ways to improve brand efficiency and effectiveness, but must also guard against making decisions that can confuse their loyal customers and undermine the brand relationships that have been built. Successful brand managers treat brands as valuable firm assets that require constant nurturing.

KEY TERMS

Advertising turnover A measure of the relationship between advertising expenditures and brand value. This measure would reflect how effectively the firm has converted advertising expenditures into brand value. Advertising turnover is calculated by dividing brand value by advertising expenditures on a year-by-year basis and examining trends.

Brand A name, symbol, word, sign, design, or combination that differentiates one or more offerings of a seller or group of sellers from the competition.

Brand architecture A complex structure of brands in a brand portfolio with a variety of different types of brand roles and relationships. The idea is that this structure is analogous to the complex structures designed by an architect.

Brand audit A comprehensive examination of the various sources of brand equity from the perspective of the company as well as the consumer.

Brand equity A set of assets (as well as liabilities) connected to the name and symbols of the brand that adds to (or detracts from) the value of the product or service to a company and/or that company's customers.

Brand health The holistic view of a brand's overall well-being using evaluations of brand leadership, brand liabilities, brand attractiveness, brand distinctiveness, and customer satisfaction with overall brand experience.

Brand idea The basic concept or meaning behind the brand. It conveys in a succinct way the nature of the brand, and it serves as the focal point for all aspects of corporate branding strategy.

Brand identity At its most basic level, the brand has a core identity, which is its essence and which remains constant; and an extended identity, which focuses on a series of psychological and physical aspects that give it nuance and texture.

Brand leveraging Where the company uses the name recognition that accompanies a strong brand to increase potential sales and profits by attaching the name to other company offerings.

Brand personality The embodiment of the personality traits of the consumer in the brand itself.

Brand ROI A ROI calculation that focuses on the brand where the normal formula (sales/investment x net income/sales) is modified, with brand sales substituted for sales, brand value for investment, and brand sales for sales.

Brand story The brand message derived from the brand idea which should be conveyed consistently in all communications and tactical decisions made with regard to the brand.

Cannibalization Where the addition of a new brand does not increase the overall sales but shifts them among a now broader range of brands, which would be unprofitable for the firm.

Co-branding The bringing together of two separate company brands to be marketed together to create a new joint-offering with additional value for the customer.

CoolBrands A list of the top brands as developed by the Superbrands Organisation that are judged by a wide range of consumers to be stylish, innovative, original, authentic, desirable, and unique.

Lovemark A move beyond branding to where the name becomes a symbol of love to the consumer. The key is that the name triggers an emotional attachment that transcends reason.

Q DISCUSSION QUESTIONS

1 What are the various benefits provided for both buyers and sellers of branding? Why is brand identity so important for effective strategic brand management? What are advertising turnover, brand ROI, and brand health, and how might they be helpful for strategic brand managers?

2 How might a brand manager assess brand value? What would you recommend?

3 What is brand leveraging, and what are the forces driving its use? What are the benefits that can be achieved through brand consolidation?

4 What is a brand audit, and why is it vital for brand revitalization?

5 How would a brand manager attempt to develop a brand personality, and how can this lead to the creation of a competitive advantage? Linked to this, what is the brand wheel, and how can it be used by brand managers for overall assessment of the brand?

6 What is a lovemark, and how does it differ from a brand? What makes a brand 'cool', and why might it matter or not?

7 Why might a brand manager consider simplifying the brand, and how might this be accomplished?

ONLINE RESOURCE CENTRE

Visit the Online Resource Centre for this book for lots of interesting additional material at: **www.oxfordtextbooks.co.uk/orc/west2e/**

REFERENCES AND FURTHER READING

Aaker, David A. (1991), *Managing Brand Equity* (New York: The Free Press).

Aaker, David A. (1996a), *Building Strong Brands* (New York: The Free Press).

Aaker, David A. (1996b), 'Measuring Brand Equity across Products and Markets', *California Management Review*, 38 (3), pp. 102–20.

Aaker, David A. (1997), 'Should you Take your Brand to Where the Action is?' *Harvard Business Review*, September–October, pp. 135–43.

Aaker, David A. (2004), *Brand Portfolio Strategy: Creative Relevance, Differentiation, Energy, Leverage, and Clarity* (New York: The Free Press).

Aaker, David A., and Erich Joachimsthaler (2000a), 'The Brand Relationship Spectrum: The Key to the Brand Architecture Challenge', *California Management Review*, 42 (4), pp. 8–23.

Aaker, David A., and Erich Joachimsthaler (2000b), *Brand Leadership* (New York: The Free Press).

Abratt, Russell, and Patience Motlana (2002), 'Managing Co-Branding Strategies: Global Brands into Local Markets', *Business Horizons*, (September–October), pp. 43–50.

Adamson, Allen P. (2007), *BrandSimple: How the Best Brands Keep it Simple and Succeed* (New York: Palgrave Macmillan).

Berg, Julie Dexter, John M. Matthews, and Constance M. O'Hare (2007), 'Measuring Brand Health to Improve Top-line Growth', *MIT Sloan Management Review*, 48 (Fall), pp. 61–8.

Berthon, Pierre, James M. Hulbert, and Leyland Pitt (1999), 'Brand Management Prognostications', *Sloan Management Review*, 40 (Winter), pp. 53–65.

Court, David C., Mark G. Leiter, and Mark A. Loch (1999), 'Brand Leverage: Developing a Strong Company Brand', *McKinsey Quarterly*, 2 (Spring), pp. 100–7.

Desai, Kalpesh Kaushik, and Kevin Lane Keller (2002), The Effect of Ingredient Branding Strategies on Host Branding Extedability', *Journal of Marketing*, 66 (1), pp. 73–94.

Devlin, James (2003), 'Brand Architecture in Services: The Example of Retail Financial Services', *Journal of Marketing Management*, 19 (9/10), pp. 1043–66.

Edmundson, Gail, Paulo Prada, and Karen Nickel Anhalt (2003), 'Lexus: Still Looking for Traction in Europe', *Business Week*, (17 November 2003), p. 122.

Henderson, Terilyn A., and Elizabeth A. Mihas (2000), 'Building Retail Brands', *McKinsey Quarterly*, 3, pp. 11017.

Herremans, Irene M., John K. Ryans (Jr), and Raj Aggarwal (2000), 'Linking Advertising and Brand Value', *Business Horizons*, (May–June), pp. 19–26.

Joachimsthaler, Erich, and David A. Aaker (1997), 'Building Brands without Mass Media', *Harvard Business Review*, January–February, pp. 39–48.

Keller, Kevin Lane (1999), 'Managing Brands for the Long Run', *California Management Review* 41 (3), pp. 102–24.

Keller, Kevin Lane (2000), 'The Brand Report Card', *Harvard Business Review*, January–February, pp. 3–10.

Keller, Kevin Lane, and Donald Lehmann (2006), 'Brands and Branding: Research Findings and Future Priorities', *Marketing Science*, 25 (6), pp. 740–59.

Knudsen, Trond Riiber, Lars Finskud, Richard Tornblom, and Egil Hogna (1997), 'Brand Consolidation Makes a Lot of Economic Sense: But only One in Five Attempts Succeeds', *McKinsey Quarterly*, 4 (Autumn), pp. 189–94.

Lane, Vicki R. (1998), 'Brand Leverage Power: The Critical Role of Brand Balance', *Business Horizons*, (January–February), pp. 75–84.

Lodish, Leonard M., and Carl F. Mela (2007), 'If Brands are Built over Years, Why are they Managed over Quarters?' *Harvard Business Review*, July–August, pp. 104–12.

McWilliam, Gil (2000), 'Building Stronger Brands through Online Communities', *Sloan Management Review*, (Spring), pp. 43–54.

Papasolomou, I., and D. Varonis (2006), 'Building Corporate Branding through Internal Marketing: The Case of the UK Banking Industry', *Journal of Product and Brand Management*, 15 (1), pp. 37–47.

Pawle, John, and Peter Cooper (2006), 'Measuring Emotion—Lovemarks, the Future beyond Brands', *Journal of Advertising Research*, (March), pp. 38–48.

Petromilli, Michael, Dan Morrison, and Michael Millon (2002), "Brand Architecture: Building Brand Portfolio Value', *Strategy & Leadership*, 30 (5), pp. 22–9.

Prince, Melvin, and Mark Davies (2002), 'Co-branding Partners: What do they See in Each Other?' *Business Horizons*, (September–October), pp. 51–5.

Rao, Akshay R., and Robert W. Ruekert (1994), 'Brand Alliances as Signals of Product Quality,' *Sloan Management Review*, (Fall), pp. 87–97.

Ries, Al, and Laura Ries (1998), *The 11 Immutable Laws of Branding* (New York: Harper Business).

Ries, Al, and Laura Ries (2000), *The 11 Immutable Laws of Internet Branding* (New York: Harper Business).

Roberts, Kevin (2004), *Lovemarks: The Future Beyond Brands* (New York: Powerhouse Books).

Roberts, Kevin (2006), *The Lovemarks Effect: Winning in the Consumer Revolution* (New York: Powerhouse Books).

Simonin, B. L., and J. A. Ruth (1998), 'Is a Company Known by the Company it Keeps? Assessing the Spillover Effects of Brand Alliances on Consumer Brand Attitudes', *Journal of Marketing Research*, 35 (2), pp. 30–42.

Superbrands (2007), *The Top CoolBrands of 2007* (London: Superbrands Organisation).

Travis, Darryl (2000), *Emotional Branding* (Roseville, CA: Prima Venture Publishing).

Vishwanath, Vijay, and Jonathan Mark (1997), 'Your Brand's Best Strategy', *Harvard Business Review*, May–June, pp. 123–9.

Ward, Scott, Larry Light, and Jonathan Goldstine (1999), 'What High-tech Managers Need to Know about Brands', *Harvard Business Review*, July, pp. 85–96.

KEY ARTICLE ABSTRACTS

Aaker, David A., and Erich Joachimsthaler (2000), '**The Brand Relationship Spectrum: The Key to the Brand Architecture Challenge**', *California Management Review*, 42 (4), pp. 8–23.

A brand portfolio can contain a variety of different types of brand roles and relationships, and this complex structure of brands can be seen as analogous to the complex structures designed by an architect. This article presents a discussion of brand architecture, and the authors present their brand relationship spectrum to help companies manage a variety of brands and sub-brands.

Abstract: This paper introduces a powerful brand architecture tool—the brand relationship spectrum. It is intended to help architecture strategists employ insight into and subtlety to sub-brands, endorsed brands, and their alternatives. Sub-brands and endorsed brands can play a key role in creating a coherent and effective brand architecture.

Herremans, Irene M., John K. Ryans (Jr), and Raj Aggarwal (2000), '**Linking Advertising and Brand Value**', *Business Horizons*, (May–June), pp. 19–26.

This paper is particularly useful in that it argues that most brand valuation has been done for the purposes of external reporting, but little has really focused on valuations for internal strategic purposes. The authors suggest that marketing investment and advertising investment are one and the same for brand valuation purposes, and they propose a new ratio—advertising turnover—which examines the relationship between advertising expenditures and brand value.

Abstract: Regardless of whether it explicitly appears on the balance sheet, most top executives would agree that the value of a company's brands—its brand equity—is one of its most important assets. This is especially true for major consumer goods companies. While all intangible assets can be of considerable importance in today's competitive environment, this article focuses on brand equity, particularly on developing performance measures of various marketing and advertising activities as they relate to brand equity.

Keller, Kevin Lane (2000), '**The Brand Report Card**', *Harvard Business Review*, January–February, pp. 3–10.

The brand audit is a comprehensive examination of the various sources of brand equity from the perspective of the company as well as the consumer. This article presents a helpful tool for effective brand auditing, the Brand Report Card, which involves ratings from one (extremely poor) to ten (extremely good) for honest answers to a series of key brand equity questions.

Abstract: Building and properly managing brand equity has become a priority for companies of all sizes, in all types of industries, in all types of markets. After all, from strong brand equity flow customer loyalty and profits. The rewards of having a strong brand equity are clear. The problem is that few managers are able to step back and assess their brands' particular strengths and weaknesses objectively. The ten characteristics that the world's strongest brands have in common are identified and a Brand Report Card is constructed. The Brand Report Card is a systematic way for managers to think about how to grade their brand's performance for each of the ten characteristics. It helps to identify areas that need improvement, recognize areas in which the brand is strong, and learn more about how the brand is configured.

Lodish, Leonard M. and Carl F. Mela (2007), '**If Brands are Built over Years, Why are they Managed over Quarters?**' *Harvard Business Review*, July–August, pp. 104–12.

This insightful article suggests that brands have lost their luster for consumer-goods companies since they are too focused on short-term data and are not concerned about their brand's long-term health. They claim that too much reliance on price promotions at the expense of advertising and long-term brand building has severely weakened a number of once powerful brands. They explain how this has happened and provide a series of helpful suggestions for adding power and value for consumers.

Abstract: Brands are on the wane. Many consumer-goods companies blame the big-box discount retailers, but research suggests that companies have damaged their brands by investing too much in short-term price promotions and too little in long-term brand building. To rescue their brands and increase profitability, corporate managers must arm themselves with long-term measures of brand performance and use them to make smarter marketing decisions. Several factors explain the shortsightedness of brand management: the increased availability of weekly, or even hourly, scanner data, which show a clear link between discounts and immediate boosts in sales; the relative difficulty of measuring the effects of advertising, new-product development, and distribution—all of which can contribute to a brand's long-term health; the short tenure of most brand managers; and the near-term orientation of Wall Street analysts.

END OF CHAPTER 6 CASE STUDY

Unilever: corporate branding for a consumer products company? Can you have it both ways?

In January of 2009, Unilever decided that it would start including its corporate logo on all of its consumer ads in the UK and Ireland. They had already been doing this in some of their overseas markets (Latin America and Asia), and it was seen as a good mechanism for creating consistency across the variety of different products that they offer. The company has decided that they need greater consistency, since the person who buys one of their products is potentially likely to buy another of its products if they know that there is a corporate connection.

If one thinks through the logic behind these contentions, this seems to be counter-intuitive since the main reason that product-branding companies use individual stand-alone product names is because the main driver of purchase at that level of consumer goods is variety and price competitiveness. It is more difficult to build strong product loyalty when dealing with products which do not have a great deal of perceived consumer risk associated with them. If consumers are deal and variety prone, then the likelihood is that Unilever will have trouble keeping them loyal; therefore, the hope is that by having an array of product offerings in each category, then consumers who want another choice will shift to another of their products. This is a rationale behind Procter & Gamble and its offering of 26 different kinds of laundry detergent. If the consumer tries another product, the likelihood is that that other product will also be one of their products. For this kind of company, a stock out is far deadlier than excess inventory since a customer who cannot get what they want will potentially buy a product from another company and never come back again. Of course, cannibalization is a potential danger when a company brings out a new product in a category where they already have offerings if they do not increase sales, but the increase does not have to be very large to reap efficiency benefits.

If the idea actually sounds like a good one with consistency and connections across company products improving the potential for selection in the mind of the consumer, think about the danger that goes along with tying a corporate brand to these individual branded products. First of all, the likelihood is that some new products will fail after introduction, and if a product fails which ties itself to a common brand, the potential is that the corporate brand will be harmed by the failure. If the product-specific brand fails, then there is no direct mental connection to the corporate brand, and the customer does not connect the failure to the corporate brand. The other downside to this is when the mixture of products is not perceived as consistent, even if the company believes that it is. Take, for example, the very different advertising approaches for Dove products as opposed to the Lynx brand. The ads run in the UK for Lynx are not at all consistent with the feminine sensitive Dove ads. The view of women as having a natural beauty all of their own and the product » only enhancing their own internal beauty and the respect for different appearances and body shapes and sizes takes an almost diametrically opposed view to the approach used by Lynx to promote the sexual animal magnetism associated with the use of the Lynx product. The idea is that when a man uses Lynx, all women will sexually throw themselves at him, and what is particularly difficult to justify would be that the women who are shown are young, fit, and attractive. Are these two disparate products consistent with each other? If not, then putting them under a common corporate brand may be really confusing for consumers who make that brand connection. Why would Unilever feel that this is a good idea?

The top ten brands for Unilever in terms of advertising expenditures according to Nielsen figures for 2007 were as follows: (1) Dove; (2) Flora; (3) Persil; (4) Comfort; (5) Lynx; (6) Vaseline; (7) PG Tips; (8) Pot Noodle; (9) Peperami; and (10) Marmite. The idea is for the company to include its corporate logo in all consumer ads for these products in the UK and Ireland. Arguments that support the corporate brand connections can be seen in the strategies of Danone to connect their array of product-specific brands to a focus on health and well-being for all of their products. This served as a clear strategic direction for Danone as the company took corrective action to divest itself of any products that did not fit with this increased health consciousness. An example of a product that was dropped was the beer, Kronenbourg 1664. This worked quite well for Danone. The key, of course, is that the consistency of the offerings that are retained must be seen as uniform as possible. Inconsistencies are apt to produce cognitive dissonance for consumers, and this usually results in negative effect.

Another company that has tried to tie its products together in this way is SC Johnson, which promotes all of its products with its company logo and a catch phrase that says that SC Johnson is a family company, promoting the family values that the name immediately instills in the consumer. The Pledge brand and Glade home fresheners are both part of this array of products, and they are connected clearly to the corporate brand. This connection gets increasingly more difficult to make, the more there are products that the company maintains in its stable of offerings since the potential for lack of consistency increases. Another problem stems from any changes over time that have been seen in its company mission and corporate marketing strategies. The strategy followed by Danone really only works if the company lives out its stated mission and strategic orientation. If Danone were to have kept the Kronenbourg 1664 brand, there would have been concern among its consumers as to whether the company really meant what it said or whether it was trying to take advantage of a short-term trend in appealing to health concerns among consumers.

The most important thing for Unilever will be to assess the meaning of its corporate brand. It will have a set of attributes associated with it that will resonate with its consumers, so the company must carefully and objectively assess what its brand really means and what it signifies, and then it must work with that as a starting point. If it likes what it finds, then it will be important to ensure that this radiates throughout its corporate literature, mission, values, and strategies; and it will mean attempting to carefully assess the fit and consistency of its array of products with that focus in mind. It will probably mean eliminating those products that are not seen as consistent, but that will be necessary, as was found for Danone, to meet consumer expectations. If, on the other hand, it does not like what it learns from the assessment process, it will be necessary to take some kind of corrective action and then hope that the company is able to communicate with and convince its consumers that it is improving its product mix for their benefit. This is what Ford Motor Company should have focused on in the US market as American consumers automatically

» connected the Ford name to only one of its product offerings, the F-150 truck model. This meant that any other types of products, sedan, sports cars, SUVs, crossover vehicles, etc. were seen as inconsistent with the automatic recognition in the minds of consumers. This signified that any other product with the name Ford connected to it would be an uphill battle for consumers. That is a serious handicap to begin with, and it should have suggested to Ford that all other types of product offerings should have been cut back or eliminated to have the best chance for success.

Often, it is difficult for companies to admit that they are not capable of being 'all things to all people'. There is a danger inherent in applying a single corporate brand to a vast array of products that have their own stand-alone brands (house of brands) since there are often aspects to these products that do not fit with each other. One wonders if this is Unilever's true direction for the future, can they then possibly support Lynx and Dove as part of the same family of products? It is difficult to see how this would ever be possible, but the important thing is to let consumers tell the company how they feel without the company second-guessing its consumers by projecting its own views and values onto its consumers. If only Daimler had had the ability to see the lack of consistency in its alliance with Chrysler, it might never have allowed the alliance in the first place. It was clearly a lack of consistency from the beginning. Of course, some alliances have much better consistency to them and work well. Once again, this depends on the perceived fit amongst the various offerings. This is something that manufacturer's branding companies already understand. Coke took almost ten years testing Diet Coke before its introduction because they knew how important it was to get the consistency with its regular Coke brand just right, and Diet Coke is now the number three best-selling soft drink (not diet drink) in the world.

Source: This case was prepared by John Ford of Old Dominion University, Norfolk, Virginia as the basis for analysis and class discussion and not to illustrate either effective or ineffective handling of an administrative situation.

QUESTIONS

1. What are the advantages and disadvantages to Unilever's use of its corporate brand on all of its product advertisements in the UK and Ireland?
2. How would you carry out a proper assessment of the meaning of the corporate brand? Be as detailed as you can and discuss methodology issues.
3. How can the Danone and SC Johnson situations be used to help with this strategic decision on the part of Unilever?
4. How would you handle the product portfolio if you were in charge for Unilever? What changes would you make and why?
5. How would you strategically approach the new corporate branding strategy for Unilever? How would you handle advertising strategy?

7

Relational and sustainability strategies

LEARNING OBJECTIVES

- Examine the importance of developing relationships with customers
- Discuss ways in which marketers can assess customer desirability, and rank customers in terms of customer value to the firm
- Identify the various ways in which marketers can build loyalty with customers
- Provide an explanation of the importance of customer relationship management (CRM) systems and understand the differences between CRM for consumer marketers (B2C) and industrial marketers (B2B)
- Present various approaches to the building of customer databases with which to strategically address customer relationship building strategies, while also explaining the potential pitfalls inherent in ill-designed and ill-conceived data-mining approaches and relationship management systems
- Explain the strategies that will help the firm to create long-term relationships with its customers that can create competitive advantage and which can be sustained

CHAPTER AT A GLANCE

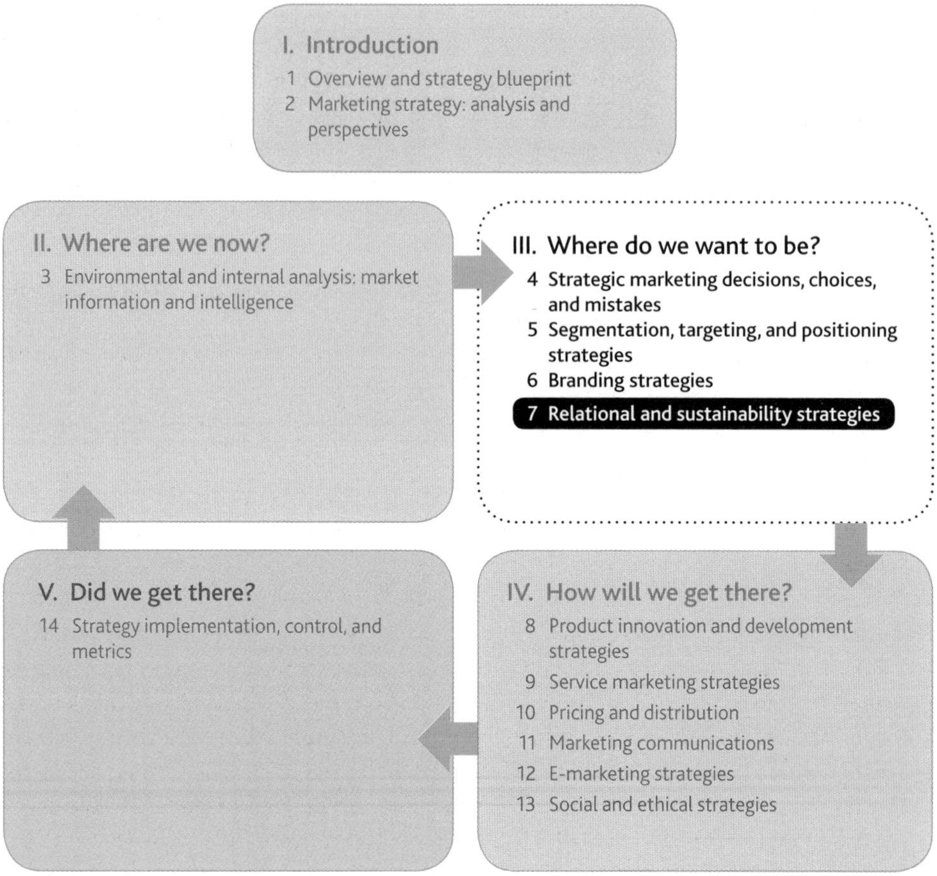

I. Introduction
1 Overview and strategy blueprint
2 Marketing strategy: analysis and perspectives

II. Where are we now?
3 Environmental and internal analysis: market information and intelligence

III. Where do we want to be?
4 Strategic marketing decisions, choices, and mistakes
5 Segmentation, targeting, and positioning strategies
6 Branding strategies
7 Relational and sustainability strategies

IV. How will we get there?
8 Product innovation and development strategies
9 Service marketing strategies
10 Pricing and distribution
11 Marketing communications
12 E-marketing strategies
13 Social and ethical strategies

V. Did we get there?
14 Strategy implementation, control, and metrics

Introduction

Marketing has gone through a rather pronounced paradigm shift over the past decade as B2C companies have changed their focus from transaction-based to relationship-centred. This has occurred as companies have slowly recognized that one-time purchases do not single-handedly keep companies in business. It is repeat purchases that are the key to success. The United States saw a number of industries during the 1960s and 1970s add significantly to their new business development capabilities, but what they did not realize was that the focus on new business development neglected the real lifeblood of the company, its loyal customers. Important accounts that are assumed to be a given are often taken for granted, and if all efforts are placed on the more fickle customers (who are also less profitable), then how much time is there left to spend paying attention to the needs of the loyal customers?

As companies like AT&T analysed their marketing activities and assessed their customer makeup, they realized that a good portion of their marketing efforts and expenditures were aimed at the smaller and more problematic accounts. They were one of the earlier companies that realized that the **80-20 rule** did have merit. This rule states that on average, an industry can expect that 80 per cent of its revenues will come from 20 per cent of its customer base. If one takes the time to consider carefully this ratio, the reciprocal suggests that 20 per cent of revenues then come from 80 per cent of the customer base. A more appropriate goal might be to spend 80 per cent of the time nurturing the relationships with that important 20 per cent of the customer base, leaving only the remaining 20 per cent of the time and effort devoted to the more problematic accounts. Support was empirically provided for this relationship by Frederick F. Reichheld in his 1996 book, *The Loyalty Effect*, in which he reported that it is five times more costly to bring in a new customer than it is to keep an existing customer.

Customer lifetime value (CLTV) has recently become a vital consideration for many companies as they recognize that happy customers are loyal customers who not only spread their satisfaction by word of mouth to friends, colleagues, and relatives, but also spend increasing amounts on the purchase of particular products/services over time. CLTV is the present value of the future profits that will accrue from the customer's lifetime purchases. The company must attempt to measure future earnings from the customer as well as be able to subtract from those earnings the cost of acquiring and maintaining the relationship with the customer. The key issue is to determine CLTV for each individual customer or group of customers so that each group can be assessed to determine the proper investments that will be necessary to make in each customer to build meaningful relationships and retain customers. This sets up an important future revenue stream that cannot be overlooked. General Motors Cadillac division analysed CLTV and determined that a Cadillac customer will spend approximately $US350,000 over their lifetime (Best, 2005). This would include both the purchase of automobiles and maintenance. One can see how problematic it can become to lose that customer early in their product purchase life cycle. Each lost customer represents hundreds of thousands of dollars of lost revenue. Best (2005) also illustrates CLTV in a description of credit card customers over a five-year period. Research in the US has shown that the acquisition of a new credit card customer costs the credit card company approximately $51 per customer. These new customers will generate an average company profit in the first year of $30, this escalates to $42 in the second year, and will grow to $55 by the fifth year. The obvious goal should be to retain the customer, since bringing in each new customer generates a loss each time.

In a recent *Harvard Business Review* article, Detlef Schoder (2007) suggests that companies be careful to make CLTV calculations based on realistic options, and he suggests that the best way to do this involves a five-step process: (1) estimate the probability of purchase and dollar amounts expected to be spent for a set of customers using the RFM (recency, frequency, and monetary value) approach; (2) then calculate costs per customer per period that are amassed; (3) both the amounts generated in steps (1) and (2) above should be used to estimate the profit contribution for each customer over the time horizon of interest; (4) then for each period, the key will be to determine whether the expected future profit contribution will be negative; and, finally, (5) to calculate the CLTV that includes the option value (i.e., the value of dropping the customer). The point is to assess with reasonable calculations what the savings might be if the customer were dropped at any particular period of time.

The purpose of this chapter is to present the various ways in which companies can build and maintain strong and profitable relationships with their customers, and the need to look beyond a short-term focus to the development of longer-term relationships with their important constituencies in order to achieve competitive advantages which are sustainable into the future.

Relationship marketing in the B2C context

What is **relationship marketing**? It is the development of long-term and intimate relationships between buyers and sellers. It involves open communications and the ability to know the customer or client so well that changes in wants and needs can be anticipated before they become critical. This means that companies really have to communicate effectively and often with their customers or clients. The problem is that all customers are not equal. One of the best frameworks in which to discuss the nature of different customers is the loyalty ladder, as popularized by Adrian Payne (2000) adapted from the original work of Raphel (1980). This loyalty ladder (see Figure 7.1) includes the following designations from least to most desirable: suspects, prospects, customers, clients (hostages/mercenaries/terrorists), supporters, advocates, and partners. This framework presents an effective mechanism for discussing relevant costs and communications strategies.

Suspects

Suspects are individuals who are not yet even mildly warm leads for the selling company. They are possibly prospects, but they are not yet interested in the selling company's products or services. These are probably not the kinds of individuals that companies should spend much time or effort on to develop relationships with. There are some industries that simply do not lend themselves to customer or client relationships and retention. In the used-car industry, the fickle

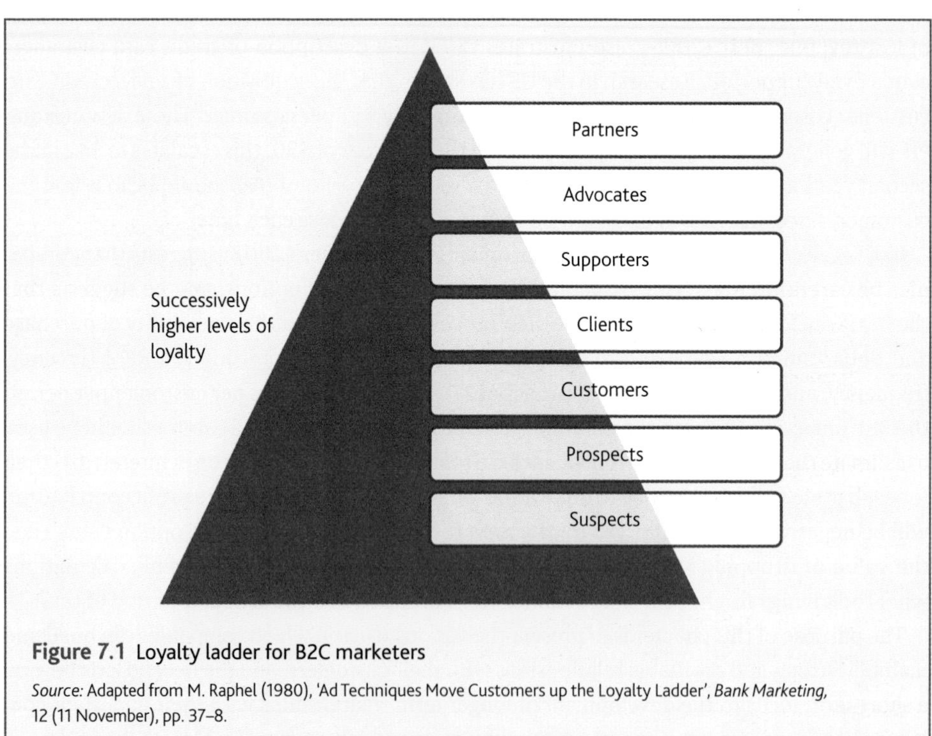

Figure 7.1 Loyalty ladder for B2C marketers

Source: Adapted from M. Raphel (1980), 'Ad Techniques Move Customers up the Loyalty Ladder', *Bank Marketing*, 12 (11 November), pp. 37–8.

nature of these customers would argue against spending time and effort building rapport and friendship since they will likely go where they get the lowest price in future transactions. The cost would most certainly outweigh the benefits. The firm must develop some kind of mechanism to determine whether the suspect is worth spending time with. One promising approach to this kind of assessment is **customer equity**, as posited by Blattberg and Deighton (1996).

Customer equity

From a financial standpoint, marketing budget setting becomes the job of balancing what is spent on customer or client acquisition with what is spent on retention. Blattberg and Deighton (1996) refer to this as the **customer equity test**, and in order to estimate this amount, the authors suggest that the firm first measures each customer's expected contribution to offsetting the company's fixed costs over their expected lifetime. Then, expected contributions to net present value are discounted at the rate set by the company as its target rate of return for any marketing investments. And, finally, the company adds together all of the discounted expected contributions across all of the company's current customers. The authors suggest that it is quite similar to assessing the value of a real estate portfolio.

An excellent overview of the relationship process was proposed by Slater et al. (2009) in a recent issue of *Marketing Management* magazine. The process is shown in Figure 7.2.

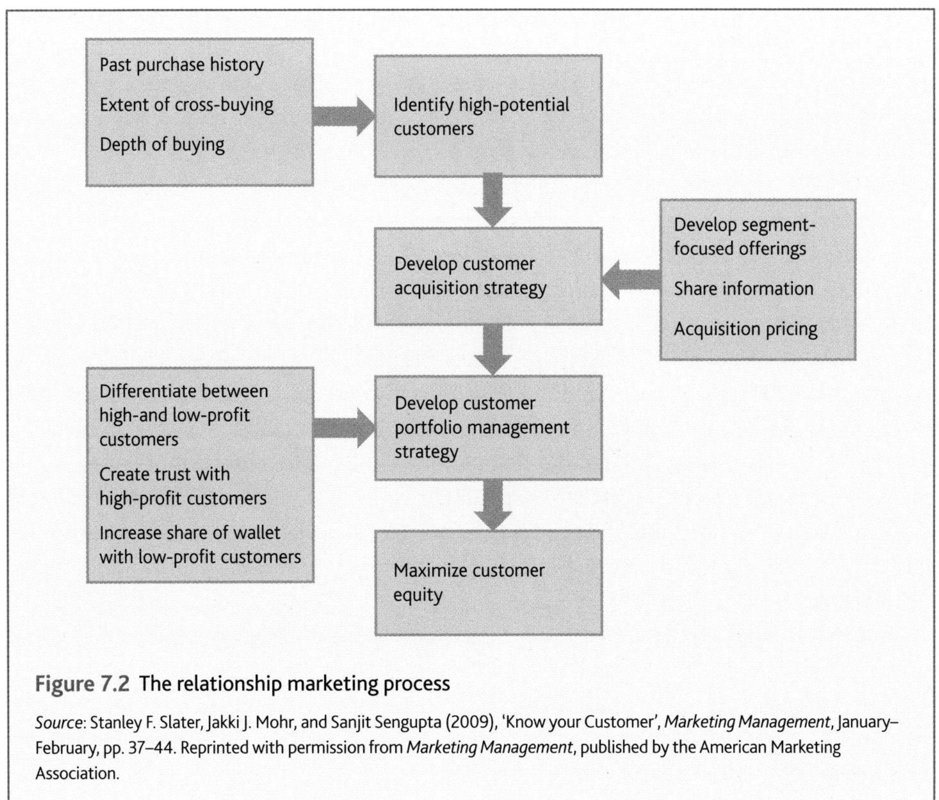

Figure 7.2 The relationship marketing process

Source: Stanley F. Slater, Jakki J. Mohr, and Sanjit Sengupta (2009), 'Know your Customer', *Marketing Management*, January–February, pp. 37–44. Reprinted with permission from *Marketing Management*, published by the American Marketing Association.

The key steps in the process are as follows: (1) **identify high-potential customer or clients**; (2) **develop a customer acquisition strategy** (Blattberg et al. (2001) identified four generic acquisition strategies that should help balance investment with returns—*(a)* full throttle or low risk/high return; *(b)* slingshot or high risk/high return; *(c)* pay as you go or low risk/low return; and *(d)* divest/restructure or high risk/low return); (3) **develop the customer portfolio management strategy**; and (4) **maximize customer equity**. Gupta et al. (2004) showed the profitability that can be found in relationship building with their demonstration that a one per cent increase in customer retention produces a three to seven per cent increase in profitability. This, of course, has shifted many companies to managing their firms as a portfolio of customer or clients rather than as a portfolio of different products/services. What Slater et al. (2009) claim is the problem, however, is that very few companies have a systematic way of identifying the best customers for relationship building and developing effective customer or client acquisition and retention strategies.

From the customer equity standpoint, the suspect is probably a poor candidate for the time and effort that would be required for acquisition, and there would be little guarantee of profitability.

Prospects

A better candidate would be found in the prospect. This is a warm lead, who has interest in your product but has not yet made a purchase. Customer equity would probably be higher for the prospect than for the suspect; however, interest is not a guarantee of purchase, and the other question that should be asked is what is the probability of purchase? This is not a regular buyer of your products or services, and the problem is that the costs of acquiring and retaining the prospect may far outweigh their potential lifetime value. The old methods of adding product selection and/or cutting prices to attract prospects may be highly problematic as adding new products/services adds to excessive inventory, and cutting prices reduces margins and intensifies competition across sellers. This argues for greater focus or expertise to increase the likelihood of attraction of interested prospects. If prospects are a major focal point for the company, direct marketing can help to reach prospects where they live. It also helps to have salespeople interact with prospects and get known and recognized. The reason for this is that relationships are based upon familiarity and trust. Spending too much time focusing on prospects as opposed to others higher on the loyalty ladder may be problematic as there is little assurance that getting them to buy will lead to a lifetime of loyalty, especially in the case of lower-level consumer products where customers or clients may be more deal and variety prone. Again, the need is to clearly identify the various levels of customers served by the firm and concentrate efforts, depending upon the value of those different customers.

Given good potential prospects, the hope is to put genuine effort into building rapport and encouraging the building of relationships with the prospect in the hopes of moving them into the customer category, but Mini Case Study 7.1 presents a discussion of the problems inherent in company employees going through the 'motions' rather than honestly and warmly approaching the relationship-building process.

MINI CASE STUDY 7.1 Faux relationships create ill will

The attempt on the part of banks to build rapport and even loyalty with their customers is something that has been at best reluctantly embraced by a number of institutions in the US and the UK as intense competition breeds the need to revisit the whole understanding of the customer service delivery process. There is nothing more enlightening for a bank than to go through the process of service blueprinting in which each step the customer might go through to obtain the bank's services is carefully examined, including the front-office personnel, back-office personnel, and behind-the-scenes processes. Why this is often so helpful is that the typical customer is dealing most of the time with the counter staff; therefore, the counter staff is the first line of impression building for the financial institution. It doesn't matter how nice and personable and trustworthy the officers of the bank are if the counter staff are difficult to deal with. Since the service itself cannot be separated from the deliverer of the service, it is important for bank officials to realize that the counter staff are the service. Each and every interaction between the counter staff and the customer is a service encounter, and the customer is affected by that encounter.

Part of the problem has been that counter staff were not jobs sought by employees as an end position in a bank. In bank management training programmes, being a member of the counter staff was often seen as a stepping stone for employees to move into the branch systems in management positions. Why this has always been problematic is that people were not joining banks to become counter staff. This would obviously create morale issues among the counter staff if they were not advancing through the system towards managerial positions at their expected levels.

If counter staff are end jobs in themselves, with sufficient reward and advancement mechanisms, then the job becomes attractive to the appropriate types of individuals, and the customer experience becomes one that is positively reinforced each time the customer interacts with counter staff that know and relate to them. Of course, this means that counter staff must be hired with people skills and empowered to a certain extent to personalize what they do, which means that bank management must have trust in their counter staff to allow any empowerment to take place. This requires a major paradigm shift as banks that are reorienting themselves to become the banks of 'choice' because they are preferred for their 'people skills' and 'customer orientation' cannot convince customers of this and change their previous perceptions unless they live out what they say in their daily treatment of the customers.

There is nothing more frustrating than entering a bank to hear the required 'Hello!' or 'Good morning!' and then to look up to return the response only to see that no one is even looking at you any longer! The point is that just by saying that you are customer-orientated does not make it so, and unless the employees really like what they are doing and enjoy the relationships that they are involved in, there will be no real warmth in the exchange. Being told that you must say 'Hello!' to each and every customer does not make a relationship happen. Another issue is that if you are lucky enough finally to build up a nice relationship with a personal counter staff, they are likely to be moved to another branch and that relationship will therefore be lost. The point is that service firms like banks should really not do something unless they truly embrace the idea completely and live it out in what they do and say, as going through the motions is far more frustrating than not even trying in the first place.

Customers

A customer, of course, is someone who has bought your product or service. The game is to try to enhance that individual or company's purchase frequency and volume over time, so that the customer becomes increasingly profitable and valuable to the company. The important question, which really must be asked, is whether all customers are 'good' customers. In the services industries, many firms have learned that customer interactions can be problematic. Services are finding that it is necessary to manage the service experience very carefully to ensure that it meets the expectations of key customers. This requires that important customers do not interact with those who might negatively affect customer value perceptions.

Imagine the restaurant that becomes an important setting for a romantic evening for an affluent couple, when the maître d' brings a loud and hard-drinking group to a nearby table. Loud voices and interactions could certainly impede the ambience for the romantic setting. The restaurant must understand who its important customers are and keep others from participating in the service who might harm the service quality perceptions of those key customers. This would mean turning some customers away. In the example above, however, it is not immediately clear which are the most important customers. The restaurant would have to have this clearly understood and handle things accordingly. If the loud and obnoxious group are regulars and spend £500 per month dining at that restaurant, they would be seen as potentially far more important than the romantic couple who come once a year and spend only £80.

This raises the question of how to deal with different and potentially incompatible consumers. Compatibility management is a concept from the services literature that is quickly gaining support for use in dealing with the mixing of different types of customers.

Compatibility management

Much depends on a thorough understanding of the target customers and spending patterns. This is referred to in the services literature as **compatibility management** and is an important consideration for service businesses where customer interactions can significantly affect the service experience. Some companies can adjust for different customers by using different pricing and different venues to keep incompatible customers from interacting with each other. Sporting events and concerts provide opportunities for wealthier patrons to separate themselves from others through differential pricing. Paying top prices allows closer access to the sports pitch or to the acts on the stage. The idea, of course, is to provide the best experiences for those who are desirable and keeping them happy.

What becomes particularly meaningful once the company has a viable customer base is to examine the variety of customers served and decide on a tiering of those customers. Especially in the B2C world of myriad customers, relationships with all customers might not be efficient or effective. If customer lifetime value (CLTV) can be calculated for each relevant customer group, then the profitability of each customer group can be assessed. As a result, one particularly relevant approach to ranking or prioritizing customers is based upon the impact which a group of customers specifically has on firm profitability. Zeithaml et al.'s (2001) customer profitability pyramid is also gaining wide acceptance.

Customer profitability pyramid

Zeithaml et al. (2001) proposed the creation of a customer pyramid based upon profitability for companies trying to improve long-term firm performance. The authors argue that tiering based upon profitability has become a high priority, especially for service firms, like FedEx, Bank of America, The Limited, Hallmark, and GE Capital Corporation. This would also have value for consumer and industrial products companies. This is a natural extension beyond segmentation that was covered in the previous chapter. The authors suggest that profitability tiering allows the company to manage the customer mix for maximum profitability. The firm can build stronger associations between service quality and profitability as well as provide an effective tool for optimal resource allocation. The point is to match up customized services and products to customer utility, ultimately producing greater customer value, which in turn would lead to higher profits.

The authors suggest that there are four necessary conditions that must be met to allow the use of customer tiers. First of all, **profitability tiers must vary and have identifiable profiles**. Profile descriptions will lead marketers to identify optimal marketing activities to reach different tiers. Second, **customers in different tiers must view service quality differently**. Different customer expectations of service quality allow the company to develop optimal bundles of attributes to offer the various tiers. Third, **different factors must drive customer acquisition and increases in purchase volume**. As a result, the company can acquire new customers and stay with them as they move to higher-profit tiers over time. They can meet perceptual service quality expectations in different ways as the customer moves to subsequently higher tiers. The point is to get the customer early and stay with them as they move up. Lastly, **improvements in service quality should have different profit impacts for different customer tiers**. Theoretically, higher tiers should see greater customer responses from improvements in perceived service quality in terms of new customer development, business volume, and the average profit level for each customer.

Using empirical data, Zethaml et al. (2001) proposed the use of a customer pyramid, with four different tiers based upon gradation in metal values. These four tiers are as follows (from the least profitable level to the highest): (1) the **lead tier** (the bottom of the pyramid—includes those customers who are costing the company money rather than bringing in any profits); (2) the **iron tier** (second tier from the bottom—provide volume for the company but do not buy enough to warrant any special treatment); (3) the **gold tier** (second tier from the top—high volume but profits may be limited due to the desire for price discounts); and (4) the **platinum tier** (top of the pyramid—customers who are heavy users, loyal, profitable, and not price sensitive).

Using the alchemy analogy, the authors suggest that strategic relationship building can move customers into higher and more desirable tiers of the pyramid. So the authors suggest that **to turn gold customers into platinum customers**, the following strategies are recommended: (1) become a full-service provider (if the customer can get everything they need from the firm, they will become better customers); (2) provide outsourcing (taking on something that the customer used to have to do themselves); (3) increase brand impact through line extensions (tying additional complementary offerings in with the company's umbrella of offerings); (4) create structural bonds (providing customized services that utilize technology and can help the customer be more productive); and (5) offer service guarantees (ensuring that the customer is always satisfied by making it right).

In order to **turn iron customers into gold customers**, the following strategies are recommended: (1) reduce the customer's non-monetary costs (reduction of search costs); (2) add meaningful brand names (adding brands to the offering lines that are perceived to be better quality than the others normally carried); (3) become knowledgeable about the customer using technology (building databases that can add customer knowledge and pinpoint recommendations); (4) become knowledgeable about the customer by leveraging intermediaries (using dealers to gather information about local needs of customers); (5) develop frequency programmes (the higher the use, the more accrued benefits for the customer); and (6) create strong recovery programmes (finding out when customers are disappointed and correcting the problem before the customer is lost).

Finally, in terms of lead customers, the authors suggest that a firm should only attempt to **move customers up from lead to iron if there is good future potential**. Otherwise, it might be best to send these customers on their way, looking for a different provider. If there is strong potential, the authors suggest the following strategies: (1) raise prices (adding prices for services that customers previously had received for free); and (2) reduce costs (find less expensive ways to deal with these customers—like remote automated sites).

One problem is that more research is needed connecting the profitability pyramid to CLTV. While there is usually strong support for the argument that higher levels of loyalty will be associated with greater customer lifetime value, there are still a few gaps in the research. In particular, it is not yet clear as to whether the advocate is any more profitable than the mercenary (client). More work is clearly needed.

Clients

Clients are regular customers. Customers become clients when they have some level of trust in the seller and believe that the seller's offerings will be beneficial to them. This is the first development of a relationship between the buyer and seller; however, it is not necessarily a relationship that will last forever, and it may not be a relationship that remains mutually beneficial for both of the parties involved. Payne (2000) raises the issue of clients who are potentially difficult or problematic for the seller. Some clients might begin to feel as though they are **hostages** to the seller due to some leverage that the seller utilizes over them. The loss of a feeling of mutual benefit raises questions about the life expectancy of that relationship, and the client may look for any opportunity to jump to another seller that appears. For a relationship to properly exist, there should be mutual benefits that are achieved by the parties to the relationship.

Another type of problematic client is the **mercenary**. This type of client is one that only appears to have loyalty to the relationship, but may hold the tenuousness of that relationship over the seller's head to maintain some kind of leverage over the seller. The idea is that this kind of client is not involved in a meaningful relationship, and, again, one sidedness in a relationship creates instability. The issue with the mercenary is that they can easily be attracted by the 'better deal' from someone else in the industry.

The other type of client that becomes a serious problem for the seller is the **terrorist**. Now the client is in a position to hold the company as a hostage rather than the reverse situation. What kind of client becomes a terrorist? An unsatisfied client! When companies can make unhappy customers pleased, they can raise their loyalty level significantly over what it was before the complaint. In the services literature this is known as the recovery paradox. The customer who has a problem but is handled successfully by the company to alleviate that problem becomes even more committed to the relationship than they were before the problem occurred. The point to be made here is that even your best customers might at one time become unhappy with you for whatever reason. The key is to open the doors of true communication with your good customers to ensure that they are remaining satisfied with the relationship. A client who has a problem, which is not immediately rectified, stands the chance of becoming a severe problem. One unhappy client can tell anywhere from seven to eleven others about their dissatisfaction, which cannot only negatively affect other existing clients, but also discourage others from becoming new clients (Pruden, 1995). Ritson (2003) found in a study of disgruntled US consumers that dissatisfied customers took steps to undermine the company involved by creating 'symbols of defiance' out of company logos. Examples include Shell's logo being changed to 'Hell', and Greenpeace's modification of Esso to 'E$$O'. These active detractors can wreak a certain amount of havoc on target companies.

Monitoring of client satisfaction becomes an important barometer to measure the potential for changes in relationships so that proper corrective action can be taken to shore up the relationship. Of course, the use of marketing for the sake of marketing is not necessarily a good way to handle this situation. As Pruden (1995) states it, relationship strategists must be careful not to let 'frequency marketing' take the place of 'aftermarketing'. Both of these can be considered as relationship marketing. Pruden (1995) defines **frequency marketing** as a strategy aimed at identifying best customers, keeping them, and increasing their expenditures through the development of intimate long-term relationships. On the surface, this would appear to mirror relationship marketing; however, Pruden suggests that there is an important difference. Pruden (1995) considers that relationship marketing should be more like 'aftermarketing', which focuses on the retention of more than just a small percentage of best customers. **Aftermarketing** involves long-term relationships being built, in which the firm actively attempts to move customers up the loyalty ladder and tries to minimize the outflow of unhappy buyers. Pruden suggests that this may not be practicable for all businesses. While direct merchants can effectively utilize frequency marketing, he suggests that aftermarketing is preferable for manufacturers of products and services who depend upon mass distribution.

Is the customer always right?

A relevant question to raise here is whether the company should rush to coddle all clients who appear to have a problem. It is possible that a client's needs may have changed over time, and that the company is not able to cost-effectively cater to that client's new needs. In that situation, it may be preferable for the company to look at outsourcing that customer rather than cater to them in a way that might prove detrimental to others of its more profitable clients. The key is to monitor continuously the relationships to see what is happening. Some customers can effectively be re-energized, while others cannot. The company is best served by realizing that some clients may no longer be as profitable and beneficial as they once were and in a positive way move them to another provider (with the hope of keeping them from becoming a terrorist). The idea is to help the customer remain satisfied while being moved to another supplier. The point is to make the transition as smooth and painless as possible.

What about unfair customers? An **unfair customer** is one who does not act in a manner in which decency, care for the welfare of others, and reasonableness are guiding principles (Berry and Seiders, 2007). These individuals can hurt the company and its employees while not engaged in behaviour which is illegal. Berry and Seiders (2007) point out five particular types of problematic customers: (1) **verbal abusers** who take their frustrations out on company employees in disrespectful and offensive ways, thereby presenting a problem not only for the service employee involved, but also for other customers within the vicinity hearing the complaints; (2) **blamers** who take aim not at the employees as much as anything that the company does and are particularly problematic in services contexts since as co-producers, they take no share in the blame for any failures; (3) **rule breakers** who handle the company and its employees using their own rules rather than following the policies and procedures established by the company; (4) **opportunists** who are also out for their own gains by creating problems and demanding compensation for their difficulties; and (5) **returnaholics** who are part opportunists and part rule-breakers creating problems excessively so that they can continually return products.

How should the company deal with these unfair customers? Berry and Seiders suggest the following strategies for dealing with them. First, they suggest that **the company should manage customers according to a standard of behaviour** (companies should have environments for dealing with anyone in which respect is an integral part and managers will need to manage customers just as they manage employees). Second, **fair customers should not be penalized** (unfair customers must be dealt with fairly but firmly in a system which is built around the fair and ethical majority). Third, **managers need to plan for possible unfair situations involving unfair actions on the part of customers and be ready for them when they occur** (this involves training employees and managers systematically how to deal with inappropriate actions). Finally, **managers need to deal fairly and firmly with customers and not allow inappropriate actions to be rewarded.**

McGovern and Moon (2007) suggest that management be prepared when assessing the potential for customer dissatisfaction by asking the following four questions: (1) **Are the most profitable customers the ones who have the greatest reason to be dissatisfied with the company's performance**? (If so, their customers are clearly not getting the appropriate level of value from the company's offerings.) (2) **Does the company have rules that they want customers to break so that they can generate excess profits** (having premiums associated with passing some procedural limit which will be important to establish)? (3) **Does the company make it difficult for customers to follow the rules and do they help the customers to violate them**? (If yes, this will lead to problems for customers that will grow over time.) (4) **Does the company rely on legal contracts to keep customers from leaving**? (This will also lead to problems.)

Supporters

Supporters are those who buy everything you produce that they can use. However, while they are supportive of your company and its products and services, and while they will spread good word-of-mouth for you, they will not necessarily be motivated to the level of an advocate (see below). They will not go out of their way to recruit others to your company. You convert a client to a supporter through the provision of great service. The idea here is to start to find ways to reward clients for their purchases and loyalty to move them to supporters. The idea is to find ways to provide extra value and benefits for the buyer. In terms of communications at this point, the job of the marketer is to avoid the danger of over-promising. The customer has to have their expectations met and surpassed, if possible. Over-promising sets up the potential for disconfirmed expectations. Strategically, however, the profitability of the supporter must not be exceeded by the cost of providing the extra value that motivates them to become more than clients.

Advocates

The advocate is a coveted position. It is the consumer who buys your products and services and actively recruits others to do the same. They are valuable commodities. These are the individuals that you particularly want to keep happy. One way to do that is with the kinds of incentives that loyalty schemes carry with them.

Loyalty schemes

Loyalty schemes are programmes that are established by companies to provide added value to the regular purchaser, as opposed to the irregular customer. It provides increasing benefits for increasing levels of company loyalty. In the UK, two particular loyalty schemes have been especially successful. One is Tesco and its use of the Clubcard, and the other is the loyalty scheme created by Nectar, which is believed to boast the largest number of cardholders in the UK. The idea is to build up points or credits for purchases, which allow the consumer to get rewards such as discounts off a series of special products or announcements about new offerings that no others receive. Frequent-flyer miles programmes for the airlines are also loyalty programmes, whereby travellers build up miles that can be used to upgrade classes of service or even for free airline tickets. There are a number of airlines and other organizations which offer their own credit cards which can build reward points that can be used every time a purchase is made using that credit card. These programmes are all designed to keep the customer satisfied and loyal and to entice them to increase their use of the company's products and services.

Loyalty schemes have their drawbacks as well. An article written by Dowling and Uncles that was published in 1997 in *MIT Sloan Management Review* raised some serious questions about loyalty schemes. The authors suggested that loyalty may not offer better returns than price cuts, a movement to the use of everyday low prices, expanded advertising programmes, or the expansion of distribution outlets. They argue that this may be due to the fact that most loyal customers are polygamous. In other words, they tend to shift back and forth across two or three favourite brands and rarely focus on one single brand. They challenge some of the norms that have been accepted regarding the use of loyalty schemes. They raise questions about whether repeat-purchase loyal customers are any less expensive to sell to, whether they buy more than others, whether loyal customers are any less price-sensitive, and whether loyalty-scheme members are willing to recommend certain sellers any more than other satisfied customers. People at the consumer-goods level tend to look mostly for variety, special deals, and availability.

The authors provide the examples of breakfast cereals, car rentals, and fast food to support their arguments. They also point out that in higher-level programmes like airline frequent-flyer programmes, customers on average belong to three different airline programmes. Most loyalty schemes appear to be focused on either big or small brands. Big brands generally have more buyers and they buy more frequently, but small brands have fewer buyers who also buy less at any one time. For these brands, the authors propose that the only way to grow market share is to get a greater number of buyers through a better distribution system, as opposed to getting current customers to buy more. The conclusion they offer is that only those loyalty schemes that build presence and encourage stocking are appropriate for the consumer marketplace. As a result, the only appropriate candidates for loyalty programmes are high-involvement products where the actual scheme enhances the value proposition of the product (a Northwest Airlines Visa card to build Northwest Airlines frequent-flyer miles). They do not believe that indirect benefits like a bank offering frequent-flyer miles are effective.

Dowling and Uncles (1997) also conclude that for loyalty programmes to be effective, they should be fully costed and the incentive to motivate the next consumer purchase should be maximized (the more spent, the higher the reward). Done correctly, loyalty schemes can neutralize competitor programmes, broaden brand distribution, and enhance brand image and increase value, but when low-involvement goods are involved, this should not be attempted other than to counter a competitors' offering.

A recent study in *Harvard Business Review* by Nunes and Dreze (2006) provides additional suggestions for those companies planning to use loyalty schemes. The authors suggest that loyalty schemes can reasonably be expected to do five things for the companies that use them: (1) keep customers from defecting; (2) win a greater share of the wallet; (3) prompt customers to make additional purchases; (4) provide insight into customer behaviour and preferences; and (5) create profit.

Nunes and Dreze (2006) also provide five key mistakes to avoid when using loyalty schemes: (1) avoid setting up a new commodity (do not just use discounting to promote greater degrees of disloyalty); (2) do not provide rewards for those who are not loyal (like grocery stores who provide their membership cards who end up merely rewarding those who own cards, rather than bringing in new customers to get the cards); (3) do not provide awards for volume and not for profitability (do not just track purchase quantity, as it does not necessarily reflect profitability); (4) avoid giving away too much (do not cut into profits if costless rewards can make the customer happy); and (5) do not promise something that you ultimately cannot deliver (the lower bounds of premium service must never look worse than standard service). The authors suggest that used correctly, loyalty schemes can still be very effective, but company management must keep a close watch on the scheme development and implementation, and they must be willing to drop the programme if it does not live up to expectations.

The point is to convert the supporter to an outright advocate. As they are important to the company, they need to be communicated with even more than the lower-level consumers on the ladder. These individuals need to feel as though they belong to the company. They are the platinum customers on the profitability pyramid. They need to be treated in a special way. If things are done correctly, the supporters will want to become advocates as they see that there are additional benefits associated with reaching that higher status on the ladder. These are also the individuals who make great testimonial spokespersons to reach others who want to be like them. Peers can significantly affect the opinions of others like themselves.

Lindstrom (2005) explains that these individuals need to be fully engaged by the company in almost every aspect of the business, from R&D to website design. This creates a personal sense of ownership which helps to make a person a true advocate for the company. The power of word-of-mouth at this level can be seen in the results of NOP World's 2004 Global Brand Advocacy Survey, which surveyed 30,000 consumers worldwide and found that the highest levels of brand advocacy in the world were for Mercedes Benz, with 59 per cent of those surveyed considering themselves 'active brand advocates'. Other brands with high levels of advocates were BMW (53 per cent), Toyota (51 per cent), Nokia (50 per cent), and Sony (46 per cent). Word-of-mouth is believed by many consumers to be the best mechanism for recommendation for a company.

A good examination of the advantages and disadvantages of loyalty programmes can be found in Mini Case Study 7.2, which compares the programme for Tesco's Clubcard and Sainsbury's Nectar.

MINI CASE STUDY 7.2 Clubcard or Nectar?

Loyalty programmes are alive and well in the UK, and the competition around the use of points and perceived value for the customer is both hot and heavy. Take, for example, the battle between Tesco and its UK Clubcard and Sainsbury's Nectar scheme. Tesco is concerned because they recently realized that many of the accrued discounts earned by the Clubcard customers were not being utilized. They launched the Clubcard programme back in 1994, and in their latest offer, they are proposing that when customers use their points many of its products prices will be cut in half. Obviously, they want people to use the accrued value and not let it just languish. Tesco runs its own programme, but Sainsbury's does not run the Nectar programme. Nectar is independent and is offered through a variety of firms besides Sainsbury's.

The problem, then, becomes management and control. How do the programmes work? Which programme is better? Tesco is perceived to be the winner in the competition with Sainsbury's. Tesco uses its programme to collect valuable consumer data, which it regularly uses to modify its marketing mix to improve its performance and focus on bringing value to its customers. They seem to understand their customers and are willing to do what it takes to make them happy, as is shown in its new stand to cut prices for programme participants to get them to use their accrued points. The way Tesco set up its programme, participants would receive one point per GB£1 spent, and the one point would have a value of one penny. What this would mean is that for every GB£100 spent, you would get a voucher that would be worth GB£1. Nectar works differently in that the customer would get two points for every GB£1 spent, but each point would be worth 50 pence (rather than 1 pence). The benefit for Nectar would be in the ability to collect points (at a variety of different rates) at a variety of retailers and other companies. When shopping online, a number of different companies offer Nectar points. So doesn't this make Nectar of greater value to customers because of variety and versatility? Not necessarily.

In recessionary times, what becomes particularly relevant is immediate savings. So, in these situations, saving money becomes more valuable than accruing a large number of points. Since people were hording points with the Clubcard membership (which they could then use for four-for-one types of deals and magazine subscriptions, etc.), Tesco realized that the best way to help people and add value was through a major cost-cutting campaign and the introduction of its new 'Double your money' campaign will »

» reap immediate benefits for its users across a vast array of products (e.g., jewellery, cosmetics, and clothing). The new plan will also allow the doubling of point totals for certain purchases bought online or in the stores, and their concern is to trigger the customers' use of the points that they have been building since it will do them immediate good in the store or online. Tesco even created what they call the 'Missing Millions' team to tell customers that they have accrued points reaching their maturity and that they had best use them.

While it appears that Nectar has more to offer, especially since there are ways to get more points quicker, the range of special offers for Nectar are not as impressive as those of Tesco. A recent example included the ability of Nectar users to get adult cinema tickets at children's prices, which is quite weak in comparison. The issue here is that just allowing points to accrue quickly is not the only thing that matters to customers, and Tesco has been able to continually monitor the effects of its offerings and maintain the perceived value for its Clubcard customers more effectively than Sainsbury's with its use of the Nectar programme.

Partners

Partners are the ultimate level of relationship as they share in everything. For the B2B situation, this is where the buyer and seller enter into a joint position of commitment where, for example, the partner modifies their way of working or behaviour to accommodate the seller. For example, a company may buy a payroll software system from a consulting firm and have to alter its processes in making payments to its staff. Obviously, this will produce the highest level of commitment to the relationship. Few B2C settings lend themselves as well to this kind of a relationship, though may be seen, for example, when Microsoft brings out a new version of Office and users have to learn new ways of working that they then get used to. An example in the B2B market is Allegiance Healthcare. The company shrink-wraps it medical supplies and labels them specifically for the destination within a hospital. This eliminates the need for hospitals to have a dedicated system to direct general incoming supplies to the relevant wards where needed. Thus, supplies are shrink-wrapped by Allegiance and sent direct to the ward that requested them.

When buyers are made to feel a part of the company, then we are verging into partnership territory. In a partnership, both parties have a vested interest in the continuation of the partnership, along with the commensurate trust and commitment made.

Relationships and loyalty in B2B markets

So how do things differ when B2B marketing is involved? When compared to B2C markets, B2B markets are characterized as dealing with fewer customers, larger transactions, customized products, negotiated prices, values are often determined by usages, and brands are not as critical as often as the relationships that are built between the buyers and the sellers. In this case, selling is far more complex as buyers may be groups instead of individuals and selling teams may be important, although there is often a key sales person who deals with a key customer. These potential relationships become critical. These target markets are often made up of one instead of thousands or even tens of thousands of individual customers. The problem is that using the same types of mechanisms as are used in B2C markets to build relationships is often not effective in B2B market situations.

Narayandas (2005) suggests that many B2B marketers are spending too much time trying to figure out ways in which they can create value for customers, rather than on communicating the various benefits that they can provide to their customers. One effective way to handle this is to develop a list of the various benefits that can be provided and a list of the corresponding key executives within the target firm that will want these benefits, and rank them in terms of importance. Practice indicates that each member of the buying group of executives will usually be looking for one specific primary benefit, so the strategic approach should be to match up the key benefit to the particular executive and make sure that he or she is effectively educated on that particular offering. In that way, the company enhances its chances of success in getting the contract and potentially keeping it over a long period of time.

One of the biggest problems faced by B2B marketers is that they seem to be focusing much too heavily on satisfaction scores, just as B2C marketers are doing; but in their case, these are misleading indicators. Narayandas (2005) warns that more than 80 per cent of B2B marketers use these scores to measure loyalty levels, but there is little correlation, if any, between satisfaction and loyalty in B2B markets. More savvy B2B marketers are realizing that better indicators would involve composite measures that include satisfaction scores, along with more reliable indicators like recommendations and repurchase ratings. The best way to address the issue according to Narayandas (2005) is to think of a B2B loyalty ladder as shown in Figure 7.3. This ladder helps by providing strategic insight that may not be gained from use of the B2C loyalty ladder as shown in Figure 7.1.

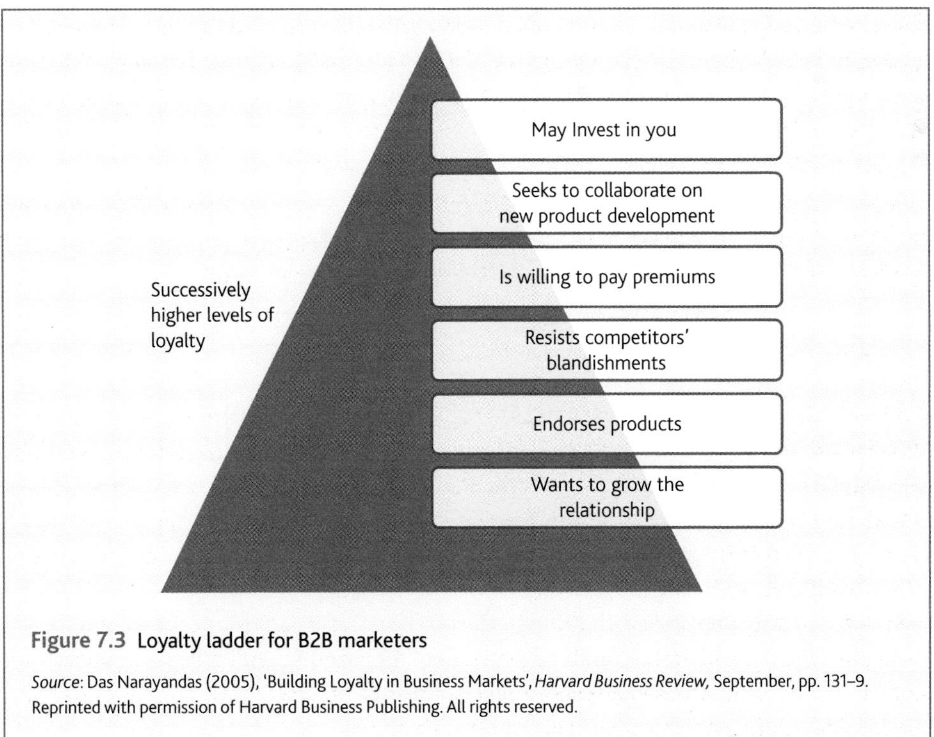

Figure 7.3 Loyalty ladder for B2B marketers

Source: Das Narayandas (2005), 'Building Loyalty in Business Markets', *Harvard Business Review*, September, pp. 131–9. Reprinted with permission of Harvard Business Publishing.

With the B2B loyalty ladder, the different segments deal with increasingly higher levels of loyalty, and the amount of time and effort spent by the company on relationship building and maintenance should be commensurate with the levels on the ladder. Beginning at the bottom and moving up the ladder, loyal customers move through a series of behaviours as they become increasingly loyal, and these characteristics must be carefully nurtured by B2B marketers. As the customer displays the next level of loyalty, the revenues will increase. Finally, Narayandas (2005) suggests that there are really four kinds of buyers (see Figure 7.4), and their position on the buyer matrix will suggest whether they are good candidates for investment, maintenance, or divestiture. Each of these customer groups will now briefly be discussed and strategic suggestions provided.

Commodity buyers are only interested in basic offerings, and are primarily interested in shopping the lowest prices. These tend to be large-volume types of customers, and the strategic focus should not be on trying to sell them on high value-added services, but to strip service costs to the bare minimum.

Underperformers tend to be those prestigious accounts that were acquired to build credibility by luring them with very low cost or even free services. The hope is that by acquiring them with low fees, they will later be able to trade them up, but this is not usually the case. The best way to deal with these accounts is either to try to move them to commodity buyers by cutting the level of services provided that are not essential, to move them to partners by having them pay more for services they need, to offer standard products, or to divest them. This is a difficult strategic choice, but it may be the best option if the customer is costing more to keep than they make up in revenue generation.

Partners are customers who want everything provided for them, since they don't have the in-house capability to handle these needs. The key is to provide them with the latest and best products available, and price premiums will not be a problem for them. They can be helpful

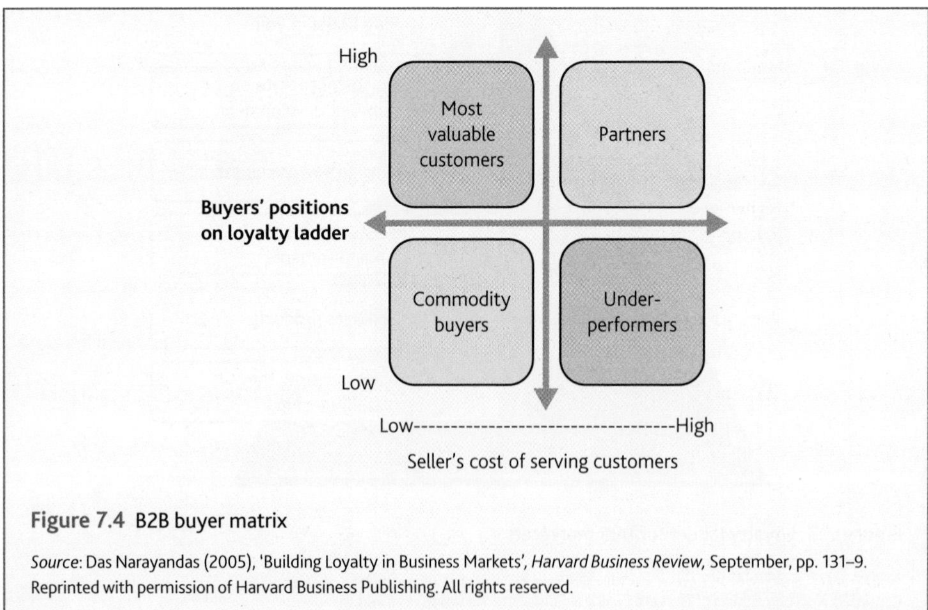

Figure 7.4 B2B buyer matrix

Source: Das Narayandas (2005), 'Building Loyalty in Business Markets', *Harvard Business Review*, September, pp. 131–9. Reprinted with permission of Harvard Business Publishing.

in new product development. The issue is that these customers can become problematic if the product evolutionary cycles are short (as in high-tech offerings), and if the supplier doesn't stay on the leading edge of product innovation, these accounts can be lost.

The final category, **most valuable customers**, are loyal and do not cost as much to maintain as the partners. Often in these cases, the customer has taken over some of the things originally provided by the supplier, but the customer is still willing to pay premium prices for the offerings in honour of past services provided. These customers will also be strong proponents for the supplier. One strategic imperative here is for the suppliers to consider moving these customers to the partner category if new technologies are created or new competitors enter the market with the offering of new services (Narayandas, 2005).

A recent creation that can be quite beneficial for the B2B marketer is the use of a tool which builds on the various aspects of relationships to assess the overall nature of the relationship. Lages et al. (2008) have developed a scale that can potentially be used to judge the nature of B2B relationships that they call the B2B-RELPERF scale and scorecard. The authors build a scale that provides a sound foundation for properly judging the nature of the relationship by

Relationship Policies and Practices (RPP)
Firm X has policies that show respect for the customer
Firm X has practices that make solving problems easy
Firm X solves my firm's problems quickly
Relationship Commitment (RCO)
Our relationship with Firm X is a long-term partnership
We would not drop Firm X because we like being associated with it
We want to remain as a customer of Firm X because we have pride in being associated with a firm that carries a technological image
Trust in the Relationship (TRUST)
In our relationship, Firm X is someone to whom I give my confidence
In our relationship, Firm X has high integrity
In our relationship, Firm X gives us reliable information and advice
Mutual Cooperation (MCO)
My firm and Firm X regularly interact
There is an open communication between our firms
Relationship Satisfaction (SAT)
Overall, we are satisfied with Firm X
We are pleased with what Firm X does for us
If we had to do it again, we would still choose to use Firm X

Figure 7.5 The B2B-RELPERF scale

Reprinted from *Industrial Marketing Management*: Luis Felipe Lages, Andrew Lancastre, and Carmen Lages (2008), 'The B2B-RELPERF Scale and Scorecard: Bring Relationship Marketing Theory into Business-to-Business Practice', *Industrial Marketing Management*, 37 (6), pp. 686–97. Copyright © 2008, with permission of Elsevier.

building on the various components that have been shown to be relevant for B2B relationships: (1) relationship policies and practices; (2) the role of trust; (3) the amount of commitment to the relationship; (4) the extent of mutual cooperation between the parties; and (5) relationship satisfaction. The scale items are shown in Figure 7.5. This allows the relationship managers for the firm to judge the various customer–firm relationships that have been established to see which are functioning properly and which have potential problems that need to be addressed.

Customer relationship management (CRM)

Having examined the nature of relationship marketing, the loyalty ladder, and customer valuation, the next logical step would involve an examination of the mechanics of relationship management. Customer retention is obviously an important goal for any company, especially in light of the costs necessary to acquire a new customer as opposed to keeping an old one. Kotler (2003) explains that there are two ways to strengthen customer retention: (1) create high switching barriers (the price of looking for another supplier, evaluating them, switching to them, and potential loss of customer discounts which are loyalty based; or (2) deliver ever-increasing levels of customer satisfaction. Kotler suggests that the latter is preferred since switching barriers are difficult and costly to erect. So, how does the company deliver appropriate levels of customer satisfaction? The corporate solution is the creation of a **customer relationship management** (or CRM) system.

CRM is a process by which a firm gathers information about the wants and needs of its customers to enable it to adjust its offerings to better fit those wants and needs. It involves data gathering, storage, and dissemination to those who need it. Often this involves the acquisition of relationship management software and data-mining techniques, which promise to track customers effectively and build large customer storehouses of data, for use by the company in building long-term relationships.

The foundation of this system is the database of information, often referred to as the **customer information file (CIF).** Winer (2004) suggests that there are five major areas of content that make up the customer information file: (1) basic descriptions of the customers (usually in terms of demographics, customer names, and addresses); (2) customer purchase histories (records of all purchases made by the customer in terms of price paid, purchase location, and product variant purchased); (3) customer contact histories (records of all customer contacts with company personnel); (4) customer response information (records of customer reactions and responses to various marketing promotions and activities); and (5) customer value (an estimate of the monetary value of the customer). The customer information file then serves as the basis for analysing customers to find out how to build better relationships and increase their profitability.

Emmy Favilla (2004) studied a series of successful companies and found that they were carefully monitoring all customer 'touch points' and finding ways to offer superior service to continuously impress their customers. Favilla (2004) provided a series of examples of companies and what they were doing to improve service levels. One example presented was Starwood Resort Hotels, which had to handle over 14 million calls each year using 900 call-centre agents across various cultures. Starwood implemented an automated customer-interaction recording and performance evaluation mechanism that created a consistent customer experience, improved reservation sales volume, helped supervisors improve call-centre productivity and improved customer-service quality ratings. Another example involved Hewlett-Packard (HP), which was trying to deal with ten to twleve different methodologies for handling common service processes, which created enormous employee frustration levels and with customers becoming confused from a variety of inconsistent responses. HP corrected the situation through the development of a single, global help-desk mechanism to improve service delivery, which reduced overall cost-per-employee and improved tracking and trend analysis. Another excellent example was that of the South African Revenue Service, which had to deal with taxpayer information kept in eight different systems. Different IT systems were utilized based upon a series of taxpayer sub-categories. To correct the situation, the company created an integrated multiple-taxpayer system through a team of companies including Accenture, IBM, and Siebel Systems. The result was a saving of almost $12 million per week and significantly improved response time to answer taxpayer questions.

One can easily see the benefit inherent in getting information in a B2B marketing situation, since industrial marketers have fewer customers to deal with on a regular basis than B2C companies. It gets trickier with companies aiming at large groups of customers, especially when there are many competitors with what appear to be very similar offerings. An article by Susan Fournier et al. was published in *Harvard Business Review* in 1998 which raised the important question of how B2C companies can build meaningful intimate relationships with hordes of individual consumers. Part of the problem that they acknowledged was that many customers of consumer goods companies get bombarded with surveys which ask for information to help the company build a database of customer information. The biggest difficulty for the consumers is that they keep giving out information but do not see anything coming back to them for their efforts. They are tired of filling out surveys and hearing nothing in return. They feel disconnected, rather than part of an intimate relationship. The authors caution that developing customer intimacy requires the company to take a holistic view to create 'life satisfaction' for the customer, rather than merely customer satisfaction. They suggest that this would require in-house controls of toll-free customer-call numbers, regular Internet monitoring, trend analyses to understand consumer lifestyle trends, and the tracking of customer perceptions to avoid negative customer backlash.

An important issue is to set up appropriate mechanisms for data collection which allow the firm to understand its consumers more effectively and to keep them trusting and committed. Davenport and Klahr (1998) discuss the importance of managing customer support knowledge and ensuring that frontline personnel get the knowledge whenever needed to help customize the offering to the needs of the most profitable customers. This kind of support knowledge would include such information as known customer problems and solutions, regular customer questions that have been asked and their answers, and customer product/service questions and a series of recommendations. Davenport and Klahr (1998) offer the following list of benefits that accrue from this kind of customer support knowledge: (1) improved solutions for the customer; (2) consistency of solutions provided; (3) improved handling of problems on the first call rather than later; (4) reduced costs per call; (5) reduced calls to the customer service support desk; (6) reduced costs of field service calls; (7) ability to hire frontline personnel for their people skills as opposed to technical expertise; (8) improved quality and speed of on-the-job training; (9) increased frontline staff satisfaction; and (10) increased overall customer satisfaction.

Davenport and Klahr (1998) offer the following knowledge-oriented technologies for use in the management of customer support knowledge: (1) **rule-based expert systems** (systems like the computer building system at the Dell website); (2) **probability networks** (relating symptoms to underlying causes and solutions in a network of probabilities); (3) **rule induction** (where examples are provided and rules are generated which are used to test situations and provide possible recommendations, which works best when example cases are complete and comprehensive); (4) **decision trees** (some products allow decision trees to be created to cover all possible symptoms and solutions, which helps novices more effectively than experts); and (5) **case-based reasoning** (a method which represents past situations or cases and attempts to retrieve a series of similar cases when a new problem is identified and helps the user to develop a solution based upon the facts and from previous solutions and then adds this new case to the case-base).

Davenport and Krahl (1998) provide the following list of managerial concerns that must be addressed in the proper management of customer support knowledge: (1) customer support knowledge is cross-functional and requires all the relevant functional areas to be included; (2) technology may raise concerns among employees as to their elimination and replacement by the new system; (3) smaller numbers of technical and product experts will be needed with the new system; and (4) customer support systems may end up taking the burden off support personnel and placing it directly on the consumer, which may not be appropriate.

Data-mining has become an important tool in customer relationship management. **Data-mining** is the analysis of consumer databases to look for new possible relationships that can provide direction for innovative customer relationship strategies. Since the early findings of synergies in reservations among airlines, hotels, and car rentals in the SABRE reservation system utilized by American Airlines, customer data have been analysed to look for possible relationships that researchers never before knew existed. The trouble is that data being gathered for the sake of having data to add to the customer knowledge system may be problematic. Davenport et al., in a 2001 article in *MIT Sloan Management Review*, report that many companies have been investing in customer transaction tracking systems which have built very large data bases, but with few helpful insights into who their customers really are. The problem is that many companies rely on raw data rather than really observing and getting to know their customers. The problems mentioned previously by Fournier et al. (1998) suggested that just asking customers for information isn't really enough, and this is what Davenport et al. (2001) are suggesting.

They interviewed personnel from twenty-four leaders in customer relationship management and found that the best companies went out of their way to combine both transaction data with human data (information about how the humans involved function). The authors found that these twenty-four leading firms had seven practices in common which should provide help for other companies looking to improve their CRM programme: (1) **focus on the most valued customers** (the company has to know which customers are worth the cost—profitability is a good mechanism for categorizing customers); (2) **prioritize objectives** (first set the customer-relationship objectives and then prioritize them according to business strategies); (3) **aim for the optimal knowledge mix** (combining transaction-focused data with consumer qualitative data to better understand, not only what consumers do, but why they do it); (4) **avoid one repository for all data** (firms should pursue many different kinds of customer information since many firms have significantly different types and groupings of customers); (5) **think creatively about human knowledge** (unconventional thinking on this is key, since the most successful companies use creative solutions, combining both explicit (documented and retrievable from storage) and tacit (observed, understood but not stored for easy access) information by having executives interact in meaningful ways with customers); (6) **look at the broader context** (many successful companies have shifted their cultures from product-oriented to customer-focused with cultural and structural changes to reflect the change in focus, but with the need to avoid focusing on only one customer type since the organization must balance generalized response systems with distinct customer types and groups); and (7) **establish a process and tools** (many firms stop after developing a management strategy, but successful firms know what they want to accomplish, create a plan, get the proper tools, and get results). The main point here is that data collected for the sake of collecting data will do very little to help the company build strong relationships with customers. These relationships must be carefully nurtured, with different types of information being collected and managed to allow the firm to best address different customer types and needs.

CRM pitfalls to avoid

Companies can easily get caught up in spending enormous amounts of money on a variety of customer relationship management schemes, but many of these will fail. In their 2002 *Harvard Business Review* article, Rigby et al. provide a series of suggestions for marketers to enhance their chances of success by avoiding a series of significant CRM pitfalls. The first of these pitfalls is **the implementation of CRM before a customer strategy has been developed**. The first step to CRM must be for the company to develop a customer strategy. This will require a clear identification of the customers that the firm wants to build relationships with. These identified customers must then be categorized into different groups ranging from the most profitable down to the least profitable, which will allow a clear delineation of actions and responses and efforts for the various segments. The authors suggest that the customer strategy must involve debates surrounding the following five questions:

1. How must our present value proposition change to gain greater customer loyalty?
2. How much customization is appropriate and profitable?
3. What is the value to be gained from increasing customer loyalty, and would this vary by customer segment?
4. How much time and money can we invest in CRM at the present time?
5. If customer relationships are important to us, why aren't we already building a CRM programme, and what might we be able to do in building customer relationships without investing in technology?

The authors warn that CRM may not be the answer if the company concludes that cost reductions or the handling of all customers in a standardized way makes more sense.

The second CRM pitfall is the **implementation of a CRM programme before the organization has become a customer-focused entity**. The danger here is that the company says that it wants a CRM programme but has not restructured its processes to better meet customer needs. Often company executives do not see the need for internal system and structure changes, since they assume that CRM affects only processes that involve face-to-face interactions with the customer. The authors claim that successful companies work for years to modify their structures and processes before ever attempting CRM initiatives.

The third peril is the **assumption that more CRM technology is always to be preferred.** Often executives will assume that CRM must be technologically intensive. But this may not be the case. It may make sense to provide incentives to motivate company employees to better track customer needs, as opposed to investing enormous sums of money into buying the latest and most complex technology. The authors suggest that excellent CRM programmes are comprised of a variety of technologies from low to high. They suggest that managers really need to ask themselves where their CRM needs fit on the technology spectrum. The best way to deal with the complexity issue is to start with low-tech alternatives and then assess whether more is needed.

The fourth and final peril is the **potential to stalk your customers, rather than woo them.** Managers often end up trying to build relationships with the wrong customers or trying to build relationships with the right customers but in the wrong way if they forget that the types of relationships will depend on what your company is and what it stands for and what types of relationships it wants to build with its customers. As the authors describe the situation, relationships involve two sides. A company may want to build stronger ties to affluent customers, but those customers may not want closer relationships with the company. It may also be that the company does not build a relationship with customers who value relationships, and these customers will undoubtedly be lost to competitors. Another challenge is building relationships with those customers who do not want them, and the company will be seen as an irritant. The problem is that the use of loyalty programmes can often fall into this pattern. Having the ability to contact customers does not mean that the company should contact them. It depends on the customer strategy mentioned earlier, rather than the CRM programme.

Developing personal knowledge banks

An interesting suggestion was recently made by Richard Watson from the University of Georgia, who argued for the development of personal knowledge banks for use in customer relationship management systems and strategies. Watson's 2004 article, published in the *Harvard Business Review* suggested that companies, which have been building databases to focus on the customer's transactions with their products and services, are missing important information. They are missing seeing the customer's interactions with the particular industry as a whole. This then leads to an inference gap.

Watson argues that the only mechanism that can provide the magic information that is needed is the customer him/herself, since they are the only ones who know all about their interactions with all companies in the industry. The only thing that makes sense, therefore, is to have the customer control and manage their own database of information that could be given to companies for use in the event that they could add value. Watson refers to this as customer-managed interactions (CMI), which have also been referred to as personal knowledge banks. These knowledge banks could be utilized to attract proposals from sellers to meet certain buying needs expressed by the customer. Watson argues that these personal knowledge banks could serve as the ultimate interface between the customer and a variety of companies for an ever-increasing range of goods and services. The problem for companies is to let the control stay with the consumer, so that they would need to earn the right to get access to consumer data. There are a variety of issues that would have to be dealt with before this use of personal knowledge banks could become practical (e.g., privacy and security, as well as rules governing access, etc.), but this new way of looking at things could be far bigger than CRM.

Sustainability of relationships and competitive advantage

The key to relationships is to convert them into long-term partnerships between the buyer and seller, whether B2C or B2B, so that the two parties become co-dependent upon each other. The hope is that the relationship will become so comfortable that the commitment level will remain as high as possible. It is the hope that switching costs will increase over time, making dissolution of the relationship no longer a possibility. Of course, this will require true trust, commitment, and confidence on the part of both partners. This will undoubtedly become more of a challenge for B2C marketers than B2B marketers, as loyalty becomes increasingly difficult as the price of the product/service decreases, but there are opportunities for those firms who nurture these relationships to shift them from short-term to long-term to create the potential for competitive advantage. The question is whether this type of advantage is sustainable or not.

Judging sustainability

In the B2B literature, recent research has proposed the imperative to manage buyer–seller relationships for the long term. Ryu et al. (2007) suggest that there has been a major paradigm shift for B2B marketers and that now relationship marketing has shifted from a short-term to a long-term focus to be effective. As a result, the measurement of the relationship management's LTO (long-term orientation) is vital for ensuring success. Practice suggests that there can be no LTO without the existence of trust. In turn, trust is affected by relational norms and satisfaction with the performance of suppliers. In this study, the authors found that the perceived level of power of the manufacturer is a moderator in the link between trust and the long-term orientation of the supplier, which underscores the fact that the power structure is important for the creation of a viable competitive advantage.

The authors also shed further light on the trust–LTO link by showing that in a turbulent resource environment, the firms involved would be hesitant to enter into long-term relationships, thinking that suppliers might not be counted on to ensure a smooth flow of needed raw materials required for the final products. Of course, the longer that the two partners have worked together and built trust in one another, the more commitment to the relationship will remain. Managerially, there is an important lesson learned from this research. Trust on the part of one partner is usually formed as a result of the proven abilities of the other partner to offer proper solutions and adapt to changing circumstances while also openly exchanging information. As a result, the supplier should regularly measure, share, and also manage all aspects of the exchange process (even what would seem to be implicit instead of explicit), so that the buyer will want to develop a long-term relationship.

But an important question which has been raised by the literature is whether trust is really enough in forging long-term relationships. Another important consideration is that for a short-term relationship to become a long-term relationship, it is imperative that the engagement between the firms or between the firm and the customer becomes an emotional one (Noble and Kumar, 2008). Obviously, this goes beyond the development of trust to a level of emotional attachment, which would be more akin to love than to mere attachment. This next level of attachment will bring with it commitment and will at the same time raise the switching costs involved, creating a situation where the customer will not want to leave the relationship, thereby creating a sustainable asset for the company. Emotional attachment is discussed in greater detail in the next section, which focuses on the latest thinking on relationships.

Latest thinking on customer relationships

Several recent developments in customer relationship management are worth reporting. One deals with taking relationships with customers to a higher plane, to engender emotional ties with customers. Another new perspective involves the promising application of Customer Experience Management (CEM), which offers theoretical advantages over CRM; and, finally, there is the use of Virtual Customer Environments (VCEs) to build strong long-term relationships with customers by significantly enhancing customer experiences with the company and the use of its products/services. Each of these will now be discussed in turn.

Building customer love

An interesting new view of customer relationships was presented in an article authored by Chip Bell, a senior partner of Performance Research Associates in Dallas, Texas, in 2002 in *Business Horizons*. Bell (2002) suggests that it is no longer sufficient just to have a relationship with your customer; you need to develop the love of your customer. This is what has made such companies as Starbucks, Ritz-Carlton Hotels, and Harley-Davidson such successful companies.

Bell (2002) suggests that there are seven important steps in building customer love (the 7 'e's; see Figure 7.6): (1) **enlistment: customers care when they share** (the key is knowing exactly when and how to include customers, since bringing them in as co-producers of a service makes them more loyal); (2) **engagement: the power of straight talk** (since customers who have a problem and complain spend twice as much as customers who have a problem and do not complain, the company must find a way to listen to and talk straight with customers in such a way that customers understand that their input made a difference); (3) **enlightenment: growing customer love** (educating and keeping customers up to date helps to build their loyalty and commitment); (4) **entrustment: affirming the covenant** (reliability is vital for trust, so to show the customer that you can be trusted, you must be seen as caring for the customer to get them to care for you); (5) **empowerment: customer control through consistency** (customers who feel in control when they have an offering that is consistent—keep the core offering intact); (6) **enchantment: making the process magical** (service which surprises adds the sizzle and not showing how keeps the mystery and builds devotion); and (7) **endearment: gifting without a toll** (showing generosity to

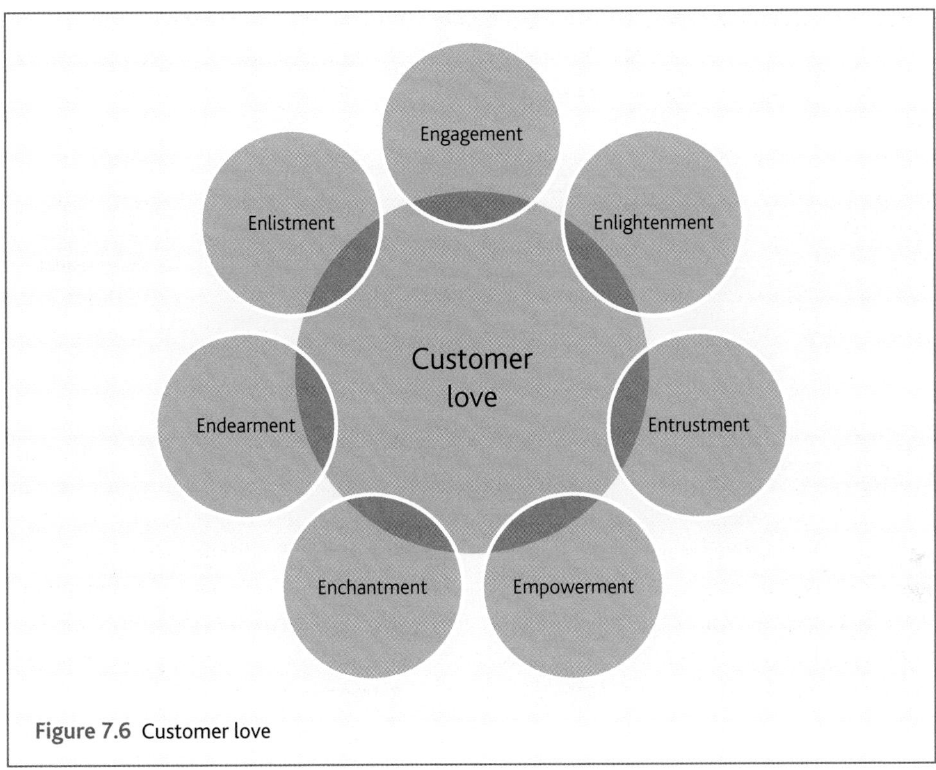

Figure 7.6 Customer love

the customer if backed by authenticity says that you really care about them without just a concern for profit).

Bell offers the following key benefits to the achievement of customer love: (1) customers who love you go out of their way to take care of you; (2) customers do not just recommend the company to their friends, they insist on their friends using the company; (3) they both forgive you for mistakes (once you have earned their love) and they try to back you up to others who have had bad experiences; (4) they will give helpful, candid, and forthright feedback when they see a problem; (5) they do not take legal action against you; and (6) they will pay more for what you offer because they feel that your offering is worth it. These are powerful benefits, and the analogy of social/human relationships applied to buyers and sellers is a helpful strategic perspective. With the bar being ever raised on customer expectations, keeping up with customers and keeping them happy in their devotion is a key to long-term viability and success.

Customer experience management (CEM)

An interesting new perspective brought to the relationship management literature involves the systematic monitoring of customer experiences in such a way that the customer is always positive about their interactions with the company and its employees across all possible touch points. CEM, as a marketing strategic tool, is presented in a 2007 *Harvard Business Review* article by Christopher Meyer and Andre Schwager (see Figure 7.7). The theory behind the system is that if the customer experience is tracked and every effort is put into ensuring that all experiences

	What	When	How monitored	Who uses the information	Relevance to future performance
Customer experience management (CEM)	Captures and distributes what a customer thinks about a company	At points of customer interaction: 'touch points'	Surveys, targeted studies, observational studies, 'voice of customer' research	Business or functional leaders, in order to create fulfillable expectations and better experiences with products and services	**Leading:** locates places to add offerings in the gaps between expectations and experience
Customer relationship management (CRM)	Captures and distributes what a company knows about a customer	After there is a record of a customer interaction	Point-of-sales data, market research, website click-through, automated tracking of sales	Customer-facing groups such as sales, marketing, field service, and customer service, in order to drive more efficient and effective execution	**Lagging:** drives cross-selling by bundling products in demand with ones that aren't

Figure 7.7 CEM vs CRM

Source: Christopher Meyer and André Schwager (2007), 'Understanding Customer Experience', *Harvard Business Review*, February, pp. 117–26. Reprinted with permission of Harvard Business Publishing.

with the company and its products/services is positive, then this type of reinforcement will create a stronger bond between the customer and the company and lead to increasing levels of profitability. **Customer experience** refers to any internal response on the part of the customer to any type of contact (either direct or indirect) by a particular company or its employees.

What is particularly new in this approach is that the key is to really get into the head of the customer and understand how they feel about their company experiences. CRM really focuses on what the company understands about the customer, rather than on what the customer thinks about the company, and as a result the mechanisms that are utilized here are different. The observational research and perceptual surveys show what the customer is thinking about the company and tracks this over time, and like the information presented about consumer franchise in the branding chapter, the point here is that a downturn in perception can be seen and addressed as soon as it is seen, rather than being missed and allowing a compounding of negative perception which, if untreated, can become a serious problem. As with consumer franchise, given the potential disconnect between consumer perception and behaviour, the problem is that by the time the consumer's concerns have shifted from benign to malignant, there may be little that the company can do at that point to retain the customer. The strategic potential here is to ensure that perceptions remain positive, rather than treating downturns in sales and share as problems in and of themselves as would be seen with CRM. The downturns in sales and share are never problems in themselves. They are always symptoms of under-lying problems. Here, the point is that CEM is an attempt to use a leading indicator rather than as a lagging indicator, and as has been noted on many occasions, reaction will always come in second to proaction!

The virtual customer environment (VCE)

This last interesting suggestion was proposed by Satish and Priya Nambisan in a 2008 *Harvard Business Review* article. The authors suggest that market winners like Nokia and

	Primary focus of the VCE: customer role				
	As product conceptualizer	**As product designer**	**As product tester**	**As product support specialist**	**As product marketer**
Nature of customer contributions	Suggestions and ideas for new products and/or for product improvement	Specification of new product design; inputs on product features and design trade-offs	Identification of product design flaws; input on product prototypes	Delivery of product support services to peer customers	Diffusion of new product information; shaping peer customers' purchase behaviour
Dominant nature of customer interactions	• Customer–customer • Customer–company	• Customer–tool • Customer–company	• Customer–tool • Customer–company	• Customer–customer • Customer–customer	• Customer–customer • Customer–tool
Typical VCE technologies	• Discussion forums • Knowledge centres • Blogs, wikis	• Virtual product design and prototyping tools • Messaging tools	• Virtual product simulation tools • Messaging tools	• Discussion forums • Knowledge centres	• Discussion forums • Virtual product simulation tools
Typical example	Ducatii's Tech Cafe	BMW's Customer Innovation Lab	Volvo's Concept Lab	Microsoft's MVP Program	Samsung's Virtual Product Launch Centre
Dominant customer experience components	• Pragmatic • Hedonic	• Pragmatic • Usability • Hedonic	• Pragmatic • Usability	• Pragmatic • Sociability	• Pragmatic • Sociability

Figure 7.8 Types of virtual customer environments

Reprinted from Satish Nambisan and Priya Nambisan (2008), 'How to Profit from a Better Virtual Customer Environment', *MIT Sloan Management Review*, Spring, pp. 53–61, by permission of the publisher.

Volvo have succeeded in part due to the fact that they have built such strong links with customers through the development of innovative customer forums that have brought customers into the process of product development and the creation of perceived value. These forums are virtual in nature and range from such activities as online discussions to product development innovation centres. In these situations, the customers are linked to new product development, and the feelings of ownership and involvement that come with these connections further enhance customer relationships with the company. As the authors have found, these VCEs mould and shape the customer relationships with the company and its various products/brands. The process is displayed in Figure 7.8. As can be seen, there are five different roles that the customer can play in his or her relationship and dealings with the company, and the company can effectively set up virtual environments to support each of these roles.

Conclusion

Once companies have gone through the process of segmentation, processing, and positioning, they must look to the creation of meaningful relationships with those customers. Customer acquisition is far more costly than customer retention, and the building of intimate relationships with key customers allows the firm to keep in step with changes in their wants and needs and be able to take corrective action in refining product and service offerings to retain those customers. But relationships with the wrong customers can be problematic, since some customers can cost far more to retain them than they are worth in additional potential revenue generation. The firm must carefully assess which customers to build relationships with and work to keep those valued relationships. The use of customer relationship management systems is an important approach to managing customer relationships, but committing to a CRM system requires careful preplanning, and a commitment throughout the organization to being customer-orientated. Putting a system in place for the sake of having a system usually leads to serious problems over time, as the system may not fit with the company outlook and environment.

Summary

Relationship marketing is important for company success. Normally, a company will not be successful trying to focus on single transactions since companies depend on repeat purchases for long-term success. Taking care of important customers is vital, especially in light of the 80-20 rule that states that in most industries, 80 per cent of the revenues come from 20 per cent of the customer base. Spending an inordinate amount of time and effort to bring in problematic customers is both inefficient and ineffective, especially since there is less time remaining to take care of the mainstay customers. The issue is that key customers must be nurtured to remain loyal to the company and continue to buy the products of the company. Relationship building requires the acquisition of relevant customer information, the storage of that information in databases, and the use of that information to adjust company offerings to build ever-stronger and more profitable customer relationships.

KEY TERMS

80-20 rule The rule which is built on the understanding that 80 per cent of the company's revenues come from only 20 per cent of its customers.

Aftermarketing Long-term relationships being built in which the firm actively attempts to move customers up the loyalty ladder and tries to minimize the outflow of unhappy buyers.

Compatibility management The management of different groups of customers to ensure that there is no interaction that could devalue the service for important customers.

Customer equity test Where the firm first measures each customer's expected contribution to offsetting the company's fixed costs over their expected lifetime. Then, expected contributions to net present value are discounted at the rate set by the company as its target rate of return for any marketing investments. And, finally, the company adds together all of the discounted expected contributions across all of the company's current customers.

Customer experience The tracking and maintenance of all responses on the part of the customer to any type of contact (either direct or indirect) by a particular company or its employees in order to ensure that all experiences with the company and its products/services is positive, hopefully resulting in a stronger bond between the customer and the company and leading to increased levels of profitability.

Customer information file (CIF) Another name for the customer database built by the firm to better understand customer wants and needs so that stronger ties can be built with the customer. The CIF contains such information as descriptions of the customer, their purchase histories, the various contacts the customer has had with company personnel, information on how customers have reacted to marketing activities, and measures of customer value.

Customer lifetime value (CLTV) The present value of the future profits that will accrue from the customer's lifetime purchases. The company must attempt to measure future earnings from the customer as well as be able to subtract from those earnings the cost of acquiring and maintaining the relationship with the customer.

Customer love Where the firm goes beyond building a relationship with its customers to the point where there is a stronger emotional bond between the company and the customer. This is where the customer believes that the firm cares about their well-being.

Customer profitability pyramid A ranking of customers in a pyramidal design, with customer groups positioned on the pyramid by profitability for the firm. The top of the pyramid contains the platinum customers, the second tier includes the gold customers, the third tier is comprised of the iron customers, and the base of the pyramid would be made up of the least profitable customers, the lead customers.

Customer relationship management (CRM) A process by which a firm gathers information about the wants and needs of its customers to enable it to adjust its offerings to better fit those wants and needs. It involves data gathering, storage, and dissemination to those who need it.

Data mining The analysis of consumer databases to look for possible new relationships that can provide direction for innovative customer relationship strategies.

Frequency marketing A strategy aimed at identifying best customers, keeping them, and increasing their expenditures through the development of intimate long-term relationships.

Loyalty schemes Programmes that are established by companies to provide added value to the regular purchaser, as opposed to the irregular customer. It provides increasing benefits for increasing levels of company loyalty.

Relationship marketing The development of long-term and intimate relationships between buyers and sellers. It involves open communications and the ability to know the customer so well that changes in wants and needs may be anticipated before they become critical.

Virtual customer environments The development of innovative virtual customer forums that can bring customers into the process of product development and enhance the creation of relationships with company employees.

DISCUSSION QUESTIONS

1. What is relationship marketing, and why might repeat purchases be so important for company success?
2. Evaluate the differences between B2C and B2B relationship marketing.
3. What is customer lifetime value (CLTV), and how is it measured?
4. Review the customer pyramid concept, and explain which customers the firm would consider retaining and which ones would make sense to offload.
5. Why is data mining important for building customer relationships? What is human data, and why might it be incorporated into a customer relationship management programme?
6. Assess the five general rules for gathering and managing data from a series of customer encounters that were presented by Davenport et al. (2001).
7. What are the pitfalls that must be avoided in the use of CRM identified by Rigby et al.?
8. Evaluate how relationships with customers might be used for sustained competitive advantage.
9. Assess how 'customer love' differs from customer relationships.
10. Compare and contrast customer experience management (CEM) and customer relationship management (CRM).

ONLINE RESOURCE CENTRE

Visit the Online Resource Centre for this book for lots of interesting additional material at: **www.oxfordtextbooks.co.uk/orc/west2e/**

REFERENCES AND FURTHER READING

Bell, Chip R. (2002), 'In Pursuit of Obnoxiously Devoted Customers', *Business Horizons*, March–April, pp. 13–16.

Berry, Leonard L., and Kathleen Seiders (2007), 'Serving Unfair Customers', *Business Horizons*, 51, pp. 29–37.

Best, Roger J. (2005), *Market-based Management: Strategies for Growing Customer Value and Profitability*, 4th edn (Upper Saddle River, NJ: Prentice-Hall).

Blattberg, Robert C., and John Deighton (1996), 'Manage Marketing by the Customer Equity Test', *Harvard Business Review*, July–August, pp. 136–44.

Blattberg, Robert C., Gary Getz, and Jacquelyn Thomas (2001), *Customer Equity: Building and Managing Relationships as Valuable Assets* (Boston, MA: Harvard Business School Press).

Bold, Ben (2004), 'John Lewis backs Card with Rewards Scheme', *Marketing*, 1 April, p. 8.

Davenport, Thomas H., and Philip Klahr (1998), 'Managing Customer Support Knowledge', *California Management Review*, 40 (3), pp. 195–208.

Davenport, Thomas H., Jeanne G. Harris, and Ajay K. Kohli (2001), 'How do they Know their Customers so Well?' *MIT Sloan Management Review*, Winter, pp. 63–73.

Dowling, Grahame R., and Mark Uncles (1997), 'Do Customer Loyalty Programmes Really Work?' *MIT Sloan Management Review*, Summer, pp. 71–82.

Favilla, Emmy (2004), '10 Strategies for Customer Service Success', *Customer Relationship Management*, 8 (6), pp. 38–45.

Fournier, Susan, Susan Dobscha, and David Glen Mick (1998), 'Preventing the Premature Death of Relationship Marketing', *Harvard Business Review*, January–February, pp. 42–51.

Gupta, Sunil, Donald R. Lehmann, and Jennifer Ames Stuart (2004), 'Valuing Customers', *Journal of Marketing Research*, 41 (1), pp. 7–18.

Kotler, Philip (2003), *Marketing Management*, 11th edn (Upper Saddle River, NJ: Prentice-Hall).

Kumar, V., J. Andrew Petersen, and Robert P. Leone (2007), 'How Valuable is Word of Mouth?' *Harvard Business Review*, October, pp. 139–46.

Lages, Luis Felipe, Andrew Lancastre, and Carmen Lages (2008), 'The B2B-RELPERF Scale and Scorecard: Bring Relationship Marketing Theory into Business-to-Business Practice', *Industrial Marketing Management*, 37 (6), pp. 686–97.

Lindstrom, Martin (2005), 'Extreme Loyalty: Show off your Brand Tattoos', *Media*, 25 February, p. 24.

McGovern, Gail, and Youngme Moon (2007), 'Companies and the Customers who Hate them', *Harvard Business Review*, June, pp. 78–84.

Meyer, Christopher, and Andre Schwager (2007), 'Understanding Customer Experience', *Harvard Business Review*, February, pp. 117–26.

Nambisan, Satish, and Priya Nambisan (2008), 'How to Profit from a Better "Virtual Customer Environment"', *MIT Sloan Management Review*, Spring, pp. 53–61.

Narayandas, Das (2005), 'Building Loyalty in Business Markets', *Harvard Business Review*, September, pp. 131–9.

Noble, Charles H., and Minu Kumar (2008), 'Using Product Design Strategically to Create Deeper Consumer Connections', *Business Horizons*, 51, pp. 441–50.

Nunes, Joseph C., and Xavier Dreze (2006), 'Your Loyalty Programme is Betraying You', *Harvard Business Review*, April, pp. 124–31.

Payne, Adrian (2000), 'Relationship Marketing: The UK Perspective', in J. Sheth and A. Pravatiyar (eds), *Handbook of Relationship Marketing* (Thousand Oaks, CA: Sage), pp. 39–68.

Pruden, Doug R. (1995), 'There's a Difference between Frequency Marketing and Relationship Marketing', *Direct Marketing*, 58 (2), pp. 30–1.

Raphel, M. (1980), 'Ad Techniques Move Customers up the Loyalty Ladder', Bank Marketing, 12 (November), pp. 37–8.

Reichheld, Frederick F. (1996), *The Loyalty Effect* (Boston, MA: Harvard Business School Press).

Rigby, Darrell K., Frederick F. Reichheld, and Phil Schefter (2002), 'Avoid the Four Perils of CRM', *Harvard Business Review*, February, pp. 101–10.

Ritson, Mark (2003), 'Brand Terrorists Offer an Insight into how the Public Interpret Ads', *Marketing*, 27 November 27, p. 18.

Ryu, Sungmin, Jeong Eun Park, and Soonhong Min (2007), 'Factors of Determining Long-term Orientation in Interfirm Relationships', *Journal of Business Research*, 60, pp. 1225–33.

Schoder, Detlef (2007), 'The Flaw in Customer Lifetime Value', *Harvard Business Review*, December, p. 26.

Slater, Stanley F., Jakki J. Mohr, and Sanjit Sengupta (2009), 'Know your Customer', *Marketing Management*, January–February, pp. 37–44.

Staff (2004), 'Brand Strategy Briefing: Land Rover Case Study—Customers at the Wheel', *Brand Strategy*, 3 November, p. 54.

Ulwick, Anthony W., and Lance A. Bettencourt (2008), 'Giving Customers a Fair Hearing', *MIT Sloan Management Review*, Spring, pp. 62–8.

Watson, Richard T. (2004), 'I am my own Database', *Harvard Business Review*, November, pp. 1–2.

Winer, Russell S. (2004), *Marketing Management*, 2nd edn (Upper Saddle River, NJ: Prentice-Hall).

Zeithaml, Valarie A., Roland T. Rust, and Katherine N. Lemon (2001), 'The Customer Pyramid: Creating and Serving Profitable Customers', *California Management Review*, 43 (4), pp. 118–42.

KEY ARTICLE ABSTRACTS

Davenport, Thomas H., Jeanne C. Harris, and Ajay K. Kohli (2001), **'How do they Know their Customers so Well?'** *MIT Sloan Management Review*, Winter, pp. 63–73.

There is a problem in customer relationship management when customer data is being gathered simply for the sake of having data to add to the customer knowledge system. This helpful article reports that many companies, which have been investing in customer transaction tracking systems, have built up very large databases, but have few helpful insights into who their customers really are. The problem is that many companies rely on raw data, rather than really observing and getting to know their customers.

Abstract: Many firms know about their customers, but few know the customers themselves or how to get new ones. Leaders in customer knowledge management go beyond transaction data, using a mix of techniques, and are not afraid to tackle difficult problems. Guidelines are presented: (1) Focus on the most valued customers. (2) Prioritize objectives. (3) Aim for the optimal knowledge mix. (4) Do not use one repository for all data. (5) Think creatively about human knowledge. (6) Look at the broader context. (7) Establish a process and tools.

Zeithaml, Valarie A., Roland T. Rust, and Katherine N. Lemon (2001), **'The Customer Pyramid: Creating and Serving Profitable Customers'**, *California Management Review*, 43 (4), pp. 118–42.

This article discusses the strategic uses of a customer pyramid based upon profitability for those firms trying to improve long-term firm performance. The authors argue that this is useful for both consumer and industrial products companies.

Abstract: Customer profitability can be increased and managed. By sorting customers into profitability tiers (a customer pyramid), service can be tailored to achieve even higher profitability levels. Highly profitable customers can be pampered appropriately, customers of average profitability can be cultivated to yield higher profitability, and unprofitable customers can either be made more profitable or weeded out. Tailoring service to the customer's profitability level can make a company's customer base more profitable, increasing its chances for success in the marketplace.

Ryu, Sungmin, Jeong Eun Park, and Soonhong Min (2007), **'Factors of Determining Long-term Orientation in Interfirm Relationships'**, *Journal of Business Research*, 60, pp. 1225–33.

The authors of this interesting article suggest that there has been a major paradigm shift for B2B marketers and that now relationship marketing has shifted from a short-term to a long-term focus to be effective. As a result, the measurement of the relationship management's LTO (long-term orientation) is vital for ensuring success. Practice suggests that there can be no LTO without the existence of trust. In turn, trust is affected by relational norms and satisfaction with the performance of suppliers. In this study, the authors found that the perceived level of power of the manufacturer is a moderator in the link between trust and the long-term orientation of the supplier, which underscores the fact that the power structure is important for the creation of a viable competitive advantage.

Abstract: Marketers have witnessed a paradigm shift in which establishing, maintaining, and forging long-term buyer–seller relationships are considered the core of marketing activities. Accordingly, investigating a long-term orientation (LTO) has become a steady research stream in the marketing literature. Building on this on-going research stream, this study confirms that an essential precursor of a manufacturer's LTO is trust that, in turn, is formed by relational norms and satisfaction with supplier performance. Interestingly, however, the seemingly strong trust–LTO path is moderated by both power asymmetry and environmental uncertainty in buyer–seller relationships. The empirical findings suggest that, regardless of emerging relationship marketing where buyer and seller are portrayed as parts of a team, power is still in use to control suppliers. In addition, a manufacturer facing uncertainty is less likely to form LTO toward its supplier for fear of losing flexibility in the time- and quality-based competition.

Nambisan, Satish, and Priya Nambisan (2008), **'How to Profit from a Better "Virtual Customer Environment"'**, *MIT Sloan Management Review*, (Spring), pp. 53–61.

This insightful article suggests that market winners like Nokia and Volvo have succeeded in part due to the fact that they have built such strong links with customers through the development of innovative customer forums that have brought customers into the process of product development and the creation of perceived value. These forums are virtual in nature and range from such activities as online discussions to product development innovation centres. In these situations, the customers are linked to new product development, and the feelings of ownership and involvement that come with these connections further enhance customer relationships with the company. As the authors have found, these VCEs mould and shape the customer relationships with the company and its various products/brands.

Abstract: In recent years, many well-known companies, including Microsoft, Cisco, Nokia, Volvo, and Nike, have forged closer links with customers in the areas of innovation and value creation by establishing technology-based customer forums. These forums, known as virtual customer environments, range from simple online discussion groups to more sophisticated product-prototyping centres. In many cases, companies incorporate organizational mechanisms to integrate customer innovation roles with internal product-development systems and processes. The benefits of engaging customers in product design and development, product support, and other related activities are increasingly visible. Research indicates that VCE initiatives can offer important (and often hidden) benefits beyond the innovation outcomes. Specifically, customer interactions in VCEs can shape their relationships with the company, as well as with the product or brand.

END OF CHAPTER 7 CASE STUDY The relationship chain

A promising new way to look at relationship building and marketing strategy focuses on the relationship chain. It involves an examination of the incremental stages required in building lifetime customer value through a loyalty marketing programme, from initial involvement to lifetime relationship. Relationship chain methodology includes an analysis of incremental sales and increasing levels of retention which can be tied back directly to the company's loyalty programme, even from the very beginning. The problem is that some approaches to analytical tools are usually involved at later stages of the chain, and, as a result, companies miss valuable information in the early stages that might have improved retention.

Higher levels of involvement/engagement for members in loyalty programmes lead to increased sales and improvements in retention rates, but companies need better indications early in the process to evaluate the effectiveness of their loyalty programmes.

Shortly after the launch of the loyalty programme, relationship chain methodology would utlize an analysis of customer activity involving such measures as increases in customer retention, levels of brand engagement, and levels of customer spending. Another important measurement would involve reductions in customer turnover. These types of measurements can then be used as helpful predictive inputs to see whether customers are properly on track to becoming loyal long-term customers with the ability to take corrective action if necessary to get customers back on track, or to let those with poorer potential fall out of the programme rather than spending too much time or money on these poorer candidates. This approach to treating relationship building as a series of incremental stages is a promising new approach. The basic idea here is that as the consumer moves from one stage to the next in the process, their relationship becomes increasingly valuable to the firm as CLTV increases and the ROI associated with the loyalty programme improves.

There are four basic stages involved in the relationship chain. The first is the stage in which the company ensures that it enrolls the right customers from the very beginning. Knowing which are the best candidates is a key step in the right direction in the proper design of the relationship chain. Who are the customers that we most value? How do we design our programme in such a way that we can grab their interest and stimulate their involvement? How will we reward them for their value to us? This starts the process rolling and helps the designers to work with specific individuals in mind who are high probability for success, and the entire programme can be designed with them in mind to enhance the chances for attraction and retention; but at least the fact that the relationship is seen as incremental in nature allows the firm to see what information it needs and when to take corrective action along the way.

The second stage involves the actual development of customer interest. The key here is to build an open communication mechanism with the customer to stimulate their response and involvement. Only through reaching customers and starting the engagement process can they be moved along the relationship chain, so the issue here is to find the right mechanisms for reaching them and actively involving them. What do we want our customers to do once they have seen our message? How do we get them to communicate with us regularly? This is where heavier uses of websites and call centres will be invaluable.

Stage three looks beyond initial contacts to regular participation in the loyalty programme. Here, the firm looks for activities that go beyond regular transactions. This would involve tracking such activities as placing of telephone orders, participation in sweepstakes, filling out of surveys, responses to pinpointed offers, bidding on items up for auction, and the number of times that the person checked their cumulative point balances. These types of activities would indicate that there is a growing interest beyond the norm, and these individuals would be seen as the prime candidates for relationship development, while others might be seen as appropriate to cull out. What can we do to give them added value? How can we cross-sell to them? Increasing participation will translate to increases in CLTV and improved retention rates.

Stage four then looks to the stimulation of multiple redemptions. So, the key is to get them to take advantage of the programme. This is where the real value is in the loyalty programme.

It is the measure of what the customer feels about the continuing value of the programme, so what is important is not just that they redeem their accrued benefits but that they do it more than once, since doing it once does not indicate engagement and commitment. If a frequent flier uses air miles once, that really does not indicate commitment to the airline, but if they do it every so often once they reach a certain level of air miles, then there is a better indication of the value of the entire loyalty programme for the consumer. The question here, therefore, is how do we get them to use the programme benefits on multiple occasions? Examples could include such things as attendance at certain members-only functions or the redemption of coupons for special discounts for better customers.

So what kinds of metrics are helpful in connection to this relationship chain? Certainly key metrics would include such measures as the amounts involved in the redemptions used by the cutomer, along with the number of times that the customer has sought redemptions, along with the time periods between redemptions. The company would also want to look at the number of non-redeemers as well. Also, the trend is important to multiple redemptions, since it will be important to determine how to predict heavier future redemption. Are there certain signs that we can use to tell when some are on the path to multiple redemptions more than others? Other important metrics would include looking at those who had actually enrolled in the programme and whether they were the ones that were the targeted audience. Also, it would be important to track those who move from one group to another along the way from enrollment to regular redemption to see if they are progressing as quickly as we have expected. Do we have different categories established from high potential to high value? Are we seeing the proper movement across these segments? Are there holdups at any point along the chain? We would also want to examine what the actual customer transaction value is on an annual basis and compare this to the chain and see if the proper improvements are being seen. If not, then we could assess why and how we might correct for the holdup. It would also be important to track cross-selling as well as trading up in sales to see again if there is any indication of value improvement. Of course, it would be important to address CLTV as well and to link it to a series of predictive measurements such as improvements in retention and increased redemptions. Finally, it would be beneficial to check the lost participants to see who is leaving the programme and attempt to determine why.

One of the most important things to remember strategically is that no single measure should serve as a panacea for everything. Relationship chain methodology should be incorporated into a series of mechanisms to get the most accurate and appropriate data for strategic decision-making. What is promising is that this may allow marketers to ensure that their efforts are paying off in the right ways and improve overall firm performance while reducing waste and inefficiency.

Source: This case was prepared by John Ford of Old Dominion University, Norfolk, Virginia, as the basis for analysis and class discussion and not to illustrate either effective or ineffective handling of an administrative situation.

QUESTIONS

Apply the relationship chain to airline travel:

1. How would you suggest the loyalty programme for the airline be structured, drawing upon the relationship chain?
2. How might you identify the different target segments for your airline?
3. What metrics would you suggest be associated with each of the stages of the chain and why?
4. Assess how you might know whether you were successful or not.

Part IV How will we get there?

I. Introduction
1. Overview and strategy blueprint
2. Marketing strategy: analysis and perspectives
II. Where are we now?
3. Environmental and internal analysis: market information and intelligence
III. Where do we want to be?
4. Strategic marketing decisions, choices, and mistakes
5. Segmentation, targeting, and positioning strategies
6. Branding strategies
7. Relational and sustainability strategies
IV. How will we get there?
8. Product innovation and development strategies
9. Service marketing strategies
10. Pricing and distribution
11. Marketing communications
12. E-marketing strategies
13. Social and ethical strategies
V. Did we get there?
14. Strategy implementation, control, and metrics

8

Product innovation and development strategies

LEARNING OBJECTIVES

- Examine the role of innovation and product development in marketing strategy
- Review the range of innovation and product development objectives
- Assess the two main adoption theories and their implications for marketing strategy
- Examine the main options for market and innovation strategies

CHAPTER AT A GLANCE

Introduction

From a strategic perspective, innovation is based upon technological superiority and posits that buyers will seek goods and services that provide the greatest interest, performance, features, quality, and/or value for money. Innovation is an integral part of marketing strategy owing to its ability to reduce costs and/or differentiate. The 'and' part of the sentence has provided one of the biggest challenges to Porter's cost-differentiation framework in that in many markets, the name of the game is to both reduce costs AND to differentiate. Buyers have become increasingly demanding and no longer see a contradiction between product innovation and development and falling prices. For example, mobile-phone manufacturers such as Nokia and Sony-Erickson offer superior products every year at similar or below previous prices. Given that most theories of business eventually become obsolete, the key competency for any organization that wants to survive in the marketplace is the ability to innovate. Drucker and Maciariello (2008) argued that, 'Because the purpose of a business is to create a customer, the business enterprise has two—and only two—basic functions: marketing and innovation. Marketing and innovation produce results; all the rest are costs' (p. 30).

Innovation often brings previously unrelated companies into competition—competitive boundaries become blurred and often companies have to trust their staff to exploit the 'small world' networks that they work within (Fleming and Marx, 2006). Take the case of telecommunications. Previously separate sectors such as computing, entertainment, telephony, and utilities are now locked in fierce competition. Thus, in the UK, BT has developed alliances with content providers to provide a variety of services over broadband, including BT Vision, which competes with Sky and Virgin media. Similarly, Siemens, Sony, and Panasonic have entered the photographic marketplace using digital technology, and Dyson has displaced the top-selling Hoover vacuum-cleaner with its 'cyclone' bagless technology.

Innovation can be used to find 'comfort zones' in the marketplace. The best strategic place for any organization is to occupy a space that rivals have no interest in or cannot easily emulate. Patek Philippe uses established technology to build classic watches, while Seiko uses innovation to produce digital watches with kinetic energy. Innovation and development only has strategic value if appropriately positioned. On the face of it, Patek Philippe has no interest in advances in Velcro strap technology!

Consider BMW's 'The Ultimate Driving Machine' pitch to the market. Here is a company saying that it will not use technology that makes driving a car like sitting on a sofa. Take the case of the controversial alcopops market, which is extremely fashion-oriented, based upon innovation with a rapid turnover of flavours. This has led to a variety of product innovation and development strategies based upon differentiation within a largely traditional sector. For example, the Hooch brand specializes in limited-edition lines such as passion-fruit flavour for St Valentine's Day and the Takara lychee cocktail from Thailand (*Marketing Week*, 2003). Product and service innovation and development offer all organizations an important means to gain a competitive advantage: innovation and development is a strategic issue.

This chapter is divided into three sections. The first looks at setting objectives for innovation and development and is then followed by one looking at targeting issues. Finally, an examination of overall product innovation and development positioning is considered. However, the first task is to examine how to define innovation.

What is innovation?

Innovation is a noun with a definition along the lines of 'the introduction of something new' or 'a new idea, method, or device', as with the iPod Nano and Persil Tablets or e-readers. In a study of corporate innovation in the US by Cheskin and Fitch, nearly 50 per cent of respondents defined innovation as delivering unmet customer needs or finding better ways of doing something (Liddell, 2004). This is not entirely satisfactory, given such definitions do not appear to provide any distance between innovation and invention, which involves designing or creating something which has never been made before such as soya ice-cream or Bluetooth Wireless Technology.

Strictly speaking, the difference between innovation and invention is that invention applies to things that are 'new-to-the-world', whereas innovation refers to subsequent changes and adaptations. An obvious example would be Alexander Graham Bell's 'electrical speech machine' of 1876. Looking back, we can see that the telephone was the precursor to the Internet, but it would be a 'stretch' to say that Bell invented the Web. So we recognize that both the telephone and the Web were new-to-the-world, despite the myriad of innovations that can be traced back to the telephone. When it comes to competitive marketing strategy, the talk is mainly of innovation rather than invention.

Disruptive business models

A disruptive technology fundamentally shifts the production paradigm and often how a product or service is used. For example, digital technology has changed a number of markets, from cameras to radios to telephony (Christensen, 1997). People still take pictures; but the dominance of the 35-mm film market has evaporated. People still listen to radios, but not solely by tuning a channel. However, in recent years, the scope of the disruption debate has been widened to include disruptive business models (Markides, 2006) such as discount shopping, low-cost airlines, and online businesses such as Expedia (see, also, Christensen and Raynor, 2003). It might be argued that there is another category: a disruptive design innovation (see Verganti, 2006; Noble and Kumar, 2008). However, design in this chapter is treated as part of disruptive product innovation. For example, the Nintendo Wii is both a disruptive product and has a disruptive design, as does the Dyson upright vacuum-cleaner.

First, a quick review of a business model is in order (see also Chapter 4). The term 'business model' arose in the early 1990s and is used to express the nature of the activities and processes a company performs to deliver goods and services to customers. Every company operates according to a business model, which may or may not be effective; for example, the different business model in terms of strategy and implementation between a high-street shop selling physical CDs compared to a website offering music downloads. A disruptive business model is the discovery of fundamentally new ways of doing business in an existing market. New business models attack existing markets by emphasizing different product or service attributes than established organizations do. The kinds of new attributes might, for example, be:

- price
- convenience
- speed of execution
- design
- selection
- location
- ease of use.

New models offering such attributes have appeared in such markets as bookshops and travel, for example with Amazon and easyJet, respectively.

Established firms often find it very difficult to respond to new business models because the 'architecture' of their business throws up a variety of barriers (Johnson et al., 2008). So, if a low-cost and no-frills competitor comes into the market, it is often not easy to respond, as it would mean renegotiating wage and supply contracts. Another issue is that new business models are seen as unattractive in the early phases of market adoption, so the incumbents often have very little incentive to respond.

There are some distinct differences to disruptive technologies; new business models rarely completely overtake the traditional ways of competing. Waterstone's still exists in face of Amazon and e-book readers have yet to make much of an inroad into the physical book marketplace (see Mini Case Study 8.1). Indeed, Markides (2006) estimates on average that new business models capture no more than 20 per cent of markets. The reason is that new business models are rarely superior to existing ones; instead, they are normally complementary and most incumbents do not find them attractive. The next section will examine disruptive products (see Figure 8.1).

MINI CASE STUDY 8.1 The future of e-books?

An e-book reader, commonly called an e-book, is a device used for the display of digital books. Generally, people tend to think of devices that are specifically designed for reading e-books but it can be something that can undertake other functions as well, such as a Personal Data Assistant (PDA). Examples include the COOL-ER, Cybook, Bookeen, Digital Reader 1000, eSlick, Ganaxa, Hanlin, iLiad, Kindle, and the Sony Reader.

The core of an e-book reader is the use of e-ink technology. This is a high-resolution active matrix display (commonly referred to as electronic paper displays or EPD displays) that are reflective and can be read in bright sunlight or dimly lit areas and can be seen from virtually any angle, just like paper, and most closely resemble the experience of a newspaper. One of the beauties of EPD is that the display only uses power when an image is changed, so that e-ink has enormous extended battery life over other types of displays. It also enables highly compact and lightweight devices.

What are the pros and cons of an e-book? The reasons for buying one are mainly as follows:

1. It's great if you travel as you have a full complement of books available at any time. Companies such as Google have expressed an interest in making e-books available. Your books can be stored online and downloaded at any time if you want to use storage for something else.
2. You can put anything you want on it, with a massive range of books, newspapers, magazines, and blogs available for download at places like Amazon and Waterstone's and across the Internet. More and more publishers are bringing out e-books by the day. Some readers can hold up to 1,500 books.
3. Prices for book downloads are lower than the physical equivalent (Amazon charges a flat rate of $9.99 for most of its e-books in the US and Waterstone's charges a few pounds (£) less for its e-books in the UK).
4. Books can be effortlessly loaded using Wi-Fi or via a usb cable to your computer and the downloads are fast (a book in often less than a minute).

5. The latest versions feel good, are well made and are so thin that they are eminently portable. Page-turning has become easier and more reliable on newer models. Furthermore, they can function without access to a computer by Wi-Fi and stay cool to touch.
6. Usability has improved considerably, with advanced bookmarking and highlighting systems and the ability to adjust the font to a comfortable reading size.
7. Dictionaries are built in and for some models are online. When you move to a word the reader provides a definition, either on the same or on a separate page.
8. Illustrations aren't perfect, but are getting better with each new model.
9. With e-ink technology, the battery life continues to improve, with most lasting for several days if continually hooked to Wi-Fi or several weeks if not.
10. Some readers can read out the book to you if you prefer, which is great for the partially sighted or, for example, if you go from reading to having to do a household chore, where you can continue the book.

The reasons for not buying an e-book are mainly as follows:

1. They don't suit study and research activities for everyone too well. They have search and annotation features but they aren't physical objects that can be moved through, skimmed, or allow for note-making on them, and things are less easy to find in an e-book than the equivalent paper version. They may be on their way to the schools in California, but they aren't quite fit for the purpose for students other than those reading novels in an English class.
2. Having a battery means it will die on you occasionally and most likely when you don't have the charger to hand.
3. They are good as reference manuals such as when working on a car or fixing electrical wiring. They just cannot emulate the ease of perusing and flicking between parts of a manual.
4. They tend to be well built but you cannot get away from the essential nature of a device with a thin screen. They cannot be thrown around and treated in the same way you might a paperback without worrying that you might break one.
5. For many people, there is just something about a physical book—perhaps something tactile—that an e-reader cannot ever replace.

There are a number of strategic issues for book publishers and retailers to consider with e-books. Publishers are generally delighted to have another channel open up but how much should an e-book cost? The digital world removes a number of the costs such as shipping and production but these aren't the main costs faced by publishers, who have to pay for intellectual permission, authors, marketing, and for running the basic business. At the moment, Amazon often takes a loss on its e-books as it buys them from publishers at the regular price and at some point it will want publishers to share the pain. It's probably unlikely, but as Amazon gathers the best data on who is buying and what they like, it is not inconceivable that they might enter the content domain and become an e-publisher. Furthermore, if e-books take off, what is to stop authors from signing directly with e-bookstores and cutting publishers? After all, Madonna and U2 deal with promoters rather than record companies.

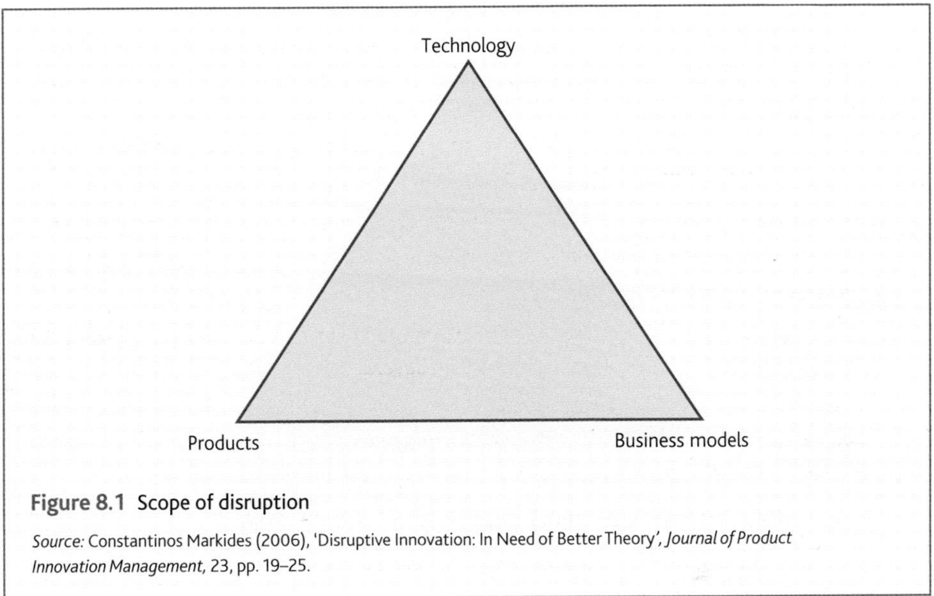

Figure 8.1 Scope of disruption

Source: Constantinos Markides (2006), 'Disruptive Innovation: In Need of Better Theory', *Journal of Product Innovation Management*, 23, pp. 19–25.

Disruptive products

Launching disruptive goods and services is a risky business, especially if the technology is discontinuous (requires a significant change in behaviour and/or in complementary technology); e.g. DVD recorders cannot play VHS tapes, as opposed to Blue-Ray, which can play DVDs. If it goes wrong, the costs can be enormous. Shortening the new product development (NPD) process can be a formidable competitive weapon. Xerox is a case in point: it recaptured its lead in the copier market by reducing its seven-year NPD process to two.

The following marketing strategies form the 'umbrella' of product innovation activities pursued by organizations and are based on the original NPD typology developed by Booz Allen Hamilton (1982) (see Figure 8.2). They are activities conducted by market leaders, challengers, and niche players who use innovation as a competitive tool in the marketplace (followers tend to introduce innovation once the risk has been reduced):

- **Additions to existing lines:** for example, when Heinz added 'Green' to its range of ketchups. Studies show additions to be about a 25 per cent of all marketing innovation and are valuable in offering new choices to loyals as well as new customers and thereby increasing overall sales.
- **Cost reductions:** cost reductions, as with the introduction of cheaper flights to Europe by easyJet and Ryanair and SouthWest Airlines in the US. These account for slightly above 10 per cent of all innovations. Such airlines have introduced new processes and ways of doing business to fill a gap in the marketplace for cheap foreign travel. Cost reductions can open up new markets for companies and provide relatively safe spaces to operate within, as long as established rivals are unable to change their processes sufficiently to match.

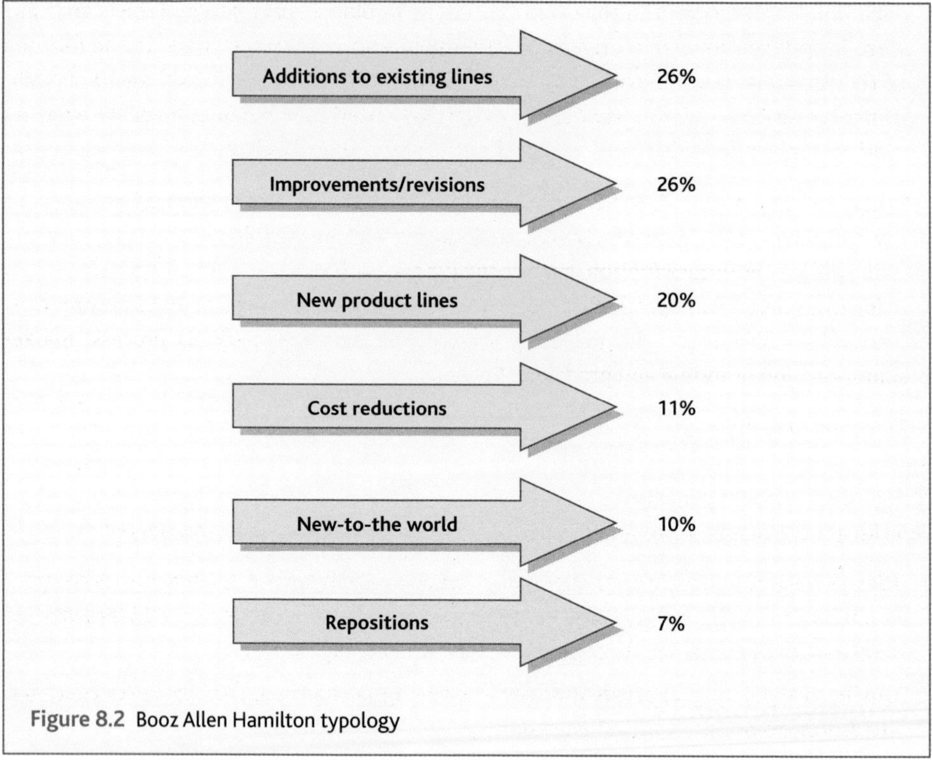

Figure 8.2 Booz Allen Hamilton typology

- **Improvements/revisions**: for example, when Kellogg's introduced a foil wrap for its cereals to improve freshness. Improvements and revisions tend to account for about 25 per cent of all marketing innovation and are particularly useful at maintaining loyalty and distancing from rival and often me-too products. Thus, in the case of Kellogg's Corn Flakes, the foil wrap distinguishes the brand from supermarket own labels.
- **New product lines:** for example, when the engineering and transport company, Atkins, added management and project services to its range of design and engineering solutions or when Asus added Eee PC netbooks to its computing range. Indications are that new product lines account for about 20 per cent of all innovations and can be successful in increasing the spend of loyals and enhancing loyalty.
- **New-to-the-world:** Motorola invented the first 'mobile' phone in 1973, but it wasn't until 1985 that they first came to market in a format that would be recognized as mobile. New-to-the-world makes up about 10 per cent of all innovations and can provide significant market advantages in the intervening space before rivals can introduce their own versions.
- **Repositions:** in its widest form, a reposition includes any kind of reposition, albeit just a change in advertising. However, more strictly related to innovation and development, it involves significant changes in at least one element of the mix—be that product, price, place, promotion, or people. For example, Lucozade was repositioned in 1985 from an energy drink for the sick to an energy replacement for sports people. The advertising

used Daley Thompson with the claim: 'Lucozade Replaces Lost Energy'. Tablets and cans were introduced to enable greater portability, but no change was made to the formula of the drink. Studies indicate that repositions account for slightly less than 10 per cent of marketing innovations a year and are especially used by companies faced with ageing markets and/or declining sales to revitalize the brand (e.g., Brylcreem).

Whatever the form, NPD and innovation are central tenets of marketing strategy for many companies. They underpin cost reductions, such as the Web delivery of insurance and banking, as well as differentiation, such as the iPhone with its various applications.

Aside from repositioning, all of the above innovation strategies require that a new product or service be developed. The following section will examine the NPD process, market preparation, and branding and product rollovers.

NPD (New Product Development)

Process

New ideas have been traditionally developed by a three-stage process (see Figure 8.3):

1. **Idea generation** involves activities like problem analysis, listing attributes and changing combinations, suggestion boxes, brainstorming, and customer requests. Ideas are then screened by their market attractiveness and market competitiveness.
2. **Business screening analysis** involves identifying positioning, creating a concept, and attempting to predict market behaviour.
3. **Development and test marketing** involves sales forecasting, product development, market tests, possible marketing mix, and break-even analysis.

Once a company has established the qualitative and quantitative nature of its objectives it has to ensure that there is a process in place to enable innovation to happen and to transplant innovative ideas into manageable projects. It may help to break the process into stages.

From an organizational perspective, the whole process might be driven **functionally**: the new product passes sequentially between departments and ends with marketing. Alternatively, a **parallel** approach might be adopted, where all the elements are developed

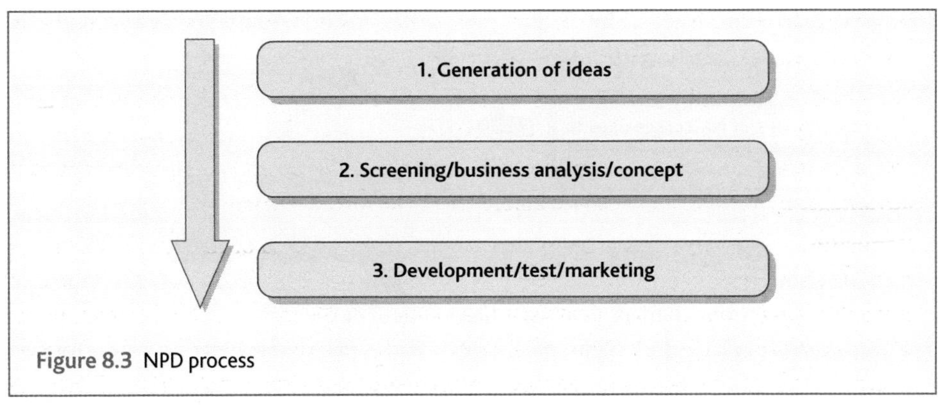

Figure 8.3 NPD process

in tandem so that marketing has involvement from the generation of the idea onwards. Alternatively, Bonabeau et al. (2008) advocate separating the early stage of NPD from the latter with two completely detached organizational structures. They argue that the first phase is for 'truth-seeking' to identify prospects or eliminate bad bets. The second is to focus on maximizing the value of products that have made it through the first stage. They broadly estimate that between 60 and 80 per cent of candidate new products will be eliminated at stage 1 and around 70 per cent will go to market launches.

Toolkit strategy

The toolkit strategy enables customers of NPD companies to undertake their own innovation and is an important example of the direction in which the NPD process is moving (see Figure 8.4). At its core, the basic problem of NPD is that the 'need information' side of the equation resides with the customer while the 'solution' information resides with the manufacturer. Take the case of BBA, which develops speciality flavours to bolster and enhance the taste of processed foods. A traditional project might start with a client requesting a single sample of a 'meaty flavour' for a soy product. The shipment is then made within six days. After three weeks, the client might respond with: 'It's good, but we need it less smoky and more gutsy' (Thomke and von Hippel, 2002). BBA then attempts to modify the flavour in two days. Several more iterations may occur before they get it right. BBA bears most of the development risks, with R&D costing from around £600 for a minor tweak to £160,000 for an entirely new flavour. Furthermore, on average, most clients only accept about 15 per cent of new flavours after full market evaluation, with 5 to 10 per cent eventually making their way to the marketplace.

In response, BBA has shifted more innovation activities to their customers. They have developed an Internet-based tool containing a dataset of flavour profiles. Customers are able to select information and manipulate it on-screen and send the new flavour design directly to an automated machine (often located at the clients' site) and the product is made within minutes. After tasting, if needed, the flavour can be manipulated and tweaked again.

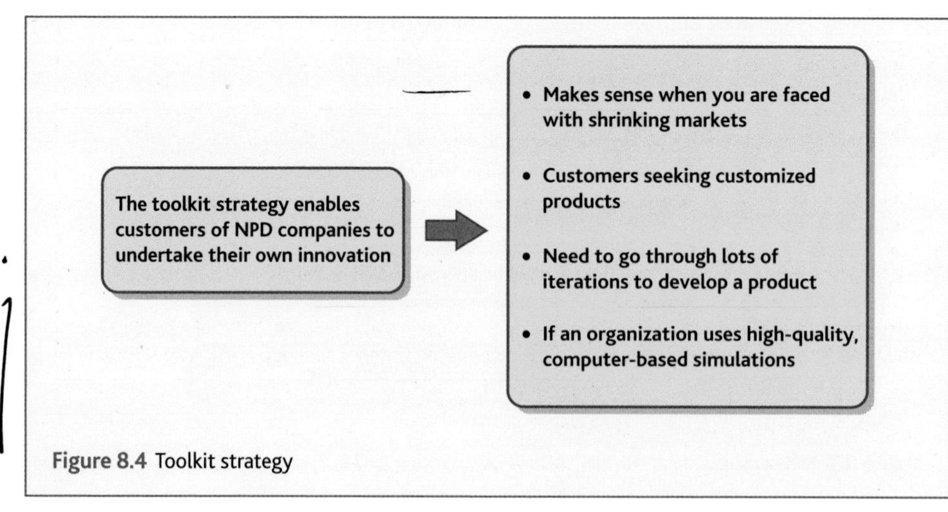

Figure 8.4 Toolkit strategy

Take another case, the custom computer chip industry. Traditionally, manufacturers were only able to undertake projects for companies wanting high volumes, given the high cost of developing bespoke chips for such uses as robotic circuitry. Companies such as LSI Logic have transformed the process by providing both large and small customers with DIY tools to design their own chips. Such developments are based on companies taking their knowledge, developed over decades, and incorporating it onto sophisticated CAD/CAM (computer-aided design/computer-aided manufacturing) programmes that contain libraries of design options to solve numerous problems using graphical interfaces. They also enable testing through computer simulations to build virtual prototypes easily and quickly. By standardizing transistor design and adding LSI's solution information, the customer toolkit can function.

When to develop such toolkits? Customer innovation and toolkits make sense when you are faced with shrinking markets and customers seeking customized products. They are also useful when you need to go through lots of iterations to develop a product. Another pointer is if an organization uses high-quality computer-based simulations to develop new products and has computer-adjustable production processes.

Systematic inventive thinking

Product developers are constantly striving for the 'innovation sweet spot'. This is the point when a new product idea is different enough from the existing product to attract customer interest and at the same time close enough to the company's existing position and capabilities so that it makes sense to customers and can be delivered by operations.

'Systematic Inventive Thinking' (SIT) provides a highly disciplined approach to new product idea generation that represents both the interests of customers and the company (Goldenberg et al., 2003) and is worth a particular mention (see Figure 8.5).

The starting point for SIT is to list all the main elements of a product in terms of physical components and attributes such as colour and expected useful life. The next stage is to identify the

Subtraction is about removing components or attributes
Multiplication involves adding elements, such as developing a double waste-bin unit that can be used for rubbish
Division is the breaking-down of an existing product into its component parts, such as the replacement of the integrated hi-fi into modular systems involving speakers, amplifier, tuner, tape, and CD
Task unification concerns assigning a new task to the product, such as when Rubbermaid placed assembly instructions for storage cabinets on the packaging rather than on a separate enclosed sheet
Attribute dependency change involves the relationship between the attributes of a product and the attributes of the immediate environment, as with the development of male and female razors

Figure 8.5 Systematic inventive thinking

Source: Jacob Goldenberg et al. (2003), 'Finding your Innovation Sweet Spot', *Harvard Business Review*, March, pp. 120–9.

immediate environment, again in terms of physical components and attributes (e.g., ambient temperature and type of user). Finally, five innovation patterns (based on the work of Russian engineer, Genrich Altshuller) may be manipulated to develop a new product idea.

The five patterns of innovation are subtraction, multiplication, division, task unification, and attribute dependency change:

- **Subtraction** is about removing components or attributes.
- **Multiplication** involves adding elements like developing a double waste-bin unit that can be used for rubbish and recycling or a double-bladed razor that lifts whiskers when shaving. (Note the need for qualitative change rather than just straight multiplication.)
- **Division** is the breaking down of an existing product into its component parts, such as the replacement of the integrated hi-fi into modular systems involving speakers, amplifier, tuner, tape, and CD.
- **Task unification** concerns assigning a new task to the product, such as when Rubbermaid placed assembly instructions for storage cabinets on the packaging rather than on a separate enclosed sheet.
- **Attribute dependency change** involves the relationship between the attributes of a product and the attributes of the immediate environment, as with the development of male and female razors.

One case was the development of a new business card for a company (Goldenberg et al., 2003). Having examined conventional business cards, it was decided to choose the pattern of 'subtraction'. A business card was developed without a job title and, instead, a hole was cut in its place. It demonstrated clearly that the company was non-hierarchical, but it presented several challenges: it undermined the primary function of a business card; it might make junior employees insecure without a title; it might seem inadvertent; and the meaning of the hole was not obvious. The next stage was 'task unification', which involved the assignment of a new task to the product. One idea was to use the hole as a window to frame additional information such as different job titles, trade association memberships, weekend activities, and intellectual interests. This demonstrated a lack of hierarchy while appearing to be innovative and offered a multifaceted view of an employee. It left a problem of how to provide a variety of role definitions. The final solution was to shrink the card to accommodate a standard rotating 'wheel' made of card that could be turned to show the multifaceted job functions, roles, relationships, and interests of the card bearer. A new product!

Market preparation and branding

Having developed a new product, market preparation is about 'warmin-up' the marketplace for the innovation. In the case of high-tech products, cooperative strategies with rivals are becoming the norm (Easingwood and Koustelos, 2000). This is because alliances and licensing helps signal to consumers that this new technology will not leave them marginalized, as happened with Betamax tape-recorders, which were overtaken by VHS despite being of superior quality. Many lessons have been learnt and operating standard agreements, which enable planning and stability, have mushroomed. For example, Psion, Motorola, Ericsson, and Nokia agreed to adopt

Psion's operating system (EPOC) as the platform for WAP. Psion's rivals knew that if they did not abandon their own systems, then Microsoft Windows CE would likely dominate. Being prepared to supply to original equipment manufacturers (OEMs) is another strand of market preparation, as, for example, IBM supplying leading-edge hard drives to rivals such as Acer and Dell.

An innovative product may have its own brand, for example, Net-Flix; or be an endorsed brand like the Asus Eee PC; or be a sub-brand such as the Sony Bravia. As such, a brand provides the potential for an organization to 'own' an innovation in the minds of buyers (Aaker, 2007), which means that even if competitors copy the innovation they will have to work harder to make an impact. Moreover, in sophisticated markets, a branded innovation says to consumers 'the benefits are such that we thought it was worth branding'. This enables a company to add credibility and legitimacy to a claim, as with Gortex linings. Brand names are highly visible and make communications more efficient. From a communications stance, PR on the forthcoming release is crucial. Intel always releases details of all its new chips, such as Celeron, which helps develop anticipation and excitement in the market. Crucially, the PR appears far enough along the process so that rivals cannot react with copycat products in time, given that Intel does not seek alliances. PR can also be used by companies to 'educate' the market about the new technology, but this is often a more long-term process. This does not mean that everything should be branded. The product innovation has to be a significant advance and newsworthy or buyers will see through it very quickly.

Product rollovers

Short product life-cycles increase the frequency of 'product rollovers', the displacement of old products by innovations (Billington et al., 1998). Ideally, existing innovation would be sold out just at the introduction of a new one, but this rarely happens. The Osborne II replacement of the Osborne I, the first successful portable computer, is a classic example. Adam Osborne announced the forthcoming Osborne II in late 1982. Market response was quite logical: people decided to cancel orders for the Osborne I and wait. However, the slump in sales for the I severely reduced Osborne's cash flow and made investment in the II hard to sustain and what is more, owing to technical problems, the introduction of the II slipped. The company eventually had to file for bankruptcy in late 1983. It is an extreme product rollover case, but it demonstrates the point that a strategy is required.

Should the old product be sold out before introducing the new one or should they be sold simultaneously? If so, should they be sold at different prices, in different geographic regions, or through different channels? The two strategic options are: *solo-product roll* and *dual-product roll* (Billington et al., 1998), as shown in Figure 8.6.

Solo-product roll aims to have the entire range of old products sold out at the planned introduction date (e.g., HP's Deskjet 510 replacing the Deskjet 500). This is a high-risk and high-return strategy. It can prove to be expensive if the old product is sold out too early or there are high inventory levels in place, as potential sales may be lost.

Dual-product roll is where both old and new products sell simultaneously for a period (e.g., the Pentium III and IV). It is less risky than the solo option, but requires the marketing of both old and new products, with the consequent risk of confusing the marketplace. Geographic rolls can reduce confusion (e.g., Mercedes first introduced the 190C in Europe

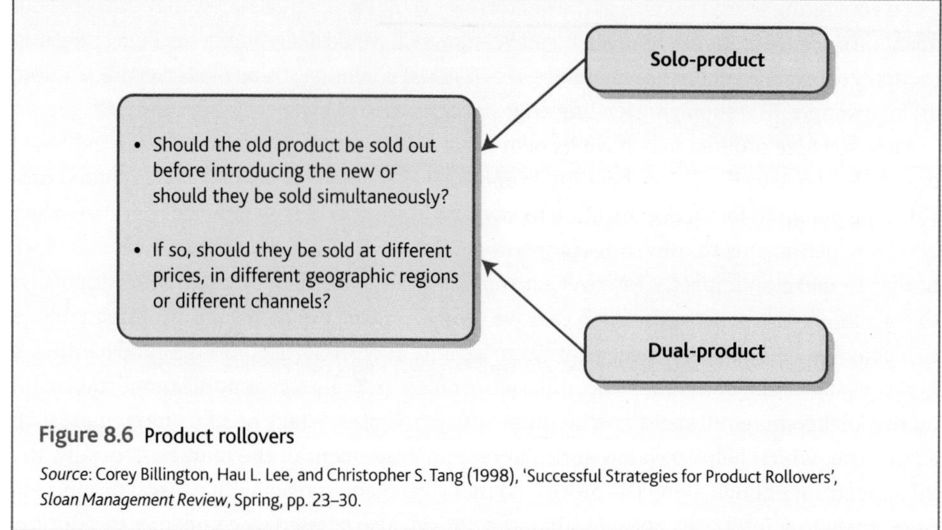

Figure 8.6 Product rollovers

Source: Corey Billington, Hau L. Lee, and Christopher S. Tang (1998), 'Successful Strategies for Product Rollovers', *Sloan Management Review*, Spring, pp. 23–30.

and then in North America). Another angle is to differentiate by channels, (e.g., Nike introducing new models at premium retailers while selling older models through discounters). Dual pricing may also be utilized, as with the aggressive pricing of older computer chips. A fourth strategy is the so-called 'silent' approach, which is to quietly introduce a new rollover without any fanfare (Sony and new Hi-Fi models). The point is to manage new products and the process of displacement of old products *jointly* rather than separately.

Disruptive technologies

The following section will examine the two main frameworks of Rogers (1983) and Moore (1999, 2004a), which address disruptive technologies.

Rogers' perspective

An innovation strategy without any idea of buyer behaviour is a non-starter. Everett M. Rogers' (1983) seminal work on the adoption of innovation was the first to compellingly categorize consumers' readiness to adopt disruptive technologies. Rogers identified five adopter types: innovators, early adopters, early majority, late majority, and laggards (see Figure 8.7):

- **Innovators:** risk-taker and willing to try new ideas
- **Early adopters:** respected opinion-leaders in the product field who are more cautious
- **Early majority:** do not seek leadership but are more likely to adopt than the average buyer
- **Late majority:** more risk-averse and will adopt an innovation after there has already been a sizeable take-up
- **Laggards:** highly risk-averse and traditional. Once an innovation has reached 'traditional status' they will come into the market.

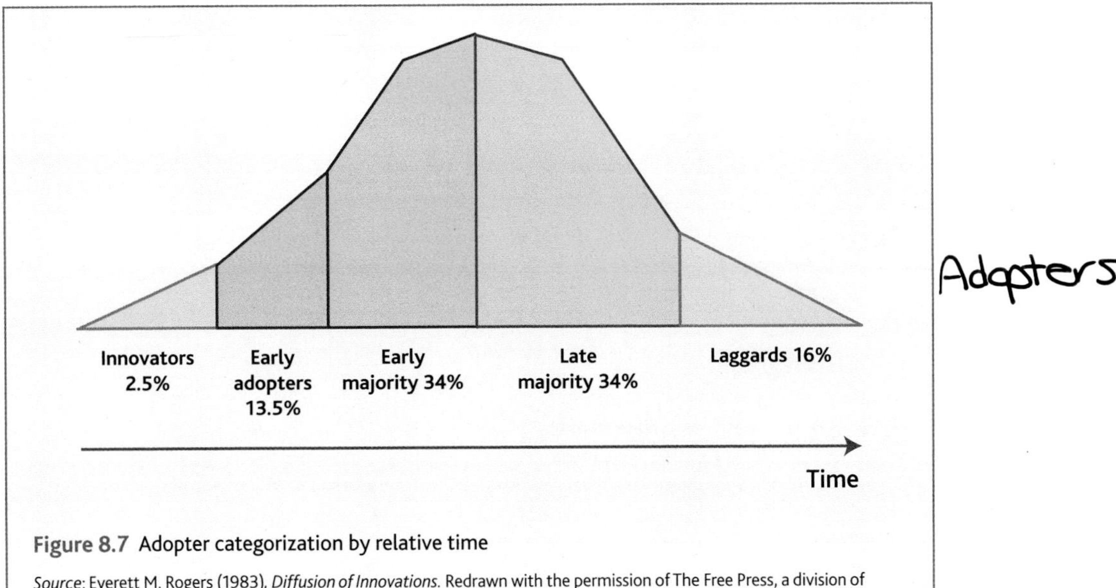

Figure 8.7 Adopter categorization by relative time

Source: Everett M. Rogers (1983), *Diffusion of Innovations*. Redrawn with the permission of The Free Press, a division of Simon & Schuster Adult Publishing Group.

There are a variety of implications arising from Roger's typology.

In order for an innovation to enter from the left of the market and move to the right it will need to have a relative market advantage. This might involve quality or convenience or anything that avoids the 'bad bits' of what it aims to supersede. For example, Recaro introduced a leading-edge child seat for Porsche and Aston-Martin drivers.

Strategically, it will also help to maximize compatibility with the existing marketplace in terms of physical space (e.g., a relatively large home-computer would no longer be a viable option for most customers); be able to hook into the current inventory of alternative; link up to other similar products; and need no or few behavioural changes. For example, attempts to introduce non-QWERTY keyboards have met with universal failure. As noted above, convergent standards are important issues. Companies introducing new digital phones increasingly make them compatible with US, Asian, and European standards. One interesting variation on this theme used by Luz Engineering installs industrial solar-heaters costing between £1 million and £3 million at no initial cost to buyers. Instead, they are required to take out a twenty-year contract at a discount rate to buy steam at 350°F with the local power company, which aids adoption considerably.

It also helps if the innovation is not too complex, can be communicated readily, and can be tried and tested. Finally, Rogers argued that perceived risk needs to be as low as possible—in particular regarding uncertainty of performance, consequences of failure, financial cost, physical health concerns, and effects on self-image.

Moore's perspective

Rogers' view of adoption largely held sway until the late 1990s, when Geoffrey A. Moore introduced his ideas of the 'chasm strategy' (1999, 2004a, and see 2004b). Moore pointed

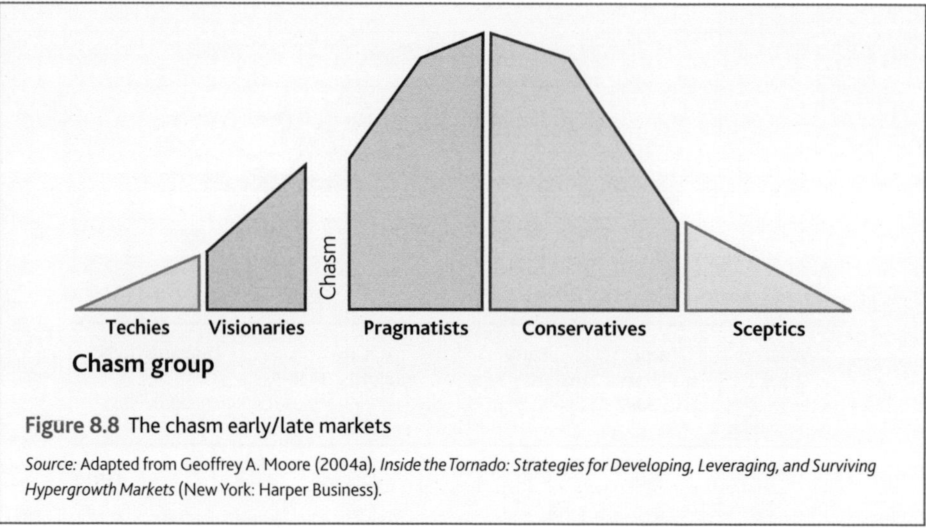

Figure 8.8 The chasm early/late markets

Source: Adapted from Geoffrey A. Moore (2004a), *Inside the Tornado: Strategies for Developing, Leveraging, and Surviving Hypergrowth Markets* (New York: Harper Business).

out that innovative products do not normally slide in from the left-hand side and work their way steadily across to the right. Instead, they often meet with failure, which he categorized as falling into 'the chasm' (see Figure 8.8).

Studies indicate that only about 10 to 12 per cent of new products make it to market. Though before going any further, the point must be made that most disappear because of internal rather than external market processes:

- about 40 per cent disappear after **business screening**
- a further 20 per cent of innovations evaporate in **development**
- around 10 per cent are dropped after **test marketing.**

Once introduced to the marketplace, around 30 to 50 per cent of all new products fail to meet with commercial success, and for high-tech products the position may be considerably worse.

Crossing the chasm

Moore has argued that the fundamental issue for success in crossing the chasm is to understand the difference between the early and late markets. His perspective is orientated towards B2B rather than Rogers's B2C view, although the implications of chasm-marketing may be equally applicable to B2C markets (see Figure 8.9):

- **Techies:** are companies that are largely motivated by technology. They do not particularly reference the behaviour of other companies and are willing to purchase high-tech products at a relatively low price and assume the risk of debugging any problems. They are not bothered if the supplier is a market leader but will need considerable training, especially with a discontinuous technology. Communications to this group should stress 'newness'.
- **Visionaries:** are companies that are looking to get ahead of rivals. They are not interested in technology for its own sake; rather, they see new technology as a way of getting ahead. They reference other visionaries, will accept relatively high pricing, and will need

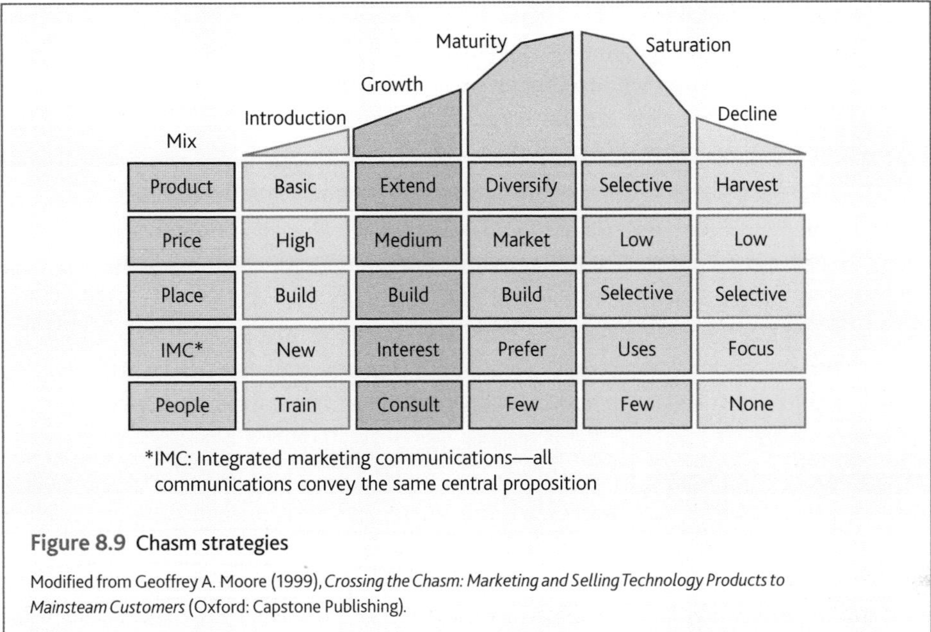

Figure 8.9 Chasm strategies

Modified from Geoffrey A. Moore (1999), *Crossing the Chasm: Marketing and Selling Technology Products to Mainsteam Customers* (Oxford: Capstone Publishing).

high levels of consulting training. Communications to this group should stress innovation rather than newness and they are likely to respond better to companies that exhibit signs of potential leadership of the new technology. If a company is unable to establish a business value for its innovation with visionaries, it is unlikely to cross the chasm.

- **Pragmatists:** on the other side of the chasm sit the pragmatists. The failure of most high-tech products rests on their inability to resonate with the pragmatic company. Pragmatists are looking to fix a 'broken business process'. Essentially, the problem posed by pragmatic companies is that if the innovation fails to fix something that they perceive as 'broken', they will simply not purchase the technology. They reference other pragmatic companies (not Techies or Visonaries), are prepared to pay a market price, and may need some training services. However, Pragmatists are looking to buy from companies that they see as strong contenders for market leadership in the technology. They do not want to be left holding innovations from companies that prove to be 'also-rans' and will need communications stressing that the technology is proven, safe, easy, and effective. If you have it, a particularly safe execution is to emphasize market leadership. The new high-tech product is launched in an 'all out' way that leaves customers in no doubt that you intend to push your product into the marketplace. Microsoft's launch of Windows was a classic case of a concentrated approach to execution, with a massive coordinated campaign across the globe, with little expense spared.
- **Conservatives:** behind the Pragmatists sit the Conservative companies that, as you can guess, are much more risk-averse than Pragmatists. They see themselves in competition with Pragmatists who they also reference. However, their risk-adversity means that they tend to wait to see whether or not the technology 'stays the course' and are waiting to see what

standards develop and which market leaders emerge. Pricing to this group needs to be at market or lower and the communications required are broadly similar to that to the Pragmatists: safe, easy, and effective. Case studies work particularly well with Conservatives. Given the penetration of the technology by this point, Conservatives need few services.

- **Sceptics:** are similar to Rogers' 'Laggards'. Sceptics are the companies at the end of the curve that have to be dragged 'kicking and screaming' into the market. They tend to buy when there is no alternative. What they have has broken down and they have to replace it and the new technology is the only alternative. For example, a small solicitors' firm may be running its business with five-to-ten-year-old computers. They do the job and there is no reason to replace them except when they are uneconomic to replace. They do not reference other companies, need low prices, will tend to buy from the leading company in the market, and are unlikely to need much in the way of communications or training services.

Two marketing campaigns

Moore suggests that the best strategy for crossing the chasm is to conduct two marketing campaigns. The early market involves Techies and Visionaries. Techies can be used to make sure the innovation works and to 'iron out any bugs'. Visionaries should then be targeted and used to develop the whole product (see Figure 8.10), including pre- and post-sales and software and peripherals. Visionaries will enable the company to find the competitive advantage within the technology and establish the basis of the appeal for the Pragmatists. For example, QR codes (short for Quick Response) were invented in 1994 by Denso-Wave, a Japanese corporation, initially to track parts in vehicle-manufacturing using bar-code technology. These special bar codes have migrated to the consumer market and allow shoppers to swipe a packet of tomatoes, for example, and can show such facts as the size and location of the originating farm. They have grown to cult status in Japan and have begun to appear in the UK but can, of course, only be read by mobile phones with cameras. The technology is poised to cross the chasm from Techies

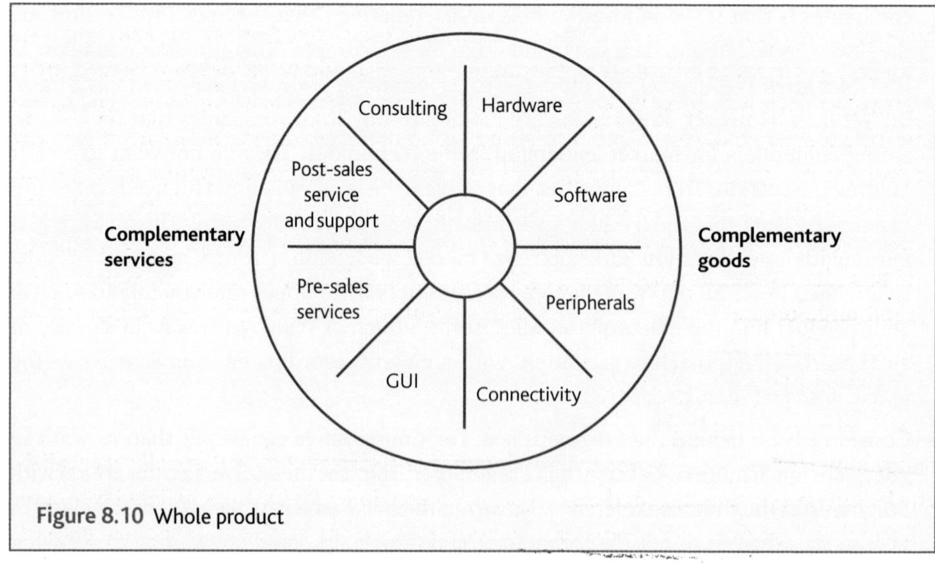

Figure 8.10 Whole product

and Visionaries to Pragmatists as Pepsi placed QR codes on 400 million products in late 2008, offering consumers access to games, videos, websites, and prizes at the swipe of a phone.

How might such technology as QR codes cross the chasm? Moore argues that as Pragmatists reference each other a 'bowling alley strategy' is required to make headway. The idea is to target and dominate a specific market that has influence over other markets—hence the bowling-alley analogy—one pin goes down and (hopefully) also knocks down several other pins too. Thus, when USDC developed an active-matrix flat-panel screen, with each pixel linked to its own transistor, it targeted the world's leading air forces which it knew had a pressing need to adopt paper-quality screens (Easingwood and Koustelos, 2000) and would influence outside commercial markets. Another example of targeting was NTT's Digital Photo System. The system enabled the transmission of digital pictures via mobile phones and was targeted at newspapers and insurance companies and later migrated out to other industries. Having penetrated the Pragmatic market and crossed the chasm, the Conservatives will then enter the market, buying from market leaders. Thus, industry opinion-leaders have been successfully used by Compaq and NEC. Doctors are commonly used by pharmaceutical companies to influence general practitioners.

Horizons of growth

An important element in managing product innovation and development is to recognize the stage of development of the business concerned. Baghai et al. (1999) have argued that there are three 'horizons' to consider: Horizon 1 (H1), Horizon 2 (H2), and Horizon 3 (H3). H1 businesses are mature and established and for most businesses provide the bulk of profits and cash flow. H2 are businesses on the rise and experiencing rapid growth. H3 businesses are emerging ones with potential.

Because each horizon has its own distinctive strategic and operational requirement, businesses encapsulating more than one horizon need more than one management system. H1 businesses need traditional management strategies and operations and can be measured by productivity and efficiencies. H2 businesses require disciplined risk-taking and significant resources to capitalize on growth opportunities and so should be judged by revenue growth and market share, whereas H3 businesses are fledgling and need to be run by champions and inspiring leaders who can create new strategies and business models. The main measure appropriate to the H3 horizon is the ability of the business to make progress in converting new ideas into workable businesses. The advantage of the approach is that it fits nicely with Moore's ideas of the chasm (H3 before the chasm; H2 at the growth stage; H1 at maturity), and provides a framework for managing innovation and development on a co-existent basis within large organizations, along with focusing management attention on the particular needs of fledgling businesses.

If you aren't the market leader

Innovation strategies that stress market dominance (Horizon 2 above) are all very well for the leading players in such markets, but what do you do if you are the smaller player in the marketplace? Quite often it is possible to be the leader in one market and the small player in another (see Mini Case Study 8.2). Yoffie and Kwak (2002) have identified what they call 'judo' strategy—an approach particularly well-suited to small players in innovative markets.

MINI CASE STUDY 8.2 Powering down the chip market

The microprocessor has been a truly disruptive technology, transforming markets and spawning a variety of new business markets. Setting aside AMD's x86-64, most of the iconic computer chips can be attributed to Intel (based in Austin, Texas):

- Intel's first, the 8080 (the successor to the 8008), was introduced in 1972 as a general purpose 8-bit processor powering the first PCs along with automated fare collection systems, video games, traffic lights, cash registers, and reel-to-reel tape recorders.
- The next milestone was the 8088, introduced in 1981. It was another 8-bit processor, but with a much faster clock speed and spawned the nascent computer industry when IBM chose it against rival offerings from its own engineers and Motorola. The personal computer was born.
- 1985 saw the introduction of the 80386 or just '386'. This became the key computer architecture and still forms the core of the programming of all current 32-bit x86 processors. It was the first processor to be single-sourced by Intel and, fortunately for the company, computer manufacturers decided against manufacturing their own versions.
- Pentium, introduced in 1993, was the first chip capable of undertaking more than one instruction per clock cycle. Fast and powerful, the truly mass market for the PC was born.
- Centrino was introduced in 2003, primarily for laptops and to enable Wi-Fi connectivity. The chip enabled laptops to rival desktops powered by the older Pentiums for performance and to operate for four to five hours on a single charge. As the Centrino chip remained relatively cool, it also enabled thinner and lighter laptops as they did not need such big cooling systems.
- 2008 saw the introduction of the Atom, offering low-power consumption rather than performance (drawing about a tenth of the power of a Centrino while offering about half the performance), and aimed at netbooks such as the Assus Eee PC, the Acer Aspire One, and the Samsung NC20.

Where should Intel's marketing strategy focus next? PC sales have proved sluggish. The biggest and fastest-growing market is consumer electronics and wireless gadgets. It's a market with some significant incumbents in places such as Nvidia, Qualcomm, and Texas Instruments. All gadgets are increasingly building in wireless applications. For example:

- Air offers positioning technology for a variety of devices. Its 'geotagging' technology can, for example, tag a digital photograph with its location.
- The Eye-Fi SD card stores photos and videos like a traditional memory card, and fits into most cameras. However, when you are within range of a configured Wi-Fi

network it can wirelessly transfer your photos and videos to your computer and/or to a photo-sharing website.

- GM's OnStar system is built into its cars and links the car in real time to a GPS tracking system that offers an automatic crash response, emergency services, stolen vehicle tracking, remote door unlock, horns and lights, vehicle diagnostics, hands-free calling, and navigation.
- Skyhook provides instant positioning based upon GPS, mobile transmitters, and Wi-Fi technology for mobile phones and personal devices.

A big player in computers, Intel finds itself the 'little guy' in consumer electronics and phones. While its culture has been gradually shifting from high-performance chips for consumer and corporate markets (e.g., the Atom), a significant shift will be required to churn out millions of low-power chips at around £10-a-piece for smart products. New thinking, new strategies, and new approaches to marketing implementation will be required to make a success for products like the iPhone. The indications are that the Intel focus on quality, power, and compatibility may not be so easily transferred. Intel might beat the competition hands down with the performance of its chips for the consumer electronic marketplace; however, is that what consumers want? Take the case of the iPhone, which runs on ARM architecture. It's great for scrolling through Web pages, but it can't run a fully compatible version of Microsoft Office. However, does anyone want it to?

Yoffie and Kwak (2002) focus on the case of Palm Inc, which they argue provides a powerful example of 'judo strategy' at work. Judo strategies rely on speed, agility, and creative thinking and make it difficult for stronger rivals to compete. Judo strategy is an approach to competition based on skill rather than size or strength and uses the three principles of 'movement', 'defining space', and 'speed' (see Figure 8.11).

Movement One of the key tactics in movement is the 'puppy dog play' Keep a low profile until you are strong enough to fight
Define the competitive space Establish the positioning of the product and keep it simple
Follow through fast Maintain innovation with a focus on design, functionality, and low prices

Figure 8.11 Judo

Source: David B. Yoffie and Mary Kwak (2002), 'Mastering Strategic Movement at Palm', *MIT Sloan Management Review*, January, pp. 47–53.

Movement

One of the key tactics in movement is the 'puppy dog play'. In essence, keep a low profile until you are strong enough to fight. Palm's first handheld organizer was introduced at a discreet and exclusive industry trade show in early 1996. It sold moderately well with 10,000 units per month for about five months but, and this was key, it sold primarily to self-rated computer experts earning $100,000 plus per annum. When they then bought it for their friends and colleagues for Christmas, sales began to take off. All the while Palm management downplayed its success: '... a little organizer that happens to connect to your PC'. By positioning it as a companion to the PC, they hoped to keep out of Microsoft's sights. Instead of a platform, the Palm was a device. According to Microsoft's CEO, Steve Ballmer, Palm didn't catch the company's attention for at least two years.

Define the competitive space

The next judo tactic is to define the competitive space. A race that pitched the PDA as the digital equivalent of a Swiss Army knife would have given ground to bigger and stronger competitors. Instead, Palm kept it simple, with a concept based on a calendar and an address book. No wireless communications or spreadsheets that would have favoured the big players were emphasized. To keep it simple, Palm integrated its software and hardware design, as opposed to Microsoft which developed the software and then 'threw it over the fence to the hardware manufacturers'.

Follow through fast

The next tactic is to follow through fast. As Microsoft began to enter the market and refine its product with Windows CE in late 1997, Palm realized that it had to maintain and, if possible, increase its lead with rivals. It did this by fairly moderate innovation but with a strong focus on design, functionality, and low prices. Typical Windows CE devices retailed for about twice that of Palm's and offered lots of features that consumers were not too bothered about and had less attractive designs. Meanwhile, Palm introduced the Professional, the Personal, and the III, IIIx, V, and VII between 1997 and 1999. Critically, by building market share, developers were encouraged to create a multitude of applications for the Palm operating system and very few others. This had been aided by the quiet introduction of a Palm software developer kit back in 1996, making the code open.

Palm is still the main player in the market and has recently merged with Treo. This is a perfect match, given Palm's marketing expertise and Treo's product competency. However, the Windows CE operating system and merging of mobile/PDA technology has left Palm slightly on the back foot compared to rivals such as HP. It will be interesting to see how their judo strategy finally plays out.

Innovation 'modes'

Despite strongly contended cases to the opposite by such companies as Sony, very little technological innovation is developed without some sense of a strategy. Once a new innovation or development has reached the market, people's perceptions and expectations are often changed (as with flat-screen televisions or photocopying) and often reshape how people live or work. Market success normally requires an overall strategic framework.

Overall, companies learn from markets, and the customers learn from new technologies. For any organization, the degree of focus on either innovation and/or the customer can vary. There are, therefore, as shown in Figure 8.12, four strategic options of low/high market orientation, matched with low/high innovation orientation (framework modified from the work of Berthon et al., 1999).

Isolate mode

The so-called 'isolate' mode (bottom left of the quadrant in Figure 8.12) is where an organization has both a low innovation orientation as well as market orientation. The flows between customer and technology are almost non-existent and technology either stagnates or is developed for its own sake. Stagnation or evolution occurs separately from the market. Such organizations are introverted and may be exemplified by the British automobile and motorcycle industry of the late 1960s and throughout the 1970s. British Leyland introduced innovations, but these were often tangential to market needs and preferences.

Follow mode

The low innovation but high market orientation organization is in the 'follow' mode of the quadrant (top left in Figure 8.12). Here, technology is used in response to the needs and

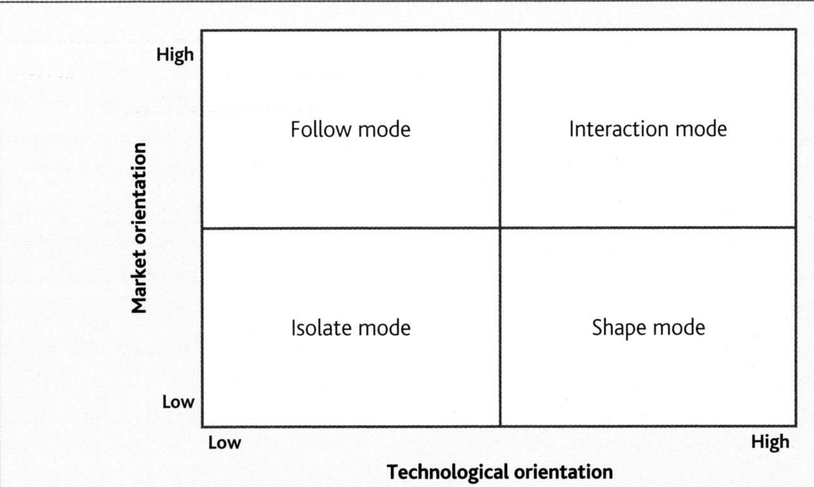

Figure 8.12 Options for innovation

Source: Adapted from Pierre Berthon, James M. Hulbert, and Leyland F. Pitt (1999), 'To Serve or Create: Strategic Orientations toward Customers and Innovation', *California Management Review*, 42 (1), pp. 37–58. © 1999, by The Regents of the University of California. Redrawn by permission of The Regents.

wants of the customer and may be seen with the development of the BMW 1 Series or the Courtyard concept by Marriott Hotels. All are examples of companies designing products based on what customers want.

Shape mode

Organizations in the high innovation but low market orientation mode are in the 'shape' part of the quadrant (bottom right in Figure 8.12). Shaping is where a company applies a technology that defines human needs and determines the nature of customer demand. A recent shaper in the market would be the Apple iPod—a technological entrant that has disproportionately influenced the criteria by which later entrants, such as the Creative Zen, have been judged. Berthon et al. (1999) suggest two distinct forms of shaping. 'Definers' lead the market, as with Chrysler's minivan of the early 1980s, and Compaq's forging of the server market in the 1990s. 'Influencers', on the other hand, shape markets but do not define the market or dominate it. For example, the Apple Macintosh shaped expectations of computers without leading the market.

Interaction mode

Organizations that achieve a high market orientation married to high innovation are in the 'interaction' mode of the quadrant (top right in Figure 8.12). This is where a true dialogue occurs between an organization's application of technology and what customers want. Such interaction occurred before mass markets arose, of course, such as with men and women's tailoring. However, interaction is being applied apace with the concept of one-to-one marketing, where companies such as Dell.com and iTunes allow customers to prepare their own specifications of computers and compilations of music CDs, respectively.

Strategic choice

Which mode to choose? It is difficult to be normative as each one has its good points—even isolation might have its proponents in some circumstances! A 'shaping' strategy would suit a rapidly evolving technology such as with genetics, but given the power of large supermarkets, suppliers of fast-moving consumer goods (FMCG) might be best to 'follow'. Overall, it is likely that interaction would win the popular vote. In particular, of the four, interaction is the most likely to maximize prices and profitability. Organizations that use technology in an interactive way and develop customized offerings reduce customer price pressures. For example, with customization, car dealers would likely reduce the need to offer discounts to close a sale. As such, this strategy will be focused upon and the factors that affect an organization's ability to offer the customization will be explored in the next section.

Customization

Customization and 'mass customization' are especially relevant to innovating and developing new services. It is worth bearing in mind that most of the product innovation and development research has been focused upon products rather than services, though products and services are on a continuum rather than on any fixed points. Nevertheless, relatively few researchers have examined the challenges of service NPD, or might it be termed NSD (New Service Development)? The difficulty is that services are fluid, dynamic, and co-produced in real time with buyers, whereas many of the invention/innovation techniques are focused on tangible 'hard' technologies (Bitner et al., 2008). In particular, Bitner et al. recommend deconstructing a service into its component parts (a technique they call 'service blueprinting'), including physical evidence, customer actions, onstage/visible contact employee actions, backstage/invisible contact employee actions, and, finally, support processes and most importantly keeping the focus on the customer throughout to find potential sources of innovation. Customization and adaptation are the foundations of NSD.

Customization from a marketing strategy context inevitably leads to an assessment of mass customization, which is similar to mass production in terms of its basic structure, with some significant differences. Instead of selecting one variety of product or service, the buyer provides unique information so that the product or service can be tailored to varying degrees. This means that the production process has to be flexible in order to tailor the product or service in the required way. Take the car industry. Only about 7 per cent of cars in the US are 'customized', or as it is known in the car industry, 'built-to-order' (BTO). By contrast, BTO cars in Europe account for about 20 per cent of all cars sold. This is partly a reflection of the smaller dealer footprints in Europe (given land prices) and the higher proportion of premium sales.

One major benefit for following a customized innovation strategy is that there are no finished goods inventories for producers. On the other hand, customers inevitably have to wait longer than they might otherwise. Technologically, the differences between mass customization and mass production are only matters of degree. The key differences are the requirements for richer information flows and added process flexibility. Unfortunately, these provide significant barriers to the growth of mass customization as a primary innovation strategy for most organizations. There are essentially four key capabilities in mass customization (Agrawal et al., 2001; Swaminathan, 2001; see, also, Duray et al. 2000), namely: 'elicitation', 'process flexibility', 'logistics', and 'inventory', that form the boundaries to any organization's strategy to mass customize.

Elicitation

Elicitation requires some means of interacting with customers to find out their requirements and is a difficult process. In order to elicit information, companies are presented with problems of enabling customers to decide what they want. Sometimes, customers are certain about what they want, but often they are not. People make selections from menus. However, depending upon the nature of the product concerned, they might find the process frustrating and give up without buying anything. This is particularly likely with low-priced and standardized everyday products. Physical measurement makes elicitation more difficult. For example, when Levi Strauss experimented with the mass customization of women's jeans, their sales staff had to take measurements in stores as body-scanning equipment is still a way away. There is some experimentation with prototypes but the technology remains fraught with difficulties. Having said that, such things as 3-D views of sofas and 3-D body images that enable people to 'try on' clothes online from catalogues have been developed (see: **http://www.myvirtualmodel.com**).

Process flexibility

Process flexibility involves the use of production technology so that the product can be tailored according to the customer's information and presents another challenge. One-dimensional processes are relatively straightforward. For example, a bicycle frame can be customized by size and easily cut as required. Two-dimensional printing and printing-like technology are also relatively easy to undertake as printing and patterns involves zero-dimension dots, one-dimensional lines, and two-dimensional patterns. However, three-dimensional processes are much less flexible. Robots are slow and expensive, so three-dimensional mass customization, such as for car parts, is a long way off.

Logistics

Logistics involves the processing and distribution stages so that the identity of each customer is maintained right through to delivery of the customized product and can present a considerable constraint to customization. Thus, Levi Strauss took several years to develop washable bar codes to customize jeans and sew and wash them in bulk, while tagging each order.

Inventory

Customization raises the question of how much inventory to carry to guarantee required service levels. How will the equipment cope with capacity? What levels of components will be needed? How do you manage the large number of suppliers required? With the shorter product life-cycles in customization, how do you manage inventory phasing, marketing, and bringing on suppliers?

On the demand side, the key implication for inventory relates to sales forecasting. Establishing aggregate demand for product A (e.g., a Toyota Corolla), is one thing, but establishing accurate forecasts for subset configurations of product A (e.g., an LX Model with air conditioning), is another. Problems mount when there are several products (B, C, D, ...) with their own possible configurations and especially when each product's sales could have an effect on the sales of others.

The car industry

The car industry presents an interesting case for customization and demonstrates the pros and cons for marketing strategy, rather than the headline cases like computers or the music business. A car company using customization as it main innovation strategy would have to leave plants idle during troughs of demand and operational changes would also be required. For example, it is standard practice across the industry for paint shops to process cars in batches for each colour to reduce costs and to minimize emissions and waste. Such economies and environmental benefits would be lost if colours were customized. Additionally, customization would also require shipping a mix of components according to individual orders rather than thousands of components as a batch.

US dealers might also resist BTO changes as they mainly feel that large numbers of cars on a lot show that they are 'healthy' and open for business. BTO would also require radical changes to labour organization and IT systems that might be painful to implement. Finally, from a customer perspective, it remains unclear as to how far they are willing to trade off delivery times of up to six months against customization.

Implementing customization

There are five primary approaches to implementing mass customization, differentiated by the degree of standardization:

- **Partial** customization is the most common approach. However, it can lead to a degree of cannibalization if noticeable. For example, two cars might share the same wire harnesses, whereas consumers would easily notice if the dashboards were the same.
- **Process** customization requires firms to store inventory in a semi-finished form to be customizsed to the specific order. For example, Honda redesigned its cars so that saloons, 4×4s, and sports models all come off the same production line.
- **Product** customization involves offering a large variety while stocking relatively few and thus being prepared to substitute higher specs. For example, Avis and other rental companies substitute higher-end cars when lower-end ones are out of supply.
- **Procurement** customization is where there is commonality in part and equipment purchasing across a wide variety of products. For example, PC manufacturers can aggregate their demand across a wide variety of products.
- Finally, an ingenious alternative is to offer **'virtual customization'** (see, Swaminathan, 2001; Papathanassiou, 2004). This involves setting up a network via the Internet or distributive channel. For example, in the case of the car industry, if customers can be offered either access to dealer's cars, cars in transit cars on the assembly line, or from cars scheduled for production, the chances are that they will find the one with the right colour and options for them. Thus, as coined by Forrester, customization or BTO is replaced by the ability to 'locate-to-order'. Customers do not care whether the product was especially built for them or not, or where the product is found in the supply chain, as long as it has the features that they want. Virtual customization via shops or the Internet may be a strategy with considerable appeal not restricted to the car industry.

Conclusion

Innovation can be a winning component of any marketing strategy. The vast majority of today's brand leaders have introduced breakthrough innovations at some point in their histories. This chapter has focused on the use of innovation and product development, but the reality is that the vast majority of companies do not see it as the panacea in the marketplace. To be fair, unplanned and untargeted innovation simply leads to what has become known as 'innoflation'—a position where new products and services are launched into the marketplace at a frenzied pace with very little impact. Consumers just get confused, company supply chains overheat, and the end result is a poor return on investment. Study after study has shown that, at heart, most consumers are loyal to a core of products and services in most markets and so, if there is to be any innovation, it needs to be focused upon existing brands. Today, too many organizations take a risk-averse stance and would rather stay with the tried and tested and buy out any competitors who appear to have hit upon 'blockbuster' innovations in the marketplace. As Airbus, Dell, Dyson, eBay, easyJet, and Tesco have shown (to name but a few) challenging or reinventing what you offer through innovation can hold the key to market success. This chapter has shown that what is required is a measured and planned approach to innovation and its potential impact on costs and/or differentiation in the marketplace. As such, it is to be hoped that more companies will reduce their concentration on immediate competitors and consider wider lateral innovation based upon new definitions of market needs and wants. For many companies, the wisest strategy would be to include innovation within their marketing strategy rather than to focus on best value alone. At the bare minimum, all companies should regularly review their innovation strategy against current and anticipated market needs and wants.

Summary

Product innovation and development can play a pivotal role in marketing strategy. Central to this is the concept of new product development (NPD), a creative activity towards which there are many different approaches, such as systematic invention thinking. Particular strategic issues to consider are market preparation and product rollovers, which can have a dramatic impact on product innovation and development. Strategic frameworks that can provide considerable insight include Rogers' product adoption curve and Moore's concept of 'crossing the chasm'. Smaller players in the market should consider the judo strategy. An organization's overall innovation mode is worth giving careful thought to. Customization is becoming an increasingly important area of marketing strategy.

KEY TERMS

Adoption patterns Differences in the propensity of customer types to adopt innovations.

Customization Tailoring products and services to suit individual needs and wants.

Disruptive technology A technology that fundamentally shifts the production paradigm and often how a product or service is used.

Innovation Subsequent changes and adaptations to 'new-to-the-world' introduction. *Innovare* is the Latin verb meaning to change or to alter.

Judo strategy An innovation strategy used by relatively smaller companies to outwit larger rivals based upon skill rather than size or strength.

Market preparation Market strategies to ensure that new-to-the-world products do not shock consumers.

New-to-the-world Significantly new product or service market introductions that are often discontinuous.

NPD New product development.

Product rollovers Displacement of existing products by new ones.

Systematic inventive thinking An NPD system based on the work of Genrich Altshuller to manipulate idea generation and stimulate relevant creativity.

Toolkit strategy Enabling customers to take significant control over the NPD process.

DISCUSSION QUESTIONS

1 Briefly outline and describe the umbrella of activities included in product innovation and development.
2 Are there any particular kinds of innovation that are more important than others or does it depend upon market conditions?
3 Toolkit strategy is a growing trend amongst B2B product developers. Do you think such an approach to innovation might work in any particular B2C markets?
4 Apply the five patterns of Systematic Inventive Thinking (subtraction, multiplication, division, task unification, and attribute dependency change) to the iPod. Can you create what you regard to be a viable new product that adds value?
5 Can you name two to three products that have recently failed to cross the chasm? To what extent do you think lack of interest from Pragmatists was the problem?
6 What are the major advantages and disadvantages of customization?

ONLINE RESOURCE CENTRE

Visit the Online Resource Centre for this book for lots of interesting additional material at: **www.oxfordtextbooks.co.uk/orc/west2e/**

REFERENCES AND FURTHER READING

Aaker, David (2007), 'Innovation: Brand it or Lose it', *California Management Review*, 50 (1), pp. 8–24.

Agrawal, Mani, T. V. Kumaresh, and Glenn A. Mercer (2001), 'The False Promise of Mass Customization', *McKinsey Quarterly*, 3, pp. 62–71.

Baghai, Merhrdad, Stephen Coley, and David White (1999), *The Alchemy of Growth: Practical Insights for Building the Enduring Enterprise* (London: Orion).

Berthon, Pierre, James M. Hulbert, and Leyland F. Pitt (1999), 'To Serve or Create: Strategic Orientations toward Customers and Innovation', *California Management Review*, 42 (1), pp. 37–58.

Billington, Corey, Hau L. Lee, and Christopher S. Tang (1998), 'Successful Strategies for Product Rollovers', *Sloan Management Review*, Spring, pp. 23–30.

Bitner, Mary Jo, Amy L. Ostrom, and Felicia N. Morgan (2008), 'Service Blueprinting: A Practical Technique for Service Innovation', *California Management Review*, 50 (3), pp. 66–94.

Bonabeau, Eric, Neil Bodick, and Robert W. Armstrong (2008), 'A More Rational Approach to New-Product Development', *Harvard Business Review*, March, pp. 96–102.

Booz Allen Hamilton (1982), *New Product Management for the 1980s* (New York: Booz Allen Hamilton).

Christensen, Clayton M. (1997), *The Innovator's Dilemma: When New Technologies Cause Great Firms to Fail* (Boston, MA: Harvard Business School Press).

Christensen, Clayton M., and Michael Raynor (2003), *The Innovator's Solution: Creating and Sustaining Successful Growth* (Boston, MA: Harvard Business School Press).

Drucker, Peter F., and Joseph A. Maciariello (2008), *Management: Revised Edition* (New York: Harper Collins).

Duray R. P. T. Ward, G. W. Milligan, W. L. Berry (2000), 'Approaches to Mass Customization: Configurations and Empirical Validation', *Journal of Operations Management*, 18 (6), pp. 605–25.

Easingwood, Chris, and Anthony Koustelos (2000), 'Marketing High Technology: Preparation, Targeting, Positioning, Execution', *Business Horizons*, 43 (3), pp. 27–34.

Fleming, Lee, and Matt Marx (2006), 'Managing Creativity in Small Worlds', *California Management Review*, 48 (4), pp. 6–27.

Goldenberg, Jacob, Roni Horowitz, Amnon Levav, and David Mazursky (2003), 'Finding your Innovation Sweet Spot', *Harvard Business Review*, March, pp. 120–9.

Johnson, Mark M., Clayton M. Christensen, and Henning Kagermann (2008), 'Reinventing your Business Model', *Harvard Business Review*, December, pp. 50–9.

Liddell, Devin (2004), 'Defining Innovation', *Brand Strategy*, December–January, p. 30.

Marketing Week (2003), 'Innovation is Key in Alcopops', 17 July, pp. 30–1.

Markides, Constantinos (2006), 'Disruptive Innovation: In Need of Better Theory', *Journal of Product Innovation Management*, 23, pp. 19–25.

Moore, Geoffrey A. (1999), *Crossing the Chasm: Marketing and Selling Technology Products to Mainstream Customers* (Oxford: Capstone Publishing).

Moore, Geoffrey A. (2004a), *Inside the Tornado: Strategies for Developing, Leveraging, and Surviving Hypergrowth Markets* (New York: Harper Business).

Moore, Geoffrey A. (2004b), 'Darwin and the Demon: Innovating within Established Enterprises', *Harvard Business Review*, July–August, pp. 86–93.

Noble, Charles H., and Minu Kumar (2008), 'Using Product Design Strategically to Create Deeper Consumer Connections', *Business Horizons*, 51, pp. 441–50.

Papathanassiou, E. A. (2004), 'Mass Customisation: Management Approaches and Internet Opportunities in the Financial Sector in the UK', *International Journal of Information Management*, 24 (5), pp. 387–99.

Rogers, Everett M. (1983), *Diffusion of Innovations* (New York: The Free Press).

Swaminathan, Jayashankar M. (2001), 'Enabling Customization Using Standardized Operations', *California Management Review*, 43 (3), pp. 125–35.

Thomke, Stefan, and Eric von Hippel (2002), 'Customers as Innovators: A New Way to Create Value', *Harvard Business Review*, April, pp.74–81.

Verganti, Robert (2006), 'Innovation through Design', *Harvard Business Review*, December, pp. 114–22.

Yoffie, David B., and Mary Kwak (2002), 'Mastering Strategic Movement at Palm', *MIT Sloan Management Review*, January, pp. 47–53.

Zipkin, Paul (2001), 'The Limits of Mass Customization', *MIT Sloan Management Review*, 42 (Spring), pp. 81–7.

KEY ARTICLE ABSTRACTS

Vorhies, Douglas W., and Michael Harker (1999), **'Capabilities and Performance Advantages of Market-Driven Firms'**, *European Journal of Marketing*, 33 (11/12), pp. 1171–202.

This is a useful paper. It places NPD and innovation within the context of the marketing mix and for assessing the relationship to marketing orientation.

Abstract: Although progress has been made in understanding market-driven businesses from a theoretical perspective, relatively few empirical studies have addressed the capabilities needed to become market-driven and the performance advantages accruing to firms possessing these capabilities. One of the barriers faced has been in defining what is meant by the term 'market-driven'. This paper develops a multi-dimensional measure useful for assessing the degree to which a firm is market-driven. The paper presents evidence that market-driven business units developed higher levels of six vital marketing capabilities (in the areas of market research, pricing, product development, channels, promotion, and market management) than their less market-driven rivals, and significantly outperformed these rival business units on four measures of organizational performance.

Hart, Susan (1993), **'Dimensions of Success in New Product Development: An Exploratory Investigation'**, *Journal of Marketing Management*, 9 (1), pp. 23–41.

This paper indicates that there is not much evidence that NPD success or failure is measured financially.

Abstract: As a key element in survival and sustaining growth, the constant development and redevelopment of products has been the subject of many academic and consulting group studies. The specific focus of these studies has often been to identify and describe those factors, which determine the outcome of new product developments, the critical success factors in NPD. In order to fulfil their objectives, the studies have focused on many aspects of the management of new product development programmes in companies, and attempted to relate them to a number of alternative outcomes. This has called for the measurement of 'success' itself. Unfortunately, there is very little consensus amongst the authors of the studies regarding how best to operationalize 'success', and researchers have employed a variety of measures, focused on different levels of analysts, sought data from different sources, and used different data-collection methods. This paper examines the performance measures used in several major NPD studies and shows how success 'measures' have been treated as financial and non-financial. In addition, attention is drawn to the problems inherent in the different definitions of success. Finally, using data from an empirical survey, the relationship between financial and non-financial outcomes is examined.

Moll, Isa, Jordi Montana, Francisco Guzman, and Francesc Solé Parellada (2007), **'Market Orientation and Design Orientation: A Management Model'**, *Journal of Marketing Management*, 23 (9/10), pp. 861–76.

This paper reminds us of the importance of design in marketing strategy. The authors suggest that if companies with a strong orientation towards design also develop a broad orientation towards the market, design orientation favours market orientation.

Abstract: Market orientation and design orientation as strategic concepts have a proven impact on business results, but the direct relationship between these concepts has not yet been analysed. This research attempts to prove the relationship by studying the managerial implication of design orientation as it relates to market orientation. After analysing twenty-eight case studies of Spanish companies well-known for their business excellence and their design orientation, a management model is proposed. The model is a management tool that offers companies a scheme for auto-diagnosis and a review of best-in-class design practices that have shown to improve business results.

END OF CHAPTER 8 CASE STUDY The charge of the electric car

Pure electric cars, as opposed to hybrids, are cheap to run and produce close to or no carbon emissions at all but are relatively expensive. Manufacturers around the world are clambering to develop them and governments are fully in support. Despite all this, there is a big stumbling block: manufacturers cannot sell them unless motorists want to buy them—and motorists have not shown any enthusiasm to buy them. In fact, in the UK, sales are pitiful at just over 160 a year, which is down from around 400 last year. By comparison, the leading hybrid model (conventional engine plus electric), the Toyota Prius, has sold over a million worldwide and sales are accelerating.

So what's the problem? The nub of it is that electric cars await better and more affordable batteries. Electric cars use lead-acid or nickel-metal hydride batteries. They have proved to be reliable and reasonably cheap for hybrids, but their limited storage capacity makes the driving range using electricity alone too short for the vast majority of drivers. A range of 50 miles, which is the common range of most electric cars (e.g the G-Wiz), will get the majority of people to work or the local train station, it will get children to school and it will get you to the shops, etc. But just about everybody with a car needs to do the occasional long-distance trip. Even the range of around 150 miles in electric cars with that capacity would be too short. Not surprisingly, London is the primary market for electric cars given the density of the population, the shorter trips, and the exemption from the congestion charge for electric cars.

Another problem is where do you recharge? There is no network of charging points and aside from people with driveways or garages, it is not feasible for people to run electric cables from their houses or flats to their cars parked out on the road. Modifications of lithium-ion batteries, the ones used in laptop and mobile phones, may hold the answer to a significant increase in range. Indeed, nearly every major motor-manufacturer is building an electric vehicle prototype using lithium-ion batteries, but the technology is expensive. The G-Wiz L-ion, made in India, incorporates lithium, which doubles its range from around 40–48 to 70–78 miles, but doubles the price from £7,995 for the G-Wiz I, to £15,795. Other lithium-battery-powered cars such as the Mitsubishi iMiEV or the Tesla sports car face similar if not higher prices. Extending the range of electric vehicles requires hefty battery packs, with the consequent loss of space. For example, BMW's Mini electric prototype has a range of 150 miles but the batteries and all the electrics take up all the space allocated to the passengers! On the upside, it only costs £1.50 to charge it overnight.

It is anticipated that electric cars will increasingly be marketed from 2011–12 onwards and so some innovative solutions are going to be needed. Governments around the world are keen to see the establishment of electric-vehicle businesses for two basic reasons: if they can encourage electric-vehicle development in their countries, there will be significant potential for, (1) exports; and (2) employment. Electric cars need a multitude of engineering companies providing components and services, so there are a great many opportunities for existing companies, along with new start-ups for cars and commercial vehicles. The second reason is a need to reduce carbon-dioxide emissions from transport to meet targets (for example, in the UK, the Climate Change Act sets a target of a 26 per cent reduction in emissions by 2020 and 80 per cent by 2050). After all, there is no exhaust pipe coming out of an electric car.

» Taking a wider perspective though, the benefits to the environment of electric cars over conventional ones are debateable, given the need to generate electricity. If you don't use technologies other than wind or solar, environmentalists have argued that there is no overall benefit. There is no doubt that if electric cars were widely adopted, it would put a massive strain on the power-generation industry and could account for up to a fifth of all the electricity generated in the world, requiring massive additional capacity.

There is no doubt that the overwhelming majority of motorists are in favour of electric vehicles to clean up the environment and lessen our dependency on oil. What is more, electric-powered vehicles have a long pedigree dating back to the nineteenth century and have been visible for many years in the UK, with the once omnipresent milk float. However, this doesn't necessarily translate to sales of cars. Consumer tests with electric cars have shown that their main concern is being stranded with flat batteries and with the 60-mile range of most electric cars, drivers start to get edgy after about 30 miles and feel the need to recharge. It's a technology waiting for what computer programmers call the 'killer application' or 'killer app' that will form the core of a proposition that people will buy.

Source: This case was prepared by Douglas West of the University of Birmingham as the basis for analysis and class discussion and not to illustrate either effective or ineffective handling of an administrative situation.

QUESTIONS

A small engineering company in Oxford, Online Ltd, is working with a major car company. Online has commissioned you to come up with a strategy to market an electric car that they are in the final stages of planning. It looks like the G-Wiz i with a slightly more streamlined body. It has a top range of 50 miles (40 miles on mixed roads) with a projected price similar to the G-Wiz i.

1. They would particularly like advice on whom to target, what might be the main value proposition to offer potential customers, and whether or not alternative business models should be considered to the conventional way in which cars are sold.
2. Before committing major funds to research and development, they also wondered if you think they are right to be developing a purely electric car rather than a hybrid. Make the case for a purely electric car.

9

Service marketing strategies

LEARNING OBJECTIVES

- Provide an overview of the nature of services
- Investigate the relationship between service quality and customer satisfaction and profitability
- Apply the service dominant logic to both services and manufactured goods
- Discuss ways in which services can streamline operations and improve productivity and profitability
- Examine the nature of the customer service experience
- Establish the relationship between customer value and sustainable competitive advantage
- Present several strategic tools for the fine assessment of the service process and the delivery of customer value

CHAPTER AT A GLANCE

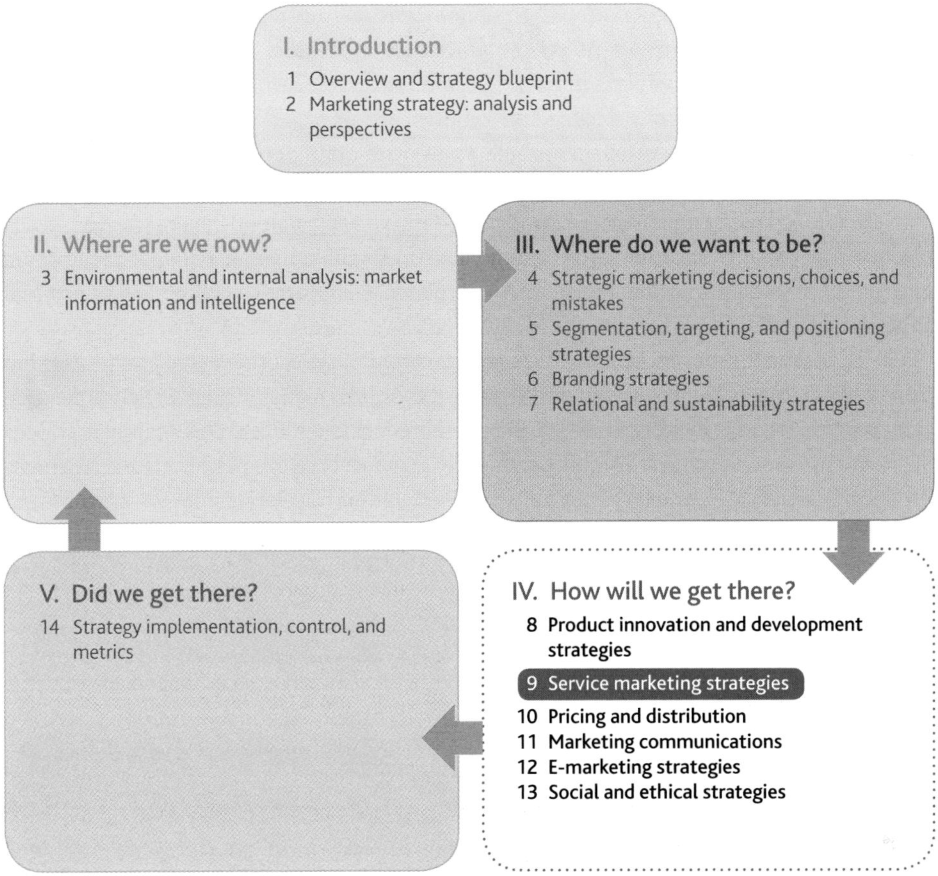

I. Introduction
1 Overview and strategy blueprint
2 Marketing strategy: analysis and perspectives

II. Where are we now?
3 Environmental and internal analysis: market information and intelligence

III. Where do we want to be?
4 Strategic marketing decisions, choices, and mistakes
5 Segmentation, targeting, and positioning strategies
6 Branding strategies
7 Relational and sustainability strategies

IV. How will we get there?
8 Product innovation and development strategies
9 Service marketing strategies
10 Pricing and distribution
11 Marketing communications
12 E-marketing strategies
13 Social and ethical strategies

V. Did we get there?
14 Strategy implementation, control, and metrics

Introduction

There is little doubt that the service sector is the fastest-growing sector of the world economy. In the OECD countries (Organization for Economic Cooperation and Development), services now account for almost 70 per cent of GDP (Gross Domestic Product), and service jobs make up the largest category of all employment opportunities, with nearly 65 per cent of all OECD country workers being employed in activities related to services (OECD, 2004). Even in the emerging economies, services are rapidly growing and often comprise more than 50 per cent of the GDP (World Bank, 2003).

Services are by nature intangible, heterogeneous, inseparable, and perishable. They create unique strategic challenges. While an understanding of industry structure can aid the service strategist to streamline service delivery and improve profitability, it is also important to achieve sustainable competitive advantage (SCA) through customer satisfaction and the creation of perceived value (Frei, 2008). Services cannot be protected in the same way as manufactured goods with property rights such as patents, so they are easily copied, unless the company has built a perceptual bond with its customers. To beat competitors, the service firm must continually meet and/or exceed customer expectations (Stuart 2006; Ford et al.,

2001). This forces the firm to continually monitor the wants and needs of its target customers and to refine strategically its offerings to enhance customer value.

The focus on customer value is not just relevant for service firms. Many global industries are presently being forced toward standardization of offerings as life cycles mature. The road to parity creates enormous strategic turbulence as firms attempt to differentiate their offerings from those of competitors. Manufacturers can differentiate through the development of value-laden complementary services (much as Saturn, a division of General Motors in the US, has done through its innovative approach to supply-chain management), but the key is to ensure that these complementary services are perceived by target customers as adding real value to the overall offering (Cohen et al., 2000).

The challenge for service firms is to create a position of perceptual value and power that cannot be easily copied by competitors. This requires a constant balancing of operational efficiency, perceived differentiation, and customer-relationship building. This chapter will focus on the nature of services, set the foundation of the general service experience, and then focus on operational efficiency and profitability and the building of relationships with customers, enhancing differentiation, and perceptions of customer value.

Services

There are four readily accepted distinguishing characteristics for services that create strategic challenges (see Figure 9.1). Each of these will be briefly examined, the seven Ps of services will then be examined, and an analysis will be made of the experience associated with the service.

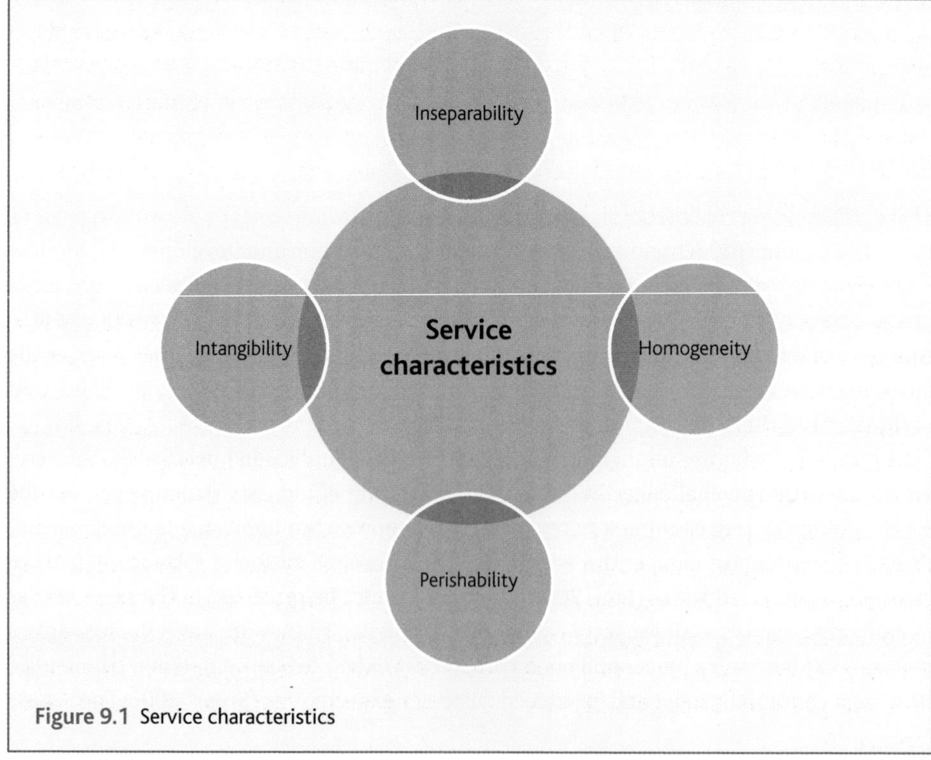

Figure 9.1 Service characteristics

Intangibility

Services are seen as being intangible so that customers cannot hold them, touch them, and try one out before buying. A key strategic issue is that even the most intangible services (pure services like consulting projects or executive seminars) have certain tangible aspects to them that can be used to convey perceptions of service quality. Consulting personnel can dress in a conducive manner to convey professionalism, the consulting offices where meetings with the client take place can be managed to convey success and professionalism through various atmospheric components (e.g., furniture, floors, walls, lighting, colour, music, etc), and the various promotional materials, communications, and the project reports can be presented in such a way as to exude quality. Even the most intangible service can be made more tangible in creative strategic ways.

Heterogeneity

This focuses on the fact that each time the service is provided there will be differences due to environmental variation or changes in attitude, mood, or emotion on the part of either the provider or the recipient. It is therefore important for the services marketer (given the heterogeneity of service interactions) to ensure as much consistency as possible. While total consistency is impossible, there are mechanisms that can be utilized to reduce inconsistencies. One involves the design of the service in such a way as to make it as uniform as possible. This might be accomplished via automation where possible or by training service personnel to follow strictly controlled guidelines. Hand in hand with this approach would go the need for an effective employee selection, motivation, and retention process. No matter how sophisticated the service is, there is no substitute for hiring the right people, training them effectively, and putting them into an environment that nurtures their success. Many service providers have found that another strategic approach is also necessary to eliminate the problems inherent in heterogeneity: the use of money-back guarantees. If the firm expects that even with tight controls, there will be the chance for a disgruntled customer, the offering of a money-back guarantee may alleviate any post-production dissonance that might arise due to service provider–customer interactions.

Inseparability

The service cannot be separated from the provider of the service in the mind of the service customer. This creates challenges. Companies can foster a more proactive involvement on the part of the customer. Another way to deal with this issue is to look at the matter of location. The production must be brought to the customer, so providing additional locations for the service provision and training personnel to handle effectively greater demand for the service. This argues for greater decentralization and employee empowerment to ensure the highest service quality level. This has helped build loyal followings for easyJet, Virgin, and Apple Computers. Another strategic approach that could help involves training service personnel to deal with problematic customers in order to reduce the potential for customer dissonance. Vocal, problematic customers can negatively affect the other customers involved, and moving them quickly out of the area into a manager's office where their difficulties can be addressed by a manager can greatly enhance the experience for all concerned.

Perishability

Since services cannot be stored in inventory, they are perishable. Dealing with the peaks and troughs of demand can only be handled either through flexing capacity or shifting demand. There are a number of ways that have been found over the years to synchronize supply and demand. These include: (1) differential pricing to shift demand to slower time periods (off-peak prices for hotel rates); (2) new services provided to customers while waiting (movies on TV screens while queuing); (3) new service opportunities in off-peak time periods (free oil-change if your car is serviced at off-peak times); (4) the use of reservations systems (keeping better track of supply and demand); (5) flexing capacity to have more staff on duty during peak times and less for slower times (like McDonald's or Pizza Hut); (6) increase the use of the customer as co-producer (customer packs up their own pots and pans before moving services arrive to pack up the rest of their household furnishings); (7) develop services that can be shared by other service providers (reservations system to help a variety of service providers).

The 7 Ps of services

In addition to the normal marketing mix elements (product, price, place, and promotion), services are usually associated with three additional mix elements: people, process, and physical evidence.

People refers to the fact that those service personnel who interact with the customer become integrally linked to the service in that interaction. These people become the service in the eyes of the customer, and it is not possible to separate the service from the service provider representative. How the customer actually feels about that service experience is shaped by the interaction, so the company must hire personnel that can do their job and enhance the customer service experience. Strategically, this focuses on hiring and retaining the best people for the provision of the service and trusting and empowering them sufficiently to allow them to provide the best customized service to meet the expectations of the customer. Service personnel are boundary spanners between the company and its customers, and they serve an important function in conveying customer expectations to management and facilitate the delivery by enabling the customer to become a co-producer of the service.

Process reflects the fact that there is a process that is utilized to provide the service to the customer. This requires the company to step back and examine that process, looking at all of the interactions between customers and service personnel to see if the process is as smooth and efficient as possible. A proper process assessment will also examine the support personnel and processes that operate out of the view of the customer to quality control the delivery.

Blueprinting is an effective mechanism for this kind of assessment, and the company is able to identify potential red flag areas when the entire delivery process is carefully examined. The point is to ensure that the customer gets the best experience as efficiently and effectively as possible when they want it. Banks can easily benefit from this blueprinting by seeing all the steps that a customer takes once they enter the bank, and they can potentially see where any stumbling blocks might be in the provision of the various offerings of the bank. What is particularly helpful is that the non-contact service personnel are also included, along with the background supporting processes (e.g., the cleaning services who come after hours, the IT support staff, the ATM maintenance personnel, etc). All aspects of the service can be examined to ensure that the service provision is smooth and error-free.

Finally, **physical evidence** focuses on the various visible attributes that affect the delivery process and customer satisfaction. This can involve the layout of the shelving and aisles in a Tesco or Waitrose store, the colours painted on the walls, the music playing in the background, the carts that are being pushed by customers for their food items, the uniforms worn by store personnel, the end-of-aisle displays, the use of posters on the walls to inform customers, etc. The point is that each of these may add to the overall service experience, and the key is to find the best experience to make the customer happy and get them to come back again.

The **servicescape** is the pictorial representation of the physical evidence associated with the service, and it provides an excellent mechanism for additional service performance evaluation. If the physical components of the service are inconsistent with the expectations of the customer, there is increased potential for service failure and customer loss. Can you imagine dirty tablecloths at a leading restaurant? Every aspect of a service environment can affect the perceptions of the quality of the service.

The service experience and service quality

In order to be successful, service strategists should try to understand exactly what the consumer is looking for when they 'experience' the service in question. Each customer will have a set of expectations regarding the service experience that must be met to ensure customer satisfaction. How is customer satisfaction ensured? Research has consistently shown that the key to service-firm success is keeping the customer happy. Fulfilment appears to be the key ingredient to the concept of customer satisfaction (Grenci and Watts, 2007). If a service meets or exceeds the expectations of the customer, the customer will enjoy a sense of fulfilment and will be satisfied with the service consumption experience. The job for the service strategist, therefore, is to determine how to measure service quality.

SERVQUAL

Parasuraman et al. (1991) have done extensive work examining the concept of service quality, and found that it is a multifaceted construct with five distinctive dimensions: reliability (dependability and accuracy); responsiveness (helpfulness and promptness); empathy (customer understanding and individualized attention); assurance (employee competence, courtesy, and trustworthiness); and tangibles (condition of physical evidence). The authors created a survey instrument to assess customer perceptions of service quality along these five dimensional lines that they named SERVQUAL, which has been used in many settings to compare the expected service delivery with the actual customer perceptions of service delivery to provide an excellent service process evaluative tool.

The various questions that make up the SERVQUAL questionnaire are shown in Figure 9.2. The way that SERVQUAL works is that there are three sections to the survey instrument. The first section asks the respondent about the various items listed in Figure 9.2 with regard to an ideal service provider of the type of service directly in question. Using 7-point scales with anchors of strongly agree and strongly disagree, respondents then indicate their perceptions

Tangibles	Reliability	Responsiveness	Assurance	Empathy
• This service has modern-looking equipment • This service's physical facilities are visually appealing • This service's employees are neat in appearance • Materials associated with the service (such as pamphlets or statements) are visually appealing	• When this service promises to do something by a certain time, it does so • When you have a problem, this service shows a sincere interest in solving it • This service performs the service right the first time • This service provides its services at the time it promises to do so • This service insists on error-free records	• Employees of this service tell you exactly when services will be performed • Employees of this service give you prompt service • Employees of this service are always willing to help you • Employees of this service are never too busy to respond to your requests	• The behaviour of employees of this service instills confidence in customers • You feel safe in your transactions with this service • Employees of this service are consistently courteous with you • Employees of this service have the knowledge to answer your questions	• This service gives you individual attentions • This service has operating hours convenient to all its customers • This service has employees who give you personal attention • This service has your best interests at heart • Employees of this service understand your specific needs

Figure 9.2 SERVQUAL survey items

Reprinted from A. Parasuraman, Leonard L. Berry, and Valarie A. Zeithaml (1991), 'Understanding Customer Expectations of Service', *MIT Sloan Management Review*, Spring, pp. 38–49, by permission of the publisher.

of the offerings of an ideal service provider across the 22 items in terms of their level of agreement with the statements. The second section of the instrument uses the same 22 items, but this time the statements are written with regard to the specific service provider being assessed. There is also a third section, in which the respondent is asked to indicate their priorities regarding the five different groupings of SERVQUAL statements, allowing 100 points to be divided up across the five groupings of items (empathy, tangibles, assurance, responsiveness, and reliability). This then indicates relative importance of each of the groupings.

The use of SERVQUAL allows the service provider to do a Gap Analysis, which allows researchers to see whether or not the customer expectations are being met. Each of the 22 items can be compared in terms of the ideal setting (or the expected level of performance) and the actual performance that they received. If the expected score is subtracted from the actual score and there is a negative number left, then the customer expectations are not being met. This is the gap in question. Of course, if the result is positive, then it means that the customer is getting more than they expected in that case. The reason for the third section becomes obvious if one considers only addressing the gaps involved, since one would assume that the statements that reflect the biggest gaps would strategically be the ones that are most in need of revamping.

A potential problem could therefore arise if the items that have the biggest gap scores associated with them are considered to be the least important in the overall assessment of the service offering. This has often been the case when SERVQUAL has been applied to university educations since the items that are often associated with higher gap scores tend to be the tangibles category (classrooms, campus, etc), while these items are considerably less important than assurance items reflecting, say, the quality of the professors and lecturers that the students are learning from. Strategically, it would not make sense in that case to put large expenditures into plant and equipment due to the limited importance that those have for the students involved. SERVQUAL research has shown many times over that perceptions of service quality lead ultimately to better firm performance.

Why is this set of relationships so important? Because perceptions of service quality lead to customer satisfaction, which in turn leads to positive purchase intentions, which leads to sales and profits. The point is that satisfied customers are likely to come back and spend more in the future while also passing the word to others. Many researchers have found that the longer a service company is able to retain its customers, the more they will spend on the services offered by the company.

Service dominant logic

Much of the early work on services focused heavily on the distinctive nature of services and the fundamental differences between services and manufactured goods. While this was helpful for service strategists at first, a new perspective has appeared in the marketing literature which takes a very different look at marketing products and services. From the definition of product in marketing, most now interpret this to mean anything that has value for the consumer. This could relate to a product, a place, a person (political candidate), a location (holiday destination), as well as a service. Assuming that products are separate and distinct from services may be somewhat of a problematic perspective since a service component

Resources	Traditional goods-centred dominant logic	Emerging service-centred dominant logic
Primary unit of exchange	People exchange for goods. These goods serve primarily as *operand resources*	People exchange to acquire the benefits of specialized competences (knowledge and skills), or services. Knowledge and skills are *operant resources*
Role of goods	Goods are *operand resources* and end products. Marketers take matter and change its form, place, time, and possession	Goods are transmitters of *operant resources* (embedded knowledge): they are intermediate 'products' that are used by other operant resources (customers) as appliances in value-creation processes
Role of customer	The customer is the recipient of goods. Marketers do things to customers: they segment them, penetrate them, distribute to them, and promote to them. The customer is an *operand resource*	The customer is a co-producer of service. Marketing is a process of doing things in interaction with the customer. The customer is primarily an *operant resource*, only functioning occasionally as an operand resource
Determination and meaning of value	Value is determined by the producer. It is embedded in the *operand resource* (goods) and is defined in terms of 'exchange-value'	Value is perceived and determined by the customer on the basis of 'value in use'. Value results from the beneficial application of *operant resources* sometimes transmitted through *operand resources*. Firms can only make value propositions
Firm–customer interaction	The customer is an *operand resource*. Customers are acted on to create transactions with resources	The customer is primarily an *operant resource*. Customers are active participants in relational exchanges and co-production
Sources of economic growth	Wealth is obtained from surplus tangible resources and goods. Wealth consists of owning, controlling, and producing *operand resources*	Wealth is obtained through the application and exchange of specialized knowledge and skills. It represents the right to the future use of *operant resources*.

Figure 9.3 Goods-dominant vs service-dominant logic perspectives: Resource use

Stephen L. Vargo and Robert F. Lusch (2004), 'Evolving to a New Dominant Logic for Marketing', 68 (January), pp. 1–17. Reprinted with permission from *Journal of Marketing*, published by the American Marketing Association.

beyond the actual manufactured product is a key ingredient in the ability to attract and retain customers. As a result, Vargo and Lusch (2004) have introduced a valuable new perspective for marketing which they call service-dominant logic (see Figure 9.3), in which the firm would use the customer as a co-producer of the service or good created. This perspective suggests that this can be used with anything that has value to facilitate the exchange process.

The key terms in this approach are **operand resources**, which refer to **resources which are acted upon or operated upon to produce an effect**, and **operant resources**, which are **resources which are used to act upon operand resources**. In other words, operant resources are resources that actually produce effects. So, from the operand resources perspective, customers are acted upon, while from the operant resources perspective, the customer becomes an actor upon something else (e.g., a co-producer). The customer is the actor rather than what is acted upon. This is an important distinction in this emerging perspective. Vargo and Lusch (2004) present eight different foundational premises which differ between goods-centred and service-centred logic:

FP1: The application of specialized skills and knowledge is the fundamental unit of change

FP2: Indirect exchange masks the fundamental unit of exchange

FP3: Goods are distribution mechanisms for service provision

FP4: Knowledge is the fundamental source of competitive advantage

FP5: All economies are services economies

FP6: The customer is always a co-producer

FP7: The enterprise can only make value propositions

FP8: A service-centred view is customer-orientated and relational.

The point behind the new paradigm is that we should not really consider goods and services as separate and distinct, as has been suggested for so long. The key is that in this era of relationship marketing, it behoves all marketers to focus on using a services-centred dominant logic to avoid the problems inherent in acting upon the customer, rather than acting with the customer to create something of perceived value. The eight foundational premises if applied to all marketing output will not only increase perceived value in the output for the customer, but will also ensure competitive advantage for the firm. A more fundamental comparison between goods-dominant and service-dominant logic can be seen in Figure 9.4, which was suggested by Lusch et al. (2006). This shows even more clearly the basic differences and further explains why the service-dominant logic approach is the higher road to take for strategic marketers to build meaningful relationships with their customers.

From the service-centred dominant logic it can be seen that what will help ensure success for service firms involves meeting or exceeding customer expectations, and it is this perceptual position in the head of the customer that serves as the basis for sustainable competitive advantage. Now, having established the key foundations of services, the chapter will focus on the strategic issues that surround services. The important questions that are raised for the needs of strategic service managers, given the Porter focus that we have adopted for this book, are: (1) how can we use our service strategy to reduce our overall costs; and (2) how

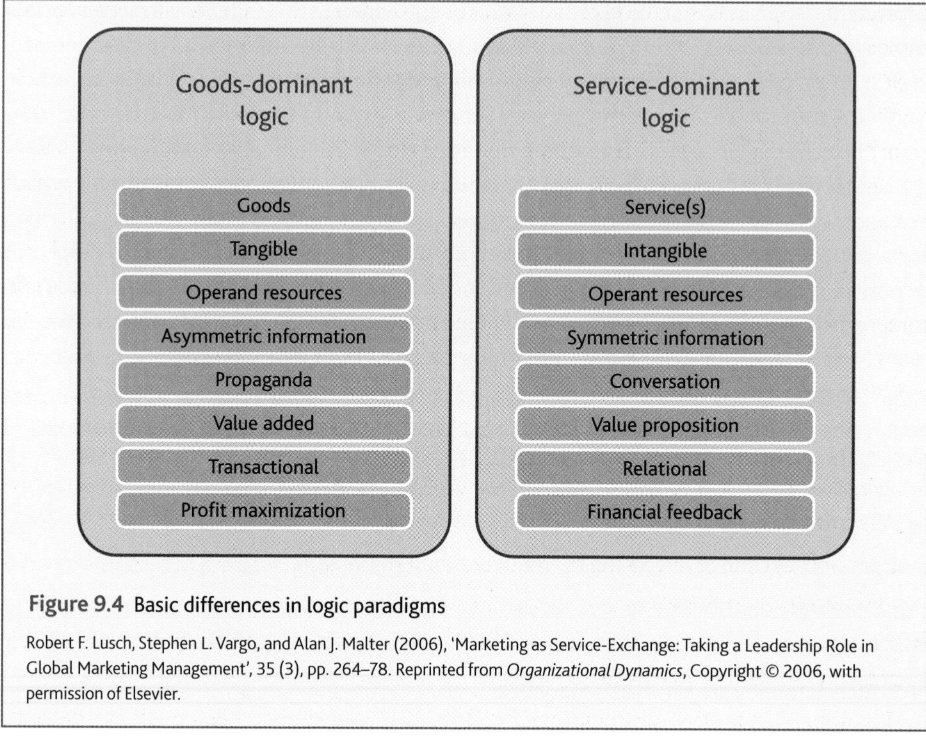

Figure 9.4 Basic differences in logic paradigms

Robert F. Lusch, Stephen L. Vargo, and Alan J. Malter (2006), 'Marketing as Service-Exchange: Taking a Leadership Role in Global Marketing Management', 35 (3), pp. 264–78. Reprinted from *Organizational Dynamics*, Copyright © 2006, with permission of Elsevier.

can service strategy differentiate our offerings and help to build a meaningful relationship with the target consumer?

Operational efficiency and profitability

Since services are basically intangible, difficult to protect legally, and have relatively low barriers to entry, they are easy to copy. Operational excellence is one way in which service firms can achieve strategic success. Operational excellence can be garnered in two important ways—streamlining and cost cutting—and also through creative strategic alliances. Strategic successes provide excellent opportunities for service firms to improve operations and raise profit margins. A series of effective mechanisms for operational improvement will now be discussed and illustrated with company examples.

Streamlining and cost cutting

Many service providers have found the need to improve operations to eliminate inefficiencies and improve profit margins. To a certain extent, customer value is enhanced when firm cost-cutting can be passed along with visible savings for the customer. Four major trends have forced service providers to focus on cost cutting: (1) ever-intensifying competition as industry regulations open competition to new and varied types of competitors (e.g., deregulation and the sanctioning of new and creative strategic alliances); (2) slowing industry growth projections; (3) increasing levels of parity across providers; and (4) increasing levels of customer expectations.

Service firms must satisfy customers at ever-decreasing cost levels (Arnold et al., 1998). Service providers have recently embraced some of the cost-cutting benefits that were experienced by Western manufacturers attempting to remain competitive with the Japanese during the 1990s (Swank, 2003). This recent use of 'lean service management' focuses on re-engineering operations to improve profitability. Swank (2003) warns service providers always to measure any improvements in performance and productivity from the customer's perspective. Whatever is attempted should not detract in any way from perceptions of customer value. Otherwise, competitiveness would be severely eroded. So what are the specific ways in which services can improve their productivity? Friedman (1998) makes the following suggestions:

1. Operate with fewer workers by providing supporting equipment and systems or helping employees do more (e.g., automation for efficiencies like scanners for supermarkets and ATMs for banks).
2. Eliminate certain elements of a process (e.g., check-in and check-out processes for hotels and car rental companies).
3. De-skill certain jobs to allow the use of a broader pool of workers (e.g., point-of-sale machines that do not require to be overseen by skilled employees).
4. Take non-customer work requirements from frontline service personnel and delegate them to others within the organization (e.g., moving international currency exchange capabilities out of neighbourhood bank branches to special regional offices).
5. Determine those tasks that must be performed close to the customer as opposed to those which can be done far away (e.g., regional customer service centres as opposed to local).
6. Offload certain work requirements to suppliers (e.g., hospitals and pre-packaged surgery kits).
7. Change customer expectations in terms of their involvement in the process (e.g., self-service gas stations and customers filling their own soft-drink cups at fast-food restaurants).

Friedman warns against the elimination of any aspects of the service that would be valued by customers. He also strongly warns against simply reducing the number of employees (since frontline personnel are critical and doing more may make them cut back on each part of the process) or asking the same number of employees to take on a greater array of tasks.

Swank (2003) provides an excellent example of service streamlining. Jefferson Pilot Financial was extremely successful in transforming itself into a lean service management enterprise by re-engineering its New Business operations. The company implemented a number of changes that improved efficiency while reducing costs. Process employees were moved into closer proximity with each other after having been previously structured along functional lines. Customer files were then more efficiently moved along from group to group. Procedures were also standardized, with all files being stored alphabetically, and process employees were housed in similar settings to ensure consistency and allow substitute employees to work efficiently when needed. It was also found that previously there had been feedback loop-backs where applications might go back to previous processing stages and cause delays. These were eliminated. Another improvement involved setting common work tempos for employees so that higher application-per-hour completion goals could be set. This type of process re-engineering proved to be extremely beneficial for Jefferson Pilot Financial as it allowed the company to charge lower premiums and handle applications more quickly.

Metters and Vargas (2000) argue that for services to streamline and improve efficiency, they must redesign the jobs of the personnel involved in the service delivery process. They suggest that, sometimes, technologies become available that allow cost cutting across the entire service while improving the level of the quality of the service provided. When these technologies exist, they should be adopted immediately. When these technologies are not available, they suggest that management should consider 'decoupling' service tasks to gain efficiencies. Decoupling involves removing certain low-customer contact tasks from frontline or front office personnel, standardizing them and moving them into remote back office locations. The authors present four different competitive approaches to decoupling(see Figure 9.5) and provide illustrative examples for each. The first category presented is the **Cost Leaders** (companies that compete on price and decouple for the main purpose of lowering costs). The focus here is to take complex jobs with multiple tasks and make them simpler through standardization with the use of specialized labour and new technologies to achieve economies of scale. The decoupling of complex jobs allows for the reduction of work variance. The discount stockbroker, Charles Schwab & Co., and the insurance company, GEICO, are firms which have eliminated localized personnel who were high-customer contact and paid by commissions, which was the standard

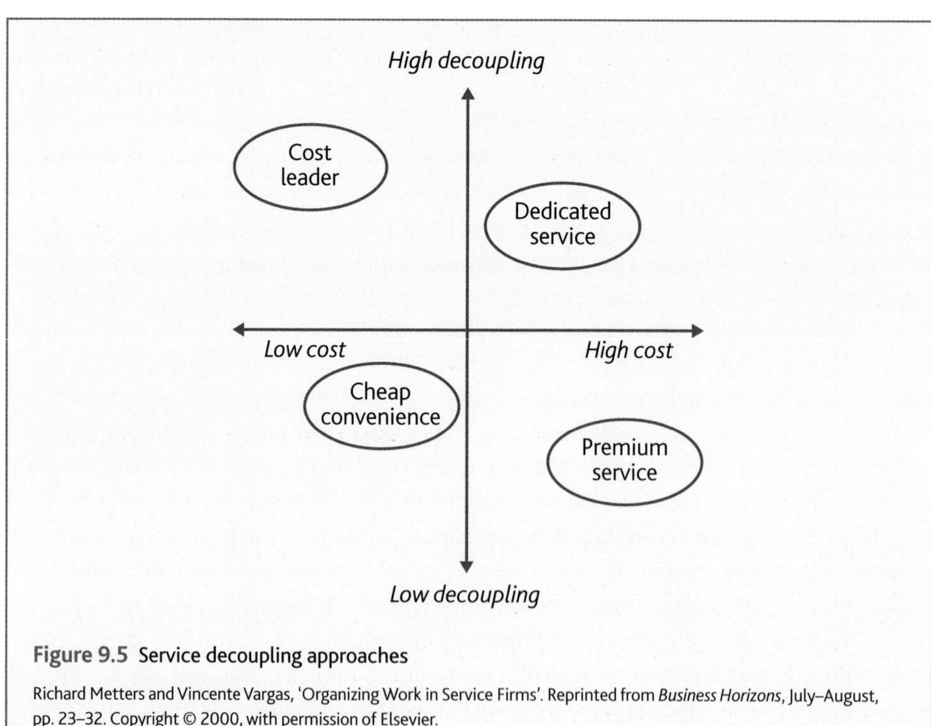

Figure 9.5 Service decoupling approaches

Richard Metters and Vincente Vargas, 'Organizing Work in Service Firms'. Reprinted from *Business Horizons*, July–August, pp. 23–32. Copyright © 2000, with permission of Elsevier.

of their industries. The standardization of certain basic components of the customer delivery process significantly streamlined operations and improved profitability.

The second type of company is the **Cheap Convenience** company, which attempts to make their service offering more convenient while maintaining a relatively low cost structure. This is known as a 'kiosk' strategy, where the firm utilizes multiple service units in different locations to provide easy customer access but offers only a limited range of services. For this type of firm, fewer, cross-trained employees are utilized doing both back office and front office work. Examples of successful competitors in this category include Dollar General, 7–11 (Southland Corporation), and Edward D. Jones stock brokerage services. These firms compete against the cost leaders by offering many convenient smaller product-line outlets. Key to success for these firms is the development of easy-to-use software and the use of tightly scripted service encounters between customers and service personnel.

The third category is the **Dedicated Service** firm that decouples to support front office personnel with cost reduction as a secondary concern. Here, tasks are separated by personality type and ability. Decoupling here allows more variety and flexibility to enhance employee morale and customer service experiences. The driving concept here is worker suitability with matching of service work to personality type. Back office tasks are centralized by region or particular back office contacts are specified for each group of front office workers. Long-term relationships are built between back office and front office to help the service delivery process flow smoothly. This approach requires more staff and potentially higher costs. Many traditional hospitals and insurance companies follow this kind of service strategy. The key here is to set up proper reward structures based on how well the back office personnel support the front office workers.

The final decoupling approach is the **Premium Service** firm, where less decoupling is used in order to maximize responsiveness and customization. Here, the strategic goal is to provide personalized service at premium prices. Intimate relationships are built between customers and service personnel. Frontline personnel are given the power to customize a variety of offerings to meet the specific needs of each customer, while back office personnel are minimally decoupled. The US firm, Krispy Kreme Doughnuts, has successfully positioned itself as a Premium Service firm in comparison to Cost Leader, Dunkin' Donuts (Metters and Vargas, 2000). A sound, differentiating device for hospitals can involve the development of specialized maternity (e.g., the Tennessee Birthing Center) or paediatric orientations (Children's Hospital of Philadelphia).

MINI CASE STUDY 9.1 Comparing and contrasting websites: value for consumers

The UK is quickly taking to the use of price-comparison websites, which makes particular sense in recessionary times, as was the case in the first quarter of 2009. One of the most popular of these comparison sites is moneysupermarket. com, which includes services from the financial industry, travel, motoring, broadband, and utilities. Estimates for visitation for the site run as high as 3 million, and with the recession forcing careful financial choices upon consumers, consumer visits are expected to climb significantly during the foreseeable future. Heavy advertising on TV is raising the visibility of competing sites like Gocompare.com, Comparethemarket.com, and Moneysavingexpert.com, to name a few. Now others

» are considering taking advantage of this opportunity and jumping into the fray. One company interested in competing is Tesco.

These sites allow consumers to see the offerings of various competitors and see what is being offered and the prices for these offerings so that they can make the best decisions. Consumers are more willing to use these kinds of platforms than ever before, and service marketers are realizing that if they don't participate, they will lose valuable customers to more creative competitors. Increasing numbers of British as well as Americans are using comparison sites as the first step in the buying process. If a company wants to have their products potentially in the consumer's choice set, they must be visible in the mix when customers start at the comparison site. This then incites company site visitation, but, in the end, the customer may return to the comparison site for final alternative evaluation and final choice. What seems to be happening here is that the lowest prices do not always get the customers to buy. If a company has the lowest price but is not known to the consumer, the customer may choose a more expensive alternative if the brand is fairly well known. Obviously, there is a reluctance to accept an offer when there are no personal experiences to draw upon.

One-stop-shopping is valuable to consumers. They are happy to see what is available and make timely comparisons, but consumers want to be able to trust the information that they see provided, a point which was of concern early on for such companies as Amazon.com, but quality controls observed by the site have eliminated consumer doubts. By expanding the mix of products and brands offered via Amazon, consumers have grown to trust the information provided. The customer-based review process helps to add credibility to these sites as consumers show their level of satisfaction, increasing consumer confidence and trust. Trailblazing was also undertaken in the travel industry with the successes of Expedia.com, Travelocity.com, and Priceline.com. How do comparison sites charge for their services? They offer space for annual or monthly rates, and some will charge by the click or by the product being offered or by the particular platform application. The point is that the marketers must pay for access on the price-comparison sites.

As more of these comparison sites become available, the marketers are being forced to consider limiting the number of sites upon which to make their product information available. Things have particularly heated up in the insurance industry, and some insurance providers have decided to try their own approach to providing comparative information. In particular, Norwich Union has actually dropped out of using price-comparison sites and has launched its own site, which provides details about its products as well as those of competitors. What is innovative about this site is that its own products may not be the lowest priced offerings, but it makes them available anyway. Several similar sites have proven to be effective marketing tools for insurance providers in the US. Progressive.com has found great success in the US by asking visitors to structure their insurance policies as they want and then compare quotes across a variety of competing offers, and the consumer sees which makes the most sense for them, given the price and their specific needs.

Why would Norwich and Progressive provide prices if their own company offerings are more expensive than other competitors? They believe that they will be seen in a better light through honesty and integrity, and that even when a competitor might undercut them, the consumer might still choose to stay with them because they project a better image and reputation than the competitors. It also provides a mechanism for outsourcing those consumers who would not be profitable for them to carry. It appears to be a win-win situation.

Creative strategic alliances

A creative strategic way to improve service profitability involves strategic partnering between different service providers, since alliances can effectively be used to strengthen brands and cut costs. These alliances can take the form of co-branding, co-marketing, outsourcing, licensing, and distribution agreements, to name a few. Examples can readily be seen in the strategic partnerings of airlines like the Star Alliance, Northwest Airlines, and KLM, and United Airlines and Lufthansa, as well as in the offering of T-Mobile Wi-Fi hotspots at Texaco stations, Starbucks coffee on United Airlines flights, and UK mobile operator 3 offering BMG music videos for download to its customers with mobile phones. These alliances offer another approach to differentiation of service offerings by allowing partners to retain their own independent brands and financial control while cutting costs and improving profits. Savings are facilitated through the sharing of assets and/or business processes or through the outsourcing of components of the offering.

Ernst and French (1996) caution that any partnerings must ensure that there is no eroding of each partner's core service concept. There are two main types of strategic alliances for services: brand-sharing alliances and asset-sharing alliances. Brand-sharing alliances involve the increase of customer benefits through joint offerings with minimal system integration. The idea is to create greater value for the consumer by offering complementary services rather than to achieve enormous cost savings. Citibank developed a relationship with American Airlines to offer its credit card users benefits in the form of frequent-flyer miles. This required only a minimum of coordination and integration, but both brands enjoyed brand enhancement. Asset-sharing alliances look to business system integration for the purpose of significant cost savings. These alliances can involve the sharing of real estate, computer systems, equipment and technology. 7–11 (Southland) has asset-sharing relationships with Citgo gas stations to share the cost of real estate. This has also been seen with the use of Little Caesar's Pizza offerings in K-Mart stores and McDonald's food offerings in Wal-Mart stores. Some of these alliances can become more like mergers than strategic partnerings as the partners become integrally linked with one another. This can be seen in the airline industry with such pairings as UsAir and British Airways with common hubs, maintenance, and ticketing facilities. It has been estimated that this alliance has resulted in cost savings and increased revenues for the partners of over $100 million per year (Ernst and French, 1996).

Instrumental to the issue of strategic alliances is the burgeoning area known as **coopetition** (Kirchner et al., 2007). This focuses on a continuum between cooperation and competition, and great promise is seen for the small service firm, particularly for non-profits and charitable organizations, which are asked to accomplish much with extremely limited budgets. In the instance of regional and local arts and cultural organizations, with extremely limited operating budgets and depending upon donations from corporations and individuals for their survival, combining forces for the creation of shared events has great potential for improving their reach and aiding in their achievement of their missions. The fact that they will share resources for event creation but not in any way for fund-raising demonstrates that these alliances are not open in all ways, thus they are both cooperating and competing at the same time.

Partnering also requires the assurance that there is a tight fit between partners in terms of customer demographics and brand image. Customers must readily see the benefit in the pairing of services. Ernst and French (1996) provide the following suggestions for managing alliances:

1. Prepare for an alliance as you would for a merger.
2. Mechanisms must be established for strategy development, organizational decision-making, and assignment of financial accountability in the new alliance culture.
3. Both partners must move quickly and effectively to manage the transition.
4. Budget sufficient time for alliance work.
5. Monitor progress on a weekly basis, at least in the beginning.
6. Build in mechanisms for conflict resolution and decision-making.
7. Consider exit options.

Another approach to alliances that can have synergies for service firms and aid in the cost-cutting process is **outsourcing**. Allen and Chandrashekar (2000) report that more than 90 per cent of all US service firms have outsourced some of their service offerings. It potentially allows firms to get goods and services at a lower cost and with a higher quality by relying on firms that specialize in certain components of service delivery. Anything that the firm believes is not part of their core competency becomes a candidate for outsourcing. This enormous trend toward outsourcing began with IT as a functional area with providers like Andersen Consulting, but it has spread to all kinds of service businesses. Hotels outsource concierge services, restaurant services, and cleaning services. Airlines outsource cleaning and maintenance and reservations services. Almost anything can be outsourced, provided that it does not potentially erode firm core competencies and confuse the customer. A good overview of outsourcing possibilities based on the levels of service provided by the service contractor can be found in Figure 9.6.

Outsourcing must be carefully managed. Allen and Chandrashekar (2000) provide a series of strategic suggestions for the proper care and handling of outsourcing. First of all, they suggest that the management of outsourcing requires a shift for managers from the management of people to the management of contracts. The wording of the contracts becomes the focal point rather than the governing of personnel. An important first step in the process should be to define clearly the expectations for the use of outsourcing. A key point that the authors make is that outsourcing should not be used as a method for eliminating a problem area for the firm if the real problem stems from something that is systematic within the firm itself. Outsourcing often involves the combination of contract workers with regular service personnel, and there is always the challenge of dealing with divided loyalties and employee-role conflict. Outsourcing managers must deal with potential conflicts between these two different types of workers. While cohesiveness of the workforce is challenging, with proper open communications and thoughtful strategic planning, outsourcing can be a powerful mechanism for service streamlining.

Streamlining service operations and improving productivity are excellent strategies for improving profitability, but the other side of the equation which is equally important is to ensure that the customer experience is the best that it can be. In order to continually meet or exceed customer expectations, it is imperative that service strategists understand exactly

Level of contractor contribution

	Labor contracting	*Mixed outsourcing*	*Complete outsourcing*
Contractor provides ...	• Some employees	Some or all of the following: • Employees • Materials • Process and system • Technology and equipment • Facilities • Management/ supervision	• Employees • Process and systems • Technology and equipment • Materials • Facilities • Supervision
Host firm provides ...	• Some employees • Process and systems • Technology and equipment • Materials • Facilities • Management/ supervision	Some or all of the following • Employees • Materials • Process and system • Technology and equipment • Facilities • Management/ supervision	• Program management

Figure 9.6 Categories of service outsourcing

Sandy Allen and Ashok Chandrashekar, 'Outsourcing Services: The Contract is Just the Beginning', March–April, pp. 25–34. Reprinted from *Business Horizons*, Copyright © 2000, with permission of Elsevier.

what the consumer expects to be delivered by the service. This next section will focus on differentiation and the nature of customer service expectations and the achievement of sustainable competitive advantage.

Differentiation and competitive advantage

Since service firms do not have the benefit of patents and other high barriers to entry, competitive advantage for service firms lies in continually exceeding customer expectations (Ford et al., 2001). If the customer believes that the quality they are receiving is the best that it can be, there is no reason to switch to the offerings of another provider. So, how does the service firm ensure that it can provide value to the customer and achieve sustainable competitive advantage? One consideration is the definition of the target customer in question. Many service firm failures point to the impossible nature of being 'all things to all customers'. Successful segmentation is a necessity for service success.

Arnold et al. (1999) found that global wireless communications companies were suffering from this 'all things to all people' malaise, and they found that the few successes that there were, were based upon clear segmentation strategies. The authors found that firm success was facilitated by a four-pronged approach to segmentation: (1) identify the most attractive customers to serve; (2) restructure business systems to cater to these customers as efficiently as possible; (3) create a basis for sustainable perceptual differentiation; and (4) establish an organizational entity that stays focused on the appropriate customer segments and applies metrics to ensure that the proper segments remain satisfied. Of course, the authors stress the importance of not differentiating for the sake of differentiating, but basing differentiation on specific sets of viable customer needs.

Internal employee culture creation and enhancement

The challenges inherent in streamlining through outsourcing highlight the importance of employees in the service mix. The front office and back office personnel are instrumental to the provision of the service and ultimately influence the customer's perceptions of quality and value. Service firms are constantly faced with employee turnover, and a lot of the problems experienced have to do with the lack of care and nurturing of these important facilitators (Frei, 2008). Poor service from internal service units within the service firm have undoubtedly forced a number of services to consider outsourcing, when a far more productive approach would involve paying more attention to these internal units and providing them with better training and support. Setting up a supportive internal culture could keep employees in these internal service units happier and more productive. Hays (1996) posits that internal service improvements can lead to dramatically increased internal service productivity (anywhere from 20 to 60 per cent gains are possible), an elevation of overall quality ceilings, and the development of new sources of competitive advantage.

Another challenge that faces service firms is the availability of service personnel. Service strategy is dependent upon the availability of appropriate employees, and service firms must change their way of thinking about service employees as the phenomenal growth of the service sector has led to a labour shortage as the number of employees has been outpaced by new job creation (Friedman, 1998; Stuart, 2006). Friedman (1998) proposes that service firms create effective value propositions for employees, tap new employee segments (e.g., older adults and the disabled), and change work structures so that they will keep good employees and be seen as the preferred employer in a particular service area. One of the most important ways in which a company can keep good employees and attract qualified candidates is to create an environment in which the employees are treated in the same way as they would treat customers. This 'golden rule' has worked exceptionally well for such service success stories as Southwest Airlines, Ritz-Carlton Hotels, Walt Disney Corporation, and Nordstrom's Department Stores.

Relationship building with customers

Service strategists are quickly accepting the importance of relationship building with customers, which can be facilitated through effective segmentation. Zeithaml et al. (2001) found that a number of successful service firms have actually created customer pyramids which differentiate customers by profit potential and recognize that different groups of customers have different sets of expectations. These firms (like Fedex and Bank of America) cater to the more profitable customers and downplay the strategic efforts to reach the less profitable segments. The authors make the following suggestions regarding when firms should utilize this customer pyramid:

1. When service resources, including employee time, are limited
2. When customers want different services or service levels
3. When customers are willing to pay for different levels of service
4. When customers define value in different ways
5. When customers can be separated from each other
6. When service differentials can lead to upgrading customers to another level
7. When the customers can be accessed either as a group or individually.

Probably the most useful lessons come from observations of the most successful service providers. Companies like Walt Disney, Southwest Airlines, Marriott International, and The Ritz-Carlton are all known for their service excellence in handling both sides of the service equation. They constantly refine and improve operational performance while continuously monitoring and providing customer value. Ford et al. (2001) studied these successful companies and identified ten lessons that can help any service firm to maximize customer value perceptions and ensure a strong perceptual position in the head of their customers:

1. Base decisions on what the customer wants and expects.
2. Think and act in terms of the entire customer experience.
3. Continuously improve all parts of the customer experience.
4. Hire and reward people who can effectively build relationships with customers.
5. Train employees in how to cope with emotional labour costs.
6. Create and sustain a strong service culture.
7. Avoid failing your customer twice.
8. Empower customers to co-produce their own experience.
9. Get managers to lead from the front, not the top.
10. Treat all customers as if they were guests.

As mentioned above, one of the ways in which companies can make customers feel more of a relationship with the service is through their greater involvement as co-producers of the service creation and delivery (Grenci and Watts, 2007). This carries with it a shift from the usual push strategies (where the sales forces and service personnel have been the forces to 'push' the service on the consumer), to pull strategies, where the consumers are more integrally involved and actively seek the service that best fits their needs or 'pull' it to themselves. Carter (2003) says that this is reflective of the shift from consultative selling to customer-driven buying, whereby the customer knows more about what they actually want, and the service person must have the expertise to work with the customer to customize the offering to the customer's expectations. The point is that customers are brought into the process more actively, and this opens the door for stronger customer involvement and the potential for stronger customer–service provider relationships being built. This is particularly promising for consumer services offered via the Internet (Grenci and Watts, 2007).

Successful service firms must understand the nature of the service experience and set up operating systems that continuously ensure that customer expectations are not only being met, but exceeded. The good news is that services of any size can gain sustainable competitive advantage if they set up effective service cultures that give the appropriate customers what they want while creating an internal environment that ensures employee satisfaction and loyalty.

One interesting new approach to providing a differentiated service can be seen in the development of a number of comparison websites that allow consumers to compare and contrast the offerings of a variety of service providers in a particular service category (see Mini Case Study 9.1).

MINI CASE STUDY 9.2 Virgin competing in low-fare air travel in the intensely competitive US market

Richard Branson is not one to shy away from competition, as has been proven time and time again. Virgin has expanded its presence into air travel, music, train travel, and broadband services. It is a multimedia and multi-industry competitive giant, and it appears that the challenge becomes a bit of a principle to the charismatic Branson. Now he is turning his attention to the fiercely competitive US air travel market, where companies have quickly come and gone (e.g., Independence Air). The air travel arm of Virgin has just celebrated its 25th anniversary, and Sir Richard is taking advantage of this milestone to aggressively expand geographic coverage. Given the state of the economy in the UK and the US in early 2009, price has become a critical determinant of air travel selection. It is competing head-to-head with such low-fare airlines as Jet Blue and Air Tran. Virgin is planning to offer better service than its competitors with better entertainment systems, hook-ups for laptop computers, and where the offering will have a distinct advantage will be in the fact that the planes that they will be using for Virgin America will be able to take off and land in worse weather conditions. Virgin will be providing in-seat entertainment screens that will be able to broadcast live television programmes and live sports matches, and the company hopes that better entertainment choices when matched with more convenient flight schedules with less dependence on good weather conditions at low prices (the expected fare for flights from New York's JFK Airport to San Francisco will be around £69) should make Virgin quite attractive to American travellers, especially business travellers who need to get to their business meetings as close to on-time as possible.

Virgin has found, however, that holiday travel will also be a big push for them in the US as well as the UK. Travellers given more for less when compared to the other providers should resonate very powerfully in light of the financial concerns of most travellers with the recession in full swing. The financial concerns of both Americans and Britons does not look as though it may abate until well into 2010 or even into 2011, and the hope is that if Virgin can build a strong 'value' image in the minds of its target markets, this will only make them more competitive when economic conditions improve. Virgin is also gearing up for the power of the Internet, as that is where most people will go to plan out their holidays, so if Virgin is readily visible in the information gathering, then brand reinforcement should work strongly for them. They are also aware that customer word-of-mouth is in addition a strong influencer, and if customer experience is positive with Virgin, then customers will pass along their experiences to others in further reinforcement of the brand.

Virgin will look to build strongly on its advertising in the US as well as in the UK. Its new 25th-anniversary adverts show an array of flight attendants walking through an airport, easily recognizable in their bright red uniforms surrounding the smiling pilot, and everyone noticing them. The use of the Frankie Goes to Hollywood classic, 'Relax', echoes throughout the ad, bringing emotional engagement with it. Richard Branson himself travelled on the inaugural flight of Virgin America, and the attachment of his powerful and charismatic personality to his new American venture should give it a good start on its way.

Customer service as differentiator

When a service company uses customer service as its sole focus for differentiation from its competition, it may face perceptual difficulties. If everyone stands for service, then there is no distinction in centring on customer service as the main foundation for differentiation. The question is whether such companies as BT, British Gas, and British Airways can build strong brands by centring on customer service in their advertising campaigns. These companies all stressed customer service in their advertisements in 2003, and Lloyds TSB is preparing to do the same thing by emphasizing relationships with its customers as the 'heart of its brand'. Most services build from the standpoint that offering great service is a foundation for creating loyal customers. If people are treated well, they should not want to go anywhere else.

So, an important question is why these kinds of major corporations would stress customer service in their advertisements. Craig Smith and Robert Gray raise some interesting questions in the 21 July 2004 issue of *Marketing*. Gray (2004) suggests that BT, British Gas, and British Airways have built differentiating positions in very competitive markets by honing their delivery of customer service. But he questions whether customer service should be the main message in all company communications. Some of the criticisms raised by industry experts include the fact that customer service is not actually a strategy in and of itself; customer service as a sole focus for differentiation may miss key elements that helped to build the company credibility and success in the first place, and research has indicated that consumers don't see customer service as particularly interesting—it is perceived to be boring and lacks imagination. Gray (2004) provides the direct comments from key personnel at BT, British Gas, and British Airways who believe that stressing customer service is the only viable way to differentiate their services. This may not be the case. As Fred Wiersema notes in his study of 5,000 companies, companies need to continually exceed their past offerings and set new standards in their offerings of customer service to stay ahead of the competition (Wiersema, 2001). Merely offering customer service is not enough; offering incomparable service is the key to success. Gray (2004) suggests that the company which stresses service must be able to deliver on its promise. Smith (2004) suggests that such catch phrases as 'the way to fly', 'more power to you', and 'do the right thing' are too nebulous to mean very much to customers. Good customer service may be a necessary requirement to be a serious competitor in a service industry, but the company had best focus on other differentiators when building their image. As Smith (2004) suggests, service should be improved to compete against strong rivals; however, service is a weak platform for true differentiation. If everyone is for excellent customer service, then no one is really differentiated perceptually. Other bases will have to be developed.

The latest thinking: great performances and emotional engagement and the Harvard Business School services model

Great performances and emotional engagement

So what is it that will make service companies profitable and ensure their success? One promising approach involves an extension of the dramaturgy concept as applied to services. Stuart (2006) argues that just any performance will not create the appropriate emotional engagement with the customer to build an emotional bond, and that the service provider must ensure that the presentation creates a 'great performance'. The idea is that customer loyalty, which is imperative for long-term profitability and gains in market share, is something which is fostered, not by perceptions of service quality but by very high levels of customer satisfaction and service reliability. This need to go above and beyond suggests that service managers look to wow their customers with the overall experience that they provide. Stuart (2006) looks to the experiences from theatre companies to find ways in which performances can be enhanced. He suggests that misunderstandings amongst service managers include the following: (1) the belief that the delivery of a memorable service experience is the same as an understanding of the customer's perception of the service; (2) the relabelling of current performance is the same as a memorable experience; and (3) making sure that they save the very best part of the service experience for the last to account for recency effects are not stand-alone mechanisms for offering great and memorable performances. He suggests that it is the ability to design a comprehensive experience which integrates a wide range of individual elements.

Stuart (2006) studied a series of successful theatre companies to see whether there were any approaches that were particularly appropriate to the consistent delivery of outstanding performances. The study found that there was a uniform process for the development of a successful theatrical offering which involved five phases: (1) development of vision and strategic focus; (2) selection of the offering to fit the vision and focus; (3) selection of the various personnel to be involved and preplanning; (4) the handling of the artistic as well as technical design for the offering; and (5) a period of integration and experimentation in which an optimal design was found and prepared for final offering. As a result of the study of theatre companies, Stuart (2006) found a great deal of consistency in the developmental process, and he offers the following seven steps for use by service managers to offer not just a good service experience, but an outstanding service experience.

Step 1 is never to lose sight of the main stage. This means that the service provider must be careful not to offer inconsistent offerings and confuse their audiences. Service managers should keep the service concept clear and focused. His firm should be careful to keep to what it knows and does best. Any offering should be challenged for fit with resource capabilities, as the firm should keep within its limits in terms of potential consistency with expectations of customers as well as the ability to maintain financial viability. The example used was Canada's low-cost airline, WestJet, which lost sight of its mission and began to experiment with inconsistent offerings like leather seats, satellite televisions, and expanded legroom.

Step 2 is to communicate extensively with visual cues. The need in this step is to create a common direction and sense of purpose as well as a shared vision among all personnel within the organization, which should be reinforced through all manner of visual cues and not just by spoken words and phrases. Vision in this case should extend beyond artistic vision to include operational aspects as well. The example, again from Canada, involved the Lieutenant Governor of British Columbia, who focused on renovating historic stable-grounds for conversion into tourist attractions but faced community resistance, but the approval of the plans was facilitated through the effective shared vision and visual cues in the form of artists' renderings of what these facilities would look like once renovated brought everything together. The consistency and appropriateness of the project was brought effectively to all involved through the actions of the individuals involved and the artists' sketches.

Step 3 is to strive continuously for authenticity and integrity. This focuses on the importance of creating a realistic and authentic environment for the service in all aspects and to develop a service delivery system and environment that is totally in synch with the service concept. The idea here is that the service firm's theme should be vital for provision of an outstanding offering. The examples provided include the mistakes inherent in many companies trying to emulate Saturn's bonds with its customers by saying that they were focused on the needs of female customers but not really living out those statements and Outback Steakhouses focusing on the authenticity of the Australian theme and experience in all facets of their offerings.

Step 4 involves integration and communication. Here, the idea is to make sure that there is integration and communication across all facets of the service delivery environment. All disciplines and functions should be integrated using both formal and informal means, with the purpose to support the needs of the frontline service personnel. There is a need for collaboration on a regular basis to ensure that the roles of all relevant people in the delivery process are understood and appreciated. The example involved the Fairmont Hotel chain in Canada and the difficult lesson that was learned when trying to focus on guest-name recognition and its impact upon customer satisfaction and the potential for repeat business, but there were inconsistencies across the various hotels in implementing this, which was further exacerbated by differences in technological capabilities and departmental structuring. A similar example involved Air Canada and the confusion caused when it attempted to eliminate travel agents and get customers to book online. The technology was problematic and consumers had great difficulties understanding how to use the website. All facets must be integrated and coordinated to make this work smoothly.

Step 5 is to use experimentation to move towards excellence. In this case, the idea is to use constant innovation and experimentation to find the best ways to delight the customer in their service experience. A great deal of this process of development is never explained or shown to the customer. It is an ongoing refinement process but important for success. The example presented involved the Canadian food service company, Tim Horton's, which tried to gain market share in the lunchtime market by offering fresh soups and sandwiches, but the company did not work through the process correctly and found many problems in terms of the nature of the soups and sandwiches and the long queues that were developing due to wide variance in service deliveries to different customers.

Step 6 is not only to play the part, but to become the part in every way. The idea is that the delivery process is not something that should be attempted without careful practice and preparation. Rehearsal becomes vital, as the delivery of the service should never be forced. It should be natural and sincere and not an obvious act. Great performances are what they say that they are, since performance is the operant word. The example provided here involves Walt Disney and their famous training programmes in which employees are encouraged to act their parts with great sincerity so that all will believe that they are who they appear to be.

Finally, step 7 is to fire the director and hire the facilitator. This means that in order to truly integrate the varying processes that are needed to deliver a memorable performance, a facilitator is really needed and not a director. This facilitator must be able to understand the realities of the business environment, who can also help the frontline personnel reach their potential, bring the artistic and technical sides together, and do everything in a fiscally responsible framework. This requires a special individual who can see beyond the superficial. This is where it all comes together, and the examples point to the dangers of not having that facilitator to bring together the disparate components of the service offering properly.

Harvard Business School services model

A very promising set of findings for services strategists can be seen in a recent study by Frei (2008). Frei (2008) reports that an extensive study of the world's most successful services has produced a model of services which is now being taught at Harvard Business School that focuses on the differences between product companies and services. This model is comprised of four critical elements.

The first is the **offering**, and the research has shown that service providers will have to decide what aspects of the service they will perform badly in order to provide superior performance on other aspects. The hard choice for the manager is to make the decision as to which service attributes will be short-changed and which will be the focus for excellence. As a result, the service must identify and target customer segments according to the types of service attributes that they most demand. The point, according to Frei (2008), is that the company must identify groups of customers with similar expectations in terms of what aspects are associated with excellence in service. The company must continually find the proper trade-offs between inferior performance for one attribute with superior performance for another.

The second element is the **funding mechanism**. The important consideration here is that to be able to excel in any service attributes, there is a cost involved; therefore, service managers must have a funding mechanism in place. There are four forms in which this funding mechanism usually manifests itself: (1) to have the customer pay for it (like Starbucks allowing people to stay and relax in its environment as opposed to pushing people through and increasing sales volume); (2) to create a positive mix of operational savings and value-added services (like Progressive Insurance in the US that provides rate quotes for themselves and their competitors to come up with the right quote for the customer, which creates the impression for the customer that the company is going way beyond the norm to provide them with exceptional service); (3) to spend money in the present to enable saving in the future (like Intuit's decision to provide free customer support when all of its industry competitors were charging for that service in the software industry, which allowed them actually to reduce the number of service calls being made); and (4) to have the customer do the work themselves (like airline frequent-flier customers who prefer using the self-service kiosks rather than the staffed positions in line to get their seats and their boarding passes).

The third element is the **employee management system**. Obviously, the service personnel can make or break a service company, as has been discussed many times in this chapter. This can be facilitated if two questions can be used for diagnostic purposes: (1) What makes the employees able to achieve excellence? and (2) What makes the employees motivated to achieve excellence? What has been learned is that if the service firm requires above and beyond 'heroism' on the part of its employees to be able to keep customers happy, there is a serious problem in the service design, since employee sacrifice is not going to be sustainable. The company must create a system in which the normal employee has the ability to be successful.

The final element is the **customer management system**. The issue here is that customers are part of the service delivery process with service employees, and their involvement in operations is at a labour rate that is less costly; therefore, if some service tasks are shifted from employees to consumers, there is a saving involved that can allow the company to pass benefits to customers in lower costs. An example is Zipcar, a very popular car-sharing service, which expects customers to clean and fuel cars before passing along to the next customer. The point here is that customers must be managed in a way that is consistent with those service attributes that the company has decided to use as their basis for service excellence.

Conclusion

Services may not be as different from manufactured goods as once thought, as the need to apply service strategies in non-service settings increases as the service-centred dominant logic perspective becomes increasingly relevant. Service consumption involves an experience that must be understood by the service strategist so that the service that is offered not only meets, but exceeds, the expectations of the customer. Customer satisfaction from a fulfilling service experience will lead to loyalty and profitability, but it is imperative for the service strategist to monitor changes in the expectations of consumers so that continuous service quality improvements can be facilitated. It is also important to streamline where possible to build on company strengths and minimize weaknesses. The firm that keeps offering the most enjoyable service experience for their customers while eliminating inefficiencies will stay ahead of the competition. It is also worth remembering that customer service as a means for service-firm differentiation may not be a viable strategy and that other defining characteristics may be more viable.

Summary

Service strategy is totally dependent upon the customer receiving the service experience that they expect. Market research examining the expectations of customers provides a necessary foundation for service design and implementation. Successful services have managers who understand the wants and needs of customers and have the courage to empower their employees to be able to adapt service offerings to the special situations faced by customers. Customer focus becomes the key strategic consideration for all service employees, and it helps when there is a supportive service culture that puts the customer first, with profits following. This is a difficult stand for management to take as profitability is such an important driver, but those willing to be bold will potentially reap the kinds of rewards that service pioneers like Virgin, BskyB, Southwest Airlines, and Marriott International have come to enjoy.

KEY TERMS

Blueprinting The mapping of all the steps that a customer takes once they enter the service, allowing service management to examine the whole process of delivery to identify any problem areas.

Coopetition The balancing between competition and cooperation that allows a sharing of assets, maximizing the impact of limited budgets; this is particularly appropriate for small service firms.

Decoupling Where the service provider removes certain low-customer contact tasks from frontline or front office personnel, standardizing them and moving them into remote back office locations. The decoupling of complex jobs allows for the reduction of work variance.

Heterogeneity The aspect of services that focuses on inconsistencies brought on by changes in mood states and emotions that can cause differences in interactions between service provider personnel and consumers.

Inseparability The service interaction takes place in a meeting of the customer and service provider personnel. The interaction creates the service experience. This means that customers are co-producers/designers of the service.

Intangibility The fact that services cannot be held in the hand, felt, and touched, presents a challenge for strategic marketing decision-making as competitive differentiation has to be experienced by users and there are really no strategies for product disposal of unsold stock.

Operand resources Resources which are acted upon or operated upon to produce an effect. From the standpoint of product-centred logic, customers and products are operand resources. They are both acted upon by marketers.

Operant resources Resources which are used to act upon operand resources. The customer works with marketers to produce value as co-producer, so the customer is not acted upon but becomes part of the action on something else to produce value.

Outsourcing Where the service provider looks to contract out service components to outside suppliers. Anything that the firm believes is not part of their core competency becomes a candidate for outsourcing. It potentially allows firms to get goods and services at a lower cost and with a higher quality by relying on firms that specialize in certain components of service delivery.

Perishability The fleeting life of a service offering. Once the service is provided, it is consumed at that time. Since a service cannot be stored, there is a need to synchronize supply and demand.

Service dominant logic The perspective that services as well as products should be thought of as being produced in the same way. The marketer in this perspective collaborates and works with the customer to create value, as opposed to being mainly an actor upon the customer to create value in the product-centred or goods-centred perspective.

Servicescape The pictorial representation of the physical evidence associated with the service, it also provides an excellent mechanism for additional service performance evaluation.

SERVQUAL A survey instrument developed by Parasuraman et al. (1988) to measure service quality which compares customer perceptions of ideal service provision to actual service delivery perceptions for a range of service process characteristics.

Streamlining Where the service provider looks to improve operations through the elimination of service inefficiencies and improve profit margins.

DISCUSSION QUESTIONS

1 Identify four distinguishing characteristics of services and explain what challenges they create for marketing strategy.

2 Compare and contrast the service dominant logic to the goods dominant logic. What are the implications of either for marketing strategy?

3 Give a basic explanation of SERVQUAL. How does it relate to the concept of the service experience?

4 Describe ways in which services can streamline and improve operational efficiency and ultimately profitability.

5 'The drama metaphor has limited application for marketing strategy in relation to services.' Comment.

6 Identify one organization that provides great service. Develop and support (in order of importance) your top five lessons for other companies that can be learnt from them. On reflection, could that top organization learn anything from a leading theatre company?

7 Identify and explain the four major elements of service suggested by the Harvard Business School model. What are the strengths and weaknesses of the model?

8 Will self-service always be important for customers when evaluating a service choice?When would self-service not be beneficial?

ONLINE RESOURCE CENTRE

Visit the Online Resource Centre for this book for lots of interesting additional material at: **www.oxfordtextbooks.co.uk/orc/west2e/**

REFERENCES AND FURTHER READING

Allen, Sandy, and Ashok Chandrashekar (2000), 'Outsourcing Services: The Contract is Just the Beginning', *Business Horizons*, March–April, pp. 25–34.

Arnold, Scott, Greg A. Reed, and Paul J. Roche (1999), 'Wireless, not Profitless', *McKinsey Quarterly*, 4 (Fall), pp. 112–21.

Arnold, Scott, Byron G. Auguste, Mark Knickrehm, and Paul J. Roche (1998), 'Winning in Wireless', *McKinsey Quarterly*, 2 (Spring), pp. 18–32.

Berry, Leonard L., and Neeli Bendapudi (2003), 'Clueing in Customers', *Harvard Business Review*, February, pp. 100–6.

Berry, Leonard L., and Kent D. Seltman (2007), 'Building a Strong Services Brand: Lessons from Mayo Clinic', *Business Horizons*, 50, pp. 199–209.

Bitner, Mary Jo, and Stephen W. Brown (2007), 'The Service Imperative', *Business Horizons*, 51, pp. 39–46.

Carter, R. (2003), 'How to Let Your Prospects Sell Themselves', *American Salesman*, 48(12), pp. 19–21.

Cohen, Morris A., Carl Cull, Hau L. Lee, and Don Willen (2000), 'Saturn's Supply-chain Innovation: High Value in After-sales Service', *Sloan Management Review*, Summer, pp. 93–101.

Ernst, David, and Thomas D. French (1996), 'Coffee and One Way to Boston', *McKinsey Quarterly*, 1 (Winter), pp. 165–76.

Ford, Robert C., Cherrill P. Heaton, and Stephen W. Brown (2001), 'Delivering Excellent Service: Lessons from the Best Firms', *California Management Review*, 44(1), pp. 39–56.

Frei, Francis X. (2008), 'The Four Things a Service Business Must Get Right', *Harvard Business Review*, April, pp. 70–80.

Friedman, David S. (1998), 'Help Wanted', *McKinsey Quarterly*, 1 (Winter), pp. 34–45.

Gray, Robert (2004), 'Customer Service is not a Strategy', *Marketing*, (21 July), pp. 32–4.

Grenci, Richard T., and Charles A. Watts (2007), 'Maximizing Customer Service via Mass Customized e-Consumer Services', *Business Horizons*, 50, pp. 123–32.

Grove, Stephen J., and Raymond P. Fisk (1983), 'The Dramaturgy of Service Exchange: An Analytical Framework for Services Marketing', in Leonard L. Berry, Lynn G. Shostack, and Gregory D. Upah (eds), *Emerging Perspectives on Services Marketing* (Chicago, IL: American Marketing Association), pp. 45–9.

Grove, Stephen J., Raymond P. Fisk, and Mary Jo Bitner (1992), 'Dramatizing the Service Experience: A Managerial Approach', in Teresa A. Swartz, David E. Bowen, and Stephen W. Brown (eds), *Advances in Services Marketing and Management: Research and Practice*, Vol. 1(Greenwich, CT: JAI Press, Inc), pp. 91–121.

Hays, Richard D. (1996), 'The Strategic Power of Internal Service Excellence', *Business Horizons*, July–August, pp. 15–20.

Hemp, Paul (2002), 'My Week as a Room-service Waiter at the Ritz', *Harvard Business Review*, June, pp. 50–62.

Kirchner, Theresa A., Edward P. Markowski, and John B. Ford (2007), 'Relationships among Levels of Government Support, Marketing Activities, and Financial Health of Nonprofit Performing Arts Organizations', *International Journal of Nonprofit and Voluntary Sector Marketing*, 12(2), pp. 95–116.

Lusch, Robert F., Stephen L. Vargo, and Alan J. Malter (2006), 'Marketing as Service-exchange: Taking a Leadership Role in Global Marketing Management', *Organizational Dynamics*, 35 (3), pp. 264–78.

Metters, Richard, and Vincente Vargas (2000), 'Organizing Work in Service Firms', *Business Horizons*, July–August, pp. 23–32.

Naumann, Earl, and Donald W. Jackson (Jr) (1999), 'One More Time: How Do You Satisfy Customers?' *Business Horizons*, (May–June), pp. 71–6.

Organization for Economic Cooperation and Development (OECD) (2004), *Innovation and Productivity in Services* (Paris: Organization for Economic Cooperation and Development).

Parasuraman, A., Valarie A. Zeithaml, and Leonard L. Berry (1988), 'SERVQUAL: A Multiple-item Scale for Measuring Consumer Perceptions of Service Quality', *Journal of Retailing*, 64 (Spring), pp. 12–40.

Parasuraman, A., Leonard L. Berry, and Valarie A. Zeithaml (1991), 'Understanding Customer Expectations of Service', *Sloan Management Review*, 32(3), pp. 38–49.

Reinartz, Werner, and Wolfgang Ulaga (2008), 'How to Sell Services More Profitably', *Harvard Business Review*, May, pp. 90–6.

Rothenberg, Sandra (2007), 'Sustainability through Servicizing', *MIT Sloan Management Review*, 48(2), pp. 83–91.

Smith, Craig (2004), 'Customer Service is no Basis for a Brand', *Marketing*, (21 July), p. 30.

Stuart, F. Ian (2006), 'Designing and Executing Memorable Service Experiences: Lights, Camera, *Experiment, Integrate*, Action!', *Business Horizons*, 49, pp. 149–59.

Swank, Cynthia Karen (2003), 'The Lean Service Machine', *Harvard Business Review*, October, pp. 123–9.

Vargo, Stephen L., and Robert F. Lusch (2004), 'Evolving to a New Dominant Logic for Marketing', *Journal of Marketing*, 68 (January), pp. 1–17.

Wiersema, Fred (2001), *The New Market Leaders* (New York: The Free Press).

World Bank (2003), *World Development Indicators 2003* (Washington, DC: The World Bank).

Zeithaml, Valarie A., and Mary Jo Bitner (2003), *Services Marketing: Integrating Customer Focus across the Firm*, 3rd edn (Boston, MA: McGraw-Hill Irwin).

Zeithaml, Valarie A., Roland T. Rust, and Katherine N. Lemon (2001), 'The Customer Pyramid: Creating and Serving Profitable Customers', *California Management Review*, 43(4), pp. 118–42.

KEY ARTICLE ABSTRACTS

Berry, Leonard L., and Neeli Bendapudi (2003), **'Clueing in Customers'**, *Harvard Business Review*, February, pp. 100–6.

One of the most successful healthcare providers in the United States is the Mayo Clinic, which has facilities in: Rochester, Minnesota; Scottsdale, Arizona; and Jacksonville, Florida. At the Mayo Clinic, the patient really does come first, and every aspect of the clinic is set up to communicate this to patients and their families, from the attitude and attire of the staff to the décor and ambience of the buildings. This insightful article addresses the effective use of evidence management to ensure that a service organization presents a consistent and effective image and set of values that is conveyed on a daily basis.

Abstract: When customers lack the expertise to judge a company's offerings, they naturally turn detective, scrutinizing people, facilities, and processes for evidence of quality. The Mayo Clinic understands this and carefully manages that evidence to convey a simple, consistent message: the needs of the patient come first. From the way that it hires and trains employees to the way it designs its facilities and approaches its care, the Mayo Clinic provides patients and their families with concrete evidence of its strengths and values and approach, that has allowed it to build what is arguably the most powerful brand in health care. A five-month study of evidence management at the Mayo Clinic was conducted. This led to the identification of best practices applicable to just about any company, in particular those that sell intangible or technically complex products. Essentially, companies need to determine what story they want to tell, then ensure that their employees and facilities consistently show customers evidence of that story.

Ford, Robert C., Cherrill P. Heaton, and Stephen W. Brown (2001), **'Delivering Excellent Service: Lessons from the Best Firms,'** *California Management Review*, 44 (1), pp. 39–56.

Companies like Walt Disney, Southwest Airlines, Marriott International, and The Ritz-Carlton are all known for their service excellence in handling both sides of the service equation. These firms constantly refine and improve operational performance while continuously monitoring and providing customer value. This article represents a study of the best service providers to determine what makes them successful. The authors present ten lessons that can help any service firm to maximize customer value perceptions and ensure a strong perceptual position in the head of their customers.

Abstract: Delivering excellent service is a challenge for most organizations. While many aspire to it, the evidence from customer satisfaction surveys indicates that too few firms are able to deliver service excellence. On the other hand, some organizations consistently deliver excellent service. This article reviews ten lessons these benchmark service organizations have learnt and shows how these organizations use them to meet and exceed the ever-rising expectations of their customers. These lessons can be emulated by any organization seeking such excellence.

Reinartz, Werner, and Wolfgang Ulaga (2008), 'How to Sell Services More Profitably', *Harvard Business Review*, May, pp. 90–6.

This insightful article suggests that even manufacturing companies are already delivering services, and this knowledge will help them to find ways in which to become more profitable in industrial services. They suggest that if firms follow a series of four steps, they can improve their profitability significantly. The steps suggested are: (1) the need to recognize that the company is already a service company; (2) the importance of industrializing the back office portion of the manufacturing business; (3) the prominence of the creation of a service-savvy sales force; and (4) the importance of focusing on the customers' processes and problems from a holistic viewpoint.

Abstract: Manufacturers frequently believe that adding value in the form of services will provide a competitive advantage after their products start to become commodities. But for every success story, at least five cautionary tales remind us that manufacturing companies will most likely struggle to turn a profit from their service businesses. Companies unsuccessful at developing service businesses have tried to transform themselves too quickly. Successful firms begin slowly, identifying and charging for simple services they already perform and using those to build enthusiasm for adding more complex ones. They then standardize their delivery processes to be as efficient as their manufacturing ones. As their services become more complex, they ensure that their sales force capabilities keep pace. Finally, management switches its focus from the company's processes and structures to the nature of customers' problems, the opportunities that customers' processes afford for inserting new services, and the new capabilities needed to deliver those services.

Vargo, Stephen L., and Robert F. Lusch (2004), 'Evolving to a New Dominant Logic for Marketing', *Journal of Marketing*, 68 (January), pp. 1–17.

This article introduces a valuable new perspective for marketing which they call service dominant logic, in which the firm would use the customer as a co-producer of the service or good created. This perspective suggests that this can be used with anything that has value to facilitate the exchange process. The authors suggest that firms deal with both operant and operand resources. From the operand resources perspective, customers are acted upon, while from the operant resources perspective, the customer becomes an actor upon something else (e.g., a co-producer). The customer is the actor, rather than what is acted upon.

Abstract: Marketing inherited a model of exchange from economics, which had a dominant logic based on the exchange of 'goods', which are usually manufactured input. The dominant logic focused on tangible resources, embedded value, and transactions. Over the past several decades, new perspectives have emerged that have a revised logic focused on intangible resources, the co-creation of value, and relationships. The authors believe that the new perspectives are converging to form a new dominant logic for marketing, one in which service provision, rather than goods, is fundamental to economic exchange. The authors explore this evolving logic and the corresponding shift in perspective for marketing scholars, marketing practitioners, and marketing educators.

END OF CHAPTER 9 CASE STUDY The luxury hotel industry: The Ritz-Carlton

The Ritz-Carlton is a luxury hotel chain, 99 per cent of which belongs to Marriot International, Inc. The company, established in 1983, currently operates 70 luxury hotels in more than 20 countries worldwide, as well as high-end spas and world-class golf courses. In order to better understand The Ritz-Carlton as a luxury hotel brand, it is important to review the company's Gold Standards found on the corporate site. The most important elements of the Gold Standards are The Credo and Motto:

The Credo The Ritz-Carlton Hotel is a place where the genuine care and comfort of our guests is our highest mission. We pledge to provide the finest personal service and facilities for our guests who will always enjoy a warm, relaxed, yet refined ambience.

Motto At The Ritz-Carlton Hotel Company, LLC, 'We are Ladies and Gentlemen serving Ladies and Gentlemen'. This motto exemplifies the anticipatory service provided by all staff members.

According to the Marriot International Inc. 2007 financial statements, revenue from luxury brands accounted for 12 per cent of total revenue. The Ritz-Carlton may face a decline in sales because of the recession and limited corporate budgets.

Target market

The luxury target market is motivated and acts differently from the average income consumers' market. In 2007, the wealthiest 10 per cent of consumers had an average household income of $359,000, whereas the median household income of Americans was $50,233. Vacation and travel is the number one category when it comes to the wealthy customer's luxury purchases. In the luxury hotel industry, these consumers are treated with specialized services and amenities above and beyond the normal hotel chain.

The luxury hotel industry provides an escape and sanctuary for their consumers from their everyday lives.

> Influenced by a fast changing world of new technology, an unstable global economy, work overload and time pressures, today's luxury consumers have new attitudes, needs and motivations for purchasing luxury goods. Less concerned with keeping up with appearances, today's affluent set makes luxury purchases in an attempt to gain control over their complicated lives and provide security for the future.

There are three segments in the luxury consumer market. Comfortably affluent Americans make up about 12 per cent of the nation's households, with an income level of between $100,000 and $150,000. Super-affluent families have an income that ranges between $151,000 and $300,000, and make up 6 per cent of the nation's households. The ultra-affluent segment of the population comprises only 1. 9 per cent of the nation's households and has an income of $301,000 and above.

The luxury hotel industry focuses on the wealthy consumer and the high-end business traveller. According to Joe Sharkey of the *International Herald Tribune*,'Luxury hotels depend heavily on high-end business travel, corporate meetings, and international visitors.' Unfortunately, in these hard economic times, this segment of the target is seeing a decline. Companies are setting mandates that executives can no longer stay at five-star resorts while travelling on business.

»

The very rich are not so easy to define because they are a mixture of instant pop stars, sportsmen, lottery millionaires, and an assortment of newly rich entrepreneurs. The number of millionaire households has grown rapidly since 1995, almost to the point where there are now three times as many millionaire households.

This target customer has strong opinions and likes to be rewarded, so hotels incorporate different strategies to reach them. Since the wealthy consumer values exclusivity and uniqueness, hotels develop loyalty programmes that centre around these characteristics. Luxury hotels also target these consumers while they are at their properties with in-room television advertisements featuring products, services, and amenities that the hotel has to offer. This will increase the amount of revenue spent during each visit and has proven to be effective.

The luxury marketer's mission and focus through good and bad economic times is the same, 'Selling a glamorous way of life to aspiring consumers'. The luxury hotel chain has to be careful during economic uncertainty to keep their brand and price integrity.

The Ritz-Carlton: economic environment

The Ritz-Carlton experienced a recession back in 1980, when many hotels were stuck with empty rooms. The Ritz-Carlton was no exception. Most of the Ritz-Carlton locations were said to require an occupancy rate of virtually 100 per cent every night of the year to make enough money to cover its debt. By July 1992, The Ritz-Carlton was more than $1 billion in debt, was in default on a loan for $70 million, and was seeking to *restructure* other debts. Today, The Ritz-Carlton has a difficult time filling rooms and the company is preparing for their toughest year since the last recession.

In November 2008, luxury hotels experienced a 15 per cent larger decline in occupancy than other types of hotels. In the first full week of January 2009, occupancy at luxury hotels fell by 24 per cent, compared with the same week last year. The other factor that affects corporate travellers is the 'AIG effect'. This refers to when the AIG company's top management spent $440,000 on an executive retreat at a California resort after being bailed out with taxpayer money. It has a major impact on the popularity of luxury hotels among the corporate traveller marketing segment.

The Ritz-Carlton downsized staff, reduced hours, and closed some dining outlets in 72 hotels. The company is keeping up the same service levels not to compromise the brand. The main focus now is on operations in terms of cost reduction and efficiency.

At the same time, The Ritz-Carlton is keeping its focus on the employees (ladies and gentlemen) and trying to save jobs whenever possible. Some of The Ritz-Carlton locations have lowered room rates by 10 to 15 per cent. As part of the company's recession survival strategy, they are offering discount packages but not having a 'fire sale'. The key to attracting guests is offering different packages and being more flexible on rates. At the chain's hotel in Philadelphia, for example, rates dropped down to $199 from $364-a-night for a stay in mid-February 2009.

Generally, when times during a recession get tough, consumer spending habits change dramatically; they require much further motivation for spending. In recessionary times, consumers not only spend less overall, but become far more selective in how they spend. The Ritz-Carlton managers realize that they must retain emotional engagement with guests by continuing their first-class service. The Ritz-Carlton executives (Michael Walsh and Vivian Deuschl) are often on the news giving interviews and generating a positive buzz for the brand.

Competitive landscape

Having a strong brand name is an important factor in the luxury hotel business. Customers look for style, service quality, amenities, and dining services, while the price is a factor in decision-making. On the other hand, competing based on price only is not enough for chains to lead. Therefore, they try to differentiate based on services to attract more customers. One example of this trend is the innovative style of W Hotels, which makes the chain popular among younger consumers.

According to the Hotel Industry Profile posted on **www.hoovers.com**, key industry trends include the following:

- The US hotel and motel industry consists of about 30,000 companies that operate 50,000 individual locations, with a combined annual revenue over $90 billion. Large US companies include Marriott International, Hilton Hotels, Carlson Hotels, and Starwood Hotels & Resorts. The industry's 50 largest companies hold about 45 per cent of the market.
- Business and tourist travel drive demand and are closely linked to the health of the economy. The profitability of individual companies depends on efficient operations—because many costs are fixed—and on effective marketing. Large companies have advantages in economies-of-scale in operations, can more easily raise capital, and have strong name recognition. Small companies can compete effectively in favourable locations and by providing specialty services. A hotel business requires large amounts of capital, and labour is a significant operating expense, requiring efficient personnel management.
- Major industry product lines are room fees and sales of food, alcoholic drinks, and merchandize. Room fees account for 70 per cent of industry revenue, food for 15 per cent, and alcohol for 5 per cent.
- Basic operations of hotels and motels consist of providing sleeping accommodation, housekeeping, maintenance, and a variety of personal services. Hotels may provide restaurants, meeting rooms, event hosting, business services, and resort services such as golf, tennis, swimming pools, and fitness centres.
- Loyalty programmes reward customers who use the same hotel or chain on repeat stays.
- Instead of trying to appeal to all travellers, hotels usually specialize in a particular market segment defined by price, service level, and location.
- Generally, hotel price categories are luxury (often over $200 per night); upscale (usually over $100); moderate (about $60 to $100); and budget (under $60). Prices vary by region, season, and occupancy rates.
- Service levels are full service, limited service, and all-suites.
- Location categories include urban, suburban, airport, and resort.
- Large hotel chains often have several brands that operate in different or overlapping segments.
- Key industry metrics, in addition to retail sales, are occupancy rates, average room prices, and revenue per available room, which is a hotel's occupancy rate multiplied by its average daily room rate.
- The industry relies heavily on travel websites like Travelocity and Expedia and on travel agents, who have exclusive access to major proprietary reservation systems. These systems have national and international reach.

- Hotel websites with reservation capability have become major marketing and sales tools, as have listings on the major reservation and travel systems. Computer and communication systems are essential for most hotels to acquire guests via the large reservation systems; provide guest services; and track reservations, guests, and room charges.
- Typical customers are business and leisure travellers: about 60 per cent are business travellers and 40 per cent are tourists.
- Due to the large proportion of business travellers and increasing use of the Internet by tourists, many hotels have installed Internet access networks, including wireless networks. With guests' greater cell-phone use, some hotels install indoor cell antennas.

Main suppliers of the industry are real estate firms, companies providing electronic reservation services, and labour. In general, the environment in the luxury hotel industry is competitive due to the following reasons: (1) maintaining high quality is essential while consumers have become more price sensitive; (2) there are lots of substitutes; and (3) switching costs for buyers is negligible.

Source: This case was prepared by Anastasia Kadantseva, Shalva Sikharulidze, and Amy Wisner, evening MBA students at Loyola College in Maryland, under the supervision of Professor Hope Corrigan as the basis for analysis and class discussion and not to illustrate either effective or ineffective handling of an administrative situation.

Additional materials to support this case

Videos

- **http://www.youtube.com/watch? v=z0q8s5pyspM**

Business source premier

- Hotels & Motels in the United States, Industry Profile, Reference Code: 0072-0520; publication date: December 2008.

National newspapers/other

- 'AIG Effect Tones Down Lavish Business Events', *USA Today online*, 29 January 2009, available at: **http://www.usatoday.com/travel/news/2009-01-26-aig-effect_N.htm**
- Bernstein, Roberta (1999), 'Navigating the Attitudes of Luxury: A New Survey from *Town & Country* Reveals the Modern Luxury Consumer and the Market's Evolving Mindset', 19 April, available at: **http://www.brandweek.com/bw/esearch/article_display.jsp? vnu_content_id=1256228**

Company websites

- **http://www.marriott.com/corporateinfo/glance.mi**

QUESTIONS

1. Watch the world travel awards video along with reading the case. Which hotel won the best luxury hotel brand in 2005, and what are the key components to success in this industry?
2. Apply Porter's Model of Competitive Forces to the luxury hotel industry (see Figure 3. 4 for the Porter Model). How can The Ritz-Carlton's top management team use the results of this analysis?

3. List three components of The Ritz-Carlton's existing recession strategy. What other techniques could be helpful during tight economic times to retain existing hotel guests and attract new visitors?
4. How could the 'AIG Effect' have a negative impact on the luxury hotel industry?
5. Graph the revenue growth of The Ritz-Carlton during2000–7, and forecast revenue to 2012. Is it growing or declining and why?

References

Bernstein, Roberta (1999),'Navigating the Attitudes of Luxury', *Brandweek.com*,19 April 1999, accessed 5 February 2009, available at: **http://www.brandweek.com/bw/esearch/article_display.jsp? vnu_content_id=1256228**

Blogs-WSJ.com, 'The Wealth Report—WSJ.com: Real Luxury is Back', accessed 15 February 2009, available at: **http://blogs.wsj.com/wealth/2009/02/13/real-luxury-is-back**

Brand Professionals count on Brandweek.com for Online Access to Branding News and Analysis, accessed 5 February 2009, available at:**http://www.brandweek.com/bw/esearch/article_display.jsp**

Census Bureau Home Page, 'US Census Press Releases', accessed 7 March 2009, available at: **http://www.census.gov/Press Release/www/releases/archives/income_wealth/012528.html**

Frank, Robert (2009), 'Real Luxury is Back', *WSJ.com*, 13 February 2009, accessed 15 February 2009, available at:**http://blogs. wsj.com/wealth/2009/02/13/real-luxury-is-back/**

Hoovers, 'Company Overview: The Ritz-Carlton Hotel Company, L. L. C.', accessed 26 February 2009, available at: **http://www.premium. hoovers.com. ezp. lndlibrary. org/subscribe/co/overview. xhtml? ID=ffffcrjshryckyrhcr.**

Hoovers, 'Industry Profile: Hotel and Motel Lodging', accessed 9 March 2009, available at: **http://www.premium. hoovers.com.ezp.lndlibrary.org/subscribe/ind/fr/profile/basic.xhtml? ID=30**

Hotel Reservations—Starwood Hotels and Resorts Worldwide—Hotel Reservations with Best Rates Guaranteed, 'Starwood Hotels & Resorts', accessed 21 February 2009, available at: **http://www.starwoodhotels.com/whotels/about/index.html**

International Herald Tribune—World News, Analysis, and Global Opinions, 'Luxury Brands Covet the Recession-proof—*International Herald Tribune*', accessed 12 February 2009, available at: **http://www.iht.com/articles/2008/03/07/sports/mluxe.php**

Kaplan, David, '"Luxury, Italian-style; Granduca's Target Market is Wealthy Long-term Guests', *Houston Chronicle*, 27 September 2006.

Loechner, Jack (2008), 'www.mediapost.com', [Weblog The View From The Top: Upscale Marketing In a Downturn], 23 December 2008, *Media Post Research Brief*, accessed 19 February 2009, available at: **http://www.mediapost.com/publications/index.cfm? fa=Articles.showArticle&art_aid=97117**

Luxury Institute Homepage, accessed 7 March 2009, available at: **http://www.luxuryinstitute.com**

News, Travel, Weather, Entertainment, Sports, Technology, U.S. & World—USATODAY.com, 'As Hotels Struggle for Business, Some Guests Find an Upside—USATODAY.com', accessed 12 February 2009, available at: **http://www.usatoday.com/travel/hotels/2009-02-05-hotels-struggle-business_N.htm**

Oliver, Mike (2003), 'Being Exclusive is Key to Selling Luxurious Items', *Marketing*, 51 (17 April), p. 20.

O'Loughlin, Sandra (2006), 'Luxury Report 2006: Net Worth', *Brandweek.com*, 20 September 2006, accessed 5 February 2009, available at: **http://www.brandweek.com/bw/esearch/article_display.jsp? vnu_content_id=1003154267**

Sharkey, Joe,(2009), 'Luxury Hotels are Feeling the Pinch', *International Herald Tribune*, 27 January.

Smith Travel Research (2008),(New York: Smith Travel Research).

'The Ritz-Carlton: About Us: Gold Standards' *Combining Luxury & Hospitality: The Ritz-Carlton Hotel Company*, accessed 23 February 2009, available at: **http://corporate.ritzcarlton.com/en/About/GoldStandards.htm**

Walsh, Michael, (2007), 'As Hotels Struggle for Business, Some Guests Find an Upside', 'General Manager, Ritz Carlton Philadelphia', interview, and Vivian Deuschl, 'Vice president of The Ritz-Carlton', interview, 7 February, available at: **http://www.abpstyle:CNews.go.com/Travel/AroundTheWorld/Story? id=6826478&page=2**

10

Pricing and distribution

LEARNING OBJECTIVES

- Examine the separate and complementary roles of pricing and distribution to marketing strategy
- Assess pricing mindsets and strategic options
- Evaluate the buyer's perspective of distribution and its implications for strategy
- Review the role of pricing and distribution amidst the drive towards the commoditization of products and services

CHAPTER AT A GLANCE

I. Introduction
1 Overview and strategy blueprint
2 Marketing strategy: analysis and perspectives

II. Where are we now?
3 Environmental and internal analysis: market information and intelligence

III. Where do we want to be?
4 Strategic marketing decisions, choices, and mistakes
5 Segmentation, targeting, and positioning strategies
6 Branding strategies
7 Relational and sustainability strategies

IV. How will we get there?
8 Product innovation and development strategies
9 Service marketing strategies
10 Pricing and distribution
11 Marketing communications
12 E-marketing strategies
13 Social and ethical strategies

V. Did we get there?
14 Strategy implementation, control, and metrics

Introduction

Pricing and distribution are distinct yet complementary elements in marketing. Strategically they are difficult to separate. A premium-priced watch cannot be sold at a discount jewellers. A tractor producer that wants a specific mark-up is going to find it difficult to control margin if it sells through intermediaries. **Pricing and distribution strategies are separate, but complimentary decisions**. This chapter will view the options individually and then examine the issues where decisions meet head-on.

Traditional marketing strategies of cost or differentiation do not provide any intrinsic logic on pricing or distribution. Porter was talking about 'cost' and not 'price'. He argued that relatively low costs provide a potential advantage over rivals in profitability. Put simply, you could charge the same price as rivals and make more money.

The price of anything and the route by which it is distributed simply **reflects its value**. Certainly, a low-cost producer is positioned to offer lower prices or discounts, but it is far from certain that it would do so. For example, Dell has attained cost leadership in the industry with its direct-to-customer Web distribution process. Nothing is built that hasn't been ordered, so inventories are reduced and with direct sales there are no intermediaries to take a share of the profit. Yet, Dell's prices are not the cheapest. What it has been able to do in a hyper-competitive market is to combine cost leadership with customized one-to-one products (the ultimate differentiation) and direct-to-customer distribution, which is a powerful value-added offering. By contrast, Sony offers greater design differentiation at similar prices, but distributes its computers via authorized dealers and its own (largely franchised) network of retail Sony Centres.

The moral is that customers look for value when they buy, rather than absolute price. Value is a perceptual concept as, for example, with the supermarket chain of Waitrose. Waitrose, given the downturn in the economy, has tried to soften their high-price/high-quality positioning in the face of intensifying price competition from Asda, Morrisons, Sainsbury's, and Tesco, and the likes of Aldi and Lidl. Middle-class shoppers, once the bedrock of Waitrose, are increasingly joining the ranks of bargain-hunters and taking a mercenary view. However, most companies approach price setting from a basis of covering their costs plus a profit mark-up and there is no denying the general logic of covering costs (at least in the longer term), however defined! For many computer buyers, a computer customized directly to their requirements provides more value than one off the shelf from a retailer. The strength of Dell's customization strategy and Sony's focus on aesthetic design will be tested as computer technology and standards converge. When all computers have Internet access, bright, flat screens, fast processors, big hard drives, CDRWs, DVDs and Blue-ray, etc., product differentiation will become less achievable and servicing and styling more important, so Sony may win out. Nothing is set, as Dell has started to introduce stylish designs with its Studio range. In this market environment, price and distribution provide a means of strategic differentiation. This chapter will review these and other issues in pricing and distribution. It begins with an assessment of pricing strategy.

Pricing

Definition

Pricing has generally been seen as **tactical** rather than **strategic** and considered much easier than creating the product in the first place. Essentially, it has been the 'Cinderella' of marketing. When it boils down to it, a price is just a number. Given prices affect sales, all things being equal, a small increase or decrease can have a disproportionate impact on profitability compared to any other marketing decision. For illustration, see Table 10.1 which shows how a 10 per cent increase in prices outweighs reductions in costs on profitability.

Pricing strategy involves deciding more than this: how much, where, when, and how a buyer will pay are the key decisions. This is what holds together individual pricing decisions based upon an organization's objectives and how they want to set their 'numbers' within the market. Most managers face enormous pressures on prices, especially during a downturn, when the pressure is generally downwards. Recessions make pricing ever more important as customers shift to lower-price alternatives or substitute one kind of product or service for another. Nevertheless,

TABLE 10.1 Effect of price changes

XYZ products			(Assume no volume change)*	
Sales	$m	**$m** *200*		$m
Materials	50		Price +10%	20
Labour	50		Materials –10%	5
Mkt & Adv	10		Labour –10%	5
R&D	10		Mkt & Adv –10%	1
Other variable	20		R&D –10%	1
Total variable	*140*		*Variable* –10%	14
Total fixed	40		*Fixed* –10%	4
Net profit		*20*		

*Falls in volume will also lead to higher profits with a 10% price increase up to a 20% drop.

customer needs may change; it is still important to align the price–benefit offering. There are several elements in pricing strategy to consider (Schindehutte and Morris, 2001), whatever market conditions prevail (see Figure 10.1):

- **Value:** price is fundamentally about value. Customers place prices within the context of perceived value. For example, when people pay more for sitting in the front row of a theatre they still see the same play as everyone else, but get the benefits of being closer to the actors. Perception is all, as with the UK positioning of Stella as an upmarket lager, despite it not being a premium lager (see Figure 10.2).

Value: price is fundamentally about value. Customers place prices within the context of perceived value

Variable: prices can be changed in a number of ways apart from the absolute level, such as by time form or terms of payment

Variety: prices can be set at different levels across multiple products and services to achieve different objectives for positioning and contribution, as with bundling or unbundling items

Visible/Invisible: prices may be open and visible or hidden and confusing for customers

Virtual: of all the decisions marketers make, a price change is arguably the easiest and quickest decision to make. It might not prove to be successful but the decision to raise or lower a price can be made quite straightforwardly in most organizations

Figure 10.1 Key elements to pricing

Source: Miner Schindehutteand Michael Morris (2001), 'Pricing as Entrepreneurial Behavior', *Business Horizons*, 44 (4), pp. 41–9.

- **Variable:** prices can be changed in a number of ways apart from the absolute level, such as by time, form, or terms of payment.
- **Variety:** prices can be set at different levels across multiple products and services to achieve different objectives for positioning and contribution, as with bundling or unbundling items.
- **Visible/invisible:** prices may be open and visible or hidden and confusing for customers. In the US, Sprint demonstrated invisible pricing when it offered 4,000 call minutes for $39.99-a-month which appears to be a-cent-a-minute (Ayres and Nalebuff, 2003). Unfortunately, only 350 are 'anytime', with the rest (3,650) restricted to evenings and weekends. Go over your 350 limit and you pay 35-cents-a-minute.
- **Virtual:** of all the decisions marketers make, a price change is arguably the easiest and quickest. It might not prove to be successful; the decision to raise or lower a price can be made quite straightforwardly.

Strategic mindset

Pricing can be a mindset issue for many companies and the consequences of the wrong decision can be dire. This has been demonstrated by Joel E. Urbany (2001) at Notre Dame in an experiment involving sixty managers. He gave these managers a straightforward choice: you sell sunglasses for $10 with a unit cost of $7 and you are thinking of cutting the price by 50 cents. According to the best sales estimate: (a) if you hold the price you will have a 100 per cent chance of selling 1,000 units; and (b) if you cut the price to $9.50, you have an 80 per cent chance of selling 1,250

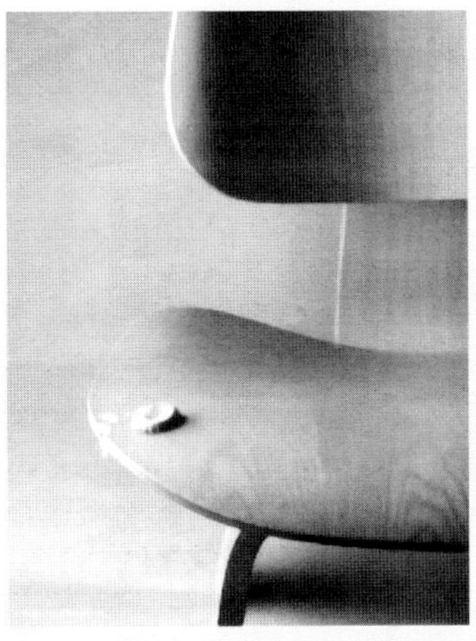

Figure 10.2 Communicating a price position—Stella Lager

units and a 20 per cent chance of selling only 1,000. Statistically, both options are identical as each produces a $3,000 profit. However, option (a) is risk-free and so might seem to be the logical choice. Despite that, most of the sixty managers opted to reduce the price. Even when they were told competitors would match the cut, they still chose to do it. Furthermore, most continued to want to reduce the price in the face of new evidence that the cut would lead to lower profits!

The case of Polaroid demonstrates (Shantanu et al., 2002) another kind of problematic pricing mindset. Polaroid was the first company to develop digital-imaging technology, but decided not to run with it. The reason was that Polaroid had relied on the 'razors-and-blade' approach to business in that it sold cameras cheaply and made money on the film. Digital imaging did not fit into this paradigm and so it gave up its lead with the technology. While this makes for an extreme case, it does demonstrate how an innovative company lost out because it lacked the appropriate pricing strategy. (Polaroid has since embraced digital technology with its Bluetooth-enabled PoGo Digital Photo Printer, which uses Zero Ink (Zink) technology.)

Strategic options

Successful pricing means that the prices set **have to complement the company's overall marketing strategy** and the whole process has to be holistic. With the latter point, prices need to be coordinated across any business. Dolan (1995) suggests eight stages to pricing strategy, as set out in Figure 10.3; this will be followed here by a review of the alternative approach of price mapping (D'Aveni, 2007), and then a discussion of several options aimed at maintaining price points.

Dolan's 8 options

Reverse cost-plus

The first stage is to reverse the traditional cost-plus-based pricing approach (see Indounas, 2006). This can be achieved by assessing the value that buyers place on a product or service which is an 'outside-in' rather than an 'inside-out' approach and requires considerable

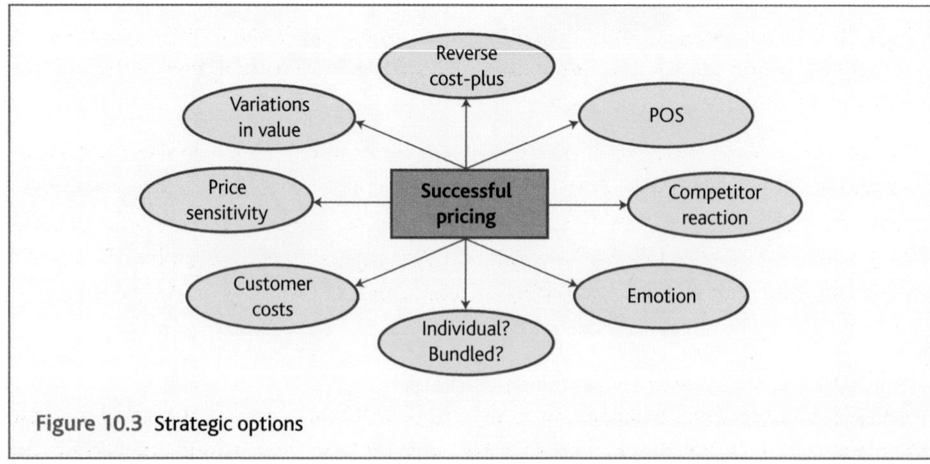

Figure 10.3 Strategic options

intelligence-gathering, either formally (e.g., market research) or informally (e.g., comments from the sales force).

Variations in value

Having considered this, it is then best to look for variations in how buyers value products. Wherever possible, try and separate markets (e.g., both companies and individuals use post-it notes and may be prepared to pay different prices) and segments (e.g., heavy, medium, and light users), and charge accordingly. Even in a recession, there are significant opportunities to apply value pricing. Performance will have different values to different buyers—pest control to a restaurant chain is more valuable than it might be to an exhaust-fitting centre.

Price sensitivity

Beneath the value that buyers place on product or service performance is price sensitivity. Buyers can differ greatly in their price sensitivity based upon their overall **elasticity**. Much will depend on who bears the cost, e.g. an individual or their company might purchase a flight. Also, what percentage of total expenditure does the product represent? Obviously, people and organizations tend to be less price-sensitive when the percentage is lower. Another factor is the buyers' ability to judge quality, as with a watch or a lawyer. To what extent can buyers compare prices and how time-critical is the purchase? Are there switching costs? A bank might increase its charges for a current account, but regular customers are unlikely to move owing to perceived high switching-costs. Thus, Napster charged its UK users nearly twice the amount it charged US citizens. Napster argued that their pricing reflected the cost of the content, and VAT was included in the UK package, unlike in the US.

Individual or multiple?

Having considered these issues, the next stage in the strategy is to identify the formal pricing structure. Should prices be single or multiple? Take the case where the optimal price for a product is £100 and there are two notional buyers, A and B:

- Buyer A is looking for five units and will buy the first one at £100, but will not buy again unless the price drops to £50.
- Buyer B is also looking for five units and will buy one at £100 and a further four if each subsequent unit is priced at a sliding discount of £10 each time (i.e., the second unit for £90 and the third for £80, and so on).

If the seller sticks to a £100 price, he or she will only make two sales for a total of £200. However, knowing Buyer B's price preferences for further units, it would be possible to sell both buyers two units for a total of £200 plus a further four units to B on the sliding scale of £300 (£90 + £80 + £70 + £60) for total sales of £500. Assuming the seller can still make a profit with the lowest sliding £60 price, bundling prices in this instance would make sense.

Competitor reaction

The key issue now is to consider how competitors will react to any price changes. Just ask this question: if the company puts up the price by 5 per cent, would competitors do nothing; match the increase; reduce their prices; or change some other element of their mix? The supermarkets have already joined the battle on the issue of forecourt prices on several occasions. A price war between the UK's top four supermarkets got under way in late 2008 after Asda, Sainsbury's, Tesco, and Morrisons announced cheaper petrol as Asda and Sainsbury's first slashed their petrol prices and Tesco and Morrisons followed and the petrol companies followed suit. In the US, when Wal-Mart began to roll out a $4 generic prescription charge in its pharmacies in 2006, Target quickly matched the price and rolled it out faster than Wal-Mart was able to. Another example from the US will suffice: Blockbuster lowered its by-post-only online movie rental plan to undercut Netflix by $1 a month and was expected, according to analysts, to enable Blockbuster to gain considerable market share. What is the moral of these examples? Competitors generally react to a lower price by lowering their prices.

Sometimes, regulation is used when predatory pricing is suspected. The European Commission fined Wanadoo in 2004 (since, renamed Orange Broadband) £6.9 million for predatory pricing, following complaints that rival ISPs were being forced out of the market. The Commission also fined Amazon £1,000 for each day that it continued to offer free delivery after action brought about by the French Booksellers' Union (Syndicat de la Librairie Française), which accused Amazon of offering illegal discounts on books—and even of selling some books below cost. Amazon chose to keep paying the fine and sending books out for free.

POS

Towards the end of the process, it is now important to monitor what prices are realized at the point of sale. If a list price is agreed within Marketing, it needs to be established whether this price is fixed or open because if list prices are subsequently reduced by Sales to close a sale, it can lead to confusion. To implement a holistic approach, it might be necessary to change the internal incentives. If you are distributing through an intermediary (e.g., Wal-Mart) there may be discounts given for early payments, rebates on volume, negotiated discounts, etc. A company may also need to consider margins in line with the product returns, service guarantees, damage claims, and so on. These should all be taken into account with the price.

Emotion

Research may be needed to assess a buyer's emotional response to a price because people develop price points over time that they see as fair. For example, British Gas, owned by Centrica, bowed to political and consumer pressure and announced in early 2009 that it was to cut its gas bills by 10 per cent after a succession of rapid price increases. On the other hand, good deals may reduce margins but produce good word-of-mouth in the marketplace. For example, the price of television terrestrial channel advertising has fallen by almost a third in real terms between 2000 and 2009 as a result of declining demand for terrestrial airtime and economic pressure on marketing budgets. On average, the cost of 30 seconds of television advertising is now £4.81 per thousand adults which, when adjusted for inflation, is 29 per cent cheaper than in the peak year of 2000.

Customer costs

Finally, wherever possible, a company needs to decide whether the returns justify the costs to serve buyers. In relationship marketing, this has led to a move by many companies to focus on whom they regard as their most profitable customers. This can be a socially and politically charged issue, as when banks have been found to occasionally send out directives to their branches on whom to encourage or discourage from opening an account. One bank advised its branches to discourage anyone aged over forty to open a current account, as by this stage of life most people had made their key financial decisions and would be less likely to provide much profit. The decision led to considerable negative publicity when the story was leaked.

Price mapping

An alternative to Dolan's eight strategic options is 'price mapping'. The idea here is to capture competitive value positions by developing positioning maps to benchmark price and perceived customer benefits. This enables the competitive tracking of prices over time. It involves five stages (D'Aveni, 2007):

1. *Define the market*: identify the consumer needs and the boundaries of the market.
2. *Choose the price*: whether to compare initial prices, prices that include life-cycle costs, prices that include transaction cost or not, or prices of bundled or unbundled offerings.
3. *Determine the primary benefit*: the benefit that explains the largest amount of variance in price (aesthetics, additional features, basic functions, durability, ease of use, serviceability, etc.).
4. *Plot positions*: draw a positioning map, plotting the position of every product (brand) in the market by price and primary benefit.
5. *Draw the expected price line*: finally, plot the line that best fits the points on the map, which will show how much on average customers will pay to gain a higher level of the benefit.

Maintaining price points

Every B2B or B2C buyer or client knows that the price paid for a product or service can vary at any time or place. It might be the result of promotions such as bonus packs, temporary price cuts, coupons, circulars, on-pack coupons or an end-of-aisle display (Davey et al., 1998). Furthermore, some policies can **mask** a price while others **highlight** it. A £10 cash transaction for a book feels quite different to a £100 one, yet the same transactions by credit card feels alike as both involve the same process with a pin number or signature. Not surprisingly, theatres find that pre-booking cash-paying customers are much more likely to turn up for shows than credit card ones!

How can a company at least maintain a price, especially in periods of deflation? Potter (2000) suggests mounting bundling benefits. As the price of the standard product falls, the price may be maintained by including previous options as standard.

One way of holding price in a market that is falling involves **bundling** benefits. As the price of the standard product falls, the price may be maintained by including previous options as standard. For example, a recent ad for the Sony Playstation 3 (PS3) Guitar Hero

World Tour offered by Amazon included, drums, a guitar, a microphone, and a Guitar Hero World Tour Game. Such bundling, in whatever format, is only a viable policy as long as the bundled benefits cost less than the price would have dropped. On the other hand, unbundling benefits is where a product or service that was a standard feature is removed and becomes an option. For example, Potter (2000) cites the case of Nissan reducing the price of one of its sports cars by 4.5 per cent but at the same time changing the T-bar roof from 'standard' to an option. Buying the T-bar increased the base price of the car higher than the price reduction!

Alternative service levels can also be offered at different price points. Lower price points can be offered without substantial service provision and may include demands for advanced payments in order to obtain savings as Marriott has done in lodging. Similarly, when a car rental company had to reduce its prices owing to market pressures, it introduced cancellation fees on bargain offers. At the other end of the scale, a new premium price point was introduced with enhanced services as there is always a segment willing to pay more.

Linking future purchases to current transactions is another strategy to explore. For example, car manufacturers often sell to rental companies with an agreement to repurchase the cars after a set period. The car rental companies get new cars at a keen price and the car manufacturers are in a favourable position to renegotiate new contracts when the rental companies rotate the cars.

Another strategy is to **change the price effectiveness period**. The aim is to lock in potentially volatile customer volume or to obtain a higher price when it is expected that prices will fall. For example, many credit card companies have lengthened the time when new customers can benefit from low levels of interest on debt. Similarly, mobile phone companies offer discounts on long-term contracts, given the likelihood of future price falls.

Having made these points, an important factor in the degree of consumption of any product or service is cost, so in the long run strategies to maintain or raise prices in themselves may cause considerable upset and disloyalty. Consumption has been found to increase the chances of loyalty and the more customers appreciate prices the more likely they are to consume. **Higher consumption helps develop long-term relationships** as customers are more likely to repeat the same patterns in the future. For example, in a field study, health club members who worked out four times a week were much more likely to renew their memberships than those who worked out once a week (Gourville and Soman, 2002). This is the phenomenon of sunk cost.

The **timing of a payment** has been found to be important as well. For example, people who pay 'upfront' large sums for memberships to health clubs tend to use the facilities regularly in the first few weeks after payment. However, as the sunk cost effects dissipate, they tend to treat their memberships as if they were free and work out less and less. Members who pay on a monthly basis are much more likely to attend regularly. It has also been found that people who buy tickets for a series of plays at festivals are much less likely to attend each play than people who buy tickets separately for each performance. By bundling, consumers lose sight of the cost of each ticket. The advice would be to introduce itemized billing as much as possible so that customers get a better sense of price.

Overall, when considering price maintenance, there are some basic elements to take into account. Rises or falls in the price of raw materials will affect a lot of organizations, especially raw materials that are widely diffused throughout the economy, such as petrol. Government policies will play a role, particularly with interest rates and purchase taxes.

Online pricing

Baye et al. (2007) suggest a number of strategies for online pricing. One of the key differences that they point out is that **online retailers increasingly compete at the product level rather than on such aspects as range, choice, and service** and so incremental costs need to be considered. Clickthroughs tend to be product-specific as people check prices across a number of sites. The fees for clickthroughs can be considerable when aggregated (they range from about 15 pence to £1) and on average only about 1 to 3 per cent of clickthroughs result in sales. This means that assuming a clickthrough rate of 2 per cent, an average of 50 clickthroughs will be needed to produce a single sale, which might cost a site between £7.50 (50 × 15 pence) and £50 (50 × £1) on top of the wholesale price. They suggest the best strategy is to **increase the mark-up when the number of competitors is low and reduce the mark-up when high**. Quite a simple proposition really.

Given that competitors can use the Web to stay constantly informed about pricing, price elasticity is a key consideration. **Keep it unpredictable**: Pixmania makes it very difficult for competitors to predict its pricing policy and so extremely hard to undercut. Pixmania's pricing of a Palm PDA (Personal Digital Assistant) was tracked and found to be highly erratic, whereas Tesco's pricing of a Samsung fridge was wholly predictable—Comet was able to undercut Tesco's every move.

Given the ease with which competitors can track prices, Baye et al. (2007) suggest a **hit-and-run** strategy by undercutting the price for a relatively short period, followed by a return to a higher price point to avoid being stuck in the middle. Companies with only slightly lower prices have been shown to achieve around 60 per cent more sales on price comparison sites such as Kelkoo. This is because slightly lower prices attract price-sensitive (mercenary) shoppers who account for just over 10 to 15 per cent of all online shoppers. If such price reductions are spasmodic (and thus unpredictable) competitors seldom see the need to respond, so a price war is rarely triggered. Yet, during the price reduction, a company can achieve an enormous increase in sales.

Setting prices slightly above the lowest price will not attract the price-conscious and margins will be greatly reduced amongst less deal-based shoppers. Comet has successfully used hit-and-run to price a Hotpoint refrigerator. It recognized it was the dominant retailer of the product and reduced its price dramatically over two fortnights with hardly any response from rivals, but was then eventually matched by rivals in the third week. A week later it 'ran' and raised its price for the fridge significantly, thereby signalling that it did not want a prolonged costly price war.

Pricing cross-subsidization on the Web also needs to be considered. Commentators have coined various terms to encapsulate the phenomenon, such as the 'free economy' or 'freeconomics' (see Mini Case Study 10.1).

MINI CASE STUDY 10.1 What's the price? It's free!

According to Chris Anderson, editor-in-chief of the Wired website and author of *Free: The Future of a Radical Price* (London: Random House) published in 2009, new business models are being developed and a new generation of consumers, mostly under thirty-five, are increasingly getting used to the idea that they don't have to pay for a lot of things.

The idea of 'free' dates back to King Gillette, who had the idea of selling disposable razor blades after finding he could no longer sharpen his standard cut-throat razor. In the first year (1903), Gillette only sold around 50 razors and 170 blades. After a series of marketing tactics, he finally bundled the razors with as many groceries as he could negotiate, including coffee, tea, and spices. In giving away the razors, he cleverly created demand for the disposable blades. Essentially, the pricing model was one of cross-subsidization and has been applied to things like mobiles and service agreements to video consoles and games.

Fast forward to today, and so much information and music is available free to a new generation of consumers that cross-subsidy pricing no longer applies. Radiohead and a clutch of other bands have offered their albums for free on MySpace. Music can be freely listened to on Spotify. An endless stream of organizations provide free news. The pricing model here is much more akin to the one adopted by commercial television and radio. By attracting an audience, income can be generated by advertisers wanting to reach that same audience. Take the case of Google—just about everything it offers including search is free (e.g., Gmail, Google Earth, and Picassa). The company is not alone: Yahoo Mail offers unlimited storage totally free and Freeview offers just under 50 TV channels to viewers and 24 radio channels for free after the purchase of the set top box. The reality is that the marginal cost of digital information is coming closer to zero as networks are reaching larger and larger audiences. A new viewer on YouTube adds nothing to the cost of the operation.

Thus, two trends are at work. On the one hand, Gillette's razor and blade subsidy-pricing model, as with Ryanair seeing itself as a travel agent rather than an airline. On the other hand, digital networks are reducing costs of transactions down towards zero, hence the drive to move people to Internet billing amongst utility companies and banks. Such services aren't really free but they are so cheap as not to matter.

Unfortunately, consumers see a big difference between incredibly cheap and free. Give something of value away for nothing and it will navigate the Web at warp speed. Charge a penny for it and the take-up is likely to be abysmal. The difference between zero and a penny, from a psychological perspective, is quite different than between a penny and two pennies. It can be the difference between a mass market and nothing at all. On the Web, winners tend to be the first ones who go free.

Giving stuff away doesn't mean that no money is being made. Marketing has traditionally viewed price as an exchange between a buyer and a seller. This basic view needs to shift to a broader view of a system, often with many parties involved and where pricing occurs between only some of them who exchange cash.

As mentioned above, this system has been around for years. Commercial television airs for free and the cover price for newspapers is heavily subsidized: advertisers pay to reach the audiences. It's a three-way market.

» On the Web, the pricing models are multifarious. For example, with Spotify, advertisers and premium subscribers subsidize listeners to their free service. Then, when it comes to free distribution of music by bands, which costs virtually nothing to distribute, the downloads are used as marketing to support live performances where the money is made on tickets, CDs, and sales of merchandize. However it appears, someone always has to pay.

New product pricing

Companies too often overplay the benefits of their new products and set unrealistically high prices (Marn et al., 2003). The first step in pricing a new product is to understand its true nature. Me-too products or services need a clear target market and pricing needs to be set in line with existing offerings. Evolutionary products or services that offer relatively small enhancements need to be priced a little higher than existing offerings to avoid a price war, whereas truly evolutionary ones that can create their own markets can price at a premium (even during a recession).

A more novel approach to new product pricing is **target pricing**. The idea is to develop products and services from the design stage and onwards with a final target price objective for a particular market (Cooper et al., 1996). The strategy was pioneered by leading Japanese electronics and car manufacturers and has since spread to Germany, the UK, the US, and beyond. Part of its benefit is that low-margin products are normally eliminated from the new product development process. However, the main benefit is that target pricing is a disciplined approach to pricing that brings the reality of the marketplace throughout the entire process, from idea conception to eventual output of the product or service. The process starts with mapping attractive segments in the market and targeting the most attractive ones. Next, the level of quality and functionality is determined for success, given a particular price. The organization finally undertakes the design, sourcing, production, and delivery process for the product or service that will enable it to achieve the desired profit level with this target market, rather than the other way around. The whole process has been developed in response to the demands of buyers in both B2B and B2C markets for not only low prices, but differentiation as well.

Camera manufacturers provide a good example of the approach. The Canon EOS Rebel SLR camera incorporates a host of cost-saving technologies to produce a camera that is around half the price of its rivals, but similar in features. Olympus is another company that has followed the practice. The company has produced a strategic plan that identifies the future mix of businesses by product line, the desired levels of profitability, and the contribution of each product to brand equity. As part of the process, Olympus undertakes continual proprietary and external technological reviews, as well as mapping of the general business environment (factors like exchange rates and changing income levels). A great deal of market research is undertaken one-to-one, in focus groups, at fashion centres, and in interviews with professional photographers to identify trends.

Target pricing is more difficult to achieve when a company does not have much control over the design and supply of components. However, Komatsu's demonstrated a viable approach in cooperation with its suppliers. In order to implement target pricing, Komatsu had to provide its suppliers with the parameters required to meet its required margins from early sub-assembly of its heavy equipment. Thus, the company 'sub-contracts' the target-pricing objectives to its suppliers to fit the overall targeted price. The idea is not to compromise the quality of the product, but rather to balance the value equation between what is produced and what buyers demand. Engineering is pressed to the limit to meet the targeted price.

Implementing pricing strategy

To implement pricing strategy, three 'capitals' are required: human, systems, and social (see Figure 10.4). Companies need to invest in all three capitals for pricing strategy to work.

Human capital

Human capital means training and hiring people who understand pricing across a range of products or services, customers, suppliers, and competitors. For example, Roche has an internal university to increase knowledge among its employees about pricing (Shantanu et al., 2002).

Systems

Systems capital relates to the hardware and software to process and implement pricing decisions. Large grocery chains have led the field by using price-sensitive tools and category-management systems to manage prices efficiently. Sophisticated systems are also used by many manufacturers in B2B markets in a variety of ways, such as helping sales reps understand the profitability of a deal. In using such systems, sales reps can quote prices to customers almost immediately instead of having go back to the office to calculate the price, which means that deals can be reached much more quickly.

Yield Management Systems (YMS) are becoming increasingly common in the service sector (Desiraju and Shugan, 1999) to fill capacity profitably using complex pricing systems administered by computer. YMS systems enable more market-responsive approaches

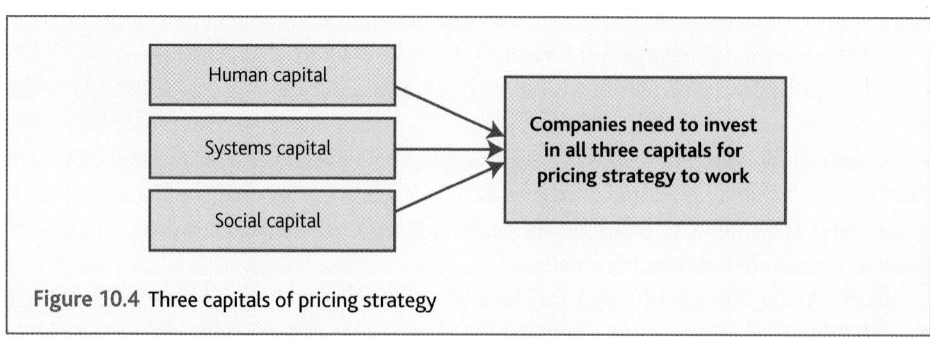

Figure 10.4 Three capitals of pricing strategy

towards pricing, such as limiting early purchase discounts and the likelihood of overbooking. These systems were first developed in the mid 1980s in the airline industry and have migrated out into other areas such as hotels, rentals, and all kinds of events. Marketers have developed complex YMS based on sophisticated mathematical computer programs. The basic objective of YMS is to adjust price over time to fill all the available capacity at a profit. In practice, it generally boils down to partitioning prices by time periods with discounts early on so that a hotel might charge £80-bookings six months away but as the hotel fills up on these dates and the space becomes more scarce, the YMS automatically raises the price. This is a further example of the impact of technology on marketing strategy, which now increasingly turns on a set of rules of behaviour rather than being based on strategic insight.

Social

Social capital is the glue that coordinates and holds together the many participants in a pricing decision. Internally, it may involve, for example, persuading divisions to accept its pricing policies. In one case, according to Shantanu et al. (2002), it took two years for the manufacturer concerned to replace divisional managers with ones who were willing to accept the pricing strategy. Sometimes, social capital is needed externally to implement pricing policy. For example, several retail chains felt that P&G was trying to dictate to them and set about undermining the then new EDLP (everyday low pricing strategy). Wholesalers were also upset and several added their own surcharge on P&G brands or stopped stocking them.

Distribution

Definition

Distribution strategy is a vital element in creating value and has a direct bearing on marketing (pricing, promotion, packaging, salesforce logistics) and delivery, installation, repair, and servicing, as well as on outbound logistics (order processing, warehousing, and inventory). Distribution is about making a supply of something available to people—be they buyers or users. It can be physical (supplying hard copy of an accounting software package for a customer in box), a service (supplying a training session for an accounting package), or virtual (downloading an accounting package via the Internet). It is intrinsically linked to pricing for most companies as the mark-up of distributors can account for a significant amount of the price, normally at least 50 per cent.

Buyer's perspective

The strategic marketing perspective on distribution is to ask the central question: what do buyers want? Of course what buyers want will vary, but some core wants are:

- availability
- speedy delivery

- reliable supply
- range of choice
- empathy when supply is interrupted
- convenience
- service and support
- a good price.

However, people are increasingly leisure 'time poor' in both B2C and B2B markets and keen to trade off shopping time against leisure, so, of all the items on the list, convenience is the primary concern of most buyers (Seiders et al., 2000). As a consequence, convenience has driven just about every innovation in retailing such as supermarkets, department stores, shopping malls, the Web, and self-scanning, in the pursuit of providing what customers want. Despite this, few managers define convenience from the customers' point of view or have a systematic convenience strategy. Instead, 'convenience' has become a generic term for a bundle of attributes such as product assortment, salesperson expertise, speed of checkouts, hours of business, service levels, layout, and parking.

From the customers' point of view, convenience means 'speed and ease'. Speed and ease consists of four elements: 'access', 'search', 'possession', and 'transaction' (see Figure 10.5). Access is about being easy to reach; search is about enabling customers to identify speedily what they want; possession relates to the ease of obtaining products; and transaction is about the ease of purchase and return of products. What is clear is that convenience is a dynamic construct: 24-hour photo-processing is no longer fast and renting a video is now seen by many as a task.

As with all aspects of convenience, **access** is relevant to both store and non-store shopping. Accessibility factors include parking, location, availability, hours of opening, and proximity

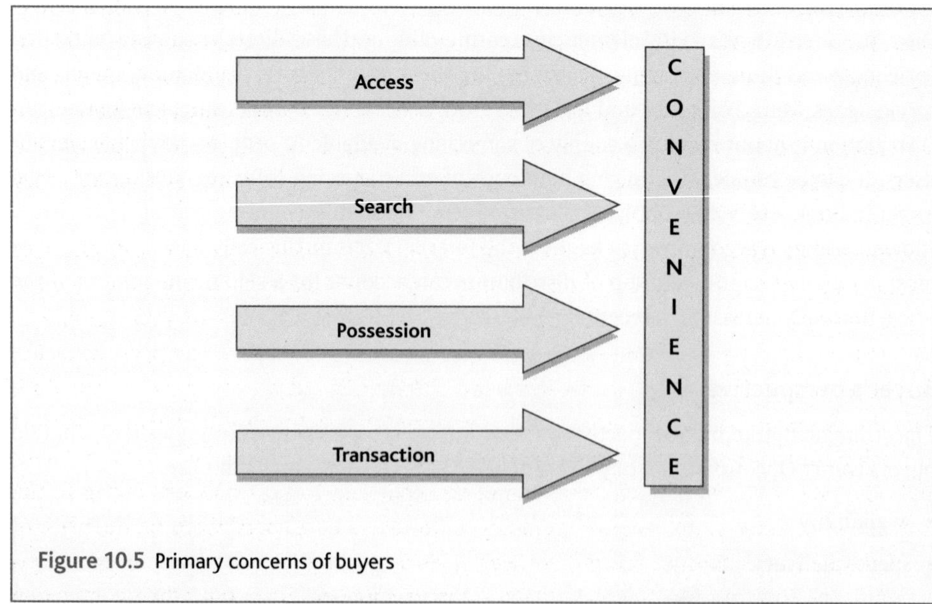

Figure 10.5 Primary concerns of buyers

to other outlets, as well as telephone, mail, and Internet. Convenience simply does not exist without access. Electrical retailer, Comet, struck a deal with energy giant Npower to offer its customers across the UK the chance to sign up for electricity and gas supplies. Comet customers will be able to obtain savings on Npower's gas and electricity dual-fuel offer. Energy companies hope such deals will reduce the cost of acquiring customers. They also see them as an alternative to the pushy door-to-door selling tactics which have given the industry a bad name.

However, access only gives distributors a good start in the process, it is nothing more than that. Customers, be they B2C or B2B, increasingly want access to products and services as fast and direct as possible with very little hassle. This appears to be a global trend, as in Japan which has seen double-digit sales growth in convenience stores offering everything from afternoon tea, evening meals, faxing and paying utility bills to buying magazines. Thus, direct shopping via catalogues and the Internet is largely being driven by time- and place-related convenience.

Search convenience, identifying and selecting the products you want, is connected to product focus, intelligent outlet design and layout, knowledgeable staff, interactive systems and product displays, packaging, and signage, be they physical or virtual. Specialist distributors are particularly apt at search convenience, given product concentrations such as telephones, bikes, ties, or office supplies. Shoppers can be confident of a good choice. Nevertheless, even the most specialist outlets could fall short with poor design and layout or staff with little knowledge. Solutions can be provided in a number of ways such as in-store kiosks, clearly posted prices, and mobile phones for sales staff linked to 'knowledge centres'. One example of good practice is the German discount chain, Modermarkte GmbH, which uses colour-coded tags to help customers quickly spot their sizes. Sound training can prepare sales staff to act more like personal shoppers by anticipating choices and matching the merchandize to the shopper. Demonstrations can also work well, as with Dixons displays of car audio systems in its larger stores, which enable customers to test out every one on display.

Possession convenience is about having merchandize in stock and available on a timely basis. For example, Nordstrom clothing store guarantees that advertised products will be in stock and Lens Crafters prepares glasses on the same day, generally in one hour. But while there are numerous examples of good practice, possession convenience has its limitations. In particular while the Internet scores highly in search convenience, it is generally low when it comes to possession convenience. Shoppers might save a trip to the store but invariably they have to wait for their purchases.

Transaction convenience is the speed and ease with which consumers can effect or amend transactions before and after the purchase. There have been a variety of innovative approaches in recent years, such as robot selection of items to self-scanning in outlets like Waitrose (the latter being a process which is perceived by shoppers as faster, despite the time it takes to scan each item). Well-designed service systems can mitigate the peaks and troughs in store traffic, as with Sainsbury's use of electronic sensors to track customer traffic to predict checkout requirements. Single queues used by banks and post offices can be effective but cannot be replicated by supermarkets owing to the lack of space. Some stores empower employees to take a customers' word on the price of an unmarked item (within reason) to keep queues moving. Transaction convenience is a significant issue on the Internet. Many Internet shoppers drop out when completing the first page of the billing form. Internet sites often require too much personal information, often designed to increase their advertising revenues. Furthermore, customers are not properly prepared for shipping and handling costs. Pure Internet retailers also have problems with returns compared to bricks-and-mortar counterparts. It is generally not that easy to return items via the post and often shoppers have to pay the non-refunded postage. Unconditional guarantees go a long way, but Internet retailers are generally at a disadvantage when it comes to returns.

Distribution options and principal channels: the buyer's perspective

Having discerned what buyers want, the strategic imperative of any distribution system should be to satisfy these wants in the most effective manner. There are a number of options for a seller to reach a buyer (more limited for services) but these can be broadly broken down into three choices: direct, salesforce, or intermediary, as shown in Figure 10.6 and in more detail in Figure 10.7.

Direct/online

Going direct to a buyer can be achieved by using the Internet, telephone, mail, catalogue, some form of direct advertising (press, DRTV or radio) or own-distribution network. Direct channels can provide a reliable supply and a good price, and can be extremely convenient by saving the physical requirement to shop. However, they are prone to problems of availability, speedy supply (no instant purchases can be made aside from digital products), range of choice (e.g., companies like Lands End offer only their own branded clothes), empathy when supply is interrupted, and service and support (especially if items have to be returned).

It is a gross simplification, but, on the whole, direct channels are best when the strategy is cost focus for niche or mass markets. Buyers are often prepared to sacrifice negatives like speedy delivery against the benefits of a lower price. Strategically, such channels may also work with highly differentiated items that cannot be obtained elsewhere. For example, when HMV offer their DVDs through direct response advertising in the *Radio Times*, it enables them to reach a large number of potential buyers cost-efficiently, compared to the alternatives.

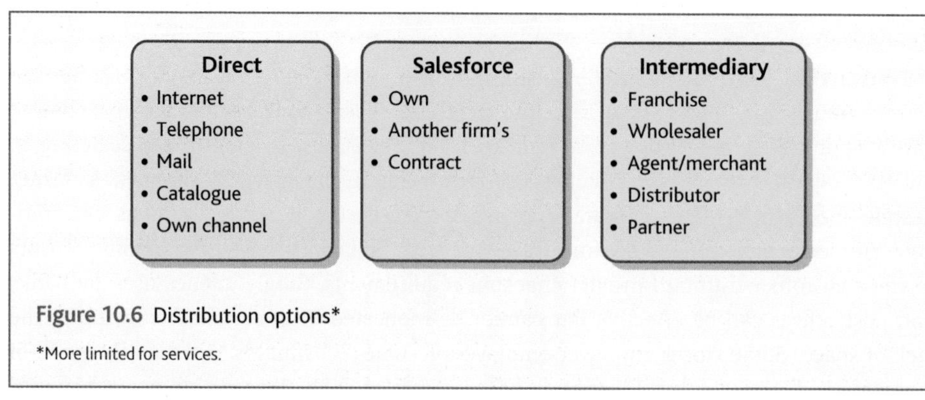

Figure 10.6 Distribution options*

*More limited for services.

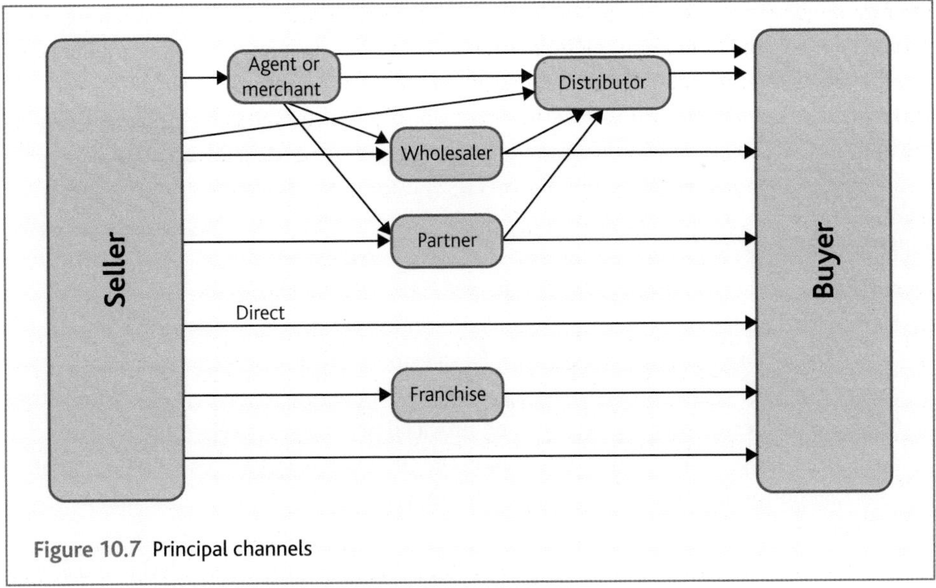

Figure 10.7 Principal channels

On the Web, shoppers can access price comparison sites and 'shopbots', which are websites for finding the cheapest online deals for a range of items. They make money by having a commercial relationship with most of the shops they list and get paid per click or via a small percentage of whatever's purchased, which means each shopbot may cover a different range of retailers. There are well-known generalists such as Kelkoo, Pricerunner, and moneysupermarket.com, as well as a number of specialists such as Quaffersoffers (wine), Find-DVD and CheapPerfumeExpert, and mySupermarket.

Online shoppers can generally be categorized into two key benefit segments, the experiential (enjoy browsing and impulse buy) and the goal-orientated (want something specific and quickly), along with a third segment blending both orientations. Strategies focused on convenience and customer care generally work well, increasing satisfaction with the goal-orientated, but value for money is key to loyalty (Souitaris and Balabanis, 2007). On the other hand, product assortment and customization have a big impact on the satisfaction of the experiential online shopper, with the character of the website having the main effect on loyalty.

From a wider perspective, going direct provides suppliers with considerable control over the mechanics of distribution and revenues and reliability of supply is directly linked to production, so there is no formal need to motivate a channel. However, it requires logistical expertise, even if many of the supply-chain relationships are contracted out (e.g., delivery) and so the investment required may be relatively high.

Having made these points, the main question with direct distribution is why would an organization choose any other way? The reason is largely down to the discrepancy of assortment—most suppliers have a small number of products and services, whereas consumers desire variety of choice and ease of purchase, especially in B2C markets. Few people would buy their groceries from individual suppliers as it would be too time-consuming (more manageable through intermediaries like Tesco). Thus, direct distribution, which has many advantages for suppliers, is largely confined to specialist single-item purchases and B2B markets where consumers are willing to trade off any disadvantages for cheaper prices or highly differentiated (or often unique) products or services. The Internet has accelerated the process by driving down transaction costs and made direct supply a lot easier for both seller and buyer.

Salesforce

An alternative to going direct is to use a salesforce. The alternatives are to: (1) set up your own; (2) use another organization's; or (3) hire on a contractual basis. The use of a salesforce in the B2C marketplace is largely no longer viable and very few companies have continued to use one. That is not to suggest that the use of a salesforce in B2C markets was ever that common; ever since the 1950s it has been largely confined to a relatively small group of industries and companies such as vacuum cleaners and financial products. There are small niche companies using salesforces in particular regions in the UK, but few large ones (The Co-operative still used agents for its financial products for the home), as even the Prudential, famous for its 'Man from the Pru' campaign, has disbanded its operation. The one major exception in recent years has been the use of salesforces by competing gas suppliers (e.g., British Gas and Southern Electric) in the newly deregulated gas market. After all, gas is an industry that is used to managing large numbers of staff to read meters. It has occasionally been highly controversial as some heavy-handed tactics have been used by a small group of unscrupulous salespeople.

The problems of using a salesforce strategy in most B2C markets have been the fragmentation of households and the rise of overall employment and the increase in car ownership, and alternative means of shopping means that door-to-door selling just does not have much appeal in B2C markets. There are simply too few people at home during the day. Added to this, few people are receptive to calls in the evening and society as a the whole is more suspicious of strangers 'at the door'. All this combined with the rise in buyers' access to information has meant that very few people will ever buy a product or service from a salesperson at the door, other than for domestic services like window cleaning.

The B2B marketplace is quite different and operates with an active salesforces across just about all markets. Sustaining a longer-term customer relationship requires developing a close personal bond between both parties. Salespeople tend to liaise regularly with a distinct and small group of senior managers, whatever the size of the company. However, the decision to select, continue, or terminate a purchase or contract at larger corporations has long been known to be the product of joint decision-making processes, involving a large number of decision-makers and influencers. Furthermore, with increasingly decentralized management structures amongst companies, many salespeople find that they are increasingly isolated from key decision-makers.

Individuals within the client company may assume one or more roles (Webster and Wind, 1972) that have a direct or indirect influence on the salesforce relationship. **Users** are the most easily identified by a salesperson. **Buyers**, senior managers, may be easily identified, but can often be more conspicuous than their 'real' importance to the decision. **Influencers** may cover a wide group of people, such as finance directors, production managers, and lawyers, who may help establish relationship criteria and direction. The **decider** may be the 'buyer', but in many organizations may involve someone removed from day-to-day activities. Their criteria are likely to be less informed and far more subjective than specialist personnel. They may also seek 'reassurance' or 'safety' by, for example, making judgements based upon a supplier's prestige. **Gatekeepers**, who control the access of information through to the buying centre (either positively or negatively), may include such people as marketers, PR, sales, and PAs/secretaries and receptionists. Senior and top managers may also channel information on rival suppliers that they have gathered.

Furthermore, Webster and Wind's (1972) industrial-buying tasks of 'new buy', 'modified re-buy', and 'straight re-buy' provide a helpful typology to appreciate the strategic issues for salespeople. Customers involved in **new tasks** will perceive a high risk so a salesperson can be effectively utilized to provide advice. With such decisions, a salesperson offers a convenient way to assess the market offering and much can be learned from discussing proposed purchases with different salespeople. However, at this stage, a salesperson can be used to provide a lot of information but may not win the business. At the new task stage, with large capital purchases the customer is generally obliged to visit the salesperson's site to see the equipment in operation (or possibly at one of their customers' premises). Service and support are also important and these can be discussed directly with a salesperson, along with queries about availability and speed of delivery. However, any individual supplier will offer a narrow range of choice, which is generally 'pieced' together by potential buyers in discussions with several competing sales people. **Modifying** a familiar purchase is often done in cooperation with a salesperson. The importance of availability and range of choice diminishes, along with service and support because, at this stage, the buyer is likely to have a greater knowledge of these aspects, given the previous experience gained. What is important is reliability, the empathy of the salespeople, and the convenience of buying.

With the **straight re-buy**, perceived client risk is minimal because the task is characterized by the repetitive actions. Here, the salesforce's role is largely one of taking the order rather than based on advice, and may be more marginal strategically. Convenience is pre-eminent in continued purchasing and in most mature markets this is the mainstay business of most salespeople.

Having your own salesforce clearly provides the optimum control and ability to motivate. But it might be more cost-effective to use the services of another organization (normally not a competitor but with the rise of global alliances it might be), or to contract the salesforce out. In either case, there will be loss of control and questions over loyalty and motivation other than monetary rewards, so generally this is not as attractive an option except for the short-term. Such decisions are often determined by the margins at stake. For example, it is not uncommon for a company like British Aerospace to employ a salesperson for five to fifteen years without making a single sale in some markets. It might take this long to develop the relationships with government agencies and other buyers and there is no prospect of contracting this person outside of the business. If a sale is made, it might be worth several billion pounds to British Aerospace and, therefore, ultimately worth the effort. Strategically, there is no substitute for a salesperson(s) in such markets.

Intermediaries

An intermediary channel has to be used when it is difficult or impossible for a supplier to 'meet' its customers. In one development, TNT Mail linked up with Express Dairies in June 2004 to launch a business-to-consumer letter and parcel distribution service in competition with Royal Mail. The move was one development in the ongoing deregulation of UK postal services, which will potentially see Royal Mail lose the monopoly it has enjoyed for hundreds of years.

There is an ownership issue here. If you own a shop and sell your products through it, it would not be classified as an intermediary. However, if you sell your products through an identical shop that you do not own, that shop would be classified as an intermediary. There are several different types of intermediary: agent, distributor, franchiser, merchant, and wholesaler. An agent acts as principal intermediary between the seller and supplier of a product or service and finds buyers without taking ownership. A merchant performs the same but does take ownership. Wholesalers stock products (not services) before the next level of distribution. Distributors do just that—they distribute the product within a market. Franchising is where a company offers a complete brand concept, supplies, and logistics to a franchisee, who invests an initial lump sum and thereafter pays regular fees to continue the relationship (e.g., KFC).

Strategically, intermediaries enable firms to offer just about everything buyers want: availability, speed of deliver, reliable supply, range of choice, empathy when supply is interrupted, convenience, and service and support. From a customer's perspective, there are few, if any, downsides aside from the kind of B2B customer identified in the previous section that is involved in a measured choice and needs to deal with a salesperson.

If intermediaries can satisfy just about all the needs of customers, the question is why do many organizations choose to go direct? What are the trade-offs and disadvantages of intermediaries? One obvious problem is the lack of control, in this respect, the opposite of the advantages of the direct channel. Suppliers are often at the mercy of intermediaries as to where their products are placed on shelves and how they are finally priced and the consequent effect on sales and margins. Competitors may offer all kinds of inducements to intermediary channels (if allowed by the channel owners) to preempt your products for shelf space, stocking, and advice. Thus, a company might run an effective advertising campaign for its lipstick, only to find when consumers go into shops to buy the product, are then advised to buy another brand which is on at a special price; or, you might launch a new shampoo, only to find a rival has usurped demand by offering bonus packs in the weeks of your launch, thereby diminishing available shelf space.

In short, for many suppliers, intermediaries are a market in their own right and require considerable resources to support and develop relationships with, hence the issue of 'push' and 'pull' and the importance of branding. Take a brand like Sony. Despite product parity in many electronic markets, Sony remains the premium electronics brand in the B2C marketplace. Any electrical retailer without Sony products is going to be less of a destination for most shoppers, as they will expect to see the brand. Sony has supplier power and can negotiate higher margins and better shelf positioning and stocking for its products than its rivals.

Multi-channel marketing

It is all very well to consider the main three channel options of direct/online, intermediaries, or salesforce, but increasingly a multi-channel marketing strategy is required for buyers who use more than one channel when interacting with an organization; for example, when customers go online for information but then go offline to complete a purchase or the process might be reversed where someone goes into a shop to get some information, but then goes online to buy it. Multi-channel shoppers are now in the majority and studies indicate they account for just under two-thirds of all shoppers and spend significantly more than single-channel shoppers. The tendency for multi-channel shopping will rise as wireless devices and mobile phones increasingly offer new ways to enter a market and associated services. Weinberg et al. (2007) suggest three cohesive courses of action for developing an effective multi-channel strategy, and each will be reviewed below.

Value proposition

Rather than take a tactical view of distribution, the idea with assessing the value proposition is to appreciate the value offered by each channel, including strengths, weaknesses, and synergies. Organizations need to review all the potential customer touchpoints and spend on the things that are working and downplay things that are not. The underlying approach is: the channels that are most valuable to the customer are the ones most valuable to the brand. For many companies, the imperative has become getting customers to use the low-cost Internet channel. However, taking a customer lifetime view, it might make more sense to encourage some high-value customers to use more costly personalized channels rather than have a uniform Internet-based approach. It just depends on what customers value. Overall, the holistic approach weaves together the best elements of the various channels to create value propositions. For example, a large number of people place items in their 'basket' and proceed through to ordering, but then leave a website without making a purchase. Might a pop up appear inviting people to talk to someone over the phone just prior to purchase to answer or advise on any issues? A holistic channel strategy requires that such touchpoints as telephone, direct mail, the Internet, and a bricks-and-mortar shop all work together to communicate a single brand image and customer experience. Bearing in mind the increasing tendency to try out products and then buy online, a number of companies are experimenting with new experiential retail outlets (see Mini Case Study 10.2).

MINI CASE STUDY 10.2 Try before you buy

The Sample Lab, which opened in Tokyo's downtown district in 2007, is a members-only shop that invites consumers to sample and test new products. Members pay around £2 for the registration fee and £6 for an annual membership fee and gain entrance to the Lab by showing a bar code stored on their mobile phone. The Sample Lab doesn't make any money from its products; instead, companies pay them to have their items stocked there so that they get consumer feedback on their items and the potential buzz.

Sample Lab offers a miscellany of products such as exercise equipment, fruit juices, cooking sauces, wrinkle creams, health foods, and stationery. Besides trying everything out in the shop, members can take home between five and ten items per visit (the restriction is no doubt to deter freebie hunters clearing out the shop), depending on the status of their membership. Sample Lab asks members to fill out surveys (in Japanese, so that

» it is not a destination for bargain-hunting tourists) about the products they've tested. Many consumers are happy to pay to be first to try out a new product and they can then spread buzz that's invaluable to brands launching new products. Indeed, the Japanese blogosphere has a number of blogs exclusively talking about the shop and the latest products on display.

Inside, the shop has shelves stocked with merchandize and a dedicated area where women can sit down to try out beauty products. The entrance opens up directly into the shop's exhibition area, where a range of products from sports drinks to the latest mini laptop are placed. Visitors can browse here or move into the 'Salon' area and relax in a modern café-like ambience. The 'Powder Room' area gives young Japanese consumers a more private area in which to try out the latest cosmetics and facial care products. When customers find something that they like, they have the option of purchasing a full-sized version or taking home more samples within their daily allocation.

Maytag provides another example. The US appliance manufacturer is enabling consumers to test-drive products before making a choice. The shops are owned by independent dealers and they display Maytag merchandize in environments that mirror people's home kitchens and laundry rooms. Potential buyers of washers and dryers can do a load of laundry, bake some biscuits, or listen to a dishwasher in action to see if it really is as quiet as they say. The shops are about the size of a department store appliance section and Maytag suggests 'try-before-you-buy' is helping to close sales. The company has plans to roll the concept out to around 30 to 40 locations.

Another example is provided by Villeroy Boch Bubble Shops in Utrecht, the Netherlands. The shop enables potential consumers to experience bubble baths in two secluded luxury rooms, along with a private outdoor area for open-air spas so that they can try out the various Aqua & Air systems or steam-shower cabins. It's free, with no strings attached and sessions in the shop can last for up to an hour, with a capacity of around four to six appointments a day.

Whirlpool's 12,000 square foot 'Insperience' shop in Atlanta, Georgia, offers a similar example to Maytag, but the intended visitor is not the end-customer. Whirlpool is more focused on the professional market of designers, architects, and estate agents, as well as its own staff, with the aim of providing training. The store houses fully equipped kitchens and family studios so that professionals can try out the latest Whirlpool and KitchenAid home appliances. Professionals are invited to see the options and how they work with a view to advising their clients when designing new homes or redesigning existing kitchens and laundry rooms.

What is the try-before-you-buy trend all about? Perhaps it is simply tapping into people's basic behaviour. People like trying things out, they love being first with new things, and they also enjoy being part of an exclusive community. Bingo! 'Try before you buy' provides the perfect fit.

Organizational structures and incentives

One of the key problems in developing a multi-channel approach is channel conflict, especially for premium and high-priced products and services. Conflicts can arise vertically, that is between sequential members in a distribution network such as agents and distributor over carrying a particular range or price increases. Horizontal conflicts may arise between the same members of a channel such as between agents or between distributors, where competition may be deemed to be unfair. Within any channel there is often collision of interests, given that all channel members naturally seek to maximize their profits and resources. For the most part, major channel conflicts are rare, but 'silos' can exist within an organization. For example, data and information may not be shared between the Internet group with the bricks-and-mortar channel. The problem is that IT systems are not necessarily designed with multi-channel markets in mind. It is very hard for many companies to obtain data that shows that 'person X' read a newspaper ad, checked on a website, and then went to a shop to buy the product. Eventually, with the introduction of Internet-enabled mobiles and loyalty cards that allow tracking, it will become easier to compile such data within the bounds of security and privacy issues. It will be key to locate cross-channel coordination at the operational level to achieve this. Incentive systems will also need to reward multi-channel behaviour. For example, Blockbuster offers a service whereby online-ordered DVDs can be returned to any of it shops and the shop concerned receives a credit from Blockbuster and has the opportunity to lever ancillary sales, and the online group can also send out the next rental faster as the return is instantly logged.

Create metrics

The third and final element suggested by Weinberg et al. (2007) is to choose the right metrics to evaluate a holistic multi-channel approach. It is a highly complicated area, given issues of loyalty, customer satisfaction, and how the metric might be used. The authors suggest that organizations measure the synergistic impact of no more than two channels at a time and focus on how well they interact, for example in the use of a website and direct mail, and once the synergies have become better understood, to then include a third channel.

Grey marketing

One final aspect to consider is 'grey marketing', where distributors purchase goods in one market, such as fluid pumps or drill bits, either from an authorized dealer or directly from the manufacturer and resell the same goods in another market at a higher price. They undercut the prices of the authorized dealers in a market and still make a healthy profit. Such activity is not necessarily illegal, but can fall foul of license agreements or be counter to trade regulations. For example, Tesco recently lost a dispute with Levi's to sell grey-sourced jeans in it supermarkets.

Companies that find that their goods are being distributed by grey marketers face a mix of problems, aside from lost profits. For a start, price discounting can affect their image and relationships with authorized dealers can become strained as they watch their markets being eroded. Furthermore, they might face legal challenges as unauthorized imports might not meet local safety or import regulations. Moreover, forward planning becomes difficult as they no longer have full knowledge of sales patterns, and their reputation may be further damaged if grey marketers fail to provide a decent level of service.

In a survey of over 400 US-based exporters (Myers and Griffith, 1999), 20 per cent felt that their exports were severely affected by grey exports. Regions particularly badly affected by grey markets are Western Europe and the Pacific Rim, followed by Latin America. Areas such as the former Soviet Union were less prominent, though this might reflect lower levels of trade activity. Within Western Europe, Germany and the UK were identified as the worst markets in terms of grey activity. In the UK, hot-spot items were: welding alloys, hand cleansers, dental-care products, electronic-ignition systems, and conveyor belts. If equalizing prices is not an option, and if the alternative of seeking a legal solution is preferred, what strategies should companies adopt to challenge grey marketers?

One worthwhile strategy is to coordinate distribution channels horizontally. What this means in practice is the sharing of information with distributors such as sales databases. If one distributor notices unfamiliar sales activities, it can both alert the manufacturer and distributors in nearby markets and thereby 'flag' potential problems. Distributors should also be encouraged to update and input data on changing regulations in their markets. This will help manufacturers and other distributors to forecast potential grey-market activity. For example, the EU might significantly change tax arrangements for a particular product between members and non-members of the community, and there may be consequences for grey markets.

Grey marketers often take advantage of differentials between goods such as colours and size or chemical compositions and emission-control systems. When restrictions occur in some markets, grey marketers often seize opportunities to supply from another region where such restrictions do not apply. In such cases, evidence needs to be gathered on specific product attributes to lobby local governments to amend their legislation.

Another consideration is to restrict the power of salespeople and lower-level managers to set different prices for particular customers. Wide price margins within markets encourage buyers to seek lower prices if they cannot access the 'deals' they see on offer. Finally, it is advisable to 'stay in touch' with your distributors. Web-based databases offer the opportunity to replace the annual or biannual meeting with a constant discussion.

Price and distribution strategies meet

Appropriate strategies for price and distribution will depend on a variety of factors, but should be synchronized. Clearly, it would be a mismatch to distribute high-priced luxury handbags in discount stores and would only confuse potential buyers. The inherent brand position and direction must be taken into account. Market position is another factor. A follower brand with a relatively small market share is likely to follow the price and distribution patterns of leaders and generally be sold at a lower price and be placed in slightly less favourable positions by distributors. The product life cycle (PLC) is also a consideration. The PLC is a tool in widespread managerial use (despite its problems), given its ability to provide some strategic insights. Depending on where an organization is on the PLC, the kinds of price and distribution decisions may vary considerably. Bearing these three points in mind, a number of observations can be made on price and distribution (see Figure 10.8).

Market leader	Market challenger
• Distribution in place • Price main weapon • Premium price • Variety of options	• Focus on flanks • Direct or indirect attack
Market follower	**Market niche**
• 'Cloning' • Set lower prices	• Stay with markets • Add niches • Premium price • Selective distribution

Figure 10.8 Price and distribution strategies

Market leader

Just about every market has an acknowledged market leader—a firm with dominant market share that sets the standards or rules in the marketplace. Obvious examples are Sony and televisions, Tesco and supermarkets, and BT and broadband. The market leader has a lot going for it, but has to be ever-vigilant to the activities of close rivals that are constantly looking to grab the top position for themselves. Leading brand names in the consumer, business, and not-for-profit marketplace have retained their leadership surprisingly well over the past thirty to fifty years and have been the subject of much academic research as to their viability and longevity.

Dominant market leaders need to expand the total market as much as possible as they are the ones most likely to benefit, given their leadership position. They can achieve this with strategies for market usage and new applications, as well as by considering developing any niche markets previously neglected. Their distribution networks are usually fully in place, which leaves price as their main armoury. They might directly attack challengers by price reductions. However, if attacked by a challenger aggressively dropping its price, a leader is generally advised to 'take stock of the situation' before deciding on the best form of counterattack. This is because market leaders normally have enough strength to wait and decide on the best response, which is often to hold off matching such drops. For example, Sony has generally been able to maintain its premier price differential in the television marketplace, despite the challenges of rivals like Samsung and Philips.

Market leaders have several attacking or defensive options in declining markets. As leaders, they have the greatest visibility in the market and by reducing their prices, they can encourage rivals to exit rapidly from the marketplace. Alternatively, they may decide to milk their position, maintain their prices, and steadily withdraw and reallocate their resources to other markets where they consider they have better prospects.

Market challenger

The market challenger is the main reason for the nervousness of the market leader. Unlike market followers, market challengers are substantial firms or institutions in their own right, with sufficient resources and skills to occupy the market leader spot. Any marketplace is dynamic and firms' fortunes can go up or down. Colgate's market leadership of toothpaste has been eclipsed by Crest, Hoover's dominance of vacuum cleaners was rocked by Dyson, and Sainsbury's lost its market leadership to Tesco. Market challengers do not normally wipe out the business of the market leader, but they can edge their way towards equality or gradually overtake the market leader. Market challengers have little alternative but to attack leaders either directly or indirectly. They need to make better use of pricing and distribution to help do this and attack the leader and strengths or its weaker spots (flanks). A concentrated all-out attack on a leader may be the best way forward to take the high ground with lower prices. Attacking other challengers, followers, or smaller niche players in the marketplace rather than leaders can launch indirect price attacks on leaders. Such tactics will result in the challenger discreetly building share without going head-to-head on price with the leader by picking off weaker geographic markets or segments in so-called 'bypass' attacks. In this way, Swatch managed to outmanoeuvre Seiko in the fashion segment. Relatively smaller challengers may adopt 'guerrilla' tactics by picking off smaller markets intermittently. But unless backed up by some wider and deeper campaign at some later point, small-scale price tactics will never dismount a leader.

Market follower

Market followers, as their name implies, make a conscious decision to chase and emulate the market decisions of leaders and/or challengers. They may clone prices and distribution and trade successfully upon the 'leftovers' of other companies. Generally, they build distribution behind leaders and challengers and set their prices somewhat lower. Their profitability emanates from their decision to forego investing in uncertain new product development or in educating consumers in new ways of thinking in favour of simply following the actions of leaders or challengers in the marketplace. Followers, by their nature, do not seek leadership or to overtly challenge a leader. They can make good profits simply by providing imitations of leader or challenger products from which the only inhibitor is legal, as with the use of patents in the drug industry. Service sectors, like banking and hotels, are particularly prone to followers, as it is impossible to copyright a service provision; as, too, are capital-intensive sectors in the business marketplace, like fibre-optic cables and steel. Typical examples of followers would be Virgin Cola, Marks and Spencer jeans, Acer laptops, Holiday Inns, and the Orange mobile phone service. By definition, a market follower needs to stick to its title. They need to follow leaders and challengers and not launch price or distribution attacks. If they launch attacks, they will become challengers and will need the requisite resources and skills to survive such combat.

Market niche

The application of the market niche brings the discussion of pricing and distribution full circle. The reason is simple: a market niche is the application of market leadership to a small and/or distinct part of the marketplace. The micro policy is based upon the macro one. Success with a niche policy is based upon the reality that market leaders or challengers have little or no interest in niches. Thus, Bang & Olufsen can survive extremely well in its high-priced, selectively distributed and upmarket, style-conscious (but not expert) hi-fi marketplace, knowing that the likes of Sony or Marantz would have great difficulty in stretching their image to challenge them. Similarly, in the brewing, fashion, and cosmetics markets, a host of small players continue to make good profits exploiting niche market opportunities that neither leaders nor challengers, or followers, would want to occupy. Thus, most major breweries are just not interested in developing products to rival micro breweries with their wheat, herbal, and chocolate beers (to name but a few!).

The secret of successful sole-niching is to operate within a niche that has very little appeal for major players in the wider marketplace. The basis of the market niche strategy, be it a sole strategy or one adopted by leaders or challengers, is to specialize. Market niche strategies may be based upon goods or services, segments, channels, or promotional images. Best practice for sole nichers is to develop more than one market niche so that the company or institution is less vulnerable to attack from a rival. It is essential that a sole nicher not be seen as a potential rival to a leader or challenger, which might result in a direct attack. An ideal position for a sole nicher would be one where just about everyone else in the marketplace regards their niche as too much effort to bother with. That way they can charge premium prices and develop selective and discreet distribution channels. A company marketing high-priced organic non-dairy chocolate products only through delicatessens and health food shops is unlikely to have much trouble from the likes of Cadbury's! Turning to leaders or challengers, they can use niches either to entrench their positions or as a form of attack. As discussed above, in the hands of leaders or challengers, a niche can provide a basis for market growth or to attack indirectly a rival's market position.

Conclusion

The reality for most marketers is that the pricing and distribution 'dice' have been 'thrown' by their companies. L'Oréal's dermatological skincare range, Vichy, was delisted by Boots because Boots preferred to stock the brand on shelves, but Vichy would rather position the brand closer to behind-the-counter products. Vichy was reluctant to compromise on its international distribution strategy, which positions the brand as a specialist pharmacy product, rather than a mass-market or premium skincare range. Thus, for the most part, strategies have to be developed in line with historic price points and distribution structures. In many markets, pricing and distribution strategies meet in conjunction with positioning and customer wants. Take the case of the petrol companies and supermarkets. Supermarkets moved into the retailing of petrol in the early 1990s, undercutting the prices of petrol companies and offering volume discounts based on how much people spent on their groceries. In response, the petrol companies transformed their garage operations into convenience stores, offering many of the same staple products as the supermarkets but with much longer opening hours. In response, several supermarkets, in particular Tesco, extended their opening hours (selective stores open for 24 hours).

Overall, intensive distribution is largely found for low-priced convenience or impulse products or services, where the opportunity to buy is important. Exclusive distribution is generally used for high-priced luxury items in order to achieve superior brand image, product support, better sales effort, and control over price. Selective distribution tends to work well for speciality producers (e.g., sewing machines) where knowledgeable dealers are needed and buyers are prepared to seek out dealers.

Undoubtedly, the Internet has provided the biggest challenge to suppliers and bricks-and-mortar channel members. For example, DSGi (previously the Dixons group) was initially reluctant to fully develop its website as the company feared cannibalization of its high-street operation. A holistic mulit-channel strategy might make sense, but there might be a conflict with the established paradigm of on-street and out-of-town shopping outlets. What to do? Ultimately, you have to follow the consumer, which is exactly what DSGi did. They placed Dixons on the Web (Dixons.co.uk) and closed its high-street shops and instead focused on Curry's as the bricks-and-mortar outlet (Dixons still remains as a bricks-and-mortar entity at airports). The group purchased a controlling interest in pixmania.com in 2006. Furthermore, they have moved into the realms of social networking, with a sponsored page for Dixons.co.uk on Facebook aimed at 18- to 24-year-olds, which was part of an advertising shift towards online. After the initial shock to the bricks-and-mortar business, the Web has been embraced.

The problems faced by marketers are that a multitude of individual and combined methods for pricing and distribution are possible and that the Internet has had a major (negative) impact on many traditional intermediaries. The key challenge for marketers in this environment is how to price and distribute in a way that supports a chosen position and fends off the drive to commoditization. This is especially, though not exclusively, what is happening in many B2B markets. Take the case of handling and storage products (e.g., hand trucks, stackers, pallet trucks) made by companies like Caterpillar, BT Rolatruc, Komatsu, and Jungheinrich. They are used to stack and manoeuvre products in warehouses and for deliveries, etc. Such products are fast approaching commodity status and traded on the Web with increasingly small margins as a result, which in turn leaves the companies with less resources to invest in R&D for future differentiation, and there is no easy solution to the problem. Given that it is less easy to evaluate a service than a product, commoditization of services is less of a problem. However, it has happened with reasonably transparent and highly competitive services such as house conveyancing, where solicitors often charge similar standard prices.

Summary

Value holds the key to both pricing and distribution. Buyers are savvy and smart, most markets are mature with products and services near (or at) parity and distribution channels are varied and largely accessible physically and/or virtually. Any strategies attempting to 'rip off' or overcharge will fail and longer-term trust will evaporate. As a consequence of these challenges, price and distribution are likely to remain key issues in marketing strategy in the immediate future.

KEY TERMS

Bundling Grouping together features or goods or services to form a single price.

Channel conflict Potential or existing disputes between different forms of distribution, for example BA airline ticket sales via its website and its travel agent network.

Elasticity A measure of the relationship between the percentage change in demand for a product or service and the percentage change in price. For example, if the price of a brand of coffee rises by 10 per cent and demand falls below 10 per cent, the brand would be inelastic. However, if the price were to rise by 10 per cent and demand fall by more than 10 per cent, the brand would be elastic.

Grey marketing Distributors purchasing products or services in one market and reselling them in another at a higher price.

Intermediary Any distributor operating between seller and buyer who may or may not take ownership of the product or service.

Multi-channel marketing A strategy for buyers who use more than one channel when interacting with an organization.

Price at POS The price realized at the final transaction between seller and buyer.

Target pricing The development of goods and services with a specific price at POS at mind.

DISCUSSION QUESTIONS

1. In what ways might an organization's pricing 'mindset' act negatively on its pricing strategy?
2. If you could only follow two of Dolan's eight stages for pricing strategy, which ones would you choose and why?
3. What is the role of price in loyalty? What pricing strategies can be used to enhance loyalty and repeat purchases?
4. Assess the impact of the Web on pricing strategies.
5. Evaluate the pros and cons of a bricks-and-mortar company offering the same or different prices on its website.
6. To what extent do you think systems-based rules will take over pricing strategy decisions?
7. Convenience has come to the fore as the key element to base distribution. Assess the arguments for and against focusing on convenience over other core wants such as range of choice.
8. Why is the salesforce so important to B2B marketing strategy and so unimportant to B2C?
9. Of the three marketing actions prescribed by Weinberg et al. (2007) for multi-channel marketing mindsets (value propositions, structures and incentives, and metrics) which one do you regard as key and why?
10. What strategies would you recommend to an organization faced with intense grey marketing distribution in one of its markets?

ONLINE RESOURCE CENTRE

Visit the Online Resource Centre for this book for lots of interesting additional material at: **www.oxfordtextbooks.co.uk/orc/west2e/**

REFERENCES AND FURTHER READING

Anderson, Chris (2009), *Free: The Future of a Radical Price* (London: Random House).

Ayres, Ian, and Barry Nalebuff (2003), 'In Praise of Honest Pricing', *MIT Sloan Management Review*, 45 (1), pp. 24–8.

Baye, Michael R., J. Rupert, J. Gatti, Paul Kattuman, and John Morgan (2007), 'A Dashboard for Online Pricing', *California Management Review*, 50 (1), pp. 202–16.

Cooper, Robin, Bruce W. Chew, and Bernard Avishai (1996), 'Control Tomorrow's Costs through Today's Designs', *Harvard Business Review*, January, pp. 88–99.

D'Aveni, Richard A. (2007), 'Mapping your Competitive Position', *Harvard Business Review*, November, pp. 110–20.

Davey, K. K. S., Andy Childs, and Stephen J. Carlotti (1998), 'Why your Price Band is Wider than it Should Be', *Mckinsey Quarterly*, 3, pp. 116–27.

Desiraju, Ramarao, and Steven M. Shugan (1999), 'Strategic Service Pricing and Yield Management', *Journal of Marketing*, 63 (1), pp. 44–57.

Dolan, Robert J. (1995), 'How do you Know when the Price is Right?' *Harvard Business Review*, September, pp. 174–9.

Gourville, John, and Dilip Soman (2002), 'Pricing and the Psychology of Consumption', *Harvard Business Review*, September, pp. 91–6.

Indounas, Kostis (2006), 'Making Effectiver Pricing Decisions', *Business Horizons*, 49, pp. 415–24.

Marn, Michael V., Eric V. Roegner, and Craig C. Zawada (2003), 'Pricing New Products', *McKinsey Quarterly*, 3, pp. 40–9.

Myers, Mathew B., and David A. Griffith (1999), 'Strategies for Combating Gray Market Activity', *Business Horizons*, 42 (6), pp. 71–5.

Potter, Donald V. (2000), 'Discovering Hidden Pricing Power', *Business Horizons*, 43 (6), pp. 41–8.

Schindehutte, Miner, and Michael Morris (2001), 'Pricing as Entrepreneurial Behavior', *Business Horizons*, 44 (4), pp. 41–9.

Shantanu, Dutta, Mark Bergen, Daniel Levy, Mark Ritson, and Mark Zbaracki (2002), 'Pricing as a Strategic Capability', *MIT Sloan Management Review*, Spring, pp. 61–6.

Seiders, Kathleen, Leonard L. Berry, and Larry G. Gresham (2000), 'Attention, Retailers! How Convenient is Your Convenience Strategy?' *Sloan Management Review*, Spring, pp. 79–89.

Souitaris, Vangelis, and George Balabanis (2007), 'Tailoring Online Retail Strategies to Increase Customer Satisfaction and Loyalty', *Long Range Planning*, 40, pp. 244–61.

Urbany, Joel E. (2001), 'Are your Prices too Low?' *Harvard Business Review*, October, pp. 26–8.

Webster, Frederick, and Yoram Wind (1972), *Organizational Buying Behavior* (Englewood Cliff, NJ: Prentice Hall).

Weinberg, Bruce D., Salvatore Paris, and Patricia J. Guinan (2007), 'Multichannel Marketing: Mindset and Program Development', *Business Horizons*, 50, pp. 385–94.

KEY ARTICLE ABSTRACTS

Avlonitis, George J., Kostis A. Indounas, and Spiros P. Gounaris (2005), **'Pricing Objectives over the Service Life Cycle: Some Empirical Evidence'**, *European Journal of Marketing*, 39 (5/6), pp. 696–714.

The service sector tends to be somewhat neglected in the pricing literature. This paper redresses the balance by assessing pricing objectives at different stages of the services life cycle and provides empirical evidence on practice.

Abstract: Purpose—to explore the pricing objectives that service companies pursue, along with the extent to which these objectives are influenced by the stage of the services' life cycle. Design/methodology/approach—reviews the existing literature and analyses data from 170 companies operating in six different services sectors in Greece in order to achieve the research objectives. Findings—the literature on pricing of services reveals the complete lack of any previous work endeavouring to examine empirically this potential influence. The study concludes that the objectives are mainly customer-orientated, aimed at improving the companies' financial performance in the market. Furthermore, the stage of these services' life cycle, along with the sector of operation, seems to have an influence on the pricing objectives pursued. Research limitations/implications—the context of the study (Greece) is an obvious caveat to the research findings, suggesting the need for further replication of the current study in different national contexts. Practical implications—the practical implications of the findings refer to the fact that managers might have much to gain by adopting a 'situation-specific approach' when setting prices. Thus, different pricing objectives should be set as a service passes from one stage of its life cycle to another, while different services also necessitate a different pricing approach.

Bray, Jeffrey Paul, and Christine Harris (2006), **'The Effect of 9-Ending Prices on Retail Sales: A Quantitative UK-Based Field Study'**, *Journal of Marketing Management*, 22 (5/6), pp. 601–17.

This paper examines the influence on the number of sales of a product rounding up prices previously set with 9-endings. Their findings oppose both basic economic theory, which suggests that sales would be lower at a higher price level, and the findings from previous experiments into 9-ending prices.

Abstract: Surveys suggest that around 64 per cent of retail shelf-prices end in 9: the preponderance of 9-ending prices is not a new phenomenon and has been the subject of much comment and discussion over the past seventy years. Despite this broad interest, very few empirically based studies have been conducted in order to assess the effectiveness of the practice; no quantitative study can be found that has assessed the reaction of UK consumers toward 9-ending prices. In this paper, the authors present the results of a large-scale store-based trial in which a selection of product prices were rounded up from the retailers' traditional 9-ending prices to round-pound prices. The results from this research suggest that the adoption of round-pound prices may be more effective, with trial sales increasing. The data yields an interesting insight into the effectiveness of the practice, and provides a clear indication of the value further research in this area would bring.

Narus, James A., and James C. Anderson (1996), **'Rethinking Distribution: Adaptive Channels'**, ***Harvard Business Review***, July–August, pp. 112–21.

This paper examines how many companies have rationalized their channels and moved from multiple to fewer distributors in an attempt to raise quality. Examples are cited for different company-types and countries. It is argued that the successful use of distribution in marketing is, to a large extent, based upon some degree of experimentation.

Abstract: To solve distribution problems, a handful of forward-looking companies are experimenting with their distribution channels to make them more flexible and responsive. Although the scope of the experiments and the specifics vary widely, each embraces a concept the authors call adaptive channels. The potential benefits of these new arrangements come from the opportunity to leverage resources and share capabilities within the channel. To learn more about innovative distribution practices, the authors conducted an extensive research study in 1994 and 1995 of twenty-seven US, European, and

Japanese organizations that are considered to be leaders in distribution. These companies' initiatives can be divided into three broad categories. In the first, the distribution channel is designed to ensure that the members are routinely able to cope with unexpected or unusual demands for products and services. In the second, the new arrangements focus on meeting customers' growing demands for broader market offers. In the third, the objective is to improve the quality of service throughout the distribution channel by substituting the superior capabilities of one member for the inferior capabilities of another.

Ross, Elliot B. (1984), **'Making Money with Proactive Pricing'**, *Harvard Business Review*, November–December, pp. 145–56.

This paper examines the concept of 'proactive pricing': taking advantage of pricing opportunities in the marketplace. Topics covered include pricing strategy and tactics, developing a pricing framework, the influence of decision-makers in pricing, changing and setting prices, and the importance of timing.

Abstract: Although the roots of capitalism stretch back many centuries, setting prices remains an inexact science. The pricing decision, one of the most important in business, is also one of the least understood. Many industrial companies, according to the author, habitually set prices reflexively on the basis of simple criteria: to recover costs, to maintain or gain market share, to match competitors. As the author shows, however, some companies have discovered the benefits of thinking more shrewdly about pricing. The rewards of a better understanding of pricing strategy and tactics can be substantial. By carefully studying pertinent information about customers, competitors, and industry economics and by selectively applying appropriate techniques, proactive pricers can earn millions of dollars that might otherwise be lost. Across a spectrum of industries ranging from lighting equipment to computer software, customers are gaining power at the expense of suppliers. Competitive intensity is increasing, causing specialty products to evolve into near-commodities. Computerized information systems enable the purchaser to compare price and performance factors with unprecedented ease and accuracy. Improved communications and increased use of telemarketing and computer-aided selling have opened up many markets to additional competitors.

END OF CHAPTER 10 CASE STUDY Taco Bell expands to India

Introduction

According to the YUM! Brands website, YUM! Brands Incorporated (headquartered in Louisville, Kentucky) boasts more than 36,000 restaurants, making it the largest restaurant company in the world. Key brands in its portfolio include Taco Bell, KFC, Pizza Hut, and Long John Silver's. While Taco Bell is primarily located in North America, KFC and Pizza Hut have both enjoyed international success. Having seen considerable growth in the global expansion of KFC and Pizza Hut, YUM! is poised to expand the Taco Bell brand beyond North America and specifically to India. In 2009, YUM! has tried to capitalize on several factors to successfully launch the Taco Bell brand in India:

- the growing popularity of Mexican food worldwide
- the low-cost appeal of Quick-Service Restaurants (QSR) in tough economic times
- the strength of YUM! Brands
- best practices learned from the successful global expansion of their own brands (e.g., KFC and Pizza Hut) and competitor brands (e.g., McDonald's).

Prior to opening the first Taco Bell restaurant in India, there are several key issues which YUM! needs to consider. Are there sales trends for Taco Bell or other YUM! brands that would help predict future consumer demand? What is the ideal pricing strategy for a Quick-Service Restaurant (and one that serves Mexican food) in India? What impact will the culture and consumer attitudes in India have on the restaurant's success? And finally, should their expansion strategy employ a global approach or a local approach?

Sales trends

According to the YUM! Brands financial data on the company website, revenues have shrunk year-over-year in the US locations. However, YUM! has been able to grow revenues abroad at a much faster rate due to an aggressive store expansion programme and cost-cutting drive (see Figure C10.1). While there are 60 stores per million people in the US, YUM! still has only two stores per million people overseas, representing a continued opportunity to expand. The International division has performed extremely well in growing sales in each of the past few years, and growth in the China division has been nothing short of remarkable.

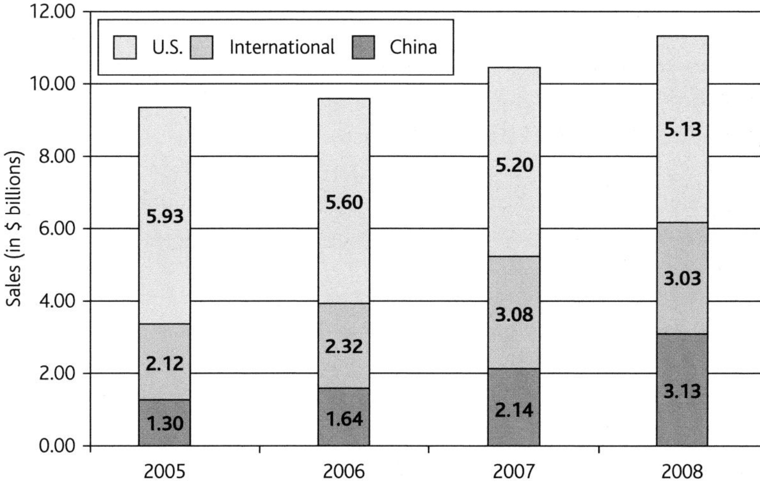

Figure C10.1 YUM! Brands sales by division, 2005–8

YUM! has topped analyst estimates by growing earnings for at least eleven straight years. Similar to sales, profits have been shrinking at a slow rate at home in the US and growing in both its China and International divisions to a point where YUM!'s overseas operations generated almost 60 per cent of group profits in 2008 (see Figure C10.2). Earnings in China have achieved an annual growth rate of more than 30 per cent since 2005, driven by the country's huge economy and consumer-spending hike, and supported by aggressive store expansions and cost-cutting measures. Until now, the overseas sales and profits have been driven by the global brands KFC and Pizza Hut. Now, Taco Bell, which is the most profitable YUM! brand in the US, is being driven overseas and specifically to India. Currently, Taco Bell has only 240 locations outside the US, most of which are located in Canada or Puerto Rico.

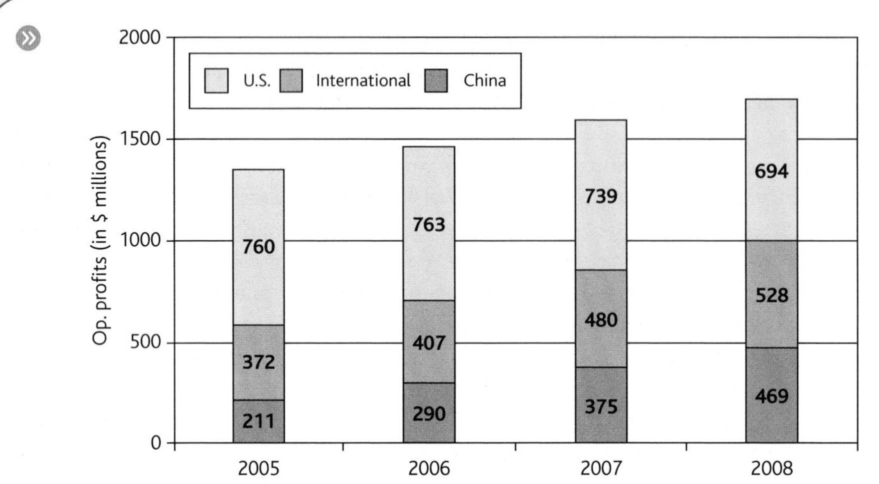

Figure C10.2 YUM! brands operating profits by division, 2005–8

Price and prestige

To understand pricing options for Taco Bell, it is helpful to look at YUM!'s previous experiences in India with their other brands. When YUM! launched both the Pizza Hut and KFC brands in India, they had differing levels of success. Pizza Hut entered with a low-cost pricing strategy in India. They turned a profit and grew quickly, driven by the availability of cheap, local ingredients. When they came out with their tandoori-style pizza in 2003, the pizzas were priced between $1.36 and $2.72. At the time, other premium-priced pizzas sold for about $2.09. The International Offices for Pizza Hut said that, 'lower-pricing strategy seeks to generate double-digit growth for the local chain'. However, KFC decided to follow a cost-plus perspective, meaning that it was priced to make a profit. Since ingredients were not so readily available in India, the brand incurred large transport costs. As a result, KFC priced itself too high in the market and sales have been slow.

It should be noted that, while Pizza Hut is keeping its prices low, it is still trying to generate a more upscale-dining experience, instead of a fast-food experience. This is a reasonable approach, given that Pizza Hut was voted 'Most Trusted Food Service Brand in India' for the fourth year in a row, according to a *Food and Beverage Close-up* article. Pizza Hut is committed to continuing its prestigious reputation by revamping its image in India (specifically in Mumbai and Delhi), and in an effort to evoke the idea of a dining *experience* over just a place to get food, it has attached the tag line, 'Stories Happen' to the makeover. The new restaurants will have expanded menus and the décor will move from an American diner-style experience to warmer lighting and earthy tones.

Culture and consumer attitudes

Anytime a company takes its business to a location outside of its country of origin, the organization's managers need to look at the culture as well as at the consumer's attitudes found in the target population in order to determine the appropriate marketing mix

» and best business strategies. With Taco Bell venturing into India, one of the most important things that needs to be looked at when starting business in this country is religion.

Since India boasts the origins of Hinduism and Buddhism, religion is extremely important to its people; as a way of life, it will have a substantial impact on an Indian consumer's purchasing decisions. Hinduism is the dominant faith, with over 80 per cent of the people in the country practicing the religion. One main aspect of Hinduism is the belief in the sacredness of all living creatures and because of this, many Hindus do not eat meat. Furthermore, the Hindus that actually do eat meat do not eat anything that comes from a cow because the cow is a sacred animal for them. This aspect of the Indian culture will impact on how Taco Bell designs their menu and markets their food.

A quick glance at Taco Bell's US menu shows that most items contain either beef or chicken. So how will Taco Bell succeed in venturing into a country where very little meat is eaten? A good start would be to look at what YUM!'s other brands have done in India to adjust the menu. For example, Pizza Hut struggled when it first went into India since its pizzas originally had Italian toppings (that contain beef and pork) which were not known to Indians. However, when it launched a vegetarian Tandoori Pizza, sales dramatically increased, since Indians were used to the flavours in the pizzas. Pizza Hut has also added new vegetarian pizzas that include toppings and seasonings that appeal to Indian tastes, such as capsicum, red paprika, red chillies, paneer, and corn.

In addition to its own brands, YUM! could also look at how other US meat-driven fast-food companies approached India's cultural barriers. McDonald's ventured into India in 1996 and now has 132 restaurants across India. McDonald's immediately recognized how diets in India are impacted on by religion. Its India website states that even its mayonnaise was specifically designed for Indian consumers and contains no eggs. The menu portion of the India website also has one side labelled 'Veg Menu' and the other side labelled 'NonVeg Menu'. The latter is suitable for religions where meat-eating is allowed, for example for Muslims, who make up a significant part of the population.

After reviewing other comparable fast-food chains that have ventured into India, Taco Bell needs to make sure it adapts to meet the cultures and tastes of India. The challenge will be in trying to keep the key aspects of its brand and name the same. Some ways that Taco Bell could achieve this would be to maintain products but remove the meat and add beans, rice, and/or potatoes instead. People in India also have a preference for spicier food, so Taco Bell may need to add more spices and chillies that are familiar to Indians.

Global vs local

Taco Bell will need to prepare much of its food to accommodate religious and vegetarian needs specific to India. While YUM! has successfully expanded its global brand in many countries by keeping the menu very stable, this new market will require a significant amount of localization in order to succeed. Considering strategies and results of previous entrants in India (KFC, Pizza Hut, and McDonald's) will be critical to achieving the right balance between a global and local approach.

The key question facing Taco Bell executives is how does it leverage existing global strengths (brand name, cost efficiencies, operations, distribution, etc.) to take advantage of growth opportunities in India while still adapting to the needs of the local culture? Co-branding with existing stores (KFC or Pizza Hut) is a possibility. This approach has » proven successful in the US, where there are KFC-Taco Bell combination chains. Unfortunately, KFC currently has only 31 restaurants in India, and with the brand still evolving, it is not as strong as the Taco Bell brand in India. An alternative to co-branding with KFC would be to co-brand with Pizza Hut, which has a strong brand image in India and 140 locations. However, Taco Bell stores are not traditionally co-branded with Pizza Hut. Lastly, Taco Bell could venture into India by building new stand-alone Taco Bells and not co-brand with any existing YUM! brands. Which approach would prove most successful given all the factors that YUM! would need to consider?

Source: This case was prepared by Allison Broglie, Mike Guest, and Corey Mull, evening MBA students at Loyola College in Maryland, under the supervision of Professor Hope Corrigan as the basis for analysis and class discussion and not to illustrate either effective or ineffective handling of an administrative situation.

QUESTIONS

1. Go to Yum.com (**http://www.yum.com/investors/restcounts.asp**) and plot the total number of stores (Total US, Total International, and Total China) for 2005–8. Your chart should look similar to Figure C10.1 on sales trends (but with different data). Describe any trends, similarities, and differences you see between your chart on total stores and the provided chart on sales. Using information from the charts as well as the additional materials, what do you expect sales and total stores to look like by the end of 2009?
2. List and define three or four possible pricing strategies that a quick-service restaurant can use when entering a new market. Which one should Taco Bell use in India and why?
3. Describe the consumer and cultural factors that Taco Bell will need to consider when developing their menu in India. Prioritize them from most important to least important and explain how a manager could choose the most important one.
4. How should Taco Bell enter India? Should they co-brand with existing KFC or Pizza Hut stores in India or open new, stand-alone Taco Bell stores? Please explain your answer.

References

Adamy, Janet, and Maria Abi-Habib (2008), 'Yum Brands Bets on Taco Bell to Win over Customers Overseas', *Wall Street Journal*, 19 November, p. B5.

AsiaPulse News, (2008), 'Pizza Hut to Invest US$11.8M in India over the Next 3 Years', 22 July, p. NA.

Bhan, Niti, and Brad Nemer (2006), 'Brand Magic in India', *Business Week Online*, 8 May,available at: **http://www.businessweek.com/innovate/content/may2006/id20060508_952455.htm**

Census of India, 2001, Ministry of Home Affairs, Directorate of Census Operations, Tamil Nadu, available at: **http://www.census.tn.nic.in/Default.htm**

Das, Debdatta (2008), 'YUM's the word', *The Hindu Business Line Online*, 14 February, available at: **http://www.thehindubusinessline.com/catalyst/2008/02/14/stories/2008021450050100.htm**

Food & Beverage Close-Up (2008), 'The Economic Times Names Pizza Hut as Most Trusted Food Service Brand in India', 26 June 26, p. NA.

Hoover, Ken (2008), 'Yum's Earnings a Tasty Morsel for Downturn', *Investor's Business Daily*, 3 November, p. B09.

MarketWatch: Food (2009), 'YUM! Brands: Taco Bell to Expand', *Datamonitor*, January, p. 16.

McDonald's India Website. 'About Us' section, available at: **http://www.mcdonaldsindia.net/about/index.htm**

Nation's Restaurant News (2003), 'Pizza Huts in India Ready New Tandoori-style Pizza,' 17 February, p. 82.

Pizza Hut India Website. 'Menus' section, available at: **http://www.pizzahut.co.in/menu_dinein.php?city_id=22**

YUM! Brands (2008), *2006 4th Quarter Earnings Release*, retrieved from: **http://www. investors.yum.com/phoenix.zhtml?c=117941&p=irol-newsEarnings**

YUM! Brands (2008), *2008 4th Quarter Earnings Release*, retrieved from: **http://www. investors.yum.com/phoenix.zhtml?c=117941&p=irol-newsEarnings**

YUM! Brands Website. 'YUM! Financial Data' section, available at: **http://www.yum.com/investors/restcounts.asp**

11

Marketing communications

LEARNING OBJECTIVES

- Assess where marketing communications sits within overall marketing strategy
- Examine the key elements in the MARCOMS process
- Provide a strategic view of MARCOMS with a focus on the creative brief
- Assess the key issues in media choice and use
- Review the operational issues in implementing a MARCOMS strategy

CHAPTER AT A GLANCE

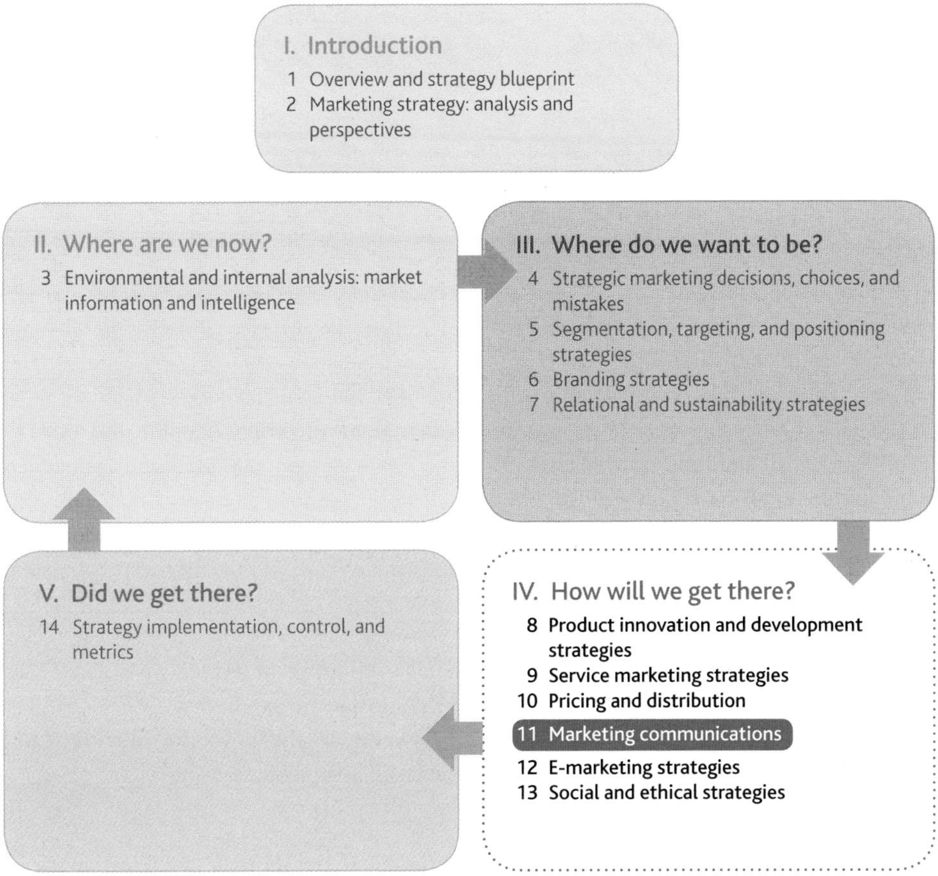

Introduction

Marketing communications (hereafter MARCOMS) are central to Porter's (1980) generic cost-differentiation focus strategies framework (see Chapter 2) and refer to four central types of media: advertising, direct marketing, Public Relations (PR), and sales promotions (see Figure 11.1). There are two layers to explore in using these four media in MARCOMS strategy relating to what the client wants to 'say' as opposed to execution, which relates to 'how' you say it. For example, the strategy for a recent campaign for Captain Bird's Eye Ready Meals has been to communicate that the products contain no artificial colours, flavourings, or preservatives. This is a message that has considerable resonance amongst their core target market, given the concerns over children's diets in the UK. The execution of the campaign shows children in a school going through the first few letters of the alphabet for the names of colours, flavourings, and preservatives. In an emphatic and unambiguous delivery of the intended message, the commercial finishes at 'n' at which point the Captain Bird's Eye character explains that the letter stands for 'Not in my food'.

Strategy needs to be clearly agreed between the client and agency (if an agency is being used) at the beginning of the campaign process. The interpretation of the strategy by the

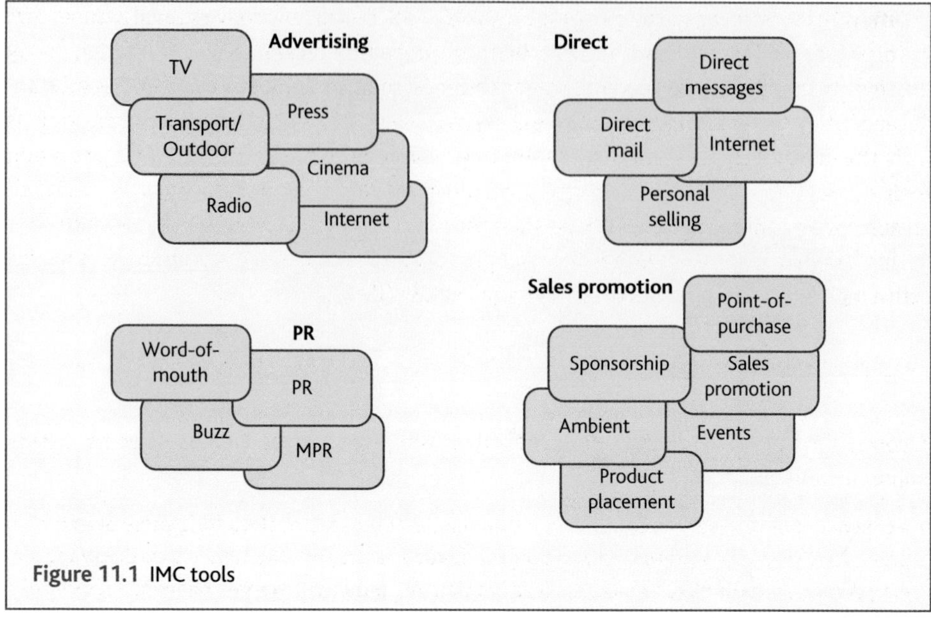

Figure 11.1 IMC tools

agency becomes the executional layer and often has to entertain or be creative in some way, to stand out from the clutter of communications that people are exposed to.

Can MARCOMS be used to reduce **costs**? The answer is largely 'No' for the short-term, but 'Yes' when a longer perspective is taken. The basic profit formula is:

Profit = (price-cost) × volume

How do MARCOMS fit in terms of a cost in the formula? In the short run, a client can spend money on MARCOMS to **help justify a price increase** or **increase volume**, but this will only add to costs. In the medium to long term, MARCOMS can support price through **brand preference** and provide some competitive protection for a brand. Furthermore, increased volume can be encouraged by pointing out **new uses** for the brand or by **targeting new markets**. Successful MARCOMS can lead to higher sales and in turn economies of scale. MARCOMS can also directly reduce costs in the medium to long term **through replacing (or increasing the efficiency) of an organization's routes to markets and in reducing market research costs**. A company with a large sales force and/or call centre may find that MARCOMS can create an environment where they can reduce the number of staff required. For example, customers can manage their accounts and track orders (CMR—customer managed relationships), fill out surveys, customize products, and find answers to their questions via advertising and direct marketing and the Web. Some commentators predict customer-managed relationships will increase a hundred times over usage today. Eventually, benefits will be designed for segments of 'one'. Additionally, successful public relations may reduce legal costs when related to crisis management and generally enhance goodwill. Even sales promotions, which largely increase costs when it involves price discounting and bonus offerings, can sometimes reduce costs. For example, by directly inducing a customer to try a product with a free sample, the adoption cycle can be fast-tracked.

Differentiation is central to spending on MARCOMS. Despite the conventional wisdom that lots of products and services are at parity, there are probably more differences in offerings today than ever before. If you take any consumer or business market, the amount of choice is substantial and often impossible for buyers to process cognitively. MARCOMS provides organizations with **the possibility of establishing their position within the market and asserting their distinctiveness.** While there are a great deal of 'metoo' communications, at heart, all organizations—be they for-profit or not-for-profit—seek to establish a point of difference.

This chapter will review and assess the primary issues in MARCOMS strategy. It begins with a look at integrated marketing communications (IMC).

IMC

According to the American Association of Advertising Agencies, IMC (integrated marketing communications) is:

> a concept of marketing communications planning that recognizes the added value of a comprehensive plan that evaluates the strategic roles of a variety of communications disciplines, e.g., advertising, direct response, sales promotion and public relations—and combines these disciplines to provide clarity, consistency and maximum communications impact.

The idea is to combine all four primary media to provide a holistic and integrated approach. Figure 11.2 provides an example of IMC integration with the 'Love Aga' campaign. The campaign utilized advertising, direct marketing, PR, sales promotion, and digital media, and sought to capture the affection and love owners display for their own Aga, making it an essential part of the home and an indispensable component of family life, and this was the unitary strategy.

Figure 11.2 Integration: Love Aga campaign

Source: By permission of Aga Rangemaster Group plc and Cogent Elliott.

One particularly important aspect of IMC is that it elevates the status of internal marketing, an oft-neglected aspect of MARCOMS. Employees, especially those interacting with customers, need to be kept informed and able to contribute towards an organizations' communications. If service quality is about reducing the gap between a customer's expectations and perceptions of service, it is generally advisable to show staff previews of forthcoming campaigns, as well as involve them in development whenever possible and appropriate. Relevant media include ambient media (e.g., sticking a notice or some such on hand-drying machines in toilets), email, intranets, newsletters, staff seminars, voice-mail, and sometimes creative placements, such as within monthly salary statements. There are several cases in marketing history where campaigns have failed because no one thought to tell the staff what was happening, such as when Clerical Medical Investments decided to reposition the brand in the early 1980s.

IMC theoretical roots

McGrath (2005) suggests that there are three theoretical foundations that support the IMC concept (see Figure 11.3):

1. IMC uses an interchange of 'push' (media exposure originating with the source of the message, e.g. a TV commercial) and 'pull' communications (media exposure originating from the receiver, e.g. the Internet), using a variety of media to **develop a relationship** between the encoder and the decoder (Schultz, 1996; Stewart, 1996; and Duncan, 2005).
2. As well as building a relationship, IMC can be more effective than other communications strategies because **a unified and consistent message is more likely to be processed effectively by the decoder** (Schultz, 1996). This is supported by evidence for 'chunking', where people have been found to integrate all the various cues from a brand into a single image in order to aid recall.
3. Finally, by coordinating the messages across different media, their individual **weaknesses are minimized while their strengths are maximized** (Peltier et al., 1992).

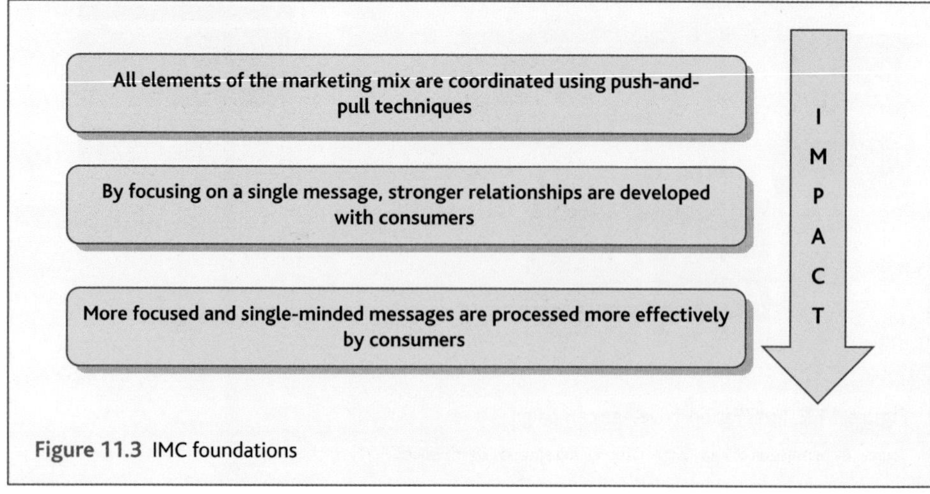

Figure 11.3 IMC foundations

Most proponents of IMC take the argument further and suggest that to be truly effective all the other elements of the marketing mix (product, pricing, place, and people) must be coordinated with communications so that the consumer is faced with a holistic brand image. For example, it would be highly inconsistent to advertise a box of chocolates as 'sophisticated' if the packaging was cheap and they were only distributed through discount supermarkets with price-off incentive sales promotions.

IMC involves message integration across a wide range of media. The concept is on a continuum rather than a fixed point. An organization with a unified message across a range of media, such as with COI's 'Big Drink Debate' (see Figure 11.4) undertook IMC through press, PR, events, and online. However, an organization with a unified message across a limited range of media may or may not be doing IMC. The distinction is that IMC is a strategic option that is managed and implemented (see Schultz and Schultz, 2004).

Having made all these points, IMC may present a number of logistical barriers that prevent its widespread adoption. For a start, it requires **considerable planning and resource allocation** to place advertising, direct marketing, sales promotions, and PR or MPR (marketing PR, sometimes called stunt marketing—a more active form of PR; see Robinson, 2006) into one unit. Take the case of General Motors, which has been one of the pioneers of IMC. As reported by Prescott (1991), GM demonstrates the administrative strain of implementing IMC for large corporations:

> At General Motors, which received a lot of publicity four years ago when it combined a portion of its PR with marketing at the corporate level, a two-tiered organizational structure was

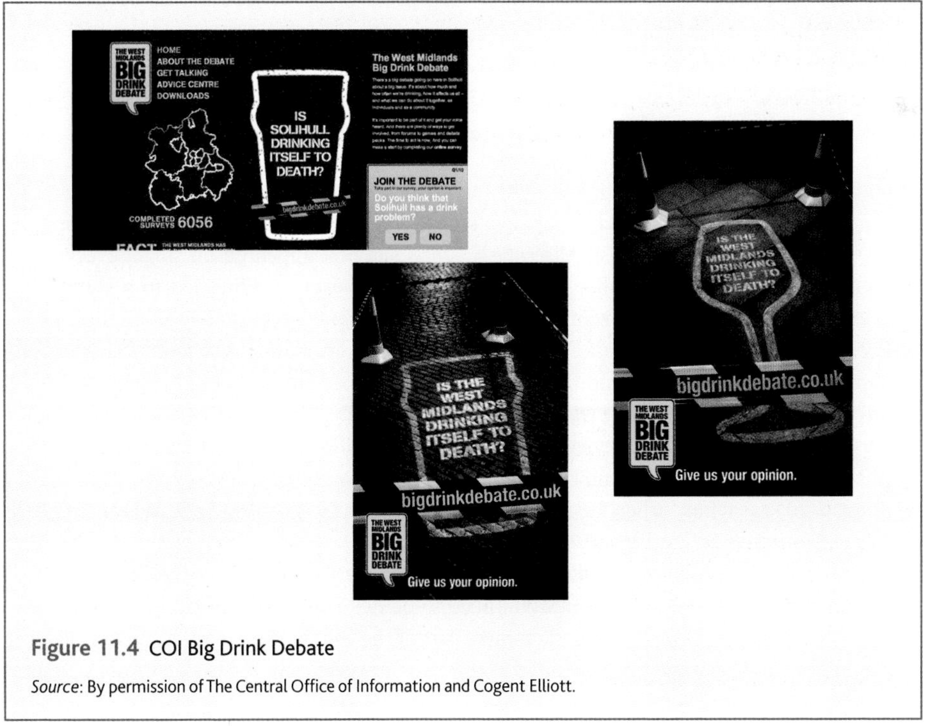

Figure 11.4 COI Big Drink Debate

Source: By permission of The Central Office of Information and Cogent Elliott.

set up to direct IMC. A Communication Council, made up of 41 communicators and directors from throughout the corporation, meets once a month and prioritizes IMC tasks. Once a task is agreed upon, the process for its execution is to appoint a Stakeholder Communication Team composed of a 'champion', a 'lead coordinator', and appropriate GM departmental representatives.

Also, the risk, as Mark Twain aptly put it, is that if you put all your eggs in one basket, 'watch that basket'. If the central message does not resonate with the audience or appears not to be genuine, **then the whole communications campaign will fail, rather than just one part**. Thus, running separate communications across different media is inconsistent and may have less impact, but it can spread the risk.

Shift from push to pull

Technology is enabling consumers to perform marketing tasks and functions which were once the preserve of advertisers and their agencies. They buy and sell on auction sites such as eBay, they advise each other on products and services such as on ePinions, and they are even redesigning and manufacturing products for themselves and others. Broadly speaking, this significant shift can be categorized as a move from 'push' to 'pull' (see Mini Case Study 11.1). Applied to MARCOMS, push is when a message is placed in order to influence members of an audience (e.g., a TV commercial), whereas pull is when the audience pulls information towards themselves, e.g. 'Googling' or in more extreme cases making their own content, such as with uploading their own versions of commercials on YouTube. As noted by Berthon et al. (2008), 'The traditional distinctions between producer and consumer and between mass communications and individual communication are dissolving' (p. 7).

MINI CASE STUDY 11.1 15MB of fame

Susan Boyle came to international public attention in 2009 after she appeared as a contestant on the UK television channel ITV1's *Britain's Got Talent* show singing 'I Dreamed a Dream' from the musical, *Les Misérables*. When she first appeared on stage, everyone seemed apprehensive about her drab appearance. However, she finished to a standing ovation and all-round praise from the judges. Her appearance, performance, and the audience and judges' reaction sparked enormous global interest, with media stories about her appearing across the world and the numbers who watched videos of her audition setting an online record. Within a few weeks, 'I Dreamed a Dream', 'Cry Me a River', and videos of her audition and various interviews with her reached millions of viewers on YouTube. Ben Rhodes, VP of marketing UK and Ireland for Mastercard was quoted in *Media Week* (26 May 2009, p. 20) as saying: 'When Susan Boyle has 100 million views on YouTube, it is no longer about 15 minutes of fame, but 15MB of fame.'

The example is symptomatic of a shift in power to consumers away from the media establishment. New marketing strategies will need to be developed to respond to the seismic changes sweeping through the marketplace. Part of the shift to digital media has involved a change in mindset that content should be free—free music, free videos, free news, and the like.

» Some players are already taking enormous gambles. Take the case of the *London Evening Standard,* which launched a risky publicity campaign apologizing to Londoners for its previous behaviour. Buses and tubes carried a series of messages beginning with the word 'Sorry'. The first one said 'Sorry for losing touch' and was followed by 'Sorry for being negative', 'Sorry for taking you for granted', and sorry for 'being complacent and for being predictable'. The billboards did not carry the *Standard* by name, but carried its Eros logo.

Why say sorry? The paper had conducted market research which suggested that Londoners and commuters saw the paper as too negative and not addressing London's needs. The *Standard*'s agency, McCann Erickson, set out to attract new readers and support existing ones by being honest and admitting to previous failings. In particular, there had been complaints that the paper was anti-New Labour and hostile to Ken Livingstone, the former mayor and credited with playing a key role in the election of Boris Johnson. The paper had also suffered circulation losses with the arrival of two free titles, *London Lite* and *The London Paper*.

The implication for brands is that they are becoming what might be termed 'conversation platforms', where consumers using websites such as Blogger, Facebook, Flickr, Tumblr, Twitter, and YouTube are influencing the behaviour of many prominent brands. For example, Unilever was forced to respond to a spoof Dove viral by Greenpeace slating the company's use of non-sustainable sources of palm oil that rapidly gained nearly 900,000 views on YouTube. Unilever announced that it would only buy palm oil from suppliers who can demonstrate that they use sustainable sources. The company may well have been going along that route anyway, but the viral is increasingly showing that credit cards are the new ballot boxes. This is not a new phenomenon, with a number of historic boycotts of brands over the past forty or so years involving banks, clothing companies, supermarkets, etc., and even countries. What has changed is the phenomenal power of consumers and NGOs to set off such boycotts with simple acts, such as the posting of viral.

The winners in the marketing communications business will be those organizations that see the digital shift of power as an opportunity rather than a threat. For example, television companies have undoubtedly lost audience share to digital media, yet companies can still help to build brands with more targeted audiences and by participating and interacting with the explosion in communities. Shows such as *Britain's Got Talent* can still set the agenda, but the business model for ITV may have to reach out to the audience beyond the basic content of the show to drive response and deliver competitive return on the investment by advertisers. Advertisers will increasingly find themselves in the content and entertainment business to help provide people with their 15MB of fame.

The result has been a general shift away from the above-the-line media of TV, press, billboards, radio, and cinema (so called because agencies 'drew a line' between media that gave commission and those that did not), towards digital and interactive media, often along with attempts to create 'buzz' (Thomas, 2004; Mohr, 2007).

The major media have fragmented at a rapid rate. Most profoundly, the role of above-the-line media has shifted to some extent from being the primary element in any campaign to playing often a supporting role; as with the use of TV commercials to point people towards websites rather than for stand-alone brand development.'Guerrilla' approaches are increasingly common to build audiences, as is done in product placement in TV shows (for example, HP placed their products in the US version of *The Office*) and films (for example, the Bond *Casino Royale* film featured Omega, Sony, and Ford), and a variety of other ways, such as attempts to raise interactivity with the use of voting for brand competitions using text messaging (though product placements are not new and date back to the nineteenth century and before). A MARCOMS campaign that does not consider the role of Google and social-networking sites like Bebo, Facebook, and MySpace would be rare today. See, for example, Figure 11.5, which shows CrossCountry Trains' Facebook application that enables people to instantly plan visits to their friends around the UK, with timetables and routes provided at a click.

Services

One particular strategy has been to abandon overt marketing messages in favour of **services**, that is, something useful or entertaining that embeds itself much deeper into everyday life and has led to communications that do not feel like traditional advertising (Bernadin and Kemp-Robertson, 2008). For example, in 2007, Fallon/London created a campaign for a new range of Sony cameras. Before airing TV commercials, they handed out one of the new

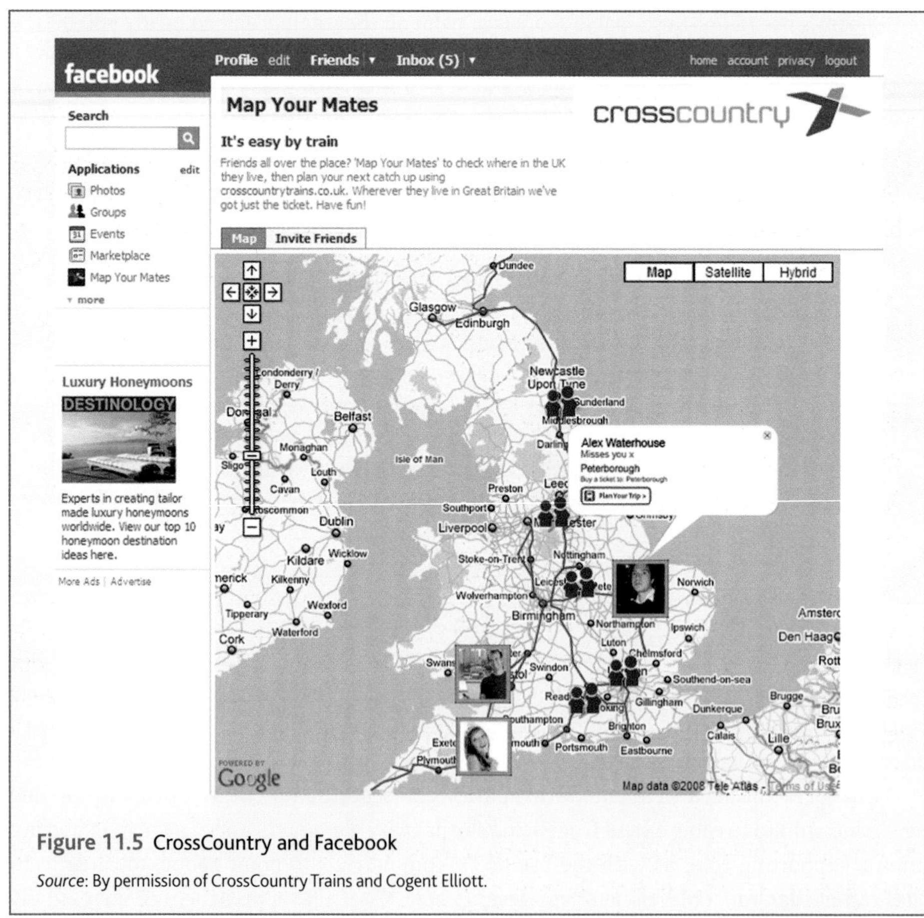

Figure 11.5 CrossCountry and Facebook

Source: By permission of CrossCountry Trains and Cogent Elliott.

cameras to each of 100 bloggers to participate in an extraordinary photograph shoot that saw 460 million litres of foam unleashed in the centre of Miami. Local residents joined in and photographs were uploaded onto Flickr.

In another example, IKEA transformed their two-dimensional catalogue cover into a three-dimensional installation by creating an exact replica of the living room that appeared on the catalogue cover. The objective was to advertise the new IKEA catalogue with an innovative consumer event that involves a lot of people and boosts IKEA's brand appeal. Their 3-D cover went on tour throughout shopping malls in 24 cities in Germany, with passersby having the opportunity to have their picture taken on the set. A few days later, participants could go back to IKEA and pick up a catalogue featuring themselves as the cover models. A total of 7,120 people had their pictures taken and 4,039 personalized catalogue were produced.

Wrangler provides another example. The brand felt it was not resonating with European youth, partly because its advertising was not in the places where its audience was spending time. In response, Wrangler set up 'guerrilla laundromats' at a number of music festivals. After leaving their dirty clothes for a free service wash, festival-goers were given Wrangler-branded jumpsuits to wear for the rest of the day until they could pick up their clean clothes.

MARCOMS strategic process

Audit

The MARCOMS strategic process can be seen in Figure 11.6. The process starts with an audit of the marketplace such as can be used with the PESTLE (political, economic, social, technological, legal, and environmental) assessment. The aim is to establish the key overall trends in the market, their importance and likelihood, and what aspects to focus upon for the MARCOMS plan.

The next stage is to examine the competitors in the marketplace. Four questions need to be answered:

1. How many competitors are there and what share does each have?
2. What positions do they take up? Why?
3. Are any doing well or badly? Why?
4. How important is their presence in this market?

A SWOT (or something similar) then needs to be carried out, detailing the strengths, weaknesses, opportunities, and threats. The key issues identified need to be related to communications such as how well or poorly first name and prompted mentions of the brand are, the brand's share of category spending, and attitudes towards the brand. Strengths and opportunities need to be leveraged and weaknesses and threats addressed.

Establishing the strategy

The next phase of the MARCOMS strategy process is to identify the central strategy (see Figure 11.6 again). Most of the following topics in the rest of this chapter feature in what

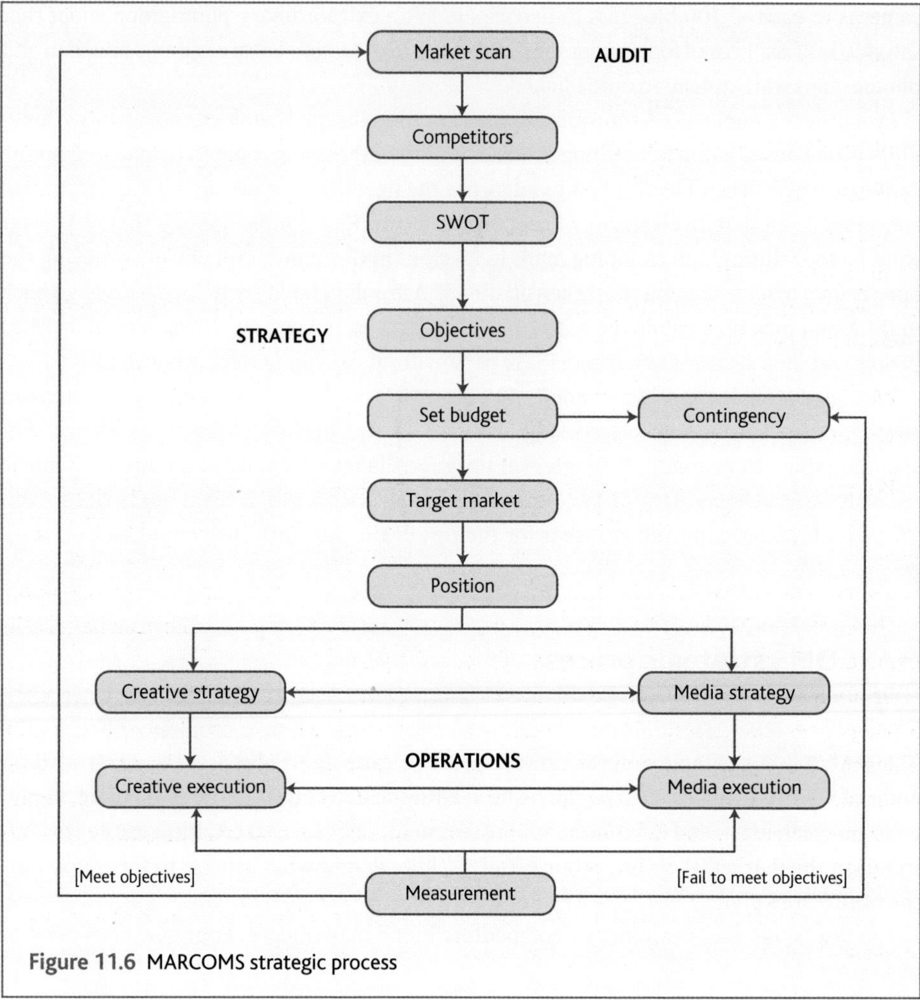

Figure 11.6 MARCOMS strategic process

agencies call the 'Creative Brief': a written summation of the MARCOMS task that will manage and stimulate the development of creative work to address that task (see Figure C11.2 at the end of this chapter for an example).

The brief generally starts with agencies isolating in a few simple sentences what the aim of the communications is—the strategic intent. Bear in mind that the creative team in most agencies (the copywriter and the art director) are not business strategists. There might be hundreds of pages of research defining and explaining the task, with an elaborate SWOT which they will never read (or ever want to read). What they want is something succinct and to the point. Tasks should be focused, measurable, and capable of inspiring the creative team to do good work (see West and Ford, 2001). Broad examples of tasks include:

- announce launch
- build/rebuild corporate reputation

- generate leads
- increase sales
- increase/maintain share
- justify a price or price increase
- stop a decline.

An example of announcing a launch can be seen in Figure 11.7 for increased destinations from Manchester Airport.

However, tasks can be articulated and a stronger direction indicated. Examples of specific tasks would be:

- Pepsi wants to be the badge of a generation
- Coca-Cola wants to be the classic choice.

Both tasks are easy to comprehend and distinct and do not need to be complicated by further elaboration. If you think about it, all the documentation and briefing in the world can be given before a major sports event, but the task for all the players is simply to win the game. In the same vein, with the Apollo programme, NASA's objective was to get a man on the moon. In the context of MARCOMS, tasks are often stated as strategic intent, which can be broadly summarized in five formats, starting with product superiority.

Product superiority could be the central strategy of the campaign. The intention of the strategy here is to communicate that a product or service can fix a problem or better fulfil a desire. There is an adage in the communications business that if you throw ten balls at someone they will not catch a single one. If you throw just one, it has a much greater chance of being caught. The implication is that objectives should be single-minded and focused; as suggested by the unique selling proposition (USP; Reeves, 1961):

> To gain a purchase, an advertiser must persuade the potential buyer that there is a unique benefit from the product.

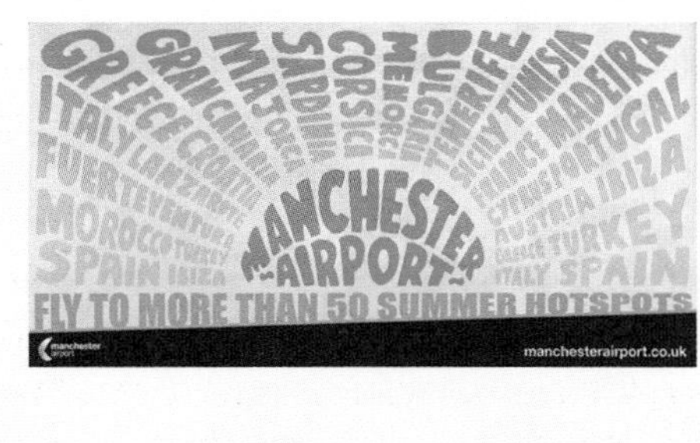

Figure 11.7 Announcing a launch

Source: By permission of The Manchester Airports Group and Cogent Elliott.

Thus, a recent campaign for the Volkswagen Passat only featured the revised breaking system of the new model—a significant benefit to focus upon. See, for example, Figure 11.8, which shows the product superiority claim of Club Med of being 'more exclusive, more inclusive'.

Tangible performance benefits such as those involving technology or design can often give an edge, but can be short-lived if easily copied. This has led to the variation of the 'ESP', which stands for **emotional selling proposition**. Thus, the Co-op, with its banks and supermarkets, adopts an ethical stance in the marketplace and communicates this through its MARCOMS. You might not get a better deal, product, or service; you feel good because your money is part of an ethically aware organization. The Nationwide Building Society, given the uncertainty over the leading banks, has advertised itself in full-page national press advertisements as: 'Solid. Stable. Dependable. Suddenly, they're the most exciting words in a saver's vocabulary.'

The **cultural identification** strategy is about making the product, service, or organization part of the consumer's world. For example, HP Sauce ran a campaign featuring the use of the sauce by various 'tribes' in the UK such as 'white van' drivers and women out on a hen night. In a similar attempt at cultural identification, Unilever's Pot Noodles brand caused considerable controversy over a campaign promoting the brand (whose main target audience is young men) as the 'Slag of all Snacks' and associating the brand with infidelity. Pot Noodle has revisited the 1980s recently with a campaign developed by Brand Manager Cheryl Caverley at Unilever (Mother advertising agency) with an un-PC TV campaign. It features two young comedians singing how they wished women were as simple as the 'just-add-boiling-water' to a Pot Noodle snack. The brand has also remained topical, with such campaign themes as the credit crunch. For an example of cultural identification see Figure 11.9 for Arriva buses, which capitalized on the general unrest at rising petrol prices.

Salience is the main concern of the **product definition** strategy. How can new products or services be made salient? Or, how can a product that has lost its salience regain it? This strategy is about finding something to say that will rekindle a brand that has lost its tarnish and esteem in the market. Perhaps one of the most high-profile cases in the UK would be Marks and Spencer. While the food part of the business continued to prosper, the clothing had lost market share to cheaper supermarket alternatives such Asda's George range and also to more design-orientated labels such as Liz Claiborne, Hobbs, Monsoon, and Jill Saunders.

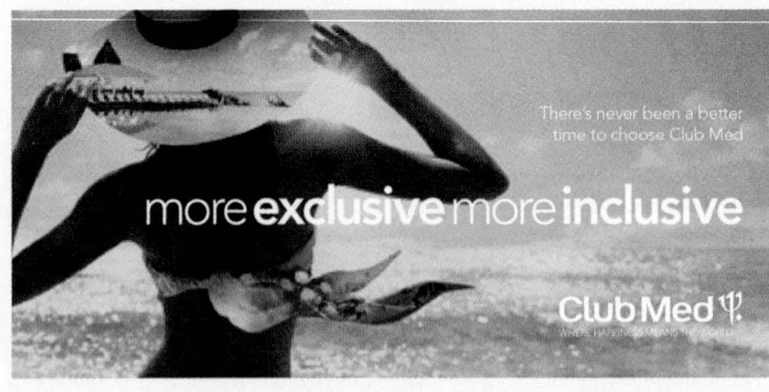

Figure 11.8 Product superiority: Club Med—more exclusive, more inclusive

Source: By permission of Club Med UK and Cogent Elliott.

Figure 11.9 Cultural identification: Arriva buses

Source: By permission of Arriva plc and Cogent Elliott.

In an attempt to re-establish salience, M&S embarked on a bold TV campaign focused on design, style, and new ranges and featuring such models as Twiggy and Erin O'Connor alongside Noemie Lenoir, Elizabeth Jagger, Laura Bailey, Myleene Klaas, and Lily Cole.

Possibly the most difficult of all strategies to engage in is the **paradigm shift**. Here, the aim is to alter the consumer's definition of a brand and/or category. One of the most successful UK attempts at a paradigm shift in recent years has been Volkswagen's campaign for the Skoda. The campaign has shown, in a variety of amusing executions, disbelief amongst the public and motor trade that the car concerned is a Skoda. The Skoda heritage may mitigate against the car being seen as the equivalent of a Volkswagen in the immediate future, yet the campaign has undoubtedly contributed towards the repositioning of the car as a sensible purchase rather than a joke.

The next stage is to translate the strategic intent into specific objectives. MARCOMS objectives are normally only applied to communications activities. Examples would be:

- 'Exposure message to ... '
- 'Create 40% awareness amongst ... '
- 'Create attitude/opinion that ... '
- 'Increase preference amongst ... '
- 'Encourage trial amongst ... '
- 'Reinforce loyalty amongst ... '

There are three levels to MARCOMS objectives: 'exposure,' 'awareness', and 'attitudes/relationships'.

Exposure represents the lowest level of objective. David Ogilvy once famously noted that: 'You cannot save souls in an empty church' (Ogilvy, 1987). Thus, exposure is simply an objective related to the desired level of OTS (all MARCOMS are only ever 'opportunities to see', as you cannot force an audience to listen and/or read your communications) and coverage to achieve the MARCOMS objectives. Most agencies seek an average of two to three OTSs amongst the target market in order to give the MARCOMS a chance to work, given that some repetition is needed for full comprehension and remembering. An example of an exposure objective might be to cover 40 per cent of the target audience with an OTS of three. Unfortunately, a campaign might effectively cover its chosen audience with the hoped-for OTS and still have little impact if people do not respond. A higher-level objective involves 'awareness'.

Awareness can be measured at two levels: 'spontaneous' and 'prompted'. Spontaneous awareness often involves open-ended questions such as:

- 'Tell me, of all the major supermarkets that you have heard of … '
- 'Any more?'
- 'Is that all?'

Prompted awareness, as the name implies, provides the prompts. For example, you might ask: 'Which one or ones of the following supermarket chains have you heard of?

- Aldi
- Asda
- Lidl
- Jeffrey's
- Marks and Spencer
- Morrisons
- Sainsbury's
- Tesco
- Waitrose.

Note that in the list there is a little known supermarket chain called Jeffrey's, though, to be honest, Jeffrey's does not exist! Quite often, a fictitious prompt is provided to gain an understanding of how seriously the questions have been answered. If 5 per cent of the sample say, 'Yes, I have heard of Jeffery's', you can broadly discount these respondents as the indications are that they would say 'Yes' to any name.

Nevertheless, you could have extremely high awareness and yet your brand might still be performing badly. Famously, the Strand cigarette was launched with a TV campaign in the late 1950s, showing Terence Brooks, a Frank Sinatra lookalike, lighting up a cigarette on a lonely street corner. The accompanying caption said, 'You're never alone with a Strand', with Cliff Adams' haunting instrumental playing in the background. The ads were hugely popular, Terence Brooks became a teenage pin-up and the 'Lonely Man Theme' was a huge hit. Yet, Strand became associated with loneliness and unsociability, and the brand soon disappeared from the market.

The highest level of MARCOMS objectives concern **attitudes** and **relationships**. Attitudes are positive or negative views of an object such as an organization, product, service, or idea that lead to the formation of relationships. Generally, marketers recognize the difference between 'opinions' and 'attitudes', between pre- and post-purchase. People hold opinions about products and services pre-purchase, but once they have tried them they have attitudes. You might feel that an Aston Martin is a great car, but not buy one because you either do not have the resources or it simply is not a priority.

Target market

The next stage is to review the various potential segments and decide upon the specific **target market(s)** that the communication is aimed at. Given the lack of business strategic background of most creative teams in agencies (West, 1993, 1994), this is not normally a technical description. What is required is a description of a person or a group that goes beyond report-format and is based upon what is, or is not, important. For example, a target description for a campaign aimed at frequent international flyers or organizational travel buyers would not point out all the details. Instead, the brief would mention such things as frequent flyers needing a good rest or sleep en route before business meetings while travel buyers are looking for deals with leading airlines and the need to justify costs. What kind of cars might such people drive?What kind of papers or magazines do they read?

Position

The next thing to consider is how to **position** the client (see Ries and Trout, 1981). A position is how potential buyers see the product and it is expressed relative to competitors. This is what you want to achieve and should be measurable and achievable, otherwise it is not worth stating. Generally, it tends to relate to rational or emotional aspects. For an MP3 player, it might be to position the product as having the capacity for the number of songs you want to carry and that it is 'cool'. The issue here is how MARCOMS might help position the player. MARCOMS might also address **repositioning**, which involves changing the identity of a product relative to the identity of competing products. There is also the potential for **de-positioning**: attempting to change the identity of competing brands relative to the identity of your own brand in the minds of the target market.

Creative strategy

Having decided upon the position required, what communications **proposition** will do this? The proposition spells out what you want to say. At this stage, agencies look for what they call 'big ideas'. The term, originating with the advertising business, has been co-opted by various groups in recent years, most noticeably by politicians. MARCOMS big ideas require collaboration and hard work, often making difficult choices and judgements, and the exclusion of product facts. They have to be sold and defended and may change (a lot) in execution, but they are central to the strategy. Some key questions to ask of a proposition to judge whether it stands up as a big idea or not are:

- Does it have staying power?
- Does it spark dramatic creative ideas?
- Is it credible?
- Is it distinctive?
- Is it focused and single-minded?
- Is the promise meaningful?

Some potential sources of a proposition are:

- Brand image characteristics
- Direct comparisons with rivals
- Disadvantages of non-use
- Generic benefits
- How the product/service is made
- Newsworthiness
- Price characteristics
- Product/service characteristics
- Product/service comparisons
- Product/service heritage
- Satisfying psychological/physiological needs
- Surprising points about the product/service
- User characteristics
- Ways of using the product/service.

The key issue to consider: is the proposition relevant?Does it relate to the target audiences' problems or desires?Strategically, is it competitively different?Can it be expressed in a single-minded execution?

You know if you have a good proposition if it **gives the creatives an 'angle' or 'way in' to develop some good creative work**. It does not need to be liberating, as restricted propositions can lead to exceptionally creative work (West and Berthon, 1997; West, 1999). It should also force a strategic choice or direction in the marketplace by being single-minded rather than all-encompassing. It goes without saying that any chosen proposition should be based on truth (rational or emotional). Thus, a recent B2B campaign by IBM extolling the benefits of on-demand processes in business used a variety of scenarios that, while fictitious in themselves (e.g., the demand for pink or white dresses being instantly fed back through the supply chain from the moment of sale at the cash register), effectively demonstrated the nature of IBM's proposition. Propositions to avoid are ones that communicate very little to the creative team such as:

- 'A wide range and good value'
- 'Stylish and modern'
- 'The best car on the market'
- 'The right food for your dog'.

None of the above would give a creative team much of a clue of what was required. However, to say that a particular mayonnaise 'takes the humdrum out of everyday food' or that a particular washing machine is 'the family workhorse', gives the team a much better steer of what is required. Bear in mind, that for many brands, the role of the proposition in MARCOMS strategy is changing with the advent of social media. Increasingly, the job is to develop audience insight and enter into so-called 'engagement', where consumers directly influence the positioning of a brand rather than respond to a proposition (see Social media in Chapter 12).

Having decided upon the proposition, it remains to consider if the claim can be **supported**. If you cannot support the proposition, you cannot have it. Why should anyone believe such a message if it cannot be supported? What are the key facts or figures that provide the evidence? None of this has to appear in the execution, but it must appear in the creative brief, otherwise the proposition will be simple puffery. Thus, if the proposition states that a tyre will continue to perform even when punctured, what is the evidence? Has it been tested and is it true? The evidence does not need to appear in the ad; however, the claim cannot be made without it.

Some potential **problems** that can arise at this stage of strategy development are:

- Confusing the client's concerns with their customers' concerns
- Lack of focus
- Lack of a meaningful target audience
- Lack of a position
- Making support of the product the promise
- Restating objectives as the proposition.

The next creative strategic issue is how to reflect the **brand's character**. This is a key strategic issue for any brand, as the wrong character may at best add little value and at worst severely damage its market standing. In the broadest sense, brand character reflects how the brand is positioned. Does the brand's character exude fun or is it serious? Does it set out to shock or reassure? Is it modern or traditional? Take the case of the highly acclaimed Walkers crisps campaign using Gary Lineker in a mischievous role in contrast to his 'Mr Nice Guy' image. However, many of the banks, such as NatWest and Barclays understandably produce campaigns with more serious appeals. Significant changes in brand character need to be conscious and well-thought through strategically. The Halifax Bank has recently dropped its upbeat campaign based upon one of its staff, Howard Brown, in favour of a more sober and serious approach, which the Bank feels is more appropriate to recessionary times. Occasionally, the brand character can become the focus of the campaign. Oliviero Toscani worked on Benetton's advertising between 1982 and 2000 and increasingly produced work that focused upon the company's values rather than its products. The communications of the brand's character became its values, as with the Body Shop.

Media strategy

In tangent and often in parallel with the development of the creative strategy, comes the development of the media strategy (see Table 11.1 for an overview of MARCOMS options). Three questions need to be answered:

1. Where is the communication(s) going to appear?
2. How frequently?
3. How much is to be spent?

The answers to these questions can vary greatly, depending upon the strategy. Media strategy is about attempting to ensure that a clients' message is seen or heard by the right people, in the right place, in the right environment, with the right frequency and weight, and at the right price. British Airways chose to wrap up a building to publicize its flat beds for Club Class passengers. Chanel N° 5 featured Nicole Kidman and produced a 180-second commercial to reposition the brand towards a younger audience. The commercial's impact and frequency of

TABLE 11.1 MARCOMS options

Medium	Definition	Horizon	Form	Scope
Advertising	A paid-for communication by an identified sponsor with the aim of informing and influencing one or more people	Mainly long-term	TV, press, posters, radio, Web, Cinema, digital, SMS	Awareness, attitudes
Direct marketing	The recording, analysis, and tracking of customers' direct responses in order to develop loyalty	Short- and long-term	Direct mail, DRTV & radio, telemarketing, press, inserts, leaflets, Web, digital, SMS	Mainly retention, but also acquisition
PR	The formulation, execution, and sustained effort to establish and maintain goodwill and mutual understanding and reciprocal goodwill between an organization and its stakeholders	Short- and long-term	Community relations/CSR, corporate advertising, crisis management, events, internal communications, investor relations, media relations, public affairs, lobbying, sponsorship, Web, digital	Credibility, visibility, and reputation
Sales promotions	An incentive for the customer, sales force, or distributor to make an immediate purchase	Mainly short-term	*Consumer*: coupons, contests, trial, mail-in offers/refunds, group promotions, self-liquidations, in-store promotions, point-of-sale, web, digital, SMS. *Trade*: dealer merchandise; contests' advertising, allowance, trade allowance/staff incentive, Web	*Consumer*: trial, re-trial, extended trial, build database *Trade*: gain a listing, increase distribution, increase inventory, improve shelving space/position

the schedule raised awareness and influenced attitudes towards the brand on a scale that a smaller spend could never have matched.

Spend has to be targeted by buyer characteristics, geography, and season. After gathering information, the classic approach is the four W's:

- **Who:** define the exact audience (e.g., '34–45-year-old women').
- **Where:** determine the geographic area (e.g., 'every major urban market').
- **When:** decide upon the time of purchase (e.g., 'prior to most house moves').
- **What:** establish creative material (e.g., 'describe the time-saving ability of a new washing-machine').

In which case, the most efficient choice might be the selection of newspapers, TV, posters, and online, focused between May and June. However, the solution is rarely that simple. Normally, a mix of media are used and media planners/buyers normally use past experience along with research. For example, sponsorship might be used to provide a direct and immediate inducement supporting the service or product to the sales force, distributors or the consumer.

Two choices need to be made in media strategy between media **classes** and media **vehicles**. A media class refers to the vertical decision involving media type, e.g. press or TV. The primary choices are:

- cinema
- directmail
- posters/billboards
- press
- public relations
- radio
- sales promotion
- sponsorship
- TV
- Web.

Operations

The final stage of MARCOMS strategy is the operational: the implementation of the strategy. This involves creative and media execution, pre-testing, contingency, and post-testing (El-Murad and West, 2003, 2004).

Creative execution

The creative execution stage is where the chosen strategy is translated into a piece of communication (West et al., 2008). If the strategy was to be based on user characteristics, perhaps a chocolate eaten by 'macho men', it would be stated as the proposition. For example, Yorkie ran a successful campaign for many years showing rugged-looking lorry drivers biting into

Yorkie bars. Nothing was said in any of the ads. They did not run headlines in the press saying, 'Macho Men Eat Chunky Chocolate!' The art of execution is to translate the stated proposition in a highly relevant and creative way without literally restating the proposition.

A variety of techniques may be used, such as the 'associative', which involves providing easy links to the proposition (e.g., a laptop side-by-side with an ant, suggesting the strength of the product), and the use of celebrities (Erdogan et al., 2001; e.g., Tiger Woods and Accenture), or simply 'show and tell' (explaining the proposition clearly and rationally). Figure 11.10 provides an example of a simple translation of a strategy to execution for Network Q, based upon the insight that buying a used car carries with it a degree of worry and uncertainty.

Finally, before the execution can be finalised **what *must* be included** has to be agreed. These rarely have any impact on strategy, as for most companies, this simply means logos, phone numbers, website addresses, and slogans (Kohli et al., 2007). However, MARCOMS strategies are constrained by legislation and the Advertising Standards Authority (ASA), which is an independent body set up by the advertising industry to police the rules laid down in the advertising codes, including broadcast, based upon its legal, decent, honest, and truthful code. Agencies and media support the use of the law and codes of practice as they recognize that the framework benefits the industry as a whole. For example, when advertising alcoholic drinks on broadcast media, the ASA code states that advertisers,

> must not suggest that regular solitary drinking is acceptable or that drinking is a means of resolving personal problems. Nor must they imply that drinking is an essential part of daily routine or can bring about a change in mood.

Media execution

Media vehicle choice concerns the choice within the chosen class; e.g., if the press is chosen, will it be *The Times* or *The Sun*? Or, if TV is chosen, what programmes will be targeted? The choice of media vehicles will depend on a number of quantitative and qualitative issues. Media planners and buyers will seek the most effective vehicles for their clients within the chosen medium. Decisions cannot be left to numbers. Thus, the numbers might suggest a

Figure 11.10 Network Q

Source: By permission of General Motors Corporation—Network Q and Cogent Elliott.

particular tabloid 'red-top' newspaper for a luxury car advertiser. However, qualitatively, the car company's brand might not benefit from the association with the 'redtop' and a quality daily (with a less cost-effective audience than the redtop) will be the preferred choice. Also, editorial content and positioning count with media vehicles. It's fashionable to write off the traditional or 'old media' from the mix, but they are not without their own digital developments (see Mini Case Study 11.2).

MINI CASE STUDY 11.2 New-old media?

The traditional, old marketing communications media of television, newspaper, outdoor, radio, and cinema are surely heading for the rust belt of the landscape in face of stiff competition from the new media. But are they? Digital technology underpins solid competition for the so-called old media, yet it may also throw them a lifeline. Let us review some of the developments occurring.

High-definition (HD) television is one such technology. There are over 7 million HD-TV-ready homes in the UK and BSkyB has nearly 800,000 HD customers and around 500,000 homes have the Virgin Media cable V+ box, which can be upgraded to HD, and Freeview will be offering HD. With a crisper and clearer picture, HD may offer more dynamic and striking commercials for advertisers. However, the take-up by the industry has been sparse, with only a handful of advertisers using the technology for commercials.

Given lots of people have various combinations of HD-TVs, DVDs, movies on demand, high-quality surround sound, and Blu-ray, Hollywood studios know that people need a compelling reason to spend out on cinema tickets, rather than watch a movie at home. **3D Cinema** has been around since the early 1950s and has tended to be associated with B movies. Now it is back! A number of films have been released in 2008 and 2009 and are slated for release in the next few years, including *Avatar*, *Bolt*, *Coraline*, *Final Destination 4: 3-D*, *Fly Me to the Moon*, *G-Force*, *Ice Age: Dawn of the Dinosaurs*, *Monsters vs Aliens*, *My Bloody Valentine*, *Piranha*, *Toy Story 3*, and *Up*. Perhaps it will be just a gimmick, with directors focusing on the 3D wow factor rather than the story. Whether 3D will go truly mainstream is a matter of debate, including who will pay for the spectacles, but the Odeon chain has stated that it intends to have about a third of its screens enabled. The problem for advertisers is that the cinema already has a high impact, so 3D won't add that much. However, if it resonates, it will deliver larger audiences.

Targeted TV advertising is a relatively straightforward technology that may, nonetheless, have far-reaching effects. The way it operates is that a comprehensive library of commercials is stored on a household's digital box or made accessible via video-on-demand services (e.g., Sky+ or Virgin Media). Audience-research panel data can then be used to tailor content to a household's demographics or behaviour. Thus, a household with a young baby might receive an added weighting of baby-product commercials. Difficulties may arise in households with mixed demographics and behavioural segmentation options (think parents and teenage children). Also, viewers may balk at issues involving any perceived invasion of privacy. People won't watch more TV because the ad breaks are more entertaining; however, the trade-off between privacy and the greater relevance of commercials may be one that people are prepared to make, given the segmentation data concerned are non-specific and broad in nature. Being able to target smaller groups will add to production

» costs, but the impact of being able to use specific messages to niche markets on advertising effectiveness could be enormous.

Finally, outdoor media have joined the digital age with digital screens, touch screens, and thin film 'e-paper' or 'e-ink displays'. While these technologies have largely dominated the thinking and the spending, **Bluetooth** short-range wireless **poster sites** have been largely ignored. There are certainly good reasons for this. Many advertisers would regard Bluetooth as too unwieldy and expensive and think that it takes too much effort and the communications produced are too creatively restrictive. The way it works is, as you pass by a Bluetooth-enabled poster, you are invited to enable your Bluetooth device and accept the download. Some of the keenest users target where people are waiting, such as railway stations or foyers (cinema chains, for example, use their 6-sheet Bluetooth-enabled sites in foyers to offer film news and deals). The beauty of the technology for outdoor advertisers is that the impact goes beyond the immediate sight of the poster. Time will tell if the potential for greater engagement and interaction will outweigh the cumbersome nature of the set-up for Bluetooth and the degree of planning required.

Overall, it may be too soon to write off the old media. Digital technology offers a number of opportunities to prolong their life further than many analysts have predicted.

Having lined up the choice of vehicle, the key decisions involve frequency and impact and each issue will impact on the other. With limited resources, agencies and their clients are forced to trade off one against the other. If you double the frequency, without the commensurate doubling of the budget, the spaces purchased will inevitably have to be halved and the impact will consequently be reduced. The key strategic issue here is the advertisers' decay rate.

The concept of the decay rate refers to the implication of stopping all advertising activity. If you stop MARCOMS tomorrow, what happens to the brand's awareness and positive attitudes? What would it look like in a week, a month, or in six months' time? Powerful brands like IBM and Max Factor would have extremely slow decay rates and would likely be well-known after years of no activity. However, lesser brands, those that are not top-of-mind in their product categories, may soon be forgotten. If awareness and positive attitudes play a major role in their sales, they will be in considerable trouble if they stop the campaign. Such brands get 'hit' twice in the marketplace. They have to maintain some presence, but the need to maintain this may mean that they have to take smaller spaces and are probably going to be less visible. Bigger brands can take stretches of inactivity, and so, not only have more resources to devote to MARCOMS, but can purchase bigger/higher-impact spaces as when they advertise in shorter bursts rather than drip feed their spends. Strategically, all that smaller advertisers can do is to attempt to maximize their creativity so that their smaller budgets may have a relatively higher impact.

Frequency

MARCOMS exposures can take some time to 'wearin', but they also eventually 'wearout' (Ray and Webb, 1986). Conventional wisdom dictates that the response function to MARCOMS tends to be concave, that is, with each subsequent impression the response is reduced (Broadbent, 1999), the idea being that most impact is made with the first impression and thereafter the impact diminishes. The implication is that wearin is fast and wearout is continuous. It is certainly commonsense that once you have paid attention to a piece of MARCOMS you are subsequently unlikely to give the same degree of attention. For example, if you read an ad in a newspaper giving details about a new camera, you would be unlikely to bother to read it again in its entirety. Strategically, it means that clients, all things being equal, need to produce a piece of MARCOMS that is so creative and entertaining that it can be seen again and again and still be enjoyed (as with the Guinness surfing commercial). Or to produce a variety of cheaper executions that support the same strategy, but provide sufficient interest so that wearout is reduced.

At a macro level, clients with high awareness can afford to use high-impact bursts of MARCOMS expenditure as they will not be forgotten in the intervening periods. On the other hand, clients with low awareness may need a more continuous ('drip') spend to maintain their presence. Timing of purchase may also play a role. Car companies face seasonality of purchases, but also know that a new car is a considered purchase so that they need continual presence in the marketplace as there is a long gestation period in decision-making. Micro-level considerations involve timings during the week or month. For example, most household goods are purchased on Fridays and over the weekend, so a lot of clients aim to reach their audiences on Wednesdays and Thursdays, just prior to consumer spending.

Measurement

It is extremely difficult to be precise about the effect of MARCOMS on behaviour using aggregate data like sales, market share, and profits or individual purchasing behaviour (see Vakratsas and Ambler, 1999). The problem is that MARCOMS effects are dependent on other factors in the marketing mix and so it is difficult to know the impact of MARCOMS alone. As such, MARCOMS measurement is normally undertaken using what are known as 'intermediate effects'—what happens to the minds of people following exposure. Aside from neurological research, there have been few radical changes in the intermediate MARCOMS effectiveness measures used in the past thirty years. The overall process of intermediate effects measurement (shown in Table 11.2) consists of:

- research prior to development
- research during development
- pre-testing
- post-testing.

Within these four stages, measures can be categorized into three groups: attention, processing, and communication.

Attention measures involve memory (recall) tests to indicate whether people paid attention to a communication and if they remember it. Recall requires the remembering of an ad without any external aid, while recognition requires identification of a previously seen ad. Recall can be category prompted or brand prompted, sometimes referred to as unaided (spontaneous recall) or aided recall (as mentioned above). Both measures can be used in

TABLE 11.2 MARCOMS measurement

Approach	Method	Objective	Type	Measure
Research prior to development	• Focus groups • Interviews	Discovery and understanding	Qualitative	• Attention measures • Little or no evaluation of the effectiveness of final MARCOMS
Research during development	• Concept testing • Consumer panels • Dummy media and copy • Readability of copy	Discovery and understanding	Qualitative	• Attention measures • Little or no evaluation of the effectiveness of final MARCOMS
Pre-testing	• Theatre/ hall testing of commercials • Physiological tests (e.g., pupil dilation, eye tracking, skin response), neurological (e.g., EEG testing) • Focus groups	Selection, development, evaluation, comparisons	Qualitative and quantitative	*Attention and processing measures*: • Likability of MARCOMS • Attitude towards MARCOMS • Credibility of MARCOMS • Brand recall • Brand recognition • Brand benefit belief • Brand attitude • Brand purchase intention
Monitoring	• Continuous tracking and testing • Recognition tests • Interviews • Questionnaires	Development, evaluation, comparisons	Qualitative and quantitative	*Processing measures*: • MARCOMS recall • MARCOMS recognition • Brand recall • Brand recognition • Brand benefit belief • Brand attitude • Brand purchase intention • Brand behaviour (purchasing)

pre-and post-tests. Physiological measures also only provide a measure of attention. Tests are done using EEG, brainwaves or by eye movements. Eye-movement measures have been shown to exhibit some relationship with brand recognition, but not with brand recall or brand attitude. Quantitative testing methods (focus groups, in-depth interviews, and such) give an insight into purchasing behaviour and generate ideas in the development of MARCOMS, but they are not appropriate when testing brand strength or evaluating effects.

Processing measures are immediate responses to a campaign and involve learning, attention, emotional responses, and acceptance. These are focused on the MARCOMS rather than the brand and should be conducted directly after exposure, which means that they are more suitable for pre-tests than post-tests as such responses are transient. An acceptance measure is when a person agrees with the benefit or claim being made in the MARCOMS or the brand. The two main measures of acceptance are cognitive response measurements and adjective checklist measures. The **adjective checklist list** (ACL) is made up of a list of descriptions from which the respondent can check which they agree or disagree with. It has been found that ACLs can be used as diagnostic tools to predict performance either in pre-tests or post-tests. The cognitive response measurement (CRM) also measures attention, but uses open-ended questions, where respondents are asked orally or in writing about their thoughts immediately after exposure and the test is widely used by practitioners.

Communication effects measures are relatively enduring mental associations connected to a brand and can be used as both pre- and post-tests. There are five effects that can be measured according to Rossiter and Percy (1997): category need, brand awareness, brand attitude, brand purchase intention, and purchase facilitation. The **category need** is when the buyer sees the category as a solution to a need, wherefore it requires a perceived connection between product and buyer motivation. **Brand awareness** is when a buyer is aware of a brand within a purchase category and is a prerequisite for purchase and for the formation of brand attitude. **Brand attitude** is an overall positive or negative evaluation of the brand relative to other brands. **Brand purchase intention** is measured by asking whether respondents have the intention of purchasing a product in a given category within a certain period of time. **Brand purchase facilitation** identifies whether there are any hindrances to purchasing the brand in the marketplace (e.g., poor distribution).

The final stage is **monitoring**, which involves tracking MARCOMS effectiveness in the market over time. It generally involves measuring the brand, competitor brands, promotions, media spending, and trade activity. Monitoring is commonly done on an ad hoc basis. Continuous monitoring is preferable and involves weekly, biweekly, or monthly interviews with small samples of buyers over the campaign period and after. This enables a relatively continuous and more sensitive measure of effect. Unfortunately, relatively few firms are prepared to devote sufficient resources to do so and receive the feedback loop to the development of the next campaign (see Figure 11.4).

International

International issues with MARCOMS strategy generally relate to advertising as few clients treat direct marketing, sales promotions, or PR from a global perspective, given the logistical problems (e.g., rules and regulations surrounding sales promotions make it virtually impossible to have standardization). Aside from setting budgets (Prendergast et al., 2006), the key perspective is the choice between the **glocal** approach of 'thinking global, but acting local' (coined by Akio Morita, the founder of Sony) in contrast to Levitt's (1983) view that the world is one global marketplace where consumers have similar needs and where companies should standardize their mix. Issues around the application of strategy remain salient. For example, campaigns showing people drinking alone or with friends can have different meanings, depending on the country and its culture (e.g., in Nigeria). This leads to the main issue facing international clients of whether to standardize or customize their MARCOMS. Most international marketing strategies have elements of both approaches.

The main argument for a localized strategy of advertising is effectiveness. Advertising may need to be localized because of powerful forces in the environment such as culture, education, and marketing elements such as the product life cycle. The main arguments for a standardization of global advertising are centred on the questions of consistency, quality control, and efficiency. However, it has also been argued that despite cultural differences, product categories have many similar characteristics (especially in business-to-business markets).

Conclusion

Advertising and direct marketing have the largest impacts on brand value by building relationships with customers, whereas PR (and increasingly MPR—marketing public relations) helps construct visibility, raising credibility, and ultimately building reputation. Sales Promotions can have strategic effects, but in practice, are largely used for short-term inducements to purchase, and the evidence suggests, with little long-term effect. The process of undertaking a MARCOMS strategy involves conducting an audit, developing the central strategy, and then deciding upon the appropriate creative and media choices. The key issue facing international organizations is the extent to which they can and should standardize or customize their communications.

Summary

MARCOMS primarily consist of four media: advertising, direct marketing, PR, and sales promotions, which can be used in marketing strategy either singularly or holistically with IMC (integrated marketing communications). While MARCOMS can enable organizations to reduce costs in the medium to long term, their main strategic use is in helping to differentiate and position.

KEY TERMS

Advertising A paid-for form of communication using a medium with an identified sponsor. Generally of long-term impact.

Creative brief A summation of the MARCOMS task in order to manage and stimulate the development of creative work to address the task.

Creative execution Translation of the proposition to a tangible form.

Direct marketing An activity involving the recording, tracking, and analysis over time of customers' responses to specific communications. Generally used to build relationships with stakeholders (key ones being customers, suppliers, and staff).

IMC A concept that recognizes the added value of a comprehensive plan that evaluates the strategic roles of a variety of communications disciplines holistically.

Medium class A type of medium such as TV, newspapers, or direct mail.

Medium vehicle A choice of medium or media within a class, such as the choice between the *Daily Mail*or the *Daily Mirror* newspapers in the UK.

Proposition A single-minded and concise statement of what is to be communicated about the product or service in the MARCOMS.

Public relations A planned activity to establish and maintain goodwill and mutual understanding between an organization and its immediate and wider stakeholders.

Sales promotions An offer or incentive of extra value for a product or service to staff, distributors, or the buyer. Generally of short-term impact.

Q DISCUSSION QUESTIONS

1 What are the pros and cons of approaching MARCOMS strategy from an IMC perspective?
2 Think of two recent MARCOMS campaigns that featured the campaigning organizations' values. What insight do you think the client had to use such an appeal from the Brand Wheel?
3 Identify three brands that you consider to have high awareness but are performing relatively badly in the marketplace. What would you recommend from a MARCOMS standpoint?
4 Select one of the leading supermarket chains and develop five different potential propositions for the brand based upon: (a) user characteristics; (b) surprising points about the service; (c) price characteristics; (d) disadvantage of non-use; and, (e) direct comparison with rivals. Which one would you choose to develop a campaign upon and why?
5 You have a local cinema as a client. Examine the case for spending their budget in a concentrated burst versus a drip campaign.

ONLINE RESOURCE CENTRE

Visit the Online Resource Centre for this book for lots of interesting additional material at: **www.oxfordtextbooks.co.uk/orc/west2e/**

REFERENCES AND FURTHER READING

Bernardin, Thomas, and Paul Kemp-Robertson (2008), 'Wildfire 2008: Creativity with a Human Touch', *Journal of Advertising*, 37 (3), pp. 131–5.

Berthon, Pierre, Leyland Pitt, and Colin Campbell (2008), 'Ad Lib: When Customers Create the Ad', *California Management Review*, 50 (4), pp. 6–30.

Broadbent, Simon (1999), *When to Advertise* (Henley-on-Thames: NTC).

Duncan, Tom (2005), *Principles of Advertising and IMC* (New York: McGraw-Hill Irwin).

El-Murad, Jaafar, and Douglas C. West (2003), 'Risk and Creativity in Advertising', *Journal of Marketing Management*, 19 (5–6), pp. 657–73.

El-Murad, Jaafar, and Douglas C. West (2004), 'The Definition and Measurement of Creativity: What Do We Know?'*Journal of Advertising Research*, 44 (2), pp. 188–201.

Erdogan, B. Zater, Michael J. Baker, and Stephen Tagg (2001), 'Selecting Celebrity Endorsers: The Practitioner's Perspective', *Journal of Advertising Research*, 41 (3), pp. 39–49.

Farris, Paul, and Douglas C. West (2007), 'A Fresh View of the Advertising Budget Process', in Gerard J. Tellis, and Tim Ambler (eds), *The SAGE Handbook of Advertising* (London: SAGE), pp. 316–32.

Kohli, Chiranjeev, Lance Leuthesser, and Rajneesh Suri (2007), 'Got Slogan? Guidelines for Creating Effective Slogans', *Business Horizons*, 50, pp. 415–22.

Levitt, Theodore (1983), 'The Globalisation of Markets', *Harvard Business Review*, May, pp. 92–102.

McGrath, John M. (2005), 'IMC at a Crossroads: A Theoretical Review and a Conceptual Framework for Testing', *Marketing Management Journal*, 15 (2), pp. 55–66.

Mohr, Iris (2007), 'Buzz Marketing for Movies', *Business Horizons*, 50, pp. 395–403.

Ogilvy, David (1987), *Confessions of an Advertising Man*, 2nd edn (New York: Macmillan).

Peltier, James W., Barbara Mueller, and Richard G. Rosen (1992), 'Direct Response versus Image Advertising', *Journal of Direct Marketing*, 6 (1), pp. 49–66.

Piercy, Nigel F. (1986), *Marketing Budgeting*(Dover, NH: Croom Helm).

Porter, Michael E. (1980), *Competitive Strategy: Techniques for Analyzing Industries and Competitors* (New York: The Free Press).

Prendergast, Gerard, Douglas West, and Yi-Zheng Shi (2006), 'Advertising Budgeting Methods and Processes in China', *Journal of Advertising*, 35 (3), pp. 165–76.

Prescott, Dan (1991), 'Public Relations at General Motors: An Integrated Marketing Communications Approach', MA, University of Colorado School of Journalism and Mass Communication, cited in Thomas R. Duncan and Stephen E. Everett (1993), 'Client Perceptions of Integrated Marketing Communications', *Journal of Advertising Research*, 33 (3), pp. 30–40.

Ray, Michael L., andPeter H. Webb (1986), 'Three Prescriptions for Clutter', *Journal of Advertising Research*, 26 (1), pp. 69–77.

Reeves, Rosser (1961), *Reality in Advertising* (New York: Alfred A. Knopf).

Ries, A., and J. Trout (1981), *Positioning: The Battle for your Mind* (New York: Warner Books/McGraw-Hill Inc.).

Robinson, David (2006), 'Public Relations Comes of Age', *Business Horizons*, 49, pp. 247–56.

Rossiter, John R., and Larry Percy (1997), *Advertising Communication and Promotion Management* (New York: McGraw-Hill).

Schultz, Don E. (1996), 'The Inevitability of Integrated Marketing Communications', *Journal of Business Research*, 37, pp. 139–46.

Schultz, Don E., and Heidi F. Schultz (2004), *IMC: The Next Generation* (New York: McGraw-Hill).

Stewart, David W. (1996), 'Market-back Approach to the Message of Integrated Communications Programs: A Change to the Paradigm and a Focus on Determinants of Success', *Journal of Business Research*, 37, pp. 147–53.

Thomas (Jr), Greg Metz (2004), 'Building the Buzz in the Hive Mind', *Journal of Consumer Behaviour*, 4 (1), pp. 64–72.

Vakratsas, Demetrios, and Tim Ambler (1999), 'How Advertising Works: What do we Really Know?'*Journal of Marketing*, 63 (1), pp. 26–44.

West, Douglas C., (1993), 'Cross-national Creative Personalities, Processes and Agency Philosophies', *Journal of Advertising Research*, 33 (5), pp. 53–62.

West, Douglas (1994), 'Restricted Creativity: Advertising Agency Work Practices in the US, Canada and the UK', *Journal of Creative Behavior*, 27 (3), pp. 200–13.

West, Douglas C. (1999), '360° of Creative Risk: An Agency Theory Perspective', *Journal of Advertising Research*, 39 (1), pp. 39–50.

West, Douglas C., and Pierre Berthon (1997), 'Antecedents of Risk-taking Behavior by Advertisers: Empirical Evidence and Management Implications', *Journal of Advertising Research*, 37 (5), pp. 27–40.

West, Douglas C., and John Ford (2001), 'Advertising Agency Philosophies and Employee Risk-taking', *Journal of Advertising*, 30 (1), pp. 77–91.

West, Douglas C., Arthur J. Kover, and Albert Caruana (2008), 'Practitioner and Customer Views of Advertising Creativity: Same Concept, Different Meaning', *Journal of Advertising*, 37 (4), pp. 35–45.

KEY ARTICLE ABSTRACTS

Barnes, Bradley, and Maki Yamamoto (2008), 'Exploring International Cosmetics Advertising in Japan', ***Journal of Marketing Management***, 24 (3/4), pp. 299–316.

This paper suggests that the Japanese market needs a greater degree of localization than might be the case in the UK. As such, agencies need to take extra care when designing cosmetics advertisements and focus more on an indirect soft sell in order to appeal to the emotional needs of the image status of the Japanese consumer.

Abstract: The Japanese cosmetics market is the second largest in the world and in 2003 was valued at approximately 1.9 trillion yen. The sector is also the largest consumer of advertising in Japan (receipts exceeding 35 million yen in 2003). Despite its size and significance, research in this area is somewhat scant. To bridge the gap, the research reports the findings of an investigation designed to explore the impact of cosmetics advertising on female Japanese consumers. The findings reveal that, despite their frequent usage in ads, celebrities fail to influence purchase decisions. Specific reference groups, including experts, friends, and female family members have varying degrees of influence. However, the sample of female Japanese respondents appears to be unconvinced when such reference sources are adopted in advertising. There was some preference for western brands and music, but not models. Magazines represent the most suitable media for influencing Japanese women, while TV is less effective, despite its relatively high cost.

Erdogan, B. Zafer, and Michael J. Baker (2000), 'Towards a Practitioner-based Model of Selecting Celebrity Endorsers', ***International Journal of Advertising***, 19 (1), pp. 25–43.

This paper reminds us that the reality of much strategic marketing is cultural and normative in scope and practice. In this case, the authors examine the process of selecting celebrity endorsers, which turns out to be a largely unceremonious process.

Abstract: Use of celebrity endorsers has become a widely employed marketing communication strategy. One of the key issues of this strategy is to decide which celebrity to employ. Even though scholars, mostly US-based, have written about the celebrity endorsement strategy and effective endorser characteristics, so far no studies have explored how advertising agencies select celebrity endorsers. To discover the process by which advertising agencies select celebrities and factors considered during this process, semi-structured interviews were carried out. Findings indicate that there is an unwritten and informal process of selecting celebrity endorsers, in which there are a number of factors affecting decisions.

Kitchen, Philip J., and Don E. Schultz (1998), 'IMC—A UK Ad Agency Perspective', *Journal of Marketing Management*, 14 (4/5), pp. 465–86.

This paper explores a number of themes related to integrated marketing communications. In particular the difficulties of measuring its effect, the problems of integrating the PR function, and its value in providing consistency, impact, and continuity.

Abstract: This paper concerns integrated marketing communications (IMC) in terms of its theoretical background, and by providing initial findings from an exploratory study of IMC within a judgement sample of UK advertising agencies (total estimated billings—£3.5 billion). We consider arguments put forward by academics and practitioners in relation to what IMC is perceived to be, and whether it offers significant value to ad agencies and their clients in the dynamic MARCOMS marketspace leading toward the next century. Research findings show that IMC is not a short-term managerial fad, nor is it just a reformulation of existent praxis. Instead, IMC offers a clear response by advertising agencies and their clients driven by a constellation of factors: new forms of information technology (including development and usage of databases), media fragmentation, client desires for interaction/synergy, and global and regional coordination. The paper concludes by stating that IMC is a fundamental, probably irreversible, shift in both the thinking and practice of ad agencies and their clients, as reflected by advertising executives. IMC is driven by technological development, customers, consumers, and by organizational drive to properly allocate finite resources to the key element of creating exchanges—marketing communications.

Percy, Larry (2004), 'Advertising and the Seven Sins of Memory', *International Journal of Advertising*, 23 (4), pp. 413–27.

Effective communication inevitably confronts the problem of memory. This paper examines Schacter's framework and provides a series of suggestions on how to overcome the hurdle. Suggestions include ensuring a consistent look and feel to your advertising over time and using distinctive cues not associated with long-term memory.

Abstract: A positive intention may be formed as a result of exposure to an advertisement, but if a memory malfunction interferes with that intention, the advertising will be ineffective. This paper considers the implications for advertisers of Daniel Schacter's 'seven sins of memory': transcience, absent-mindedness, blocking, misattribution, suggestibility, bias, and persistence. Each of the 'sins' is explained in detail and advice provided for advertisers on how to avoid these pitfalls.

END OF CHAPTER 11 CASE STUDY dothetest

Nigel Hanlon of Transport for London (TfL) went into his office in Victoria with a nagging worry. He had just been briefed by his clients (Road Safety Unit and Surface Transport) with the aim of reducing the number of cyclist KSIs (killed or seriously injured), whilst attempting at the same time to grow the number of cycling trips in London by 400 per cent by 2025. His worry was that by increasing the number of cyclists on the roads, the number of KSIs would increase. Despite the falling KSIs in recent years, the evidence suggested that people felt cycling was an increasingly unsafe thing to do and reports of cyclist deaths in London's press continued to raise awareness of the dangers. TfL wasn't advocating cycling just in the busy centre of London, as much as cycling in general in the boroughs, where the roads were generally wider and there is less traffic and, in particular, fewer lorries (which are a key problem for cyclists).

Nigel also wanted drivers to reappraise their behaviour and to take extra account of cyclists. However, it was also brought to his attention by his clients that cyclists also 

need to re-evaluate their behaviour and understand that they were not always easy to see and, rightly or wrongly, cyclists often got a bad press when they jumped lights or cycled on the pavements. While a lot of this occurred because cyclists often felt under pressure from drivers, it nevertheless gave a general impression that cyclists were uncontrollable.

WCRS

Two days later, Nigel went across London to see Fergus Adam at the WCRS advertising agency near Oxford Circus tube station, who was appraising the problem with a view to conducting an advertising campaign for TfL. Fergus was Group Account Director with overall responsibility for managing and briefing the team at WCRS (Planning Director: Giselle Okin; Head of Digital Planning: Laurence Parkes; Art Directors: Kit Drayman, Vince Chasteauneuf; Copywriters: Tom Spicer, Simon Aldridge). He began with the idea that, overall, Londoners and commuters needed more confidence in cycling. Fergus argued that the perception of the likelihood of having an accident on a bicycle was far greater than the likelihood of it happening to anyone.

Road safety campaigns

Road safety campaigns have a well-trodden path involving showing an accident or the aftermaths of an accident. One area that kept surfacing in the discussions between Nigel and Fergus was why, when cyclists even wore bright florescent clothing (though a good number do not), drivers frequently said that they just did not see them. However, the Road Safety Unit at TFl isalways interested in looking at new angles to help drive behaviour change and Nigel was aware of other work being undertaken by TfL Marketing colleagues on motorcyclist safety that was based on research that drivers were very good at judging the speed of large objects, but very poor at judging the speed of small ones. How good were they at seeing cyclists?

Attention blindness

As part of the research process, Fergus came across a variety of research studies (for a summary, see Lawton, 2007) that showed a common 'attention blindness'—when you concentrate on one particular thing, you tend to miss other things. For example, Lawton cites a study where a passerby asked a stranger for directions. As the stranger spoke, two workmen rudely barged between them carrying a door. Then, in the moment that the passerby was behind the door, he switched places with one of the workmen. The stranger was left giving directions to a different person, who was taller, wearing different clothes, and had a different voice. Do you think you would notice? When researchers at Harvard University played this trick on 15 unsuspecting people, 8 of them failed to spot the change.

Thus, both Nigel and Fergus agreed, for such a message to have any impact, it had to be experienced rather than told. However, they were keen to avoid the usual 'path of blame', where either the cyclist or driver is deemed to be at fault. Why? Because attention blindness is the reality and it is incredibly easy to miss a cyclist, whatever they are wearing and however bright their lights are. At the root of the problem are the primary concerns of drivers. Most drivers are worried about larger vehicles. Car drivers worry about vans; van drivers worry about heavy goods vehicles (HGVs); HGV drivers worry about lorries; lorry drivers worry about artic lorries. Consequently, the cyclist is at the bottom of their concerns.

Nigel appreciated the idea of attention deficit straight away when Fergus showed him the campaign. The 'eureka moment' was recognizing the application of attention blindness to cycling safety. Nigel took the attention blindness idea to his marketing colleagues and clients (Road Safety Unit and Surface Transport) at TfL who loved the idea. They could easily see how this technique, backed up by the scientific methods, would make a strong point to both cyclists and drivers without attaching any blame to either party. The project was agreed.

The campaign

The commercial was called 'dothetest'. It took as inspiration some of the earlier studies on attention blindness. It was directed by Chris Palmer for Gorgeous Production. The target group was skewed towards the young but encompassed just about everyone who cycled or drove or did both. One of the risks was that it broke the traditional mould of road safety campaigns, with no bicycles or accidents involved. The campaign was pre-tested by WCRS, including with their own staff, who were asked not to mention the concept to anyone prior to broadcast. It was clear straight away that the ad was working well. People were experiencing attention blindness for themselves.

The budget was limited to £300,000. Because the commercial only needs to be watched once for maximum impact, most of the media budget was spent on five prime-time TV slots placed by MEC, the TfL media planning and buying agency. In essence, the TV commercial launched the campaign, with online and viral work providing the mainstay.

In order to give the ad a sense of an event as it had such a limited showing, TFL needed to create some buzz around the ad and so the TV commercials were preceded by a two-day teaser press campaign in the London newspapers to 'drive' people to the TV spots. On the day of the campaign, people dressed in basketball clothing waited at busy London thoroughfares and handed out flyers to travellers. No press releases were provided. However, TV was not going to provide the coverage required, and so, given the relatively small budget, there was an extensive digital media plan by social media experts at WCRS involving seeding on a number of community and video sites (such as YouTube), with the intention of highlighting it to motoring and cycling bloggers. It was also planted as a pay-per-click social ad on Facebook, targeted towards London-based cyclists and motorists. TFL also utilized posters at bus stops to drive additional traffic to the online campaign.

The result?

Within the first six months, 22 per cent of Londoners reported seeing it and, most importantly, had changed their behaviour by looking out for cyclists more carefully and cyclists became more aware of the driver 'blindspot'. The media coverage amplified the campaign with stories in such papers as *The Observer* with features on BBC London and London Tonight on ITV1 and even as far afield as ABC News in the US. In terms of hits, the campaign has generated over 13 million views online (and rising) and more than 6,000 people rated it, hundreds of people have loaded up the commercial and posted it as their own and many have done their own version of 'dothetest'.

The campaign has had a phenomenal impact, especially for such a small media spend. The central creative leap was to connect attention blindness to cycling safety. In recognition of this, the campaign has started to win accolades such as at the Cannes Gold and two Golds at the Kinsale awards, and a New Media Age award for best use of viral marketing. TfL was voted 'Advertiser of the Year 2008' by the leading advertising trade *Campaign* (partly for this and partly for other work undertaken: see the Exhibit in Figure C11.2).

Source: This case was prepared by Douglas West of the University of Birmingham as the basis for analysis and class discussion and not to illustrate either effective or ineffective handling of an administrative situation.

QUESTIONS

TfL has no intention of resting on its laurels. Nigel and Fergus have put a meeting in their diary to discuss how to capitalize on the success of the campaign and to keep the momentum going. They are less concerned about execution than making sure that the central message has impact and remains real. Shortly before the meeting, Nigel sends Fergus an email asking:

1. What should be the next stage of the communications strategy?
2. Should we do more of the same or should the strategy change with a move away from awareness blindness?

References

Lawton, Graham (2007), 'Mind Tricks: Six Ways to Explore your Brain', *New Scientist*, 19 September, pp. 34–41.

You can see the TfL commercial (and the follow-up commercial) at: **http://www.dothetest.co.uk/**

You can see the University of Illinois at Urbana-Champaign attention blindness demonstration at: **http://www.viscog.beckman.uiuc.edu/grafs/demos/15.html**

Marketing communications brief

0435—Cycling Safety

1. Is this brief:

- A new campaign ☐
- An update to, or extension of, an existing piece of communication ☐
- An ad hoc specific request, ☐ if so, please detail: ____________

2. Which business objective will this activity contribute to?

- Surface Transport Strategic Goal is to: Make travel more accessible, safe and secure to users
- Road Safety Priority is to support the Government and Mayor of London's target to reduce Pedal Cyclist casualties by 50% by 2010
- Surface Transport Marketing priority is to: increase security and safety and reduce road casualties.

3. Describe the relevant background to aid proper understanding of this brief.

- Pedal cyclists have the second highest casualty rate per 100 million vehicle kilometres after powered two-wheelers. It is therefore a key priority within Surface Transport and TfL to reduce this in line with the mayor's objective. A number of initiatives have been developed over the years to try to tackle this problem and this umbrella brief has been written to develop a more structured and integrated programme of activity.
- In 42% of fatal collisions the pedal cyclist was in collision with a car and in 32% with a heavy goods vehicle.[1] The aim of this campaign is to change attitudes and behaviours of all current and potential cyclists to actively reduce casualties.

Figure C11.1 WCRS brief for TFL

1. Pedal cyclist casualties in Greater London April 2005 Fact sheet.

Figure C11.2 Exhibit: examples of TfL campaigns, including 'dothetest'

- The number of cyclist fatalities decreased from 21 to 19 between 2005 and 2006; however, they were still above the 1994–1998 average. They show a year-on-year fluctuation. These changes should be seen in the context of substantially increased cycle usage especially in central and inner London. (Stats available to highlight this information.)
- Customer insight research conducted into Londoner's attitudes to cycling showed that safety is a key issue as to why people do not cycle in London. A third of cyclists do not feel safe from accidents during the day (with little alteration between night and day). This perception may be exacerbated by media reporting of cycle fatalities.
- 85% of Londoners feel traffic makes people afraid of cycling in London.
- Whilst we need to highlight the dangers to ensure cyclists cycle safer and smarter, we also need to be careful that we do not scare people into being too afraid of getting on their bikes in London.
- As well as this, it has been noted that due to the increasing numbers of cyclists on the road there is a need to educate those new to this mode about cycling safety.
- *A campaign already exists that has aimed to engender respect between cyclists and other road users.*

4. **What is the overall strategic direction for the parent brand?**

   TfL wants to be seen to deliver better transport in London, provide a comprehensive service, be inclusive and equitable, and striving to achieve the highest standards.

5. **Who are we targeting?**

   - Motorists and other road users (specifically cars and HGVs)—to be aware of cyclists on the road and their vulnerability.
   - Cyclists (current and potential). 79% of all KSI cyclists are male (age report breakdown available for frequency of casualties)

6. **Is this to persuade, inform or tell?**

   - Persuade ☐ Inform ☐ Tell ☐

   And what is it that we want them to do, think, or know as a result of this activity?
   Cycling can be safe if the right responsible steps are taken to understand the dangers of travelling near to, or alongside cars, HGVs, and other large vehicles.

7. **How will this activity contribute to achieving our social inclusion aims?**

   This activity will be aimed at all road users, irrespective of race.

8. **What is the single-minded proposition?**

   Are you closer than you think?

9. **What supports this?**

   Other vehicles were the primary cause of collision in the majority of cases; in 42% of fatal collisions the P/C was in collision with a car and in 32% with a heavy goods vehicle.
   - The most common fatal P/C collision (32%) involved the P/C and other vehicle travelling alongside each other.

Figure C11.1 cont.

- 16% involved the P/C moving from the nearside to the offside across the path of the other vehicle.
- 11% were killed when either hitting or swerving to avoid a door being opened into their path.

(All these statistics sourced from Pedal cyclist casualties in Greater London LRSU April 2005 Fact sheet.)

Recently, Surface Transport in partnership with others has been working on a Share the Road campaign tackling some of these issues.The campaign highlights issues around cycling on pavements, vehicles, and cyclists making room for each other and cyclists stopping at red lights.The London Road Safety Unit several years ago pioneered an ongoing initiative to highlight the dangers faced when HGVs [were] turning left.Working in partnership with hauliers, lorry posters and leaflets have been produced giving cyclists and drivers reminders about lorry blind spots.

A lot of work has also been done on increasing levels of awareness on the road for both cyclists and HGVs as this is a high cause of collisions and injuries amongst cyclists.

10. What tone of voice should be used?

Bold, honest, direct, and caring.

11. What operational, seasonal, legal, or environmental factors need to be considered?

Safety is still the main barrier to persuading people to consider or reconsider cycling. It must steer clear of adopting a moral stance in judging any particular road user or by apportioning 'blame' to any particular party.

12. Mandatory inclusions/exclusions?

- Communication should engage with its target audience whilst reflecting London's diversity, both in terms of its people and its places. Avoid tokenism, deliver the right balance overall. Show parts of London people enjoy and aspire to make this attainable rather than elitist. Unless it is a specific requirement, do not show 'tourist London'; focus on modern, everyday London. Do not show only the city centre; outer London is just as important.
- Develop materials as part of the campaign to support LRSU and the educational team, including the yellow HGV stickers and relevant leaflets.
- For this campaign to carry weight it must be seen to have the support of road user organisations involving links with FORS and CCE.
- Every use should be made of free media such as DR bus/Tube/Tram circuits, Metro, and The Londoner, as well as the TfL website.The Tfl press office should be worked with closely to ensure press coverage is as widespread as possible.

13. How is the effectiveness of this activity to be measured?

Using STATS 19 to measure a reduction in cyclist KSIs towards the 2010 target of 50% from the baseline.

Use LRSU Accstats data to provide statistics on the number of pedal cyclist casualties by severity.

Figure C11.1 cont.

14. When is the activity to appear in the marketplace?

Spring 2008.

15. Budget (split design/production/media as appropriate)?

To be confirmed.

16. What are the key dates/milestones for this project?

Activity must be booked and in the marketplace prior to March 31st, 2008.

12

E-marketing strategies

LEARNING OBJECTIVES

- Provide an overview of e-marketing strategy
- Examine the impact of e-marketing strategy on industry structure and profitability
- Assess the role of e-marketing on competitive advantage
- Review global issues related to e-marketing

CHAPTER AT A GLANCE

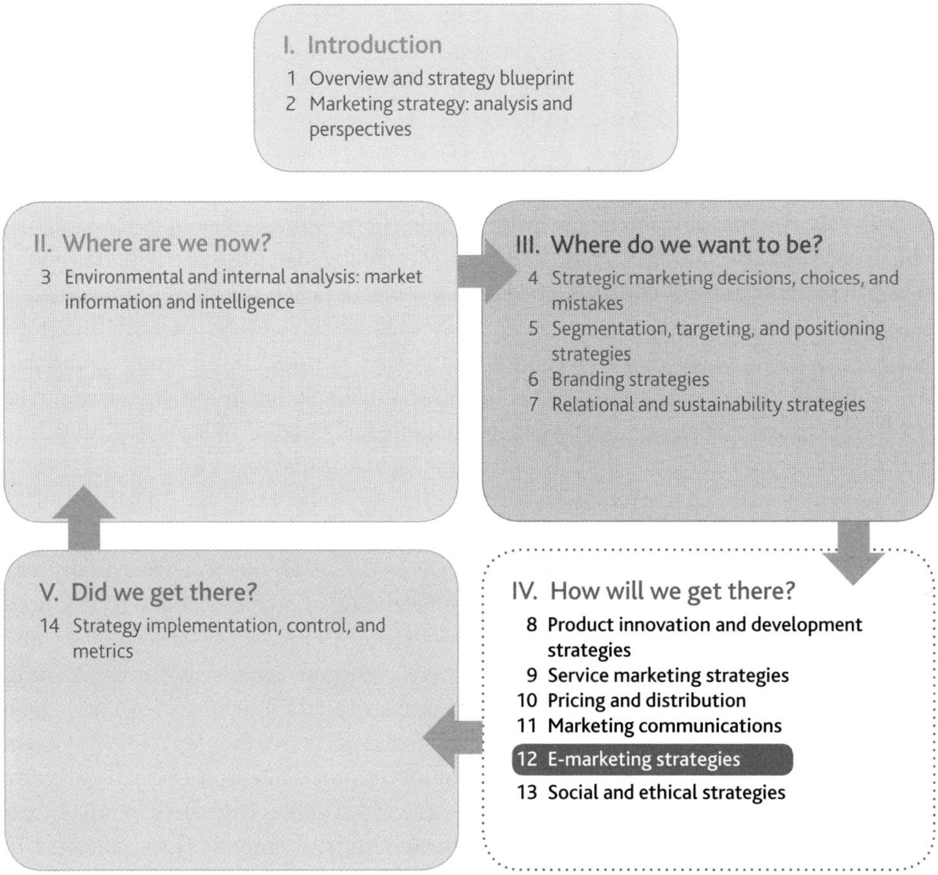

Introduction

Rosenbloom (2002) has suggested that many of the 'new paradigms' attached to e-marketing have been disproved and Porter (2001) has forcefully argued that the fundamentals of strategy remain unaltered. He argued that e-marketing can only be used to create value if companies focus on: (1) industry structure, which determines profitability; and, (2) find a sustainable competitive advantage (SCA), which will allow a company to outperform the average. (Industry structure is determined by the five underlying forces of competition: rivalry, the bargaining power of suppliers and buyers respectively, barriers to entry for new competitors, and the threat of substitutes.)

When it comes to industry structure and profitability, many of the trends from Internet technology are negative. For example, buyers have more information, there is a reduced need for a sales force or established channels, barriers to entry are reduced, and there is the potential for greater substitution and intensive rivalry with the open system of the Internet.

However, on the positive side, the Internet has dampened the bargaining power of channels as companies go direct to customers and as overall efficiency has increased, many markets have expanded. The problem is that while markets have expanded, many companies have found that Internet technologies have made it more difficult to capture the profits. For example, in the PC market, customers have more information and choice, but pure-play online sellers find it extremely difficult to differentiate as they often lack retail outlets, service departments, or personal selling.

Turning to competitive advantage, the Internet offers considerable scope for operating at a lower cost, commanding a premium price or doing both. Thus, Oxfam introduced its first online newsletter to cut costs on postal services. Meanwhile, the monthly newsletter sent to several hundred-thousand donors is personalized to match closely the interests of individual supporters. However, Internet operational advantages are often easily copied and so there has been considerable convergence. There is no durable advantage from Internet operational efficiency. Thus, strategic positioning has become increasingly important. If you cannot be operationally more efficient, the only way to generate higher levels of economic value is to gain a cost advantage or price premium by competing in a *distinctive* way.

Thus, strategy goes far beyond best practice. The Royal Opera House (ROH) uses SMS (short message service—texting) and the Internet to boost theatre attendance. As part of the plan, the ROH encourages visitors to 'My Royal Opera House' at: **http://www.roh.org.uk/myroyaloperahouse/index.aspx** to build a profile and set of preferences and receive notifications of forthcoming events and free open air events, TV broadcasts, special offers, and promotions. In the housing market, rightmove (**www.rightmove.co.uk**) uses an e-CRM facility, which automatically notifies customers with 'property alerts' by email when a new home becomes available that exactly matches their specified criteria (see Figure 12.1). The system is designed to take over the house-hunting process for customers by ensuring that they receive only information which matches their exact needs. It also allows customers to refine their property searches to specific price bands and precise locations, property types, and sizes. In such ways, organizations can use e-marketing tools to deliver a tailored and integrated value chain. In the UK, the top uses of the Internet are email, finding information about goods or services, travel and accommodation, Internet banking, and reading news and magazines.

According to Porter (2001), the way to use Internet architecture is to customize packages based on a company's unique strategic position by providing a common IT delivery platform across the value chain. Out-of-the-box packages on the Internet will not work—competitive advantage rests on tailoring. Overall, the indications are that organizations that treat the Internet as an **evolutionary** force outperform organizations that see it as a **revolutionary** one. A good example would be Avis, Europe's largest car rental company, which has developed newsletter templates used by regional offices across fourteen European countries to boost online reservations and reduce costs.

To sum up, the impact of the Internet on marketing strategy has been as follows:

- bargaining power of channels has been dampened
- barriers to entry have been reduced
- buyers have more information
- efficiency has increased
- there is greater substitution and intense competition

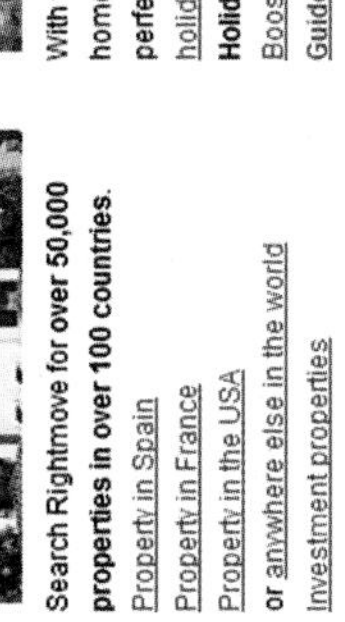

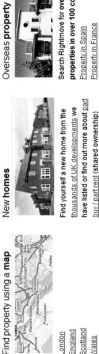

Figure 12.1 Rightmove

Source: By permission of The Rightmove Group Ltd.

- many markets have expanded
- it is more difficult to capture profits
- there is more scope for operating at a lower cost, commanding a premium price, or doing both
- there is reduced need for sales force or established channels.

E-markets

Customers

The numbers of people with access to the Internet has grown significantly. Take the case of the UK. Just 9 per cent (2 million) of households in 1998 could access the Internet. This had risen to 46 per cent (11 million) by 2002 and grew further to 65 per cent (16 million) by the end of 2008 (see Figure 12.2).

The most successful B2C companies at adapting 'bricks to clicks', such as Tesco, have an ability to integrate marketing, customer service, and use of information and technology in order to deliver a profitable long-term market share or niche strategy (Willcocks and Plant, 2001). But what are the key characteristics of e-markets? One of the key characteristics of the e-marketing environment is that it is largely 'smart' (Glazer, 1999), as opposed to 'dumb' static markets, which are fixed and where information is poor. Smart markets are dynamic, turbulent, and information-rich and are based on new kinds of products, competitors, and customers. As such, some kind of distinctiveness is required to build a sustainable competitive advantage (SCA) in e-marketing (Krishnamurthy, 2006). Brand creation can also be achieved, as with Prudential Assurance and Egg, and depends upon consumer motivation and preference.

According to Wolfinbarger and Gilly (2001), consumer motivation on the Web falls into two categories: (1) 'experiential' for fun; or (2) 'goal directed' for efficiency (see Figure 12.3 for

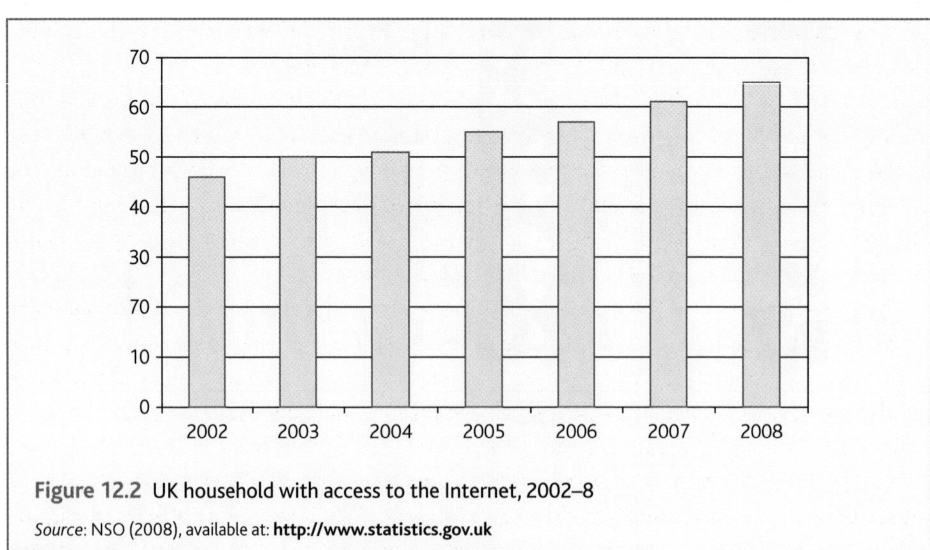

Figure 12.2 UK household with access to the Internet, 2002–8

Source: NSO (2008), available at: **http://www.statistics.gov.uk**

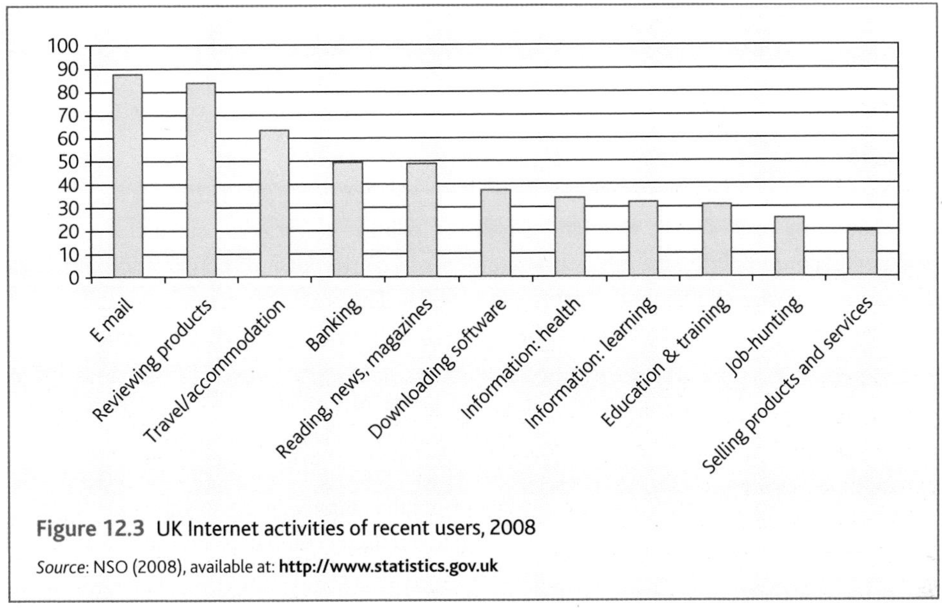

Figure 12.3 UK Internet activities of recent users, 2008

Source: NSO (2008), available at: **http://www.statistics.gov.uk**

the top uses of the Internet in the UK). Experiential behaviour tends to occur when shoppers have a continuing hobby interest. This is all about the 'thrill of the hunt' as much as acquiring items. Goal-orientated shopping is task-orientated, efficient, rational, and deliberate. In terms of numbers, a Harris survey found that just over 70 per cent of online shoppers said that their most recent purchase had been planned, with the remainder saying that they had been browsing and bought on impulse.

Goal-orientated shoppers like convenience and prefer the anonymity of the Web. Experiential behaviour is quite different to goal-orientated. Experiential shoppers are motivated by surprise/excitement/uniqueness, positive sociability, deals, and product involvement. The implications for e-marketing strategy are that shoppers use offline to touch and feel items and enjoy the experience of being 'out', but they might then buy online. The other key thing to note is that only experiential shoppers are interested in the strategies of content and community (and even so, they are the minority). Most shoppers just want the commerce. The goal-focused shopper wants a site that is easy to navigate, packed with information, and has easy transaction processes and quick delivery. However, Zona Research Inc. suggest that after waiting for a Web page to load for just eight seconds, 30 per cent of customers will exit and by twelve seconds, a further 40 per cent will have gone.

The one Achilles heel of the Internet is delivering physical products at the right time. When shoppers need products in a hurry, they head for the bricks-and-mortar outlets, rather than their Web counterparts. Moreover, certain experiences cannot be delivered, in particular goods that need touch, such as clothing and furniture, and shoppers that enjoy the social experience of shopping are unlikely to trade this in for their computers.

Despite this, many service-focused organizations have successfully harnessed the Web to offer a variety of value-added practices to consumers. They have 'personalized', as with BT Yahoo! which enables users to tailor their interface, and with the use of such things as tiered service levels like Dell's 'platinum' services. They have collected information to provide enhancements, as with FEDEX's package tracking and they 'keep it simple' and respond to what customers 'do not like', as with Direct Line's online car insurance quotes.

Judo

Another distinctive characteristic of e-markets is the use of 'Judo'. There are similarities in e-marketing to its use by relatively small companies undertaking product innovation and development. Judo strategy is commonly used as the form of competition amongst e-marketing rivals (Yoffie and Cusumano, 1999). The analogy is made to the art of judo because players attempt to use the strength and weight of their opponents to gain advantage, rather than to exchange blows directly. Sumo matches ('wrestling' each other 'face-to-face' to force the opponent to the ground or 'out of the ring') are what Internet companies try to avoid, as only relatively small players tend to lose in sumo.

Judo strategy is where e-marketers set out to turn to their own advantage their rival's size, strength, and resources using three key principles. Firstly, 'judo players' must be able to move rapidly to uncontested market spaces to avoid direct combat. Next, they must recognize superior force in the market and give way when attacked, rather than 'stand and fight'. Finally, and this is the essence of judo strategy, they must use the weight and strength of their opponents against those same opponents. It might be argued, for example, that President Barack Obama effectively utilized the Internet against initially stronger rivals within the Democratic Party and then against the Republican Party candidate, John McCain. Similarly, Microsoft may have strength in not releasing its underlying code, but if a smaller rival decides to release this code, this action can turn Microsoft's strength into a weakness. Other developers, such as Linux, can then get involved.

Yoffie and Cusumano (1999) illustrate the case with the Netscape Navigator. It was just about the best browser in the marketplace by 1994, but not by very much. Its spectacular early success was based on the first judo principle and moving the battle to where Netscape had an advantage compared to rivals. Netscape's decision was to target early adopters—sophisticated users who already had a high degree of experience of the Internet. By comparison, their rivals offered a complete stack of tools such as dial-up Internet access, a browser, and email. Netscape gave the product away by allowing free educational and non-profit use and many people who downloaded it for a trial period of 90 days never paid for it. This facilitated a rapid market penetration. Its final use of Judo principle #1 was to post a beta version of Netscape on its home page and invite Internet users to try it out and file their comments and complaints. Microsoft was quick to learn Judo principle #1 and released its own browser, Explorer, as a free product bundled with Windows 95. However, Microsoft upped the ante by making Explorer free to all users, including corporations. Netscape responded by using principle #2, being flexible and giving way when attacked directly by a superior force. They decided to target the intranet, and later the extranet markets, and built a deeper e-commerce strategy to shelter from Microsoft's assault. Furthermore, when Microsoft announced it had done a deal with the *Wall Street Journal* to offer special access to Explorer 3.0 users, Netscape rapidly signed up dozens of content providers to deliver interactive Web pages directly to a user's email address.

Moreover, when Netscape realized by late 1996 that it could not continue to develop its own platform against Microsoft, it decided to 'embrace and integrate' with all Microsoft's technologies and servers.

Again, Microsoft demonstrated that it, too, was a master of judo strategy and willingly adopted numerous Internet technologies that Java and Netscape had pioneered, even when they conflicted with Windows. Perhaps the best demonstration of this was Microsoft's decision to bundle AOL online services with Windows 95 in 1996 and undercut the market for its own Microsoft Network (MSN). Later, all online services were given open access to Windows 95.

Finally, principle #3 represents the essence of Judo strategy: use the weight and strength of opponents against themselves. Microsoft's greatest strength was its dominance of the PC operating system market, which enabled it to offer Explorer free on every new PC or network sold in the world. The strategy was to make the operating system, interface, and browser inseparable. One flaw in the strategy was that users with older PCs or networks were unable to use the latest version of Explorer. Thus, Netscape positioned itself as the only browser that supported the entire installed base of Windows—a cross-platform support that included Unix users. In 1998, in another classic judo strategy move, Netscape decided to give away the source code to its new browser, Communicator 5.0. This was akin to Coca-Cola giving away its formula! The only proviso was that anyone using the code had to register any changes with Netscape developers. Being unable to match Microsoft's research base, going to the Web potentially provided Netscape with access to thousands of developers, as with Unix. Microsoft was unable to respond in kind because if it opened up its proprietary code it would lose its market hold.

Netscape was finally purchased by AOL in late 1998. One more judo player was counted 'out'. The basic lesson here is that judo strategy can also be used by opponents and that Microsoft is, despite its sumo image, a masterful exponent. As well, judo strategy may be extended beyond the Internet to other markets, wherever the potential exists to turn a rival's size and strength against itself.

Navigation

At the heart of differentiation is navigation. Navigation is the process of steering between the mass and variety of information in cyberspace. Of course, navigation also occurs in physical commerce. For example, no one reviews all the possible options in buying a shirt or pair of shoes. Instead, consumers rely on suppliers and retailers to help them navigate. However, applied to e-marketing, navigation takes a different form. Over the Internet it is possible to search extensively at negligible cost. Navigation and selection occur independently of physical warehousing and distribution and bricks-and-mortar companies have only a very few advantages (principally in those categories where, as mentioned above, people still prefer to physically shop, such as in the case of clothing). Electronic retailers can focus on navigation and outsourcing and 'pure' navigators like Google, Yahoo!, and Lycos can simply help people make sense of the information (see Mini Case Study 12.1) without being party to any transactions at all, aside from the paid-search element (Laffey, 2007).

MINI CASE STUDY 12.1 Choose your words carefully

The evidence suggests that spending on search continues to be growing as consumers use the Internet to find deals. The world's top search engines, AOL, Ask, Google, ixquick, Sogu, and Yahoo! continue to be popular because advertisers know that they are essentially only talking to people who might be interested in what they have to offer and their campaigns can be updated and measured relatively straightforwardly.

However, it's rarely a short-term fix. It takes considerable planning and application. Another issue to consider is that, as it has become more popular, CPC (cost-per-click) prices have increased, which has meant more detailed analysis of which keywords are providing the highest conversions and which ones to avoid.

Experts in the industry expect the buying of generic keywords like 'cheap hotel' will be replaced by deeper search terms such as '4-day breaks in 3-star hotels in New York'. Instead of buying several hundred-thousand key words, experts foresee a trend for clients to buy several million deeper key words. Increasingly sophisticated analyses are able to correlate particular search words with the requisite phases of the buying cycle. For example, people searching for a washing machine will likely start with broader and inclusive words when they set out to explore the market and may be looking for review sites, etc., and then hone down and be more specific when they are closer to a particular purchase.

The basic requirement is to keep testing words and phrases over and over again until you understand exactly how people search for your products and services. This will bring PPC (pay-per-click) rates down over time, which comes in at about £5 per customer for organic search and considerably more for sponsored search.

Search engine services will develop in unexpected directions, given the myriad of opportunities people's search terms offer. For example, Google's 'Flu Trends' uses certain search terms that are deemed good indicators of flu activity. By geographically aggregating people's search terms, flu outbreaks can be estimated up to two weeks faster than traditional systems and health authorities alerted where specific areas are experiencing outbreaks so that resources can be allocated more effectively.

In another Google example, the company has partnered with UK Trade & Investment (UKTI), HSBC, Royal Mail, Institute of Export (IoE), and Applied Language to form the 'Google Export Adviser' in order to help guide UK SMEs in overcoming barriers to exporting with useful tools and grow internationally. Companies visit the website and type in the name of their product or service and the technology creates a map showing countries where people are actively searching for and talking about it using Google and other sites. The point is that a lot of SMEs are interested in doing business overseas but are put off by the scope of the various markets. They simply cannot match the millions spent by larger companies on market research to investigate international markets. Search technologies offer simple means to identify where smaller companies might have some success. Often, the results are quite unexpected, with Italians having a taste for Stilton cheese and Germans a liking for tartan. For a small fee, Google and its partners will offer to translate websites and offer advice on tax, duty, and customs issues.

Search engines will undoubtedly remain incredibly powerful. However, as social networks such as Twitter and their archives grow, the value of searching for information via an extended social network may start to offer stiff competition. If you are looking for some 

information on a car, advice shared by a leading motor correspondent on Twitter might well be more relevant and valuable to you than sifting through the top search results from your favourite search engine. Successful businesses in the future may well have millions of Facebook, MySpace, and Twitter followers whom they interact with and spend millions on, rather than traditional advertising. What will they do? There are already signs that Twitter will be used to involve customers in brainstorming new products, offering first access to new products, and live customer service. Words will always need to be chosen carefully.

Navigation is the key to profit potential. For example, Amazon.com started out as an online bookseller but has broadened its offering to include music, DVDs, games, electronics, computing and office, homes and gardens, toys, children and baby, jewellery and watches, clothing and shoes, sports and leisure, health and beauty, and DIY and tools. Where will it end? Amazon had its roots in the publishing industry; the unknown limits to the domain in which Amazon.com is the preferred navigator is the reason why the company is now worth more than the entire publishing industry.

Navigation has four dimensions: 'reach', 'affiliation', 'richness' (Evans and Wurster, 1999), and 'range' (Wells and Gobeli, 2003) as shown in Figure 12.4.

Reach

'Reach is the degree to which a firm can manage its value chain activities to connect its customers to an accessible product/service offering' (Wells and Gobeli, 2003). In other words, it is not only the ability of customers to reach the firm but also the firm's ability to reach the customer with its products and services. For example, the music industry for many years marketed, sold, and distributed its product offering while ignoring the digital transmission element. Napster.com seized the initiative by leveraging the opportunities of reach ignored by the record companies for so long. While Napster was seen as a threat, record companies at first failed to appreciate that the model of providing digital downloadable music offered a win-win for both the industry and consumers, given the lowered costs for the companies and the ability for consumers to customize. Where reach is limited through physical

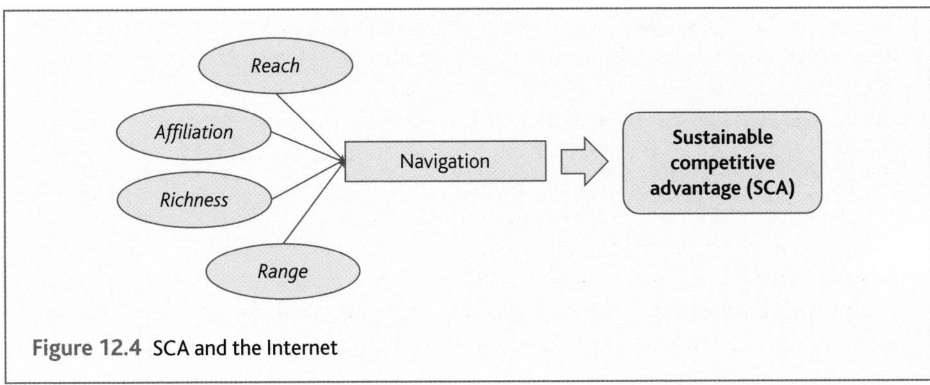

Figure 12.4 SCA and the Internet

incompatibilities, as many supporting processes as possible should at least be digitalized, such as supply-chain management and payment. The collective failure of the music business to see the threat of downloads as an opportunity has resulted in Apple's domination with its iTunes business. Thus, a computer manufacturer, unencumbered with the baggage of seeing music downloads as a threat, won out.

Internet reach is phenomenal. The average music shop carries 30,000 to 50,000 titles, whereas companies like HMV.com offer 100,000s of CDs, DVDs, and games. However, the explosion of reach crosses conventional boundaries with a click of the mouse. E-commerce companies that just mimicked conventional physical retailers found that they lost out to wider navigators. For example, CDNOW.com, one of the earliest e-tailers founded in 1994, carved out a dominant reach-based position on the Internet, only to lose it eventually to Amazon.com which eventually purchased the brand in 2001. With hindsight, it is clear that consumers do not see CDs as a discreet category and the same may be true for many other categories in the traditional physical marketplace. Indeed, many physical retailers of music have branched out into other areas of entertainment based upon digital technologies.

For many suppliers, especially the relatively smaller ones, Internet reach is just fine. Small winemakers have increased their business with wine.com and small bookshops have applauded the success of abebooks.co.uk. Most small suppliers do not want to be in the navigation business, so expanded reach is a blessing for them. By contrast, large suppliers have traditionally used navigation tools, like branding and promotion, in the physical marketplace, to good effect. To lose them to Internet retailers is not a welcome move, but they have to participate in the world of e-commerce. The problem is that, whenever the reach extends beyond a supplier's offering, they will always lose. Thus, no book publisher can match Amazon.com. for reach.

One strategy for the individual supplier to achieve critical mass is to form alliances, as when Universal and BMG (two of the world's largest music companies) formed GetMusic.com. CDs were offered from their own as well as rival companies. Solo efforts would have no chance of succeeding against the likes of Amazon. Reach has to be pursued in its own right and the lines and identity of the site must make intuitive sense to consumers.

Affiliation

Affiliation is based upon trust. It is a by-product of Internet culture and the greater transparency that comes with the visibility of e-commerce with such things as product reviews and price and product comparisons. However, the difference online is that customers cannot tangibly evaluate the physical space of the shop or office concerned (Reichheld and Schefter, 2000). Images and promises are all that they have, and if they do not trust the company concerned, they will shop elsewhere. Moreover, when a customer does trust an online company, they are more likely to share personal information and this information can be used by the company to form a more intimate relationship by providing bespoke goods and services.

Amazon.com has come to dominate e-tailing by creating one of the most reliable and trustworthy of B2C sites. Customers, in their millions, allow Amazon to store their names, addresses, and credit card details so that they can then make repeat purchases with just the click of a mouse. If customers did not trust Amazon to protect their personal details and data, its dominance of the business would be threatened. However, book publishers have long promoted particular books in bookshops and no one has uttered a murmur. But when Amazon.com allowed publishers to pay for superior Web-page placement, the consumer indignation was so strong that the company was forced to publish the details of these arrangements on its home page (Evans and Wurster, 1999).

The issue of affiliation has been compounded by reach. Give a sales agent one sales line and he/she will push it aggressively but as the range increases, the propensity will be to present the range more neutrally. Give the customer the ability to compare sales agents and the propensity to please the customer more than the supplier will increase as, for example, with honestjohn.co.uk and autos.msn.com, which provide buyers with reviews and the information to compare alternate cars on objective criteria. Both sites maintain an objective arms length and are not affiliated to any particular dealers or manufacturers.

Pure navigators are best poised to exploit affiliation. Motley Fool is in a better position to navigate mutual funds than Fidelity because it is not in the business of selling funds. Product suppliers will always lose when it comes to affiliation. However, affiliation is an issue on the Internet as e-commerce runs on the engine of the 'clickstream' (Carr, 2000). For example, an army of owners of specialized content sites that cover a myriad of interests and topics such as football, cosmetics, and dieting make money from click-throughs. For example, the specialist financial website moneysavingexpert.com notes on its website:

> Articles are written purely from a 'what's the best way to save money' stance. Yet, once they're finished one of the team has the job to see if any 'affiliate links' to the top products can be found. While these look and work the same way as normal links; if someone clicks through, the link is tracked and it may generate a payment to the site (sometimes for the click, per user, per application, per accepted application or any combination) ... Where do the links come from? They come from finance comparison sites like Moneysupermarket, MoneyExpert, Uswitch, Moneyextra, Find, Smartquotes or affiliate sites such as Tradedoubler or Commission Junction. Their links are used and then if someone clicks through, this site gets a split of their revenue.

The second types of intermediary that make money are the infrastructure companies that provide the search engines, the advertising networks, the affiliate networks, and the so-called 'backbone' providers, such as Ask.com, Yahoo!, and, most notably, Google. Scale is important to their profits as every click will only deliver a small amount of revenue. However, these businesses quietly collect substantial revenues.

One strategy for product suppliers is to evolve beyond product categories and to use the Internet to offer consumer solutions. The idea is to provide objective data and decision-support software about content unrelated to your own business to mitigate the sense of affiliation. For example, Dell has widened its sales presence with a much broader offering that navigates from the core computer business to peripherals with the provision of objective information about them. Overall, the proposition cements affiliation to Dell while preserving its own product base. Of course, the savvy consumer may use Dell's site for choosing peripherals and the peripheral alliance to choose computers. To preserve their own businesses, sellers may increasingly commoditize each other.

Richness

'Richness is the degree to which a firm can facilitate the exchange of information to deliver products/services that match customers' exact wants and needs' (Wells and Gobeli, 2003). For example, the interaction between a local tailoring shop and its customers is extremely rich as they can easily observe preferences and produce a customized product. The challenge is to identify the attributes conducive to the digital medium and lever them effectively. Timbuk2 is a good example (see Figure 12.5). Manufacturing custom-made messenger bags leveraging IT, Timbuk2 offers customers control over product design, order entry, and production planning. Only bags designed and purchased are manufactured, which lowers their overheads while at the same time providing customers with a customized product. Another example is the Swedish 'Tailorstore' (**www.tailorstore.co.uk**), which offers made-to-measure shirts in a variety of fabrics.

Physical retailers have always had the ability to collect and use information about their customers, but the Internet greatly enhances this aspect. For example, 1-800-flowers.com maintains a customer-specific file with anniversary and birthday information and a record of gifts sent. Customers can be alerted as to an impending birthday and suggest particular flowers. Furthermore, data-mining techniques can be applied to browsing behaviour, as well as purchasing history and building relationships. Purchasing behaviour can be compared

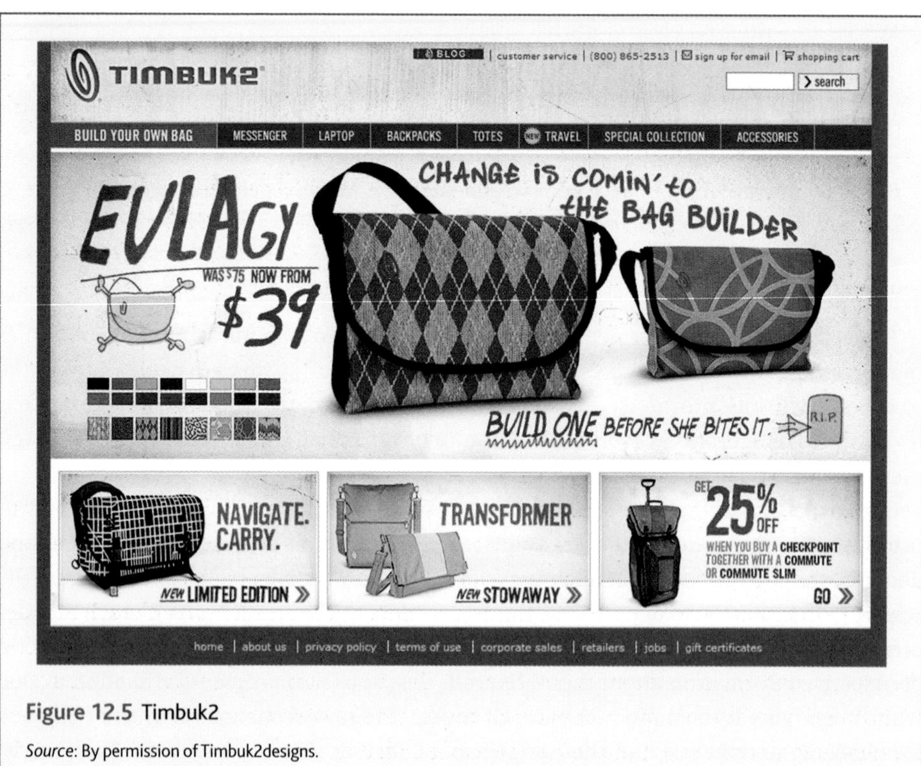

Figure 12.5 Timbuk2

Source: By permission of Timbuk2designs.

between similar customers. Thus, Amazon.com uses 'swarming' technology to compare the titles purchased between two similar buyers and suggest the different titles purchased by each one to each other. Limitations to richness will evolve, especially with legislation on privacy, and the increasing ability of consumers to manipulate their own information (for example, customizing their own estimation of net worth, and possibly selling it). Furthermore, no single player is likely to have the ideal database.

Richness is one area where producers have an edge when related to customer information. Retailers, be they physical or electronic, have most information on consumers, but no one knows the goods or services better than suppliers. For example, in the music industry, it is the record companies that are best at developing information-rich performer biographies, discographies, recording histories, and chat rooms. Much of this information can be placed on websites, provided to retailers or placed on enhanced CDs or DVDs. For example, reviewers often complain that Amazon does not give enough information about a CD or DVD or Blu-ray Disc.

Cross-selling is helped as well as building the brand image of performers. Whether such sites will ever become 'hot' is doubtful as many buyers seem to prefer funky anti-establishment sites. Supplier sites that could become 'hot' are ones involving innovation and rapid product development such as mobile phones, hi-fi, and computer technology. But when objectivity and comprehensiveness matter more, they are unlikely to succeed. Furthermore, hot news and excitement about such product categories as groceries are improbable.

Range

The final issue is range. 'Range is the degree to which a firm can offer its customers a value proposition containing a breadth of products/services' (Wells and Gobeli, 2003). It might be category-specific (narrow) as with Dell, which can offer high customization. It might be cross-category (broad) like Currys, which offers breadth but minimal specialization or customization. Integrating the digital attributes along the product/service offering is the key to strengthening e-strategy with range. The digital medium allows the seamless integration of complementary products and services that were previously difficult or impossible to manage. Thus, travel portals like ebookers.co.uk can offer tickets, car rentals, and hotel reservations in one cohesive package.

IIDC strategic process

Being able, and willing, to change behaviour towards a customer based upon what they tell you, and what you already know about them, is the central strategic process to differentiation in e-marketing (Pingjun, 2002; about one-to-one marketing, see: Peppers et al., 1999). E-marketers have a better opportunity, through technology, to get smarter with each transaction and increasingly customize their offerings to a customer. Eventually, even if a rival has the same capabilities, a customer is unlikely to defect, as they would have to teach a rival everything they have already learnt. For example, via the Web, Brompton Bicycles customers can choose between options for the type of handlebar, gears, colour, rack, mudguards, seat pillar, saddle, tyres, luggage, lights, pedals, and some elements of how it will fold.

The company can learn what an individual customer wants and use such information to aggregate the direction of the market.

There are four key steps to consider which collectively form 'IIDC': (1) identify your customers; (2) interact with them; (3) differentiate them; (4) customize your product to fit their needs (see Figure 12.6). Bear in mind that the reality of the process is iterative rather than linear-sequential, as suggested by IIDC.

Identification

Identifying customers requires being able to locate and contact a number of customers directly, or at least a large chunk of the most valuable ones, and understand their behaviour. This involves habits and preferences as well as the obvious addresses, phone numbers, and so on, which must be logged at every contact point. This might mean hiring an outside service for scanning or data entry, drip-irrigation dialogue with customers (asking only one or two questions in each transaction), and a periodic review of the integrity of the list. The basis of identification in e-markets is to use an individual 'CIF', a customer information file. A CIF classically covers: customer characteristics; what, when, where, how, and why they buy; what they bought and the cost of goods or services sold; and the potential profit of each customer. For example, train operator c2c offers special local and London online promotions to boost its database in a bid to better serve its passengers. The data gathered are used for tailored campaigns.

Interaction

The Internet enables organizations to adapt or respond to the environment as they interact with customers. One organic food e-tailor overhauled its site in a rapid response to discovering that people often logged on to make the same order. It decided to incorporate a 'repeat

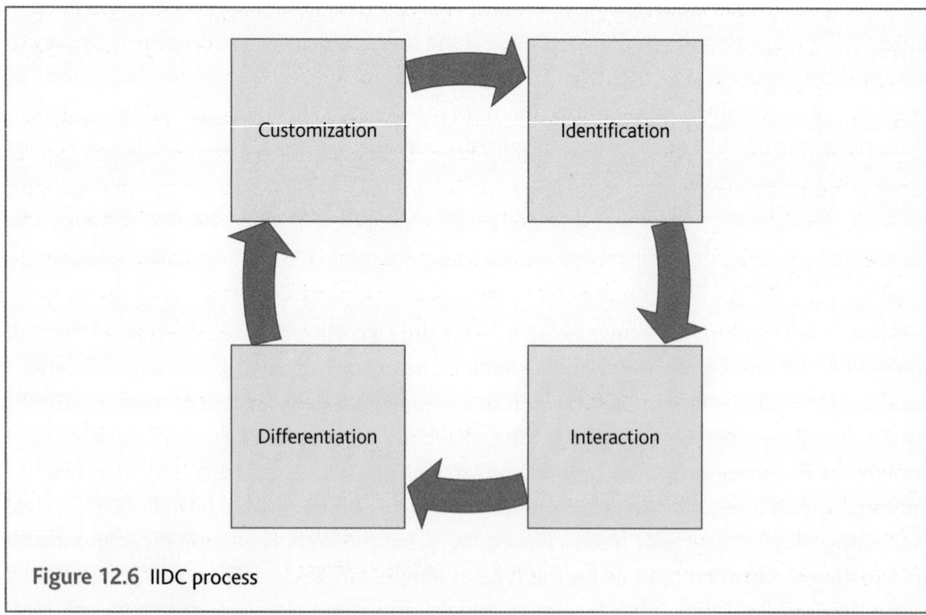

Figure 12.6 IIDC process

order system' (branded as a 'shopping list'), which enables visitors to have their organic shopping delivered without having to return to the site.

Customers are also continually changing and require constant information updates. They want convenient one-stop shopping, participation in design, production, and delivery of goods and services, and for companies to anticipate their needs. Thus, P&O Cruises encourage interactive activity and one-to-one communications through its website at: **www.pocruises.com/Home.axd**, which includes a community section and the ability to choose the cruise most suited to your needs by destination, ship, time of year, or special interest.

The term 'Web 2.0' underlines much of the new interactivity on the Web. Web 2.0 describes a change in how the Web is used rather than any technological development. For example, when Facebook was first introduced in 2004, users could do little more than place a 'police dossier' level of information: name, date of birth, domicile, a few interests and hobbies (*Information Today*, 2008). Today, the site's users have a host of applications (such as calendar to-do lists, book reviews, Shakespearian insults, maps of where users have been, and online scrabble). To some extent, Web 2.0 is just jargon, but the 2.0 view of the Web is one where applications and services are built around the unique features of the Internet and where much of the activity is open source or may be termed 'perpetual beta'. This has provided a richer user experience, more dynamic content, and greater participation.

Many leading bricks-to-clicks companies see Web 2.0 as central to their strategies as part of a network-centric information-gathering business environment. They are not so much concerned by the technology itself as by what it means for information collection, storage, analysis, and application. Furthermore, they realize that their businesses have to operate non-stop all year round and that their websites need constant updating. Learning is quick and they are ready to shift focus. They generally adopt a top-down route, where the top team focuses on the goals and the integration of Web technology, as with Direct Line. Critical business thinking is applied to e-business processes. Companies like Tesco use the Web as part of their multi-channel strategies built upon their established brand and existing business strengths, as with Tesco's entrance into the financial marketplace which caught many established players off guard.

Interactivity on the Internet is part of a larger investment. Thus, Ford and Motorola have made substantial investments in intranet, extranet, and supply chain applications, not just the front-end. Friends Provident provides an interesting example. It has launched an online 'Friends Provident Advisor' website solely for Independent Financial Advisors (IFAs). The new service provided an entirely paperless transaction for IFAs for new business, and existing business, along with an 'info' centre, a breakdown of the funds, and the ability to update profiles. Such interactive online services and products reduce costs for IFAs by eliminating a great deal of administration and paperwork.

One development has been 'virtual advisors' (Urban et al., 2000), which are programmed to behave just like an experienced human advisor and will likely become more popular in the future. They can ask questions, record responses, and make recommendations on the basis of these responses. Clearly, not all goods and services need an advisor. Advisors are more likely to be needed when purchases have a high price, are complex (financial planning), have a need for new learning (e.g., digital cameras), and are subject to rapid change (e.g., PCs) or involve risk (e.g., health care).

Differentiate customers

A differentiation strategy requires recognizing customers' different levels of values and needs. This is invaluable for deciding on the best e-marketing strategy in any given situation. People will do business with sites that make their lives easier and are prepared to pay a premium. Of course, this does not mean that they do not care about price—simply that they are prepared to trade it off against convenience. Brand choice influences another large group of customers on the Web and like the convenience-seekers, these customers are also looking for longer-term stability in their exchanges on the Web. Take the case of John Lewis, a successful UK departmental group: its website does not cater for everyone, but is instead squarely aimed at the middle classes, which form the core of its customer base. The site is comprehensive, well organized, and carries the same goods and services at the same prices as the shops. Its website is helping to build loyalty as much as gain new business. The key is to use technology to enhance the customer experience.

The Web enables organizations unprecedented ways of differentiating customers based on their observed behaviour compared to physical markets. Web portals such as AOL and Yahoo! and search engines such as Google provide good examples of companies that carefully monitor customer behaviour (Iyer and Davenport, 2008). When they upgrade their software they analyse the key drivers of customer loyalty. For example, finding that customers were more likely to maintain their accounts when they used AOL as part of their daily routine, the company enhanced the software's calendar, scheduling functions, and stock-portfolio tracking capabilities.

Customization

The essence of customization is to add value. Having identified, interacted, and differentiated a customer or a client, now what are you going to offer them? If customization is used effectively, both B2B and B2C markets can be populated by highly loyal customers. An example of the former has been the financial services forum tank!group (**http://www.taskgroup.com**) which launched an e-marketing group that keeps participating senior managers abreast of key e-marketing and direct marketing issues, such as response rates, legislative updates, and case studies.

E-marketing enables customers to become co-producers (or more correctly, co-designers of products and services), as exemplified by 'choiceboards' (Slywtotzky, 2000). Choiceboards are online systems that interact with customers so that they can design their own goods and services from a menu of features. Instead of having to haggle over the price of fixed product lines, the Internet changes commerce and enables consumers to describe exactly what they want. Furthermore, suppliers are able to deliver bespoke goods and services without compromise or delay. Examples include Dell's online configuration, Mattell's 'My Design Barbie', My Virtual Model Inc's 'My Virtual Model' (see Figure 12.7), and Schwab's mutual fund evaluator. Customers go onto choiceboard sites and configure their products as they would like them. In doing so, choiceboards collect precise information about consumer preferences which enable companies to continually monitor and increase their knowledge and understanding of consumer needs and preferences. In a sense, they do not need market research. They do the whole IIDC process in one go. The knowledge gained from choiceboards can be used to

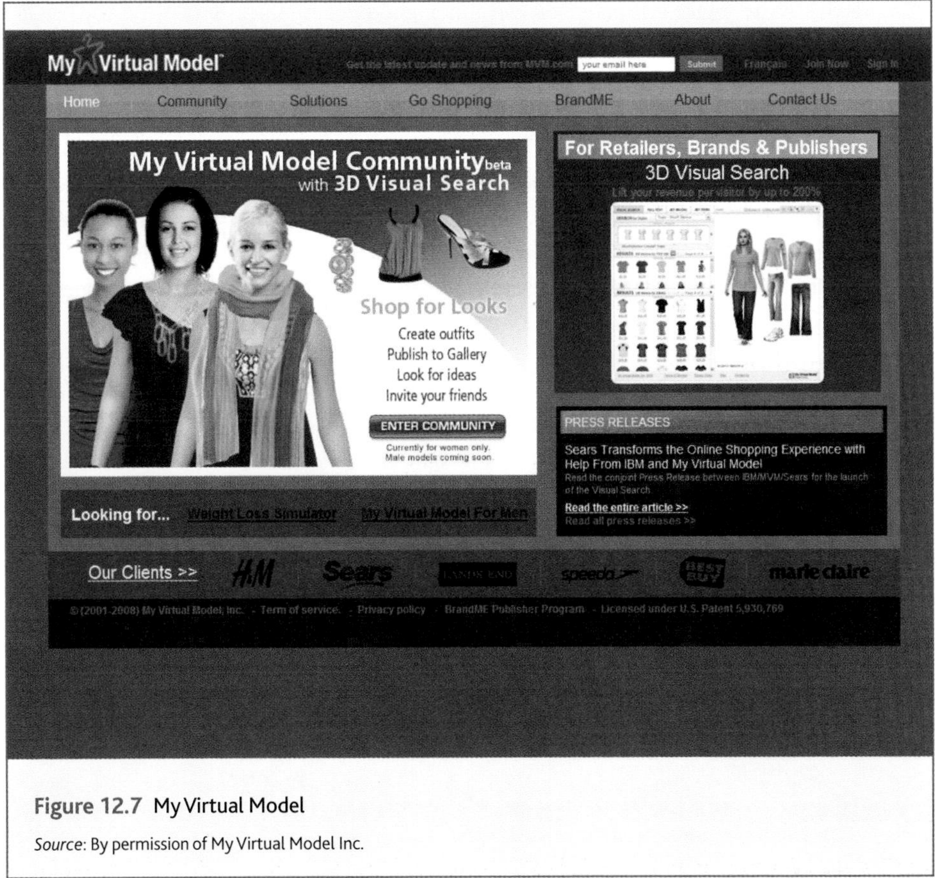

Figure 12.7 My Virtual Model

Source: By permission of My Virtual Model Inc.

customize the website interface, as well as to potentially point the way for the evolution of entire product lines. Competitors, without matching knowledge, find it hard to compete with choiceboard players. Furthermore, choiceboards act as magnets for suppliers who appreciate accurate information about demand and customers' preferences.

Two kinds of choiceboard competitor have developed. Companies like Dell and Schwab are the first kind—individual manufacturers. Secondly, and probably the most threatening kind, have been intermediaries. Choiceboards are simply design tools, so they need not be controlled by producers. Thus, Point.com uses a choiceboard to help consumers find and buy mobile/cell phones, service plans, and accessories, but does not make anything it offers. Intermediaries are particularly effective in industries where producers have failed to develop choiceboards. Intermediaries have the potential to dominate markets as they offer unequalled richness and range.

Communities

There is a straightforward logic to social networking: if Bill knows Jane and Jane knows Harry, then Bill can make contact with Harry. Software can analyse each person's contacts and facilitate Bill asking Jane for an introduction.

Using this basic logic, a number of consumer goods companies have tried to develop 'community brands' which enable consumers to communicate with each other, with the aim to build differentiation through relationships (McWilliam, 2000). Leading examples include Pentax and Shell. With the 'Pentax User Club' (**www.pentaxuser.co.uk**), users are offered the latest information about Pentax products and features, as well as advice, seminar programmes, special offers, competitions, local group news, free classified advertisements, and photography holidays. Shell, with their LiveWire forums and groups (**www.shell-livewire.org/**), offers opportunities to discuss any issues related to the company and the wider environment. Ensuring that brand activity is relevant to the core audience of a social network is crucial if a brand wants to establish a dedicated site (Brown et al., 2007). For example, Sunsilk's community (**http://www.gangofgirls.com**) has over 500,000 members who can discuss their shampoos, boyfriends, make-up, music, sports, etc., play games, and try out new hairstyles digitally and receive advice on hair care (see Figure 12.8).

People like online social networks as they can easily socialize without much effort, especially in not having to leave their home or invite people over and it provides considerable expressive freedom. They also seem to be a considerable leveller as it has been found

Figure 12.8 Gang of Girls

Source: By permission of Sunsilk/Unilever.

that opinion leadership within Internet social networks is not a function of expertise or charisma so much as a function of human nature—influence is something that we all seem to have when it comes to a social network on the Internet (Smith et al., 2007). Cova et al.'s (2007) edited collection of work provides a compelling case for **tribalism** as a phenomenon beyond the usual conventions of sub-cultures, brand communities, and cultures of consumption. Consumer tribes arise where consumers collectively determine, largely on the Web, to what extent they will be manipulated or manipulate brands. The book paints a picture of a delicate 'game' between consumers and corporations, for example, the tribe of Star Trek bootleggers' copyright disputes with Paramount and the industry surrounding gothic gatherings.

User groups, of course, have been around for years, especially in B2B markets like banking, insurance, and property. Outside of B2B, enthusiasts have formed a variety of clubs, especially around car and motorcycle marques (most notably, Harley-Davidson, at: **www.harley-davidson.com**). In Harley's case, some of the indigenous Harley chapters (clubs) threatened the image of the company and so they formed the official Harley Owner's Groups (H.O.G.s). While spontaneous and independently formed—user groups pose a risk—they do offer a number of attractions. Such groups can be contacted for opinions on things like new designs, product enhancements, and for product tests. As well, they can act as important opinion leaders.

The interactivity of social network sites has proved particularly appealing to companies such as HMV who focus on music, gaming, and entertainment. Another element is escapism. This is particularly the case with virtual worlds such as 'Active Worlds' and 'the Second Life® virtual world' (see Figure 12.9), where people create avatars of themselves which, surprisingly, it has been argued, may be marketed to in their own right in addition to the

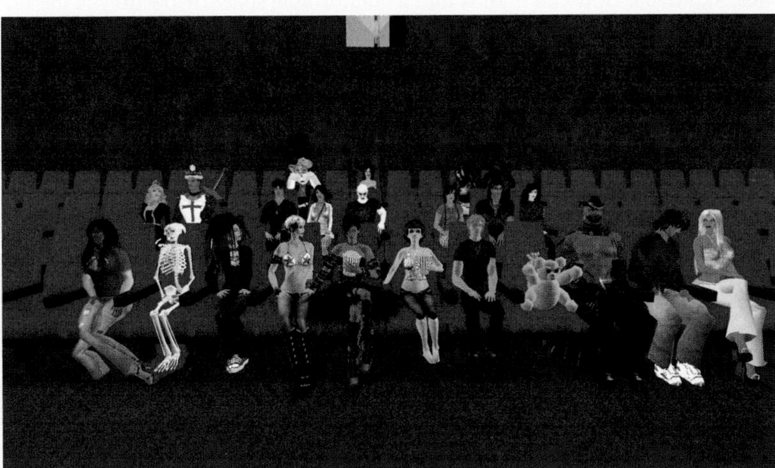

Figure 12.9 Second Life

Source: Second Life is a trademark of Linden Research, Inc. Certain materials have been reproduced with the permission of Linden Research, Inc.

people behind them (Hemp, 2006). Two leading forms of online communities have emerged (and may co-exist): (1) real-time 'chat rooms'; and, (2) asynchronous discussions that take place over days, weeks, or months. The great thing is that these exchanges provide brands with free content and consumers appreciate the ability of meeting like-minded people. The content and exchanges act like magnets and draw people back frequently and regularly. Tools using fuzzy logic, neural networking, and standard statistical analyses (**www.artificial-life.com**) can turn such electronic discussions into useful managerial information.

There are two points of view to successful community sites—the participants and the managers. From the consumer perspective, one key aspect is that a site should provide a forum for the exchange of common interests. For example, women's portal iVillage UK (**www.ivillage.co.uk**) has message boards covering such topics as money and finance and working at home, along with a social network where women can upload their profiles and make contacts.

Consumers like sites that provide a 'physical sense' of space with set codes of behaviour. It must be a community where people easily grasp what is on offer, what the community norms are, and what is expected of them. Additionally, sites need to promote dialogues and relationships that flow casually and colloquially as in face-to-face contact (see, Mini Case Study 12.2). Finally, it is important to encourage participation by everyone. Too often, communities fall into the hands of cliques who dominate the conversation, act as gatekeepers to 'outsiders', and leave most people simply reading the messages rather than participating.

MINI CASE STUDY 12.2 Social media and brands

Many brands have looked and wondered at the social media phenomenon led by Facebook, MySpace, and Bebo. How can brands find a comfortable space? How do you get it right? Social media have not been set up for use by brands so they have to fit in rather than manage. Adding value and minimizing intrusiveness appear to be some of the key elements.

Coca-Cola, Nutella, and Pringles have all built communities of over a million on Facebook, mainly by taking a long-term view and offering value to users. Coca-Cola's site is particularly interesting as the group was first established completely independently of the company as a space where people could talk about the brand and the drink. Coca-Cola took over the running of the site when it reached 1.5 million and has since expanded it to 3 million. The success of the site was in essence based upon the existing buzz about the brand. Companies have also begun to provide links wherever possible, particularly by linking Twitter to Facebook groups with micro blogs. For example, Skittles has experimented with—and gained wide press coverage in so doing—replacing its home page with a live Twitter feed, along with content from YouTube, Flickr, and Facebook. It's a learning curve, though. Skittles had to abandon the idea after two days after the site was bombarded by stupid and irreverent tweets!

One of the first stages in social media engagement has to be to understand what people are saying about the brand on the street. For example, Dell has had a policy, along with many other firms, of identifying the influential bloggers and forums in their market and entering into an honest and frank engagement with them about Dell's products and services. »

» It has also launched IdeaStorm on the main Dell website, where people can comment on the offerings and suggest improvements or new products and services.

Take the case of Orange on Facebook and Bebo. The brand has been associated with film for many years, with its Orange Wednesdays promotions and its advertising in cinemas, but the take-up has been relatively low. By setting up film clubs on Facebook and Bebo, the brand has started to attract an active online community and the prospect of establishing a strong relationship between Orange, films, and younger audiences. Another brand viewing social media from the 'added value' perspective has been Fly Thomas Cook. It has a relatively small marketing budget compared to its bigger rivals, so its engagement with social media offered a David and Goliath payback. It offered a widget that travellers could download that gave a countdown clock to the start date of their holiday, regular updates on the weather at their destination, and other elements such as the ability to upload holiday photos. This was a genuinely useful widget (well, compare it to the Carling iPint! and its free iPhone game playable while downing a virtual pint of beer!) and an example of the basic principles of keeping it simple, offering something people want to engage with, and not overtly pushing the brand.

There have been some stunning examples of how not to do it, though. One in particular noted in the media trade press were the efforts of Chevrolet to engage with people by offering user-generated advertising content. People were welcomed onto Chevrolet's site and, using the video content and audio and text tools provided, could create their own commercial for the Chevy Tahoe 4x4 and upload it onto the site. Unfortunately, the missing mechanism from the process was a moderator. Depending on everyone's goodwill proved a mistake as users generated commercials that blamed such large 4x4s for things like global warming and killing thousands of people driving smaller cars, and pedestrians, and cyclists. Not quite what the brand had in mind.

From a managerial perspective, the first requirement is to attract people to the site. Some product groups, like power tools and photography, benefit from their high involvement status and have less trouble attracting people, such as Disney's 'DIBB' (Disney Information Bulletin Board) for parents planning holidays. Other product groups may not be so lucky, so another approach is to focus on associated interests. For example, Canada's Molson brewery (**http://www.molson.com**) attracts ice-hockey fans with information and gossip in the 'Life and Style' tab. However, first-mover advantages occur with such sites as there are only so many associated interest sites that are viable. Anonymity is a thorny issue. It is known that some brands use their own moderators to pose as members of the public. Furthermore, members of the public often create false identities for themselves in chat rooms.

Another issue for managers is that large communities can lose intimacy, so sub-segments might be encouraged. The biggest problem is often that thousands of members simply 'lurk' and do not participate, so a large community may be needed to produce the critical mass of exchange. One thorny issue is whether or not there should be links to other sites or not. Such links might interest the community, but are they in the brand's interest? Allied to this is the extent to which the brand should control content.

The difficulty is that the brand's personality could be adversely affected by 'ugly' comments. But then, again, transparency has its attraction and if people are going to be ugly about your brand it might be best to have it happen on your own website which is linked to the growth in blogging.

Blogging originated amongst project management techie companies in the 1990s to facilitate cooperation between teams. The practice has now spread widely and the blogosphere (the collection of all blogs on the Internet) is made up of over 65 million plus individual blogs. Blogging might be regarded as a kind of viral marketing tool as it uses social networks, is user-generated, and uses interactivity to spread the message (Singh et al., 2008). For example, the Dalai Lama and Britney Spears all Twitter and the UK celebrity, Stephen Fry (**twitter.com/stephenfry**) regularly reaches audiences of over 100,000-a-day (see Figure 12.10). Video blogging is on the horizon (see, for example, **www.seismic.com**). When it comes to organization, firms that blog enhance their relevance to customers and appear more differentiated within a market (see, for example, Bzz Agent's 'BeeLog' at: **www.bzzagent.com/pages/Page.do?page=Blogs**). Blogs are used by companies such as Boeing, Microsoft, and Garmin (see, for example, **http://garmin.blogs.com/**) for internal and external communications and feedback, to conduct market research, gather competitive intelligence, generate new product ideas, and supplement promotions.

Companies by no means dominate the community space on the Internet. In the UK, the top three sites are not affiliated to companies: Facebook, MySpace, and Bebo (the latter of which is aimed at a younger audience). Collectively, they dwarf the efforts of companies to develop communities. People join such networks largely by choosing people similar to

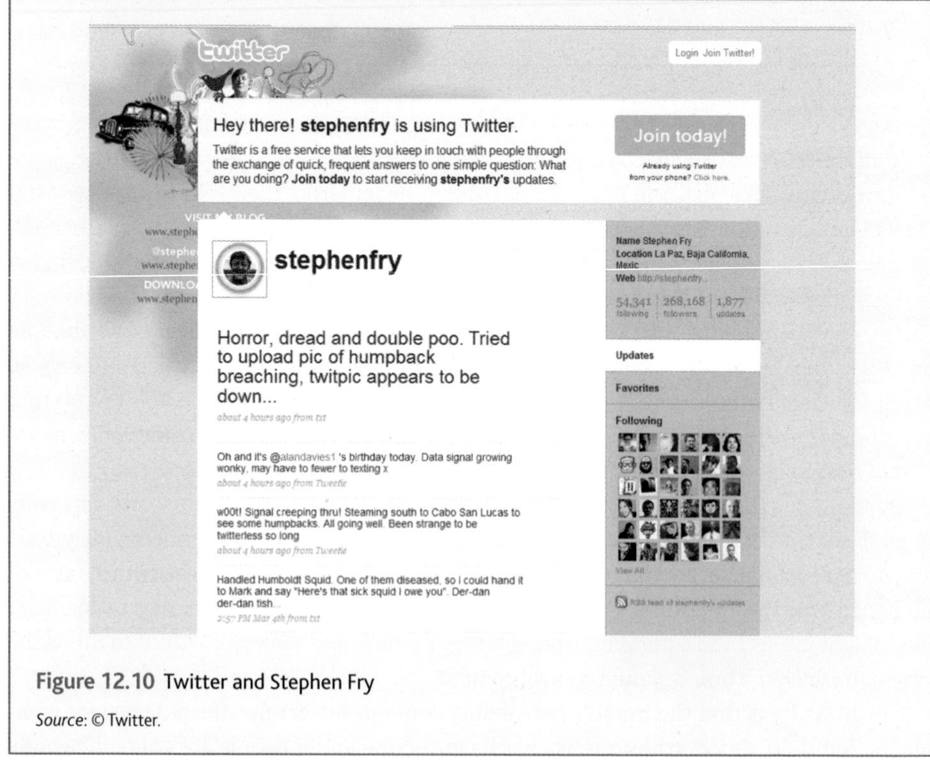

Figure 12.10 Twitter and Stephen Fry

Source: © Twitter.

them (homophily) and so social network sites vary in popularity by regions of the world as people opt for people similar to them, for example Friendster in Asia, Orkut in Brazil, and IRC-Galleria in Finland (see Figure 12.11). People often choose those who know more than them (expert power) to join their networks (Dwyer, 2007). After all, the content generated in a network is the main draw, with little regard to who the originator was.

Professional social networks offer a different type of value to users and are based on relevance. They enable people to search specific criteria such as industry type, a specific company, or people interested in a particular topic. Professional networks are especially valuable for event planners, recruiters, suppliers, venture capitalists (e.g., putting entrepreneurs in contact with financiers), as well as all groups whose businesses rely upon the ability to capitalize on relationships such as accountants, consultants, and lawyers. LinkedIn is a professional network for business people with about 8 million members and a projected revenue in the region of about $80 million. Another prominent professional network is ryze.com, founded in 2001, which has about 500,000 members (see Figure 12.12). However, it differs from LinkedIn as the site is mostly used by people in their thirties and forties who are entrepreneurial and it does not have a referral mechanism. Another professional site, Hoover's Connect, uses its enormous company records database in conjunction with its network. The 'connect' button

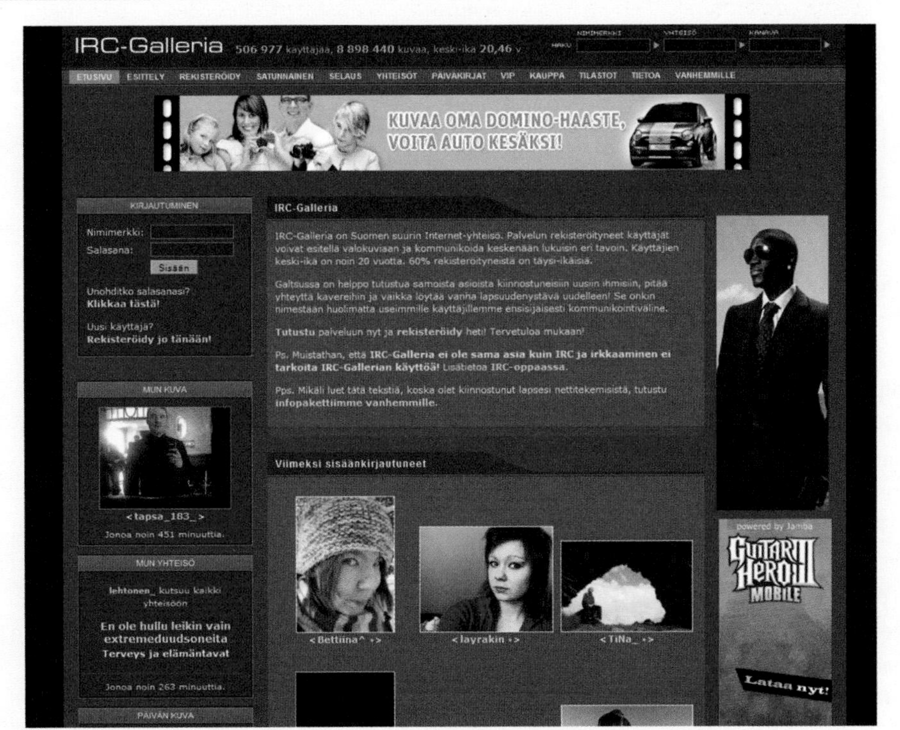

Figure 12.11 IRC-Galleria Social Network, Finland

Source: © IRC-Galleria.

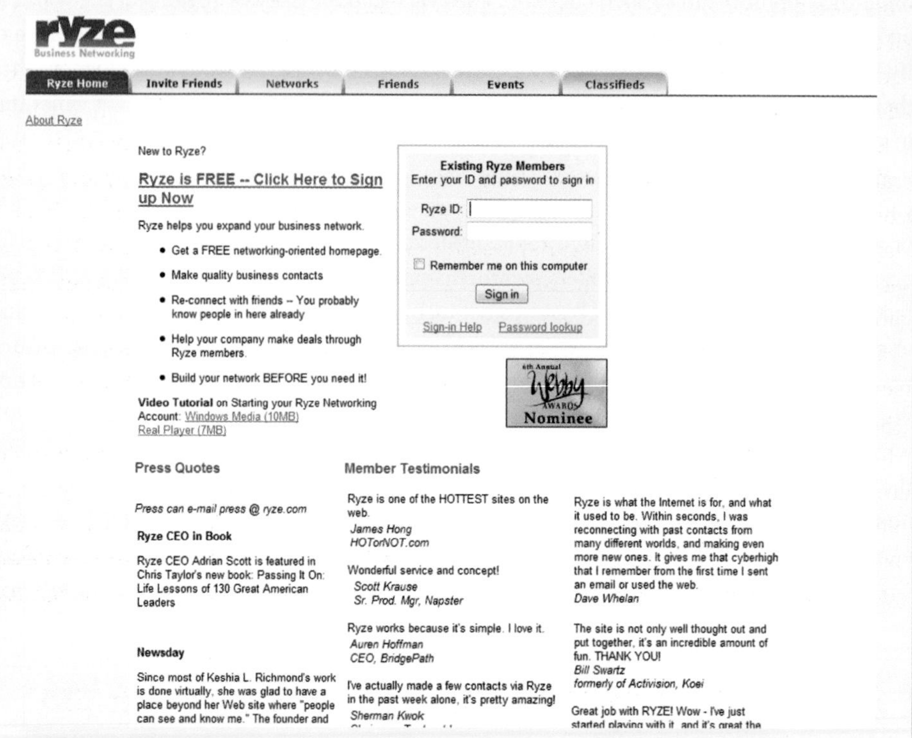

Figure 12.12 Ryze business network

Source: © By permission of Ryze.

offers various referral paths that highlight the strongest path within that user's network. The service allows users to build up their networks by inviting colleagues to join as well through an Outlook plug-in that applies social-networking algorithms to automatically rate relationship strengths within the database. A slightly different approach is taken by **http://www.FDCareers.com**, which is aimed at students and young professionals and attempts to combine career-focused sites like LinkedIn with the Second Life® virtual world, as it enables brands to interact with potential employees.

The same web-spider technology that powers search engines like Google is used by social-networking sites, except that the engines are focused inwards. Where Google uses weighting to provide relevance to a search, the same technology is applied within the network to make the most relevant connections between people. The software looks at the 'length' of a path to reach a contact, as well as the 'strength' of that path.

Professional social-networking is not foolproof. Mistakes are made and even when it works it can only take you so far. A social network cannot make a poor salesperson any better. Privacy is key and most people do not want to be bothered by too many introductions (though people who do not respond to introductions are likely to have networks routed around them). Personal information should always be under the final control of the user who placed it and agreed to share it. Control is, indeed, a major factor in the success of all types of social networking sites and, therefore, it is not surprising that most users have been resistant to having advertising placed on their profile pages unless they had picked the advertiser (Nutley, 2007, p. 18).

Social-networking sites have changed the nature of the game because users largely generate the content. It seems that people are not against marketing per se; they are against irrelevance. People engage with products and services either by recommending them or warning against them, as demonstrated by the numerous company 'fan' sites on Facebook such as the one for Sears (see Figure 12.13). Instead of formal pathways and structured navigation, social networks provide users with hyperlinked and unstructured navigation.

Software can automate the process of filtering the message traffic in any network and identify the information that attracted the most traffic and the members who provided it (Doyle, 2007). This presents a dilemma to social-networking sites. In 2008, for example, when Facebook launched Beacon (software that sends data to external websites to enable targeted ads), it had to withdraw it within days. Even if individuals cannot be identified, people in social networks do not want anything that may be seen as intrusive. Communities coalesce around ideas and relationships and are largely self-regulated. They do not want any external control or what they see as intrusion. YouTube faces a similar dilemma. Google, the

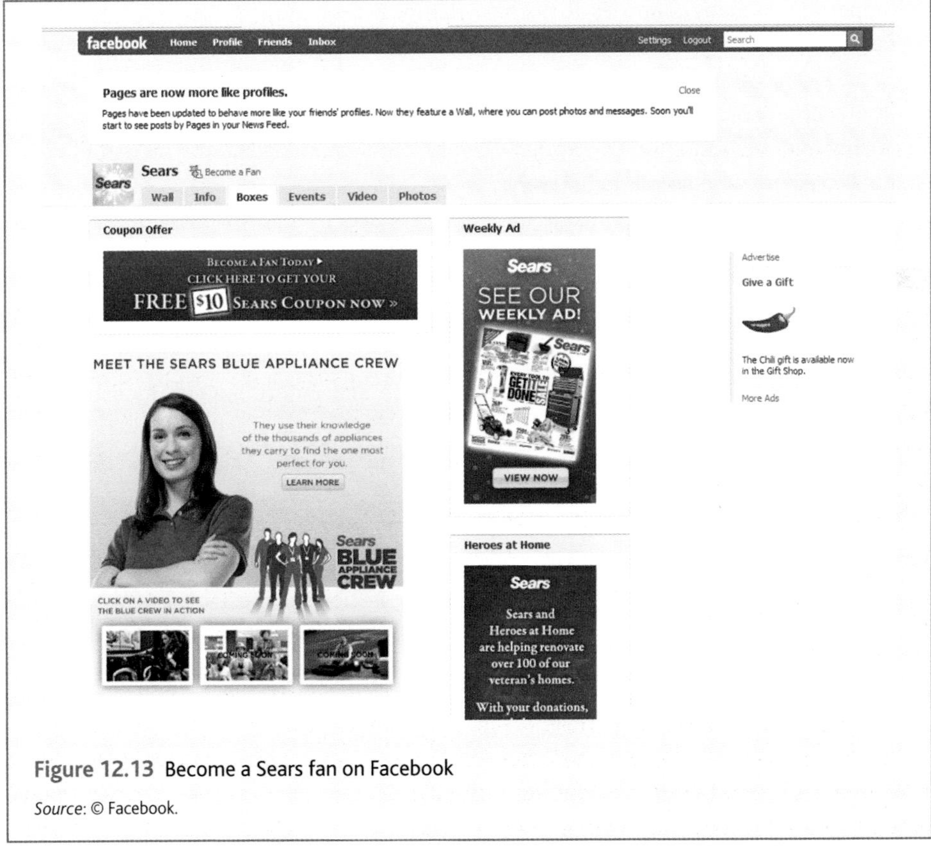

Figure 12.13 Become a Sears fan on Facebook

Source: © Facebook.

site owner, wants to make revenue from it but charging brands to advertise around video clips will likely put off users (*Marketing Week*, 25 February 2009, p. 18).

What is the best strategy if a company cannot develop its own community site. For example, we may love the brand, but very few people will want a Heinz Beanz site. One is to develop commercial stand-alone sites that capitalize on the brand's equity with alliances (see: Chatterjee et al., 2006) such as MySpace Music, which is jointly operated by Universal, Sony, and Warner. Another is to accept the chaos of social networks and try to provide solutions and services, instead of trying to 'push' the brand. That will provide value, which in turn will drive advocacy and positive word-of-mouth, and eventually a 'pull' for the brand. Staff should be encouraged to blog and critics of the brand should be given an opportunity to 'vent', along with advocates.

Global issues

The World Wide Web has not proved to be as 'global' as was first anticipated (Guillén, 2002). Global standardization on the Web does not deliver the highest profits. For a start, telecommunications and Internet infrastructures differ markedly from country to country. International bandwidths vary considerably between countries, which greatly affects the speed of downloading pages. Websites often need redesigning for particular countries. Limited ownership of PCs and a lack of access is another issue, as, too, are government controls. Local costs are also important, as many countries do not have flat-fee access rates.

Geographic distance may not be an issue for the Internet, but it is when it comes to delivering products. It can cost up to £120 to deliver a £20 CD to certain destinations. Not surprisingly, nearly 50 per cent of foreign orders to US websites are never shipped. It is not just distance—processing and restocking return products can be problematic, given the myriad of cross-national consumer regulations in the world.

Another factor is that buyers like to purchase products in their own language. Translation objects and browser translation tools provide only partial fixes and do not compare with bespoke local websites. Most search engines and directories are country-specific and operate in one language only. E-business may require staff to handle emails, faxes, and phone calls from people in other languages.

Buyer behaviour varies in such markets as leisure and entertainment, foodstuffs and clothing and with such aspects as holidays and festivals. User characteristics vary, too; for example, women make up only 10 per cent of users across Latin America but are close to 50 per cent in North America or Europe.

E-commerce is largely dependent on the widespread use of credit cards. Even so, it can still prove a challenge in many countries that have a high usage of credit cards, as distrust of using them on the Web can run very high, as in Japan. Thus, 7–Eleven has established a store-wide system whereby Japanese customers can settle their e-commerce bills in person.

How to quote prices is also a problem. Successful US auction sites have found it hard to compete with local competitors in places like the UK, Germany, France, or Sweden, where local currency sites dominate. Currency conversion engines help, but they often frustrate potential buyers. One other consideration is that the time lag between the order and processing often exposes e-businesses to currency risk.

National origin effect is a factor, too. It is not that well understood, but it is becoming clear that consumers make judgements about websites partially on the origin of the site. This is particularly so for companies selling financial services or running auctions. However, for many branded goods, their origin will likely remain more important than the origin of the site.

Conclusion

E-marketing strategy is here to stay and will play an increasing role in both B2B and B2C marketing, as is increasingly happening in C2C. The Internet has not changed 'everything', as popularly thought. The construction industry is a case in point. E-marketing has enabled architects, builders, engineers, and general contractors to easily transmit information and drawings amongst multiple firms at different locations. However, materials procurement has hardly changed. Most contractors are small businesses with a regional focus and purchasing is typically handled by project managers in the field rather than by purchasing departments. Over 20,000 distributors provide materials to customers at a local level the same day or the next and are generally ordered by mobile. The idea of placing orders via the Internet would have required on-site computers, would not have increased efficiency, and would have required significant training amongst the workers. In this case, the pay-off was not there and it has not happened.

However, the Internet has significantly affected industry structure by intensifying rivalry and empowering buyers. Many B2C and B2B markets (such as forklift trucks) have become commodity markets in the process. The key to a successful e-marketing strategy is to compete effectively on reach, affiliation, richness, and range. Ultimately, the goal is to develop above-average performance through a sustainable competitive advantage. With e-marketing strategy, this will be most likely achieved through some form of identification-differentiation-interaction-customization process, as with one-to-one marketing and/or the development of a community or working with a social network.

Summary

E-marketing strategy is rooted in the classic elements of the Five Forces and sustainable competitive advantage. Any e-marketing strategies should be based on businesses run like bricks-and-mortar companies, using classic metrics such as gross margin and size of order. However, to achieve e-marketing success, it may often be necessary to break down mentally the current business model into its components, understand the new e-business models, and take some risks. Schwab famously reinvented itself when it halved its brokerage fees, committed to navigation as its core business, and started selling its competitors products. For most companies, such a change would be too big a gamble.

KEY TERMS

Bricks and mortar An organization with a physical presence in the market.

Clickstream A series of mouse-click choices between websites, often leading to a purchase and generating income for each mediator.

Community A group who communicate with each other via a particular website.

Co-production The concept of enabling customers to co-design products and services.

E-business An all-embracing term that describes how an organization uses the Internet such as intranets, knowledge management, and payroll services.

E-commerce This is transactional and relates to using the Internet to facilitate transactions (business-to-business, business-to-consumer, and consumer-to-consumer).

E-marketing solely relates to the use of the Internet to undertake marketing.

E-tailer A retailer without a physical market presence.

Hypermediation The series of mediation on a clickstream.

Internet Global network of computers enabling communication and the sharing of and access to information, as well as the ordering and payment for products and the movement of digital products.

Judo strategy Using the Internet strength of a market rival against itself.

Navigation Steering between the mass and variety of information on the Internet.

Smart market A market based on customization, the exchange of information, and constant monitoring of change.

Stickiness: The degree to which a website holds the attention and clicks of a user.

DISCUSSION QUESTIONS

1 Evaluate the impact of e-marketing on the traditional Five Forces analyses.

2 What has been the impact of e-marketing on sustainable competitive analyses (SCA)?

3 What factors might limit the success of e-marketing judo strategy (i.e., turning a rival's size and strength against itself)?

4 To what extent do you agree with the proposition that e-marketing is more about differentiation than cost advantage?

5 Why is navigation central to developing SCA with e-marketing?

6 Do you agree with Slywtotzky that the future of e-marketing customization belongs to the 'choiceboard'?

7 Considering the perspectives of users and site owners, what are the pros and cons of external companies gaining access to personal data on social networks?

ONLINE RESOURCE CENTRE

Visit the Online Resource Centre for this book for lots of interesting additional material at: **www.oxfordtextbooks.co.uk/orc/west2e/**

REFERENCES AND FURTHER READING

Barsh, Joanna, Blair Crawford, and Chris Grosso (2000), 'How E-tailing can Rise from the Ashes', *Mckinsey Quarterly*, 3, pp. 98–109.

Brown, Jo, Amanda J. Broderick, and Nick Lee (2007), 'Word of Mouth Communication within Online Communities: Conceptualizing the Online Social Network', *Journal of Interactive Marketing*, 21 (3), pp. 2–20.

Cart, Nicholas G. (2000), 'Hypermediation: Commerce as Clickstream', *Harvard Business Review*, January–February, pp. 46–7.

Chatterjee, Dbabroto (Dave), Albert H. Segars, and Richard T. Watson (2006), 'Realizing the Promise of E-business: Developing and Leveraging Electronic Partnering Options', *California Management Review*, 48 (4), pp. 60–83.

Cova, Bernard, Robert Kozinets, and Avi Shankar (2007), *Consumer Tribes* (Oxford: Butterworth-Heinemann).

Day, George S., Adam J. Fein, and Gregg Ruppersberger (2003), 'Shakeouts in Digital Markets: Lessons from B2B Exchanges', *California Management Review*, 45 (2), pp. 131–50.

Doyle, Shaun (2007), 'The Role of Social Networks in Marketing', *Database Marketing & Customer Strategy Management*, 15 (1), pp. 60–4.

Dwyer, Paul (2007), 'Measuring the Value of Word-of-mouth and its Impact in Consumer Communities', *Marketing Science Institute Report*, No. 06–118.

Evans, Philip, and Thomas S. Wurster (1999), 'Getting Real about Virtual Commerce', *Harvard Business Review*, November–December, 84–94.

Glazer, Rashi (1999), 'Winning in Smart Markets', *Sloan Management Review*, Summer, pp. 59–69.

Guillén, Mauro F. (2002), 'What is the Best Global Strategy for the Internet?' *Business Horizons*, May–June, pp. 39–46.

Hemp, Paul (2006), 'Avatar-based Marketing', *Harvard Business Review*, June, pp. 48–57.

Higson, Chris, and John Briginshaw (2000), 'Valuing Internet Businesses', *Business Strategy Review*, 11 (1), pp. 10–21.

Information Today (2008), May, pp. 1 and 46.

Iyer, Bala, and Thomas H. Davenport (2008), 'Reverse Engineering: Google's Innovation Machine', *Harvard Business Review*, April, pp. 59–68.

Krishnamurthy, Sandeep (2006), 'Introducing E-MARKPLAN: A Practical Methodology to Plan E-marketing Activities', *Business Horizons*, 49, pp. 51–60.

Laffey, Des (2007), 'Paid Search: The Innovation that Changed the Web', *Business Horizons*, 50, pp. 211–18.

McWilliam, Gil (2000), 'Building Stronger Brands through Online Communities', *Sloan Management Review*, Spring, pp. 43–54.

Nutley, Michael (2007), 'How to Win Friends and Influence People—the Social Networking Way', *Marketing Week*, 19 June, p. 18.

Peppers, Don, Martha Rogers, and Bob Dorf (1999), 'Is your Company Ready for One-to-one Marketing?' *Harvard Business Review*, January–February, pp. 151–60.

Pingjun, Jiang (2002), 'Exploring Consumers' Willingness to Pay for Online Customisation and its Marketing Outcomes', *Journal of Targeting, Measurement & Analysis for Marketing*, 11 (2), pp. 168–84.

Porter, Michael (2001), 'Strategy and the Internet', *Harvard Business Review*, March, pp. 63–78.

Reichheld, Frederick F., and Phil Schefter (2000), 'E-loyalty: Your Secret Weapon on the Web', *Harvard Business Review*, July–August, pp. 105–13.

Rosenbloom, Bert (2002), 'The Ten Deadly Myths of E-commerce', *Business Horizons*, 45 (2), pp. 61–6.

Shama, Avraham (2001), 'E-coms and their Marketing Strategies', *Business Horizons*, September–October, 44 (5), pp. 14–20.

Singh, Tanuja, Liza Veron-Jackson, and Joe Cullinane (2008), 'Bloggin: A New Play in your Marketing Game Plan', *Business Horizons*, 51, pp. 281–92.

Slywtotzky, Adrian J. (2000), 'The Age of the Choiceboard', *Harvard Business Review*, January–February, pp. 40–1.

Smith, Ted, James R. Coyle, Elizabeth Lightfoot, and Amy Scott (2007), 'Reconsidering Models of Influence: The Relationship between Consumer Social Networks and Word-of-mouth Effectiveness', *Journal of Advertising Research*, December, pp. 387–97.

Urban, Glen L., Fareena Sultan, and William J. Qualls (2000), 'Placing Trust at the Center of your Internet Strategy', *Sloan Management Review*, 42 (1), pp. 39–48.

Wells, John D., and David H. Gobeli (2003), 'The 3R Framework: Improving E-strategy across Reach, Richness, and Range', *Business Horizons*, 46 (2), pp. 5–14.

Wheale, Peter R., and Amin L. Heredia (2003), 'Bursting the dot.com "Bubble": A Case Study in Investor Behaviour', *Technology Analysis & Strategic Management*, 15 (1), pp. 117–37.

Willcocks, Leslie P., and Robert Plant (2001), 'Pathways to E-business Leadership: Getting from Bricks to Clicks', *MIT Sloan Management Review*, 42, Spring, pp. 50–59.

Wolfinbarger, Mary, and Mary C. Gilly (2001), 'Shopping Online for Freedom, Control and Fun', *California Management Review*, 43 (2), pp. 34–55.

Yoffie, David B., and Michael A. Cusumano (1999), 'Judo Strategy: The Competitive Dynamics of Internet Time', *Harvard Business Review*, January–February, pp. 70–81.

KEY ARTICLE ABSTRACTS

Brown, Mark, Nigel Pope, and Kevin Voges (2003), **'Buying or Browsing? An Exploration of Shopping Orientations and Online Purchase Intention'**, *European Journal of Marketing*, 37 (11/12), pp. 1666–84.

This paper points out that shopping online is about more than convenience. As such, the marketing strategies of e-tailers need to take into account other factors affecting purchase intention, such as whether the product or service had been purchased previously.

Abstract: Consumer selection of retail patronage mode has been widely researched by marketing scholars. Several researchers have segmented consumers by shopping orientation. However, few have applied such methods to the Internet shopper. Despite the widespread belief that Internet shoppers are primarily motivated by convenience, the authors show empirically that consumers' fundamental shopping orientations have no significant impact on their proclivity to purchase products online. Factors that are more likely to influence purchase intention include product type, prior purchase, and, to a lesser extent, gender. Findings indicate the existence of similar shopping orientations as in other retail spheres and a possible experience relationship with the intention to purchase. The authors suggest that the Internet is very similar to other forms of non-store retailing. There are challenges to online retailing and profitable Internet retailers are said to be among the minority. Rather than conceptualizing the Internet as a purely convenience-orientated patronage mode, retailers may be better served by taking a more holistic approach with their marketing strategies.

Hoffman, Donna L., and Thomas P. Novak (2000), '**How to Acquire Customers on the Web**', *Harvard Business Review*, May–June, pp. 179–88.

This paper highlights CDnow's pioneering 'pay-for-performance' marketing strategy which has been emulated by the likes of Amazon.com, REL.com, Dell.com, and Barnesandnoble.com. CDNOW offers a revenue-sharing arrangement with affiliated sites: when a customer clicks through from an affiliate's website to the CDNOW website and buys a CD, CDNOW gives 3 per cent of the revenue from the sale back to the affiliate. In effect, CDNOW has turned its affiliates into a virtual commissioned sales force.

Abstract: Online retail companies, or e-tailers, are finding that it takes enormous marketing expenditures to acquire customers. For most of these companies, the average customer acquisition cost is higher than the average lifetime value of their customers. The authors studied online marketing for seven years, and note the success of the music retailer, CDNOW. CDNOW, currently the most powerful online music brand, was one of the first to develop a multifaceted, integrated customer acquisition strategy that reflects a sophisticated understanding of the economics of an online business. The company's BuyWeb program was the first application of what has come to be known as 'affiliate' or 'associate' marketing programs. CDNOW currently acquires customers using its Cosmic Music Network, which allows unsigned artists to put up a Web page at the CDNOW site. In addition, the company also uses radio, television, and print advertising, online advertising, strategic partnerships, word of mouth, free links, and public relations. As sophisticated as CDNOW's strategy is, the company is finding that, over time, its pure CPM (the number of people who would see an advertisement) buys are disappearing. And this trend will likely affect other e-tailers. CDNOW's experience shows the power of the Internet as it applies to marketing, but it is impossible to say what the best marketing strategy is.

McGoldrick, Peter J., Kathleen A. Keeling, and Susan F. Beatty (2008), '**A Typology of Roles for Avatars in Online Retailing**', *Journal of Marketing Management*, 24 (3/4), pp. 433–61.

The evidence of this study stresses the importance of providing choice in whether or not, and how, to interact with an avatar. Most people perceive some positive roles for them emphasizing friendliness. Others appear to lean towards a more functional avatar, adopting a more specialist sales role as a 'virtual personal shopper'.

Abstract: Avatars are now appearing as online assistants on transactional websites, yet their scope is still limited. This paper explores their potential roles in providing assistance, a friendlier interface, and purchase recommendations. As avatars are at the early stages of implementation, the conceptual framework draws upon human–computer interaction research, plus cognate literature on salesperson roles and the use of synthetic characters in other contexts. The empirical study involved two longitudinal panels of online buyers and an international, online survey of 2,114 Internet users. Following split-sample principal components analysis and k-means clustering, four categories of role preference are identified. The results inform decisions on the appropriateness of avatars, their adaptation to customer needs and buying contexts, and their possible roles. Hypothesized relationships with age, gender, and online buying experience are tested, suggesting scope for avatar role segmentation. Suggestions are offered for marketers and website designers considering deploying avatars, and for future research directions.

Varadarajan, P. Rajan, and Manjit S. Yadav (2002), '**Marketing Strategy and the Internet: An Organizing Framework**', *Journal of the Academy of Marketing Science*, 30 (4), pp. 296–312.

This paper provides an assessment of the role of the Internet within marketing strategy. They examine the key drivers and outputs and point out that building relationships with customers is difficult on the Internet without offline contact.

Abstract: In a growing number of product markets, the competitive landscape has evolved from a predominantly physical marketplace to one encompassing both the physical and the electronic marketplace. This article presents a conceptual framework, delineating the drivers and outcomes of marketing strategy in the context of competing in this broader, evolving marketplace. The proposed framework provides insights into changes in the nature and scope of marketing strategy; specific industry, product, buyer, and buying environment characteristics; and the unique skills and resources of the firm that assume added relevance in the context of competing in the evolving marketplace.

END OF CHAPTER 12 CASE STUDY Bust Loose

Introduction

In the beginning, all Glenn Fawcett wanted was a free trip. At the time, the 23-year-old University of Calgary commerce student had just slogged through final exams in 1983 and he wanted a cheap place to let loose before starting his new job. Mexico sounded like a great spot, but he didn't want to spend $750 to $800, the going rate for airfare and hotel packages.

So, he rounded up a large group of his classmates and planned his own holiday. Fawcett took advantage of contacts he had made while he was president of his high school and university ski clubs to arrange a fun-filled two-week trip to Puerto Valarta through Delta Airlines. The vacation cost the 68 other book-weary students only $599 each, but because he'd reserved so many seats with the airline, the canny Fawcett's fare was free.

After the holiday, he settled down to what he thought would be a typical corporate career as a market analyst at Gulf Canada Corp. But his phone would not stop ringing. On the line were old campus chums thirsty for another taste of tequila.

Bust Loose

Several years later, his phone was still ringing. In the 1980s and 1990s, Fawcett founded his company, Bust Loose, and airlifted 4,000 students seeking post-exam fun and sun to Cancun, Puerto Valarta, and Mazatlan. Glenn Fawcett has since sold his shares in the business. However, Bust Loose continues to thrive with a specialization in off-season student travel.

Breaking travel industry rules has created a novel market niche for Bust Loose. 'If one had done a marketing study five or six years ago,' Fawcett said, 'and asked when it was a good time for students to travel, the last time one would have picked is the end of final exams, when most of them are broke.' In fact, the first to sign on for Fawcett's tours late in 1983 were those who had the cash. But when word got around about the good time to be had, others started to save for the trip. 'It's almost like a relocation of financial resources,' he says. 'We've created a demand for travel.'

Niche market

In the Canada/Mexico travel business, Bust Loose is seen as a market innovator, offering its holidays across Canada and Mexico. A manager at the Carleton University office of Travel Cuts, a Toronto-based discount travel agency catering to students across Canada, says Bust Loose has no direct competition. 'Bust Loose is a completely different ball game,' she says. 'They specialize in spring holidays.'

Bust Loose flies into Mexico during April and May. 'At that time of year, travel to Mexico is not that busy,' says Delta Airlines' Claude Latour. 'From Easter to the 15th of June, we're 

sort of in a valley.' Seats are booked on regularly scheduled flights because Bust Loose has to move most of its customers over a three-week period between the end of exams and the start of the job season. If they chartered their own aircraft, it would mean costly deadheading (flying empty) of the planes back to Canada to pick up more passengers.

There's another advantage to flying commercial flights. For every 15 seats that Bust Loose books on Mexicana Airlines, for example, they get one free. And if you have a lot of people coming, in you get group airfares, which are typically $25 less per person than the regular lowest price. Plus, you get a percentage or two above the regular (10 per cent) travel agents' commission.

Mexican hotels, too, are happy to fill empty rooms with Bust Loose's crazy Canadian students at half the regular-season rates because they can make up the differences on food and bar bills. 'In a short time, Bust Loose has become the largest producer for Mexicana in Canada,' says Bert Parada, Mexicana Airlines' Western Canada district sales manager. 'We are very impressed they have put together such a classy product. The hotels are extremely happy.'

Target market

And how does Bust Loose sell the tours to the 18-to-35-year-olds targeted? By appealing to people's inner desire to have fun. Air Canada's Calgary passenger sales manager says, 'Bust Loose's quite a promotional company. They have some excellent posters in strategic places around universities.' Images alone, though, aren't enough. To stir up interest during dreary winter months, Bust Loose serves up free promotional parties at pubs frequented by students. A limbo or two, a tequila smash contest (the first drink is free), and potential clients are intoxicated with that 'Mexican feeling'.

Organization

Sales rely on 300 representatives, who are, for the most part, students. Finding eager reps has never been a problem. The carrot: free airfare and accommodation if they get 25 to 30 others to sign up and they have to be willing to play host on the trip. In the beginning, reps were Fawcett's friends and family members. Today, paying customers are approached about working on the next year's trip.

Though 'wild' might be the operative word to describe the Mexico trips, things do not get out of hand. The reason: before they get their tickets, would-be revellers must sign a waiver acknowledging individual responsibility for damages incurred. The sun has a bit of a mellowing effect. In the past five years, there's only been $216 in damage claims. And before departure, the amateur tour-guides (Bust Loose has about 50 paid staff in Mexico to supervise arrivals and activities) are treated to seminars that teach them how to handle everything, from exchange rates to first aid. On location, early morning meetings get everyone thinking about guests' needs and the day's activities. Iguana races, burro polo, tequila drinking, and sand sculpture contests enliven the participants' stay.

Two weeks of three-star hotels and airfare—plus activities—are competitively priced. Bust Loose attributes the ability to keep costs down to economies of scale and an extremely devalued peso. One out of three people who make the Mexico trip return the next year, a fact Bust Loose credits to good party organization and solid customer service. Survey forms reveal what guests did (and did not) find enjoyable.

Bust Loose Plus

The realization that people cannot drink tequila forever led to the inception of packages to a wider range of destinations (most notably Asia), shorter break packages within Canada (Calgary Stampede, Halloween, and New Year), and the hire of 'party buses'.

Source: This case was prepared by Douglas West of the University of Birmingham as the basis for analysis and class discussion and not to illustrate either effective or ineffective handling of an administrative situation.

QUESTIONS

Bearing in mind issues of navigation, the IIDC strategic process, and communities:

1. Examine the Bust Loose website at: **http://www.bustloose.com** and critically evaluate their current e-marketing strategy.
2. Identify and defend some strategic suggestions for the future.

13

Social and ethical strategies

LEARNING OBJECTIVES

- Examine the nature of social marketing and its implications
- Provide a comparison between the interests of shareholders and those of the firm's stakeholders
- Discuss environmental/green marketing and social marketing as firm initiatives
- Discuss ethics and moral judgement and the firm's actions as a morally responsible organization in society
- Explain the various facets of corporate social responsibility
- Explain philanthropic activities and initiatives and cause-related marketing strategic choices
- Illustrate the ways in which a firm can get involved in socially responsible activities to improve its standing as a hands-on and caring community citizen
- Examine the ways in which the corporate social responsibility (CSR) strategist can make social responsibility meaningful for the firm by making it a strategic imperative as opposed to an act of compliance
- Discuss ways in which social responsibility can be measured and evaluated
- Examine the newest initiatives for CSR strategists to improve their performance, involving the Virtue Matrix and the addressing of global poverty through partnerships between corporations and NGOs

CHAPTER AT A GLANCE

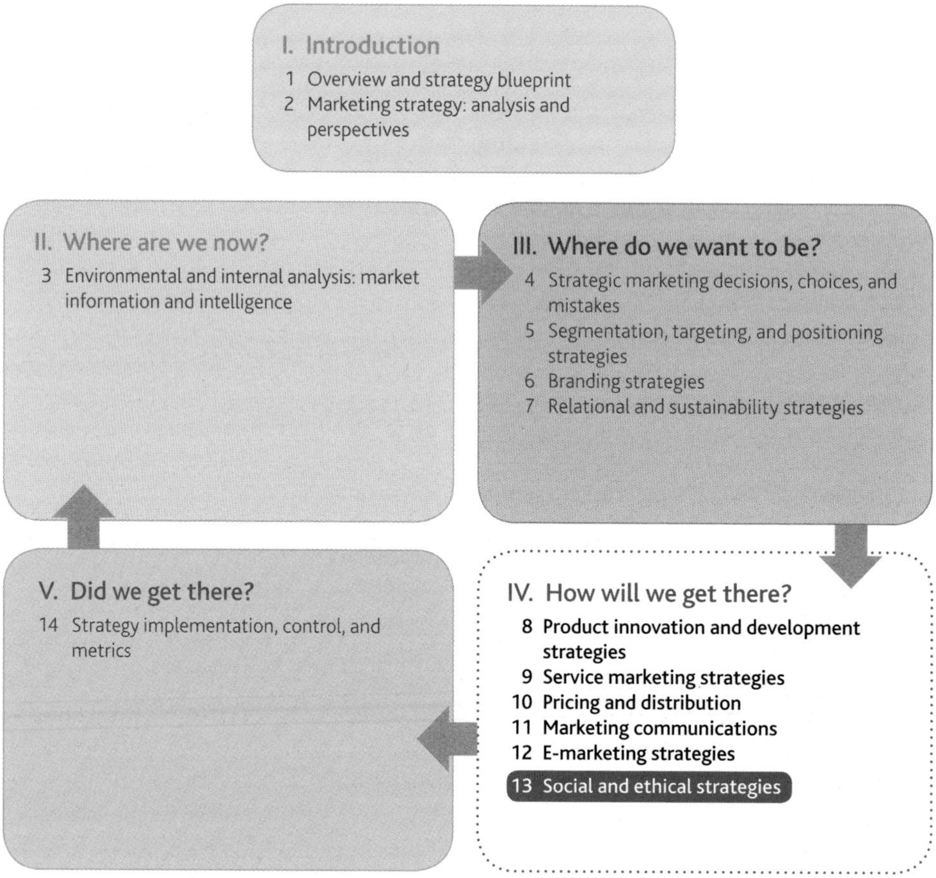

I. Introduction
1 Overview and strategy blueprint
2 Marketing strategy: analysis and perspectives

II. Where are we now?
3 Environmental and internal analysis: market information and intelligence

III. Where do we want to be?
4 Strategic marketing decisions, choices, and mistakes
5 Segmentation, targeting, and positioning strategies
6 Branding strategies
7 Relational and sustainability strategies

IV. How will we get there?
8 Product innovation and development strategies
9 Service marketing strategies
10 Pricing and distribution
11 Marketing communications
12 E-marketing strategies
13 Social and ethical strategies

V. Did we get there?
14 Strategy implementation, control, and metrics

Introduction

In the world of today, the company does not compete against other firms in a vacuum. The wants and needs of society and the importance of doing business in an ethical and non-harmful manner are important contextual considerations. Firms must not only produce excellent goods and services and keep customers happy, but must also be concerned with their relationship with society at large as well as the environment. The marketing concept has evolved into market orientation, and firms are more heavily focused on wants and needs of consumers, but this is no longer sufficient. There is a broader context in which the firm operates, and the health and well-being of society and consumers must be taken into consideration for the firm to be seen as a good community citizen. Consumers expect that corporations will not only operate legally and fairly, they also want them to act ethically, help charitable causes, clean up the environment, and improve conditions for citizens locally, regionally, nationally, and in some cases, internationally.

The firm and its role in society

An important starting point for understanding corporate responsibilities in a societal context is the determination of whom the firm is actually serving with its operations. Is it the shareholder or is it a wider variety of publics? This determination will lead the company to undertake very different strategic initiatives.

Shareholders vs stakeholders

One can see in all of this a potential conundrum in that, on the one hand, there are those who follow the philosophy that the social responsibility of the firm is to make the most money that it can for its shareholders within legal means. But, on the other hand, the argument is that being a good citizen and giving money to needy organizations or undertaking community improvement projects by nature reduces profits or forces firms to increase retail prices to cover the incurred costs. To understand the potential benefits of CSR, one has to be careful to examine all of the relevant constituencies affected by the firm's actions (Snider et al., 2003). The important distinction here really lies in whom the firm sees as its important constituencies. If shareholders are the only public that they are concerned with, then all actions undertaken must be done in a way that will maximize return for shareholders. This perspective would argue strongly against any expenditure without proven profitability. One could argue that any community investment expenditure or donation to a charitable organization would be seen as a potential drain on company financial performance. If, on the other hand, the firm considers that there are a variety of publics that must be considered, then it might strategically make a very different set of choices.

Stakeholders are all those groups or publics that interact with and are affected by the operations of the firm. These publics include employees, partners, suppliers, customers, community members, governmental agencies, and social activist groups. If the firm takes the view that all of these groups have a stake in the operations of the firm, then their concerns must also be considered in corporate strategies and CSR initiatives. It may be that value perceived by some of these stakeholder groups may precede and in some cases drive improvements in shareholder wealth (Snider et al. 2003). As a result, stakeholder theory serves as a better framework for examining how the corporation can effectively position itself in its social context. The various stakeholder constituencies are shown in Figure 13.1.

Social issues with regards to marketing have three important facets, which will be discussed in this chapter: the use of marketing to reduce societal problems (social marketing); the need for the firm to operate in an ethical manner; and the importance of the company and its representatives acting in socially responsible ways (corporate social responsibility). Each of these will be discussed in detail.

Social marketing

Social marketing is the application of marketing principles and practices to help with the resolution of public health and social problems. This involves the use of marketing to help public-policy makers change public behaviour and practices considered to be harmful

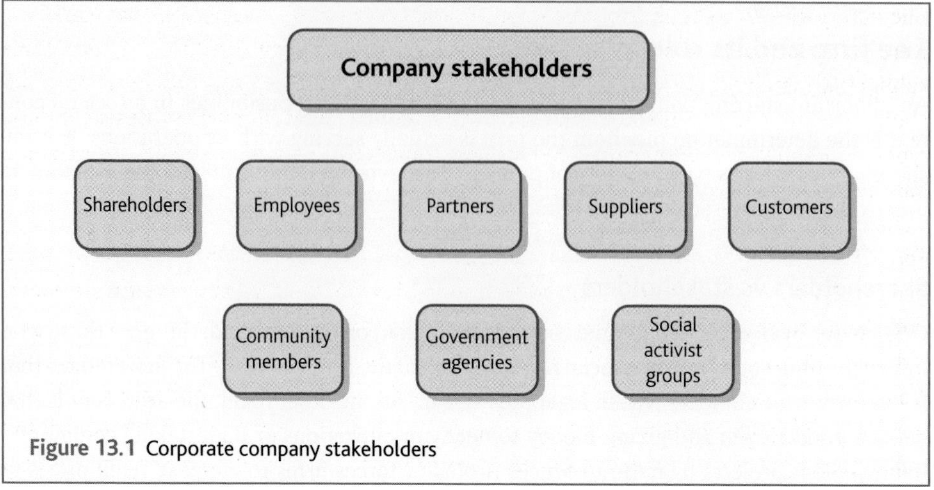

Figure 13.1 Corporate company stakeholders

to health and societal well-being. The first suggestions for this appeared in the marketing literature in the early 1970s, and today there are a vast number of public awareness and improvement campaigns in evidence in many different countries. Public service announcements (PSAs) abound in the UK, the US and Australia, to name a few. In the UK, for example, media audiences are constantly being exposed to campaigns which raise awareness of various health issues like cancer risks and the need for self-examination, the dangers of drink driving, the problem of teenage pregnancies, the need for children and adults to exercise and eat healthily to stay fit, and the harm associated with drug use. These are common societal problems, and public-policy makers in these countries have turned to marketing tools to get their messages to their constituencies to encourage healthier lifestyles and improved living conditions. Why has this come about? Two driving concerns for businesses have been dictated by public-sector policy-makers concerned with safety and well-being. These concerns are the health and well-being of the consumer and the protection of the environment.

Consumerism and environmentalism

Two important facilitators for social improvements have been the internal pressures in a variety of countries to address consumerism and environmentalism. In the 1950s, when the marketing concept first appeared in the literature, the concern was to shift the focus to satisfying the wants and needs of consumers to be able to differentiate one firm from its competitors and ensure consumer choice. This made appealing to the consumer a first priority, but major criticisms of the marketing concept centred around the fact that profit was the overriding purpose, rather than considering the welfare of the consumer. Consumerism became an important topic after a variety of books appeared touting the potential harm to the consumer that could be brought about by corporate mistakes. The book, *The Hidden Persuaders* (1957) by Vance Packard, discussed the potential manipulation of the consumer by marketers to affect the choices of consumers with such unsavoury methods as subliminal manipulation (affecting consumer perceptions when they were not consciously aware that this was happening).

The outcry about the book from the public in the US led to the suggestion that marketers were potentially able to brainwash consumers to do what they wanted them to do. While subliminal manipulation was never proven to significantly affect subconscious consumer choice, the mere idea was so onerous that any evidence found supporting the use of these types of methods would force marketers to stop their activities immediately. Self-regulation has therefore taken over, not only in the US, but in the UK as well and is still in effect.

The Hidden Persuaders was later followed in 1966 by Ralph Nader's book, *Unsafe at any Speed*, which touted the dangers inherent in the use of the Chevrolet Motors Corvair, which had caused injuries or death for a number of users. The point is that consumers were potentially being harmed by using unsafe products or being manipulated by companies to do their bidding. This was grounds not only for concern but in a number of countries, governmental watchdog agencies were established to protect consumers from these 'untrustworthy' corporations. How has this helped the consumer? This vigilance on the part of companies and public-sector policy-makers has raised the quality of consumer goods and made the safety of consumers a primary issue.

This wave of building consumer protectionism was further fuelled by concerns over the environment during the 1960s and 1970s. The pumping of pollutants into the environment and the use of non-biodegradable materials in packaging caused further outcry from the public about the damaging practices of corporations. Environmentalism then began to take hold as a major governmental concern, and, again, watchdog agencies were created to monitor the activities of companies in terms of their potentially damaging effects upon the environment. Companies were therefore held liable for actions which would potentially harm the environment, and green marketing or environmentally sound marketing became a major strategic initiative.

Environmental/green marketing

Environmental/green marketing involves the actions undertaken by the firm or donations that are aimed at improving or preserving the environment surrounding the firm. Green marketing focuses on the idea of keeping the environment clean and green. This often entails reducing or eliminating corporate pollution. There is certainly support for the statement that 'It pays to be green'. One can see many examples where the concerns of the environment are being strategically built into corporate plans. Take the visible example of McDonald's. McDonald's was criticized for using styrafoam packaging for its hamburgers that were not biodegradable. Strategically turning to improvement of its image, McDonald's began to replace the plastic packaging with paper packaging so that they were seen as more environmentally friendly. The New Zealand Government decided that since it was already known for its clean and green environment, anything made or connected with New Zealand would benefit from that association, so fruits, vegetables, lamb, agricultural equipment, and other products were automatically tagged with the 'made in New Zealand' label, which signalled environmental responsibility. There was great synergy strategically in undertaking this, since New Zealand found that its competitive advantage lay in its excellent agricultural industry.

Recently, Kia attempted the green strategy in the UK with the offering of a free bicycle with the purchase of a Sedona (Staff, 2005a). Since most car trips in the UK were found to be less than one mile in distance, Kia's concern was to give a free bicycle so that any short trips could be done on the bicycle, while longer trips could be handled using the Sedona. Kia also utilized a 'walking bus' campaign to promote escorting children to school, but while the company was able to take 1 per cent of the competitive car market, its cars were not seen by the public to be environmentally responsible, so the company was forced to use an aggressive pricing advertising strategy. The mistake here was that its product did not live up to its green strategic orientation, due to poor fuel efficiency ratings and perceived emission problems, thereby raising concerns with consumers that the image was inconsistent with their actions.

A more successful example could be seen in the environmentally responsible campaign undertaken by ABB Corporation. ABB invented a variable-speed drive unit that could allow a factory to operate in much the same way as a hybrid automobile, by slowing the emissions output and saving energy when the plant was not needed at full capacity production. In 2002, ABB ran a global campaign that touted that it could stop 50 million tons of carbon dioxide from being produced, and the campaign was quite successful, allowing the company to repeat the campaign in 2005, but it can now suggest that it can stop 68 million tons (Staff, 2005a).

Corporate strategists have taken particular notice of the Toyota Corporation World Food Programme. Toyota has put its brand soundly behind the United Nations' World Food Programme by supplying fleets of trucks to help with food deliveries. They just did this and did not promote it to the maximum. This has been one more piece of evidence of its environmental concern, and it has long supported this UN initiative. A clear partnership was formed which works to the benefit of both parties. The UN is aided by the use of the trucks, and Toyota gains increasing credibility for its environmental stewardship. This is an example of a win-win proposition. But what makes this so successful is that this activity is perfectly consistent with Toyota's mission, image, capabilities, and strategic context (Staff, 2005a).

The move to being seen as Green and environmentally friendly has picked up considerable corporate interest over the past ten years. Many companies now look to ensuring, not only that their own practices are environmentally sound, but that their suppliers and customers should be environmental stewards as well. This may spell the difference when considering the choice of different suppliers for potential long-term contractual relationships. In 2005, Ford Motor Company took the high road in attempting to address environmental issues by eliminating cardboard boxes when shipping materials from one plant to another and creating a plastic shipping container that not only reduced greenhouse gas emissions, but also reduced the number of shipments and used the containers in recycled form to create splash shields for its F-150 truck line. This saved almost 25 per cent in shipping costs and addressed a pressing environmental problem (Stoiber, 2006). Recently, Tesco has begun requiring its suppliers to provide labelling information reflecting the extent of their product's carbon footprint. Other good examples involve the decision by Coke to work towards ensuring clean water accessibility in many countries in which it sells its products, along with the recent environmental initiatives undertaken by UPS and FEDEX (see Mini Case Study 13.1).

MINI CASE STUDY 13.1 UPS and FEDEX are improving the environment

How do companies really live out their social responsibilities? Two global package delivery companies have both made significant commitments to social initiatives in both word and action. UPS and FEDEX have both made significant contributions to improving the environment and sustainability. United Parcel Service (UPS) has committed to launching delivery trucks with ordinary exteriors but very special interiors with completely experimental hydraulics systems which will attempt to replace many standard truck components with more efficient and less environmentally destructive alternatives. Several prototypes are already in production, and if they prove to be successful, they will be mass-produced and replace the existing truck fleets. The main purpose of the innovative componentry is to significantly reduce carbon emissions and provide capabilities for trucks that would rival the type of hybrid systems available for the Toyota Prius and Honda Civic, with the trucks drawing energy when the brakes are depressed, which will at the same time provide new pressure for the already used hydraulic fluids. UPS expects that the prototype trucks, which will cost somewhere around US$7,000 (£4,350) more per truck, will save the company in excess of US$50,000 (£31,050) over the lifetime of the truck, while reducing carbon emissions by as much as 30 per cent.

FEDEX (Federal Express) is also committing to social responsibility. FEDEX has recently released a Global Citizenship Report, which describes the company's plans for committing resources and manpower to make significant impacts upon communities in which it operates around the world. FEDEX is committed to reduce carbon emissions in particular from its fleet of aircraft by as much as 20 per cent, as well as improve its aircraft fuel efficiency by 20 per cent by the end of 2010. Using aircraft with cleaner-burning turbines will help to make this happen, and the company already expects its workforce to have a positive impact in every area of the world where they have plant and equipment, and they are well on their way to making this happen. FEDEX also recently launched a citizenship blog (**blog.fedex.com**) in conjunction with their Global Citizenship Report to highlight their plans to carry out the management's pledge to make the company a responsible world community member and improve sustainability. This will allow a regular interaction between FEDEX management and citizens/investors to facilitate this pledge and improve the process. The Global Citizenship Report discusses the various company social initiatives and accomplishments during the previous year (2008) and presents the goals for the upcoming year (2009). The company sets its objectives in terms of five different areas of social responsibility (benefits for the environment, aid for particular communities, improvements in economic performance and efforts on behalf of economic development, improving the lives of people both within the company and those affected by the company, and, finally, responsible handling of corporate governance).

These global companies believe that they can make a difference and they are doing much more than just talking good citizenship.

Forest L. Reinhardt, in a 1998 *California Management Review* article, outlined key strategic considerations when attempting to use environmental product differentiation. Reinhardt presented the following requirements for both industrial and consumer marketers:

- Will the customer pay a premium for this environmental product differentiation?
- Do the customers have credible information regarding the claims that you are making about these environmentally responsible products?
- Are there sufficient barriers to imitation to keep competitors from eroding the perceived advantage of your environmentally responsible products?

But environmental causes and actions on behalf of consumers may not by themselves be sufficient or fit with corporate strategy. Companies will not only need to act as stewards of the environment and protect consumers, but must also ensure that they act in an ethical manner.

Corporate ethicality

At one time, being a good corporation meant that you operated in a reasonable manner, adhering to laws and regulations, but as corporations like Enron, MCI, Parmalat, and Credit Lyonnais were seen as violating public trust, the issue of ethicality was added to the set of firm requirements. Charles Handy, in a 2002 article in the *Harvard Business Review*, discussed how serious this loss of trust had become in the US and the UK. He reported that a 2002 Gallup poll found that 90 per cent of Americans surveyed felt that those running corporations could not be trusted to look after the best interests of their employees. In this same study, it was also reported that only 18 per cent of those surveyed believed that companies made a significant effort to look after their shareholders, and 43 per cent perceived that senior executives were only concerned with their own well-being. Seeing the enormous amount of salaries being paid to senior executives when their companies were seriously underperforming presents supporting evidence of this problem. In fact, Handy reports that a British survey found that 95 per cent of those British respondents surveyed believed that senior executives were looking out for their own self-interests.

A more recent study by Ronald W. Clement (2006) found that when studying US business news reports for the period of 1 January 2000 until 30 June 2005, there was evidence found that as many as 40 of the *Fortune 100* most important US businesses had committed actions that would be considered to be unethical. These actions included antitrust behaviour, various types of fraud, discriminatory practices, infringement of patents, making unreported payments to executives, and various other ethical as well as legal infractions.

What these studies tell us is that this is representative of a serious problem, and the first step in eliminating the problem involves companies taking a harder stand on acting in an ethically responsible manner.

What is ethics? It is the set of moral principles or values that shape the actions of either an individual or a group of individuals. Ethical principles therefore set a standard for behaviour in a society. Legality sets the foundation for which behaviour are seen as lawful or unlawful, but ethics focuses more on moral judgement, and the focus becomes whether something is the right thing to do from a moral standpoint, as opposed to whether it is lawful or not. The difficulty is that certain activities that are seen as lawful may not actually be seen as ethical or morally appropriate, and certain activities that are seen as unlawful may not be morally inappropriate.

Why do we need ethics? Because there are a number of examples of businesses that have acted in ways that have damaged public trust. Scandals throughout the global business community have served to weaken consumer trust and belief in big business. Ethicality and the adoption of codes of ethical conduct serve to signal to the public that the companies that adopt them will not abide by unethical behaviour. With ethics, the question is not whether an action is legal or not, but whether the action is morally right or wrong. Morals are basically sets of rules derived from cultural norms. **Moral judgement is the framework of beliefs upon which the individual makes judgements on whether action is morally appropriate or not.** Different cultures have achieved different levels of moral judgement, which affects their views on whether certain actions are ethical or unethical. Cultural differences in ethical predisposition can be seen clearly when collectivist cultures are compared to individualistic cultures (Ford et al., 1997). Japanese managers coming from a collectivist orientation must undertake actions that benefit the group as a whole before they can even think about their own personal aggrandizement. Individualistic American managers look towards benefiting themselves first and secondarily look to benefit the group.

These differences in perspective and expectation can create difficulties when addressing the issue of ethicality of certain actions. As an example, a Japanese firm may use individuals to do intelligence gathering about competitor actions using any means necessary to find information that will help their company, but if the organization is put in a better position as a result of the information gathering, even if the actions were not morally defensible, the group benefits, and the individual benefits because the group benefits. The danger would be that if the Japanese employees were actually caught in the act of using inappropriate means to get the information, they would actually bring shame upon the company and be fired. This shows the potential complexity in the determination of right or wrong when judging the ethicality of certain actions or practices. Does the end justify the means, or do the means justify the end? These are fundamental philosophical arguments, and different cultures may approach ethical responsibility from different perspectives. In some cultures, if the group benefits as a result of the action, that is the only thing that matters. In other cultures, doing things the right way will ensure that the outcome is also morally defensible. What is ethical is a complex subject.

So how does a company approach ethical actions and ensure that it acts in an appropriate manner? It sets up a set of ethical guidelines for behaviour. All employees of the organization are asked to adhere to these guidelines in their actions. These guidelines often become formalized into a code of ethical conduct. It is expected that all individuals who are employed by the company will follow the code. Lamb et al. (2005) suggest that developing ethical guidelines or codes of conduct provides companies with the following advantages:

1. Employees learn to identify what the company recognizes as acceptable business practices.
2. The guidelines can serve as an effective internal behavioural control mechanism.
3. A written code eliminates any confusion as to whether a practice is ethical or not for decision-making purposes.
4. The formulation of the code of ethical conduct allows for the discussion among the firm's employees as to what is appropriate or not and produces better decision-making.

But is being ethical sufficient? Firms may need to actually get out into the community and 'make a difference'. How would this be achieved? The firm must act in a socially responsible manner.

Corporate social responsibility

So what exactly is corporate social responsibility? Is it corporate philanthropy? Is it helping the local community? Is it helping Third World countries? The answer is that all of these are examples of CSR tactics, but each may be insufficient on its own. It is a multi-faceted construct that is more complex than once thought. It is really all things that the firm can do to be a good and responsible citizen of the world community, and it incorporates everything previously mentioned in this chapter, along with a series of additional strategic choices to ensure that the company is a caring and contributing member of society. **Corporate social responsibility is the actions of the company to act in a socially responsible manner to protect and enhance the various stakeholders that have an interest in the company, the community in which it operates, the environment which surrounds it, and society.**

The various components of corporate social responsibility are shown in Figure 13.2. Two of these were previously discussed in this chapter, and the additional two will now be discussed. One important caution for global companies at this point is that different cultures may have different perceptions of the use of the importance of different levels of corporate social responsibility initiatives. A recent article by Nabil Ibrahim and Faramarz Parsa (2005) found that there were significantly different CSR responsiveness orientations when comparing American and French managers. The authors found that in general, American managers were more legally and ethically driven in terms of their orientation towards corporate social responsibility, while the French were found to be more driven by the economic and philanthropic components. These types of cultural differences can have a significant bearing on the success of global CSR initiatives, and understanding the potential for differences in perceptions helps prepare CSR strategists for alliances with foreign firms and organizations. Clearly, this research is in its infancy, and with the growing importance of CSR, more research is needed. The two initiatives that will now be discussed are corporate philanthropy and social activism.

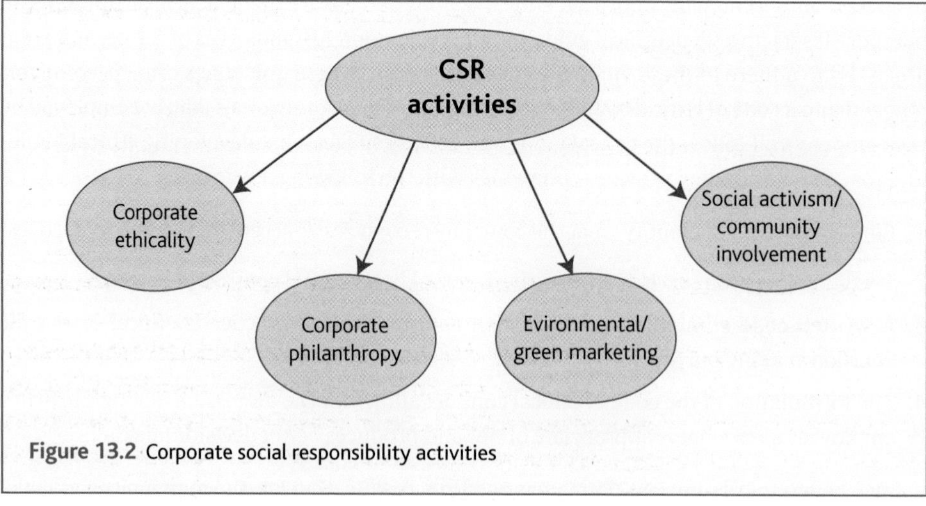

Figure 13.2 Corporate social responsibility activities

Corporate philanthropy

Corporate philanthropy is primarily focused on corporate giving to charitable organizations. Michael Porter and Mark Kramer (2002) suggest that, while most companies feel that they should give to charities, most do not know how to do it well. They argue that what is considered to be strategic philanthropy by many corporations, is often far more opportunistic than strategic, or worse, done for the sake of doing it rather than tying giving to anything meaningful. They suggest that philanthropy is actually more like public relations or advertising that works to enhance a company's image by attaching the name to cause-related marketing or charitable sponsorships. Porter and Kramer ask the question of whether corporations should even consider giving philanthropically. If by philanthropy one is referring to a variety of small cash payments to local charities or universities, this may not be appropriate, especially if the giving is more a function of the interests of certain executives in the organization. What is needed is the connection of these payments to a series of sound social or business objectives.

What Porter and Kramer (2002) suggest is that charitable giving can be used to improve their 'competitive context', which entails the actual quality of the business environment in the locations where the company does business. They suggest that philanthropy be used to merge social goals and economic goals, which would allow the company both to give money and also to leverage relationships and capabilities in the active support of charities. To accomplish this, there are changes that would have to be made in the way that the business approaches charitable giving. The company needs to refocus where it should spend its money as well as how.

The first requirement is to choose the best grantees for charitable donations. Who will benefit most from the company's donations? Who fits with the company's mission and capabilities? These are important questions to be answered first, before anything else is attempted. The second step entails signalling other funders as to what organization is a good recipient for donations, and by attracting the interest of other donors, overall philanthropic spending can be increased but also spread more effectively across a number of givers. Step three involves the improvement of recipient performance, which will not only benefit society but will also increase the impact of the monies given. This will then lead to the fourth step, the advancing of knowledge and practice, setting up what Porter and Kramer identify as a 'virtuous cycle'.

Another variant of charitable giving is what has become known as cause-related marketing or CRM (not to be confused with customer relationship management). **Cause-related marketing involves a linking up between the corporation and a particular charitable cause. There are two ways that this can happen: the company can make unconditional donations on a regular basis to a particular charitable cause, or it can link its donations to customer purchase behaviour.** The company that makes a donation to charity once a consumer has made a particular purchase allows the company to receive its benefit before the charitable organization receives its donation. Intuitively, one would expect that this could leave the consumer feeling that the activity is not as altruistically motivated as unconditional donations would be. However, a study done in 2003 (Dean, 2003/2004) found that when consumer perceptions of conditional and unconditional donations to charitable causes were compared, there was little negative effect found for the use of conditional donations. This study also examined the idea of whether long-term relationships with charitable cases and corporate donations were more important than single donations to charities, and the findings indicated that:

- Firms with excellent reputations for social responsibility gain little from single-instance charitable donations.
- Firms with poor reputations for social responsibility may significantly improve consumer perceptions from single-instance charitable giving.
- Firms with average reputations may or may not see improvements in consumer perceptions with single-instance giving.
- Firms that are perceived to be irresponsible socially will not be thought of as excellent community citizens with a single charitable donation. This will take time and effort to change significantly.

Ultimately, if the firm is interested in charitable giving, it must note that there are concerns associated with donations (Endacott, 2004). One is that causes like products or services may be subject to changing consumer preferences. What is the hot cause or charity today may lose resonance with your consumers tomorrow, so the donor company must be careful to track the perceptions of its consumers periodically to see if their feelings have changed towards a particular charity or cause. Significant events like hurricanes, tsunamis, terrorist attacks, and other disasters can divert consumer interests and force the company to shift its focus to a different charitable organization. The selection of a cause must be done carefully, since the cause or causes must resonate with your consumers and have a logical association with your company brand. Finally, for multinational companies, there are very few global charities but there are many global causes, so the multinational must be careful to choose wisely and realize that consumers in different countries may have significantly different perceptions of the same charitable organization or cause.

Sasse and Trahan (2007) suggest that corporate managers should carefully consider the basic trade-offs before committing any valuable corporate resources to social causes. They suggest that executives should follow four key guidelines when considering philanthropic activities:

1. Managers should be wary of any philanthropic expenditures that have unclear values or methods for determining pricing.
2. Managers should never underestimate or overestimate the benefits to company reputation that can be accrued through philanthropic spending (in particular, overhyping CSR can foster cynicism, as opposed to goodwill).
3. Managers should realize that even for very large corporations there must be clear spending limits set for philanthropic endeavours.
4. Managers should determine whether the philanthropic activities being considered limit the individual choices available for primary stakeholders (like diminishing individual volunteerism). The point is that if philanthropy is truly a strategically sound initiative, then it needs to be incorporated into business activities, but if it is only discretionary, then it should be offered to individuals rather than made a company-wide priority.

But merely giving to or lining up in an affiliation with a charitable organization may not be sufficient in this day and age. Another possibility involves focusing on improving the environment. This may certainly have social consequences, but the concern is for the improvement of the environment. Strategically, this may be a better choice for companies that have been criticized for polluting the environment or cutting down forests. It may be a necessary step to improving a damaged image. A unique example of this type of initiative can be seen in how Pernod-Rocard is trying to tie its Malibu Rum to sustainability in the world's coral reefs (see Mini Case Study 13.2).

MINI CASE STUDY 13.2 Rum and reefs?

Here is a new twist on corporate citizenship. Ads for Smirnoff have run recently in the UK with the image of clear and clean water and clarity of the purity of the vodka that is inside the bottle of Smirnoff, and over the course of the TV ads that have been running, everything is being rejected by the sea that has fallen into it over the course of history, leaving it pure once again like the product in the bottle of Smirnoff. The mental connection is pretty clear here, but now the French alcoholic beverage company, Pernod-Ricard, is taking this connection between water and its product to a completely different level in terms of its concern over the environment and the sustainability of global resources, by tying its Malibu Rum brand to actual efforts to protect and replenish coral reefs around the world.

There is certainly a nice perceptual connection between rum and Caribbean Islands, sun, sand, and surf, and fruit-and-rum island drinks, and Pernod-Ricard is seeing an effective way to tie itself to environmental sustainability through its building relationship with Reef Check, which is a non-profit organization focused on saving endangered coral reefs around the world. In order to make this connection, Pernod-Ricard is not only donating money to Reef Check to help with their cause, but is also adding Reef Check's logo to some of its Malibu Rum bottles to further solidify the connection. This type of corporate philanthropy is an interesting variation of the corporate social responsibility orientation. It makes a perceptual connection between a for-profit and a non-profit and makes its social initiatives tangible. This takes social activism from words to actions.

In this economically challenging period, the problem is that when charitable giving is involved, charities that are not faith-based are all in jeopardy as donors will prioritize what are key charities to them for giving purposes. Since donors will give more purposefully, some charities will fall out of their choice set, and this will hurt many smaller and less visible charities unless they find corporate benefactors. This type of alliance should be a win-win situation for Pernod-Ricard as it will be seen as doing its part for the environment while helping a small but meaningful charity in the fight against depletion of the world's resources. It will also help Pernod-Ricard in the sense that market research in the United States has shown that a large percentage of alcoholic beverage consumers would consider switching from a brand that does not align itself with a social cause to one that does. The special bottles will not only include the Reef Check logo, but will also have the charity's website and information on how consumers can potentially enter into a training programme to become actual reef monitors. Pernod-Ricard hopes that this will help it to build a long-term relationship with its consumers. This could be an interesting step in the right direction, provided the connection becomes clear enough to potential consumers.

Social activism and community involvement

One important type of CSR activity involves the firm in an activist role in attempting to improve the community in which it operates. **Social activism includes the actions undertaken by a firm, individuals or a group that are aimed at making the quality of life in society better for all the inhabitants. From a firm strategy perspective, this would often involve some kind of proactive role in improving the community in which the firm operates.** An important approach to this can be seen in what is known as corporate social initiatives or CSIs. Many companies in the UK as well as in the US are now focused on building corporate images as good community citizens. A great deal of financial resource is being invested in community involvement projects. These projects range from locally focused education and training for youth and adults to improve their employment potential, to global projects involving aid for developing countries. The various levels and mechanisms for corporate social activism are found in Figure 13.3.

A pointed example of social involvement can be seen in the US in the efforts of Home Depot to bring company employees into community service. In 2004, a donation of 2 million hours of community service was made by 50,000 of Home Depot's 325,000 employees (Grow et al., 2005). Home Depot's CEO, Robert L. Nardelli, is trying to encourage other companies to follow Home Depot's lead. In May 2005, he invited executives from 24 different companies and foundations to come to Home Depot's headquarters in Atlanta, Georgia, to discuss community service initiatives. In September 2005, these executives kicked off a 'Month of Service', a plan developed with a community group known as the Hands-On Network, which entails 2,000 different community projects across the United States using corporate volunteers. This is certainly a reflection of the importance of changing the focus from shareholders to stakeholders, as Nardelli argues that the firm must be accountable to its suppliers, customers, employees, community members, and social activists.

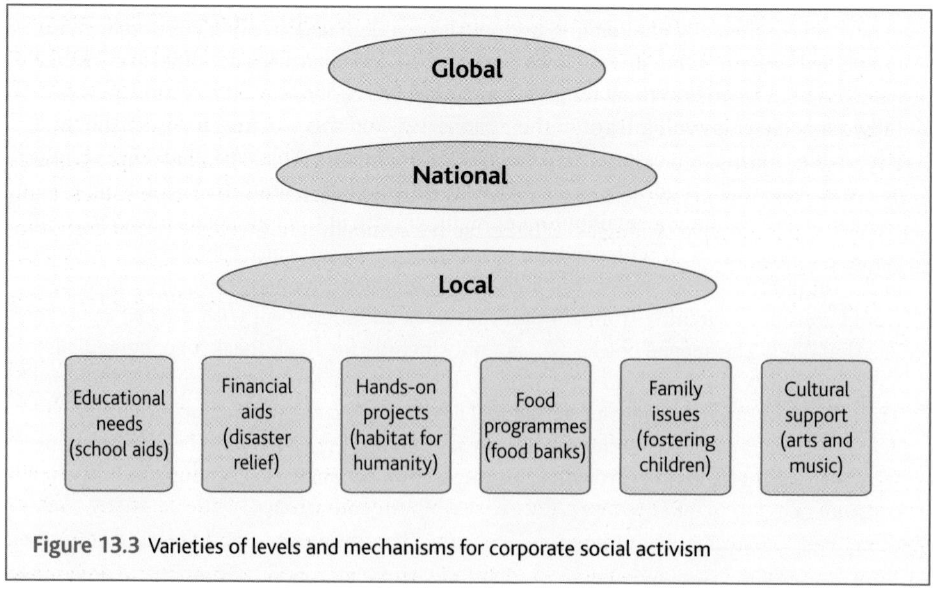

Figure 13.3 Varieties of levels and mechanisms for corporate social activism

The use of the Hands-On Network is reflective of the fact that there is an increasing importance to the partnering possibilities with NGOs (non-governmental organizations). **NGOs are organized around shared values, principles or beliefs (Spar and LaMure, 2003). They are activist organizations that work for particular causes of interest. Examples include Greenpeace, Earthwatch, PETA (People for the Ethical Treatment of Animals), and the Free Burma Coalition. These organizations can bring strong pressure to bear upon target organizations.** When faced with NGO pressure, companies have three strategic options: (1) pre-emption; (2) capitulation; and (3) resistance (Spar and LaMure, 2003). Some firms become proactive and develop a dialogue with NGOs which can lead to a partnership, while others give in to pressures or fight. The costs of resistance can be high from the standpoint of financial costs as well as potentially damaged images. A good example of a company partnering with NGOs is that which was recently announced between Cadbury Schweppes and two NGOs to work together on a project to improve biodiversity levels of cocoa farms in Ghana and help the country establish its first cocoa farm eco-tourism initiative (Staff, 2005b).

The key to success for these kinds of proactive partnerings is to understand what each party wants to get from the partnership and see how this can be accomplished. Cadbury paired up with Earthwatch and the Ghana Nature Conservation Research Centre (NCRC), and the three worked together to find a common ground. The partnership helped ensure benefits for each of the three partners. It helped develop strong relationships for Cadbury with cocoa farmers in Ghana, improved the conditions for the farmers, fostered agricultural improvements that aided the environment, and created new natural habitats for wildlife. All around, it was seen as a beneficial relationship. It seems clear that social activism, social projects, and community involvement are important mechanisms for CSR.

Hess et al. (2002) argue that these new social projects are a significant departure from previous community relations projects, which were often opportunistically undertaken. The authors suggest that these new corporate social initiatives, or CSIs, as they call them, are actually closely tied to core competencies and long-term corporate strategies. They cite such companies as United Parcel Service (UPS), which has collected packaged food products from Europe and the United States, stored these donated products in distribution centres and then delivered those goods to aid refugees and natural disaster victims in impoverished countries. This type of corporate aid represents a major shift from the isolated philanthropic gestures of the 1980s when firms made donations without truly building on their core values, competencies, and long-term strategies. What effective companies now realize is that corporate investments in community development build strong community trust, goodwill, and partnerships, which in turn lead to stronger local economies as well as corporate profitability. It is definitely based upon their public profile due to their charity work.

Hess et al. (2002) examined a number of recent successful CSIs and found that they had three things in common: (1) they were all connected to core values of the firms involved; (2) they were all built upon the core competencies of the firm; and, (3) the CSI programmes undertaken were systematically reviewed, evaluated, and were reported regularly to all relevant firm stakeholders. This represents a shift from the sole importance of the company's shareholders to all relevant stakeholders (e.g., communities, employees, and governments). The authors argue that the change has been driven by three factors: (1) competitive advantage (community involvement and the resulting positive image creates a new source of less tangible and hard-to-imitate corporate competitive advantage; (2) the new moral marketplace (companies must adhere to the moral expectations and standards of their stakeholders); and, (3) the comparative advantage of private firms (intense competition has enabled private firms to be better positioned than either governments or non-profits to assist in solving social problems).

The authors caution that firms designing corporate social initiatives should be aware of possible criticisms that they may face. Shareholders (rather than stakeholders) may raise concerns surrounding the costs inherent in CSIs that might reduce potential dividend payouts. Even some of the firm's stakeholders may be concerned with the particular causes that are chosen. Finally, they caution that CSIs may involve difficult judgements on such things as the actual reaction of consumers to the initiatives, as well as the actual nature of the expected market impact. Will the consumers buy into the cause? Will they buy more of the company's products and services as a result?

Hess et al. (2002) present four critical suggestions for companies when approaching the development of corporate social initiatives:

1. The firm must connect the CSIs to its mission statement and core values, with top management integrally involved in the CSI programme development, implementation, and evaluation.
2. Firm management must be in sync with marketplace expectations of social responsibility so that alienation and reputation loss will not occur.
3. CSIs must be tied directly to the core competencies and primary resources of the company.
4. The company must set clear objectives for CSI programmes and have specific mechanisms for measuring the success of these programmes.

So how do we measure and communicate our successes in terms of our CSR initiatives? We must be careful to do it thorough social audits. There is a growing concern in Europe as well as in the United States over the need for social auditing, accounting, and reporting (SAAR). This is a necessary evolutionary development as there must be measurement of firm success in terms of social performance to be able to report effectively that performance to stakeholders. Social reporting improvements have recently been seen in the creation of the Global Reporting Initiative (GRI) and the Institute of Social and Ethical Accountability (ISEA). These types of initiatives will help companies better communicate their successes with important stakeholders.

But if CSR is so important and widespread, why is there still so much confusion? Because too many firms are doing it to say that they do it, and they do not have any true commitment to it. CSR must be made an integral part of the strategic planning process.

Moving CSR from compliance to strategic imperative

If the company is to move beyond the use of CSR to playact at being a community citizen, it becomes imperative to find ways in which the firm can truly practice what it is preaching. This, like strategic planning itself, can be done so that the organization can say that it has completed the process to tick off one more box on the list of things to do. As has been discussed previously in this chapter, CSR is not just giving money to charitable organizations. It incorporates such important issues as human rights, environmental stewardship, family-friendly work conditions, and community development and nurturing. It is a multifaceted construct which should be thought of as an integral part of business strategy. What firms are now finding is that corporate citizenship leads to competitive advantage. Marc J. Epstein and Bill Birchard present a convincing argument for this in their groundbreaking 1999 book, *Counting What Counts: Turning Corporate Accountability to Competitive Advantage*. The authors suggest that intense competition in a variety of industries presents companies with the possibility that all of them will be seen as comparable, potentially undermining perceived competitive advantages. A reputation for good corporate citizenship serves as an effective point for differentiation. One can certainly argue that firms like Ben & Jerry's and The Body Shop have made names for themselves with their corporate citizenry. As the authors argue, good reputations attract investors, customers, and better job candidates, and nurturing environments help keep employees from leaving. There are also tax benefits that can accrue to those good corporate community members, and, above all else, a strong reputation is not easily undermined by competitors.

Well, how do we know that corporate citizenship really pays? Epstein and Birchard (1999) tried to find some evidence to support these claims. They discuss the results of two surveys that were done in 1998 to demonstrate the relevance of CSR. The first was done in the UK by MORI, and the main finding was that one-third of the analysts and institutional investors that were surveyed believed that community citizenship does positively affect financial performance. The other survey was done by the Conference Board in New York City which involved interviews with 25,000 consumers across 23 countries and found that two-thirds of the consumer respondents felt that businesses should address social issues. Even more enlightening was the fact that 23 per cent of the respondents actually took personal actions to punish those companies that they believed were not being socially responsible.

The problem is that even though this argument has been made, many managers still seem to remain somewhat sceptical about the importance of CSR. The Conference Board went further in their assessment and found that in the period from 1995 to 1997, those asset management firms that were socially conscious and invested accordingly grew by 227 per cent as opposed to only 84 per cent for assets managed across all funds (Epstein and Birchard, 1999). There is at least evidence that being a responsible corporate citizen can be a profitable strategy. What is helping presently is that there are increasing numbers of firms that are actually touting their financial successes from pursuing social responsibility initiatives. In a recent *Marketing Week* article (5 May 2005), Sainsbury's CEO, Justin King, was reported as telling their investors that the company's support for Comic Relief's Red Nose Day generated an extra 0.3 per cent sales in the first quarter of 2005. People were visiting Sainsbury's to actually buy a red nose (he reported that almost 4 million were sold) and remaining in the stores to buy other items. As a result, Sainsbury's, which had been struggling financially, was able to increase store sales while also raising £6.5 million for Comic Relief's charities. It seems as though it is resonating much more visibly with consumers as well.

If community citizenry is to help the firm gain a competitive advantage, CSR must be integrated into everything that the company does. Epstein and Birchard (1999) examined a number of companies and found that the following steps were important in ensuring that this integration actually takes place within the firm:

1. Engage the stakeholders through dialogue. (What would they like us to do?)
2. Define and codify values, codes, and policies. (What does citizenship entail?)
3. Assign executive responsibility. (Who will champion the process?)
4. Integrate social issues into strategic planning. (Is it really important to the company?)
5. Communicate and train. (Are our people on board and committed?)
6. Measure what really counts. (What are meaningful measures for social performance?)
7. Report and verify. (Have we effectively told our story to our stakeholders?)

Companies are increasingly reporting that the pursuit of CSR initiatives is paying back in significant ways. An analysis was carried out by the Work Foundation and The Virtuous Circle in the UK in 2003 to assess whether CSR activities generated higher performance, and the report published from this study on 25 March 25 2004 called, *Achieving High Performance: CSR at the Heart of Business*, indicated that high-performing businesses did show a strong correlation between CSR activities and stronger performance in terms of productivity, as well as profitability when compared with other firms (Staff, 2004). The key, as has already been demonstrated, is to make CSR a part of corporate planning so that it is pursued meaningfully, carefully, and synergistically.

Probably the most persuasive argument presented for the value of CSR is that of Porter and Kramer (2006) in the *Harvard Business Review*. In a follow-up to their insightful article from 2002 (previously discussed), the authors argue that there are now four prevailing justifications for CSR: (1) moral obligation (it is the duty of good citizens to act in a morally responsible way); (2) sustainability (we should be good stewards of our environment and our communities); (3) license to operate (we must get formal approval from governments and other important stakeholders to operate as a business entity); and, (4) reputation (if we improve our company image through good works, we will improve our image, our morale, and our stock value). They argue, however, that all four of these justifications are limited since they centre more on the discrepancies between the business and society than on the codependency of the two. As a result, no single justification is sufficient from this list. Porter and Kramer (2006) suggest that in order to really advance CSR, companies must recognize that they and society are interrelated and that if they do well, society will do well, and vice versa. The most important point made by the authors is that the real test for whether a social initiative makes sense to pursue is whether it presents the chance to create some kind of shared value. This requires a meaningful benefit for society that is also valuable to the company. **An appropriate social agenda for a company should not try to solve all of the problems faced by society, but should fit with and reinforce company strategy through social advancement.** This is the key to success.

In order to examine various social issues, Porter and Kramer (2006) suggest that the firm think of social issues as divided into three different classifications, which will affect their priorities. These are shown in Figure 13.4. **General social issues** are those that are important for society but have little effect upon the company and its competitiveness or are little influenced by how the company does business. **Value chain social impacts** are those that are affected by what the company does in its business operations. **Social dimensions of competitive context** are those factors that affect company competitiveness. In order for the company to create an effective social agenda, it must rethink the purpose of its CSR. Responsive CSR where the company acts as a good corporate citizen is not the real answer. The real answer is in elevating CSR to strategic CSR, where the company chooses a unique position for itself,

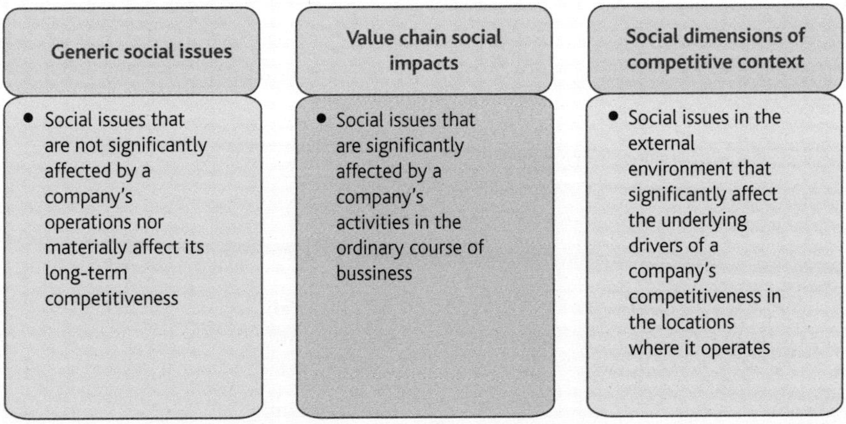

Generic social issues	Value chain social impacts	Social dimensions of competitive context
• Social issues that are not significantly affected by a company's operations nor materially affect its long-term competitiveness	• Social issues that are significantly affected by a company's activities in the ordinary course of bussiness	• Social issues in the external environment that significantly affect the underlying drivers of a company's competitiveness in the locations where it operates

Figure 13.4 Prioritizing social issues

Source: Michael E. Porter and Mark R. Kramer (2006), 'Strategy and Society: The Link between Competitive Advantage and Corporate Social Responsibility', *Harvard Business Review*, December, pp. 78–92. Reprinted with the permission of Harvard Business Publishing.

which improves company performance from an internal operations perspective as well as an external perspective, not only in better serving its customers but also in making incremental improvements for society and interconnecting themselves with society. This cannot be a short-term fix used by a company as a stopgap measure. In terms of the move to strategic CSR, Falck and Heblich (2007) argue that the only meaningful way to do this is to make a long-term commitment to strategic CSR, since any meaningful action is an investment in the company's future and as such should be carefully planned, supervised, and evaluated.

A study published in 2007 by Husted and Allen provided an interesting follow-up to the suggestions of Porter and Kramer (2006). Their comparison of traditional CSR, strategic CSR, and traditional strategy is found in Figure 13.5. They address the differences across five important strategic dimensions: visibility (the extent to which social actions can be seen by stakeholders); appropriability (the ability of the firm to gain economic benefits from the social activity); voluntarism (taking into consideration the differences between market activities and CSR projects); centrality (the connection to the core business mission); and proactivity (the extent to which the company is forward thinking and acting, rather than reactive). This adds nuance to the suggestions of Porter and Kraner (2006) that can help businesses shift more effectively from traditional CSR to strategic CSR.

Finally, given the current economic problems, the danger is that with recession and economic uncertainty comes a shift from long-term to short-term planning horizons. The tendency to shift initiatives as the situation changes may lead a number of companies to forget that the important benefits to be accrued from strategic CSR will require a continued focus on the long term. Short-term knee-jerk reactions to environmental shocks will potentially undermine the incremental investments that have been made and reputational benefits that have begun to accrue for the businesses involved. Staying the course will be the key to riding out the rough economic times so that serious backtracking is avoided.

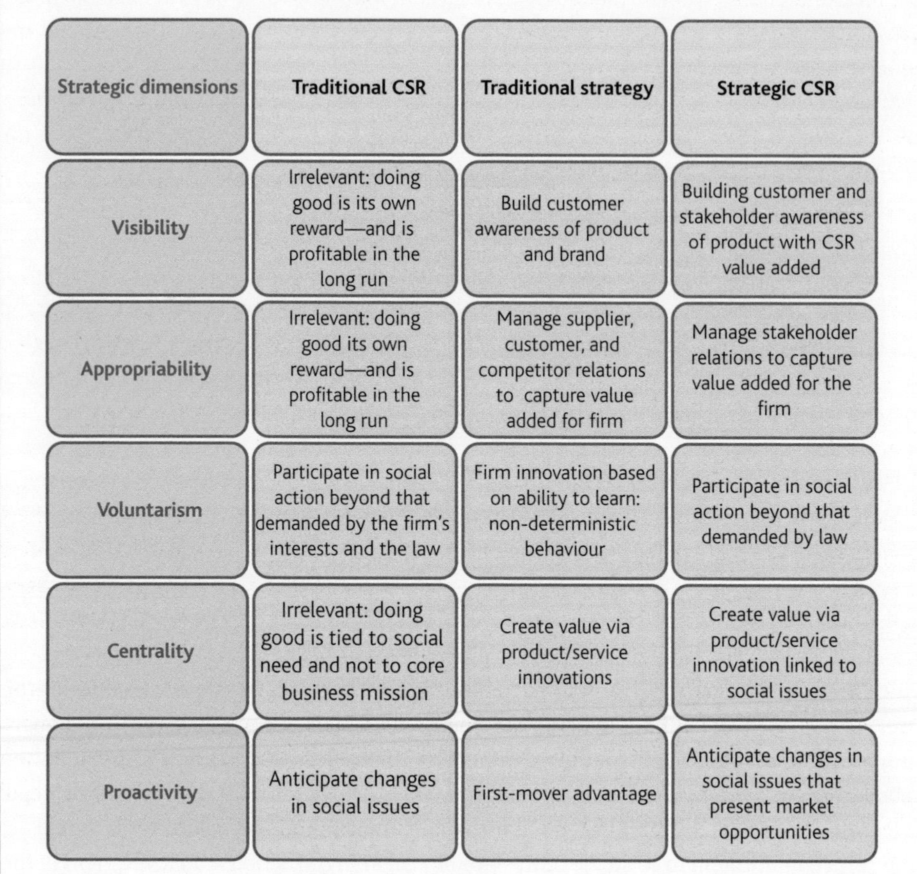

Strategic dimensions	Traditional CSR	Traditional strategy	Strategic CSR
Visibility	Irrelevant: doing good is its own reward—and is profitable in the long run	Build customer awareness of product and brand	Building customer and stakeholder awareness of product with CSR value added
Appropriability	Irrelevant: doing good its own reward—and is profitable in the long run	Manage supplier, customer, and competitor relations to capture value added for firm	Manage stakeholder relations to capture value added for the firm
Voluntarism	Participate in social action beyond that demanded by the firm's interests and the law	Firm innovation based on ability to learn: non-deterministic behaviour	Participate in social action beyond that demanded by law
Centrality	Irrelevant: doing good is tied to social need and not to core business mission	Create value via product/service innovations	Create value via product/service innovation linked to social issues
Proactivity	Anticipate changes in social issues	First-mover advantage	Anticipate changes in social issues that present market opportunities

Figure 13.5 Comparison of traditional CSR, strategic CSR, and traditional strategy

Source: Bryan W. Husted and David B. Allen, Strategic Corporate Social Responsibility and Value Creation among Large firms: Lessons from the Spanish Experience, *Long Range Planning,* pp. 594–610. © 2007, with permission of Elsevier.

Lessons learned by key CSR practitioners

An insightful article was published in *Corporate Responsibility Management* that provided important strategic lessons learned from five experienced CSR practitioners (Longshaw et al., 2005). Paul Longshaw is a CSR consultant who has worked with a number of major corporations, including British Petroleum, Cancer Research UK, Orange, Oxfam, and Vodafone. One particularly relevant lesson related to his experiences with BP, which tasked him and three others with the responsibility to implement a global volunteering initiative for 100,000 employees. He found out that it was not possible to do this virtually through the intranet and that this kind of communication really had to be done face-to-face. He had to be able to convince the employees, but this could not be done from a distance. He also recommended that global programmes of this kind have to allow for cultural adaptations, since different cultures have different ways of dealing with community involvement. The last recommendation that he made was that if a company attempts this kind of global initiative rollout, it should heavily utilize the backing of senior management. Their names and endorsement should be readily visible.

Another practitioner interviewed in the article was Anita Roper, who was hired as the director of sustainability at Alcoa. Her recommendation involves taking the time to talk to the relevant stakeholders. Nothing is better than outright personal consultation, but the process takes time and should be planned for. All relevant stakeholders should be included and given sufficient time to understand the issue and give their informed opinion.

The third practitioner interviewed in this article was Brendan May, head of CSR at Weber Shandwick, a UK public relations company. May suggests that the greatest lesson he learned was to actively engage NGOs. The people who work for NGOs work for low salaries because they are so heavily committed to the cause that they are focused on. They tend to be much trusted by the public, and entering into dialogue and eventual partnerships is the best approach to take.

The fourth practitioner interviewed was Michael Hastings, head of corporate social responsibility for the BBC. He provides three main lessons learned: (1) it is essential to get ownership of the CSR agenda you are interested in undertaking from the CEO; (2) CSR is most importantly about ingraining processes into an organization rather than a PR proposition; and (3) if the process is to be incorporated into the fabric of the organization, you have to show people how it will improve performance.

The fifth and last interviewee was Lynn Patterson, senior manager in charge of CSR at RBC Financial Group. Her suggestion for CSR practitioners is to be careful to slow things down a bit since there are quite quick changes going on in CSR. She suggests that rushing in may be a mistake because fads come and go, and implementing an initiative without knowing who all the key players are and without a network of trusted sources may be disastrous.

The latest thinking: the Virtue Matrix and the New Social Compact

The Virtue Matrix

Roger L. Martin, in an article in the *Harvard Business Review* (2002) provided an excellent tool for corporate strategists to allow them to calculate the potential profitability of acting socially responsibly. He called this tool the Virtue Matrix. Martin argues that corporate management must deal with a series of obstacles when attempting to position their companies as better community citizens. If companies commit to community projects that are not undertaken by competitors, they risk losing their competitive position. If they welcome the involvement of the government in overseeing the projects, they face the possibility of new regulations being passed forcing the company to spend a considerable amount of money in compliance with limited social benefits being realized. Finally, if companies adopt wage scales and working conditions that match those in developed nations, they may force jobs to be outsourced to countries with less restrictive standards. Martin presents corporate social responsibility as a product or service that is subject to market forces, and his Virtue Matrix allows the user to understand the forces that affect supply and demand.

Martin (2002) divides corporate social responsibility into two components: instrumental and intrinsic. Instrumental CSR involves such activities as the support of charities and arts/cultural organizations, either by choice or by regulation, that serve both the interests of shareholders and the interests of society and the community. Intrinsic CSR includes those actions and initiatives that are altruistic by nature but which may or may not resonate with shareholders. These are actions which are undertaken because management believes that they are the right thing to do but may not sufficiently serve shareholder interests. As a result, by incorporating both of these aspects into the matrix, Martin provides a better framework for managers to evaluate CSR opportunities.

The matrix is divided into four quadrants. The two lower quadrants of the matrix comprise the **civil foundation**, which incorporates laws, regulations, customs, and norms. The lower-left quadrant includes conduct that is undertaken **by choice** to adhere to norms or customs, while the lower-right quadrant includes those actions that are mandated by regulations or laws. These actions are therefore labelled as actions of **compliance**.

In his article, Martin (2002) suggests that many CSR actions begin by entering in the bottom-left quadrant, but as they become more the norm rather than the exception, they eventually become the basis for laws or regulations and move to the lower-right quadrant. Martin suggests that the key aspect to the civil foundation is that the upper limit is not fixed. It will move over time. In developed economies, it may be expected that new social initiatives will often become norms and are later codified. The point is that the upper limit will move. In developed economies, it may be expected to move upwards, while it might actually move downwards in less healthy economies.

The upper quadrants involve those activities that are intrinsic by nature, which may or may not be seen as beneficial by shareholders over time. These actions are undertaken because management feels they are the correct actions to take. Certainly it would be expected that if these are seen as valuable to shareholders, other companies would imitate those behaviours, and as a result upper-quadrant initiatives may move downwards into the civil foundation over time. The upper-left quadrant is the **strategic frontier**, which includes activities that may actually add to shareholder value if those actions are supported by customers, employees, and governmental agencies. The upper-right quadrant is the **structural frontier**, which includes those actions that are intrinsic and clearly not in the interests of shareholders. Here, the idea is to bring benefits to society rather than immediately to the company. The line separating these two upper quadrants is shown as a wavy line because some CSR initiatives fall in the middle between those actions that would be seen as beneficial and those that would be seen as inappropriate. It becomes clear when examining the matrix that there would be potentially innovative and beneficial initiatives that would be stifled because management would not want to take the risk to attempt something which competitors would not emulate and which shareholders would not value.

Martin (2002) argues that the biggest barrier to corporate virtue is the lack of vision inherent in company management, but this can be corrected by providing support for businesses and leaders who undertake innovative and risky actions. Martin suggests that **consumer agitation** can help in this regard. Consumer pressure can support corporate actions. Martin also suggests that **peer encouragement** can help, as businesses that achieve success can communicate that success and encourage other companies to follow suit. Martin also argues that the lack of any economic incentives is problematic regarding corporate initiatives that fall in the structural frontier because, here, the rewards are not necessarily visible to consumers, so consumer agitation will not help and peer encouragement will not be found since the risks may appear to be too high. As a result, it may have to be governmental agencies that step in and validate the actions undertaken to help initiatives shift from the upper quadrants to the lower quadrants.

The Virtue Matrix is one of the most interesting and innovative approaches that have been developed to help corporate managers understand the forces inherent in positioning their companies as good community citizens. Companies and their innovative managers can indeed find ways in which to better both society and their own shareholders, as well as create for themselves a competitive advantage and greater profitability if they understand the forces involved and the potential barriers that have to be overcome. The Virtue Matrix provides an excellent tool for strategic decision-making.

The New Social Compact

Another recent innovation that is of interest to strategists is the New Social Compact, as proposed by Brugmann and Prahalad in a 2007 *Harvard Business Review* article. The authors argue that companies and social activists are beginning to work together in meaningful ways to develop completely new business models that will help to improve companies and the poor globally. They suggest that there are great synergies between major corporations and NGOs in relation to their particular competencies, infrastructures, and understanding of what is happening in low-income areas of the world. They found effective examples in the partnerships between Microsoft and the NGO Prathau to provide personal computers to villagers in low-income areas of India. They also found that Nestlé was working with health officials and NGOs in Columbia, the Philippines, and Peru to provide educational programmes for the poor and to provide healthier food products to the poor in those countries. Another example involved the partnership between Danone and Grameen Bank in Bangladesh to create and sell vital, yet affordable, dairy products. What is important is that these organizations are working to help those at the bottom end of the income scale. Working together, these companies and NGOs can develop new business models that will help customers to move out of their poverty level. The benefits are clearly social and environmental and will improve company financial performance at the same time. Putting real strategic CSR into action will produce a myriad of benefits for the companies themselves, along with society at large. Great strides are being made as social initiative is interwoven into business mission and strategy.

Conclusion

Companies must carefully consider their place in the world around them. What role will they play in society? What social initiatives must they undertake to be considered a good community citizen? These are important questions that must be answered. Firms can no longer think of themselves in isolation from the forces and publics around them. Gone are the days of just satisfying shareholders. The company of today must pay attention to a number of relevant publics, including employees, suppliers, partners, community groups, and social activists.

CSR managers must weave initiatives into the basic fabric of the organization, and CSR must be a process that is endorsed by top management. When done the right way, not only will it improve the image of the firm, but it will also improve productivity and profitability. Good corporate citizenship is well worth the effort, but it must be tied to the skills, abilities, competencies, and values of the firm.

Summary

Corporate social responsibility is comprised of a number of important components. The firm has an economic responsibility in that it must maximize shareholder value. The firm also has a legal responsibility to operate according to society's rules and regulations. Beyond law and economics, social responsibility also encompasses ethics. The firm must act in a fair, just, and moral way in its operations. Finally, corporate social responsibility entails a discretionary/philanthropic level that entails such diverse social responsibilities as donating money and hands-on help to charities, the community, the environment, and in some cases to developing nations. Being a good community citizen carries great responsibilities with it. It signifies being a good steward of the investments made by the shareholders; it means operating within the legal system of not only the location of the headquarters but also wherever else the firm has operations; it entails ensuring that the firm, its employees, and its management always do what is fair and morally defensible; and it demands that the firm act in a responsible way to help the local community, make the environment cleaner and safer, and protect community citizens.

But being a good citizen is not just doing things that appear to be altruistic for the sake of being able to say that you are a good community citizen. The things that are done, the aid given, the corporate presence in different activities and initiatives, must be tied to the mission, values, and essence of the organization and its leadership. Corporate social responsibility must be treated as an integral part of strategic market planning. Only when the company sees itself as a vital member of its various communities will it act in the most appropriate ways and ensure its viability. Hopefully, with the strategic knowledge that this text provides, the reader will be more prepared to make better-informed decisions as the firm operates in its various markets.

KEY TERMS

Cause-related marketing (CRM) The commitment of a corporation to a particular charitable cause. There are two ways that this can happen, the company can make unconditional donations on a regular basis to a particular charitable cause, or it can link its donations to customer purchase behaviour. The company that makes a donation to charity once a consumer has made a particular purchase allows the company to receive its benefit before the charitable organization receives its donation.

Corporate philanthropy The act of giving to charitable organizations. This might include donations of monies, physical labour, or marketing expertise.

Corporate social responsibility (CSR) The activities of the company undertaken for the purpose of acting in a socially responsible manner to protect and enhance the various stakeholders that have an interest in the company, the community in which it operates, the environment which surrounds it, and society.

Environmental/green marketing The actions undertaken by the firm or donations that are aimed at improving or preserving the environment surrounding the firm. Green marketing focuses on the idea of keeping the environment clean and green. This often entails reducing or eliminating corporate pollution.

Ethics The set of moral principles or values that shape the actions of either an individual or a group of individuals. Ethical principles therefore set a standard for behaviour in a society. Legality sets the foundation for what behaviour are seen as lawful or unlawful, but ethics focuses more on moral judgement, and the focus becomes the right thing to do from a moral standpoint, as opposed to whether it is lawful or not.

Instrumental CSR The types of activities undertaken by the company in support of charities and arts/cultural organizations, either by choice or by regulation, that serve both the interests of shareholders and those of society and the community.

Intrinsic CSR Actions and initiatives that are altruistic by nature but which may or may not resonate with shareholders. These are actions which are undertaken because management believes that they are the right thing to do but may not sufficiently serve shareholder interests.

Moral judgement The framework of beliefs upon which the individual makes judgements on whether an action is morally appropriate or not.

Non-governmental organizations (NGOs) Enterprises organized around shared values, principles, or beliefs. They are activist organizations that work for particular causes of interest. Examples include Greenpeace, Earthwatch, PETA (People for the Ethical Treatment of Animals), and the Free Burma Coalition. These organizations can bring strong pressure to bear upon target organizations.

Shareholders Those individuals who have purchased stock in the company. They have a vested interest in the operation of the firm. They expect the company to be a good steward of their investments.

Social activism The actions undertaken by a firm, individuals or a group aimed at making the quality of life in society better for all the inhabitants. From a firm strategy perspective, this would often involve some kind of proactive role in improving the community in which the firm operates.

Social marketing The application of marketing principles and practices to help with the resolving of health and social problems. This involves the use of marketing in a great many countries to change public behaviour and practices considered to be harmful to health and societal well-being.

Stakeholders All the groups or publics that interact with and are affected by the operations of the firm. These publics include employees, partners, suppliers, customers, community members, governmental agencies, and social activist groups.

Q DISCUSSION QUESTIONS

1 Evaluate the difference between company shareholders and stakeholders. Why might the difference matter when determining appropriate CSR strategy?

2 Give an example of a judgement. Explain how it might affect marketing strategy decision-making.

3 How do French and American managers differ in their views of corporate social responsibility, and why would this be important for a CSR strategist?

4 What is cause-related marketing? Assess the two variations of cause-related giving that were discussed in the chapter.

5 Evaluate the three primary requirements for using environmental product differentiation as suggested by Forest L. Reinhardt.

6 What are corporate social initiatives? Evaluate the key considerations when they are being developed.

7 Does corporate social responsibility create firm profits? Provide reasoned arguments and support for them.

8 What is the Virtue Matrix? Explain how it works, and why is it important for the CSR strategist.

ONLINE RESOURCE CENTRE

Visit the Online Resource Centre for this book for lots of interesting additional material at: **www.oxfordtextbooks.co.uk/orc/west2e/**

REFERENCES AND FURTHER READING

Brugmann, Jeb, and C. K. Prahalad (2007), 'Cocreating Business's New Social Compact', *Harvard Business Review*, February, pp. 80–90.

Clement, Ronald W. (2006), 'Just How Unethical is American Business?' *Business Horizons*, 49, pp. 313–27.

Dean, Dwayne Hal (2003/2004), 'Consumer Perception of Corporate Donations: Effects of Company Reputation for Social Responsibility and Type of Donation', *Journal of Advertising*, 32 (4), pp. 91–103.

Endacott, Roy William John (2004), 'Consumer and CRM: A National and Global Perspective', *Journal of Consumer Marketing*, 21 (3), pp. 183–9.

Epstein, Marc J., and Bill Birchard (1999), *Counting what Counts: Turning Corporate Accountability to Competitive Advantage* (New York: Perseus Books).

Falck, Oliver, and Stephan Heblich (2007), 'Corporate Social Responsibility: Doing Well by Doing Good', *Business Horizons*, 50, pp. 247–54.

Ford, John B., Michael S. LaTour, Scott J. Vitell, and Warren A. French (1997), 'Moral Judgment and Market Negotiations: A Comparison of Chinese and American Managers', *Journal of International Marketing*, 5 (2), pp. 57–76.

Grow, Brian, Steve Hamm, and Louise Lee (2005), 'The Debate over Doing Good', *Business Week*, 3947 (15 August), p. 76.

Handy, Charles (2002), 'What's a Business for?', *Harvard Business Review*, December, pp. 49–55.

Hess, David, Nikolai Rogovsky, and Thomas W. Dunfee (2002), 'The Next Wave of Corporate Community Involvement: Corporate Social Initiatives', *California Management Review*, 44 (2), pp. 110–25.

Husted, Bryan W., and David B. Allen (2007), 'Strategic Corporate Social Responsibility and Value Creation among Large Firms: Lessons from the Spanish Experience', *Long Range Planning*, 40, pp. 594–610.

Ibrahim, Nabil, and Faramarz Parsa (2005), 'Corporate Social Responsiveness Orientation: Are there Differences between US and French Managers?', *Review of Business*, 26 (1), pp. 27–33.

Joachimsthaler, Erich, and David A. Aaker (1997), 'Building Brands without Mass Media', *Harvard Business Review*, January–February, pp. 39–50.

Kayes, D. Christopher, David Stirling, and Tjai M. Nielsen (2007), 'Building Organizational Integrity', *Business Horizons*, 50, pp. 61–70.

Lamb, Charles W. (Jr), Joseph F. Hair (Jr), and Carl McDaniel (2005), *Essentials of Marketing*, 4th edn (Mason, OH: South-Western Publishing).

Longshaw, Paul, Anita Roper, Brendan May, Michael Hastings, and Lynn Patterson (2005), 'What I've Learned as a CSR Practitioner', *Corporate Responsibility Management*, 1 (5), pp. 34–7.

Martin, Roger L. (2002), 'The Virtue Matrix: Calculating the Return on Corporate Responsibility', *Harvard Business Review*, March, pp. 68–75.

Nader, Ralph (1966), *Unsafe at any Speed: The Designed-in Dangers of the American Automobile* (New York: Pocket Books).

Packard, Vance (1957), *The Hidden Persuaders* (New York: Random House Inc.).

Porter, Michael E., and Mark R. Kramer (2002), 'The Competitive Advantage of Corporate Philanthropy', *Harvard Business Review*, December, pp. 56–67.

Porter, Michael E., and Mark R. Kramer (2006), 'Strategy and Society: The Link between Competitive Advantage and Corporate Social Responsibility', *Harvard Business Review*, December, pp. 78–92.

Reinhardt, Forest L. (1998), 'Environmental Product Differentiation: Implications for Corporate Strategy', *California Management Review*, 40 (4), pp. 43–73.

Ritson, Mark (2005), 'Nike Shows the Way to Return from the Wilderness', *Marketing*, 20 April, p. 21.

Sasse, Craig M., and Ryan T. Trahan (2007), 'Rethinking the New Corporate Philanthropy', *Business Horizons*, 50, pp. 29–38.

Snider, Jamie, Ronald Paul Hill, and Diane Martin (2003), 'Corporate Social Responsibility in the 21st Century: A View from the World's Most Successful Firms', *Journal of Business Ethics*, 48 (2), pp. 175–84.

Spar, Debora L., and Lane T. LaMure (2003), 'The Power of Activism: Assessing the Impact of NGOs on Global Business', *California Management Review*, 45 (3), pp. 78–102.

Staff (2004), 'CSR Activities Generate Higher Performance—Official', *Women in Management Review*, 19 (5/6), p. 280.

Staff (2005a), 'Brands that Play the Green Card', *Campaign*, 15 July, pp. 26–7.

Staff (2005b), 'Communication Key to Cadbury-NGO Partnership', *Corporate Responsibility Management*, 1 (4), pp. 8–9.

Staff (2005c), 'Corporate Social Responsibility: Show them you Care', *Marketing Week*, 5 May, p. 41.

Stoiber, Marc (2006), 'Growing Green: The Mainstreaming of Sustainability', *Strategy*, December, p. 74.

KEY ARTICLE ABSTRACTS

Hess, David, Nicolai Rogovsky, and Thomas W. Dunfee (2002), **'The Next Wave of Corporate Community Involvement: Corporate Social Initiatives'**, *California Management Review*, 44 (2), pp. 110–25.

Many organizations are finding that corporate community involvement is a key to success. This helpful article discusses the concept of corporate social initiatives, or CSI, for guiding community involvement. Critical factors for success are presented to help companies achieve the most effective community image.

Abstract: The practice of corporate philanthropy has evolved significantly over the past few decades and has now become an integral part of corporate strategy. This article identifies an emerging form of corporate community involvement called corporate social initiatives (CSI). CSI programmes differ from their predecessors in that they are connected to the firm's core values, and have clear objectives and means for measurement. This article explicates the drivers behind the increased interest in CSI, relates CSI to changes in the environment of social expectations for business, reviews potential challenges to CSI programmes, and suggests critical factors in the design of successful CSI programmes.

Martin, Roger L. (2002), '**The Virtue Matrix: Calculating the Return on Corporate Responsibility**', *Harvard Business Review*, March, pp. 68–75.

This insightful article provides marketing strategists with a tool for assessing the possible returns from being socially responsible. The Virtue Matrix is presented as an effective mechanism for balancing the costs of social responsibility with the opportunities.

Abstract: Many consumers and investors, as well as a growing number of business leaders, have added their voices to those urging corporations to remember their obligations to their employees, their communities, and the environment, even if they pursue profits for shareholders. But executives who wish to make their organizations better corporate citizens, face significant obstacles. If they undertake costly initiatives that their rivals do not embrace, they risk eroding their competitive position. These dilemmas, which have long bedeviled business thinkers, were the focus of discussion among a group of executives, academics, and public-sector policy-makers, including Martin, who gathered at the Aspen Institute in Colorado under the auspices of its Initiative for Social Innovation through Business. It would be going too far to say that the group arrived at any solutions to these urgent problems. But prodded by the discussion, an analytical tool that helps executives think about the pressing issue of corporate responsibility is presented.

Porter, Michael E., and Mark R. Kramer (2006), '**Strategy and Society: The Link between Competitive Advantage and Corporate Social Responsibility**', *Harvard Business Review*, December, pp. 78–92.

This insightful article suggests that in order to really advance CSR, companies must recognize that they and society are interrelated and that if they do well, society will do well, and vice versa. The most important point made by the authors is that the real test for whether a social initiative makes sense to pursue is whether it presents the chance to create some kind of shared value. This requires a meaningful benefit for society that is also valuable to the company. In order for the company to create an effective social agenda, it must rethink the purpose of its CSR. Responsive CSR, whereby the company acts as a good corporate citizen, is not the real answer. The real answer is in elevating CSR to strategic CSR, whereby the company chooses a unique position for itself which improves company performance from an internal operations perspective, as well as an external perspective, in not only better serving its customers, but also making incremental improvements for society and interconnecting themselves with society. This cannot be a short-term fix used by a company as a stop-gap measure.

Abstract: Governments, activists, and the media have become adept at holding companies to account for the social consequences of their actions. In response, corporate social responsibility has emerged as an inescapable priority for business leaders in every country. Frequently, though, CSR efforts are counterproductive. In this article, the authors propose a fundamentally new way to look at the relationship between business and society that does not treat corporate growth and social welfare as a zero-sum game. They introduce a framework that individual companies can use to identify the social consequences of their actions; to discover opportunities to benefit society and themselves by strengthening the competitive context in which they operate; to determine which CSR initiatives they should address; and to find the most effective ways of doing so. Perceiving social responsibility as an opportunity rather than as damage control or a PR campaign requires dramatically different thinking—a mind-set, the authors warn, that will become increasingly important to competitive success.

END OF CHAPTER 13 CASE STUDY
Managing packaging and production for environmental sustainability

Introduction to environmental sustainability

Environmental sustainability is a term that can describe various efforts to protect and continuously improve the environment. However, a broader definition is the maintenance of processes in a system (biological, ecological, or other) that can be sustained well into the future, keeping the system intact for generations to come. The current trend is in the businesses environment, possibly utilizing 'green' packaging, and/or efficient or renewable energy.The recent changes are perceived by many environmentalists and advocates as overdue responses to our own carelessness, and some environmentally aware consumers feel that 'green' packaging is too little, too late.

According to the United States Environmental Protection Agency (EPA, 2009), the organization originally acted 'primarily as the nation's environmental watchdog, striving to ensure that businesses met the legal requirements in the area of pollution control'. However, as time passed, many environmentalists, businesses, and the EPA realized that the best defence was not pollution control, but pollution prevention. As interests grew, 'a new generation of innovative approaches to environmental protection' was born. The practices initially included building and development measures, storm-water management, reduction of CO_2 emissions, regulation of point-source dischargers into waterways, voluntary and mandatory recycling programmes, and a host of other programmes and practices. Currently, 'the EPA aims to make sustainability the next level of environmental protection drawing on advances in science and technology, application of diverse government regulations and policies, and promoting green business practices'.

Product packaging is a very specific component of environmental sustainability. Plastic is just one substance used for product packaging, but it accounts for a large percentage of package and container material. In many ways, plastics can do more with less. According to the American Chemistry Council Plastics Division, 'When it comes to packaging, plastics often enable manufacturers to ship more products with less packaging material.' This process, 'called light-weighting, can play an important role in boosting the environmental and economic efficiency of consumer product packaging'.

There are several benefits to creating lighter-weight and/or smaller-sized packaging. For example, many consumers prefer products that are more compact, which can be used/consumed on the go. Portability is a significant factor in many purchase decisions, and consumers appreciate any small convenience.

Lighter packaging can also lead to a reduction in shipping and transportation expenses. In addition, the amount of material waste that must be disposed of once a product is consumed decreases. Therefore, the overall amount of non-recycled packaging (which thus enters the solid waste stream) declines. The changes even make an impact on the level of waste at landfills. Regardless, recycling is still an essential aspect of overall sustainability. Fortunately, many plastics are recyclable and can often be reused.

Proctor & Gamble's strategy to protect the environment

Procter & Gamble (P&G) has been a global leader in the production of consumer products since 1837. The company began as a small candle and soap manufacturer, and has developed into a global giant. Despite this growth, P&G continues to maintain excellence, and as stated on the corporate website, strives to continuously uphold its overall 'purpose of providing products and services of superior quality and value'. As the company grew, it also recognized the need to give back, both to the community and to the environment, taking a strong stance in support of sustainability, product safety, and social and environmental responsibility.

P&G's green efforts began over half a century ago, when the company started fundraising for various US charities. During this time, the company also started conducting research on the effects of surfactants (wetting agents), like detergents, on the environment. A water-quality lab was subsequently established in 1964. The lab even conducted environmental audits of its manufacturing plants, starting in 1970, and conducted tests that were published and later developed into the Ready Biodegradability Test (1973). P&G also initiated efforts to reduce its use of packaging materials, and in 1983, it developed a triple-concentrated version of its Downy fabric softener, Downy 3x.

In addition, P&G developed an Environmental Quality Policy, ensuring its stance as a leader in the shift towards sustainability. The effort led to the development of innovative, practical solutions, particularly regarding the environmental issues related to its own products, packaging, and processes. Throughout the past few decades, P&G has maintained its support of sustainable practices, and continues to share its learning experiences and developed expertise with those with the goal of achieving environmental sustainability.

Liquid laundry detergent

A couple of developments that made a significant impact on both P&G and the 'green' industry were the concentration of liquid fabric-softener and laundry detergent. Making the formula stronger (adding less water) yielded positive, sustainable results from a variety of aspects. P&G was able to reduce the amount of packaging and as previously mentioned, most likely saw a reduction in logistical related expenses. Consumers were given a more manageable way to do laundry.

The sustainable packaging of laundry detergents/fabric softeners was an area of innovation that P&G sparked in the 1960s and continuously worked to improve. Advancements slowed for some time; however, the company was given a significant push forward when a competitor, Unilever, launched its own concentrated laundry detergent (All Small & Mighty). Wal-Mart had also increased its own sustainability efforts during this time by setting a goal to reduce packaging materials by least 5 per cent, which would impact all suppliers.

P&G's managers reacted quickly and reduced packaging on the entire $4 billion liquid-detergent portfolio. The results were viewed as an environmental breakthrough, requiring '44 per cent less water and at least 22 per cent less packaging'. Tide, for instance, evolved from 1x concentrate to 2x concentrate. Tide's new packaging was extremely beneficial to consumers because it made doing the laundry a little easier. The bottle was given a lighter, smaller design, and featured a built-in handle to make it more convenient to carry, pour, and store.

The new packaging was also advantageous to P&G since it reduced production and distribution costs. According to Tony Burns, Associate Director of Sustainability for P&G's Global Package and Device Development, the concentrated formulation saves more than '500 million liters of water, 100,000 metric tons of CO_2, 40,000 truck shipments, and

15,000 metric tons of packaging materials'. In addition, the reduction in product materials helps P&G reduce costs and improve its green appearance. In fact, the manufacturing process became so efficient that 96 per cent of raw materials get converted into finished products. The small amount of residual waste is usually non-hazardous, and can typically be recycled into other products, such as soaps and perfumes.

Consumer perspectives

While sustainability may be the new buzz word in package design, the concept is not impervious to shifting consumer beliefs and misleading assertions. Many individuals are aware that environmentally friendly packages 'provide key end-benefits to users such as the ability to see the products, and/or improved product protection'; however, they neglect to follow through with the purchases. There are two likely reasons for the disconnect between the consumers' interests and their purchasing habits. One is that they might not believe that they are knowledgeable enough to select the most sustainable packaging. The other is based on the belief that price-conscious consumers tend to make purchase decisions based primarily on cost, thus minimizing the importance of environmentally friendly products and packaging. To these individuals, being 'green' may simply not be worth the extra dollar at check-out.

One of the fundamental concerns surrounding eco-friendly packaging is whether consumers really know which packages are better for the environment. According to a survey conducted by *Brand Packaging Magazine*, which questioned this exact uncertainty, packages of hard plastic and paperboard were seen as preferable because they could be easily recycled. Respondents also indicated that they lacked the knowledge necessary to properly evaluate other packaging materials, such as glass and metal. Therefore, the magazine concluded that the tendency to rate these materials unfavourably as recyclables was due to a lack of consumer awareness and education. Since the findings confirmed that 'environmental ratings did not consistently correlate with purchase preferences' it became evident that the industry would need to shift consumer perceptions in order to create mainstream demand.

P&G has reduced its packaging by more than 15,000 metric tons a year; however, many consumers do not view this as a basis for their purchasing habits, as underscored by the study by *Brand Packaging*. With this in mind, P&G should put more effort into its communication regarding what it is doing to help the environment through its packaging, processing, transportation, and operations. For example, many individuals might not know that P&G always strives to establish and maintain 'green' buildings and grounds. Informing consumers about any sustainability strategies could help build upon brand value and strengthen trust in the company. Through this, consumers might choose to purchase a P&G product over the competition, simply because they respect the company and realize its products do less damage to the environment.

Regulating the impact on the environment and environmental claims

The US Environmental Protection Agency (US EPA) is the federal arm that sets policy for the nation's environment, including air, land, and water quality. According to the EPA website, 'Today, EPA aims to make sustainability the next level of environmental protection drawing on advances in science and technology, application of diverse government regulations and policies, and promoting green business practices.'

The US EPA has passed a number of acts that regulate industries. The ones most applicable to P&G's laundry detergent packaging relate to: (1) the plastics that enter the solid-waste stream and end up in landfills; and, (2) CO_2 emissions from plants that create the packaging. To a lesser degree, a P&G product (especially in some foreign markets) reduces the rinse cycle, therefore decreasing the amount of water that gets sent to waste-water treatment plants. The CO_2 emissions that are expelled during shipping, which P&G successfully reduced with the advent of light-weighting, are not regulated by the EPA at this point in time.

The Federal Trade Commission (FTC) regulates corporate use of environmental benefits as marketing claims. It ensures that companies do not make false claims that might mislead consumers about eco-friendly practices. (6)

Cost management

Aside from any concerns about customer education about environmentally friendly packaging, companies should evaluate whether or not consumers are willing to pay more to be green. According to Young's article (2008), Bart Becht, CEO of Reckitt Benckiser (a multinational company specializing in household, health, and personal-care products) said, 'environmental concerns don't necessarily drive purchase intent'. However, he also indicated that an overwhelming, 85 per cent of consumers believe that manufacturers should be willing to incur the costs of eco-friendly packaging, without passing the costs along to the consumer. The mind-set of these individuals creates a dilemma. Companies should evaluate their customers to decide if environmentally friendly packaging is a justifiable expense, and if the current packaging could be altered to better meet the needs of consumers and the company.

In many cases, manufacturing costs can be cut by making product packaging more eco-friendly. In an instance such as this, the change would not only help the bottom line, but also help to align the products with consumer values. It could even improve consumer perceptions of other products or brands.

For example, if a (non-loyal) consumer who cares about the environment, realized that P&G had created eco-friendly packaging for its laundry detergents, it might appeal to his green side and influence the likelihood of a future purchase. P&G increased its raw materials from recycled sources by approximately 7.8 times its total from 2007 to 2008. The company also generated more than $2 billion in sales in 2008 by launching seven sustainable innovations. These sales may not have been reached if P&G hadn't aligned the corporation's focus with that of the consumers' values. Despite the high initial costs that the company faced, the decision helped them become a leader in sustainable manufacturing, packaging, and everyday operations. Other companies look to P&G as a guide, and consumers rely on the company to provide high-quality, sustainable products.

Source: This case was written by Kathryn Cook, Pamela Mooring, and Christine Zeitschel, evening MBA students at Loyola College in Maryland, under the supervision of Professor Hope Corrigan as the basis for analysis and class discussion and not to illustrate either effective or ineffective handling of an administrative situation.

QUESTIONS

Briefly describe how you have seen products and packaging change over the past few years to become more eco-friendly. In addition, please provide at least five examples of sustainable products.

1. How does a company show sustainability in its products and various initiatives?
2. What does consumer uncertainty about eco-packaging mean for P&G's marketing strategy as they strive towards creating more eco-friendly packaging, given that many competitors have not taken this leap?

3. Discuss specific marketing mix elements and how you would use them to convince consumers that you are really concerned about the environment and not just paying lip service to the concept of eco-friendliness.

References

American Chemistry Council, Plastics Division (2009), website, 21 February, available at: **http://www.americanchemistry.com/plastics/sec_content.asp?CID=1078&DID=4232**

Butschli, Jim (2009), 'Sustainable Packaging: P&G Provides Leadership in Sustainable Packaging Journey', retrieved from *Packaging World Magazine*, February, pp. 55–61, available at: **http://www.packworld.com/article-27005**

Environmental Protection Agency (EPA) [2009], accessed 19 February, available at: **http://www.epa.gov/osw/conserve/materials/plastics.htm**

Environmental Protection Agency (EPA) (2009), 'Sustainability', 19 February, accessed at: **http://www.epa.gov/Sustainability/basicinfo.htm#sustainability**

Guides for the Use of Environmental Marketing Claims, 21 February 2009, available at: **http://www.ftc.gov/bcp/grnrule/guides980427.htm**

Mininni, Ted (2009), 'A New Revolution in Packaging', *Brand Packaging Magazine*, available at: **http://www.brandpackaging.com/Archives_Davinci?article=1032**

Murray, Alan (2008), 'Environment (A Special Report); Waste Not: Wal-Mart's H. Lee Scott Jr on What the Company is Doing to Reduce its Carbon Footprint—and those of its Customers', *Wall Street Journal*, 24 March, p. R.3.

Proctor & Gamble (2007), 'Our Heritage', accessed 18 February 2009, at: **http://www.pg.com/company/who_we_are/ppv.shtml**

Proctor & Gamble (2008), 'Our Commitment', 16 February, available at: **http://www.pg.com/company/our_commitment/index.shtml**

Procter & Gamble (2008), 'Sustainability', accessed 21 February 2009, at: **http://www.pg.com/innovatingsustainability/index.shtml**

Procter & Gamble [2009], 'Sustainability', video, available at: **http://www.youtube.com/watch?v=Hy2yi7r5-Ts**

Procter & Gamble (2008), 'Purpose, Values and Principles', accessed 16 February 2009, at: **http://www.pg.com/company/who_we_are/ppv.shtml**

Ratushny, Claire (2008), 'Pre-thinking Recycling: The New Eco-consciousness', *Brandchannel*, 22 September, available at: **http://www.brandchannel.com/brand_speak.asp?bs_id=202**

SPI-Sustainability, 21 February 2009, available at: **http://www.plasticsindustry.org/Sustainability/**

Sustainability Report (2008), 16 February, available at: **http://www.pg.com/innovatingsustainability/PG_2008_Sustainability_Report.pdf**

Young, Scott (2008), 'Packaging and the Environment: The Shoppers' Perspective', *Brand Packaging*, January–February, pp. 24–7.

Wal-Mart Sustainability Spotlight, KNWA-TV, available at: **http://walmartstores.com/Video/?id=1290**

Part V Did we get there?

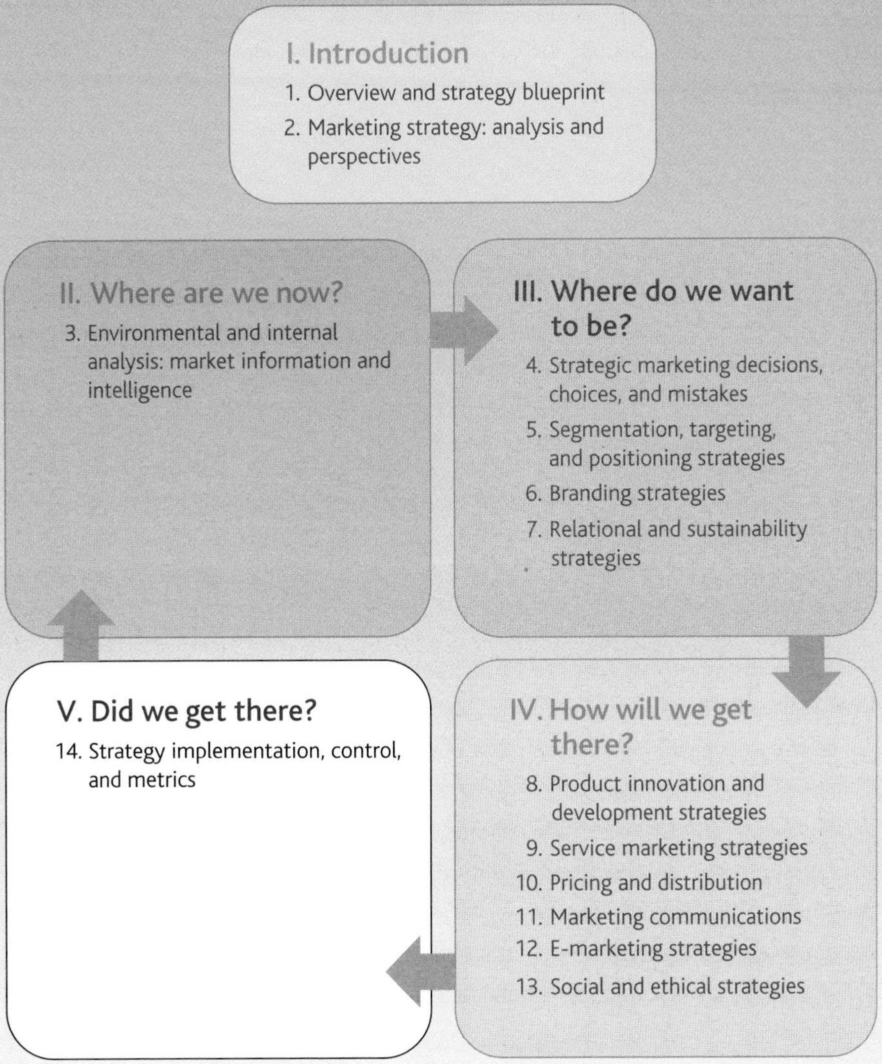

I. Introduction
1. Overview and strategy blueprint
2. Marketing strategy: analysis and perspectives

II. Where are we now?
3. Environmental and internal analysis: market information and intelligence

III. Where do we want to be?
4. Strategic marketing decisions, choices, and mistakes
5. Segmentation, targeting, and positioning strategies
6. Branding strategies
7. Relational and sustainability strategies

V. Did we get there?
14. Strategy implementation, control, and metrics

IV. How will we get there?
8. Product innovation and development strategies
9. Service marketing strategies
10. Pricing and distribution
11. Marketing communications
12. E-marketing strategies
13. Social and ethical strategies

14

Strategy implementation, control, and metrics

LEARNING OBJECTIVES

- Understand the nature of managerial control in a marketing context
- Appreciate the importance of implementation of marketing strategy and why it is frequently the reason for organizational and strategic failure
- Conceptualize competitive advantage as an ongoing process that needs to be measured, managed, and controlled
- Calculate customer lifetime value as an outcome of a competitive advantage process
- Understand the notion of customer equity as a guiding objective for the evaluation of marketing strategy
- Recognize organizational culture and structure as a factor that either helps or hinders the implementation of marketing strategy

CHAPTER AT A GLANCE

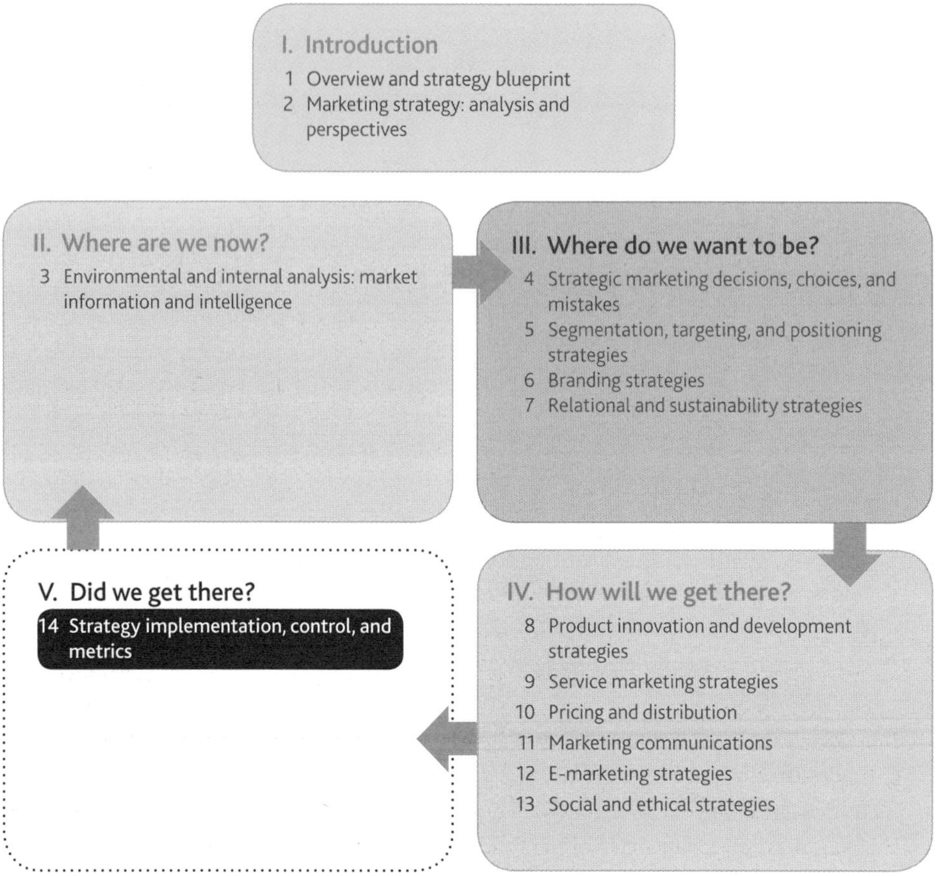

I. Introduction
1 Overview and strategy blueprint
2 Marketing strategy: analysis and perspectives

II. Where are we now?
3 Environmental and internal analysis: market information and intelligence

III. Where do we want to be?
4 Strategic marketing decisions, choices, and mistakes
5 Segmentation, targeting, and positioning strategies
6 Branding strategies
7 Relational and sustainability strategies

IV. How will we get there?
8 Product innovation and development strategies
9 Service marketing strategies
10 Pricing and distribution
11 Marketing communications
12 E-marketing strategies
13 Social and ethical strategies

V. Did we get there?
14 Strategy implementation, control, and metrics

Introduction

There is every indication that in the future, a firm's marketing success will hinge not so much on having a good strategy, but on how well this strategy is implemented and controlled. The managerial act of control involves four steps:

1. Set targets of performance (these are typically in the form of goals or objectives).
2. Evaluate the reality of what occurs against these steps, i.e. failure or success.
3. Take corrective or reinforcing action where required.
4. Establish new targets in light of the situation at step 3.

These steps are illustrated in the marketing example in Figure 14.1. Assume a firm sets a market share objective of 25 per cent, which is step 1 in the control process. At the next step, the manager compares reality against the standard and either fails to achieve 25 per cent or achieves/overachieves 25 per cent. At the third step, the manager either takes corrective or reinforcing action. If the market share achieved was only 15 per cent, then the manager would attempt to correct whatever aspects of marketing strategy caused this to happen. On

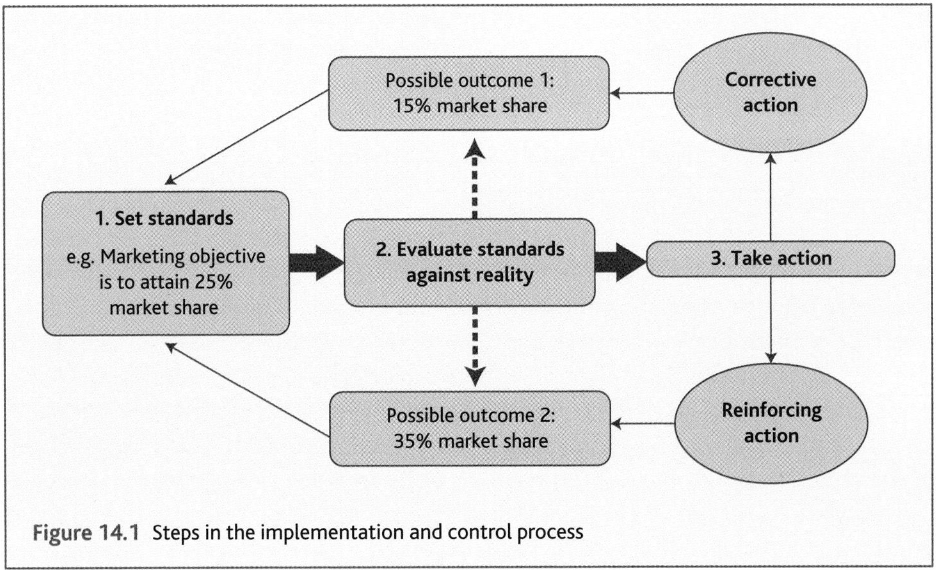

Figure 14.1 Steps in the implementation and control process

the other hand, if the market share really achieved was 25 per cent or more, the manager would seek to reinforce whatever actions caused this to happen. Though note, overachievement can often present its own problems. For example, owing to supply logistics, it may be extremely difficult to meet increased demand, which might lead to some kind of rationing or price increases (consider how demand rapidly outstripped the supply of the Wii when it was first launched and the product achieved a higher than retail price on eBay). The final step is to establish the next set of targets in light of the outcomes of actions in Step 2.

Having made these points, it must be emphasized that control is a process rather than a linear and sequential series of steps—the corrective and reinforcing step in turn becomes the source of information for the setting of subsequent standards. **Time** is a critical dimension. In reality, outcomes may be either higher or lower than the target figure set, or the objective set established, so most astute managers usually assign a time frame to an objective. For example, 'Our firm sets a market share objective of 25 per cent to be achieved within a year.' Managers will then monitor achievement against this standard on a monthly, quarterly, or annual (or whatever is deemed appropriate) basis and it is at this time that the control process and related actions will be undertaken.

The act of implementation is the accomplishing of or carrying into effect; it is the executing of a plan or strategy. Marketing strategy implementation consists of 'doing' the strategy. When strategic marketing failures occur, it is usually strategy formulation that is blamed: managers say things like, 'Our strategy was wrong.' Too often, they overlook the fact that there may have been nothing wrong with the strategy, but that the execution was flawed. As one executive ruefully put it, 'Our thinking was right. But we did it wrong!' For example, when Tesco entered the US market (Arizona, California, and Nevada) with its 'Fresh & Easy' chain in late 2007, it had high hopes. Being a savvy marketer, Tesco undertook extensive qualitative research, rigged up a mock store in California and developed clear and concise behavioural segmentations and positioning. Unfortunately, its mid-price point positioning proved a mistake. A great strategy, but not when American consumers were tightening their belts and looking for deals.

The implementation of marketing strategy

The problem with poor implementation of strategy is that it is difficult to diagnose. This dilemma was recognized some years ago by Harvard Business School Marketing Professor Tom Bonoma (1984), who argued that **marketing managers trying to put marketing strategies into practice often confront structural and personnel problems**. The structural problems of marketing involve marketing functions, programmes, systems, and policy directives. Marketing functions often fail because of faulty management assumptions or inattention to marketing basics, while programmes are often contradicted by a lack of functional capabilities or insufficient management attention. Systems are limited by errors of ritual and politicization, and marketing policies regularly suffer from the lack of a marketing theme and culture. However, good interaction, allocation, monitoring, and organization skills can overcome poor marketing practices. Bonoma suggests that marketers consider two aspects of their strategy when diagnosing (or indeed, controlling for) its success or failure, which are mapped out in the grid in Figure 14.2.

The two dimensions on the grid in Figure 14.2 consider **strategy formulation and strategy implementation**, which can range from poor to adequate. Bonoma's suggestion is that managers should use the grid to map the formulation of their own marketing strategy, and its implementation. When strategy is well formulated and implemented, then it is likely that **success** will follow. Similarly, when strategy is poorly formulated and implemented, then, not surprisingly, it generally results in **failure**. It is when one of the other two situations on the diagonal in the grid in Figure 14.2 occurs that marketing managers are faced with a dilemma.

Strategy that is adequately formulated but poorly implemented, leads to **trouble**. This is because very often, poor results will be blamed on the strategy, not on its implementation. 'Our strategy was wrong,' managers will say and 'we shouldn't have done that.' However,

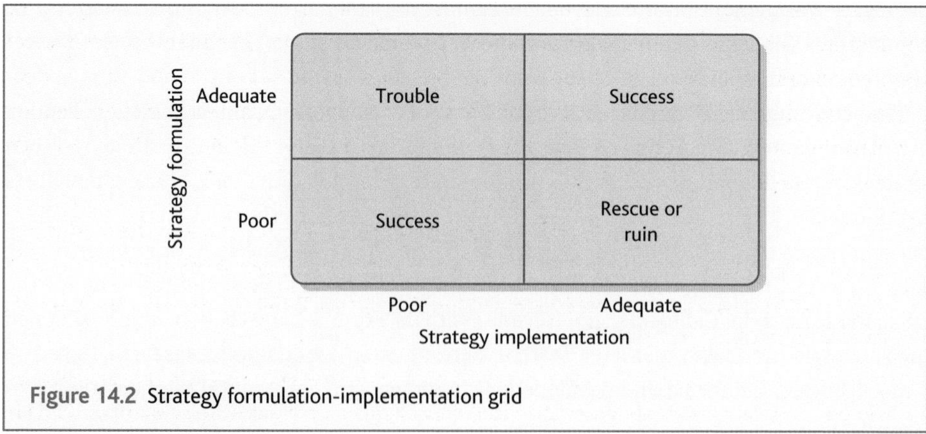

Figure 14.2 Strategy formulation-implementation grid

what they might be saying after some introspection would be something like, 'We had the right strategy, but we implemented it poorly.'

For example, a major consumer goods marketer in Brazil recognized that, while they were poor, the consumers in Rio de Janeiro's *favelas* (hillside slums) represented an attractive market segment for the products that the firm made. The marketing team formulated a strategy that involved designing innovative new products targeted at this market, paying particular attention to issues like packaging (products needed to be portable, durable, and storable). They were also able to price the product range affordably. An innovative approach to promotion involved a tie-up with a popular local soccer team, which produced good results in market research. In order to distribute the products, the firm would rely on the many informal neighbourhood shops (many of which were run from people's homes) that served the slum areas, rather than on large supermarkets that were often far from the consumers. However, six months after the implementation, the results in the target market were most disappointing. Rather than simply blame the strategy, the marketing director and his team undertook an in-depth analysis of implementation. It was discovered that the small informal shops frequently did not carry the products, and those that did were often out of stock. Further analysis revealed that the sales team seldom visited the stores concerned, either because they believed that individually, the small stores didn't matter, or because they were in areas salespeople preferred not to enter. Second, deliveries to the stores were unpredictable and intermittent. Many of the *favelas* are situated on steep hillsides, and truck drivers simply chose not to deliver to them because this was difficult to do. So, a good marketing strategy failed because of implementation issues.

Returning to the grid in Figure 14.2, Bonoma suggests that strategy that is poorly formulated but well implemented, leads to **rescue or ruin**. This is a particularly complex situation, because the consequences can frequently be dramatic and unpredictable. On the one hand, this situation can rescue a firm's poor marketing strategy because a well-implemented strategy can overcome weaknesses in formulation. On the other hand, effective implementation of a bad strategy can hasten a firm's downfall. In simple terms, if an idea is really stupid, and you do it really well, it shouldn't be surprising that disasters occur!

Deighton's (2002) article on the birth, demise, and resurrection of the soft drink brand, Snapple, provides a good example of a 'rescue or ruin' (in this case, ruin) situation. Quaker purchased the Snapple brand from its founders in 1994 for $1.7 billion. The thinking behind this strategy (its formulation) was that Snapple would be a good complement to Quaker's Gatorade brand of sports drinks. Whereas Snapple was strong in convenience stores, delis and lunch restaurants, Gatorade was strong in supermarkets. If Quaker's marketers had formulated their strategy more carefully, they would have realized that Snapple's success was built on certain key issues:

1. **The theme of being 'natural':** While not a health drink, Snapple contained few additives and was seen as an alternative to cola drinks. The natural theme was enhanced through quirky advertising and the use of unconventional spokespersons for the brand, including 'shock jock' radio DJ Howard Stern.
2. **Snapple's range included dozens of different flavours**, some with rather bizarre mixes. While not all of these were successful in terms of sales, product development costs were

very low, and the range of flavours made the product interesting in the eyes of the market, and customers always wondered what the next new Snapple flavour would be. The product was also packaged in heavy, chunky, glass bottles, not cans.

3. **Snapple was sold at a premium price,** which consumers typically didn't perceive, as the drink was usually purchased as part of lunch. So, rather than notice that they were paying $2 or $3 for a soft drink, consumers spent $8 on lunch, which would typically include a sandwich and a Snapple.

When it was sold through supermarkets, Snapple's new marketing strategy quickly unravelled. In order to cut costs, Quaker ceased the natural and quirky promotional theme, including dropping Howard Stern, who, as a consequence, called the drink 'Crapple' on his radio programme. As supermarkets do not tolerate lots of different product variations, the Snapple range had to be ruthlessly pruned, which caused the brand to lose its consumer interest factor. Consumers who considered purchasing Snapple in a supermarket quickly realized that a six-pack of bulky glass bottles was heavy and difficult to carry. Furthermore, when they were buying Snapple in isolation and in comparison to other soft drinks, they also recognized it was expensive—something they had overlooked when they had purchased it as a component to lunch. Gatorade also didn't sell well in the convenience/deli channel, as consumers did not want to drink a sports drink with their sandwiches.

Quaker had implemented its Snapple strategy ruthlessly and well. **The problem was that the strategy's formulation had been exceptionally poor.** So poor in fact, that the Snapple brand was sold off for $400 million (a brand equity write-off of $1.3 billion). Not a rescue situation in this case, but very much a ruin. (TriArc turned the Snapple brand around and subsequently sold it to Cadbury Schweppes. It achieved the turnaround by returning to the original Snapple strategy and implementing it well.) Thus, a poor implementation often obscures the effectiveness or ineffectiveness of the marketing strategy; so, marketing practices should be examined before adjustments are made to strategy.

Why are marketing strategies not always implemented well? The reality is that it is often easier to develop a new strategy than to implement it. In too many organizations, marketing strategy is implicit and resides only in the minds of senior marketers. These individuals may have trouble explaining their strategy, so most of the other people in the marketing function are forced to guess what the strategy is, and they may guess wrongly. Marketing executives often develop their strategy in isolation, leaving people without ownership and with no understanding of the rationale behind it. As many members of the marketing function as possible should be involved in developing a strategy in order to achieve accurate understanding and proper execution. A good strategic marketing process will help management identify and proactively manage the implications of the strategy for the organization's products, markets, customers, and structure. According to Robert (1991), there are a number of barriers to the implementation of strategy that deserve brief consideration.

The marketing strategy is implicit, not explicit, and people cannot implement what they do not know: when strategy resides in the head of the senior marketing executive, others in the marketing department are forced to guess what it is—and they may guess wrong. This may be referred to as 'strategy by groping' because the strategy only becomes clear over a long period of time, as people test what the strategy might be by trial and error. **Implication:** make the marketing strategy explicit!

The marketing strategy is developed in isolation—and people cannot implement what they do not understand: often, marketing strategy is developed by a senior marketer or a few senior marketing executives, usually at a retreat at some exclusive resort. Others in the organization, and especially the marketing function, feel divorced from the marketing strategy, and also do not understand it. **Implication:** involve as many people as possible in the formulation of marketing strategy in order to achieve accurate understanding and proper execution. Also, consider appointing a CSO (Chief Strategic Officer) to work alongside the CEO. CSOs act as 'mini CEOs' and have the mandate to walk into any office and say: 'What we've been doing isn't in line with the company's strategy—and we need to fix that' (Breene et al., 2007).

Not everyone is a good strategic marketing thinker: many individuals within the marketing function are involved in day-to-day marketing activities. So, they don't spend much time thinking strategically, and have difficulty coping with strategic issues, especially when these are sprung on them. If they are encouraged to understand the differences between strategic processes and everyday operational marketing issues, they will be better able and more willing to implement the formulated marketing strategy. **Implication:** encourage the participation of key marketing subordinates in strategy formulation, even if only for its educational value.

The marketing strategy is developed by an external consultant: many firms employ consultants to formulate their marketing strategy for them. While there are roles for consultants in organizations, including conducting marketing audits, conducting research, and other specialist advice, the formulation of marketing strategy probably should not be one of them (certainly not in isolation). The problem caused by having an external consultant(s) formulate marketing strategy is that most members of the marketing function are not committed to this strategy because it is not their strategy. By engaging external consultants, organizations lose out on the commitment that comes from participation. At worst, this will often lead to so-called 'white-anting' (an Australian term for the process of internal erosion of a foundation—to subvert or undermine from within), whereby people actively work against and sabotage a strategy that they perceive to be someone else's. **Implication:** do not normally use external consultants to formulate marketing strategy—people will not implement a strategy they are not committed to.

The marketing strategy has unanticipated consequences: when formulating strategy, many marketers do not think it through carefully enough to be able to foresee all the implications the strategy might have. When the strategy is then implemented, people who initially supported it often begin to say things like: 'If we'd known that would happen, we wouldn't have supported it.' A good strategic marketing planning process will anticipate, identify, and proactively manage the implications of a marketing strategy on the organization's products and services, markets, customers, organizational structure, and personnel. **Implication:** identify strategic implications beforehand so that people don't give up on a strategy whose repercussions have not been foreseen.

Marketing budget

Having made these points, sometimes the issue is simply that the allocated budget is inappropriate. Setting an appropriate budget is crucial for two reasons: if too much is spent, short-term finances are stretched (Farris and West, 2007). However, if the budget is too small, longer-term opportunities may be lost and competitiveness eroded. A variety of methods are used to set budgets and most firms use multiple methods (circa 2–3 methods on average). Here is a snapshot of the leading methods being used:

Judgemental methods

- *Arbitrary*: solely determined on the basis of what is 'felt' to be necessary to implement the strategy.
- *Affordable*: the organization determines what it can spend on other areas such as production and operations and then decides how much it can afford for marketing.

Objective and task

- Spending is in accordance with what is required to meet the marketing strategy objective(s). Ranked by importance, objectives are set, tasks agreed upon to meet these objectives, and then costs estimated. If the strategy cannot be afforded, lower-importance objective(s) are eliminated until the budget can be afforded.

Measurement

- *ROI*: marketing is considered an investment and money is spent to the point where the ROI is diminishing.
- *Incremental*: the budget is allocated in an incremental series of tests. Spending is increased or decreased in line with the results achieved.
- *Quantitative models*: computer simulation models are used involving statistical techniques such as multiple regression analysis.

Percentage of sales

- *% of last year's sales*: set percentage of previous financial year's sales.
- *% of anticipated sales*: set percentage of the firm's anticipated sales.
- *Unit sales*: the organization allocates a fixed percentage of unit price for marketing and then multiplies this amount by projected sales volume (e.g., 5% unit price x 200,000 cars sales forecast).

Competitive

- *Competitive absolute*: the budget is set in line with the closest rival.
- *Competitive relative*: all the competitors in the market spend in line with their market share.

In terms of the methods used, indications for the US and UK broadly show that:

- about 25–30 per cent of budgets are set by judgemental methods
- about 25–30 per cent of budgets use objective and task

- 20 per cent use measurement
- approximately 15 per cent use percentage of sales
- about 5–7 per cent use competitive methods
- around two to three methods are combined on average.

Controlling marketing strategy

It is useful to distinguish three kinds of control with regard to managing marketing strategy:

1. **Annual plan control:** the objectives set in the annual marketing plan are evaluated against the results achieved. Corrective or reinforcing action is taken when necessary (see Figure 14.1).
2. **Financial or expense control:** considers the financial parameters and objectives set by a firm in its annual marketing plan, and the corrective or reinforcing actions needed to attain these. So, for example, a firm with a lower than budgeted return on sales may find there was excessive discounting by the sales force. Management would need to take steps to ensure less discretion by sales staff with regard to pricing. In another example, a firm may have budgeted £100,000 for a trade exhibition, but only spent £80,000 and still achieved the planned results. A review of how the exhibition was managed might reveal that the reduction in spending was due to the judicious management of free samples and brochures through careful targeting. Management then ensures that the procedures adopted are reinforced throughout the marketing department for implementation at future exhibitions.
3. **Strategic control:** the purpose of strategic control is to ensure that the organization maximizes the opportunities in its environment. Strategic control often takes the form of a marketing audit. A marketing audit is a structured and in-depth examination of all the firm's marketing activities undertaken to identify those areas of marketing in which the firm is not performing to full potential, as well as those in which the firm is doing well. In order to ensure objectivity, many firms will choose to employ outside consultants to conduct a marketing audit.

Organization

Every organization has its own unique culture or set of values, whether it has consciously tried to create this or not. Usually, the culture of the organization is created unconsciously, based on the values of the top management or the organization's founders and it forms a major factor in control. As already noted, writers such as Bonoma (1984) have noted that one of the most important reasons for the failure of marketing strategy is an inadequate corporate culture. Often, members of an organization will be heard to say things like, 'In order to implement that strategy, we would have to change our culture', as if culture can be changed easily and quickly, like bed linen. The reality of organizational culture is that it is usually very deep-rooted. Sometimes, it may be easier and better to try to understand the organization's culture, and to work with it, rather than change it—and this has wide and significant implications for the implementation of marketing strategy.

Culture

Marketing academics have long been interested in the effects that an organization's culture has on its ability to formulate, and more importantly, to implement, marketing strategy. Badovick and Beatty (1987) found that shared organizational values (one aspect of culture) significantly impacted on strategic marketing implementation. Tse et al. (1988) investigated the relationship between national culture and marketing decision-making, finding that an executive's home (national) culture had a significant and predictable effect on decision-making. Qualls and Puto (1989) found that the cultural climate affects choice behaviours by influencing the decision-maker's reference points and decision frames. Webster (1991) investigated cultural consistency within service firms, and found that an employee's position influenced their attitudes towards their firm's actual and ideal marketing culture. Narver and Slater (1990) and Slater and Narver (1992) found that market orientation (a construct comprised of three elements: customer orientation, competitor orientation, and inter-functional coordination) was linked to business performance, and the authors use the concept of organizational culture to explain the relationship (see Mini Case Study 14.1).

Webster (1994) and Deshpandé et al. (1993) found a direct link between organizational culture and business performance, while arguing that market orientation was a sub-component of culture. They investigated the relationship between culture and business performance in Japanese companies and found that companies with cultures that stress competitiveness (market cultures) and entrepreneurship (adhocracy cultures) outperform those with cultures that stress internal cohesiveness or rules. More recently, Berthon et al. (2001) looked at the influence of organizational culture and memory development on managers' perceptions

MINI CASE STUDY 14.1 Customer satisfaction

Customer satisfaction has been one of the key end points of marketing strategy for some years. To some extent, the measurement of satisfaction could be bypassed by new Web processes. As noted in Chapter 12, customers have become co-designers of products and services, as exemplified by 'choiceboards', which enable them to design their own goods and services from a menu, and brands can deliver goods and services based on exactly what consumers want. Examples include 'My Design Barbie', My Virtual Model and the Schwab's mutual fund evaluator. In configuring products as customers would like them, the brands concerned can collect precise information about consumer preferences to use to develop strategies and tactics based upon future needs and preferences. In this regard, they do not need to take any measurements as they do the whole process of finding out what consumers want in one go. Well, that's the theory anyway. In practice 'It ain't necessarily so.'

Take the case of Dell, a $37 billion company. When Michael Dell returned to take over as CEO from Kevin Rollins in 2007, he was facing a number of problems. The stock was stagnating, profits were down by a quarter, and the company had a reputation for lack of innovation and poor customer service. What a turnaround. Dell had been famous for a culture of exceptional service, but as sales ballooned it seemed to lose touch with the customers who were at the heart of the business. It set up a self-serving process that didn't place the customer at the centre of activities and it came across as being rather arrogant and aloof as a brand. »

» The irony is that the Web technology underpinning choiceboards has enabled consumers to discuss brands. Networks that link people via blogs, consumer forums, Facebook, MySpace, and Twitter, etc., and these outlets have given Dell a complete pasting online, with the brand seen as having some of the worst customer service going. Dell has rapidly overhauled its reputation and is now rivalling HP and Gateway when it comes to customer satisfaction. How did it achieve such a rapid turnaround in its service culture?

For one, the company has built better products. In part, this has been achieved with the Dell IdeaStorm site that enables people to sign in and vote consumer-generated ideas up or down. Feedback on the site was used by Dell's engineers, for example, to add a keyboard that lights up Latitude laptops in the dark.

The company also recognized that putting its own house in order was only part of the equation, albeit an important part. Research indicates that 50 per cent of people consult blogs or consumer reviews or forums before making a purchase, and potential customers spend 99 per cent of their time online trawling the Web for information. Dell signed up with Buzzlogic and Radian6—companies that specialize in monitoring Web conversations—identifying key bloggers and influencing debates. It's definitely a 'tread lightly' area as it isn't about finding mentions of your brand or trolling for your competitor's customers and fans in social media and pitching. Rather, the idea is to connect and build relationships and find relevant conversations from within communities and understanding how those impact your business.

As well, Dell has introduced its own team of just over 40 staff, who engage with people on social media. Post a comment on Dell online and there is a good chance someone from the company will join in within a few hours, if only to say to people that the company cares and is looking into it. Blogs and message boards have been added to the site and customer reviews of products are posted for all to see, whether good or bad—much better for people to gripe about their problems to Dell than to the entire Internet. They have also launched a self-help site where customers can post and have their problems potentially solved by other customers, with thousands of fixes posted and several million views recorded. This not only involves customers, but also reduces servicing costs.

of role-related problems. They found that both organizational culture and memory influence managers' perceptions, with externally focused cultures emphasizing strategic problems, and organic process cultures emphasizing unstructured problems (see, also: Handy, 1978; Quinn, 1988; Campbell and Freeman, 1991; Goffee and Jones, 1996).

Structure

Organizational structure plays a key role in control. There has been a great deal of interest over the years into the ways in which organizations maintain their internal and external viability in light of market competiveness. If organizational culture is akin to an individual's sense of self, then organizational structure is akin to the biological functioning of the body to make a viable human being.

Organizations can take on a number of different marketing structures. Figure 14.3 illustrates a basic **functional** organization which offers the specialization in task activities to develop skills, with marketing tasks and responsibilities clearly defined. The **disadvantage** is that excess levels of hierarchy may reduce unity of control and direct lines of communication may be ignored and so conflicts may emerge, leaving integration a major problem for the chief marketing executive (CME). As such, functional structures are best suited to simple marketing operations where there is a single primary product or market.

Figure 14.4 and Figure 14.5 illustrate specialization in **brand organization and services/ products**, respectively. Such an organization enables greater management attention to the specific marketing requirements of different brands/services/products and a faster reaction to brand/services/products related changes. The key disadvantages are the need for dual reporting, potentially too much product rather than market emphasis, and more management levels and costs. It fits best where there are wide product lines sold to homogeneous groups of customers, and where there is sharing production/marketing systems.

A **market** organization (see Figure 14.6) provides a fast reaction to market-related changes. However, as with brands and product structures, the **disadvantage** is the duplication of functions, the need for greater coordination, and more management levels. It is perhaps best suited where there is a limited, standardized, homogeneous product-line sold to customers in different markets.

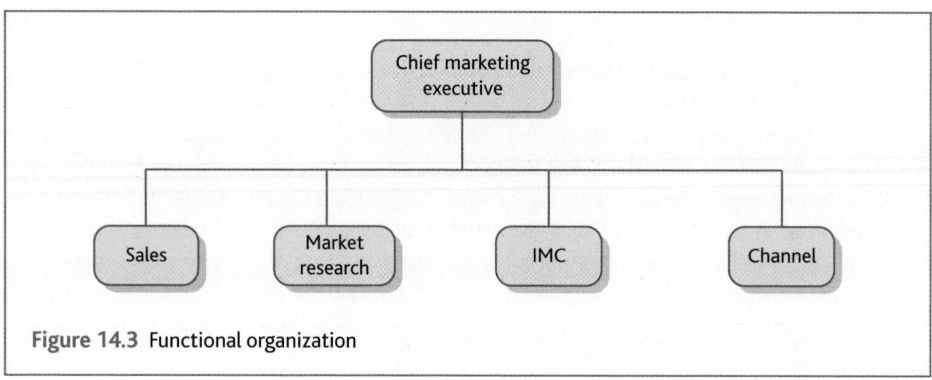

Figure 14.3 Functional organization

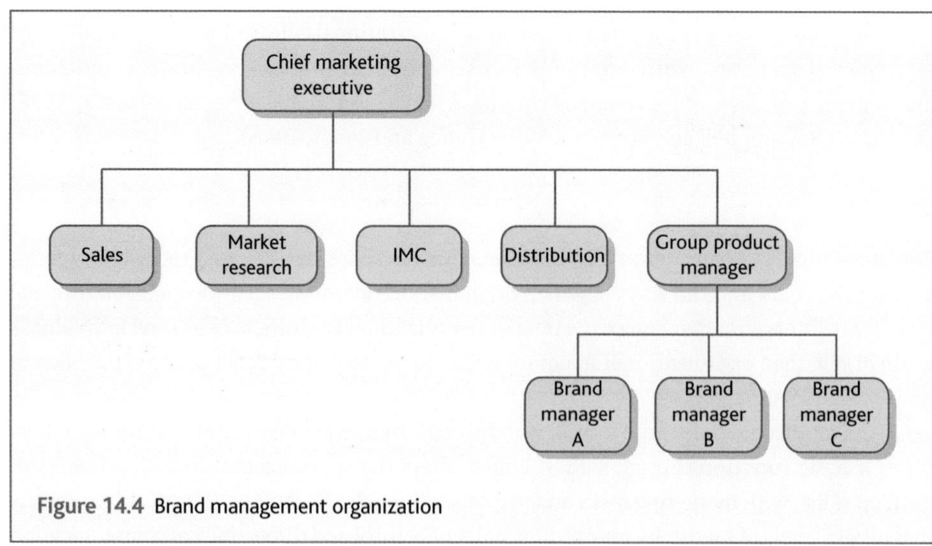

Figure 14.4 Brand management organization

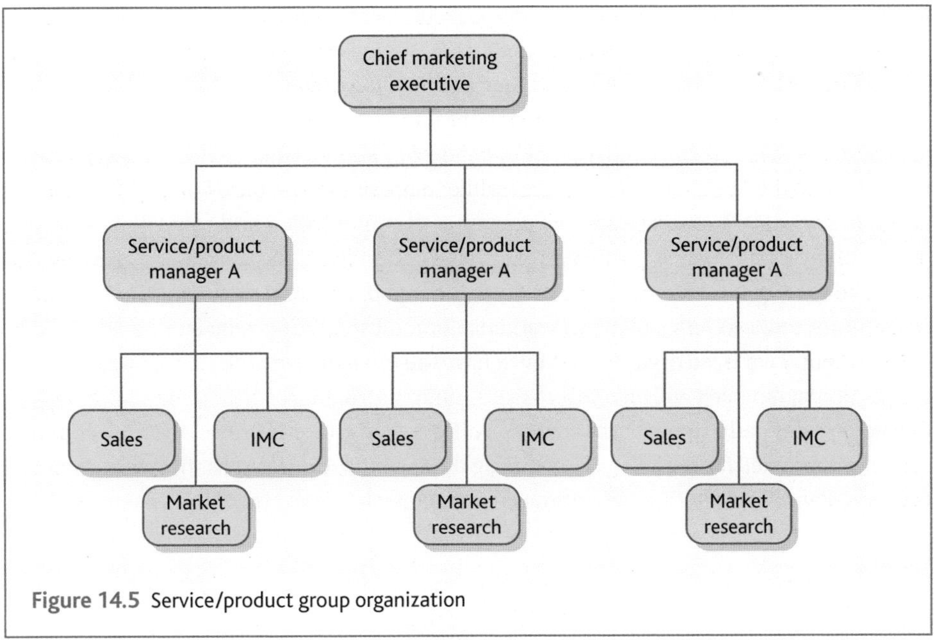

Figure 14.5 Service/product group organization

Finally, Figure 14.7 shows a **combined service/product/market** organization which offers the advantage of functional services/products and market specialization integration. The **disadvantages** are that allocations of responsibilities are difficult and there will inevitably

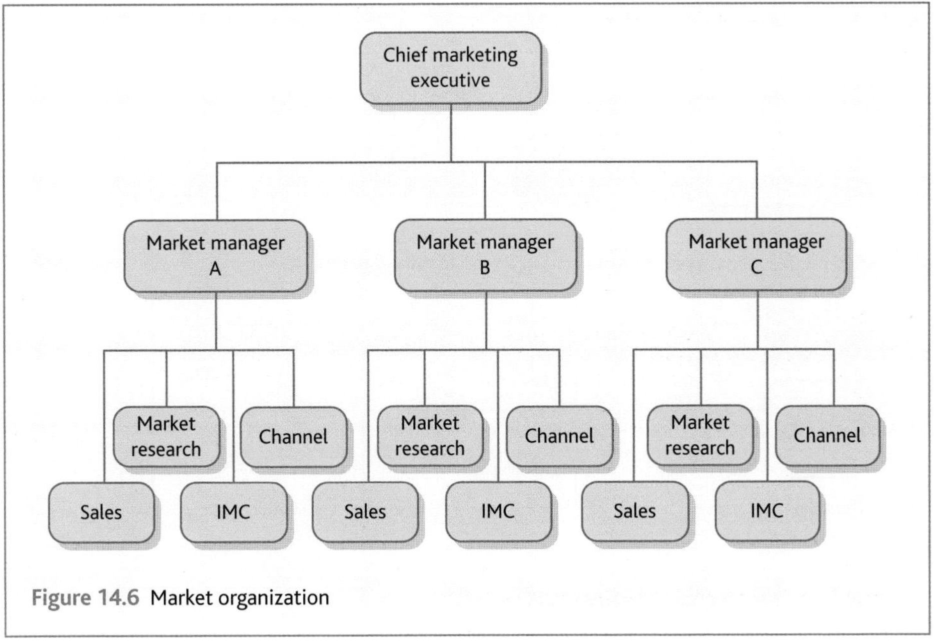

Figure 14.6 Market organization

be duplication inefficiencies. However, it is probably the best structure for a company facing multiple products and multiple markets.

The traditional analyses of organizational control along the lines of function, brand, service, product, or market lines often misses the reality that organizations control their actions along a series of interconnected activity systems and that rules and procedures are needed to coordinate the use of scarce resources while maintaining standards of quality (Bruning and Lockshin, 1994). Cybernetics, the science of communication and control in organisms and machines, has made a particular contribution here with the concepts of **variety** and **requisite variety** (Jackson, 1988). Variety is the number of events or scenarios in an environment. In order to be viable, every organization must develop requisite variety with its environment. That is, an organization must have the capacity to match changes in its operating environment which will enable it to exert some control.

The founding father of cybernetics was W. Ross Ashby (see Brocklesby and Cummings, 1996), who worked for the US military during the Second World War. Ashby was particularly concerned with anti-aircraft and anti-missile systems. He argued that for a system to be viable, it had to go as low, and as high, and as fast, and as slow, at the objects in its environment in order to 'match' or 'destroy'.

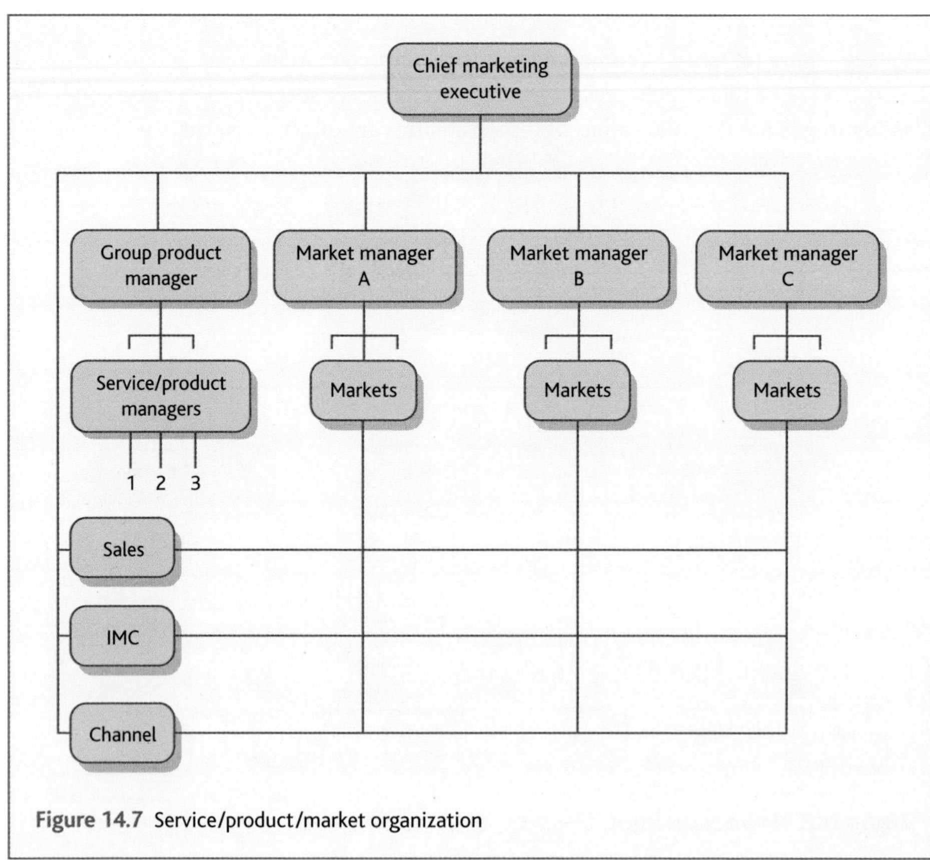

Figure 14.7 Service/product/market organization

Ashby's ideas were further developed by Stafford Beer (1979, 1981, 1985) who argued that any organism would only remain viable if it matched all the life-threatening varieties in its environment. For example, to use an analogy, the worm goes underground to escape the bird, and the bird goes into the air to escape the cat, and the cat jumps up a tree to escape the dog (Brocklesby and Cummings, 1996). Thus, organizations have to match variety with variety and this is the essence of successful control. Figure 14.8 depicts Beer's Viable System Model (VSM) with its five major systems:

- **System 1:** basic work unit(s) where the services/products/brand coordination is undertaken
- **System 2:** main regulatory centre
- **System 3:** operating management control centre
- **System 4:** intelligence and information-gathering centre
- **System 5:** overall strategic direction.

The environment includes all the suppliers, regulatory bodies, customers, media, and legislators, etc., that have an impact on the organization.

Beer's VSM model certainly has it critics, particularly those who say that it gives little, if any, role to culture or power in organizations. However, from a marketing strategy perspective, it enables individuals to define their purpose with respect to their relevant unit and to

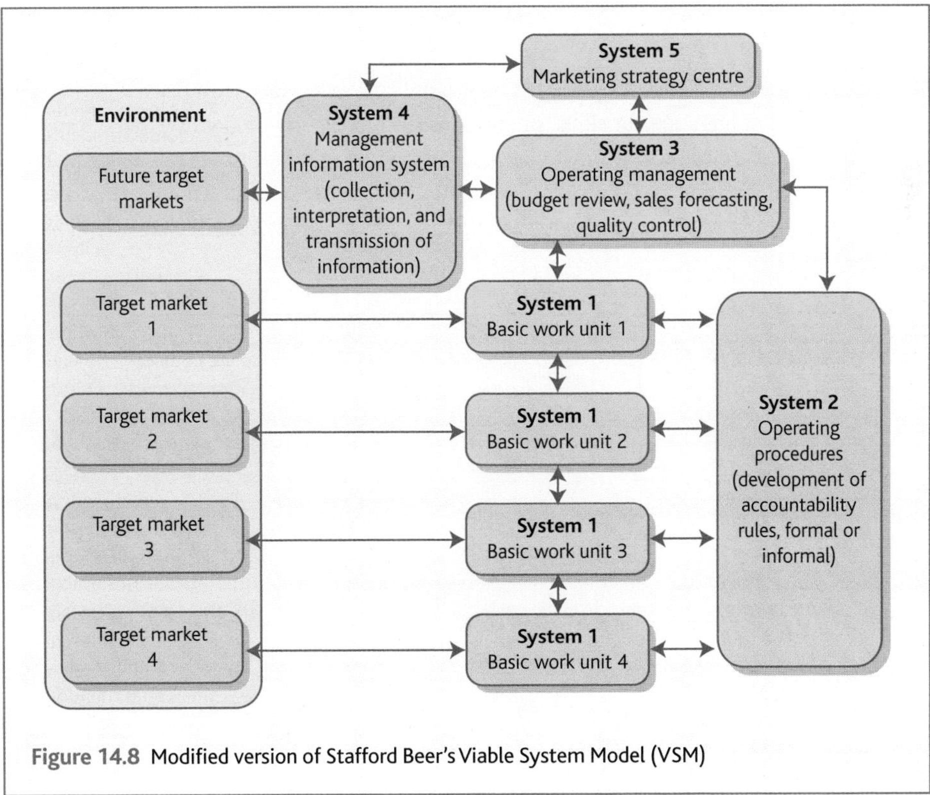

Figure 14.8 Modified version of Stafford Beer's Viable System Model (VSM)

those units with which they are connected. Beer also pointed out that the whole system could be placed within a business unit so that each unit could have its own sub-set of the operating procedures, operating management, information gathering, and strategy. His model has been used by governments in Chile and in the UK (the Scottish Parliament, Welsh Assembly, and Northern Ireland Assembly can all be seen as 'work units' within the framework of the UK Government), and companies such as Shell. For a specific example of its application, see Brocklesby and Cummings' (1996) discussion of Telecom (NZ). It might also be argued that the root cause of failure of such companies as Woolworths has been an inability to develop the requisite variety needed to survive in the environment. Woolworths was viable during the good years, but its market weaknesses and lack of focused position were exposed during the recession.

Metrics

Culture and organization are key elements in control, but Day and Wensley (1988) have alerted us to the management of competitive advantage as a process and hinted that the aspiration to a competitive advantage that was 'sustainable' was probably unrealistic for most firms (see, also, Montgomery (2008) on the importance of getting the strategy right rather than focusing on competitive advantage). A slightly modified version of Day and Wensley's model of the process of competitive advantage is shown in Figure 14.9.

Sources of competitive advantage

According to Day and Wensley (1988), there are only two sources of competitive advantage for a firm: it either has superior skills, or superior resources, and, hopefully, both. 'Superior skills' is an all-embracing phrase for greater resources with regard to human talent, know-how, abilities or competences. 'Superior resources' implies greater stocks of financial and other capital, better productive capacity, better location, access to supply, and the like.

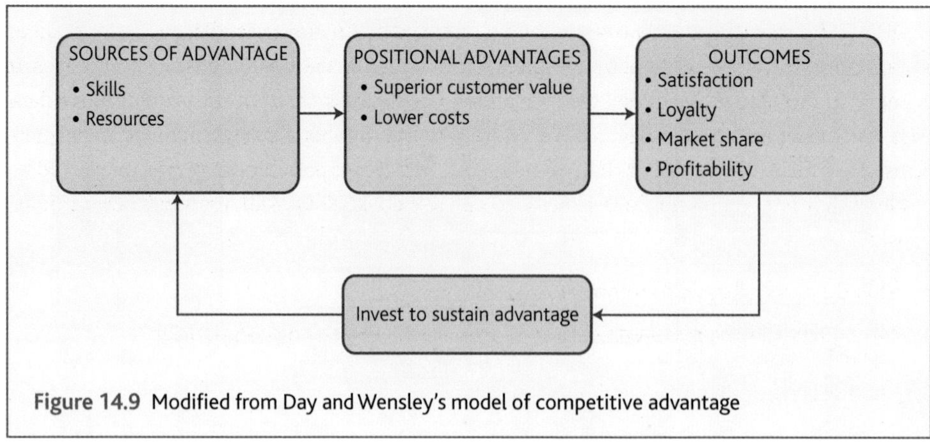

Figure 14.9 Modified from Day and Wensley's model of competitive advantage

Positional advantage

These sources of competitive advantage are used to achieve one of two positional advantages or ways of competing. Following Michael E. Porter (1985), the authors identify two generic competitive strategies: the position of low relative cost or superior customer value. Supposedly, the low-cost competitor is able to produce and deliver the product or service at the lowest cost, with the advantages of margin and pricing flexibility that this confers. For those competitors who are unable to achieve the low-cost position, the only other course of action is to offer superior customer value. That is to say, these competitors must, for example, make the product or service bigger, smaller, faster, more colourful, better quality or in a wider range. In short, they must differentiate their offerings in ways that will bestow superior customer values that people are prepared to pay a premium for. Porter (1985) implied that the two strategies are mutually exclusive and that to attempt to be a low-cost differentiator is to court the disaster of being stuck in the middle—increased costs without real differentiation. While that might have been true for the late 1970s and early 1980s, more recently, developments such as flexible manufacturing technologies have made these choices less clear-cut. Indeed, recent examples of firms such as Dell and Amazon.com might mean that it may not only be desirable to strive after both positions, but in many situations it may be the key to survival and success.

Performance outcomes

When a firm exploits either of the two generic strategies of lower relative cost and/or providing superior customer value with some success, according to Day and Wensley (1988), the outcomes will be evident in a number of variables and these variables form the foundations of marketing control; they are measurable.

Financial measures

Performance will manifest itself in financial productivity, measured by a return on investment (ROI)—or for that matter, any of a number of financial acronyms. Indeed, the development of a marketing strategy would not be complete without an overview of the business's finances. It is important to note at the outset that the analysis is always sterile without comparative data (see, for example, Rosenzweig, 2007). Moreover, the financial analysis will prompt questions about the business rather than give answers. Wherever possible, comparisons should be made with other companies in the sector to gauge 'best in class', and, amongst other things, to ask:

- What do we need to do to improve our position?
- How can we maintain our current position in the face of strong competition?

Key issues

There are three interrelated issues which need to be considered in the context of a marketing strategy:

- Profits and long-term profitability
- Cash and long-term sustainable cash flows
- The value of the business and how the business creates value.

The initial financial analysis will show how these issues stand currently and one key objective of the marketing strategy will be, inter alia, to optimize and improve all three in order to create shareholder value. Figure 14.4 illustrates the connections between the principal financial statements. It shows that shareholder return rests upon the ability of any business to generate cash to pay dividends and long-term profits and cash flows to grow investment in the business and subsequently the value of the business.

An example

There is a myriad of measures and analyses which could be used to understand a business's finances; however, a few key measures and techniques will give an initial picture of the business. Assume that the contents in Table 14.1 are extracts from the accounts of Oxtma plc (a fictitious company), which will be used to illustrate the analysis.

TABLE 14.1 The accounts of Oxtma plc

	£M
Revenues: the total value of all goods and services sold to third parties in the normal course of trade	25.00
EBITDA: earnings before interest, taxation depreciation, and amortization	3.10
Operating profit: the profit after the deduction of all expenses (business overheads) other than interest and taxation (also known as profit before interest and tax)	2.50
Operating cash flow: the cash effects of transactions and other events relating to operating or trading activities	3.00
Total assets: the sum of all the assets, i.e. fixed and current	15.00
Total liabilities: the total financial claims of lenders and others who supply money, goods, and services	7.00
Shareholders' Equity: the sum of share capital and **reserves** less any issued preference shares. Equity represents the ordinary shareholders' interest in the company	6.00
Trade debtors: people or businesses who owe money to the business; also referred to as **receivables**	5.00

The operating margin

The margin measures the profitability of sales revenues, as it reflects the combination of the cost and pricing structures of the business. Margins differ between sectors: for example, a supermarket might achieve between 2 and 5 per cent, whereas a pharmaceutical company might make between 20 and 30 per cent. Where the information is available, other margins can also be calculated as a ratio of sales revenues. Taking the example of Oxtma plc:

$$\frac{\text{Operating profit \%}}{\text{Revenues}} \quad \frac{2.50}{25.00} = 10.00\%$$

Revenues to total assets

Revenues to total assets (or asset turnover), which is a prime measure of efficiency, shows the intensity with which the total assets are employed in the business. The level of margin often depends upon the efficiency of investment in the business and the scale of revenues. The higher the ratio, the more efficient the business is in utilizing its assets. Highly capital-intensive businesses (e.g., power generation) will have relatively low ratios (i.e., below 1:1); on the other hand, low capital-intensive businesses (e.g., supermarkets) could have ratios of above 2:1. In the case of Oxtma plc, it is:

$$\frac{\text{Revenues}}{\text{Total assets}} \quad \frac{25.00}{15.00} = 1.67:1$$

Return on total assets (ROTA)

The third key measure is a return on investment (ROI). Return on total assets (ROTA) gives a good indication of profitability and the efficiency of management by highlighting the relationship between the assets employed in the business and the profits that the business has generated by using those assets. ROTA is closely connected to the return to shareholders (after taking account of debt and other liabilities); therefore, a key strategic objective is to optimize this figure through improved margins and efficiencies. Comparison with other companies and with previous years is essential, but a return in the region of 10 to 20 per cent should be expected, depending upon the riskiness of the business. Companies with high operating margins often have low revenues to total assets and vice versa. Oxtma's ROTA would be:

$$\frac{\text{Operating profit}}{\text{Total assets}} \quad \frac{2.50}{15.00} = 16.67\%$$

Cash conversion

The ability to generate cash (cash flow) or to convert profits into cash (cash conversion) is key to the survival of the business. Cash conversion is important because businesses often fail primarily through lack of cash rather than poor profitability. Operating cash flow to EBITDA measures the relationship between cash flow and profit. A strong indicator of possible cash-flow problems is when operating cash flow is less than EBITDA. A ratio of less than 90 per cent might give rise to concern, especially when there is a trend over a number of years. Using the example of Oxtma plc, cash conversion would be:

$$\frac{\text{Operating cash flow}}{\text{EBITDA}} \quad \frac{3.00}{3.10} = 96.77\%$$

Days sales outstanding (DSO)

Poor cash conversion might result from rapid revenue growth, poor receivable collections, or a number of other factors. Days sales outstanding (DSO) is a crude calculation which often highlights the cause of cash conversion issues. A difficulty with this measure, as with others which associate an annual 'flow' figure with a year-end 'temperature' figure, is that the latter may not be typical of the level experienced throughout the year. This is especially true when a business is expanding or contracting rapidly. Oxtma's DSO would look like this:

$$\frac{\text{Trade Debtors}}{\text{Revenues}} \quad \frac{5.00 \times 365}{25.00} = 73 \text{ days}$$

Gearing or leverage

Where a company has borrowed funds to finance the business, the drain on cash resources through interest payments and debt repayments can be an important issue. The level of debt can be assessed by comparing debt and equity. Debt to equity (gearing or leverage) measures the proportion of a business funded from borrowing or other non-equity sources of finance. If there is a high proportion of 'prior charges' (i.e., capital other than equity), then the gearing is high. There are no hard and fast rules, but levels of debt above 40 to 50 per cent might be a cause for concern, especially where there are cash flow problems. Oxtma plc's gearing would be:

$$\frac{\text{Debt}}{\text{Equity}} \quad \frac{2.00}{6.00} = 33.33\%$$

Shareholder value

The final part is to understand the impact of the marketing strategy on the current value of the business (see Koller et al., 2005; Doyle, 2008). Shareholder value can be created by growing the value of the business and destroyed by shrinking it (see Figure 14.10). Value can be measured in different ways, but, in each case, the principle of value creation remains the same. Some alternatives are:

- the value of the shareholders' equity in the business
- the total assets of the company
- or, for listed companies the market value or market capitalization.

In each case, value ultimately depends upon the ability of the business to generate long-term sustainable cash flows and profits.

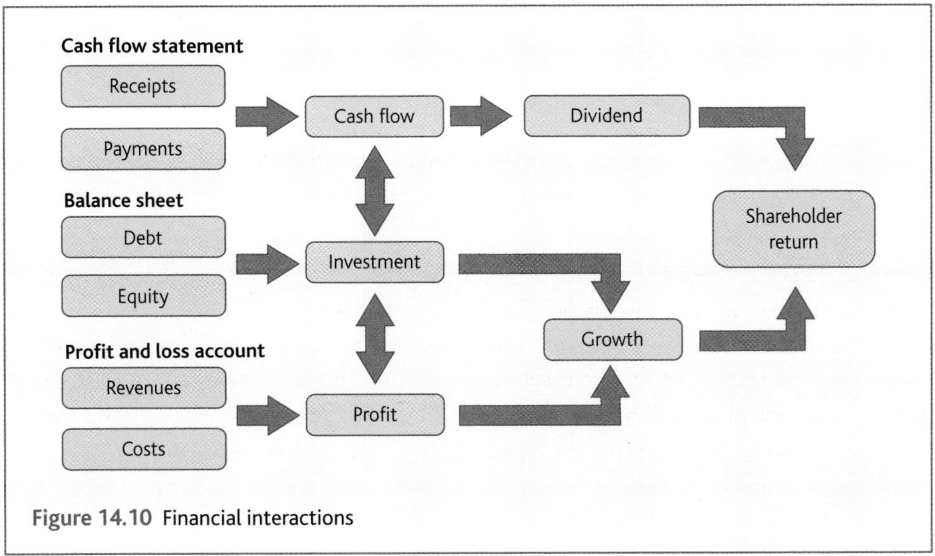

Figure 14.10 Financial interactions

Market share

Aside from financial measures, the successful competitor's performance will also be manifested in the form of increased market share, or at the very least, a maintenance thereof. There are two other outcomes of achieving a position of competitive advantage. One is customer satisfaction: a firm that offers customers the benefits of a differentiated offering, or passes on some of the rents achieved by lower cost, will satisfy customers, all things being equal. The other is loyalty: satisfied customers tend to remain loyal to the firm that really fulfils them, and, given the choice, refrain from patronizing competitors.

Most managers give more attention to the outcomes of market share and financial productivity for two obvious reasons: these outcomes tend to be easier to measure, and managers are typically rewarded directly for improvements in them. Managers are also inclined to agree that customer satisfaction and loyalty are important and that they (as loosely implied in the sequence in the diagram in Figure 14.11) lead to market share and ROI (or other measures). However, they will likewise contend that these concepts are vague and less easy to measure.

To a large extent, they are right. While the attempts by consumer psychologists and marketing researchers to improve the measurement of customer satisfaction (cf. Anderson et al., 1994) and service quality (cf. Parasuraman et al., 1985, 1988) have been most laudable, it should not be forgotten that what they are trying to achieve is daunting, indeed. Getting 'inside the heads' of customers and assessing complex human cognitive processes such as satisfaction using tools like five- and seven-point scales is not easy.

What makes market share and financial productivity measures appealing as outcomes of a position of competitive advantage is the fact that they are 'hard'—expressed in numbers that can be easily calculated, compared, and tracked. The main problem, however, is that they are historical—a good way of tracking the past, but not necessarily an indication of the future. They are not good diagnostics of strategic health. While customers may be capricious

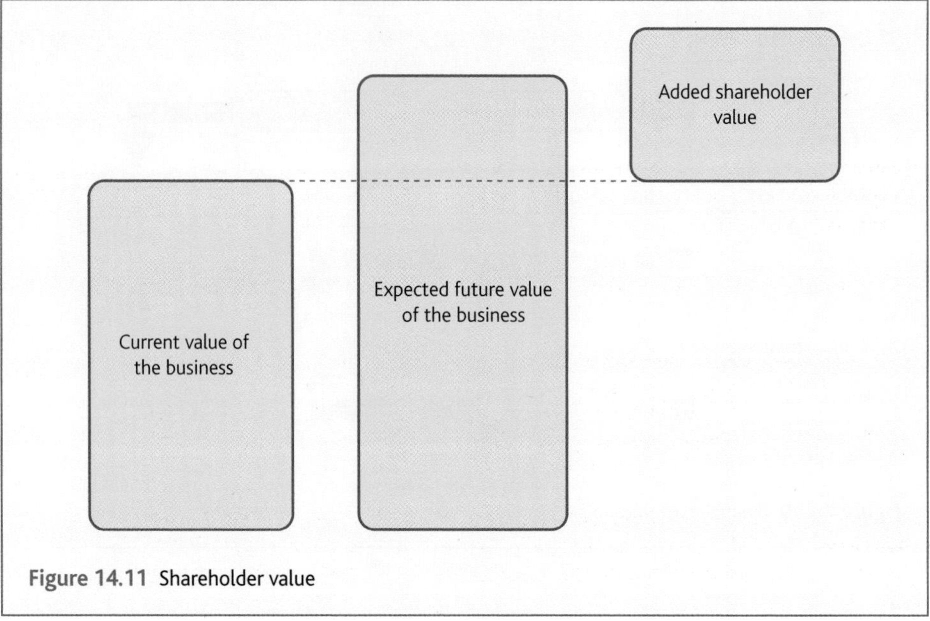

Figure 14.11 Shareholder value

at times, all things being equal, they are not so fickle as to be satisfied today and dissatisfied with the same good offering tomorrow, or change the loyalty horse in midstream. Indeed, most customers are probably more tolerant of marketers' shortcomings than the latter would give them credit for, and only downgrade ratings or shift allegiances as the result of gross dereliction. Again, the problem with most measures of customer satisfaction and loyalty is that they are soft and impression-based. They are, however, about the future.

The logic of the process model presented in Figure 14.9 is that the astute firm will reinvest the financial outcomes of competitive advantage in the sources of competitive advantage itself, namely, superior skills and/or superior resources. This activity closes the loop in the model, and suggests that managing for competitive advantage is a process that is continually renewed, revived, and refreshed. Certainly, a marketing strategist's skills may well be distinguished by his/her knowledge of what sources of competitive advantage to invest in, what position(s) to adopt, and the ability to determine the outcome of the process effectively—what was referred to earlier in this chapter as 'control'.

The variables which can be measured and controlled in the outcomes in the model in Figure 14.9 are illustrated in Table 14.2.

Customer equity

While the two sets of outcomes in the Day and Wensley model presented in Figure 14.9 each have their own particular strengths, each set also has its limitations (Pitt et al., 2000). The outcomes of ROI and market share are hard, but historical, and the outcomes of customer satisfaction and loyalty are future-orientated but soft. The ideal marketing control variable would be an outcome that is both hard (a number that can be expressed financially) and

TABLE 14.2 Metric variables

Outcome	Operationalization	Typical measure
Customer satisfaction/ dissatisfaction	Customers' overall satisfaction with an organization's products or services	Customer satisfaction survey, requiring customers to rate satisfaction or various aspects of it on an interval scale Focus groups, user-group forums, blogs, observational studies
	Difference between customer's expectations of the quality of a product or service and their perceptions of a particular product or service (also known as 'disconfirmation')	Service quality studies using instruments such as SERVQUAL (Parasuraman et al., 1988)
Customer experience	Customers' internal and subjective response to any direct or indirect contact with an organization	Surveys, targeted studies, observational studies, 'voice of customer' research (Meyer and Schwager, 2007)
Customer loyalty	The extent to which customers would be willing to choose an alternative over the organization's offering, given availability	Surveys of loyalty
	Customer churn (also known as customer retention rates, or conversely, customer defection rates)	How many customers who are in an organization's customer base at the beginning of a period (usually a year) are still in it at the end of a period? An indication of **retention** How many customers who are in a firm's customer base at the beginning of a period (usually a year) will not be in it at the end of a period? An indication of **defection**? (See: Reichheld and Sasser, 1990; Reichheld, 1993; Page et al., 1996; McGovern and Moon, 2007)
Market share	The percentage or proportion of the total available market or market segment that is being serviced by a company Increasing market share is one of the most common objectives used in business. The main advantage of using market share is that it abstracts from industry-wide macro-environmental variables such as the state of the economy, or changes in tax policy	Can be expressed as: • a company's sales revenue (from that market) divided by the total sales revenue available in that market or • a company's unit sales volume (in a market) divided by the total volume of units sold in that market

(Continued)

TABLE 14.2 *(Continued)*

Outcome	Operationalization	Typical measure
Measures of financial productivity	All of the measures below assess the ability of the organization to make a profit	
	Sales growth Analysis: look for a steady increase in sales If overall costs and inflation are on the rise, then you should watch for a related increase in your sales—if not, then this is an indicator that your prices are not keeping up with your costs	**Percentage** increase (or decrease) in sales between two time periods Formula: Current year's sales – Last year's sales/Last year's sales
	COGS to sales Analysis: look for a stable ratio as an indicator that the company is controlling its gross margins	Percentage of sales used to pay for expenses that vary directly with sales Formula: Cost of Goods Sold/Sales
	Gross profit margin Analysis: compare to other businesses in the same industry to see if your business is operating as profitably as it should be. Look at the trend from month to month. Is it staying the same? Improving? Deteriorating? Is there enough gross profit in the business to cover your operating costs? Is there a positive gross margin on all your products?	Indicator of how much profit is earned on your products without consideration of selling and administration costs Formula: Gross profit/Total sales where Gross profit = Sales less cost of goods sold
	SG&A to sales Analysis: look for a steady or decreasing percentage, indicating that the company is controlling its overhead expenses	Percentage of selling, general, and administrative costs to sales Formula: Selling, general and administrative expenses/Sales
	Net profit margin Analysis: compare to other businesses in the same industry to see if your business is operating as profitably as it should be Look at the trend from month to month Is it staying the same? Improving? Deteriorating? Are you generating enough sales to leave an acceptable profit? Trend from month to month can show how well you are managing your operating or overhead costs	Shows how much profit comes from every pound of sales Formula:Net profit/Total sales

TABLE 14.2 *(Continued)*

Outcome	Operationalization	Typical measure
	Return on equity (ROE) Analysis: compare the return on equity to other investment alternatives, such as a savings account, stock, or bond Compare your ratio to other businesses in the same or similar industry	Determines the rate of return on your investment in the business. As an owner or shareholder this is one of the most important ratios as it shows the hard fact about the business—are you making enough of a profit to compensate you for the risk of being in business? Formula: Net profit/Equity
	Return on assets (ROA) Analysis: ROA shows the amount of income for every pound tied up in assets Year-to-year trends may be an indicator—but watch out for changes in the total asset figure as you depreciate your assets (a decrease or increase in the denominator can affect the ratio and doesn't necessarily mean the business is improving or declining)	Considered a measure of how effectively assets are used to generate a return (this ratio is not very useful for most businesses) Formula: Net profit/Total assets

future (customer)-orientated. Customer lifetime value (CLTV), which in turn leads to customer equity, is arguably that single appropriate outcome. Traditional accounting systems have viewed customers as sources of revenue. Increasingly, firms are beginning to use their accounting systems to view customers as assets, especially if they have access to Web analytics (see Mini Case Study 14.2), and are basing their decisions on customers much as they would base their decisions on investments.

MINI CASE STUDY 14.2 **Using Web analytics**

The ability to measure ROI (return on investment) has been one of the key features in the success of the Web. Finance directors have long dreamt of being able to measure the impact of marketing investments and the Web has certainly done that. Marketers can trace, track, and monitor every move beyond what was possible with traditional direct response marketing such as direct mail. That's the theory. Unfortunately, the reality of wading through masses of Web analytics data showing where customers are coming from and tracking their behaviour when they arrive at your site can be daunting. The evidence is sketchy, but the indications are that only about a fifth of organizations are linking Web analytics to their marketing strategy.

Site and external analytics are critical to improving acquisition, retention, and cross-selling. The base level of approach to Web analytics is to ask: how well are we selling

» products and services online? Firstly, look at your own main website microsite, which is a cluster of pages within the main site around a theme, and the landing page, which is where a visitor arrives when they click on an ad or a search engine. With PPC/CPC (pay per click/cost per click) or CPA (cost per action, be it a sale or registration), the landing page can be customized to measure the effectiveness of relative clickthroughs—the software can be crunched to show the best inward routes such as online display, affiliate schemes (content-rich sites that provide hyperlinks to brands such as: **http://www.epinions.com**), and search. Search engine optimization (SEO) is a black art that attempts to manage the routes to landing pages organically so that key phrases and words are used that best lead to specific landing pages. Thus, the marketing spend can be optimized by focusing on the routes providing the best return.

Such Web analytics can provide an organization with a good understanding of what appears to be working and, accordingly, what to do more of and what to do less of. But what does it have to do with marketing strategy?

Incorporating Web analytics into marketing strategy takes a more holistic perspective of ROI, with a different set of questions and a wider range of ROI analytics. Standing back from the Web component, marketers need to develop strategies based upon the synergies with wider marketing activities. Take the case of the T-Mobile TV 'flash mobbing' commercial, which featured hidden filming of 350 undercover dancers dancing to Lulu's 1965 hit 'Shout'. The dancers were surreptitiously positioned amongst surprised commuters at Liverpool Street Station. The dance routine was carefully choreographed and the work of intensive training. Strategically, the commercial provided a concise personification of the brand's positioning of 'Life is for sharing'. The ad reached the crucial and media-fragmented 18–24 audience and at the time of writing, has attracted nearly 16 million views on YouTube.

Yes, it is possible to measure the Liverpool Street Station commercial with the effect on the T-Mobile website in terms of clickthroughs, PPAs, and CPAs. Some other useful measures would be the amount of time dwelt on the site and the number of times the commercial was passed on (viral). However, such Web analytics won't provide much insight into the effect of the campaign on the engagement with the brand. For example, should T-Mobile spend more or less on search when a big campaign is running? To gain a better strategic picture, qualitative research can be useful, for example discussions on social networks and word-of-mouth and blogs. What is more that old-fashioned technique of the focus group may also prove its worth.

Customer lifetime value

Customer lifetime value (CLTV) is the net present value (NPV) of the profit that a firm stands to realize on the average new customer during a given number of years. This is illustrated in the calculations shown in the spreadsheet in Table 14.3. It can be calculated using the formula:

$$\mathrm{CLTV} \underset{i=1}{\overset{n}{=}} \Sigma (1+d)^{-i} \pi_i$$

Where:

π_i = sales profit from this customer in period i + any non-sales benefits (e.g., referrals) − cost of maintaining the relationship in period i

d = discount rate
n = final period, estimated to be lifetime horizon for customer.

The spreadsheet in Table 14.3 might be typical of a firm marketing a specialist academic journal subscription. If it is assumed that the firm sells 1,000 new subscriptions in Year 1 at £150 each, then the calculation of net revenue and also of net costs at 50 per cent of revenue, are both simple procedures. A further important issue is retention: in simple terms, how many of the customers at the beginning of a year are still subscribers at the end of the year? What has been done in Table 14.4 is to assume a retention rate of 40 per cent at the end of Year 1, and then increase this gradually over the five-year period. Thus, 400 customers are still subscribers at the beginning of Year 2 (0.4 × 1000), 180 at the beginning of Year 3 (0.45 × 400), and so forth.

The revenues and the costs for each year are functions of the number of customers at the beginning of that year. Calculation of gross profit is a subtraction procedure and what follows is perhaps the only, albeit slightly, complex calculation in the entire process. As in all investments, the returns for a customer five years from now are not worth what they are today. Therefore, there is a need to discount gross profits. The discount rate chosen in Table 14.3 is 4 per cent. This figure is discretionary, and its choice will vary from firm to firm; some may choose a premium bank rate, others an internal rate of return, still others some minimum rate of investment acceptability. This is not critical to our discussion, for the principles remain the same. This discount rate is used to calculate the net present value (NPV) of the cumulative gross profit over the years. The final calculation is a simple one: what is the CLTV of a customer who was put on the books in Year 1? The answer is the NPV of the cumulative gross profit for the year divided by the number of customers (in this case 1,000) in Year 1. Thus, the CLTV of one of these customers in Year 4 would be £122, and in Year 5 £126, and so on.

An obvious application of this type of spreadsheet is its use in the calculation of 'What happens if we increase CLTV by x%?' The decision-maker can change variables such as price, costs, the discount rate, the number of years an individual will be a customer, and of course the retention rate, to determine the effects these will have on CLTV. For example, Table 14.4 uses the same data from Table 14.3 with a hypothetical 5 per cent increase in retention. It can be seen in Table 14.4 that the final NPV increases from £126 to £129.

In more general terms, however, it is worth considering what can be done from a marketing strategy perspective to **maximize** CLTV—what marketing strategies need to be formulated? **Control** is another issue to consider—CLTV is a very powerful control variable that can be used to assess the success or otherwise of a marketing strategy and its implementation. Not only is the overall number a useful metric, but it can be broken down into its components and be calculated not only by customer group or target market, but right down to the level of the individual customer.

In summary, CLTV can be increased by:

1. increasing lifetime either by increasing retention rate, or increasing customer life (i.e., the number of years a customer can remain a customer)
2. increasing sales to, or as a result of, a customer, either by increasing the firm's share of the customer's purchases, or by increasing the customer's referral rate (the number of times they refer others to the firm's products and services)
3. cutting the costs of serving a customer.

TABLE 14.3 Example of the calculation of CLTV

			Year 1	Year 2	Year 3	Year 4	Year 5
Revenue							
Customers	(A x B/100) t–1	A	1000	400	180	90	50
Retention rate (%)		B	40	45	50	55	60
Customer spend		C	£150	£150	£150	£150	£150
Total revenue	(A x C)	D	£150,000	£60,000	£27,000	£13,500	£7,500
Costs							
Cost %		E	50	50	50	50	50
Total costs	(D x E)/100	F	£75,000	£30,000	£13,500	£6,750	£3,750
Profits							
Gross profit	(D–F)	G	£75,000	£30,000	£13,500	£6,750	£3,750
Discount rate* (4%)		H	1.00	1.04	1.08	1.12	1.17
Net present value profit	(G/H)	I	£75,000	£28,846	£12,482	£6,001	£3,206
Cumulative profit (NPV)	(I) t1–5	J	£75,000	£103,846	£116,328	£122,328	£125,534
Lifetime value (NPV)	(J/1000)	K	£75	£104	£116	£122	£126

*D = (1 + i)n, where D = discount rate, i = interest rate, and n = number of years you have to wait for return.

TABLE 14.4 Example of the calculation of CLTV + 5% Increase in Retention

			Year 1	Year 2	Year 3	Year 4	Year 5
Revenue							
Customers	(A x B/100) t–1	A	1000	420	197	105	50
Retention rate (%)		B	42	47	53	58	63
Customer spend		C	£150	£150	£150	£150	£150
Total revenue	(A x C)	D	£150,000	£63,000	£29,610	£15,693	£7,500
Costs							
Cost %		E	50	50	50	50	50
Total costs	(D x E)/100	F	£75,000	£31,000	£14,805	£7,847	£3,750
Profits							
Gross profit	(D–F)	G	£75,000	£31,500	£14,805	£7,847	£3,750
Discount rate* (4%)		H	1.00	1.04	1.08	1.12	1.17
Net present value profit	(G/H)	I	£75,000	£30,288	£13,688	£6,976	£3,206
Cumulative profit (NPV)	(I) t1–5	J	£75,000	£105,288	£118,977	£125,952	£129,158
Lifetime value (NPV)	(J/1000)	K	£75	£105	£119	£126	£129

*D = (1 + i)n, where D = discount rate, i = interest rate, and n = number of years you have to wait for return.

Pitt et al. (2000) use a number of cases from well-known firms to illustrate these principles:

- **Increasing retention rates:** loyalty programmes operate in industries, ranging from airlines to restaurants and supermarkets to hotel chains. Their objective is to raise switching barriers for customers, thereby encouraging their loyalty. Tesco's Club Card in the UK, FlyBuys in Australia, and the Click's Card in South Africa are some excellent international examples of this strategy.
- **Increasing customer lifetime value:** Huggies disposable nappies developed a product extension branded 'Pullups' or 'Trainer Pants' in various international markets. The disposable pants were targeted at infants who were almost potty-trained, but whose parents still required the certainty that accidents could be avoided. The product added about 6 months to the life of a Huggies customer. While this may not seem like much, 6 months on a life of two years adds 25 per cent to CLTV!
- **Increasing sales of the same product:** Tia Maria is a liqueur usually consumed in small shot glasses after a meal, which limits its sales. The brand has since published recipe booklets encouraging the use of the product in cocktails, as a sauce over ice cream, and as an ingredient in desserts.
- **Increasing the sales of other products to the same customer:** while Amazon.com began its life in book sales, it quickly moved on to sales of music and DVDs and on to clothing, DIY and tools, jewellery, etc., as it understood its customers more effectively.
- **Exploiting customer referral rates:** Apple's iPod has been one of the most successful digital products in history. Yet, Apple spends relatively little on promotion. The product is sold almost entirely on WOM (word-of-mouth) as owners enthusiastically advocate it to their friends.
- **Cutting the costs of serving customers:** the Internet has provided marketers with a wide range of applications to reduce the costs of serving customers without lowering service levels. Customers do their banking online, purchase and check in airline tickets, and check their frequent-flyer miles. Most customers welcome the control this gives them over the purchasing situation, yet for the institutions involved, being able to rely on technology and the customer to do the work means very significant cost savings.

From CLTV to customer equity

It is important to note that the simple spreadsheets presented in Table 14.3 and Table 14.4 represent the CLTVs of 'average customers'. Yet, all customers have their own CLTVs. In different markets each day, there are attempts by marketers to capture the data to enable them to get closer to calculating the CLTV of an individual customer, e.g. customer databases, databases of loyalty cards and warranty registration schemes, and the like. If these CLTVs were then summed, the total value of the firm's customer base may be calculated—a process Blattberg and Deighton (1996) call **customer equity**.

Potentially, customer equity could be the ultimate marketing control measure: every marketing decision would be evaluated by whether or not it increased customer equity. For example, when thinking about customer acquisition and retention, the decision should be based on where the next marketing pound (or euro, dollar, or yen, or whatever) would be better spent, on getting new customers or keeping the existing ones. The answer: whichever one of the two strategies has the greatest effect on customer equity. Some companies have used customer equity analyses as the basis to decisions either to migrate their customers to a new provider, normally a partner, but who may also be a competitor, or to terminate the relationship with the customer altogether (Mittal et al., 2008). This is normally because the company no longer views the customer as profitable (e.g., insuring a home in a flood zone).

Rather than merely allocate marketing and advertising budgets according to such variables as media selection and spend, or territories, or even customer markets, in the future managers may wish to consciously split the budget between customer acquisition and customer retention activities. Customer equity becomes the basis upon which this decision can be made. Firms may even wish to consider organizing themselves along the lines of acquisition and retention, and to evaluate the performance of these divisions on their ability to contribute towards customer equity (Blattberg and Deighton, 1996).

Wachovia, a financial subsidiary of Wells Fargo, is a leading example of a company that has done this (Hanssens et al., 2008). In the absence of readily available tools to link marketing budgets to customer equity goals, the company set about building a model of customer equity based upon the three key elements of:

1. Customer acquisition
2. Customer retention
3. Cross-selling to existing customers.

The company built a market-response model with the aim of working out how marketing inputs affected the customer equity output and included a variety of variables such as historic advertising expenditures, changes in the branch network, and levels of customer satisfaction and linked it up to acquisition, retention, and cross-selling amongst its customers grouped by household.

The analysis showed that the inputs indicated in Table 14.5 have the greatest impact on Wachovia's customer equity.

TABLE 14.5 Primary inputs on Wachovia's customer equity

Directly controlled by marketing	Indirectly controlled by marketing	External
• Media advertising • Internet advertising • Direct mail • Sales employees per branch • Rate ratios • Sponsorships	• News coverage • Customer satisfaction • Brand equity	• Leading economic indicators • Seasonality • Identified shocks (e.g., economic or social)

Their model is not simple, for it has to calculate the impacts of thousands of different combinations of marketing allocations by media, market, and segment and with a variety of constraints on budgets and outcomes. What they have found, though, is that there are no uniform effects on customer equity. For example, a marketing mix designed to maximize acquisitions in the short term would differ significantly from a mix designed to maximize long-term customer equity. Wachovia appreciate that the model is not infallible and so it is used as just one contribution to the overall discussion about the strategy.

Conclusion

Most firms spend an inordinate amount of time and effort on the formulation of marketing strategy and it is likely that the reason for many strategic marketing failures and problems lies in implementation, rather than in formulation. The problem with the implementation of marketing strategy is that it can easily mask formulation. When a well-formulated marketing strategy fails, the blame is frequently given to poor formulation, whereas poor implementation might have been the cause. Likewise, when marketing strategy is poorly formulated, good implementation can have two very different possible outcomes. On the one hand, good implementation can disguise a poorly formulated strategy and make it look good by leading to short-term success. On the other hand, when a poorly formulated strategy is well implemented, it can simply hasten the downfall by accelerating the impact of the weakness.

The managerial task of control lies at the heart of successful strategic implementation. If marketing objectives and goals are carefully and skilfully articulated and then regularly and systematically compared to performance, then corrective action can be taken in time to bring strategy back on track.

The successful implementation of marketing strategy involves many behavioural issues within the organization. It has been demonstrated empirically that successful implementation of marketing strategy is influenced by the culture of the firm. Managers should, therefore, strive to understand the cultures of their organizations and the impact this will have on the successful implementation of marketing strategy.

Summary

This chapter defined control as a managerial task that sets targets, evaluates performance against those targets, and then takes corrective or reinforcing action where necessary. Control generally takes three forms: annual plan control, profitability control, or strategic control. Implementation is the act of execution of an endeavour and in the future it is likely that organizations will become as good at strategy implementation as they are at formulation. A number of causes of the inadequate implementation of marketing strategy within organizations were identified.

The implementation of marketing strategy in organizations was viewed through the lens of managing a process of competitive advantage. This process consists of identifying superior skills and superior resources and turning them into positions of competitive advantage, either a low-cost position or superior value. If a firm enjoys a position of competitive advantage, this will result in measurable and consequently controllable outcomes, principally customer-satisfaction loyalty, market share, and measures of financial productivity. The logic of the process of competitive advantage is that the superior returns enjoyed will be reinvested in the sources of competitive advantage. A significant change in marketing has been a shift from these four measures to the single yardstick of customer lifetime value (CLTV), which has become a critical measure to use to evaluate and control the successful implementation of an organization's marketing strategy. The summation of an organization's CLTVs is known as customer equity.

The successful implementation of a firm's marketing strategy is also partly a result of an organization's corporate culture, defined simply as 'the way we do things around here'. Three approaches were considered in this respect, looking at corporate culture: Handy (1978); Deshpandé et al. (1993); and Goffee and Jones (1996).

KEY TERMS

Control The managerial task of setting standards, evaluating these standards against reality, and the taking of corrective or reinforcing action where necessary.

Corporate culture The moral, social, and behavioural norms of an organization based on the beliefs, attitudes, and priorities of its members.

Customer equity The sum of all of the CLTVs of the customers estimated from an organization's customer database.

Customer lifetime value (CLTV) The net present value of all future cash flows from a customer over their lifetime.

Financial analysis The assessment of the effectiveness with which funds (investment and debt) are employed in a firm.

Implementation Executing an activity, or putting a plan into action.

Marketing budget The financial statement and programme put before top management for approval for spending on marketing in order to meet set objectives.

Process model of competitive advantage An approach to competitive advantage and the implementation of marketing strategy which views competitive advantage not as something static, but as an ongoing process which has to be formulated and controlled.

Strategy formulation-implementation grid A tool for the diagnosis of the successful or otherwise formulation and implementation of marketing strategy.

Viable System Model (VSM) A tool for anticipating, planning for, and implementing strategy.

DISCUSSION QUESTIONS

1 Briefly outline and describe the steps a marketing manager could take to ensure control of marketing activities at different levels.

2 What are the possible consequences for marketing strategy when a poor strategy is well implemented? Can you think of examples of this occurring, other than those mentioned in the text? What are the

consequences for marketing strategy when a good strategy is poorly implemented? Can you think of examples of this occurring, other than those mentioned in the text?

3 List some of the reasons why marketing strategy is often not implemented successfully, and think of practical examples of this in organizations with which you are familiar.

4 Choose an organization with which you are familiar, and set up a process model of competitive advantage for it. What are the sources of its competitive advantage? How does it compete? What are the outcomes of this process for the organization? What skills or resources will it have to invest in the future if it is to survive and prosper?

5 Set up a simple spreadsheet and use it to estimate the lifetime values of:

- an infant wearing nappies for two years
- the credit card customer of a bank who takes a card at the age of 20 and is projected to live to the age of 75 (assuming this is a middle-income customer).

6 Now, use your spreadsheet to predict what might happen if:

- the above organizations could extend the lifetimes of their customers either by starting them earlier or ending them later. How might this be achieved?
- the above organizations could get the customer to use more of their products
- the above organizations could get customers to use their other products or services.

7 To what extent do you agree with the premise that the measurement of marketing success or failure is always sterile without comparative data?

ONLINE RESOURCE CENTRE

Visit the Online Resource Centre for this book for lots of interesting additional material at: **www.oxfordtextbooks.co.uk/orc/west2e/**

REFERENCES AND FURTHER READING

Anderson, Erin, Claes Fornell, and Donald R. Lehmann (1994), 'Customer Satisfaction, Market Share, and Profitability', *Journal of Marketing*, 58 (July), 53–66.

Badovick, G. J., and Sharon E. Beatty (1987), 'Shared Organizational Values: Measurement and Impact upon Strategic Marketing Implementation', *Journal of the Academy of Marketing Science*, 15 (1), 19–26.

Beer, Stafford (1979), *The Heart of Enterprise* (Chichester: Wiley).

Beer, Stafford (1981), *Brain of the Firm*, 2nd edn (Chichester: Wiley).

Beer, Stafford (1985), *Diagnosing the System for Organizations* (Chichester: Wiley).

Berthon, Pierre R., James M. Hulbert, and Leyland F. Pitt (1997), 'Brands, Brand Managers, and the Management of Brands: Where to Next?' *Commentary Report*, 97–122 (November) (Cambridge, MA: Marketing Science Institute).

Berthon, Pierre R., Leyland F. Pitt, and Michael T. Ewing (2001), 'Corollaries of the Collective: Effects of Corporate Culture and Organizational Memory on Decision-making Context', *Journal of the Academy of Marketing Science*, 29 (2), 135–50.

Blattberg, Robert C., and John Deighton (1996), 'Manage Marketing by the Customer Equity Test', *Harvard Business Review*, July–August, 136–45.

Bonoma, Thomas V. (1984), 'Making your Marketing Strategy Work', *Harvard Business Review*, March–April, 69–77.

Breene, R. Timothy S., Paul F. Nunes, and Walter E. Shill (2007), 'The Chief Strategy Officer', *Harvard Business Review*, October, pp. 84–93.

Brocklesby, John, and Stephen Cummings (1996), 'Designing a Viable Organisation Structure', *Long Range Planning*, 29 (1), pp. 49–57.

Bruning, Edward R., and Lawrence S. Lockshin (1994), 'Marketing's Role in Generating Organizational Competitiveness', *Journal of Strategic Marketing*, 2, pp. 163–87.

Campbell, J. P., and Sarah J. Freeman (1991), 'Cultural Congruence, Strength, and Type: Relationships to Effectiveness', in R. W. Woodman and W. Pasmore (eds), *Research in Ozzal Change and Development*, Vol. 5 (Greenwich, CT: JAI Press).

Day, George. S., and Robin Wensley (1988), 'Assessing Advantage: A Framework for Diagnosing Competitive Superiority', *Journal of Marketing*, 52 (April), 1–20.

Deighton, John (2002), 'How Snapple Got its Juice Back', *Harvard Business Review*, January, 47.

Deshpandé, Rohit, John U. Farley, and Frederick E. Webster (1993), 'Corporate Culture, Customer Orientation, and Innovativeness in Japanese Firms: A Quadrad Analysis', *Journal of Marketing*, 57, 23–7.

Doyle, Peter (2008), *Value-based Marketing*, 2nd edn (Chichester: John Wiley & Sons).

Farris, Paul, and Douglas C. West (2007), 'A Fresh View of the Advertising Budget Process', in Gerard J. Tellis and Tim Ambler (eds), *The SAGE Handbook of Advertising* (London: SAGE), pp. 316–32.

Goffee, Rob, and Gareth Jones (1996), 'What Holds the Modern Company Together?' *Harvard Business Review*, November–December, 133–49.

Handy, Charles (1978), *The Gods of Management* (London: Pan).

Hanssens, Dominique M., Daniel Thorpe, and Carl Finkbeiner (2008), 'Marketing when Customer Equity Matters', *Harvard Business Review*, May, pp. 117–23.

Jackson, M. C. (1988), 'An Appreciation of Stafford Beer's 'Viable System' Viewpoint on Managerial Practice', *Journal of Management Studies*, 25 (6), pp. 557–73.

Koller Tim, Marc Goedhart, and David Wessels (2005), *Valuation, Measuring and Managing the Value of Companies*, 4th edn (New York: John Wiley & Sons).

McGovern, Gail, and Youngme Moon (2007), 'Companies and the Customers who Hate them', *Harvard Business Review*, June, pp. 78–84.

Meyer, Christopher, and Andre Schwager (2007), 'Understanding Customer Experience', *Harvard Business Review*, February, pp. 117–26.

Mittal, Vikas, Matthew Sarkees, and Feisal Murshed (2008), 'The Right Way to Manage Unprofitable Customers', *Harvard Business Review*, April, pp. 94–102.

Montgomery, Cynthia (2008), 'Putting Leadership Back into Strategy', *Harvard Business Review*, January, pp. 54–60.

Narver, John C., and Stanley F. Slater (1990), 'The Effect of a Market Orientation on Business Profitability', *Journal of Marketing*, 54 (October), 20–35.

Page, Michael J., Leyland F. Pitt, and Pierre R. Berthon (1996), 'Analysing Customer Defections: Predicting the Effects on Corporate Performance', *Long Range Planning*, 29 (6), 821–34.

Parasuraman, A., Valarie A. Zeithaml, and Leonard L. Berry (1985), 'A Conceptual Model of Service Quality and its Implications for Future Research', *Journal of Marketing*, 49 (April), 41—50.

Parasuraman, A., Valarie A. Zeithaml, and Leonard L. Berry (1988), 'SERVQUAL: A Multiple-item Scale for Measuring Customer Perceptions of Service Quality', *Journal of Retailing*, 64 (Spring), 12–40.

Pitt, Leyland F., Michael T. Ewing, and Pierre R. Berthon (2000), 'Turning Competitive Advantage into Customer Equity', *Business Horizons*, September–October, 11–18.

Porter, Michael E. (1985), *Competitive Advantage: Creating and Sustaining Superior Performance* (New York: Free Press).

Qualls, William J., and Christopher P. Puto (1989), 'Organizational Climate and Decision Framing: An Integrated Approach to Analyzing Industrial Buying Decisions', *Journal of Marketing Research*, 26 (May), 179–92.

Quinn, Robert E. (1988), *Beyond Rational Management* (San Francisco, CA: Jossey-Bass).

Reichheld, Frederick F. (1993), 'Loyalty-based Management', *Harvard Business Review*, March–April, 64–72.

Reichheld, Frederick F., and W. Earl Sasser (1990), 'Zero Defections: Quality Comes to Services', *Harvard Business Review*, September–October, 301–7.

Robert, Michel M. (1991), 'Why CEOs have Difficulty Implementing their Strategies', *Journal of Business Strategy*, 12 (2), 58–60.

Rosenzweig, Phil (2007), 'Misunderstanding the Nature of Company Performance: The Halo Effect and Other Business Delusions', *California Management Review*, 49 (4), pp. 6–20.

Slater, Stanley F., and John C. Narver (1992), 'Superior Customer Value and Business Performance: The Strong Evidence for a Market-driven Culture', *Marketing Science Institute Report*, No. 92–125 (Cambridge, MA: Marketing Science Institute).

Tse, David K., K.-H. Lee, Ilan Vertinsky, and D. A. Wehrung (1988), 'Does Culture Matter? A Cross-cultural Study of Executives' Choice, Decisiveness, and Risk Adjustment in International Marketing', *Journal of Marketing*, 52 (October), 81–95.

Webster, Cynthia (1991), 'A Note on Cultural Consistency within the Service Firm: The Effects of Employee Position on Attitudes towards the Marketing Culture', *Journal of the Academy of Marketing Science*, 19 (4), 341–6.

Webster, Frederick E. (1994), *Market-Driven Management: Using the New Marketing Concept to Create a Customer-Oriented Company* (New York: John Wiley & Sons).

KEY ARTICLE ABSTRACTS

Noble, Charles H., and Michael P. Mokwa (1999), **'Implementing Marketing Strategies: Developing and Testing a Managerial Theory'**, ***Journal of Marketing***, 63 (4), pp. 57–73.

This paper develops a model that includes important factors which influence the implementation of marketing strategy. The authors have tested their model at mid-level marketing management.

Abstract: Implementation pervades strategic performance. It is a critical link between the formulation of marketing strategies and the achievement of superior organizational performance. Research conducted in this area has generally suffered from a lack of conceptual and empirical grounding. Furthermore, implementation research often ignores the mid-level managers, who are intricately involved in most implementation activities. The authors integrate a broad literature review and a grounded theory-building process to develop a model of important factors that influence the implementation of marketing strategies from a managerial perspective. They test this model in a study of mid-level marketing managers in two different organizations. The results provide insights into the nature of implementation in marketing and suggest future research opportunities.

Dickinson, Sonia J., and B. Ramaseshan (2008), **'Maximising Performance Gains from Cooperative Marketing: Understanding the Role of Environmental Contexts'**, ***Journal of Marketing Management***, 24 (5/6), pp. 541–66.

Co-marketing strategic implementation has been largely neglected. This paper plugs the gap and examines the issue of cooperative marketing in particular and its impact on performance.

Abstract: Understanding the situational relevance of strategy is vital, given that strategies have varying utilities under different environmental settings which result in performance variations. Research remains silent regarding the situational relevance of cooperative marketing strategy implementation whereby performance outcomes are maximized. Through quantitative survey results, we explore the relationship between cooperative marketing and performance outcomes across varying environmental contexts (internal and external environments). While past studies acknowledge the importance of an open system's perspective and the influence of the environment on strategic outcomes, they fall prey to key shortcomings such as a reductionist perspective and inadequate measurement. The authors provide an insight into the environment-strategy-performance relationship by using a holistic environmental approach and detail the environments conducive to co-marketing strategy implementation. Managerial implications and future directions for research are also provided in the paper.

Lane, Nikala (2005), **'Strategy Implementation: The Implications of a Gender Perspective for Change Management'**, ***Journal of Strategic Marketing***, 13 (2), pp. 117–31.

This is a very interesting article, which examines how the managerial style of strategy implementation varies between male and female sales managers.

Abstract: The implementation of strategic marketing plans remains an elusive goal for many organizations, with many managers knowing what to do but not how to do it. A relevant question relating to the implementation capabilities of managers regards the characteristics of successful implementors. This question highlights several interesting issues, including the impact of manager gender. The current paper reveals the role of female managers in implementing new management techniques in sales organizations, namely the introduction of behaviour-based management control strategies as an indicator of a possible gender dimension in more general implementation capabilities. The authors summarize the findings from single-company and multi-company studies where the implementation capabilities of male and female field sales managers are examined. The provocative conclusion is that superior implementation capabilities are shown by female sales managers in the implementation of behaviour-based control strategies. The authors suggest this finding may provide insight into implementation capabilities in strategic marketing and more generally.

Raps, Andreas (2004), **'Implementing Strategy'**, ***Strategic Finance***, 85 (12), pp. 48–53.

This paper highlights the low rate of success when it comes to strategy implementation. It encourages business organizations to pay more attention and invest more resources to develop and improve strategy implementation skills as they've done before for developing strategic planning skills.

Abstract: If your company has successfully implemented a strategic plan, then you're definitely in the minority. The real success rate is only 10 to 30 per cent. This low rate is discouraging, especially since a growing number of companies in recent years have invested considerable resources to develop strategic planning skills. Companies obviously need to improve strategy implementation activities but the pace of these activities and the implementation itself have many problems. Traditional strategy implementation concepts overemphasize structural aspects, reducing the whole effort to an organizational exercise. Ideally, an implementation effort is a 'no boundaries' set of activities that doesn't concentrate on implications of only one component, such as the organizational structure. You should concentrate on four key success factors: (1) culture;

(2) organization; (3) people; and, (4) control systems and instruments. It's worth the effort. An efficient strategy implementation has an enormous impact on a company's success.

Piest, Bert, and Henk Ritsema (1993), 'Corporate Strategy: Implementation and Control', ***European Management Journal***, 11 (1), pp. 122–31.

This is an interesting article, which suggests incorporating the implementation process of corporate strategy into the control system in order for organizations to achieve its strategic objectives more effectively in the dynamic environment.

Abstract: Implementing and controlling corporate strategy is not an easy matter. What is called for is flexible control, combining individual creativity and direction without turning into rigidity. In a dynamic environment, change is the only constant factor. Therefore, possibilities of changing the corporate strategy should be incorporated into the control system. This sets specific demands concerning the process of controlling a strategy. Some of the basic issues with regard to implementation and control are discussed. These issues are: (1) using the business mission as a management instrument; (2) developing a control system that is directed towards the future; (3) discovering the limited value of financial figures; (4) finding information that is really meaningful; and, (5) making 'What if?' analyses. Regarding the implementation of these management instruments, the control system should be kept simple and the company should be segmented into various entities.

END OF CHAPTER 14 CASE STUDY A stitch in time

Note: This case is fictitious; any resemblance to personal or business names is purely coincidental.

Brad Clothing Ltd
Charlotte Street
Kingston
UK

MSC Marketing Research
Henry Street
Kingston
UK

5th January

Dear Consultant,

As discussed, we, the management of Brad Clothing Ltd, Kingston, would like you to consider how to cope with our difficulties. We have been spending 5 per cent of sales on marketing over the past two years. Our seven-year-old company has built up enough business to support a staff of 32, sales for the year look as if they will surpass £1 million. But despite these healthy signs, we are facing a loss for the third consecutive year. Please consider our brief which we have attached.

Yours sincerely,
Sheila Merrit and Valerie Spingle

Product: Specialized clothing

We make garments which have such features as larger openings and Velcro fastenings which make dressing easier for people with fading vision, limited dexterity, or motor-control problems. Also, we make back-opening clothing to help healthcare workers and others who dress people unable to do it themselves. Thirdly, we make alterations to ready-made clothing to adapt them to people's needs: even older people who can dress and undress independently need to adjust fasteners and buttons as they commonly have difficulties moving their fingers at will. On the other hand, those who cannot dress and undress by themselves have difficulties passing their elbows and arms through sleeves. Thus, they require improvements in the design of clothes. Such people want clothes to be adapted so that they are easier to put on, using the original ready-made design. Estimates indicate that approximately 90 per cent of people with motor impairments wear ready-made clothes. With an ageing population, and a growing sensitivity to its needs, the concept of the company is surely right. We see opportunities in expanding into footwear and luggage. There has also been some talk amongst us about possibly adapting fast fashion brands such as H&M, Top Shop, and Zara for younger people suffering motor-control problems.

History

We were founded seven years ago as a not-for-profit, job-creation project funded by local government and administered at the research phase by a local college. We were hired to do the feasibility study, and were the logical choices to run the enterprise after the government approved it, even though neither of us had any business experience (we were teachers in design and textiles at the College).

A local government grant provided £225,000 in start-up money to cover wages and benefits, rent, consulting services, and other overhead costs. We did not avail ourselves of a consulting service. The allocation of funds for rented premises was generous—we had 232 m^2 that we originally could not fill—but since funds were tied to the number of employees, we had to hire more people than required in order to get the variety of equipment needed; i.e., we deliberately hired more people than we needed in order to get enough money to buy the variety of equipment required. The local government money continued to be received, in diminishing amounts, for three years. In year four, with £178,000 in sales and a £15,000 profit, Brad was incorporated, and we were confident that we could continue on a regular business footing. There were no other garment manufacturers like us locally (to our knowledge), and we knew of nothing comparable to Ease (our brand name) in the UK needle trade.

We considered taking management courses given by the Textile Institute but decided that conventional industry wisdom was not pertinent to our unconventional situation. We think the formula for success in the textile industry is one product, one fabric, and lots of it. Orthodox garment manufacturers, overwhelmingly based outside the UK, employ pieceworkers and simply regard seasonal layoffs as business as usual. That is not us. Our line is very diverse, and our market is specialized. We pay by the hour considerably over the minimum wage—and try to maintain steady production through the year. When incorporation papers were finalized, annual sales had reached £300,000 and the small profit had held steady. Preferred shares, redeemable a year later, and equal to half the £160,000 in assets held by the company, were issued to us and the five employees who had been with Comfort for at least a year.

Problems

After incorporation came an unexpected change of fortune. Although sales continued to grow, the company also began to show steadily growing losses. In year five, the loss was £2,800 on sales of £784,800. In year 6, however, the deficit grew to £27,500 on sales of £957,682. We realized we had problems:

- Morale is low and our staff feels overworked.
- We have a cash-flow crisis.
- Our marketing lacks a focus and is essentially opportunistic.
- Under-capitalized from the start, our equipment requirements continued to get short shrift since the return from increasing sales is being used to finance further growth and past losses.
- Our rapid growth has made the firm's IT systems obsolete and our management, which has lost track of the costs of doing business, is inexperienced in standard business practices. We have an excellent product, but have possibly grown too fast.
- June is the maturity date of the original preferred shares. If even a few of the shareholders redeemed on 30 June, Comfort will be in very deep trouble.

Opportunities

As we see it, in order to get back on track again, our opportunities appear to be to develop the UK market as a whole and to develop new opportunities in the EU and possibly North America. We think we have a good overall value proposition, but we are unsure about how to make our marketing implementation and control effective and so whether our planned future strategies will work. We don't know whether we should focus or adopt broad strategies and markets. Goals are rarely set other than 'let's grow the business'. Budgets are generally agreed without much precision and media (mainly the Web, trade journals, direct mail, conferences, and digital) are used without planning or assessment. Our pricing is unscientific and little attention is paid to strategies for customer acquisition and/or retention. In essence, we are clueless as to how to use our limited resources for marketing wisely. We don't expect any details from you at this early stage.

Source: This case was prepared by Douglas West of the University of Birmingham as the basis for analysis and class discussion and not to illustrate either effective or ineffective handling of an administrative situation.

QUESTIONS

1. Provide Brad Clothing Ltd with a short-point checklist for their marketing in terms of key issues for implementation, key controls, and most useful metrics, and defend your choices.

End-of-book case studies

Introduction

In order to give you a chance to apply the concepts covered in this text, a set of three end-of-book cases are provided. These cases cover particular sections of the book. The cases are set out in the order of the various phases of the strategic marketing process and Figure I shows the four phases. Phase One (Audit) focuses on the question, 'Where are we now?' The funnel depicted in the figure is wide at this point, since the firm is taking in such a wide array of information, which is then funnelled down as the firm determines its strategic position during Phase Two (Strategy), which deals with the question, 'Where do we want to be?' The funnel then opens up wider again during Phase Three (Translation) as the firm utilizes its marketing mix in the implementation of its strategy, which addresses the question, 'How will we get there?' Finally, the funnel narrows again during Phase Four (Evaluation), when the firm attempts to assess its performance against the strategy with the use of specific marketing metrics and measurements.

Case I

The first Case, Case I, is entitled, 'Concept of protected areas and ecotourism: the challenges for three developing countries'. This case fits well with Phase One of the funnel diagram, which is concerned with the question, 'Where are we now?' Figure II provides an overview of the particular elements of Phase Two covered in this case. In analysing this case, it would be best to concentrate on the material in Chapters 2 and 3.

Case II

The second case, Case II, is entitled, 'Sitting Pretty: Managing Customer-Driven Innovation at Faurecia Car Seating'. This case lends itself to Phase Three of the funnel diagram ('How will we get there?'), and Figure III shows the focal elements of Phase Three. Our suggestion would be to review the materials in Chapters 8 to 12 when analysing this case.

Case III

The third case, Case III, is entitled, 'Marketing strategy of Changhong, a leading Chinese TV manufacturer'. While this case provides an excellent illustration of Phase Four (see Figure IV) of the funnel diagram ('Did we get there?'), it really allows you the opportunity to go back and integrate all of the phases of the book to assess the position of the company. In analysing this case, it would be advisable to concentrate on Chapters 13 and 14, but as the case reflects the entire marketing strategy process, a thorough integrative analysis of all the chapters should be undertaken.

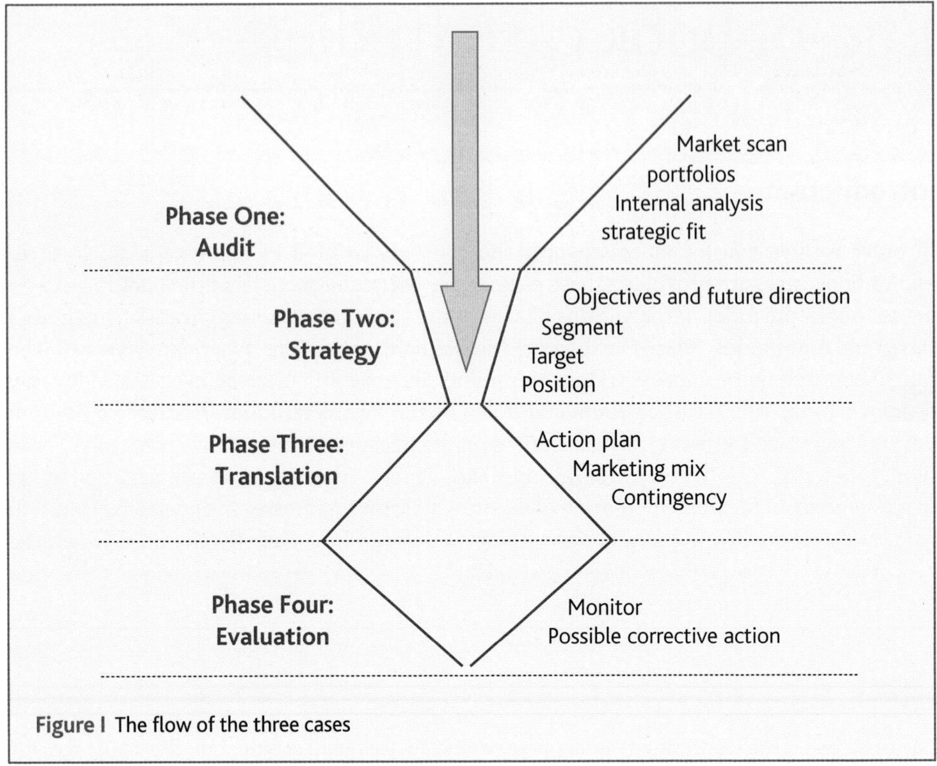

Figure I The flow of the three cases

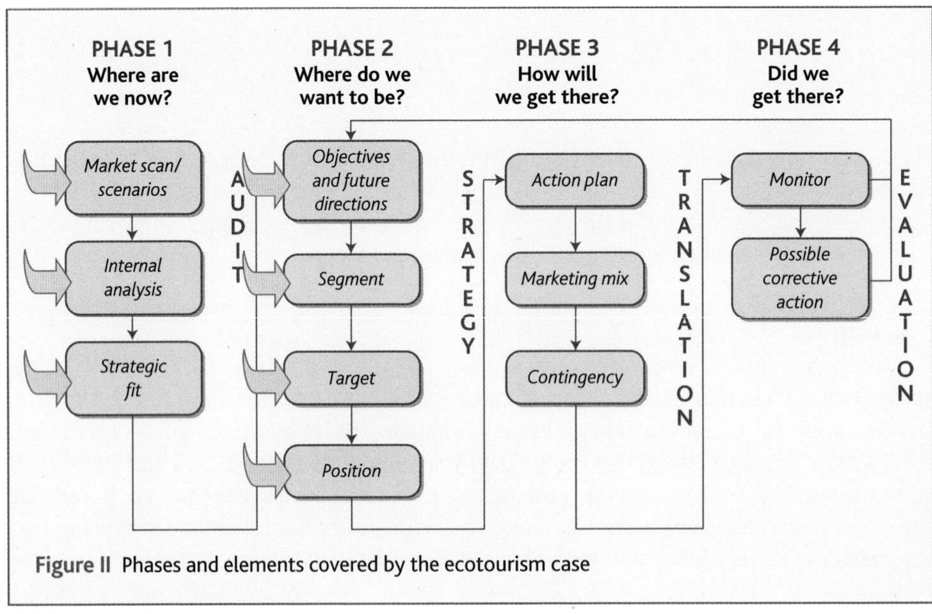

Figure II Phases and elements covered by the ecotourism case

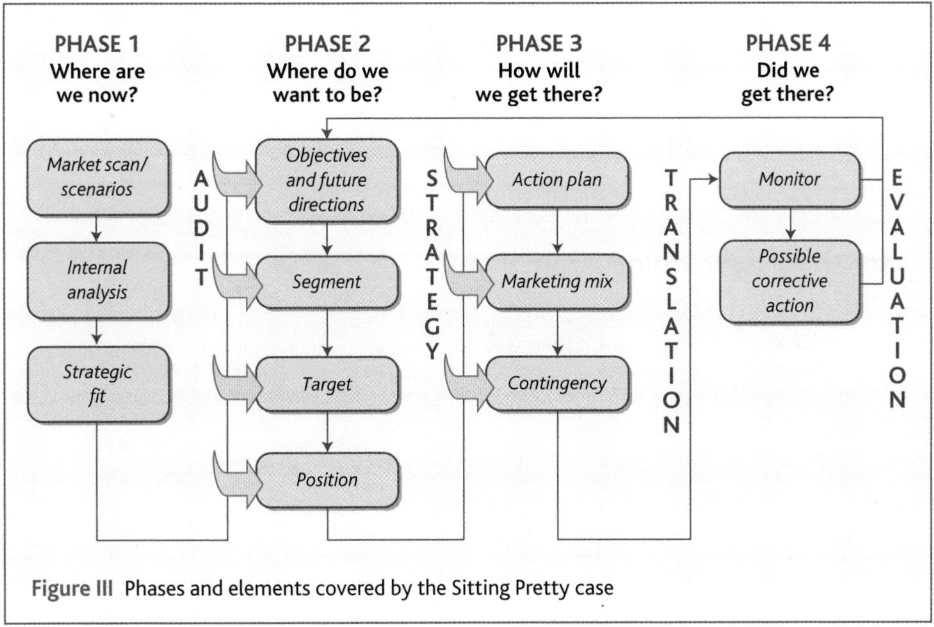

Figure III Phases and elements covered by the Sitting Pretty case

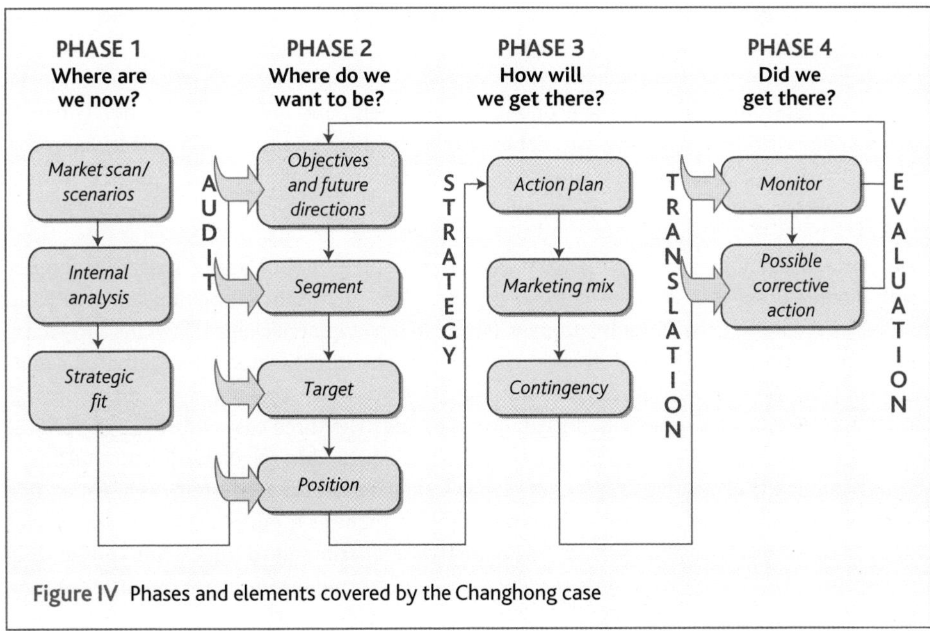

Figure IV Phases and elements covered by the Changhong case

End-of-book Case I

 Concept of protected areas and ecotourism: the challenges for three developing countries

Source: This case was prepared by Lavanchawee Brahmopala Sujarittanonta of Chiang Mai University, Thailand, Rajeev Raghavan of St Albert's College, Kochi, India, Philip Williams and Hy Martin of International Consultancy Europe BV, Bangkok, Thailand, and Thanaphat Payakkaporn of the Wild Animal Rescue Foundation of Thailand, as the basis for analysis and class discussion and not to illustrate either effective or ineffective handling of an administrative situation.

Introduction: tourism destination competitiveness, ecotourism management, and sustainable economic development

Three real-world cases are used to demonstrate how flora and fauna can be strategically managed, both profitably and sustainably. These three cases illustrate how natural ecosystems could be capitalized upon as an advantage-generating resource from which tourism destination competitiveness is derived. By comparing the case of voluntourism in Thailand and ecotourism in Cambodia, and considering India's potential to develop a similar business, the three cases explore how natural habitats can be managed in various ways to produce differing results. The three cases also highlight the critical importance of strategic marketing to create a win-win situation for consumers and all stakeholders, be they humans, flora, or fauna.

Natural resource management can bring about not only natural resources conservation, but also poverty alleviation, sustainable economic development, and tourism destination competitiveness. This is in line with alternative economic models which present a more holistic approach to development, compared to the mainstream neoliberal perspective.

The potential and challenges of ecotourism management

Ecotourism is a rapidly growing industry where developing nations are increasingly popular destinations (Gossling, 1999). International organizations such as the World Bank also see a role for tourism in fulfilling the United Nations Millennium Development Goals (Hawkins and Mann, 2007). Tourism destination competitiveness models also highlight factors that promote sustainable economic development through ecotourism. Ecosystems are seen as a country's natural capital, from which economic benefits can be generated. The three cases illustrate the critical importance of partnership and cooperation among all stakeholders in generating mutual financial and non-financial benefits for each other, based on maintaining ecosystems as a sustainable source of revenue. However, ecotourism management requires a multifaceted approach. Not only is it necessary to ensure that derived benefits are distributed to local communities, it is also necessary to conduct awareness campaigns to educate and encourage cooperation among stakeholders.

For example, visitors to African protected areas happily pay more for a wildlife experience (Moran, 1994; and Barnes and de Jager, 1996). If the local communities could receive economic benefits from ecotourism to offset the opportunity costs of foregoing income from harvesting wildlife (Moran, 1994), then their attitudes towards conservation would be changed for the better (Infield, 1988). Past cases have shown that economic interests need to form the basis of conservation efforts for it to be successful. For example, the case of the conservation of African wild dog Lycaon pictus derived sufficient economic benefits from ecotourism to offset the costs of three wild dog conservation options (Fanshawe et al., 1991; Lindsey et al., 2005).

The competitiveness of nations is said to be influenced by climate, morals, power of the state, cultural values, and moral discipline (Franke et al., 1991; World Economic Forum, 2002). Crouch and Ritchie (1999) also added historical and cultural resources for the tourism context. Competitiveness of a nation also stems firm-specific factors that lead to competitiveness and should be identified at the macro level as well (Rumelt, 1984; Porter, 1985; Barney, 1991; Grant, 1991; Waheeduzzan and Ryans, 1996). Moreover, even subjective perceptions by the tourists of the reality of the destination matters to destination competitiveness.

Thus, the management of ecotourism also has to focus on 'development and maintenance of meaningful assets and skills, the selection of strategies and competitive arenas to exploit such assets and skills' (Aaker, 1989). For example, for ecotourism to be sustainable, tourism activities have to be controlled in order to ensure eco-efficiency of destinations (Becken and Gnoth, 2004; Kelly et al., 2007), since tourist high-visitation levels can also negatively impact the ecosystem (Ashforth, 1992). Tools have been developed to identify sustainability indicators, e.g. the Ecological Footprint (EF) method (Wackernagel and Rees, 1995; Wackernagel et al., 1999; Rees and Ecological Economics, 2000; Monfreda et al., 2004).

Concerns towards a sustainable economic development

Neoliberalism proposes that economic objectives are best left to be driven by market forces. However, this does not work when the commodity is non-renewable, as with the case of endangered species. Past cases have shown that hidden environmentally damaging subsidies which have a very large negative impact on the environment exist on a global scale (de Moor and Calamai, 1997; Myers, 1998; Roodman, 1998; and van Beers and de Moor, 2001). These 'perverse' subsidies encourage activities that leave both the environment and the economy worse off.

National development is about improving the quality of life, which entails matters that are far more delicate and complex than the dollar amount of a person's salary or numerical percentage increase in national productivity. Various qualitative aspects have been addressed by alternative approaches to development, by taking into consideration critical concepts that provide a more holistic view and offer more balance. Thus, by supplementing the predominant neoliberal development policies which focus on quantitative development measures like GNP and personal income, other development approaches make it possible also to measure qualitatively the progress of development. A variety of supplementary approaches are available—from the UN's Sustainable Development, which is universally accepted and practiced, to insightful formulations by academics, such as Amartya Sen's Capabilities approach to socioeconomic valuation (Sen, 1985, 1999, 2000, 2002).

Thailand has been implementing the King's sufficiency economy philosophy alongside the neoliberal development policies, to address concerns such as resource constraint, good governance, human capacity, poverty alleviation, environmental conservation, etc. Other countries have implemented alternatives such as India's Gandhian self-sufficiency path to development in the past, to Bhutan's unique Gross National Happiness (GNH) or the Middle Path of development (Uddin et al., 2007) to balance the pressures of society, economy, politics, culture, and the environment.

The successful case of Thailand and Cambodia demonstrate that it is possible to sustainably capitalize on the ecological, financial, and social capital of the local community and its project partners. In contrast, the case of Kerala's endangered ornamental fishes in India is presented to illustrate the real-world complications that the government faces. When endangered species of freshwater fishes are seen as a commodity, the short-term income generated from this dwindling resource cannot be sustainable in the long term for forest-dwellers, who actively destroy the very natural habitat that they are currently making a decent living from. Over-harvesting by poachers for short-term gains leads to species extinction and the destruction of the habitat, very possibly leaving the forest-dwelling communities with no commodity to make a decent living from in the near future.

I. Case of relationship management and sustainable revenue from 'voluntourism' in wildlife habitat conservation: the Wild Animal Rescue Foundation (WARF) of Thailand

The following case about Thailand describes how an NGO, the Wild Animal Rescue Foundation (WARF), established a business structure (Gibbon Rehabilitation Project, Forest Fire Protection Project, Volunteer Network Program) to generate income from arduous conservation activities involving the caring of wild animals and their natural habitat. This highlights the collaboration of stakeholders and the creation of sustainable benefits (financial and non-financial) for all parties involved, and the implementation of an education programme alongside the ecotourism operation.

Despite the current economic downturn, the work of the Wild Animal Rescue Foundation (WARF) of Thailand has proven to generate sustainable revenue streams from 'voluntourists', or ecotourists who pay a fee to work voluntarily with the locals, caring for wild animals at sanctuaries by the nature reserves. The foundation has also been successful in incorporating nature conservation into the vision and mission of various agencies and organizations in Thailand, be they governmental, non-governmental or private.

The strategic business structure that was set up by WARF generates income from arduous conservation activities involved in the caring of wild animals and their natural habitat, and demonstrates how stakeholders can enjoy a win-win for all when they come together to protect flora and fauna in a sustainable way.

The setting

WARF is one of Thailand's leading advocates for nature conservation. Its work focuses on providing housing and care for rescued wild animals and returning them to the wild. Thus, wild-animal habitat conservation is critical, since the survival of the rescued wild animals depends on the conditions of the natural environment back into which they are released. All this would not have been possible without the collaborative effort of others, whose participation generates mutual benefits that are both financial and/or non-monetary.

Establishing and maintaining relationships with stakeholders

Maintaining good relationships among stakeholders is the key to success. Initially, the foundation had started out in the garden of its founders' house in Bangkok in 1992. Today, WARF has expanded its operations to include several projects and four wildlife sanctuaries across Thailand by developing close ties with government and non-governmental agencies.

For example, joint operations with the Royal Forestry Department at Krabok Koo, 150 kilometres east of Bangkok, now shelters gibbons, macaques, Asiatic black bears, and Malayan sun bears that were abandoned or confiscated by the authorities. WARF's rescue centre and zoo, 120 kilometres north of Bangkok in Lopburi Province, was established in cooperation with the Royal Thai Army, and houses over 300 animals. WARF's Forest Fire Protection project was established in association with the Forest Fire Control Division and NOK Flying Club, where pilots and members of the flying club are invited to participate in reporting outbreaks of forest fires in Chiangmai and Lamphun Provinces to the Forest Fire Control Division. Highland Farm, a sanctuary in Tak Province, now houses 20 gibbons, thanks to the owners of the Mae Sot Experimental Fruit Farm. Donations from Ford and by the Royal Society for the Protection of Animals (RSPCA) made it possible for WARF to operate rescue operations throughout Thailand with their Mobile Animal Clinics (MAC).

WARF's close relationships with stakeholders are maintained through joint activities. To illustrate in more detail how everything fits together to create a win-win for all, selected WARF projects are highlighted in this study, namely the Gibbon Rehabilitation Project (GRP) in Phuket, and the Volunteer Network Program, which operates across the country.

Gibbon Rehabilitation Project (GRP)

The very southern tip of Thailand, at Bang Pae Waterfall, Tambon Pa Klok, Phuket is where WARF and Asia Wildlife established the Gibbon Rehabilitation Project (GRP) in 1990. The project is also a tourist attraction in Phuket, and is featured prominently in brochures, magazines, and websites that cater to tourists.

The island of Phuket is a major tourist destination in Thailand. In the past, gibbons were poached from infancy, so that tourists can be photographed with them in exchange for a small fee for the gibbon owner. However, these gibbons eventually grew up and were simply abandoned, since they were no longer cute. The GRP rescues gibbons that are exploited or abandoned. As part of the rehabilitation process, gibbons are successively moved further and further from humans, both geographically and in terms of human contact. Once a pair of gibbons are deemed fit to survive on their own, they are released back into the remaining protected wilderness on the island.

Thus, educating the local population in Phuket is essential for the successful running of the project, in order that exploited gibbons are reported, and rehabilitated gibbons do not get poached and exploited again by the locals to make money from tourists. GRP runs the Gibbon Rehabilitation Educational Project (GREP) to educate not only foreign visitors, but also the local community about the protection of gibbons and their rainforest habitat. This programme builds communication links between GRP and the local Thai community at all levels—primary and secondary schools, community groups, and universities.

The Volunteer Network Program

WARF depends on donations and assistance from its partners. However, manpower is needed for the day-to-day tasks in caring for the rescued animals and running education programmes in schools and communities. These duties require dedicated personnel who are knowledgeable, but who would be expensive to hire. WARF found a solution by creating an educational 'product' to serve the research needs of researchers, particularly students who have almost completed their studies for a degree in biology, ecology, primatology, or veterinary science. This offers an opportunity for them to become fee-paying volunteers who get to conduct research on animal behaviour and disease, an opportunity to be in close contact with the wild animals, and immerse themselves in the animals' natural habitat at WARF's sanctuaries set up close to the nature reserves.

These fee-paying ecovolunteers are recruited by travel agencies and by publicity via the Internet. The Volunteer Network Program not only provides WARF with a constant source of income for the latter's projects, but also supplements WARF with dedicated personnel.

II. The case of sustainable financial structuring, allowing for international investment in an endangered ecoregion, Cardamom Mountains, Cambodia

The comprehensive conservation project in the Cardamom Mountains in southwestern Cambodia involves poverty reduction and species protection through the development of sustainable revenue streams, notably ecotourism. This case demonstrates the potential for detailed financial structuring, project management, and careful due diligence to bring international investments and other varied stakeholders into complex conservation programmes, with ecotourism as a flagship component.

The setting

The Cardamom Mountain range (roughly 4.4 million hectares) is located in southwestern Cambodia, with the Thai border along its western edge and the Gulf of Thailand along its southern edge. The area is classified as an endangered ecoregion and, as a former Khmer Rouge stronghold, many sections of the forest remain unexplored. The mountain range is one of the few ecoregions left in Indochina with intact rainforests that still have the potential for landscape-level conservation actions. The region contains a number of endangered and threatened species, including the Asian elephant, the Indochina tiger, the Malayan sun bear, the pileated gibbon, the Irrawaddy, and humpback dolphins, the Siamese crocodile (last remaining population), and the Royal turtle. It also appears that local endemism is significant. The local Cambodian population is relatively spread out and lives in extreme poverty. This poverty creates a driver for activities that have put pressure on the forest; the past decade saw increased levels of illegal logging, wildlife poaching, and forest fires from slash-and-burn agriculture.

Stakeholders

In order to create a sustainable protection plan for the Cardamoms as well as develop alternative livelihoods for the local population, ICEBV has worked with Wildlife Alliance, the University of Victoria, Jetwing Eco Holidays, and the Royal Government of Cambodia. Wildlife Alliance, an NGO with local knowledge, is responsible for conservative strategy, community development, and the most project implementations. Professor Philip Dearden from the University of Victoria is responsible for scientific input, design, and implementation. Jetwing Eco Holidays is responsible for managing ecotourism operations, facilitating Community Based Ecotourism (CBET), and marketing the overall project. The Cambodian Government handles certain aspects of the region's conservation, as well as community development and implementation. ICEBV is responsible for financial structuring, developing payment for ecosystem services, and overall management of the comprehensive project.

The lack of revenue streams limit financial possibilities for stakeholders

While the Cambodian government and Wildlife Alliance had the will to preserve the forest, the two stakeholders were financially unable to do so. This financial roadblock held up the project by several months, at which point ICEBV was brought in to develop a financial solution. ICEBV was able to find financing through a combination of equity investment, revenue from payment for ecosystem services, and sourcing grants. It took one year for the consortium to design the project and another year for ICEBV to raise the funds. Project implementation began in August

2008 and will run until August 2043. Revenue streams set up by ICEBV (mainly reforestation and ecotourism) will provide returns to investors by August 2010. All revenue streams are located on land privately owned by ICEBV, mainly on the edges of the forest. ICEBV is continuing to develop and research additional revenue streams from payment for ecosystem services, including payment for watershed services and biodiversity offsets. ICEBV, Wildlife Alliance, and Jetwings Eco Holidays created an agreement by which the revenues are divided up amongst the three stakeholders and directed towards the appropriate aspect of the project plan.

The importance of ecotourism in sustainable revenue streams

Through developing eco-tourism assets in developing markets, the ICEBV team has found it essential to ensure the complete private and public investment of the projects. By supplying thorough financial structuring of the project activities, the company has successfully sourced private financing for the development of two discount ecotourism lodges. This financial structuring includes the innovative aspect of including all potential revenue streams in the revenue calculations. Such ecological-specific revenues include:

- mountain-bike tours of local wildlife reserves
- biodiversity hotspot viewing by motorized vehicles
- alternative use of lodges during low-occupancy months; and
- discounted cost of sustainable timber from community forests.

These revenues, and cost reductions, are in addition to the classical tourism revenue streams (room rental, food, and beverage). This specialized financial structuring allows outside investors to understand more fully the financially innovative sections of their investment.

The next crucial step in developing a successful ecotourism asset is the early creation of a comprehensive project team. Before launching the project, ICEBV shored up its team by assembling an internationally renowned small- to medium-sized hotel operator, an architecture team focused on the ecological design of tourist accommodations, and internal management to ensure that project benchmarks were met in a timely manner. By developing this well-respected team from the beginning of the project, ICEBV found it much easier to source early capital for these burgeoning environmental investments, not well-known amongst traditional financiers.

Lastly, ICEBV has found it imperative to conduct thorough due diligence and market research on the region in which ecotourism projects are to be developed. In identifying the niche market from which the asset will produce revenue, the company was able to tailor its approach to the overall project. Originally, ICEBV planned to create two high-end lodges in Koh Kong Province, Cambodia, but upon further research, the team found that two luxury resorts would far exceed demand for such services. In response, the organization is developing only one high-end lodge and two discount lodges, catering towards the more economical traveller. This deviation from the original project planning has allowed the portfolio of investments to diversify, thus ensuring a safer investment for the respective financiers.

These three steps of successful ecotourism asset creation again included: (1) the enumeration of all potential revenue streams (specifically ecological); (2) the early establishment of a full project team; and, (3) thorough due diligence and ecological-specific market research. By following these principles of ecotourism development, ICEBV is working to grow the ecological, financial, and social capital of the local community and its project partners.

III. The case of the endemic and endangered freshwater fishes of Western Ghats biodiversity hotspot, Kerala, India

A real-world case example of native ornamental fisheries in Kerala, India, involving endangered and endemic species can be used to illustrate the delicate micro-level complexities that exist amidst the macro-level influences of: socioeconomic incentives of international trade; the government's development vision and objectives for a non-renewable natural resource that is found at the regional level; and individual stakeholders such as forest-dwelling communities.

The setting

The riverine ornamental fisheries of the Western Ghats (WG) in the South Indian state of Kerala is widely considered to be among the most prized in the world (Ramachandran, 2002), with the presence of more than 100 species. Since the early 1990s, the forest dwellers made their living from collecting and exporting native ornamental fish, starting with 10 fish species exported at the beginning of this decade (Kurup et al., 2003) to more than 100 at present (Anon, 2005). There is a high demand for these fish in the markets of Southeast Asia, the Far East, and Europe, commanding exceedingly high prices (Ramachandran, 2002), with some species (e.g., Puntius denisonii) fetching as high as $US30 per piece (Anon, 2006a, 2006b).

As a result of this lucrative trade, the exploitation and trade of native ornamentals has been a sunrise industry that has developed rapidly over the past few years, and the government of Kerala is actively promoting the trade in native ornamentals and is urging locals to do more to cash in on the current boom in tropical fish exports (Clarke, 2007). This attitude from the government is highly discouraging and negatively impacts the biodiversity of the region. There is also poor understanding of legal issues of ownership and harvest in this part of the world. The fishery for the native ornamentals is an open access fishery devoid of any quotas or restrictions. No regulation on either catch or effort is in place, nor are there policies specific to native ornamental fisheries. Adequate time and expertise for monitoring and research has also been unavailable, which adversely affects the planning and implementation of conservation and management strategies for these native ornamentals.

Stakeholders

The WG is home to a large population of tribes and forest-dwelling communities who for centuries have depended on the natural resources of the area, including fish, for their livelihoods. These tribes and local communities living in the forests of WG are an important link in the native ornamental trade, as they carry out the fishing and collection of the native ornamentals and supply the wholesalers or directly to exporters. Ornamental fish collection has therefore become the livelihood option for hundreds of such local communities residing along forest streams.

Captive breeding as a conservation tool: the impact on the fish market

Captive breeding is widely considered as a key tool for the conservation of threatened and endemic fish (Philippart, 1995). However, captive breeding and small-scale aquaculture may act as an alternative to wild collection and/or fishing only if it is able to provide sufficient incentives in the form of returns to 'displace and not supplement' the wild collection. In addition, local communities collecting marine-reef fishes for the ornamental trade are known to be unsupportive of aquaculture initiatives and have been known to oppose a shift from wild-fish collection to captive rearing (Pollnac, 1982, 1990; Watson, 2000). Furthermore, captive production is often associated with a shift from a rural setting (where collection is normally carried out) to a more developed urban region, as seen in the Amazon (Gerstner et al., 2006). The urban regions have better facilities for breeding and marketing, including the presence of international airports.

In Kerala, many forest-dwelling local people earn their livelihoods from collecting native ornamental fishes and would be negatively impacted by any mass adoption of captive breeding and rearing technologies, as this would increase supply and drive the prices down. Hence, a detailed understanding of the existing socioeconomic conditions of local communities and ensuring their participation are vital prerequisites for popularizing the captive-breeding technology of native ornamentals of this region.

Towards sustainability: possible conservation and management solutions

The conservation of endangered species in a developing country is an expensive task and the opportunity costs of both *in situ* as well as *ex situ* conservation strategies could be high (Damania and Bulte, 2007). This makes it imperative that strategies such as protected areas and ecotourism ventures be promoted to conceive holistic resource management strategies, so that it would benefit both the natural resources and the communities whose livelihood depends on these resources.

It has been suggested that based upon the understanding of the nature of the native ornamental-fish exploitation and trade in this region, management practices that are implemented will need to direct the fishery and trade into a sustainable enterprise. Fishery management strategies based on input and output control, technical measures, ecologically based management, and indirect economic instruments can be used with necessary modifications to suit local needs. Regulating catch and effort through granting licenses and access rights can be one of the most successful strategies that can be enforced in the present scenario.

The process of granting export licences and collection permits should be streamlined and the number of such orders issued have to be strictly regulated by the government agencies concerned. As suggested by Woods (2001), a meaningful way of reducing overall collection pressure and maintaining a status quo is by limiting the volume of stock that can be exported. However, this can be successfully enforced only after a detailed stock assessment of this species in the rivers of this region is carried out. Results of such studies can subsequently form a baseline for setting up restrictions on export volumes in the future.

Q QUESTIONS TO BE ANSWERED

1. Based on the description of Cambodia's ICEBV project, identify and describe the groups of consumers for ecotourism in Cambodia. What motivates ecotourists?
2. Based on the description of the Wild Animal Rescue's (WARF) project in Thailand, identify and describe the groups of consumers for voluntourism in Thailand.
3. What motivates customers of voluntourism to volunteer and pay to work?
4. Currently, who do you think are the consumers whose behaviours are endangering the fish population in the rivers of Kerala, India?
5. Are there any other potential consumer groups for the endangered fish habitat of Kerala, India, besides ecotourists or voluntourists who would enjoy the natural ecosystem where the endangered fish live?
6. Based on the characteristics of the consumer groups for each of the three cases, suggest marketing channels to reach the market segments for the ecosystems of Cambodia and Thailand.
7. Considering the characteristics of the potential consumers of Kerala, India's, natural ecosystem, suggest strategies to promote nature conservation among consumers of the endangered fish.

8. Considering the stakeholders in the cases of Cambodia and Thailand, what were the strategies used by ICEBV and WARF to promote nature conservation among the stakeholders, and what made them successful?
9. What were the marketing strategies that ICEBV and WARF used to market nature conservation to its target customers?

REFERENCES AND FURTHER READING

Aaker, David A. (1989), 'Managing Assets and Skills: The Key to a Sustainable Competitive Advantage', *California Management Review*, 31, 91–106.

Anon (2005), 'List of Freshwater and Brackishwater Ornamental Fishes that are Being Exported at Present from India', *MPEDA Newsletter*, July, 10–17.

Anon (2006a), accessed 21 April 2006, available at: **http://www.practicalfishkeeping.co.uk/pfk/pages/show_article.php?article_id=137**

Anon (2006b), accessed 11 April 2006, available at: **http://www.aquahobby.com/gallery/e_Puntius_denisonii.php**

Ashforth, G. J. (1992), 'Planning for Sustainable Tourism', *Town Planning Review*, 63 (3), pp. 325–30.

Balmford, A. et al. (2002), 'Economic Reasons for Conserving Wild Nature', *Science*, 297, pp. 950–3.

Barnes J. I., and J. L. V. de Jager (1996), 'Economic and Financial Incentives for Wildlife Use on Private Land in Namibia and the Implications for Policy', *South African Journal of Wildlife Research*, 26, pp. 37–46.

Barney, Jay B. (1991), 'Firm Resources and Sustained Competitive Advantage', *Journal of Management*, 17 (March), 99–120.

Becken, S., and J. Gnoth (2004), 'Tourist Consumption Systems among Overseas Visitors: Reporting on American, German, and Australian Visitors to New Zealand', *Tourism Management*, 25, pp. 375–85.

Caughley, G., and A. Gunn (1996), *Conservation Biology in Theory and Practice* (Oxford: Blackwell Science).

Chao, N. L. (2001), 'Fisheries, Diversity and Conservation of Ornamental Fish of the Rio Negro River, Brazil—A Review of Project Plaba (1989–1999)', in N. L. Chao, P. Petry, G. Prang, L. Sonneschien, and M. Tlusty (eds), *Conservation and Management of Ornamental Fish Resources of the Rio Negro Basin Amazon, Brazil, Project Piaba* (Manaus: Universidade do Amazonas), pp. 161–204.

Clarke, M. (2007), *Practical Fish Keeping Magazine*, Web version, accessed 4 March 2007, available at: **http://www.practicalfishkeeping.co.uk/pfk/pages/item.php?news=793**

Constanza, R. et al. (1998), 'The Value of the World's Ecosystems Services and Natural Capital', *Ecological Economics*, 25, pp. 3–15. [Also available at: **http://www.ecy.wa.gov/programs/wr/hq/pdf/naturepaper.pdf**]

Crouch, G. I., and J. R. Brent Ritchie (1999), 'Tourism, Competitiveness, and Societal Prosperity', *Journal of Business Research*, 44, pp. 137–52.

Damania, R., and E. H. Bulte (2007), 'The Economics of Wildlife Farming and Endangered Species Conservation', *Ecological Economics*, 62 (3/4), pp. 461–72.

de Moor, A., P. Calamai (1997), *Subsidizing Unsustainable Development: Undermining the Earth with Public Funds* ([Toronto]: Earth Council); avaiable at **http://www.evict.org.au/file/subsidizing Development.pdf**

D'Harteserre, A. (2000), 'Lessons in Managerial Destination Competitiveness in the Case of Foxwoods Casino Resort', *Tourism Management*, 21 (1), 23–32.

Dwyer, Larry, and Kim Chulwon (2002), 'Destination Competitiveness: A Model and Determinants', available at: **http://www.ttra.com/pub/uploads/007.pdf**

Fanshawe, J. H., L. H. Frame, and J. R. Ginsberg (1991), 'The Wild Dog—Africa's Vanishing Carnivore', *Oryx*, 25, pp. 137–46.

Franke, Richard H., G. Hofstede, and M. Bond (1991), 'Cultural Roots of Economic Performance: A Research Note', *Strategic Management Journal*, 12, pp. 165–73.

Gerstner, C. L., H. Ortega, H. Sanchez, and D. L. Graham (2006), 'Effects of the Freshwater Aquarium Trade on Wild Fish Populations in Differentially Fished Areas of the Peruvian Amazon', *Journal of Fish Biology*, 68, pp. 862–75.

Gossling, S. (1999), 'Ecotourism: A Means to Safeguard Biodiversity and Ecosystem Functions?' *Ecological Economics*, 29, pp. 303–20.

Grant, Robert M. (1991), 'The Resource-based Theory of Competitive Advantage: Implications for Strategy Formulation,' *California Management Review*, 33 (Spring), pp. 114–35.

Hassan, S. (2000), 'Determinants of Market Competitiveness in an Environmentally Sustainable Tourism Industry', *Journal of Travel Research*, 38 (3), pp. 239–45.

Hawkins, Donald E., and Shaun Mann (2007), 'The World Bank's Role in Tourism Development', *Annals of Tourism Research*, 34 (2), pp. 348–63.

Infield, M. (1988), 'Attitudes of a Rural Community towards Conservation and a Local Conservation Area in Natal, South Africa', *Biological Conservation*, 45, pp. 21–46.

Kelly, J., W. Haider, P. W. Williams, and K. Englund (2007), 'Stated Preferences of Tourists for Eco-efficient Destination Planning Options', *Tourism Management*, 28, pp. 377–90.

Kurup, B. M., K. V. Radhakrishnan, and T. G. Manojkumar (2003), 'Biodiversity Status of Fishes Inhabiting Rivers of Kerala (S. India) with Special Reference to Endemism, Threats and Conservation Measures', in: R. L. Wellcome and T. Petr (eds), *Proceedings of LARS2*, 2nd Large Rivers Symposium, Phnom Penh, 11–14 February (Bangkok: FAO Regional Office for Asia Pacific (FAO/RAP)), pp. 163–82.

Lindsey, Peter A. et al. (2005), 'The Potential Contribution of Ecotourism to African Wild Dog Lycaon pictus Conservation in South Africa', *Biological Conservation*, 123 (3), pp. 339–48.

Mercy, T. V. A. (2006), 'Status of Development of Captive Breeding Technology for the Indigenous Ornamental Fishes of the Western Ghats of India', in *Souvenir: Ornamentals Kerala* (Cochin: Department of Fisheries, Government of Kerala), pp. 71–5.

Monfreda, C., M. Wackernagel, and D. Deumling (2004), 'Establishing National Natural Capital Accounts based on Detailed Ecological Footprint and Biological Capacity Assessments', *Land Use Policy*, 21, pp. 231–46.

Moran D. (1994), 'Contingent Valuation and Biodiversity: Measuring the User Surplus of Kenyan Protected Areas', *Biodiversity and Conservation*, 3, pp. 663–84.

Myers, N. (1998), *Perverse Subsidies* (Winnipeg: International Institute for Sustainable Development).

Philippart, J. C. (1995), 'Is Captive Breeding an Effective Solution for the Preservation of Endemic Species?' *Biological Conservation*, 72, pp. 282–95.

Pollnac, R. B. (1982), 'Sociocultural Aspects of Implementing Aquaculture Systems in Marine Fishing Communities', in L. J. Smith and S. Peterson (eds), *Aquaculture Development in Less Developed Countries* (Westview Special Studies in Agriculture/Aquaculture Science and Policy) (Boulder, CO: Westview Press), pp. 31–52.

Pollnac, R. B. (1990), 'Socio-cultural Aspects of User Conflicts in Aquaculture', paper delivered at the 21st Meeting of the World Aquaculture Society, 10–17 June, Halifax, Nova Scotia.

Porter, Michael E. (1985), *Competitive Advantage: Creating and Sustaining Superior Performance* (New York: The Free Press).

Porter, Michael E. (1990), *The Competitive Advantage of Nations* (New York: The Free Press).

Ramachandran, A. (2002), 'Freshwater Indigenous Ornamental Fish Resources of Kerala and their Prospects for International Marketing', In M. R. Boopendranath, B. Meenakumari, J. Joseph, T. V. Sankar, P. Pravin, and L. Edwin (eds), *Riverine and Reservoir Fisheries of India* (Kochi: Central Institute of Fisheries Technology and Society of Fisheries Technologists), pp. 109–35.

Rees, W. E., and Ecological Economics (2000), 'Forum: The Ecological Footprint', *Ecological Economics*, 32, pp. 341–94.

Roodman, D. M. (1998), *The Natural Wealth of Nations: Harnessing the Market for the Environment*, The World Watch Environmental Alert Series (New York: W.W. Norton and Company).

Rumelt, R. P. (1984), 'Towards a Strategic Theory of the Firm', in Richard B. Lamb (ed.), *Competitive Strategic Management* (Engelwood Cliffs, NJ: Prentice-Hall), pp. 557–70.

Sen, A. (1985), 'Well-being, Agency and Freedom', *Journal of Philosophy*, 82, pp. 169–221.

Sen, A. (1993), 'Capability and Well-being', in: M. Nussbaum and A. Sen (eds), *The Quality of Life* (Oxford: Clarendon), pp. 30–53.

Sen, A. (1999), *Development as Freedom* (New York: Oxford University Press).

Sen, A. (2000), *Development as Freedom* (Oxford: Oxford University Press).

Sen, A. (2002), *Rationality and Freedom* (Cambridge, MA: Belknap).

Souza, M. (2001), *American Zoological Association Communique*, 8–9 January, p. 50.

Uddin, A. N., R. Taplin, and X. Yu (2007), 'Energy, Environment and Development in Bhutan Renewable and Sustainable Energy Reviews', 11 (9), pp. 2083–103.

van Beers, C., A. de Moor (2001), *Public Subsidies and Policy Failure* (Aldershot: Edward Elgar).

Wackernagel, M., and W. Rees (1995), *Our Ecological Footprint: Reducing Human Impact on the Earth* (Gabriola Island: New Society Publishers).

Wackernagel, M. et al. (1999), 'Natural Capital Accounting with the Ecological Footprint Concept', *Ecological Economics*, 29 (3), pp. 375–90.

Waheeduzzan, A., and J. Ryans (1996), 'Definition, Perspectives, and Understanding of International Competitiveness: A Quest for a Common Ground', *Competitiveness Review*, 6 (2), 7–26.

Watson, I. (2000), The Role of Ornamental Fish Industry in Poverty Alleviation National Research Institute, Kent, UK, Project No. V 012 (Kent: National Research Institute).

Woods, E. (2001), 'Global Advances in Conservation and Managementof Marine Ornamental Resources', *Aquarium Science and Conservation*, pp. 65–77.

World Economic Forum (2002), *The Global Competitiveness Report 2001–2002*, available at: **http://www.weforum.org/en/initiatives/gcp/Global%20Competitiveness%20Report/PastReports/index.htm**

World Economic Forum and IMD International (1992), *The World Competitiveness Report* (Lausanne: IMD International), available at: **http://www.worldcompetitiveness.com/online**

End-of-book Case II

Sitting Pretty

Managing Customer-Driven Innovation at Faurecia Car Seating

Case study
Reference no ESMT-606-0057-1

This case was written by Professor Francis Bidault and Alessio Castello, ESMT European School of Management and Technology. It is intended to be used as the basis for class discussion rather than to illustrate either effective or ineffective handling of a management situation. The case was made possible by the co-operation of Faurecia.

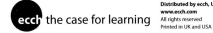

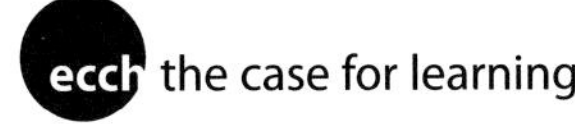

Distributed by ecch, UK and USA
www.ecch.com

Printed in UK and USA

North America
t +1 781 239 5884
f +1 781 239 5885
e ecchusa@ecch.com

Rest of the world
t +44 (0)1234 750903
f +44 (0)1234 751125
e ecch@ecch.com

ESMT-606-0057-1

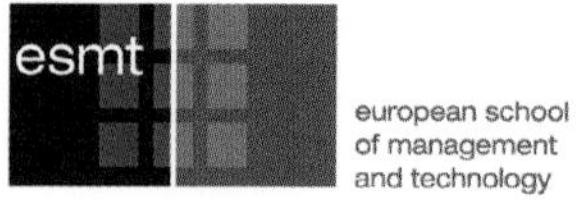

March 29, 2007

ESMT Case Study

This Sitting Pretty: Managing Customer-Driven Innovation at Faurecia

This case study was written by Francis Bidault and Alessio Castello.

Introduction

It was a late afternoon in November 2003, and the twilight flooding the countryside around Narita airport gave an impression of harmony and peace. But peaceful, the minds of Faurecia managers were not. Aboard the Japan Airlines 747, a team led by Mr. Gaston Jacques, R&D director of the automotive seating business unit, was returning home from a study trip to visit customers and competitors. Despite the excellent weather, the team's mood was gloomy; as Mr. Louis Pourdieu - Vice President Manufacturing, Automotive Seating – later on summed up:

> "We realized that we had a double digit productivity gap relative to our competition, that our development cost was much higher, that we had bigger ergonomic issues in our just-in-time plants and that we needed to still improve our quality standards".

Being less efficient than the competition in the car industry was simply not allowed as automotive suppliers faced a formidable and growing array of selection criteria imposed by their customers. These criteria incorporated cost competitiveness, quality, technology, logistics capabilities, and others associated with being a full-service supplier such as R&D, product development and engineering resources. Frequently, all of these demands had to be met in a context of annual unit price that declined through a model programme life cycle. For suppliers, survival, let alone growth and modest prosperity, was difficult in such an environment and they had to adopt the best possible strategies to compete in the global market.

Faurecia's top management decided that it was time for reviewing the company's approach to the car seating market and that innovative solutions would be required to keep the company among the three largest players worldwide.

Faurecia: A world leader in car seating

Faurecia was incorporated in 1998 following the merger of Bertrand Faure and Ecia (a subsidiary of Peugeot-Citroen) that led to the creation of a world-class player in the automotive components sector. Faurecia was active in four main activities: automotive seating, vehicle interior, exhaust systems and front-end module.

Since its incorporation, Faurecia's revenues had been steadily growing to 10.7 billion euros in 2004 (refer to **Exhibit 1**). The company had reached a multinational status with 60,000 employees in 28 countries, 160 industrial sites and invested 600 million euros in R&D every year.

By 2005 Faurecia was the ninth largest parts supplier to the car industry worldwide and the third largest player in car seating. Over the years, it had become clear that a truly global supplier to the automotive industry needed not only to be technologically advanced, but also that manufacturing excellence and cost competitiveness were required to fully satisfy the car industry needs.

Automotive seating was Faurecia's largest division with sales of nearly 4.8 billion euros in 2004. It was one of the most integrated seat suppliers in the world, hence able to cover the widest range of orders from car makers. In addition it was the world leading supplier of seat mechanisms and intended to stay that way. Historically, the main focus of the company for car seating was on metallic structures and mechanisms, as this corresponded to customers' demand: originally the seat assembly was done by carmakers. However, with the trend towards increasing outsourcing, the car seating division had gradually expanded its offering.

At the turn of the century, one of Faurecia's key strengths was its expertise in all aspects of car seating. It had in-house capabilities to design and manufacture components for its own assembly lines as well as those of its customers. Faurecia was especially strong in adjustment mechanisms, frames, recliners and tracks. Since recently, it also made foam pads and trim covers (refer to **Exhibit 3**). Faurecia had expertise coordinating and managing for just-in-time (JIT)[1] delivery of complete seats and operated JIT facilities around the world.

The company's vertical integration was certainly among its key strengths; yet, in an evolving market requiring innovative business models, product development and offering had to be fine tuned to satisfy the customers' needs.

In the car seating industry there was both intense competition and extensive cooperation. Faurecia, like the other suppliers, delivered frames both to its and the competitors' assembly plants and assembled seats to car manufacturers using its own as well as its competitors' metallic structures.

The car seat industry

All companies supplying parts to the car industry were entirely dependent on the automotive market. To understand the components market it was therefore crucial to analyze the car industry.

The car market

Since the early 80s, the car industry had turned into a mature one. Yet, competition never seemed to cease and new players continued to enter the market to challenge the existing leaders. Competition had become global as new entrants either started production or exported their models into the large European and North American markets. Market shares were always moving, generally down for the Western car makers, and up for the Asian ones.

The challenge of global competition had forced the Western competitors to review their strategies and operations to try to match the "best in class" (the leading Japanese makers in particular). This resulted in drastic revisions of the manufacturing processes, with "lean operations" (minimum inventories), greater reliance on suppliers (outsourcing) and a special emphasis on quality (Total Quality Management). As car makers (known also as OEMs – Original Equipment Manufacturers) changed the scope of their operations, suppliers had to redefine their business. Many suppliers

---

1 Manufacturing functions organized in such a way to enable the shipment of goods exactly where and when needed thus permitting a drastic decrease of inventories

took responsibility for activities that OEMs gradually gave up, but competition was fierce and car makers also put pressure to reduce the number of their supplier base.

In 2004, after a few years of moderate growth, the global automotive market had grown 5.2% year-on-year to reach 60.9 million units, despite the convergence of many adverse external factors hitting the industry. Asia and Eastern Europe contributed the most to the sales increase observed in 2004. In the three largest regional markets, Western Europe was the main growth catalyst, with car sales rising 3% to almost 16.5 million units whereas the US market grew by a timid 1.4% to 16.8 million units and the Japanese market was flat.

The world's top 12 OEMs controlled 83.1% of global market (refer to **Exhibit 2**). With some 8.633 million vehicles sold worldwide, GM's global sales grew 3.3% over 2003, giving the US carmaker a 14.9% global market share. At the same time, Toyota's global sales increased 10.3% while Ford only managed to push sales up 1.7% in 2004. Toyota had zoomed ahead of Ford, securing a 900,000 units lead over the world's second-largest carmaker whilst reducing its lag behind GM to 1.160 million units. Other Asian brands also performed above industry average in 2004, and Hyundai reported the strongest sales growth among the top 12 carmakers, with car sales soaring 11.6% over 2003 to 3.147 million units. In 2004, Toyota not only had the industry's largest market capitalization but also generated the highest net profit and had the second best operating margin.

Already afflicted by overcapacity, the automotive industry and its main players were expected to face further challenges, some set to linger on for some times such as fluctuating currency markets and uneven economic growth, others being more immediate, like the sudden rise in raw material costs seen in the second half of 2004. Global carmakers were pressured to respond appropriately to these external factors while securing growth in new booming markets and continuing to invest in new technologies and meeting more stringent regulations to ensure that they maintained an upper hand on new players. As of 2005, and although it was still described as a mature industry, car manufacturing was attracting a new set of new entrants, the majority being located in China.

Western car makers, therefore, also faced real pressures to seek out growth prospects outside traditional mature geographic and product markets. At the geographic level, the pressure was on to seek out areas of growing demand, with China clearly at the top of the list for most, and other countries in Asia not far behind. At the product level there was a constant search for the next niche (such as the SUVs – Sports Utility Vehicles, in the 90s) that would generate significant competitive benefits, at least for the period before competitors would follow suite and degrade margins.

The suppliers to the car industry[2]

For suppliers to the automotive industry, the drivers of globalization and the redefinition of the value chain were fairly straightforward. The opportunities were huge, as OEMs left entire businesses to be taken over. But, strategic risks were also considerable as several suppliers realized later on.

High-profile corporate failures in North America, most notably Meridian Automotive Systems, Tower Automotive, Delphi, Dana Corporation and Collins & Aikman, all of which had filed for Chapter 11 protection (to avoid bankruptcy), highlighted how things could go wrong. Although exacerbated by recent cyclical downturns at major customers, the demise of all five reflected the costs of facing the challenges outlined above.

Global trends were hard for suppliers to ignore, especially those at the so-called "tier one" level, e.g. those supplying directly to car manufacturers, and coordinating a set of sub-suppliers (nick-named "tier two"). Through the growth of overseas purchasing offices, virtually all carmakers had access to a wealth of information on global procurement and pricing. With this knowledge, they could pressure suppliers to meet these prices, or move offshore.

Besides, with the need to discount all but the most popular models and the resulting profit squeezes at carmakers, suppliers had to accept an era of annual price declines for their components, systems, and modules. Given the increasing costs associated with greater product development and logistics responsibilities, suppliers faced the continuous threat of declining profitability and margins. The possibility of a new wave of consolidation among OEMs was, of course, not a scenario that suppliers appreciated.

Suppliers were left with the option to join in innovative programs which car makers launched in an effort to outrun their competition. These were typically aiming at niche products (such as new hard top convertibles), which, if successful, would allow the car maker to charge decent margins and, in turn, accept to reward nicely its suppliers for their support. However, getting in this type of programs required substantial engineering efforts to support the OEMs' innovations. This is what Faurecia succeeded to achieve with the Toyota Verso program for which they designed a very innovative back seating system which could fold with the pressure of a single finger!

The car seating industry

The relationships between OEMs and their seat suppliers had undergone substantial changes since the mid-80s, with the outsourcing of a growing portion of the seating modules to suppliers.

In the late 80's, after a period during which OEMs designed and made seats entirely in house, carmakers started outsourcing the manufacturing of the metallic parts of seats, e.g. frames, tracks and mechanisms. Therefore a number of suppliers from the steel industry, among which Bertrand Faure, who previously supplied metal pieces for OEMs to assemble seats, started to ship seat

2 Adapted from "Challenges and forward strategies for the global automotive supplier sector", 2005 – Just-auto.com

frames (the "skeleton" of the seat) to OEMs who covered them with foams and textile. The model adopted was the so-called "build to print", through which OEM designed the pieces required and suppliers received detailed plans and volumes of parts to be manufactured.

Back then, seat suppliers worked on customers' specifications and their role was to deliver on time a limited variety of products with some possibility of inventory at client site. Their main activity was the processing of metallic parts and the equipments used were metal working tools.

In the late 90s, carmakers, first in the US and then throughout the world, began to outsource the whole seat manufacturing and assembly (sometimes even design) to tier-1 suppliers. This move implied a change of position in the value chain for metal parts manufacturers like Bertrand Faure who moved from tier-1 to tier-2 (thus loosing contact with OEMs).

Also, the delivery procedure of complete seats was radically different from the one used until then for seat frames and metal parts: carmakers expected to reduce inventory and cost of supplies by streamlining shipments. The concept of Just-In-Time delivery was adopted, meaning that OEMs expected their suppliers to assemble the seat minutes before it was to be mounted on the car in their assembly line.

OEMs realized that this approach towards supplying seats had multiple advantages: it moved the development cost to the supplier, it reduced the engineering skills required in-house and it cut the investment required to launch a new model (production tooling and development cost were paid as a fraction of each part supplied and not when incurred); essentially, outsourcing the seat manufacturing reduced the OEM's risks. Following this trend, the French Peugeot-Citroen group spun off its car seating division that merged with Bertrand Faure to create Faurecia.

The new company decided that its place ought to be in the "tier-1", hence supplying complete seats. This meant that it not only had to acquire new skills (among which assembly techniques and dealing with a large number of suppliers), but also to adapt to new ways of interfacing with customers for shipping parts.

The cost structure of frame suppliers who decided to become seat manufacturers changed dramatically as the cost of assembly appeared into the equation and had to be optimized.

Since the early 2000s, in an industry facing strong economic challenges, a further new trend began to appear: OEMs started to impose to tier-1 suppliers to source components from tier-2 suppliers selected and qualified by them. Also, with the intent of increasing pressure on suppliers, carmakers divided the seat and its frame into small subsystems, and, according to this scheme, OEMs could order the cushion frame, the backrest frames and the reclining mechanisms from three different suppliers; plastic covers, foams and other parts from other suppliers and then have contracted still a different company to do the assembly and coordinate the whole process. This scheme was called the "unbundling" of the seat.

As a consequence, roles in the supply chain were changing fairly radically and the control on the value chain and consequently on profit margins started shifting. The challenge for suppliers was to keep growing as they concentrated on these new roles. Supplier were redefining their positioning, ranging from attempting to do everything to narrow specialization. In short, suppliers needed to adopt different roles, competencies and strategies, and this could result in new business models.

With the unbundling of the seat, Faurecia, having the competencies and capability to address virtually all blocks of the seat supply chain, had to adapt to an increased variety of customers' demands. Its activities varied from designing and making entire seats to supplying some parts to a competitor's JIT through assembling seats using competitors' parts.

The car seats market in 2005

The world market for car seats reached 27.5 billion euros in 2005. There were about 30 suppliers, a large majority of which had a limited geographical scope or addressed specific niche segments (refer to **Exhibit 4**).

The industry was dominated by three main players: Johnson Controls Inc with about 28% market share, Lear Corporation with around 21% and Faurecia with about 10% market share. Each of these three companies had operations in at least four continents, and altogether they represented about 60% of the global market.

In-house manufacturing (e.g. seats made by car manufacturers directly) represented a small 4% of the market. In other words, 96% of the seats manufactured were outsourced: the seat's increased complexity coupled with strong pressure for cost containment favored large manufacturing companies who could benefit from economies of scale, in particular for R&D spending, quality improvement programs and manufacturing excellence.

Throughout the 90s, seat suppliers had demonstrated that they could innovate and bring to production high-technology systems that increased vehicle comfort, safety and, most importantly, attractiveness to the end consumer. Car seats had evolved from simple objects on which the passengers sat to devices that contributed dramatically to the safety, comfort and aesthetics of the car and that could help differentiate one car model from another. It was estimated that seats represented approximately 5% of a car's value.

Seats were a source of constant technical change, with electronics and flexibility in use at the forefront of this change process. It was in the most advanced technical areas, e.g. heated, ventilated or cooled seats, memory seats, fold-flat and fully reclining seats, that the major changes were taking place.

Over time, new features were being added and many were fitted as standard; customers wanted added comfort and features once considered luxury. As these features became standard, they lost the differentiation appeal they had offered. The effective commoditization of some technologies simply reinforced the pressure on the suppliers to apply new technologies to differentiate one carmaker's seats from another.

In 2005 the price of a car seat set varied from 200 euros for a very simple model to 2500 for a full options leather set, with an average price of 480 euros per vehicle.

Capital investments in the industry had become extremely high. Acquiring a new customer or a new program for an existing customer was very expensive: not only the selection, qualification and set-up processes could last up to three years during which heavy investments were required, but it could also mean the construction of a new JIT plant. Logistics imposed that the factory supplying complete seats had to be located only a short distance from the car assembly line. As an example, Faurecia had an impressive 160 industrial sites to supply parts to its customers!

Even if an existing plant was suitably located for the new program, major modifications to the manufacturing lines were required to host the new model. The required investment per program from the first discussion with the potential customer to the beginning of seat manufacturing could reach tens of million euros. Only very large and cash rich companies could afford these kinds of investments and mistakes were extremely expensive.

For tier one suppliers, being the partner of choice for a particular component was a key competitive position. While this could be founded on identification of business opportunities and anticipation of customer needs at very early stages of vehicle design, it also increasingly required suppliers to have global engineering and R&D capabilities and global manufacturing facilities so as to be able to serve a large number of customers in as many countries as possible.

The technology and manufacturing of car seats

A car seat, especially a front one, was a concentrate of technologies with many different components (refer to **Exhibit 3**).

The development of a car seat

When a carmaker decided to develop a new car model or to renew an existing one, the process normally included the design of new seats.

To do so, the car manufacturer had two options: either they had the skills and resources to design and manufacture the seats in house (but this happened in only 4% of the cases), or they opened a tender and contacted several seat suppliers. In the second case, two further options were available. There were car manufacturers who designed the seat in house and others who just presented the desired functional specifications (performance, volume and costing) and let the supplier do the entire development.

The typical interval from the request for proposals to suppliers to the beginning of manufacturing was three years. During this time, several steps took place (refer to **Exhibits 5**):

- The carmaker issued the call for proposal
- The suppliers presented a "proof of concept" to the client, normally CAD designed models that included computer estimated functionalities and security checks
- In parallel price negotiations took place

- The supplier was then selected, the program awarded and the actual seat design work could start; in this phase sub-suppliers were identified and selected (eventually by the carmaker)
- Upon customer agreement, the final details of the design were completed and the tooling for volume production manufactured
- The actual manufacturing started at the same time as the car production so that the first seats arrived at the car manufacturing line right on time with the first models of the new car.

Once in production, a car model was manufactured for six years on average and sales peaked after 18 months. During this time, carmakers normally did not change seat supplier; the relationship was therefore a long lasting and mutually binding one.

The making of a car seat

A car seat had essentially two main components: the metallic frame and the "soft" parts that included foams, fabric texture and color, air bags, plastic covers, electric motors and other options.

The manufacturing of the frame and the final assembly of the seat were always done in different plants and potentially by different companies. Therefore there were frame plants that delivered metal structures (that included all the metal parts and the recliner mechanisms) and "Just-In-Time" (JIT) plants, always located close to the car manufacturing factories, which coordinated and received parts from all suppliers and did the final assembly and on-time delivery.

JIT plants were required by the nature of the car industry. Carmakers accepted only a few minutes of inventory, and parts for the exact model moving along the line had to arrive at the right place at the right time. OEMs actually adopted a build to order strategy according to which a particular car was assembled upon a final customer order: when a customer ordered a car with a given set of options, the OEM launched its manufacturing. JIT delivery was required to enable the OEM to ship the car to the end-user within a reasonable delay.

Around the world there were far more JITs than frame plants, as the extremely short lead-time imposed the JIT to be close to the customer plant. Hence, metal structures had to be shipped from the frame plant to the JIT (refer to **Exhibit 6**) located near (and sometimes inside) the carmaker's factory for the assembly of the various seat components. The metallic structure could be delivered either in one or two parts (sometimes even more according to the recent unbundling of the seat by carmakers), in which case the cushion frame was separated from the backrest one; recliner mechanisms were usually attached to the cushion and, once bolted to the backrest, served as link between the two parts of the frame.

1-part vs. 2-part seats: a strategic choice

Until 2002 almost all structures delivered by Faurecia were in one part. This was essentially due to cost reasons: manufacturing structures in one part was less expensive as the recliner was welded on both the cushion and the backrest directly in the frame plant. Since welding was never performed in the JIT factory, shipping frames in two parts would have implied modifying the recliners in order to allow bolting the cushion to the backrest during assembly. As a consequence, the cost of the frame would have increased. This approach was also quite consistent with Faurecia original position as a supplier of "seat frames" to car makers who previously controlled the final assembly of seats and with a dense regional manufacturing footprint.

The situation changed with the evolution of the business model and the decision by Faurecia to operate JIT factories thus delivering complete seats to its customers wherever located. In this case, the total cost was not only the one of the frame, but also its transportation, the assembly and the tooling required to perform it. New contributions to the total cost had to be considered that impacted drastically the final result.

Furthermore, with the unbundling of the seat required by carmakers, suppliers had to develop subsystems to suit customers' demands while trying to standardize product offering: the supplier's goal was to contain costs wherever possible and reducing the number of products was a way to achieve it. In product terms, this meant the development of a set of standard "plug & play" modules that properly combined fulfilled customers' needs. The seat was therefore becoming a customized product made assembling standard subsystems.

The difference between one- and two or more-part seat frames was considerable as it had numerous industrial implications and, therefore, moving from one to several parts was a strategic decision requiring a deep analysis.

The role of the JIT plants

Once in manufacturing, there could be up to 2000 different types of seats that fitted a single car model (e.g. Citroen Picasso), depending on fabric color, texture and other options.

Carmakers gave forecasts to seat suppliers about five days in advance, while the firm purchase order was placed no more than four hours before the seats had to be ready on the car assembly line. In other words, the supplier had just four hours to receive and process the order, assemble the full set of seats for a given car model and deliver it to the carmaker.

The supplier was responsible for JIT delivery, and shipment in advance was not permitted. In case of missed or wrong delivery, the supplier had to cover the costs of the delays induced along the line. If the line had to stop because of a supplier, the same supplier would have incurred serious penalties that included the wages of the operators whose work had been delayed.

Therefore a full set of countermeasures had to be put in place by suppliers to avoid any such event. A line manager at Faurecia's factory near Rennes, France, said:

> "Our worst nightmare is to slow down the car manufacturing line. We have spare parts and alternatives for all our tools; we have planned alternative routes to ship our parts in case of heavy traffic or issues on the road. We are ready to clear the roads in case of snow, and we have spare trucks in case of accidents. We are ready to ship individual parts and even mock ups of seats to keep the car line moving."

Some of these precautions were not needed in the JIT plants integrated in the carmaker's factory, such as the Faurecia factory in Leipzig, Germany, located in the BMW plant. There seats were directly brought to the assembly line on the conveyor belt system of the factory.

Tight deadlines and the willingness to contain inventory at the JIT induced seat manufacturers to strive to push diversity from one seat type to the other as downstream as possible in the seat assembly process. Having interchangeable plug & play modules for the frame certainly contributed to reach this goal.

Logistics and ergonomics issues

A metallic seat structure was a big and heavy object (refer to **Exhibit 7**) that needed to be packaged and shipped and then received, inspected and stocked before assembly. Despite the studies done to reduce the shipment volume and therefore cost, a Faurecia manufacturing manager working in a plant producing one-part seats said:

> "We have been trying very hard to optimize the seats' packaging, and yet, in our trucks, we deliver quite a lot of air with some metal in it. The issue is becoming critical if we want to meet the costing structure required by our customers".

Also, once in the JIT, the inventory of components for assembly needed to be optimized and seat structures took up the largest part of the warehouses. From a logistics standpoint, it was therefore essential to address the issue represented by these bulky objects.

As to JIT plants, using one-part seat frames was becoming less and less practical with the increased complexity of seats and the more recent assembly techniques in use.

Historically the shop floor in an assembly factory was organized in islands where the frame was put on a pedestal that allowed rotations in all directions for the operators to fit it with the required components. The frame remained set on the same device until the accomplishment of the seat assembly. Therefore, the operators had to learn to perform all the operations required to assemble a full seat from the bare frame to the delivery to the car manufacturer. This required a lot of training, long set-up times and resulted in quality differences from one seat to another coming from a different island. Also, pedestals had to be customized for each type of frame; the tooling cost for the launch of a new manufacturing line was becoming prohibitive.

With the evolution of car seats and the increased number and variability of parts to be assembled on one seat, the number of operations to be performed during assembly increased and the JIT shop floor changed from islands to continuous flow lines: the frame entered the shop floor on one side of the line and kept moving on assembly lines on which operators, working in teams, added parts until it was ready to be shipped to the car manufacturer.

Each operator performed a limited number of operations and could focus on optimizing its tasks with a dramatic decrease in processing time.

Parts to be assembled on the frame were available in front of the operators within arm's length; workers did not need to turn or bend to take them.

A bare seat frame could weigh up to 12 kilos; the weight increased while the seat moved along the line and a complete seat weighed up to 25 kilos. Having abandoned the pedestal, the stress on operators who had to lift or rotate the seat could be huge; robots had therefore been introduced on the lines to perform this operation.

Seat assembly was thus a very labor-intensive manufacturing process with severe ergonomic issues that could result in potentially harmful effects on the operators and have costly consequences for the company.

Design For Assembly at Faurecia

In 2004, the automotive seating business unit of Faurecia launched an ambitious program that was bound to have a major impact on the seat design and manufacturing process: a Design For Assembly (DFA) team with the goal of optimizing the assembly process, had been created to support all the steps of product design, development and manufacturing.

The rationale was simple: two products with an identical number of parts may differ in required assembly time by a factor of two or three. This is because the actual time to grasp, orient and insert a part depends on the part geometry and the required trajectory of the part insertion.

Not only the time required was critical, but also operators' comfort during their job was mandatory. Musculoskeletal troubles that cause health problems were a major concern in the JITs. In mere economic terms, the consequences were evident; not only were stressed workers generally less productive, but also the cost of absence due to health reasons was quite high.

DFA was a transversal process aimed at optimizing the activity and comfort of operators.

Mr. Pascal Connesson, DFA manager, said:

> "We want to influence the design of our products in order to optimize the assembly process; we have designed the ideal assembly line for the JIT, one that optimizes ergonomics and assembly costing, and we want to adapt the product design to fit it. This is a dramatic revolution for Faurecia, as the focus had always been on the technical side, somehow neglecting the assembly process during manufacturing. Given the nature of car seat assembly, our target is to move the connection between the cushion and the backrest as far as possible in the assembly line."

Program development at Faurecia

When a new program was started, the development team was typically composed of a program manager, nominated by and reporting to the Division Program Director, a finance controller to analyze product costing, a product engineer for the metallic structure and a manufacturing engineer to provide JIT expertise; sales, purchasing and quality experts were also part of the program core team.

The document that circulated in the team and that captured all the information about the product under development was called "Master Principles". Since the introduction of DFA, a new column had been added to the Master Principles to collect comments about the process.

DFA recommendations were sometimes as simple as the reminder not to leave sharp edges in the metallic structure that could harm the operator during assembly but could also consist in a deep ergonomic analysis of the operations to be accomplished in the JIT.

DFA's mission was to optimize operators' safety, comfort and quality of work, and their comments were highly considered all along the design chain. A red flag from DFA automatically implied a modification to the design of the product.

The early involvement of DFA was extremely important as, once the design was frozen and production tooling launched, only minor modifications were possible.

Among the scopes of DFA, there was the reduction and, possibly, the elimination of musculoskeletal troubles in manufacturing plants; the focus was therefore on ergonomics and physical efforts. As a consequence, DFA was strongly in favor of assembling the seats starting with two or more part frames and connecting the cushion and the backrest as far in the JIT assembly line as possible.

Organizing for product development

On December 31, 2004, the executive committee of Faurecia met to review the priorities for the upcoming year. At the top of the agenda was the need to redefine the product development process for the whole of the Faurecia Group. As the company gained market share, its engineering resources were becoming stretched and a new development process was required in order to maintain the momentum.

The challenges faced by car seating were actually quite illustrative of the type of issues confronting the whole company.

Certainly, the strategic move undertaken by Faurecia to become one of the world leaders in car seating was paying off. By 2005, Faurecia had become a global player with operations in all regions with significant car production. Its client list increasingly read like the who's who of the car industry: Toyota, BMW, VW, Renault, PSA, among others.

Also Faurecia's wide set of competencies, thanks to its presence in most activities of the car seating value network, meant that it had an increasingly rich contribution to its customers development.

Finally, as car became more complex systems incorporating a larger number of technologies, the role of car seating was becoming quite challenging. Not only was Faurecia supposed to stay abreast of the latest technology introduction, but it was expected to design faster a growing variety of seats.

It resulted that Faurecia had also become a "development" machine, pursuing simultaneously the engineering of a large number of car versions for a given model, at a time when it was engaged in support engineering for numerous programs for a large number of OEMs. The resources of car seating got inevitably strained under the overwhelming pressure from engineering needs. The system was quickly approaching its limits and incidents started to occur which required management time to fix:

- Some projects had suffered delays, causing costly catch up to prevent penalties imposed by contractual clauses
- The allocation of resources (especially development engineers) for product development programs was not optimal, as it was the result of the relative bargaining power of project leaders rather than "objective needs"
- Problem resolution was not always as good as expected due to project team dynamics where some departments were more successful than others in imposing their "best solution"
- Sometimes, teams suffered from the "Not Invented Here" syndrome where suggestions from suppliers were simply ignored, making decisions on product development less effective.

It was clear that product development had become a key process and that Faurecia needed to set up a policy in line with best practices world wide.

Exhibit 1: Faurecia's sales by business segment

Sales by business segment

(in € millions)	2004	%	2003	%	2002	%
Vehicle Interior Modules						
- Automotive Seating	4784.7	58	4353.2	55	4031.6	54
- Vehicle Interiors	3500.9	42	3505.7	45	3462.8	46
	8285.6		7858.9		7494.4	
Other modules						
- Exhaust Systems	1714.9	70	1587.9	70	1777.7	75
- Front-end	719.0	30	675.9	30	593.4	25
	2433.9		2263.8		2371.1	
Total	**10719.5**		**10122.7**		**9865.5**	

Source: Faurecia

Exhibit 2: Top 12 car manufacturing groups by sales

Top 12 Manufacturing Groups By Sales									
	2004			2003			2002		
	Sales	Market Share	y/y Change	Sales	Market Share	y/y Change	Sales	Market Share	y/y Change
General Motors	8,633,626	14.9%	3.3%	8,354,406	14.4%	-1.2%	8,456,682	14.9%	-1.6%
Toyota	7,470,442	12.9%	10.3%	6,770,427	11.7%	9.1%	6,206,621	11%	4.5%
Ford	6,570,131	11.3%	1.7%	6,460,421	11.1%	-0.5%	6,496,060	11.5%	-4.8
VW Group	5,006,651	8.6%	2.4%	4,887,743	8.4%	0.5%	4,861,839	8.6%	-2.5
DaimlerChrysler	4,159,385	7.2%	2.6%	4,053,126	7%	-3.4%	4,194,326	7.4%	-2
Nissan	3,202,349	5.5%	9.2%	2,933,831	5.1%	8.6%	2,700,425	4.8%	5.7
Honda	3,189,001	5.5%	9.3%	2,917,516	5%	2.6%	2,844,756	5%	6.5
Hyundai	3,147,812	5.4%	11.6%	2,821,302	4.9%	2.6%	2,750,682	4.9%	9.3
PSA Group	3,118,380	5.4%	0.1%	3,115,868	5.4%	2.3%	3,045,577	5.4%	4.7
Renault Group	2,397,246	4.1%	4%	2,305,842	4%	-0.4%	2,316,024	4.1%	-0.2
Fiat	1,992,356	3.4%	4.4%	1,908,933	3.3%	-8.3%	2,081,977	3.7%	-12.5
Suzuki	1,785,422	3.1%	10.1%	1,621,837	2.8%	8.9%	1,489,527	2.6%	4.6

Source: Global Insight

Exhibit 3: Structure of front seat

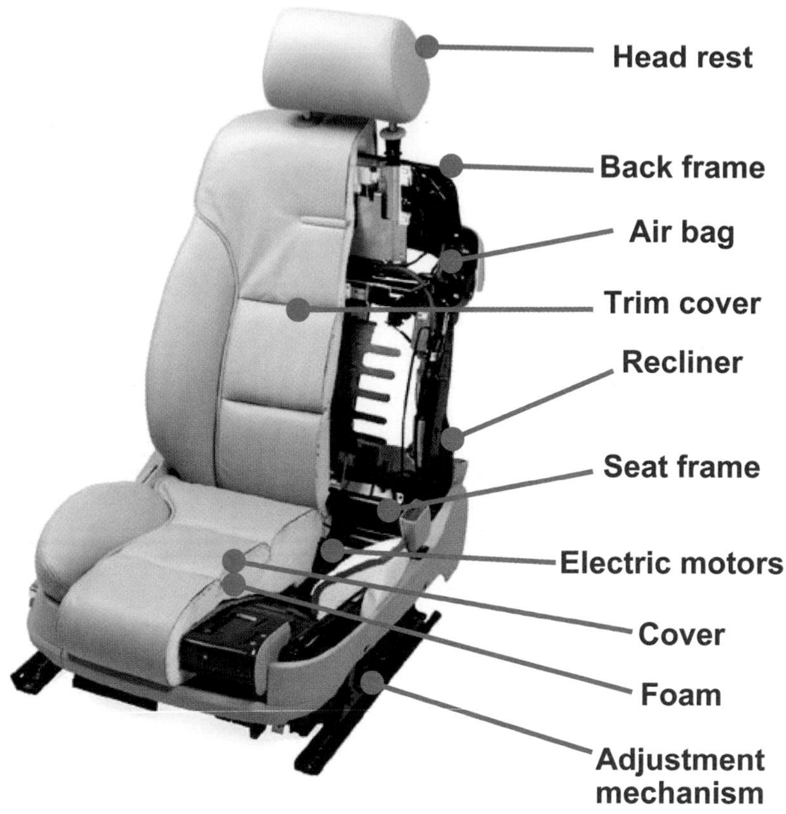

Source: Faurecia

Exhibit 4: 2005 worldwide car seats market share

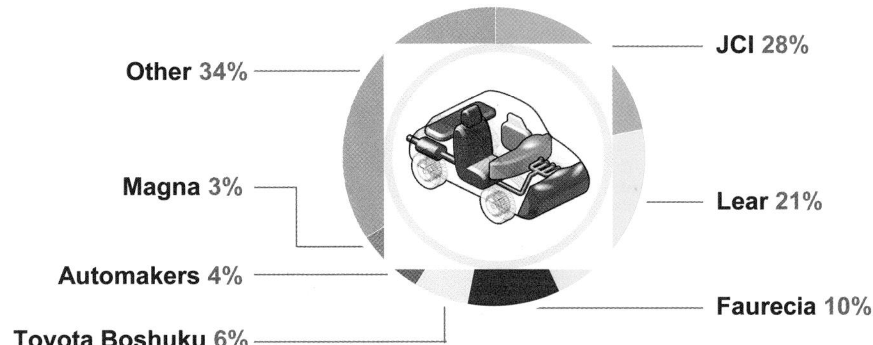

Europe		
1.	**Faurecia**	**30%**
2.	JCI	29%
3.	Lear	25%
4.	Carmakers	11%

North America		
1.	JCI	38%
2.	Lear	33%
3.	Magna	10%
4.	**Faurecia**	**3%**

China		
1.	JCI	59%
2.	Lear	16%
3.	**Faurecia**	**4%**

Source: Faurecia

Exhibit 5: The lifecycle of a car seat

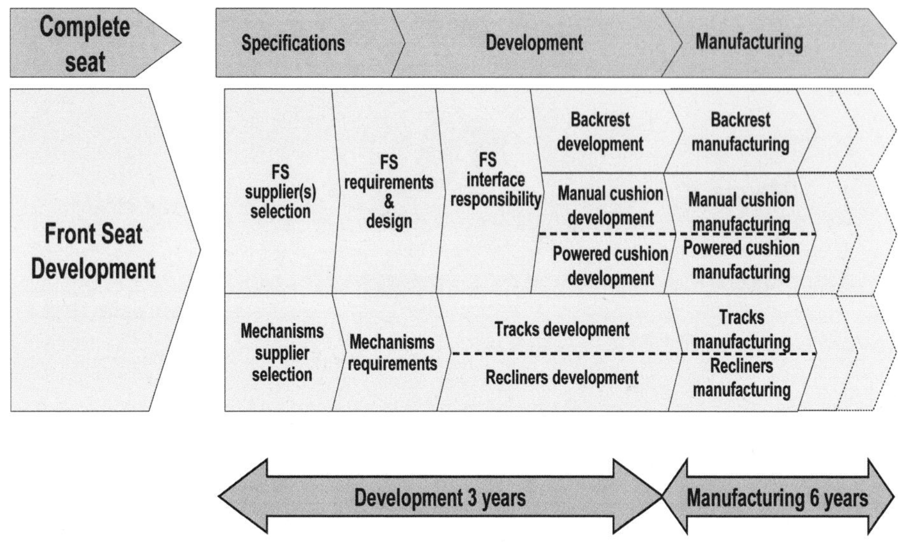

Source: A.T. Kearney

Exhibit 6: Typical shipment scheme

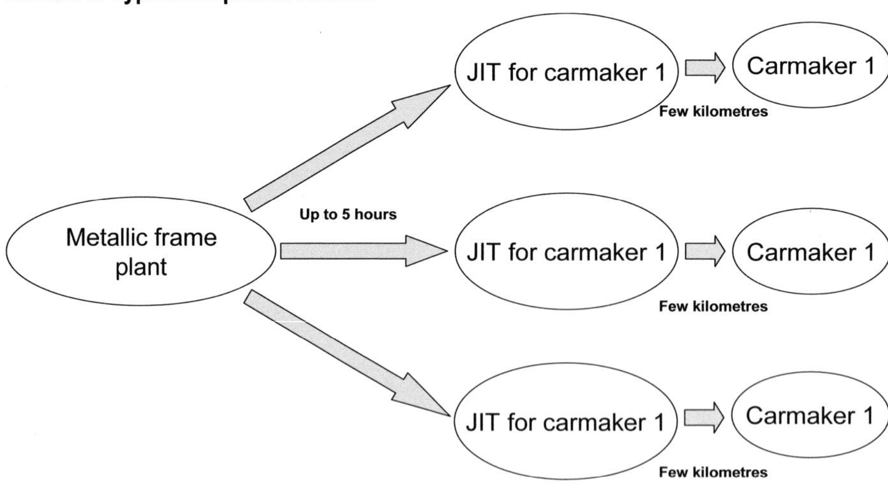

Exhibit 7: Front seat tracks and structure

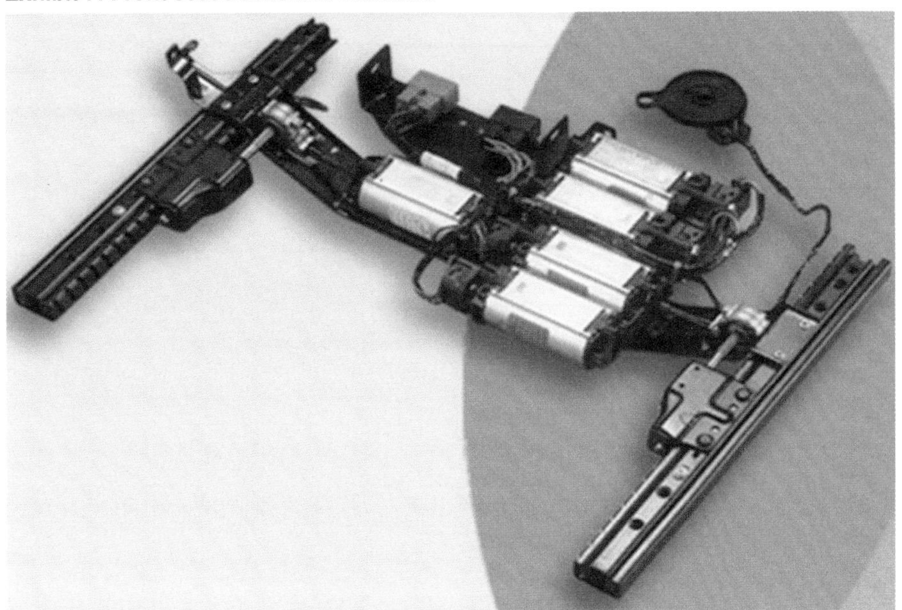

Source: Faurecia

QUESTIONS TO BE ANSWERED

1. What were the problems facing Faurecia at the beginning of the case?
2. What changes occurred in the industry prior to 2005?
3. How did Faurecia respond to the conditions that it faced?
4. Discuss Faurecia's approach to product management.
5. How would you recommend that Faurecia move forward, given the changes that have taken place?

End-of-book Case III

Marketing strategy of Changhong Electric Company, 2009; a leading Chinese TV manufacturer*

* *We would like to thank the Alexander von Humboldt Foundation for sponsoring parts of this research.*

Source: This case was prepared by Marc Fetscherin and Paul Beuttenmuller of the Crummer Graduate School of Business, Rollins College, as the basis for analysis and class discussion and not to illustrate either effective or ineffective handling of an administrative situation.

Changhong Electric Co., Ltd (Changhong), a manufacturer of colour televisions in China, had seen its sales multiply from the mid 1980s through the late 1990s, as China and its markets experienced record economic growth. The firm had a solid position as the colour television industry's market share leader in the domestic market. But, beginning in 1998, Changhong experienced a series of setbacks, ultimately leaving it with an RMB 3.68 billion loss in 2004. Facing intense competition, that year the company replaced its chairman, Ni Runfeng, with its general manager and executive president, Zhao Yong. Zhao Yong was charged with reshaping the company's strategy and tactics to strengthen the brand. He needed not only to maintain Changhong's dominant position in the domestic market but to expand the brand worldwide.

Changhong's major competitors include Today China Lion (TCL) and Konka, as well as several 'no-name' manufacturers that periodically enter the market. This latter group prices its televisions much lower than the industry average, leading to volatile price fluctuations, and even, for some types of televisions, to price erosion (see Table I below).

The lack of a single technology standard has encouraged shoppers to delay purchases as they anticipate the emergence of a clear-cut standard in either liquid crystal display (LCD) or plasma display panel (PDP) televisions.

Confronted with a variety of strategic decisions, Changhong's chairman, Zhao Yong, must determine the appropriate response to these dynamic competitive conditions. He must stem the company's recent decline in profits and reorganize to become a global leader within the television manufacturing industry.

TABLE I Average retail prices of televisions (RMB)

Type of TV	2002	2003	2004	2005	2006	2007	2008
Cathode ray tube	2,020	1,960	1,970	1,870	1,660	2,050	1,770
Flat panel	N/A	N/A	7,100	10,420	8,770	8,280	7,790
LCD	10,080	9,600	9,540	9,950	8,740	8,130	7,630
Plasma	38,330	35,340	26,690	18,170	11,560	10,430	9,620
PRTV	2,730	2,560	2,460	2,570	2,620	2,820	2,920

Source: Access Asia Limited (2009), *Televisions in China 2009: A Market Analysis*, January, accessed June 2009, at: **http://www.accessasia.co.uk/showreport.asp?RptId=12**

Changhong (China)

Changhong was founded in 1958 as a state-owned military-radar factory in Mianyang, with the assistance of the former Soviet Union, as part of China's first Five-Year Plan. When the demand for military products started to decline in the mid 1970s, the firm shifted toward developing and manufacturing civilian products, notably colour televisions. In 1979, the Changhong factory signed a technical collaboration agreement with Matsushita Electric Industrial Co. of Japan to build a colour-television assembly line in Mianyang. Changhong independently constructed an additional TV production line, increasing the firm's annual production capacity to over 10,000 units by 1980.

Ni Runfeng was appointed chairman of Changhong in 1985 and transformed the military-radar maker into the top television manufacturer in the country. Within a year, output skyrocketed to 320,000 units, including 196,000 colour televisions by emphasizing mass production, quality, and after-sales service. In October 1987, they established a Holding structure (Changhong Electronics Holdings Co., Ltd), making way for the joint-stock system transformation of state-owned Changhong. Hence, (Sichuan) Changhong Electric Co. was founded in 1988 with the parent company of Changhong Holdings (see Figure I below), which was supervised and administered by government officials of the city of Miangyang.

Just three years later, in 1988, Changhong emerged as a large-scale enterprise, with annual television production reaching almost a million units. In 1994, it was listed as a publicly traded company on the Shanghai Stock Exchange and, by 1995, was recognized as China's largest television manufacturer at the 50th International Statistics Conference (Li and Mao, 2007).

As the nation's market share leader since the mid 1990s with a market share of 15 per cent in 2007, Changhong has been identified as China's sixth most valuable brand for 2008 (RMB 65.59 billion) according to the study by World Brand Laboratory (Access Asia Limited, 2009).

Changhong (International)

Changhong's growth strategy consisted of a three-tiered approach, starting with Sichuan Province markets. Once the company had captured a majority of the local market through a low-price strategy, the chairman, Runfeng, shifted his attention to the domestic Chinese market outside

Figure I Control and ownership structure of Changhong Company, 2006

Source: Changhong Company Website, available at: **<bb>www.changhong.com.cn**

Sichuan Province. Changhong launched two separate price wars, one in 1989 and the second in 1996. By 1996, it had 35 per cent of the overall market and had increased its sales volume to nearly 5 million units per year.

At a 1999 board meeting, Ni Runfeng and other company leaders decided to build an international brand image by exporting televisions and opening overseas sales offices. This became the third tier of the strategy. Changhong established colour television production lines in Russia (1999), Indonesia (2000), and Algeria (2003), while exporting to other countries such as the US and Europe.

Changhong's television export volume reached almost 4 million units in 2002. Despite this success, however, the firm encountered several setbacks, particularly in the US. Changhong was charged with a 26.37 per cent anti-dumping tax and its relationship with its primary American importer, Apex Digital, Inc., deteriorated. These negative events, combined with a poor country-of-origin effect, have prevented Changhong from building its brand image in global markets, especially in the US.

Today, Changhong markets its products in over 90 countries in regions as diverse as South East Asia, the Middle East, Europe, and South America. Indonesia is one of Changhong's most profitable markets as the company was able to capture 20 per cent of the market within the first five years of entering it. In other regions, such as Russia and the Ukraine, Changhong exports components and parts, and production technology for colour televisions. To areas that include the US, Europe, the Middle East, and Africa, the company mainly exports product parts in order to expand its market share, taking advantage of economies of scale. Some products are sold with the Changhong brand while others are sold as a 'no-name' under Original Equipment Manufacturer (OEM).

Changhong's setback and the appointment of Zhao Yong

When China adopted its reform policy in 1978, there was a single television manufacturing company, with an annual output of approximately 3,800 units. By 2006, China produced more than 90 million televisions, making it the world's largest television-producing country, with over 50 per cent of global production. China manufactured nearly 38 million colour televisions in the first six months of 2007, with over half going to the domestic Chinese market to fulfil the increasing consumer demand of China's emerging middle class.

While extreme income disparities exist between urban and rural regions, average per capita gross domestic product purchasing power parity (GDP PPP) increased from $3,600 in 2000 to about $6,000 in 2008. This rising consumer wealth is driving increased domestic demand. Per capita television ownership rose from 2 persons per 1,000 in 1985 to over 300 per 1,000 in 2003, but there is clearly room for domestic growth. As new technologies emerge, consumers want to upgrade their TV, resulting in evolving product portfolios of television manufacturing companies.

From 1990 through to 1998, Changhong's distribution channel began with the manufacturer and passed through a huge wholesaler and retailer network before reaching the end consumer. Changhong could not obtain adequate feedback, as the company had no real idea who its customers were. Runfeng, the chairman, could not respond to changes in the marketplace in a timely manner. In 1999, however, he altered the distribution channel so that products went from Changhong to a chain retailer and then the end consumer. While this allowed prompt feedback, it resulted in huge marketing and sales expenses and large inventories. These increasing costs, along with growing competition and changing technologies, impacted Changhong's financial stability. In 1998, alone, inventory rose from RMB 3.55 million to RMB 7.71 billion and net profit

EXHIBIT I Changhong's net profit, 1994–2005

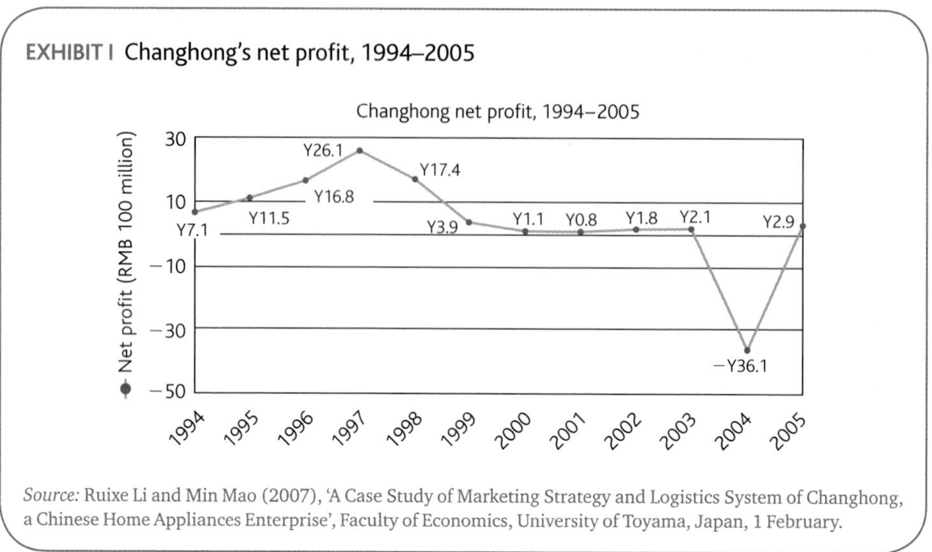

Source: Ruixe Li and Min Mao (2007), 'A Case Study of Marketing Strategy and Logistics System of Changhong, a Chinese Home Appliances Enterprise', Faculty of Economics, University of Toyama, Japan, 1 February.

dwindled to RMB 0.38 billion from RMB 1.70 billion. The company recorded historic lows in 2004, when it lost RMB 3.68 billion (see Exhibit I and Exhibit II). Although Runfeng responded by expanding internationally, Changhong's financial situation didn't change. The company's gross profit margin continued to decrease, and revenue declined. It became evident that, in order to maintain its leadership position in the industry, Changhong had to revamp its strategy and marketing approach under a new leadership.

Zhao Yong and Changhong's reorganization

Zhao Yong had served as general manager and executive president of Changhong from 2000 to 2001, but he resigned in May 2001 to become deputy mayor of Mianyang People's Government. When Changhong collapsed in 2004, its board, seeking a turnaround under a distinguished leader, appointed Zhao Yong as its new chairman. Yong immediately focused his attention on technological innovation at the company core and restructured the company to align with this new strategy.

Yong believed that improving Changhong's technological capabilities would transform the company from a scale-oriented declining enterprise into a technology-oriented efficient one. When he rejoined Changhong, a variety of obstacles existed that prevented the company from succeeding either domestically or internationally. First, it was operating under a centralized (hierarchical) organizational structure with no clear functional definition for each management level, overlapping functions, and a marketing and sales system with a weak reaction time to the rapidly changing market. Second, Changhong's logistics system was inefficient. With more than 40 raw material storehouses, 50 finished product storehouses, 200 sales storehouses, and 1,000 freight vehicles in Mianyang city alone, the company's costs were unnecessarily high compared to the industry average. No cross-functional coordination existed, and inventory remained alarmingly high due to poor logistics and ineffective supply chain management. Finally, the supply chain operated under a typical push system, resulting in massive inventories and increased costs.

EXHIBIT II Changhong's gross profit margin, 1994–2005

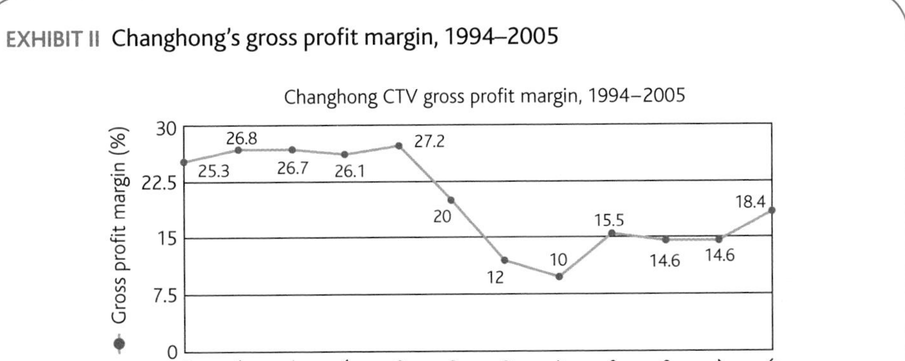

Source: Ruixe Li and Min Mao (2007), 'A Case Study of Marketing Strategy and Logistics System of Changhong, a Chinese Home Appliances Enterprise', Faculty of Economics, University of Toyama, Japan, 1 February.

Yong addressed each of these obstacles with his management team. In late 2004, he launched the largest reorganization in Changhong's history. He first created a decentralized organizational system with powerful marketing functions based on the products. With the assistance of a consulting firm, Yong reorganized the organizational structure, under which headquarters would make decisions on national and global issues, but not regional ones. The idea was to have a bottom-up approach, where the decision authority was spread throughout a reduced number of sub-companies. The sales and marketing department was reorganized, as illustrated in Figure II.

Yong next sought to improve logistics operations by reducing inventory and establishing cross-functional coordination. He restructured the company's logistics through five initiatives: improving its overall IT applications; introducing an Enterprise Resource Planning (ERP) system; rebuilding the warehouse management system; retooling the logistics network and logistics flow; and remodelling the logistics operational management. This resulted in finance/cost control, material management, improved inbound and outbound inventory management, decreased rent expense, and cross-functional coordination. These actions significantly improved Changhong's efficiency, as rent expenses decreased by 50 per cent, logistics costs dropped by RMB 130 million, four central distribution centres and 66 regional distribution centres were established (replacing dozens of storehouses), and the inventory of raw material goods fell by 61 per cent.

Finally, Yong implemented a strategy to fulfil his promise of transforming the company into a technology-orientated enterprise. For example, Changhong developed a state-level technology centre and a first-rate scientific research workstation while establishing R&D centres in Shanghai and Shenzhen in China, Silicon Valley in the United States, and another centre in Japan. Yong obtained government support to establish joint R&D labs with high-tech firms such as Microsoft, Philips, Toshiba, GE, Samsung, LG, and Sanyo, among others.

Perhaps the most critical element of Changhong's technology-based transformation occurred in 2006, when the company teamed up with a technology consulting firm to implement the IBM product innovation management model. This model focused on the principles of integrated

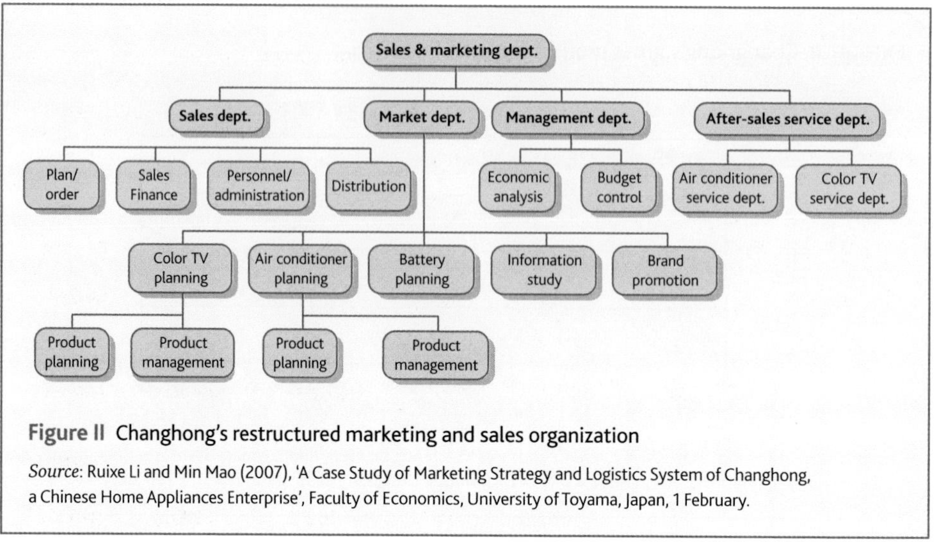

Figure II Changhong's restructured marketing and sales organization

Source: Ruixe Li and Min Mao (2007), 'A Case Study of Marketing Strategy and Logistics System of Changhong, a Chinese Home Appliances Enterprise', Faculty of Economics, University of Toyama, Japan, 1 February.

product development, market planning, emerging business opportunities, and research and technology management. Together with the consultants, Changhong's management restructured the entire organization, as well as process flows. As a result, the firm achieved significant cost reductions, increased its capacity for continuous innovation, and reduced its time-to-market for new products by 25 per cent.

Yong tapped into the high-end television market—LCD, flat panel, and PDP televisions—through the company's investments in upstream parts and components. While the market for high-end televisions remains relatively small in China, Changhong is placing its bets on future demand for these products, with potentially higher margins and a larger market share in the long term (see Exhibit III). Yong realizes that this strategy, like that of his predecessor, is high-risk, but by strengthening its technology and innovative capabilities, Changhong can differentiate itself from the competition more distinctly and position itself for broader international growth.

The domestic television manufacturing industry

Ten years ago, the Chinese colour television industry was in a slump: overcapacity stalled growth, market competition was fierce, and none of the manufacturers were in control of the core technologies, making it impossible to lower costs. Due to excess supply, price wars were the norm, as firms relied on high volumes to maintain profitability. Zhao Yong realized that Changhong could not survive with this strategy.

While Changhong, Konka, and other leading manufacturers were under pressure to lower prices, several small, 'no-name' manufacturers were producing high-tech sets and selling them at very low prices. Smuggling colour sets into the country was common, creating a large grey market. Changhong faced even greater pressure as prices fell further.

In mainland China, Changhong's competition includes not only domestic brands such as Konka, Today China Lion (TCL), and Hisense, but foreign brands such as Sony, Matsushita, Toshiba, and Sharp. In fact, the world's top ten manufacturers of consumer electronics all have production facilities in China and are investing heavily there. Competition is now shifting towards the

EXHIBIT III Forecast of growth in the high-end television sector

'000 units	2009	2010	2011	2012	2013	Growth (%)
CRT	27,655	26,615	26,289	25,478	24,771	–10.43%
Flat panel	12,208	13,891	15,981	19,779	19,779	62.01%
LCD	11,001	12,621	14,611	16,384	18,248	65.88%
Plasma	1,189	1,350	1,549	1,726	1,912	60.74%
PRTV	17.8	0	0	0	0	–100%
Total	*39,864*	*40,507*	*42,271*	*43,309*	*44,550*	*11.75%*

RMB (billions)	2009	2010	2011	2012	2013	Growth (%)
CRT	51.96	47.13	44.12	40.72	37.86	–27.15%
Flat panel	101.05	108.35	118.13	125.52	133.14	31.76%
LCD	89.15	96.38	105.75	112.92	120.27	34.91%
Plasma	12.16	13.01	14.15	15.01	15.9	30.73%
PRTV	0.06	0	0	0	0	–100%
Total	153.01	155	162	166	171	11.75%

Source: Access Asia Limited (2009), Televisions in China 2009: A Market Analysis, January, accessed June 2009, at: **http://www.accessasia.co.uk/showreport.asp?RptId=12.**

high-end market originally dominated by foreign companies. After purchasing the television-manufacturing unit of the French Thompson Group in 2003, Today China Lion became one of the nation's largest manufacturers. Together, the top five companies in the Chinese colour television industry account for over 65 per cent of total market share. Table II provides key financial data for China's largest domestic television manufacturers.

With the shift towards high-definition and digital television, Chinese manufacturers are scrambling to adopt new technologies in order to remain competitive. The race to gain expertise and competitive advantage through technology has driven firms to invest heavily in R&D.

In the past, manufacturers relied on price wars to build market share. Before 2001, Chinese domestic television manufacturers had significant cost advantages over foreign competitors, but as the costs of production for newer technologies have risen, and international competitors also produce in China, this edge disappeared. As a result, overall industry profitability has fallen and the average profit margin for domestic LCD makers is only 2.3 per cent, compared with the electronic industry's overall profit margin of about 3.5 per cent. Greater consumer awareness and improved manufacturing capabilities are fuelling price wars among competitors today, further eroding the average selling price and profit margin of a television unit.

Despite this difficult environment, Zhao Yong's restructuring of Changhong in 2004 brought earnings into the black. In 2005, annual turnover hit $2.2 billion (RMB 15 billion) and the gross

TABLE II Competitive financial analysis of Chinese TV manufacturers, 2008

	Total revenue, million RMB	Gross profit, million RMB	Employees	Stock market code
Changhong	27,930	4,787	30,000	SH 600839
TCL	22,731	3,622	50,000	HK 1070
Hisense	13,407	2,327	10,800	SH600060
Skyworth	12,294	2,631	5,200	HK 0751
Konka	12,205	2,361	17,000	SZ 200016

Source: Compiled from Reuters Financial Statements (2009), available at: **http://www.reuters.com/finance/stocks**

profit margin increased from 14.61 per cent in 2004 to 19.60 perc ent in 2007 (see Exhibit II and Exhibit IV). By 2008, the company's brand was estimated at over RMB 61.5 billion.

Changhong's improved sales and financial stability were a result of several factors in addition to its leadership. First, the company had diversified through manufacturing IT products, audio and video products, refrigerators, air conditioners, mobile phones, batteries, and network products, allowing it to profit from economies of scope. Second, Changhong was one of the first colour-television manufacturers in China to offer superior after-sales service as a way to stand out from the crowd. It set up toll-free lines, mobile service vehicles in major cities, and currently maintains over 1,000 service centres worldwide. But while Changhong had great success domestically competing against multinationals such as Sony, Sharp, and Matsushita, the company still faces hurdles. It needs to make substantial investments in research and development, expand internationally, and strengthen its brand image.

Government regulation, imports, and market entry

The colour television industry, with over 120 manufacturers in the 1990s, took a leap into the global marketplace when the Chinese Government lowered import tariffs on colour televisions from 35 per cent to 23 per cent in 1996. The industry went through a massive consolidation as foreign-manufactured televisions flooded the Chinese market, leading to the elimination or consolidation of over 30 manufacturers. Since China joined the World Trade Organization in 2001, further liberalization has increased foreign trade and reduced barriers to entry to the Chinese domestic market. Consequently, consumers have a vast number of choices among televisions distributed through many different retail channels, giving them unprecedented bargaining power.

Competing in the consumer electronics retail market is now more problematic than ever, with additional consolidation likely. Availability of substitutes, overcapacity, diminishing profit margins, and high start-up costs have created a relatively unattractive market for new entrants and existing companies face similar obstacles.

International markets are difficult to enter as foreign governments increase barriers to entry for Chinese television manufacturers. For example, after US television manufacturers filed an anti-dumping petition in 2003, the US Department of Commerce (DoC) levied heavy dumping duties on the leading Chinese manufacturers in 2004. Levies applied to televisions of 21 inches

EXHIBIT IV Changhong key financial data (in RMB millions)

	2004	2005	2006	2007	2008
CRT	11,539	15,061	18,893	23,249	27,930
Gross profit	1,634	2,409	2,952	3,620	4,787
Net income	–3,681	285	229	370	31
Total assets	15,649	15,824	16,780	24,552	28,725
Current assets	11,912	12,329	11,940	17,190	17,084
Total liabilities	6,194	6,033	7,681	15,225	19,739
Current liabilities	5,975	5,755	7,286	12,698	14,892
Total equity	9,455	9,791	9,099	9,327	8,987

Source: Compiled from Reuters Financial Statements (2009), available at: **http://www.reuters.com/finance/stocks**

and larger and were set at 26.37 per cent for Changhong, 21.25 per cent for TCL, and 9.69 per cent for Konka. The US also mandated that any television sold after March 2007 had to meet the strict technical specifications designated by the US Advanced Television Systems Committee (ATSC). Currently, five of the 170 ATSC standard patent holders are demanding that Chinese exporters pay $10 per unit shipped to the US.

In the European market, environmental regulations pose similar challenges. The Restriction of Hazardous Substances in Electrical and Electronic Equipment Directive, imposed by the European Union (EU) prohibits the use of six substances in manufacturing. The directive applies not only to goods produced in the EU, but to all goods sold in the EU as well, resulting in higher production costs for many Chinese television manufacturers, who now face yet another entry barrier to foreign markets.

In response to these trade restrictions, China's Government has offered major support to Changhong and other top television manufacturers to promote their brands in the international market. The Ministry of Foreign Trade and Economic Cooperation issued a list of industries it wanted to promote globally. The leading firms in these industries received access to loans from domestic banks and financial institutions to assist in overseas ventures. The government also granted many manufacturers permission to establish manufacturing and assembly facilities abroad in order to promote exports from mainland China.

Changhong has directly benefited from the government-supported financial packages. Thanks to a tame Chinese inflation rate and favourable interest rates, the cost of debt-financing is low, and Changhong has borrowed heavily. The China Development Bank, for example, has committed to give Changhong a loan of over RMB 1 billion to fund technological improvements and aggressive expansion, both domestically and internationally. The Bank of China granted the firm another RMB 1 billion loan. Yong acknowledges the benefits Changhong has received from the Chinese Government, and the importance of cooperation from governmental and financial entities for the future.

Looking into the future

Changhong has already distinguished itself as a top-selling brand in the Chinese market. As its exports continue to increase, the firm is moving towards its goal of becoming a world-renowned television manufacturer like Sony or Samsung. But Yong knows that pursuing a low-cost entry strategy in international markets and trying to establish the brand name simultaneously will be very difficult. Since the company's entry into international markets, it has relied on price reduction and original equipment manufacturer production to increase market share. But results have been mixed, as the company continues to encounter setbacks. The share of revenue from colour televisions has decreased in tandem with the diversification of the company's product line (falling from 74.45 per cent in 2004 to 47.27 per cent in 2007). Overseas operations suffered a similar decline (24.88 per cent in 2004 to 11.55 per cent in 2007), and the company disclosed a net profit decline of 91.6 per cent, to RMB 31.3 million, in 2008 (see Exhibit IV).

Changhong's key hurdle in expanding internationally is to create a strong brand image, thus generating awareness and sales. Is Yong capable of transforming the company into a new technological giant, similar to Japanese and Korean multinationals? It appears that he has steered Changhong down the right path, having restructured the organization, its logistics operations and distribution channels, while investing in the high-end sector for the future. But Yong's challenges are far from over as competition continues unabated and margins fall. In this context, what is the appropriate marketing strategy and marketing mix for Changhong?

QUESTIONS TO BE ANSWERED

1 How attractive is the domestic Chinese market compared to international markets for Changhong? Where should the company compete?

2 What is the source of Changhong's competitive advantage and how should the company compete?

3 Were Zhao Yong's changes sufficient to maintain Changhong's position for the long term? How should the company's performance be measured?

4 What type of marketing organization would work best? Should the company take a different approach in the future?

REFERENCE AND FURTHER READING

Access Asia Limited (2009), *Televisions in China 2009: A Market Analysis*, January, accessed June 2009, at: **http://www.accessasia.co.uk/showreport.asp?RptId=12**

Asia Pulse (2005), *Chinese TV Makers Pressure Foreign Rivals*, retrieved March 2009 from: **http://www.atimes.com/atimes/China_Business/GK23Cb02.html**

Beyer von Morgenstern, I., and C. Shu (2006), *The Great Electronic Wars*, retrieved March 2009 from: **http://www.mckinsey.com/locations/greaterchina/mckonchina/industries/high_tech/electronics_war.aspx**

Chang, Agrin (2009), 'China's Sichuan Changhong to Double '09 LCD TV Output', *Reuters Business Briefing*, 2 June, available at: **http://IN.reuters.com/article/rbssConsumerGoodsAndRetailNews/idINTP20086520090602**

Chen, Zhiming (1999), 'Changhong Sparks New Television Price War', *Business Weekly*, 2 May, pp. 3–8.

China Daily (2006), 'As Nation Opens, TV Sector Booms', retrieved March 2009 from: **http://www.china.org.cn/english/BAT/189754.htm**

Chung, O. (2007), 'Picture Wobbling for Chinese TV Makers', *Asia Times Online*, accessed June 2009, at: **http://www.atimes.com/atimes/China_Business/IH25Cb01.html**

CIA World Factbook (2008), Available at: **https://www.cia.gov/library/publications/the-world-factbook/geos/ch.html**

Dang, N. (2003), *China Systems Market Share: Local Brands Dominate Chinese TV Sets Market*, iSuppli Corporation, El Segundo, CA, July, accessed June 2009, at: **http://www.isuppli.com/Abstract/P5187_20030722135605.pdf**

Hoover's Company Records [2009], *Sichuan Changhong Electric Co., Ltd.*, retrieved June from: **http://www.proquest.umi.com.ezproxy.rollins.edu:2048/pqdweb?index=0&did=913611331&SrchMode=2&sid=1&Fmt=3&VInst=PROD&VType=PQD&RQT=309&V Name=PQD&TS=1245703724&clientId=394**

IBM Corporation [2009], *Changhong: Adopting a Culture of Innovation and Surpassing Expectations*, retrieved June from: **ftp://ftp.software.ibm.com/software/solutions/pdfs/ODC03086-USEN-00.pdf**

LexisNexis Academic [2009], Sichuan Changhong Electric Co. Ltd., retrieved June from: **http://www.lexisnexis.com.ezproxy.rollins.edu:2048/us/lnacademic/search/companyDossiersubmitForm.do**

Li, Ruixe, and Min Mao (2007), 'A Case Study of Marketing Strategy and Logistics System of Changhong, a Chinese Home Appliances Enterprise', Working Paper No. 213, Faculty of Economics, University of Toyoma, Japan, 1 February, accessed June 2009, at: **http://www.scribd.com/doc/2620449/WorkingPaperNO-213**

Reuters Business Briefing (2009), 'China's Changhong Electric '08 Net Profit Falls 92 pct', 25 April, accessed June 2009, at: **http://www.reuters.com/article/companyNews/idUKSHA36885420090425?symbol=600839.SS**

Reuters News Service (2004), 'China's TCL to Move Output to Avoid US Levy', accessed March 2009, at: **http://www.forbes.com/technology/networks/newswire/2004/05/18/rtr1375167.shtml**

Reuters Stock Quote [2009], 'Sichuan Changhong Electric Co., Ltd.', retrieved June from: **http://www.reuters.com/finance/stocks/overview?symbol=600839.SS**

Shanghai Daily (2007), 'LCD TV Production Booms, but Cost Jump Trims Earnings', retrieved March 2009 from: **http://www.en.ce.cn/Industries/Consumer-Industries/200710/08/t20071008_13153476.shtml**

Sichuan Changhong Electric Co., Ltd. Company Website (2009), retrieved June from: **http://www.changhong.com/changhong_en/changhong_global.htm**

Index

C

D

E

J

K

L

M

N

Q

R

S